AF664454

Swami Vivekananda

The Complete Biography

Volume 1: Before his Visit to the West

SRI ANANDA

PUBLISHERS & DISTRIBUTORS(P) LTD

7/22, Ansari Road, Darya Ganj, New Delhi
Tel.: +91-11-4077 5252, 2327 3880
E-mail: orders@atlanticbooks.com
Web: www.atlanticbooks.com

Reprint 2025

Published by Atlantic Publishers & Distributors (P) Ltd.

Printed & bound in India by Atlantic Print Services

Swami Vivekananda

To

My revered teacher,
Swami Prameyananda (April 1933 - October 20, 2011)
former vice president of the Ramakrishna Order.

Author's Note To The First Edition

Since 2008 I started writing articles on different aspects of varied ideas of Swami Vivekananda in different Bengali magazines, and in course of writing I realized that many Bengali people, except few learned parsons, have little knowledge about this great philosopher and his works. When I began to search the reasons behind it, I found that most of the books are classic for they are written by the scholars, and due to the highly scholarly features of these books, ordinary people do not feel easy to grasp the subject, and get disappointed which forces them to avoid the study. They have learnt only to admire Swami Vivekananda, but do not feel enough courage to plunge into the depth of the subject. In fact, most of his lectures and literary works were in English and they were later translated in Bengali and other languages. Revered translators, no doubt, had done a great work by virtue of their excellent command in language, but they hardly thought about the ordinary readers. But, the articles and letters, written by Swamiji himself in Bengali, are very much comprehensive and lucid.

Books, as I think, are not printed only for the high educated society; there live a large number of ordinary men and women whose contribution to the world of mankind cannot be ignored. They, too, have every right to read good books, which can help them to learn more for shaping their lives better by knowing the noble aspects of great ideals like Swami Vivekananda. I highly appreciate the classic literatures, and admire their authors for they have done great jobs. Yet, I think, when the subject of a book is religion and spirituality, and concerning to the man-making mission of Swami Vivekananda, it must be the most comprehensive and written in a lucid manner so that it can reach a large number of readers.

Many books were printed interpreting the biography of Swami Vivekananda, but they are unable to provide a complete picture of his life and works. I, therefore, have made an effort to ensure the readers' satisfaction incorporating sufficient knowledge on Swamiji's life and teachings.

I would like to express my gratitude to revered Swami Ekavratananda, the secretary of the Ramakrishna Mission Calcutta Students' Home, Belgharia, Kolkata, without whose constant inspiration it would have been impossible for me even to think of doing such a hard work. After the success of my previous work *Adwitiya Vivekananda* (in two volumes), the most comprehensive biography of Swami Vivekananda in Bengali, published by Parul Prakashani, Kolkata, Revered Swami Ekabrotananda Maharaj-ji encouraged me for writing the same subject in English. Considering his suggestion as an ardent member of Sri Ramakrishna order, I plunged into the work, and by the grace of Lord it has been possible to get it done. While I was writing the book, Mr. Dilipkumar Chattopadhyay, a senior friend of mine and retired English Professor, had carefully read it and made all required corrections, and, thus, he has made me grateful to him forever. Mr. Saroj Upadhyay, my another friend and a Professor of Economics, also helped me in this work, encouraging me all the way, giving his wise opinion, and drawing my attention to many valuable points. I shall remain ever indebted to his great contribution in making this work successful. I am also grateful to Mr. Ranadev Bhattacharya, who helped by giving me the voluminous book *Swami Vivekananda in the West, New Discovery*, and inspired me in this work. Mr. Indranath Bandyopadhyay, as a friend, always stood by me with his best wishes.

And finally, I want to express my gratitude to my great hearted publisher and all those who have expressed their well-wishes and worked hard to bring out this beautiful voluminous book.

Sri Ananda

Preface

Since 1893, Swami Vivekananda is well-known to the world as a great spiritual teacher. On 11th September, 1893, Swami Vivekananda, a young monk of thirty years from India, appeared on the platform of the World Parliament of Religions held in Chicago, America, and addressed the learned audience saying, "Sisters and Brothers of America", which indeed was his address to the world. With these five words he established almost the whole of Vedanta philosophy. He, in fact, meant to say that all of us are members of one family of one world; each person is either sister or brother to an-other, for we are children of One God.

People may speak in different languages and practice different religions. God may be worshipped in different name in different lands, but He is One. We may pray in different style but to whom we pray is One and what we pray is the same. There are many religions but every religion follows one Sun and one Moon. Churches, Mosques, and Temples are identically different for their different architectural structures, but they all are made up of same materials. We all drink water, but call it by different names. Biologically too, there is no difference between two persons of two different land. This is absolutely true that we all are children of One God. Difference among us is only in language, colour, and culture. Yet we see a group of people fights with the other and even gets pleasure by killing another. Swami Vivekananda had tried to find out the root of this problem.

In every nation, there have been perfected souls who, after reaching the highest state of Realization, have become the guidelines to all spiritual aspirants. People began to worship these God-men and, thus, they have become the common feature in religions. Along with this, the worship of name and of symbols becomes common. "So we find," Swamiji said, "that in almost every religion, these are the three primary things which we have in the worship of God—forms or symbols, names, God-men". The words or teachings of these prophets are recorded in texts, considering them the very words of God and very sacred. Thus, in the world, there have been several religions and certain books followed by them like Vedas, Bible, Koran, etc., which are considered to be the aids to spiritual growth by all religions.

There is a great similarity on many points in different religions, and that is why Swamiji remarked, "So startling is this likeness, at time, as to suggest the idea that in many particulars the different religions have copied from one another.... The language of the soul is one, the languages of nations are many; their customs and methods of life are widely different. Religion is of the soul and finds expression through various nations, languages, and customs. Hence, it follows that the difference between the religions of the world is one of expression and not of substance; and their points of similarity and unity are of the soul, are intrinsic, as the language of the soul is one, in whatever peoples and under whatever circumstances it manifests itself. The same sweet harmony is vibrant there also, as it is on many and diverse instruments".

Many of us believe that religions are of no use in society. But, Swamiji, with great stress on its application to the whole society, said:

> Of all the forces that have worked and are still working to mould the destinies of the human race, none, certainly, is more potent than that, the manifestation of which we call religion. All social workings of that peculiar force, and the greatest cohesive impulse ever brought into play amongst human units has been derived from this power.... It is the greatest motive power that moves the human mind. No other ideal can put into us the same mass of energy as the spiritual. So far as human history goes, it is obvious to all of us that this has been the case and that its powers are not dead.... Religion is the greatest motive power for realising that infinite energy which is the birthright and nature of every man. In building up character, in making for everything that is good and great, in bringing peace to others and peace to one's own self, religion is the highest motive power.

Yet, it is the religion that has caused the hatred and dimmed out the true sight. Instead of hearing its sweet music of harmony, we here only strain of conflict. Instead of sticking to the fundamentals of religion, instead of understanding the true import of its essentials, we put emphasis on the difference between the non-essential elements of religion, namely, ritual and mythology. The different religions essentially concern themselves with the practical life of men by formulating codes of conduct and spiritual disciplines. These doctrines or various paths call upon their followers to pray to the One and the same God. But the paths are different and the details they pronounce vary, which creates the divergence.

Till the real aim of religion is not grasped, quarrels between different religions will continue. Every religion consists of three parts, namely, philosophy, mythology, and ritual. Describing these three parts of religion Swamiji said, "philosophy presents the whole scope of that religion, setting forth its basic principles, the goal and the means of reaching it. The second part is mythology, which is philosophy made concrete. It consists of legends relating to the lives of men, or of supernatural beings, and so forth. It is the abstractions of philosophy concretized in more or less imaginary lives of men and supernatural beings. The third part is the ritual. This is still more concrete, and is made up of forms and ceremonies, various physical attitudes, flowers and incense, and many other things that appeal to the senses. In these consists the ritual."

These are accessories to religion and are necessary for all except rare cases. "Temples or churches, books or forms, are simply the kindergarten of religion, to make the spiritual child strong enough to take higher steps, and these steps are necessary if he wants religion."

Explaining the third part of religion Swamiji says, "Even the expression through mythology, the lives of heroes, is not sufficient for all. There are minds still lower. Like children they must have their kindergarten of religion, and these symbologies are evolved—concrete examples which they can handle, grasp, and understand, which they can see and feel as material something."

The third part of religion is philosophy and every religion has its own philosophy. Though philosophy is to be the central theme of religion and mythology and ritual as only the outer sheaths, certain problems appearing round individual spiritual experiences and approaches create disagreement even in philosophies. Commentators have exhausted all their dialectic skill in proving their own positions, and have, thus, reduced the scriptures to a bundle of dry, obscure, and philosophical speculations. It was left for Swamiji, who had plunged into the depths of realization, to prove that the various doctrines are only progressive stages on the path of realization. He taught that man is not travelling from error to truth, but from truth to truth, from lower to higher truth.

Swamiji had prescribed the four *Yogas* (*Raja-Yoga*, *Karma-Yoga*, *Jnana-Yoga*, and *Bhakti-Yoga*) as the different paths of spiritual disciplines to meet the needs of men of different temperaments. He tried to show that each path is effective if pursued with sincerity, good intent, reason, non-attachment, and renunciation, though he had repeatedly made it clear that none of these paths is exclusive.

More than once he said, "There is not really so much difference between Knowledge (*Jnana*) and Love (*Bhakti*) as people sometimes imagine. We shall see, as we go on, that in the end they converge and meet at the same point. So also is with *Raja-Yoga*, which when pursued as a means to attain liberation...leads us also to the same goal." And of *Karma-Yoga* he said, "Work, endless work—without looking at results, and always keeping whole mind and soul steadfast at the lotus feet of the Lord! ...this is *Karma-Yoga*...you must harmonise the four different *yogas*; otherwise how can you always keep your mind and heart wholly on the Lord?" Blending of all the four modes of practice would go a long way to build an ideal character. With this view he wished that the spiritual disciplines to be followed in his organization should be based on the synthesis of the four *yogas*. He realized that the vision of the *Paramatman* is obtained by the union of these four *yogas—Raja*, *Karma*, *Jnana*, and *Bhakti*. This note of harmony has been heard in its unbroken strain all along in the Hindu religious consciousness. The conception of the supreme spiritual unity of God is as old in India as the *Rig-Veda*. The Vedic Prophets saw this reality in different lights and spoke variously about it, and yet did not lose the consciousness about its underlying unity.

Swamiji had clearly seen that his mission in life was to spread this spirit of harmony which he saw in the very being of Shri Ramakrishna, who, with his vast and rich spiritual experience, could declare that all religions and all creeds lead to the same goal, namely God-realization, and, hence, all were true.

Swamiji called Hinduism the 'mother of religions' at the Parliament of Religions held in Chicago in 1893. He also declared there, "I am proud to belong to a religion which has taught the world both tolerance and universal acceptance. We believe not only in universal toleration, but we accept all religions, as true."

"Truth", asserted Swamiji, "has always been universal.... Just so with religion. If one creed alone were to be true and all other untrue, you would have a right to say that religion was diseased; if one religion is true, all others must be true. Thus, the Hindu religion is your property as well as mine." And again speaking on the same subject he said, "We Hindus accept every religion, praying in the mosque of the Mohammedans, worshipping before the fire of the Zoroastrians, and kneeling before the cross of the Christians, knowing that all the religions, from the lowest fetishism to the highest absolutism, mean so many attempts of the human soul to grasp and realize the infinite, each determined by the conditions of its birth and association, and each of them marking a stage of progress. We gather all these flowers and bind them with the twine of love, making a wonderful bouquet of worship."

By harmony Swamiji meant unity, and not uniformity. Harmony cannot be obtained by a combination of different views about God. It is difficult for the ordinary run of men to grasp the absolute Truth. According to the knowledge, intellect, mind, and view of a man, only partial or relative truths are revealed to him. The greater the number of sects, therefore, the greater the number of people who are benefited.

Swamiji still had spoken about an ideal Universal Religion. He himself explained it as, "What then do I mean by the ideal of a universal religion? I do not mean any one universal philosophy, or any one universal mythology, or any one universal ritual, held alike by all; for I know that this world must go on working, wheel within wheel, this intricate mass of machinery, most complex, most wonderful. What can we do then? We can make it run smoothly, we can lessen the friction, we can grease the wheels, as it were."

Understanding this universality practice is of more importance than that of the intellectual assent. Only through faith and struggle one can be convinced that God expresses Himself in many ways. And this conviction alone can lead one to understand Swamiji's ideal of the harmony of religions and universal religion.

Swamiji says that "Vedanta, and Vedanta alone can become the universal religion of man and that no other is fitted for that role." ... "Through all these various conceptions run the golden thread of unity, and it is the purpose of the Vedanta to discover this thread." ... "The duty of Vedanta is to harmonize all these aspirations, to manifest the common ground between all the religious of the world, the highest as well as the lowest."

Swamiji coupled Vedanta with science, and, thus, empowered his Vedanta with intellectual vigour, progressiveness, comprehensiveness, and practicality. He preached the philosophy of the unity and solidarity of all existence, ensuring happiness and welfare of all beings.

In America, his mission was the interpretation of India's spiritual culture, especially in association with the rational and humanistic teaching of Vedanta philosophy and, thus, he tried to enrich the religious consciousness of the Western world. As a spiritual teacher, he pleaded eloquently for better understanding between India and the New World. He intended to create a healthy synthesis of East and West, of religion and science.

He, as a lover of mankind, made every effort to promote peace and human brotherhood on the spiritual foundation of the Vedantic Oneness of existence. He often presented his ideas in the soul-stirring language of poetry. His mind, like that of his Master, Shri Ramakrishna, was to soar above the world and forget itself in contemplation of the Absolute.

Swami Vivekananda had left his mortal body on 4th July, 1902, after living a short life of thirty-nine years, five months, and twenty-four days, of which only ten years were devoted to public activities, and those, too, in the midst of acute physical suffering—he left for posterity his four classics—*Raja-Yoga, Jnana-Yoga, Karma-Yoga,* and *Bhakti-Yoga*—all of which are outstanding treatises on Hindu philosophy.

Swami Vivekananda spoke of himself as a "Condensed India". His life and teachings are of inestimable value to the West for an understanding of the mind of Asia. William James, the Harvard Philosopher, called him the "Paragon of Vedantists". Max Müller and Paul Deussen, the famous Orientalists of the nineteenth century, held him in genuine respect and affection. "His words", writes Romain Rolland, "are great music, phrases in the style of Beethoven stirring rhythms, like the march of Handel choruses. I cannot touch these sayings, of his, scattered as they are through the pages of books, at thirty years' distance, without receiving a thrill through my body like an electric shock. And what shocks, what transports must have been produced when in burning words that issued from the lips of the hero."

On the day of his passing away, Swamiji held a class on Sanskrit Grammar at Belur Math in the afternoon, in course of which he gave his last message to his motherland, "India is immortal, if she persists in her search for God. But, if she goes in for politics and social conflict, she will die."

In the prelude of his book, *The Life of Vivekananda*, Romain Rolland writes, "It was impossible to imagine him in the second place. Wherever he went he was the first". Swamiji, too, spoke of himself, "the one without a second".

Swami Vivekananda is now a well known name to the world. His awe-inspiring personality is highly admired by the civilized society of different countries irrespective of caste and creed. Many books have been published incorporating several facts of his life and teachings. But, many of them seem to have failed in giving sufficient accounts with reference to their authentic sources. They only have highlighted some parts of this many-sided geniuses. Thus, they reflect many contrasting facts about this great personalty. If one wishes to understand Vivekananda, he needs to study a number of books, and even then there is a possibility of missing some books which could have been found more important works containing authentic account of swamiji. Without having a vast knowledge on any subject it is very hard to come to a valid conclusion. But, to my knowledge, there hardly such a book is available, in which his [Swami Vivekananda's] vast knowledge of Eastern and Western culture as well as his spiritual insight, fervid eloquence, brilliant conversations, inspiring lectures and letters, unparallel compassion, colourful personality, manifestation of divine character, and his everyday activities have been explained in comprehensive and lucid manner. The present endeavour, therefore, considering all these significant features, tries as much as possible to present multifaceted available information from all probable authentic sources and reconcile them to give a shape to the most comprehensive biography of Swami Vivekananda. It includes almost all the lectures delivered by Swamiji in America, Europe, and India, and accompanied by their consequent reports appeared in several newspapers, quotations from several articles written by those who had opportunity of seeing the great monk and having a chance to make conversation with him. If this effort is found to be successful in touching the hearts of the readers and can reach up to the mark of their expectation, I shall consider that it has been possible only by the grace of Ramakrishna-Vivekananda, and the holy Mother, the holy trinity who ushered a new era in the world of religion and a new element of livelihood in the human civilization.

Sri Ananda

Contents

VOLUME 4

1
Ancestry

With due respect to the readers of this book, we would like to acknowledge the limits of power of our understanding before we venture to write the spiritual life of Swami Vivekananda. The task is hard and hardly to be accomplished with full satisfaction. Yet we dare to share the pleasure that we fortunately felt in course of reading many books on him. Words fail to express the depth of his realization, yet we wish to help the readers to have the taste that we have experienced from his vast struggle in his short span of life for a period of 39 years, 5 months and 24 days. His Eastern and Western Disciples say, "...the world must know the greatness of the life that has thrilled it through its Eastern heart and Western mind."

As we know, childhood is the beginning of every life, it is better to start the review of one's life from the time he was born. It is also not very unusual to be seized with curiosity to know about the family where he took birth. It becomes more important to look into his childhood where the great personality like Swami Vivekananda was hidden.

The World's Parliament of Religions was a gathering held in connection with the World's Fair at Chicago in 1893. There, on 19 September, Swami Vivekananda in his "Paper on Hinduism" said:

> We cannot deny that bodies acquire certain tendencies from heredity, but those tendencies only mean the physical configuration, through which a peculiar mind alone can act in a peculiar way. There are other tendencies peculiar to a soul caused by its past actions. And a soul with a certain tendency would by the laws of affinity take birth in a body which is the fittest instrument for the display of that tendency. This is in accord with science, for science wants to explain everything by habit, and habit is got through repetitions. So repetitions are necessary to explain the natural habits of a new-born soul.[1]

Swamiji, being appeared as a human being on the earth, also had inherited some tendencies. Hence, before we start the review of his boyhood, we should better try to look into the historical background of his family, and I believe it will help us to know the reason behind his inclination to the life of a monk.

Dutta Family of Simulia

Only the families of worldly people have always been conferring monks to the human society. No one is monk by birth. Shankaracharya and Vivekananda too had to take birth in their families.

Shankaracharya quitted his family at the age of only sixteen and Vivekananda at twenty-four years. Before that both of them had to learn walking and talking under the loving shade of their families.

The family, where Swami Vivekananda was brought up as Bilu, or as Vireswar or as Narendranath, was the famous Dutta-family of Gaur Mohan Mukherjee Street at Shimla, North Calcutta (presently called Kolkata). Once this place was called Simuliya. Viswanath Dutta was his father. Viswanath's father was Durgaprosad Dutta. Durgaprosad's father was Rammohan Dutta.

Duttas once used to live at Deretona village of Kalna in Burdwan district of Bengal. Ramnidhi Dutta, of clan Kashyap of Dakshin Rarhi, came to Garh Govindapur (Kolkata) along with his son, Ramjivan and Ramsundar, his grandson. Later the Dutta family had to quit the place when the fort was built on that land. They shifted to the Shimla or Simuliya at North Kolkata and built a new house in Madhu Roy Lane. Ramsundar, son of Ramjivan, was a dewan (financial steward) of a Zamindar (landowner). Ramsundar had five sons; of whom one was Rammohan Dutta. This Rammohan Dutta was the great-grandfather of Vivekananda.

Behind the huge property of the Duttas was their hereditary legal practice. In a word, the Duttas of Shimla were a group of lawyers and attorneys. Rammohan Dutta was a famous 'Persian lawyer' at the highest Court of the land. He used to work as a managing clerk in an office of an English attorney. The huge property, good reputation, and prestige for Dutta family, was earned by him only. He had two villas at Shalkiya and a lot of land at Khidirpur. The new house at 3, Gaur Mohan Mukherjee Street, Kolkata, was also built by him. There was a huge land of about one and half Bigha (1 Bigha = 14,400 sq. ft.) inside that house. A huge lawn could be seen by entering the house through the big southern gate made up of teak. To the east there was a beautiful west-facing Panchphukuri—means a hall called Thakur Dalan with five brick-built arches on brick-built rounded pillars. This hall (Thakur Dalan) was used for worshiping God. On the first floor of the Thakur Dalan, there were many big rooms towards the south. There was big drawing room to the north and a room called Thakur Ghar (temple) to the south. To the south side of the house there was a room at ground floor. This room was called Bodhan Ghar (invocation). To the west of the outside lawn there were a square-shaped platform and a cowshed. There were two lawns to both sides of the gynaeceum and to the back side was a pond used by women. Outside of that house Rammohan Dutta had a stable on a land of about 2880 sq. ft. at 2, Gour Mohan Mukherjee Street. Drawing room was decorated with different kinds of chandeliers of that period. Beside these, different types of paintings made its wall beautiful to look at.

It was an aristocrat joint family. After the new building was built Rammohan told everybody to come and live in that house. Three of his brothers came to him, but the third brother didn't join them. He decided to live separately. After Vishwanath Dutta got married everyone agreed to sell the old house.

Rammohan died of cholera when he was a young man of only 36 years. Splendid development by legal profession and total destruction of the family by frequenting to the court for the settlement of disputes among the partners—both were the remarkable characteristics of Dutta family. Vivekananda also studied law and served apprenticeship in an attorney office. But he couldn't be pleased when Mahendranath, his younger brother went to London for learning law.

Rammohan Dutta had two sons and seven daughters. When he died, he left one widow daughter and two little sons. Durgaprosad Dutta, the elder son of Rammohan, was the grandfather of Vivekananda. The other son was called Kaliprosad. Pramathanath Basu, in his book *Swami Vivekananda*, said, "grandfather's name was Durgacharan." But, Bhupendranath Dutta, brother of Vivekananda, said, his grandfather was Durgaprosad, not Durgacharan, because, there was a paper signed by Durgaprosad in 1883-84, when the property was being divided at court. Durgaprosad

Dutta got married with Shyamasundari, the younger daughter of Rajiblochan Ghosh, dewan of north Kolkata. He was also at legal practice, and was as successful as his father was in both money and good reputation. He was wise in Sanskrit and Persian languages, and an expert in music too. Durgaprosad was virtuous and liked the association with saints and ascetics. Once, at the age of only 25 years, he left his legal practice and his family, and finally became a saint.

Strife among partners of a joint family was a common feature of that time. We came to know that Durgaprosad left his family when he found his wife being insulted by the relatives. Even after becoming a saint Durgaprosad used to come to his disciple-son at Shimla Street by riding a pony. Once he was kept locked in a room, but three days later he was found seriously ill with his mouth foaming. Later he was allowed to move away wherever he liked. Since then he never returned home.

Bhupendranath Dutta has informed, "Durgaprosad, on his visit to the Ganges, used to come off and on to one of his Brahmin disciples at Simla Street, and then Biswanath also used to go there. Last time when he came, Shyamasundari being advised by her relatives went there to massage her husband's feet. Durgaprosad moved aside and cried, 'a Chandal (a lower caste) has touched me.' Since then he never came to Kolkata."[2] According to *Lilaprosango*, "Although he left home, Durgaprosad twice saw his wife and relatives briefly by the will of Providence." However, we think, his attraction to the spiritual life had forced him to renounce the worldly life.

Shyamasundari, Durgaprosad's wife was beautiful and wise too. She wrote a book of verse titled *Gangabhakti Tarangini*, but it was lost before it published. She had only two children. First child was a daughter, she died at seven only. We know nothing about her. Durgaprosad when twenty-five years old renounced the worldly life leaving his only son and wife to his relatives. This son, Viswanath Dutta, was then only two or three years old. Revered Swami Gambhirananda said, "Viswanath Dutta was then only of six to seven years old at his *Annaprasan*, when he was given tasting rice for the first time, Durgaprosad renounced the worldly life and left his home at the age of 20 to 22 years." This Viswanath Dutta is the father of Swami Vivekananda.

After renouncing the family life Durgaprosad visited many places for five to six years and then reached Varanasi. In those days there was no railway service in this country. One had to walk or had to ride a boat for going to Varanasi. Viswanath was then only a boy of about eight years. Shyamasundari, wife of Durgaprosad, set out for Varanasi on a boat with her eight years old son Viswanath. Pramathanath Basu has informed that Viswanath was then a boy of eight years. But, Reverend Swami Gambhirananda has told that Viswanath was a boy of three years, when all the members of his family went to Kashi-Dham (a holy place) by boat. One day Viswanath, while playing on the boat, fell into the river. According to Bhupendranath—"Someone cried, the boat is sinking, and Shyamasundari jumped into the river with her son." Mahendranath Dutta also has supported the incident of sinking of the boat.[3] However, Shyamasundari, a loving mother, jumped into the river to save her son without knowing how to swim, and without caring about her own life. The unconscious mother was seen clenching a hand of her son when they were taken out of water. Viswanath had a mark of his mother's hand on his hand for a long time.

Reverend Swami Gambhirananda has told that Shyamasundari jumped into the river and clenched her son's hand and tried to save him. Umapada Gupta, an Ayurvedic physician, was on that boat. He used to stay at Dutta House. Realizing the dangerous situation, the physician jumped into the river and caught hold of her hair and pulled her on to the boat. Thus, the mother and her son were rescued.

Reverend Swami Saradananda said:

> When his (Durgaprosad) son, Vishwanath, was two or three years old, Durgacharan's wife and relatives went to Varanasi—perhaps in search of him—and stayed there for some time. There was no railroad in those days, so wealthy people went on pilgrimage to Varanasi by boat, and Durgacharan's wife joined a group of pilgrims. On the way, Vishwanath fell into the Ganges. When his mother saw this, she jumped into the river to save him, although she could not swim. After a great effort, both were rescued. People saw that the unconscious mother still had a firm hold on her son's hand. Thus Viswanath's life was saved by the limitless love of his mother.[4]

Reaching Varanasi Shyamasundari Devi felt the peace of mind by visiting many idols of deities. One day she fell in front of the temple of Visweswara while walking on the road after a sudden shower. A monk saw her falling and cried out, "*Maiji gir gai*", then, soon he rushed to her for helping her to stand up. Shyamasundari caught sight of the face of monk, and asked to herself with startle—"Who is this monk?" The monk carefully lifted her up and took her to the step of the temple, their eyes meet together. What a wonder! They looked at each other motionless and felt a strange shuddering within themselves. This is called the wheel of fortune. The ascetic was none other than Durgaprosad.

As soon as Durgaprosad recognized that the lady was his wife, he left the place at a brisk pace saying—"*Maya Hai, Maya Hai*". In a moment he became out of sight. Though after a long time Shyamasundari Devi felt a little relief by seeing her husband's face, yet the idea of forcing him to return home didn't arise in mind of the self-denying lady. After going around the temple she offered a handful of flowers at the feet of Lord Viswanath and returned home with her son.

But we are informed by Reverend Swami Gambhirananda that the lady, who fell down that day on the drenched road in front of the Viswanath-temple, was Durgaprosad's sister, not his wife. Durgaprosad carefully helped her standing again. Though he was in a dress of monk, his sister recognized his voice and looking at his face she asked, "Are you Durgaprosad?" Ascetic Durgaprosad replied disgustfully, "Here too you have come to disturb me!" Then he swiftly left the place. According to Bhupendranath and Mahendranath, the lady was a relative of them. Bhupendranath said that the road was slippery due to rain. Mahendranath has informed that the road was extremely heated under the sun.

There is a custom among ascetics that after renouncing the worldly life one has to visit his motherland at least for once. Following this custom after twelve years Durgaprosad returned to Kolkata, and instead of his own house, he took shelter in one of his friends' house. He requested his friend not to disclose the news of his returning to anybody of his family. But the friend didn't follow his request and exposed the news secretly to Dutta-house. As a result, what happened was very much usual. People from Dutta-house appeared there, and forcefully took him with them to his own house. Viswanath heard that an ascetic has come, and he rushed to see him. But the ascetic didn't take the boy up on his lap. He only raised his right hand blessed the little boy. Durgaprosad came to know that his wife had gone to heaven a year ago. Family it was decided not to allow the monk to move away. They locked him in a room and requested him repeatedly for coming back to the worldly life. But how could an ascetic, who once had tasted the pleasure of freedom, be ready to be caught in the cage of worldly life? He closed his eyes and suffered the bondage without retaliation. Continuous fasting made him appeared on the threshold of death. Then, the relatives unlocked the door of his room. Next day he was found disappeared, nobody knew where he had gone.

Had he ever remembered his wife or ever thought of his son? The answer is unknown to us. Pramatha Nath Basu has remarked, "Perhaps, he didn't consider the child as his son, rather he dedicated the child as an offering at the feet of the father of world." Durgaprosad, the ascetic went away. Hence, he was never seen by anyone.

Parents of Vivekananda

After the renunciation of worldly life by Durgaprosad, Kaliprosad, his brother became the head of the family. He didn't have earnings by his own. Hence, the expenditure of the family was met out of the money saved earlier. Many relatives had been taking shelter there. A daughter of Rammohan and her children were living in this family for the last four generations. Savings amount gradually touched the bottom, and the Dutta family became poor. Moreover, we have come to know that Kaliprosad was a selfish person. Viswanath Dutta and his family had to suffer a lot for this Kaliprosad. Such a hint is given by Bhupendranath Dutta—"Durgaprosad renounced the worldly life to avoid the misery of life and for making his soul free from all bondage; but, he left his wife and son under the custody of hungry and ferocious wolves, and those wolves and their next generation didn't allow them to live in peace till 1903."

Reverend Swami Gambhirananda has claimed that Bhupendranath Dutta has blurred his readers with illusion by mixing two miserable situations of the family—the situation after the renunciation of worldly life by Durgaprosad, and the situation after the death of Viswanath Dutta. He has also tried to establish the cause of his claim. He said, "Renunciation of worldly life by Durgaprosad made his wife and her son encumbered, but they didn't have any pecuniary hardship, and it appears such by their pilgrimage. Renunciation by Durgaprosad was not responsible for the hardship that they had to face later; rather, it would be more justified to blame the custom of living in a joint family. However, it is easily understood that Viswanath, being deceived from his father's love, didn't have any reasonable care from the brother of his grandfather. Moreover, Shyamasundari died when Viswanath was only of twelve years old. Viswanath was then an orphan and had been treated also as an orphan. Yet, he was such a noble-minded, that after being adult, he had a great respect for the brother of his grandfather though he knew that in every step he had been beguiled by him."

Viswanath Dutta, father of Narendranath, used to live as an orphan depending upon the kindness of Kaliprosad, his uncle. As he grew up, he became scholar in different languages. After having the degree of graduation, he followed the footprints of his ancestors and started practicing law.

Viswanath studied in the school of Gaurmohan Adhya. Rasik Chandra was one of the teachers of that school. His second son renounced the worldly life and became known as reverend Swami Abhedananda.

Being unsuccessful in legal practice Viswanath Dutta accepted the job of an articled clerk under the attorney Charles F. Peter on 11 April 1859. Later, on 29 January 1861 he joined the office of attorney Henry Jorge Temple as an articled clerk and continued the job till 10 October 1864. Then on 14 March 1866, he sent an application to the bench of the chief justice Sir Barnes Peacock, where he wished to work as an attorney or as a proctor. With this application Viswanath Dutta attached two certificates issued on same date (7 January 1865), one was issued by Sri Garish Chandra Bannerjee and the other by Sri Digamber Miter. Mr. Justice Walter Morgan granted the application on the same day. Later, Mr. Morgan became the Chief Justice of North-West Frontier. To everybody around the court Viswanath Dutta was known for his company named 'Dhar & Dutta'. Ashutosh Dhar was his partner. Probably, after passing the exam of Attorney he opened this company along with Mr. Ashutosh Dhar.

Bhupendranath Dutta has informed that his father, who was a devotee to literature, wrote a novel, but he hadn't enough money to publish the same. The book was published in the name of Gopal Chandra Dutta, younger brother of his grandfather and then working at a post office. But he couldn't tell us the name of the book.

With reference to the above information Reverend Swami Gambhirananda, in his book titled *Jugonayak Vivekananda*, said, "He (Viswanath Dutta) wrote a book titled *Sulochona*, and after being printed in 1880, it was well appreciated by the people. In 1882 he wrote another book titled *Sistachar-Padhyati* (*Method of Civility*) in both Bengali and Hindi, and it was printed by some other person. In the last book, he wrote that he had travelled all over this country except the southern India. He found that our society being damaged by many kinds of superstitions. The second volume of this book couldn't be published due to his premature death" (translated by the present author).

Vivekananda also had to suffer from such ill-luck of publishing his writings in the name of another person. Before becoming a monk, he had to allow publishing some of his books in the name of publisher only in exchange of a little amount of money. A book on music, a book on spoken English, and a book translated in Bengali were among the above books.

The description of Viswanath Dutta's economic condition, that we get from the book titled *Swami Vivekananda* written by Pramathanath Basu, is different from the above information.

Viswanath Dutta was an attorney at the High Court. He earned fame in his profession and even the people from different rural areas had faith on his talent. He was very much intelligent. Besides jurisprudence he was a scholar in many other subjects. He was fond of reading history and liked to investigate the causes of rise and fall of different nations. Alongside his knowledge, intelligence, and vast experience, he was a sensual person. His concept of living was to enjoy life to the full. If a person wants to live a worldly life, he should try to satisfy all his desires, and should have extreme pleasure in every moment of life. A human life is gratified only when the person can live like a king by earning money and spending them for having extreme pleasure with family and friends. He led his life in accordance with his thought. He didn't like to live an unostentatious life of the poor. He had earned a lot and was bountiful too in spending them all. His friends were innumerable. He was generous enough to make friendship with any stranger in a short time. Viswanath Dutta was a simple-hearted and humorous person. He liked to have delicious food and also wished to share the same with everyone around him. He was not less expert than a good cook. A man like him, who liked cooking and serving out delicious meal to his guests, was very rare. Every now and then he used to make experiment of cooking new spicy dishes in his kitchen and serving out that food to his guests was a great pleasure to him.

That was a transition period. A new civilization that grew up by mixing the Hindu and the Muslim cultures was coming up at an irresistible speed, and it was also the beginning of being influenced by the European civilization. Indian society of educated people was endowed with the influencing power of these three types of culture. Viswanath Dutta, as usual, was also one of them. The influence of these three religious cultures forced him to have faithful adherence to each of them. He had many European friends. He used to follow the old Hindu and Muslim customs in wearing, drinking, and eating, and in forms of manners. He, in his daily life, was also seen to imitate the English like those people of educated society of that period. But in observance of religious rules and rites he used to follow the traditional orders. Brahmins were given gift by him and Muslim saints were also not deprived. He was never seen in any movement of social reformers. But he agreed with Vidyasagar in supporting the practice of early marriage. Once there was a loud uproar in an issue of early marriage near Dutta house, when Viswanath Dutta and his wife approved the marriage. So, we see that in customs and practices Viswanath Dutta followed the other Hindus but was hostile of narrow-mindedness. He considered the convictions of each religion with much respect. So, he was seen interested in reading the Bible, Dewan-e-Hafiz, etc. After his death, a 'Bhagavat' written by someone with the surname of 'Bharat' was found in his private library. With reference to this context Mahendranath Dutta has informed that Viswanath Dutta was a regular subscriber of *Srimatbhagavat* published by Upendra Chandra Dutta.

Viswanath was a liberal person, but never followed any doctrine indiscriminately. Once Narendranath was influenced with Brahmoism and used to take vegetarian diet. Once at dinner he raised objection to eating a vegetable curry only because of its being touched by a bowl of fish. Swarnamoyee, his elder sister, was serving out the meal. When Viswanath Dutta came to know the cause of quarrel between brother and sister, he shouted from bathroom: "His fourteen generations had been eating shell-fish, and now he has become a Brahmo demon who doesn't eat fish." It proves how much was he influenced by Brahmoism. With reference to this context Reverend Swami Gambhirananda said, "Though Viswanath Dutta had passed the above remake, but never he interfered in the liberty of his son. Even it is known that every now and then Acharya Shibnath Sastri, a leader of Brahmo society, used to come to the Dutta house, and was welcomed with due honour."

Viswanath Dutta was also inclined to travel. He liked to visit different places. Sometimes he didn't have any fixed destination. All of a sudden he used to decide a place to go and set out on a journey. He lived for few days at Lucknow in north-west India and at Lahore, the places mostly populated by the Muslim community, as a result of which he was interested in customs and rituals of them. He was fond of Muslim food. So fashion of eating pilau, highly spiced dish of rice and meat boiled in clarified butter, was in vogue in his family.

In a word, he used to live a poetic life. He was a luxurious person with a very soft heart. He couldn't help crying if ever any person was seen in misery. He used to donate liberally for the welfare of others. He was a fosterer of many relatives. Nobody was ever sent back disappointed by him. With reference to this context Mahendranath Dutta said, "His charity perhaps became a disease to him. He would say, 'I don't need to think of my sons, they will look after themselves; but these poor people are not so strong. Hence they need help.'" Viswanath maintained a large family that included many distant relatives, lavishly spending money on food and other necessities. Some of them were even addicted to drug or drinking. Narendranath, being grown up, could not tolerate these relatives. If ever he would reproach his father and would say that to award an unworthy person is nothing but a misuse of money, he would reply, "How can you now understand the great misery of human life? When you feel the depth of their suffering, you will sympathize with the unfortunate ones who are trying to forget their sorrows even for a moment by using intoxicants." He would consider that it is better to let a man try to reform himself by his own experience than to correct him forcefully. It is not possible to realize any higher knowledge till we have attraction for any little worldly matter. Interest in thinking of higher knowledge arises in mind only after a person is satisfied with all worldly pleasures.

Main ambition was of keeping his family happy. He didn't think of his sons, especially for Narendra he didn't worry at all. He believed that his sons will be good human being in future. He believed that children should be given well nutritious food; otherwise their brain will not work fast. It is not necessary to build a huge saving for children; rather they should be given well education and should be introduced to higher quality of life so that they can help themselves live a creditable life. A huge saving can easily be destroyed by a stupid man. Viswanath Dutta's confidence in his ability to earn money and his experience to live in a joint family and the inefficiency of his relatives forced him building such an angle of vision towards human life. He had seen Kaliprosad Dutta, son of wealthy Rammohan Dutta, not to earn anything, but ready to spend unscrupulously. Whereas Viswanath Dutta was brought up like an orphan and became wealthy on his own.

We are surprised to know his concept of religion. He believed that spiritual knowledge is not found anywhere as deep as it is found in the Bible, the Christian scripture, and in the verses of Persian poet Hafiz. Every day he used to read the Bible and the Dewan-i-Haphiz, and sometimes he liked to read them to his wife and sons. It shows that he had a great respect for Christianity.

In reference to this context Reverend Swami Saradananda, in his book *Lilaprosanga*, said:

> Although Narendra's grandfather, who became a monk, had great faith in the Hindu scriptures throughout his life; his son, Narendra's father, fell under the influence of Western education and the doctrine of freethinking, and lost that faith. He believed that the culmination of spirituality could be found in the mystical poems of the Persian poet Hafiz and the teachings of Jesus as recorded in the Bible. Narendra's father was drawn to those books to satisfy his spiritual appetite because his ignorance of Sanskrit kept him away from studying the Bhagavad Gita and other Hindu scriptures. We heard that once when Narendra's father saw him studying religious books, he presented Narendra with a Bible and told him, "If there is any religion to be found, it is in this book only."[5]

According to *Lilaprosango*, Viswanath Dutta might have read those books, but they didn't influence his life with any spirituality. Rather he followed the society of those people who were scholar in Western education of that period. He was busy in making himself happy and trying to please everyone around him with all worldly pleasures. In those days materialism and worldliness of Western countries made the educated society doubtful about religion and infidel in many ways, and very few people could save themselves from being influenced.

Bhupendranath also agreed that Viswanath Dutta was interested in Hafiz's poetry and in the Bible, but he was not ready to accept his father's ignorance in Sanskrit. He had no proof in support of his sentence, because he was then only a child of three years old when Viswanath Dutta died (23 February 1884). According to Bhupendranath, his father had completed his study of preuniversity, and hence he must have studied Sanskrit. Moreover, Viswanath Dutta studied in the school of Pandit Kalicharan Bhattacharya, who had been living in Dutta house for a short period. Viswanath Dutta studied astronomy and could make horoscope too. He wished to mention that after his father's death the *Srimadbhagavat* was found in his private collections. With all these above arguments Bhupendranath has denied his father's ignorance in Sanskrit.

But we cannot ignore the opinion of the author of *Lilaprosanga*. Because we hardly can believe that Reverend Swami Saradananda may comment such without knowing the truth. He had unlimited regard for the parents of Swami Vivekananda. Hence before coming to any conclusion more investigation is necessary.

Here we have a beautiful pen-picture drawn by reverend Swami Saradananda. He has described the social conditions of that period.

> Western materialism, which is based on the idea that earthly life is everything, had created a terrible scepticism—and sometimes even atheism—in the mind of people like

> Narendra's father. Those who propagated this materialism constantly tried to prove that there was nothing to be gained from our ancient rishis and scriptures except for weak-mindedness and superstition. As a result, many people lost their faith in religion and lost their moral strength. They harboured one idea inwardly but behaved differently and thus became selfish and hypocritical. For a short time, the Brahmo Samaj, established by Raja Rammohan Roy, tried to hold back the tide of materialism that swept the country, but due to Western influence and conflicts within the group, it split into two and was weakened. There is also some evidence that the members of both factions also succumbed somewhat to that materialism.[6]

Viswanath Dutta was well known for his sweet behavior. He was soft-hearted but knew how to become serious. He was very much aware of how to behave with whom, and how to teach someone. His system of teaching was beautiful and extraordinary. Once Narendranath, his son, asked him, "What have you done for me?" In reply Viswanath Dutta pointed his finger to a big mirror hanging on a wall and said, "Go, and look at yourself in the mirror, and then you'll know." Nothing was there to say any more. Narendranath didn't have any problem to understand what his father indicated. One more incident is known to us—Narendranath was arguing with his mother on some topic and had blurted some indecent words. Viswanath Dutta heard about this but didn't scold his son directly. On the door of a room, where Narendranath used to have friendly talks with others, he wrote with a piece of charcoal: "Today Narendranath has told these words to his mother—" adding the words that he had used. Narendranath felt ashamed and shriveled for a long time since his friends saw that note.

Once Narendranath asked his father, "How shall I conduct myself in the world?" Viswanath Dutta replied, "Never show surprise at anything." Probably with the effect of this advice Narendranath, at home and abroad, could enter the palaces and huts without any discrimination.

We also have come to know that Viswanath Dutta was fond of music. Once he learnt music from a music-teacher. Bhuvaneswari Devi, Narendra's mother, also was a good singer, and often used to sing lyrics from *Krishnayatra*. If ever a beggar would come to their house, she would request him to sit down so that she could learn his songs. Many of us know that Narendranath was also a famous singer of those days. Narendranath perhaps inherited the talent in music from his parents. Many times, he sang to Sri Ramakrishna on his request. It was seen many times, while Narendranath was singing, Sri Ramakrishna became overwhelmed with divine ecstasy and went in *Samadhi*; he seemed motionless, even breathless.

According to the rule of joint family, the eldest person is considered the head of the family. In accordance with this rule Kaliprosad Dutta was the head of the family. Viswanath Dutta, though used to earn more, was obedient to Kaliprosad for his seniority in family.

Taraknath, son of Kaliprosad, also started practicing law after he completed his education, and began to earn money. Family condition didn't allow Viswanath Dutta to own any property for his own children. Whenever he got an extra property, Kaliprosad grabbed it on the pretext of leadership in the family. Once Kaliprosad, due to paucity of fund, had mortgaged some gold ornament of Bhuvaneswari Devi; in lieu of transfering some property in her name. But, when she took possession of the property, the paper was found full of errors and omissions. Hence, she couldn't get the property. Viswanath and his wife, both were tenderhearted. Once, Viswanath Dutta bought his wife a piece of land from a Muslim. One day the Muslim descendants came to him and said, "We are too poor to pay the rent." Viswanath Dutta replied, "I'm not the owner of that land, it belongs to my wife." Then they went to meet Bhuvaneswari Devi, and listening to them she released them from paying tax. Sometimes it happened that Kaliprosad wanted to take possession of the property, which belonged to Bhuvaneswari Devi. Even he didn't hesitate to say, "Why won't you leave the property? Is it belonging to your father?" Bhuvaneswari Devi immediately signed the deed of conveyance.

These are the variety of causes for the financial downfall of Viswanath Dutta. Before a short period of his death Viswanath Dutta was very tactfully forced to live separately, so that they could grab his property. Then Viswanath Dutta went to a rented house at 7 Bahirav Biswas Lane with his family. According to Bhupendranath, Narendranath was then getting ready for B.A. exam.

According to the register of Kolkata Corporation, Viswanath Dutta died on 23 February 1884. But according to the appeal by Bhuvaneswari Devi to the High Court the date was 24 February 1884. At the time of death his resident was at 3, Gour Mohan Mukherjee Street. He felt a pain in his chest and had a cardiac attack. But the death certificate says that his death was caused by diabetes. That night Narendranath was in one of his friends' house, and, when he got the news, he rushed directly to the crematorium. His signature is found in the register of the crematorium.

Bhuvaneswari Devi, mother of Swami Vivekananda, was born in 1841. Nandalal Basu was her father and Raghumoni Devi, her mother. At the time of marriage Bhuvaneswari Devi was only a child of ten years and Viswanath Dutta, her husband, was of 16 years. Bhuvaneswari was the only daughter of her parents. In respect of merit and beauty she was a very good match for Viswanath Dutta. People, who saw her, would say that a lady like her was very rare on the earth. She was extremely beautiful, intelligent, good singer, virtuous and expert in various works. In all works for such a big family she managed time to sew, sing, and enjoy other pursuits. Her memory and intelligence were very much sharp. Her education did not beyond reading the *Ramayana* and the *Mahabharata*. She learned many things by listening to her husband and sons. It was hard to believe, during conversation with her, that she had learnt those things without reading any book. She had prodigious memory and great power of understanding. She could repeat anything after hearing it only for once; and she remembered everything that she had heard of or experienced long ago as though it had taken place the day before. She used to read the *Ramayana* and *Mahabharata* regularly. It is exceptionally good of Vivekananda and his two brothers that they all inherited the sharp memory from their mother.

It cannot be ignored that the influence of Vivekananda's parents was behind his becoming a good writer. Bhuvaneswari Devi, his mother, was also fond of composing poems and reading books. Her practice of reading books regularly continued till her death on 15 July 1911. A European lady used to come and teach her English. Vivekananda had his first lesson of English from his mother. She was moderate in her speeches, sweet in her behaviour and reserved in her manners. Other women felt elated by talking to her and while living in her sweet company.

Bhuvaneswari Devi taught her sons, "Always maintain purity in your life, defend your dignity, and never disrespect anybody. Try to maintain peace, but have strength of mind, if necessary."

Vivekananda said, "He, who cannot literally worship his mother, can never become great." He could say so, because he was the son of Bhuvaneswari Devi, a great mother.

Bhuvaneswari Devi had ten children—seven daughters and three sons. Vivekananda was the sixth of them. Her first child was a son, but no one could say much about him as he died at the age of only eight months. The beauty of this son was explained by the mother for a long time. His face was more or less similar to that of his grandfather. Next child was a daughter and died in infancy. Her name is not known to us. People say that she died at the age of two and a half years only. Haramoni, the third child, lived only for twenty years, and we know nothing more about her. Sarnamoyee Devi, the fourth child, lived a long life of 72 years. Bhupendranath Dutta has told that on every birthday of Vivekananda she used to send Rupees ten to Belur Math till her death. Bhuvaneswari Devi started this donation, and it was continued till the direct disciples of Sri Ramakrishna were in existence. Her fifth child was also a daughter, died at the age of only six years, and her name is unknown. Sixth child was Narendranath, lived for a short period of 39 years, 5 months and 24 days [1863-1902]. Seventh child was Kiranbala, lived for 18/19 years. Eighth child, Jogendrabala, lived for 25 years. Ninth and tenth children are respectively known as Mahendranath and Bhupendranath. Mahendranath lived for 88 years [1868-1956] and Bhupendranath died at 81 years [1880-1961].

After the death of her first son Bhuvaneswari Devi had four daughters, two of them died in childhood. Thereafter she became restless for having a son. Every day and night, at the time of worship, she used to express her sorrow to her deity. An old woman, her relative, lived at Varanasi. Bhuvaneswari Devi requested her, in a letter, to visit the temple of Lord Vireswara Siva regularly on behalf of her and pray on her behalf to God to fulfil her wish of having a son, the crowning glory of her family. In compliance with that request the old lady used to go to the temple of Vireswara to offer worship, and every day she prayed on behalf of Bhuvaneswari to grant her a son. Bhuvaneswari was blessed by God and she became the mother of three sons, but none of them ever got married.

We know very little about the daughters of Bhuvaneswari Devi. Detailed descriptions are not available. Some people had to be given new flats for their rehabilitation when the possession of the house, where Vivekananda was born, was transferred to the Ramakrishna Math and Mission. They are the descendants of Vivekananda's sisters.

It is known from a reliable source, while Vivekananda was wandering as an ascetic; Jogendrabala, his sister, committed suicide in her husband's house at Simla hill. Bhuvaneswari Devi had to take care of her two under-aged granddaughters (Jogendrabala's daughters). According to another source, when Bhuvaneswari Devi was afflicted with grief, this son-in-law, after his second marriage, came to meet her, and she received him with cordiality. Helpless mothers of this pitiable country can only have patience in each unbearable pain and maintain their duties silently.

How the daughters of Bhuvaneswari Devi got married and how much duty towards his daughters was carried out by Viswanath Dutta in his lifetime or what their brothers did for their marriage after their father's death, nothing is known to us. But it is known that Narendranath's elder sister was educated in English in Bethune School and two of his sisters got education in Christian Missionary School. Miss Kamini Shil, the principal of Bethune College, used to come home for teaching English to Jogendrabala, and Mrs. Macdonald was her second private tutor.

Bhuvaneswari Devi though dignified but was an afflicted woman for a long time. One after another premature death of children, suicide of a daughter, premature widowhood, and lawsuit with relatives, etc.—miseries came in succession.

Taraknath Dutta was the second son of Kaliprosad Dutta, Viswanath Dutta's uncle. Hence, Taraknath in relation with Vivekananda was his uncle. He was a famous lawyer of Kolkata High Court. Taraknath died on 25 February 1886. Gyanodasundari, the widow of Taraknath, was Vivekananda's aunt and she was at the centre of the above lawsuit. In July 1886, she brought up a case against Bhuvaneswari Devi. She lodged a complaint that the properties, registered in the name of Bhuvaneswari Devi, were all bought with the money earned by Taraknath, her husband. She also claimed that Viswanath Dutta, husband of Bhuvaneswari, never earned so much money that he could purchase any property. Even she said that Viswanath's family in Kolkata was also maintained with the money of her husband. But we know that Viswanath had been living a luxurious life with his family. His princely style of living, eating and drinking did not indicate that he had any financial problem. The period (1880-84), when the monthly income of an educated person of middle class was only Rupees 15, the monthly expenses of his family veered round Rupees one thousand.

Huge expenditure of court-case swallowed all the savings of Gyanodasundari, and she became as poor as a beggar. When she was near to the end of her life, she had to meet Vivekananda and ask for help. God didn't joke little less with Bhuvaneswari Devi; she had no end to her suffering for this Gyanodasundari. After the death of Swami Vivekananda, his aunt (this Gyanodasundari) used to visit Belur Math and shade tears.

Bhuvaneswari Devi was the only beloved child of her mother Raghumoni Devi. She was another amazing lady. She lived for 90 years and a helpless eyewitness to many mishaps. She had seen Bhuvaneswari being harassed in her husband's house, expelled from joint family, premature widowhood with a number of children, unexpected misfortune, etc.; and even she couldn't avoid seeing the premature death of Bilu, the only grandson, dearer than her life. She was the only daughter of Ghosh-family of Beadon Street, her father's name was Gopal Chandra Ghosh, and the year of her birth was 1825. Raghumoni was a true Vaishnava [devotee of Lord Vishnu].

One of the daughters of Bhuvaneswari Devi lived a completely helpless life in solitude, although she was married in a large joint family. After the premature death of her husband Bhuvaneswari had no source of income; the eldest son became a monk, the middle one was rambling continuously here and there, and the youngest son, when grown up, was engaged in fighting for the freedom of his country; once he was locked in jail, and as soon as he became free, he left the country and voluntarily exiled himself. In this terrible situation, Raghumoni Devi, grandmother of Swami Vivekananda, always stood by her and became the only shelter. This lady, a true Vaishnava, lived till the death of her daughter in 1911, and died on the day after next day. Bhuvaneswari died of meningitis on 25 July 1911, and Raghumoni Devi expired on 27th July just at the interval of a single day. At the time of death she was a resident of Nimtala Gangayatri Niwas. It was Mahendranath, the only relative, who signed the register of crematory. Bhupendranath, in his book, has given some different dates; we have mentioned the record of corporation.

Helpless Bhuvaneswari Devi had to take shelter in her mother's house. Narendranath, her eldest son, used to go there frequently. This house at Ramtanu Bose Lane is the witness of many touching events. Another resident of this house was Raimoni Devi, great-grandmother of Vivekananda, who started staying here with her daughter after her husband's death.

Bhuvaneswari Devi had only a dwelling-house and a land of about two kathas (1 katha = 720 sq. ft.) as her parental property, which was to be inherited by her sons. Viswanath Dutta, Vivekananda's father, was gifted a farmhouse by his grandmother. But Bhupendranath, Vivekananda's younger brother, said, "Viswanath's second uncle (mother's second brother) suddenly appeared there, and convinced him to sign a paper to transfer the property to his hand. I heard this story from my mother. She also supported her husband in signing the paper. She said that if he would not sign the paper his uncle (father's brother) would have grabbed the same. At that time everyone of the family was trying to sell the house of Madhu Roy Lane. Viswanath signed his part of the property in the name of his uncle."

With reference to his mother, Bhuvaneswari Devi, Swami Vivekananda said, "The love which my mother gave to me has made me what I am, and I owe a debt to her that I can never repay."[7] He was proud of his mother's controlling power. He said, "Once my mother had fast for fourteen days." We have seen the reflection of such power in his life. Sometime before his death he didn't drink water for twenty-one days following the advice of a physician.

Who doesn't want to see his son getting married? Bhuvaneswari Devi also wished to see the marriage of her son. The next day of the of the death of Viswanath Dutta was fixed for going to select a bride for Narendranath. Bhupendranath Dutta wrote that Viswanath Dutta had a friend, who was an attorney at Calcutta High Court. He proposed the marriage between Narendranath and his granddaughter, and on condition of that marriage he promised to bear the expenditure of the court-case.

Mother's line of Vivekananda was Vaishnav [devotee of Sri Krishna] and father's line was Shakto [devotee of Kali], and Viswanath Dutta was fond of the Bible. Every morning Raimoni, great-grandmother of Vivekananda, used to sing Krishna-Katha [divine play of Sri Krishna] so long she was alive. Mahendranath was influenced by the Vaishnava culture. He didn't eat or drink anything without offering water to the Tulsi plant [a sacred plant in Hindu belief]. No onion was used in cooking. Even he had to eat cow dung. Western cauliflower was not allowed to enter the kitchen. Once they all went to Raipur with Viswanath Dutta. Let us listen to Mahendranath, when he said, "On the way, at Ghoratala, meat was cooked. I won't eat that. Elder brother thrust a piece of meat into my mouth and started striking on my back with fists and forced me to eat. What next? I did the same as a tiger does after having the taste of blood."

Vivekananda had been really a hero since his childhood. He is awarded as the Divine incarnation of the age, because he never haggled with the truth. The foundation of this firmness in his character was built by Bhuvaneswari Devi, his mother. With reference to this context we remember a remarkable incident. One day in school, when he was Narendranath, a geography teacher punished him because he thought that his answer was not appropriate to the question. Narendranath reproached, "I am not wrong at all, what I told was very much correct indeed." At this reproach the teacher became much angry and beat him hard with stick. Narendranath returned home with eyes full of tears and expressed everything to his mother that had happened in school. Mother heard him and said, "My child, what does it matter, if you are in the right path? Always follow the truth without caring about the result. Very often you may have to suffer injustice or unpleasant consequences for holding to the truth; but you must not, under any circumstances, abandon it." Thus, Bhuvaneswari Devi, the mother, taught his eldest son Narendranath and inspired him in leading a hard and brave life of Vivekananda. Here we must say that the teacher, who punished Narendranath that day, realized his fault later and acknowledged his mistake too.

Vivekananda had acknowledged the kind influence of his mother in all good works done by him. In a lecture in abroad he referred to the selfless love and the divine character of his mother. He said, "I am indebted to my mother for efflorescence of my knowledge."

When Viswanath Dutta was alive, monthly expenditure for maintaining his family was Rupees one thousand, but after his death Bhuvaneswari Devi had to manage her family with only about Rupees thirty for a month. This downfall of monthly expenditure easily shows the amount of misery that she had to suffer. With reference to this context Reverend Swami Saradananda has reported:

> When she was in deep poverty after her husband's death, she developed patience, perseverance, courage, and other noble qualities. ...she was never disheartened. She managed her little family with that meager income so efficiently that people assumed her monthly allotment to be much higher than it was. ...she had no guaranteed income with which to maintain the family, but she nonetheless had to support her mother and children who had been brought up in opulence, and she had to meet the children's educational expenses. Instead of helping her, the relatives who had been making good money with her husband's assistance now took the opportunity to attempt to deprive her of her legitimate right to her property and possessions. Although her eldest son, Narendra, had many good qualities, he could not find a job despite his best efforts. Moreover, he had become disgusted with the world and was slowly to renounce it forever. One cannot help but appreciate and respect Bhuvaneswari as one considers how she performed her duties calmly and steadily in that terrible situation.[8]

It is necessary to mention here a scene of a play that was played by God with Bhuvaneswari Devi. One day she along with her son, Mahendranath, went to Cossipore garden house to visit Sri Ramakrishna. We would like to know the rest of it from Mahendranath Dutta. He said, "Mother took me to the room of Ramakrishna. It was a large and specious room on the first floor, where on a bed at the middle of the room Sri Ramakrishna was sitting in a posture of half-laid down leaning back on a dumpy bolster. As we entered the room, he looked at us and said, 'Doctor has forbidden me for talking, but I must have to talk to you. It's good that you have come. Take Naren back to home with you. Girish and others together forced him to put on the dress of a monk, but I at once reproached and said—how is that possible Naren? You have a mother, who is widow, and have a little brother, who is too young to take care of himself. You cannot become a monk.' After that Narendranath set out for home with me and my mother. On the way, while we were sitting in a carriage, my mother said to Narendranath everything that she was told by Sri Ramakrishna. Narendranath replied, 'He says the thief to steal, and advices the family man to be alert.'"

We cannot help but become surprised to see that how can He, who says the thief to steal and advices the family man to be alert, become so kind to help someone keeping himself hidden.

Bhuvaneswari Devi used to wear a silk cloth while she did her daily prayer to God. But her cloth was no more wearable. She said to Naren, "I need a new cloth for my daily prayer." Narendranath silently bent his head down and left the place as he didn't have sufficient money for buying a new cloth for his mother. By that time a devotee came to Sri Ramakrishna to give him a new cloth. The Master took the cloth and said to Naren, "Take this cloth for your mother; she will wear it for her daily prayer." Narendranath didn't receive the cloth. Later on the Master sent someone to Bhuvaneswari Devi to give her the cloth. Who can understand His divine play!

Vivekananda had faith in God that He will maintain his family. This is very much clear in his speech. One day, when Narendranath used to visit the Master regularly, Bhuvaneswari Devi asked him, "What is this? Wandering day and night without any aim! Do you have any idea, how this family will be maintained?" Narendranath replied, "Who am I to maintain the family? He, who is the father of everyone, will do His duty."

Again in relation with the family, we heard Bhuvaneswari Devi teaching moral lesson to his sons, "Worldly life is always full of trouble, but to neglect the moral character is to pollute you."

Co-disciples of Vivekananda looked after Bhuvaneswari Devi and her mother till the last day of their life. They went to visit many holy places along with Vivekananda's mother. Bhuvaneswari

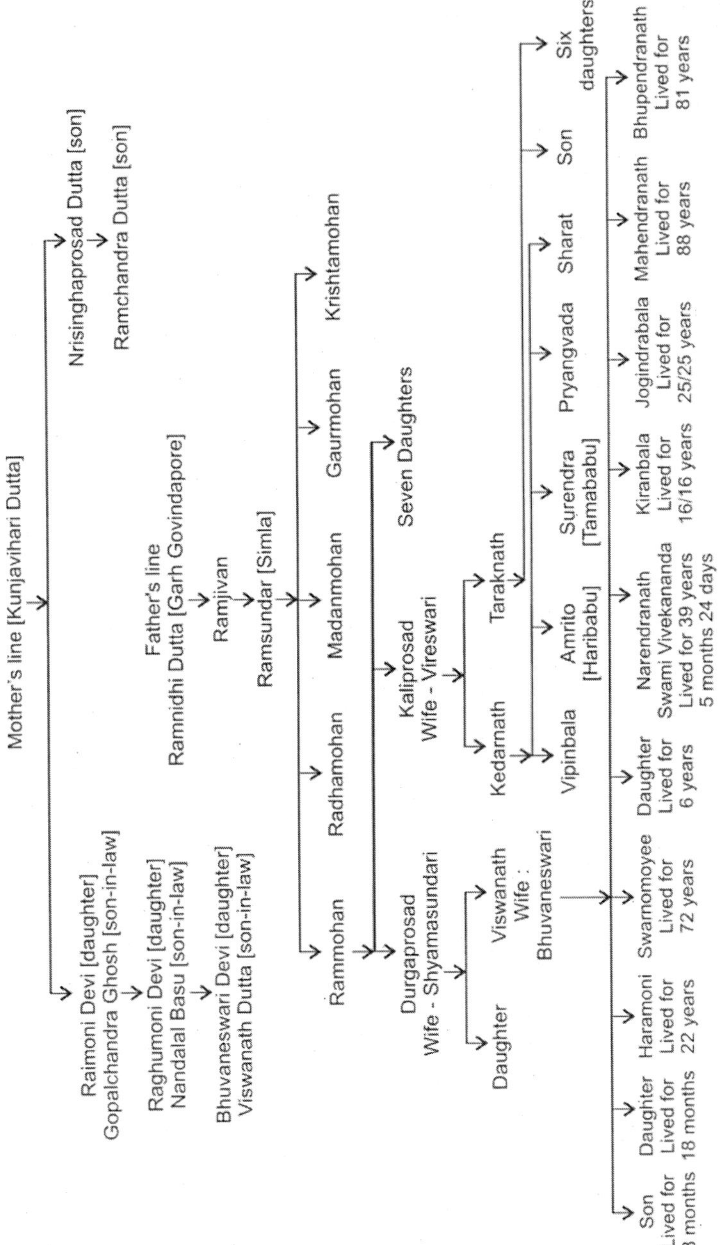

Devi went on pilgrimage last to Puri in 1911. Returning from there she was attacked with meningitis. She was treated by Dr. J.N. Kanjilal. She died on 25 July 1911. Bhupendranath Dutta has written in his book that on that day he was in New York and dreamt that his mother was dead.

Bhuvaneshwari Devi (1841-1911)

The only picture of Swami Vivekananda's mother, daughter of Mr. Nandalal Bose & Mrs. Raghumani Devi

Raghumani Devi

(The metarnal grandmother of Swami Vivekananda)

Vivekananda's ancestral house (foreground) 3 Gour Mohan Mukherjee Lane Calcutta

Vivekananda's ancestral house as it is today

2
Birth and Childhood of Vivekananda

When two out of four daughters died in young age, Bhuvaneswari Devi became restless for a son. She didn't have peace. Day and night she was praying to God sitting in front of the idol of Lord Shiva. We have already told about an old lady, who used to visit the temple of Lord Vireswara at Varanasi daily following the request of Bhuvaneswari Devi. Every day she used to offer worship and prayed for a son on behalf of Bhuvaneswari.

The days passed by, Bhuvaneswari Devi had concentrated her faith on the God. She started meditating Lord Shiva every day and night. She didn't stop chanting the holy name of Shiva even when she was busy in her household work. Shiva is said to be pleased with the Bel leaves. Shiva is also easier to be pleased than any other God or Goddess. He fulfills the wishes of His devotee. Bhuvaneswari Devi also had such a faith in God, and she absorbed herself in the worship of Shiva for the gratification of her desire.

Some days later many family-members began to say—"She (Bhuvaneswari) has become more beautiful. Her face has been glowing more and more, a wonderful light has been radiating from her body. One day Bhuvaneswari Devi was found absorbed in worship in her private room for prayer, and she didn't have any sense how the day had passed and the evening melted in dark. That night she dreamt that Lord Shiva came out of his divine trance and arrived in front of her with the form of her son. She enjoyed the beauty of Shiva and felt her heart full of joy. Suddenly, she woke up and chanted "Shiva! Shiva! Shiva..." She began to think with wonder—is it only a dream? Or is it a wave of light of the truth? Who knows when this dream will come true!"

It was 12 January 1863. Early morning of Monday, 6 hours and 49 minutes, the lunar day of Krishna Septami, star—Hasta, point of time—Capricorn, zodiac sign—Virgo, clan—Dev, class—Sudra. It was holy day of *Paus Sankranti* (according to the Bengali calendar it is the last day the month Paus). *Paus Sankranti* is a Hindu festival, also known as *Pausparvan* or *Makar Sankranti* (marking the transition of the sun from Sagittarius to Capricorn, in Magh). It is commonly believed that a dip in the Ganges on this day washes away all sins. It is also the time to begin the vow of *Dadhi Sankranti*. In some areas it is the time for a new crop festival marked by making cakes in every home. An unprecedented flash of light came from Varanasi and touched the land of Simla in north Kolkata, when Vivekananda was born as a beautiful child as a partial incarnation of Lord Shiva lightening the lap of Bhuvaneswari Devi. Sri Ramakrishna saw in a vision a streak of light flash across the sky from Varanasi towards Simla, at north Calcutta. In a great joy he exclaimed, "My prayer has been granted and my man must come to me one day."

Everyone, who saw the new-born baby, was surprised and said, "He looks mostly like Durgaprosad, his grandfather." Someone said, "Durgaprosad couldn't forget his family, and therefore, has arrived again with a new body." At the time of giving a name to the new-born baby most of the family members said, "Let's call him Durgadas." But Bhuvaneswari Devi didn't like that name. She looked deeply into the eyes of her son, as if she was trying to find out something there. Thus, after gazing at her son for a long time she thought for a while and said, "Name? His name is Vireswar." Nobody had any objection to such a good name. Since that day everyone called him by the name Vireswar or Bile. Bhuvaneswari called him 'Bilu' with most affection. No doubt 'Bilu' was good to call as a nickname, but there should be another beautiful name for outsiders. The other name was decided as 'Narendranath'. 'Bilu' had another nickname. A quarter to six feet high Vivekananda was also called 'Bente Shala' by his fourth grandfather. It means Vivekananda was shorter than other men of Dutta-family.

One day Bhuvaneswari Devi came to Belur Math and standing on the ground she called Vivekananda with a loud voice, "Bilu…u…u…" As soon as Vivekananda heard mother's voice, he rushed to the ground and talked to her with his calm, heavy and sweet voice.

This is he, whose uncontrollable naughtiness forced his mother to say—"Wished to have Shiva, but He has sent a Ghost." Overwhelming with love every mother on this earth is heard to make an expression like this.

Mahendranath, Vivekananda's brother, said, "One day while Bilu was crawling on corridor, an old Brahmin lady had been gazing at him for a long time. She said, "This son of Viswanath must be an incarnation of God, he is having a beautiful body and sweet manner like that of God. If he remains alive and grows up, he will work like God." Saying this she passed her hand with love on his head and blessed him a lot.

Days went on in its course. Narendranath became three years old. But his restlessness had no end. Almost from every corner was raised complaint against him for breaking peace. Mother couldn't control his son, he was very much obstinate. He must do what he once decides to do. None can restrain him. Everyone was impatient with his naughtiness. Scolding, prattling or frightening—everything was useless. If there was anything that he didn't like, he became angry immediately. His mother would say, "I had prayed and made a special offering to the Lord Vireswara of Varanasi for a son, but perhaps He sent me one of His demons instead." When Naren was found angry for some reason, his mother found it extremely hard to control him. However, she found that even when Naren grew extremely restless, if cold water was poured on his head at the same time chanting the name of Shiva in his ear, the child would quiet down. Some time she frightened him and said, "If you again play a mischievous trick Shiva will not let you go to Kailash." What a surprise! He at once would stop shouting and would calm down in a moment.

Although Narendranath was a crazy boy, he had a good quality too. He considered everyone as his relative. If anyone would call him politely, he at once would be ready to ride on his lap. Narendranath was always obedient to sweet behaviour; he could never tolerate any hard word.

Whenever the Western disciples of Swami Vivekananda would hear these stories from his mother, they couldn't keep their laughter concealed. They would say, "Well, then in his childhood Swamiji too was a naughty boy!" "Of course, he was." Mother would reply, "There were two maid-servants always to take care of him." She would often chat, "From his childhood onward, Narendra had a terrible weakness. If he became angry for any reason, he completely lost control and destroyed furniture and other things in the house."

Whenever *Sadhus* (monk) visited their house, he would rush to see him. No one could control him. If a monk would ask him for anything, he didn't feel well till he could give him the same.

As a result the elders of the house some time would feel very uneasy. Once he gave a piece of new cloth which he was wearing to a *Sadhu*. *Sadhu* blessed him and went away.

In those days *Sadhus* used to visit the Dutta house every now and then. Viswanath Dutta had a great respect for *Sadhus* and *Fakirs*. He liked to entertain them at his best. Since they had experienced earlier about Naren's behaviour, his parents locked him up whenever *Sadhus* came to the house. But it was hard to control him; whenever Naren could see the *Sadhus* he would throw things to them through the window. Thus, he felt a great joy by being able to harass his elders. Now and then he said that he would become a *Sadhu* himself someday.

One more thing was noticed in Narendranath. Often in course of his playing with his friends—suddenly he was found stop playing and stand still on the ground. His friends got surprised to see that strange behaviour of Naren and asked him, "Hallow brother! What happened to you?" But they were afraid to touch him. Everyone watched that he was no more as before; as if he was a stranger. But after a little while he became as before. Again he started playing. He was such a natural meditative person since his boyhood.

He also liked to play at meditation. He would sit with some of his friends in front of an image of Sita-Rama or Shiva. Then they all would meditate and think about God. He would get lost in his thoughts about God and for a while he would not see or feel anything around him. Once a cobra came gliding along the ground. The other boys were frightened and ran away, but Naren stayed unmoved. They shouted at him, but he didn't hear them. After some time the snake went away. Later his parents asked Naren why he had not run away. He replied, "I didn't know anything about the snake. I was feeling very happy."

Narendranath was not much friendly with his sisters. He never left any opportunity to harass them. When they tried to catch Naren, he would run away and stood near garbage or by a dirty drain, wherefrom he would make faces at them with a bright smile. None of his sisters could go there to touch him. He didn't care any profanity. He made faces with a smile and said, "Catch me if you can."

Narendranath was fond of animals and birds. He liked to play with pet animals. Western rat, monkey, goat, peacock, cockatoo and pigeon, etc. were his playmate. He loved the cow which was kept as a pet in their house. He often used to decorate her with a garland and mark a dot with vermilion on her forehead, and some time would chat with her.

He was very much friendly with the valets of his house. In his childhood he had a strange hobby, he liked to hear the sound of carts running on the road of Kolkata. Whenever he could hear the sound of a cart, he rushed out of the house to watch it running. It seemed to him that a coachman was a person of high class. They were not ordinary persons. It would be a great pleasure to him, if he could be able to move around the city, sitting with the coachman in his box at the top of the cart.

One day Naren was on a tour with his parents by a carriage. He was sitting on his mother's lap and asking so many questions to his father. His curiosity had no end. In the meantime father asked him, "What do you like to be in future?" Little boy at once replied, "I would like to be a coachman." As if he had no doubt that there was no other profession as great as that of a coachman. Being influenced with the above idea he often would go to stable to see the horse. That was his favourite place. He liked to go there often because he liked horses.

The coachman of the house influenced him with a dream, "Look Bilu babu, one day I'll teach you to ride a horse, and the horse will take to the roof of the house and a sound like Tog..

Bog.. Tog.. Bog.. will arise by the hoofs of it. The horse will fly in the sky. There is a winged horse which can fly above the cloud." Bilu promised to buy a winged horse.

Although he finally didn't have any winged horse, yet fortunately a white horse was arranged. Young Narendranath learnt riding horse. He used to run here and there of the city with his horse. No such photography of his riding horse is available, but the description of such event is found written by many authors. Aswinikumar Dutta is one of them who had experienced about Vivekananda riding a horse.

It was probably May or June of 1897. Aswinikumar went to Almorah. One day he heard his cook saying, "A strange Bengali *Sadhu* has come, speaks English, moves around on a horse like a king." Aswinikumar guessed who might be the *Sadhu*, and he went out in search of that heroic monk. He asked a man about the monk. The man replied, "Swami Vivekananda? Who is that fellow? I don't know him. Oh! *Sadhu*, who rides a horse? There he is on his horse."

Aswinikumar saw that a man with a cloth dyed with red ochre was riding a horse and running it very fast. The horse stopped in front of a house and a European person caught the horse while the monk got down.

Narendranath after becoming Swami Vivekananda rode horse for several times. With reference to this context we may quote some lines from his letters—"I would have given you a surprise if you had seen me bounding from rock to rock like a chamois, or galloping might and main up and down mountain roads."[1]

"It is a beautiful mountain park I am living in now. On the north, extending almost all along the horizon, are peak after peak of the snow-clad Himalayas forests abounding."[2]

"I am getting exceptionally adept in riding and do not feel the least pain or exhaustion even after a run of twenty or thirty miles at a stretch."[3]

"I began to take a lot of exercise on horseback, both morning and evening. Since then I am very much better indeed. I was so much better the first week of my gymnastics that I have scarcely felt so well since I was a boy and used to have *kusti* (wrestling) exercises. I really began to feel that it was a pleasure to have a body. Every movement made me conscious of strength—every movement of the muscles was pleasurable. That exhilarating feeling has subsided somewhat. Yet I feel very strong. In a trial of strength I could make both G.G. and Niranjan go down before me in a minute."[4]

Naren's mother told him stories from the *Mahabharata* and the *Ramayana*. He loved to hear the story of Sri Rama. The story of *Ramayana* influenced him with the character of Sita and Rama. Somehow he managed to save a small amount of money. One day he went to market along with Hari, his local friend, and bought a small clay image of Sita-Rama. Both of them went to the garret and locked the door from inside. Naren put the image of Sita-Rama somewhere on the floor and began to worship it with flowers. Naren closed his eyes sitting in front of the image and absorbed himself in meditation; he lost his sense of time and place. On the other side elders of the family started searching Narendranath as they didn't find him for hours long. Everyone in the house indulged in a tumultuous affair. The little boy was found nowhere in the house. In the meantime someone said, "We have not yet gone to the roof. I think we must go there, isn't it?" When they went there, the door of the roof was found locked from inside. They called him by his name loudly but got no reply from the other side of the door. Finally, it was decided to break the door. When they broke the door, Hari was found sitting in a corner. He was afraid of seeing the people at large and immediately ran away from there. But Narendranath was sitting silently with his eyes closed. He lost himself in meditation. When he was pushed hard, he came back to his sense.

Narendranath, as we have said, used to visit the stable every now and then. One day a funny matter was happened. A good friendship was established between Naren and the all-knowing syce. Whenever Naren wanted to know something, he would go to ask him. That day the syce seemed to have promised himself to raise a storm of hard realism in the innocent mind of young Narendranath. Somehow his conjugal life was filled with unhappiness, so he had no affection with any married life. He, in course of conversation, said to Naren, "It is very bad to marry." He also referred to his experience and tried to convince him that a married life is full of trifling, arguments, anger and many other problems. It increases the number of dependent for maintenance. It increases the number of relatives, who are very selfish. In short, marriage makes a man unhappy and slave. Naren heard him and felt that he was right, then at once decided not to marry in his life. But he simultaneously felt a terrible problem. What should he do with the idol of Sita-Rama? They, whom he had been worshiping for a long time, are also a married couple. He heard from his mother that there was an extraordinary love between Sita and Rama. It was a heavenly love with endless joy. But the syce has made a contradictory image in his mind. His mind was vacillating on account of doubt. He couldn't make himself calm and, therefore, began to weep again and again. What is wrong and what is right—he couldn't discriminate. He felt sorry for Sita-Rama. He went into the house and expressed his sorrow to his mother. Mother, on hearing everything, said, "Bilu! So what? You worship Lord Shiva."

Narendranath, as the evening covered with darkness, went to the garret and sat silently for a while. He looked at the image of Sita-Rama with a sigh. Then he lifted up the idol and threw it on the road. The clay image broke into pieces as it fell on the hard road. Next day he went to market and bought an idol of Shiva. He put the idol of Shiva in place of Sita-Rama and absorbed himself in meditation sitting in front of it.

Although the above solution was nothing but a childish game, yet he had felt peace in his mind. But later we will see him not losing his respect towards Sita-Rama, his devotion was beyond compare. The story of the *Ramayana*, that he heard sitting on the lap of his mother, had never been faded in his mind, although the story of the groom was full of his bitter experience of a married life. Rather it became stronger by the experience of Western culture. Especially, the character of Hanuman of the *Ramayana* attracted him in his childhood. Sri Hanuman, the strange worker, and the heroic devotee of Rama, was his ideal; he never missed to watch the divine play of the *Ramayana* whenever he would get any news of the same. He liked to listen to the reading of the *Ramayana*. One day he heard that Hanuman lived in banana grove. He asked the reader, "Can I see him if I go to a banana grove?" The reader laughed at the boy and said, "Better you may go there and see him with your own eyes." There was a banana grove near his house. On his way to return home he went to the banana grove and stayed for a long time, hoping to see Sri Hanuman. When, after waiting for a long time, he couldn't see Sri Hanuman, he returned home with broken heart and expressed his sorrow to the elders. They tried to console him, "Hay Bilu, perhaps he has gone somewhere else to do some urgent work, and that is why you couldn't see him." This assurance made him calm down.

Vivekananda, since his childhood, was inclined to the life of ascetics. One day he was loitering wearing a small piece of ochre cloth tied around his waist, his mother saw that and asked, "What is this?" Little Narendranath screamed with joy, "I am Shiva." He heard elders saying if someone meditates continuously like a sage, he develops a mass of matted hair that reaches the ground. Boys are naturally innocent. As he sat at meditation, motionless, he sometimes opened his eyes to see whether his hair had become matted and grown long enough to plunge into the earth like the roots of a banyan tree. When he found his efforts were in vain, he rushed to his mother and said, "Why is it so! I meditated for a long time but couldn't see my hair growing long and matted!" Mother consoled him and said, "It is not a matter of an hour or of a day. You need a long period for that."

Elders usually saw Narendranath sitting at meditation either lonely or with some of his friends. No one knew what the boy was thinking! Whenever he was at meditation, he had no sense of what was happening around him. He became so much absorbed in meditation that no one would get any response to his call. Here we would like to mention a strange event in this connection. Let's know the event as he said:

> One day when I was still seated after meditation, the room filled with a divine effulgence and the striking figure of a monk suddenly appeared, standing before me at a little distance. He wore and ochre cloth and held a *Kamandalu* [water pot] in his hand. His face was calm, serene, and indifferent to the world, and its contemplative expression captivated me. He walked towards me slowly, fixing his gaze on me as if he wanted to say something. But I was so seized with fear that I couldn't keep still. I got up, opened the door, and quickly stepped out of the room. The next moment I thought, 'Why should I be afraid?' I boldly returned to my room to hear what the monk had to say, but he wasn't there, though I waited for him a long time. I sadly asked myself, 'Why did I foolishly run away without listening to him?' I've seen many monks but never have I seen such an extraordinary expression on any other face. That face was imprinted on my heart forever.[5]

However, he never saw the face again, and couldn't find out the truth. He said, "I may be wrong, but quite often I think that I was blessed on that day with a vision of Buddha."

Another strange thing was his sleep. He couldn't sleep like others. He used to lie on his bed in the way people bow down touching the ground with their foreheads. He sued to see all his life a wonderful point of light between his eyebrows, as soon as he closed his eyes in order to sleep. He would observe its various changes. The point of light kept changing its colours and increasing in size, and it became gradually converted into a form of a ball, and bursting at last, covered his body from head to foot with white liquid light. As soon as it happened, he got asleep. He believed that it happens naturally with all people, so he didn't disclose the matter to anyone. Later, when he grew up and practiced daily with a few friends according to the instructions of Maharshi Devendranath, he asked his friends whether they could see the same during meditation. He came to know that they never had such vision of a light, and none of them went to sleep in that way. Later in 1882 Sri Ramakrishna, when heard of such vision, said, "They, who are perfect in meditation, only can see this light." Narendranath had experienced the vision throughout his life, though towards the end it was not so much prominent.

One day after a long period a brother disciple of Vivekananda requested him to show him the vision of light. Swamiji touched his forehead, and immediately the brother disciple saw—everything of the material world was completely changed, he started seeing only an overwhelming ocean of light.

Narendranath, from his childhood and onward, had love for his friends as well as indomitable courage. Therefore, he could take the role of a leadership in his student life and later when he became head of the Ramakrishna Order. When he was only a boy, he became the leader of the boys who were almost similar to his age. Once, on the day of *Makar Sankranti*, he requested his father to allow worshiping the Ganges with some of his school-fellows. With reference to this context Mahendranath said that in those days there was a custom of worshipping the Ganges followed by singing in adoration about her beauty and wonderful qualities. On the day of *Makar Sankranti*, Viswanath used to offer new dresses to the teachers and some of his students, and he allowed them playing musical instruments and singing in adoration while they go to worship the Ganges, the holy river. He offered them sweets when they would return home. Boys used to sing in one voice while going in a procession all along the road till they reached the bank of the river. They offered flowers and lamps to the holy river. Lamps they offered on bark of banana tree floated on the wave of water and went as if to the ocean when the shadow of evening melted in darkness.

Narendranath in his childhood usually took the role of a king while he played his favourite game—'Raja-Kotal' [king and police] with his friends. The corridor of the worship room of Dutta house was as high from the ground as the height of a man. The court was held on a flight of stairs leading from the courtyard to the worship room. Naren, of course, used to sit on the top step and ordered two of his friends to sit on the lower steps, and said, "You are the prime minister, and you are the commander-in-chief"; rest of the boys were ordered to sit on the lowest step according to their rank as they were the general members of his court. When the king arrived, his workers would salute him lying down on the ground. The king asked, "Minister, how is the empire?" Sometime the minister would say, "My Lord, people are very happy", or sometime he said, "A dacoit is making mischief." The king at once ordered, "Kill him soon." Then and there a group of ten to eleven boys became busy to punish the dacoit. The dacoit didn't surrender himself, he rushed to the main gate of the house, and the policemen ran after him. Servants of the house were getting a nap after having meal at noon. They couldn't sleep in piece as the boys ran around them. Servants woke up and ran after the boys to punish them. But they couldn't catch any one of them, and finally being tired they would sit together and grumble. Narendranath sitting on his throne used to enjoy the scene and would smile silently.

Narendranath liked to play different games on different days. In those days gas-light was newly introduced in Calcutta. Soda-lemonade was sold in shops. Narendranath managed to gather machineries and made an imitation gas-works and a factory for producing gas and soda-lemonade. Even the railway system was also arranged. The factory was established on the lawn of Dutta house, and some pipes made up of zinc, clay pitchers and some dry thatches were its machineries. When the thatches were set on fire it produced smoke that would come out through the pipe and spread in the sky. Narendranath looked at the sky with his hands at his waist and felt pleasure for that successful discovery while he watched everything seriously like a wise man. Sometime if everything was not according to his direction he said to his friends, "There is something wrong, fire is not sufficient, go on puffing more; I need to see more gas."

About the gas-works his younger brother writes as follows:

> With old zinc tubes, earthen cooking-pots and straw he made his gas-works in the outer courtyard of the house. The straw when lighted gave out a peculiar smoke, but to his mind it was a miniature gas-works, which lighted the whole city of Calcutta. It was amusing to see his gas-works and himself as he stood with arms akimbo, gravely looking at his contrivance as the smoke issued forth. Sometimes, however, he would express disapproval by turning up his nose—a family peculiarity—and impatiently ordering his

playmates to put more fuel on the fire, or to blow more fiercely whenever the smoke rose up too sluggishly.[6]

Viswanath Dutta had a Muslim client, who loved Narendranath very much. Narendranath called him 'Chacha'. Whenever he would come to meet Viswanath, Naren rushed to him and listened to the account of his journey—how he had travelled places like Punjab, Afghanistan, etc. that are difficult to access by riding camel or on a horse. The story had neither any point of beginning nor any end. But Narendranath never felt tired of listening to those stories. Chacha used to bring sweets for Narendranath, and he took them with pleasure. When other clients saw Narendranath eating sweets brought by a Muslim, they considered it as a depraved practice and made faces with irritation. Viswanath, when entered the room, could understand the situation, but didn't say anything to his son because he was very much liberal in eating and drinking.

One day that Muslim gentleman was sitting in the drawing room and telling the story of the king Akbar. Suddenly, a loud cry was heard from inside the house—"Narendranath has fallen rolling down the staircase leading to the Thakur-Dalan [worship hall] and he has become senseless." Doctor came, and after a long struggle of an hour Narendranath got his sense back. Doctor said, "The wound is deep, but there is nothing to be worried." Since that day Narendranath had a mark of that wound till the end of his life. Later Sri Ramakrishna, when heard of the incident, remarked, "In a way it was a good thing. If he had not thus lost some of his blood, he would have created havoc in the world with his excessive energy."

In those days untouchability and caste-distinction was a common practice. Two men of different castes sitting with each another was could not be thought of. One, if touched by someone of lower caste, had to take bath. People of higher caste got afraid of being outcast by eating anything given or cooked by a man of lower caste. Naren's father, as we have said, was a lawyer. Many clients came to see him. He entertained them and offered them tobacco to smoke. There were many pipes for different castes in the drawing room of Viswanath Dutta. No one touched the pipe for another caste. Narendranath heard and also saw this system but couldn't find any solution of this mystery. Why was a member of one caste not ready to eat with members of other caste? Why were there different tobacco pipes for the different castes? Would there be an explosion? What was the reason they were afraid of? Would the roof fall down? Narendranath didn't know any answer to these questions. He decided to find out for himself. One day, when there was no one in his father's drawing room, he went there and took a whiff from one pipe. Nothing happened. He tried all pipes in turn and took whiff from each of them. Still he found nothing to happen. He found no change in anything of the world. In the meantime, his father entered the room, and got surprised to see the madly action of his son. He asked Naren, "What are you doing?" "O father!" Naren replied fearlessly, "I was trying to see what would happen if I broke caste." His father was startled by seeing that wonderful experiment and the strange technique of finding out a solution; he couldn't help but burst out into a laughter and went out of the room saying—"Naughty boy!"

We have heard of his leadership. But it doesn't mean that he was infatuated with any kind of domination for being a boss. He would never be tired of repeating a proverb—"*Sirdar to Sardar*—The giver of the head is alone the leader", that means, he alone can be a leader who is ready to die for others. It is true that he could be a leader of his friends because he was always seen ready to sacrifice his life for them. He was then only a boy of six years old. One day Naren along with his playmates went to visit *Chadaka/Chaitra Mela* [a festival of worshipping God Shiva]. There he bought a clay image of Shiva. One of his friends fell behind while they were returning home in the dark of late evening. Suddenly, Narendranth realized a carriage was proceeding towards them from behind. He looked back and saw his friend was about to go under the hoof of horse. People, who walking on the road, cried, "He'll die...will die." No one came to help him. Narendranath, keeping the image of Siva under his arm, rushed to his friend and saved his life by pulling his hand with all his strength. People, who witnessed the incident, resounded with a compliment to Narendranath. Narendranath didn't pay much attention to them, he returned home and said everything of that to his mother. Mother blessed him a lot and said, "Bravo! You have really done the work of a man. Always try to be proper human being."

In another incident Narendranath was seeded to save a mother and her son. Once he went to see the fort near esplanade with twenty to twenty-five boys. One of them suddenly became ill. Other boys didn't take his illness seriously, and they walked ahead. Narendranath was also walking gladly. Suddenly, he remembered the boy who was sick. He turned back and found the boy was sitting by the road and he looked very tired. He at once rushed to him and found the boy had been suffering from high fever and trembling too. Naren immediately helped him to get into a car and brought him to home.

Since his childhood onward, Narendranath had compassion for his friends and he was tremendously brave. It was an incident when he was only a boy of seven or eight years old. One day Naren and his friends hired a boat at Chandpal ghat for a trip to Metiabruz to visit the Zoological Gardens of Wazid Ali, the former Nawab of Lucknow. During their return trip one of the boys felt sick and couldn't help but vomit in the boat. The boatman became annoyed very much and stopped rowing his boat little before reaching at the Chandpal, he said, "I shall not allow anyone to leave until the boat is cleaned up." The boys offered to pay to have someone else clean it, but the boatman didn't agree to this. He threatened the boys, "I shall not anchor the boat at the ghat." The argument and threatening gradually was about to turn into a fight while other nearby boatmen joined and prepared to assault the boys. Most of the boys became frightened and could decide what to do.

Narendranath was the youngest among them, and while the quarreling was going on, he cleverly stepped aside and jumped on the shore. The boatmen considered him a little boy and, therefore, didn't try to stop him. Naren stood on the shore and saw that the situation was going to be serious. He was thinking how to save his friends. Meanwhile he saw two English soldiers walking along the street. He rushed to them, greeted them, and caught hold of their hands. Despite his deficiency in English, he tried to explain them the situation with a few broken words. The soldiers were pleased with the behaviour of this handsome little boy. They understood the situation, and said, "All right my boy, don't worry." They immediately reached near the boat and ordered the boatmen to release the boys. The boatmen got terrified at the sight of British soldiers and anchored the boat soon to release the boys. The soldiers were very much pleased with the courage of Narendranath, and they invited him to accompany them to the theatre. But Narendranath thanked them and declined, taking his leave.

In another story of Narendranath, we found his quality of bravery and his ability of judgment. There was a Champak tree [a flowering tree of Magnolia Family] in the compound of his friend's house. Naren often used to climb this tree and swing from its branches. He would hang from a branch by his legs, swing back and forth and finally somersault to the ground. One day Ramtanu Bose, grandfather of his friend saw Naren swinging from the branch of Champak tree. He found the game was risky; the boy might break his hands or legs by falling down on the ground. Branches of Champak tree is very soft and may break any time. He requested Naren not to play such game, for it was risky. Naren didn't agree with him, and said, "Why is it risky?" The old man realized that they boy would not obey his request, and hence he found it was better to frighten him. He said, "There is a ghost in that tree. A Brahma-daitya lives there. If you disturb him, he will break your necks. Beware that you don't climb that tree again."

This was enough to frighten other boys, but Narendranath didn't find any truth in his sentence. As soon as the old man was out of sight Naren climbed the tree again. His friends said, "How dare you do that again? Didn't you hear what the old man had said? Brahma-daitya will break your neck."

Naren laughed and said, "What assess you all are! See, my neck is still there. The old man's story is simply not true. Don't believe what others say unless you yourselves know it to be true."

With reference to the above context we came to the father of the friend who was very kind to him. He believed that Narendranath would be a famous person in future. Once, when he saw Naren swinging from a branch of Champak tree, he said, "You are found to loiter and be busy in game all the day! Do you study at all for you school?" "Yes sir." replied Naren, "I do both—play and study." He wanted to take a test, and asked Naren many questions on different subjects—geography, mathematics, reciting of poems, etc. Naren took not much time to answer them all. Then the examiner was very pleased and said, "Good, very good. Well, who looks after you? Your father is living at Lahore."

"Yes, you are right that my father is at Lahore," Naren replied, "but my mother is living here with me. She instructs me all what I should do, and I study that all myself."

The gentleman didn't say anything more, but told himself, "You must shine in life, I bless you my boy." Since then he had his eyes on Narendranath and tried to know his every movement.

Many events in Narendranath's early life exemplify his tremendous courage, and it will not be irrelevant to mention one of them. He was then about twelve years old when the emperor, Edward VII, visited India as the Prince of Wales. At that time the Syrup, a gigantic British warship, was docked at the port of Calcutta. Many people had passes to take tours of it. Narendra's friends forced him to visit the warship with them. Narendranath agreed and filled out an application for a group pass and took them to the office on Chowringhee Road [now Jawaharlal Nehru Road]. As he stood near the door gatekeeper didn't allow him to enter. He saw the people leaving with passes. He thought how he could meet the English officer who was issuing passes. He watched that people were going to the corridor on the second floor of the office building. He began to search for another way to enter the building. Suddenly, he found a spiral staircase at the rear leading to the back room of the corridor. He guessed that the stairs were used only by the servants. There was a chance to be humiliated if someone caught him, but he gathered his courage and reached the second floor by riding those stairs. As he entered the corridor, he saw that applicants gathered around the officer, who was bent over the desk signing applications. Narendranath stood at the end of the line. When he had his group pass signed, he saluted the officer and left the building through the front staircase along with others. He showed his group passes to the gatekeeper with a big smile. Gatekeeper was surprised to see Narendranath and asked him in Hindi, "*Tum upar kayse gaya tha*? [How did you enter the office?]" Narendranath flattered the gatekeeper in Hindi, "Ham jadu janta hay [I am a magician]." Next day he visited the warship with all his friends.

Narendranath was very much fond of mockery and fun. He said, "He, who doesn't know how to make a new fun every day, is dull headed; and cannot develop his brain."

The sky in the morning mostly can say how the rest of the day will be, and many a time the forecast is found correct. Thus, the childhood of a person can give us a picture of his future, and most of the time it comes true. In case of Narendranath his future was clearly indicated by each of his activities in childhood. He looked beautiful since he was a child, no one could help loving him. Everyone treated him with cordiality. People say, "A good beginning makes a good end." Well-shaped body, wide and bright eyes, fair complexion, long hand, a wide forehead, a genius in appearance—each of these qualities of Narendranath indicated that he would be a saint in future. Endless love, sharp brain, indomitable courage and enthusiasm, unlimited working power, power of concentration, amazing ability of judgment, meditation, etc.—a sum-total of these qualities is found in Swami Vivekananda since his childhood. He is a metaphor by himself. And again he is beyond any metaphor.

Narendranath Dutta

This is probably the first photograph of Swami Vivekananda taken in 1886

3
Vivekananda as a Student

Human brain starts developing since one lives in mother's womb, and after birth learns the first lesson of life from mother. There was no exception to it in the case of Narendranath. Narendra's future personality was influenced by his generous and gifted father and his resolute but saintly mother. Both of them kept a chastening eye upon him. He received his early education from his mother, who taught him Bengali alphabet and his first English premier and also told stories from the *Ramayana*, and the *Mahabharata*. His education and purification was always fleshed through his lectures at different places.

At the age of only six years, he memorized an entire musical composition on the *Ramayana*. He attended all recitals of the Puranas, held at close quarters. One day a singer, who was performing the *Ramayana*, forgot a part of the composition. Narendra immediately prompted him the line, whereupon he was appreciated by the singer and rewarded with some sweets.

In 1869, Kaliprosad, the head of the Dutta house, was on his deathbed. He, before his death, wished that someone of the young members of his family would read the *Mahabharata* in his ears. But everyone felt sigh and didn't come forward to fulfil his wish. Finally, Narendranath lifted up the *Mahabharata*, the heavy book, by his little hand and appeared before Kaliprosad. He read few pages from the *Mahabharata* in his sweet and clear voice with proper pronunciation. Kaliprosad opened his eyes wide and looked at Naren with a passion and breathed his last breath saying—"Brother Bilu, you will be a great person in life." Mahendranath said, "Not only for that day, Kaliprosad many a time had listened to Naren reading the *Mahabharata*."

Initiation into Study and First Schooling

Narendranath began his studies at the age of six. He went to a primary school in an unbleached cloth, with a wooden pen thrusting at waist, and a mat at armpit. Sometime before that the family priest initiated him into writing with a piece of chalk—"This is '*Ka*', this is '*Kha*'..." Naren repeated the same imitating his pronunciation "This is '*Ka*', this is '*Kha*'..."

Environment of a house is far different to that of a school, where students come from different houses of different culture and assemble at a common place. One day he uttered at home some of the ugly words that he had learnt from his classmates. Within a few days he had learnt some words that are out of dictionary and very much unusual in any cultured society. His parents heard him uttering those ugly words and took exception to it. They took him out of the school and appointed a private tutor for him. At first Naren didn't like this bondage under the rule of a home tutor. There in school he had many friends and would practice writing many new words on a palm-leaf. His parents, therefore, invited some other children of the neighbourhood to join the classes conducted by the private tutor in the worship hall. Naren started learning his lessons in that private school.

Naren was always pleased with polite words; he could never stand any hard word. No one could teach him anything without his consent. His method of study in childhood was quite different to that of other boys. He could learn any subject on first hearing about it and keep it in his memory for ever. When he was admitted to school, a tutor was appointed to help him with his studies every day. He would bring his English and Bengali books to his teacher, showed him each section that was to be read that day. Then he sat or lie down quietly. The teacher taught the spelling, pronunciation, and meaning of the words from the section of those books, as if he was learning them himself, and then went away. That was enough for Naren to learn the lessons.

Thus, his education was going on but, as usual, what he had been learning from his mother did not stop. Bengali alphabets, English First Book by Pyaricharan Sarkar—he learnt from his mother.

Reverend Swami Saradananda, in his book *Lilaprasanga*, said, "From his childhood onward, Narendra's many-faceted talents manifested themselves in various fields. Before he reached the age of five, he could recite all the aphorisms of Sanskrit grammar in the *Mugdhabodha*. Every evening an elderly relative taught him the names of his ancestors, hymns of gods and goddesses, and those Sanskrit aphorisms." This 'elderly relative' was Nrisingha Dutta, father of Ramchandra Dutta, a devotee of Sri Ramakrishna. Nrisingha Dutta was then living at Narendra's house with his son.

In this way Narendra's talents were manifested in various fields with the help of his mother, elder relative and his teachers.

Young Naren at School and his Education

Sister Nivedita used to say that those who knew Swami Vivekananda understood that he was one who had experienced in his own life all the truths about which he spoke. Swamiji knew that education plays a vital role in curing the evils in society and is critical in shaping the future of humanity. In order to understand his view, we should first consider his oft-quoted definition of education: "Education is the manifestation of the perfection already in man."[1]

The word 'manifestation' implies that something already exists and is waiting to be expressed. As Vivekananda said, "What a man 'learns' is really what he 'discovers', by taking the cover off his own soul, which is a mine of infinite knowledge."[2] It means spontaneous growth, provided the impediments, if any, are removed.

Next important expression in Swamiji's definition of education is—'already in man'. This refers to one's potential, which means the abilities and talents of a man that he owned by birth.

The word 'perfection' in the above definition is also very significant. Our every act is connected with learning, training, etc. It is the part of a process directed towards an end. The English word 'perfect' implies completion, or something being made whole.

Swamiji said: "The education which does not help the common mass of people to equip themselves for the struggle for life, which does not bring out strength of character, a spirit of philanthropy, and the courage of a lion—is it worth the name? Real education is that which enables one to stand on one's own legs."[3]

Swami Vivekananda envisioned a society with a new type of human being in whom knowledge, action, work, and concentration were harmoniously blended, and he proposed a new type of education for achieving this.

If we consider civilization to be the manifestation of the divine in human beings, as Vivekananda conceived it to be, no society has made much progress so far. This is why we find that mildness, gentleness, forbearance, tolerance, symhathy and so forth—the signs of healthy civilization—have not taken root in any society on an appreciable scale. Vivekananda prescribed 'man-making and character-building education.' His thoughts on education ought to be seriously re-examined today. Here, in this book, we will try to find out what kind of life he lived and what message he tried to convey to us for making a truly civilized society.

In 1871, when Swamiji was eight years old, he was sent to the Metropolitan Institution, which was started by Pandit Ishwar Chandra Vidyasagar. In this connection Bhupendranath Dutta said, "According to the receipt of admission fees, it is known that in 1871, Narendranath was admitted to ninth class [class II] in English section. At that time Prasanna Chandra Roy was the headmaster of that school." The building, where the school was established, is now Laha house at Sukia Street in north Kolkata. His exceptional intelligence was soon recognized by his teachers and classmates. He was reluctant to read English at first and said, "It is a foreign language, why should I learn it? It is better to learn our own language." Everyone tried to convince him—"English is a good language, and you must learn it." Who was able enough to force him to do a thing that he once decided not to do? He was completely against learning of English. Nrishingha Dutta, the elderly relative, tried his best to make him understand the necessity of learning English, but all his efforts turned in vain. Suddenly, one day Narendranath started showing his interest in learning English, and everyone was surprised to see his progress within a very short period.

No one knows how the wheel of fortune is regulated by the God. Although Narendranath was very much reluctant to learn English at first, later he taught the world in that language, and declared the cause of his appearance on the earth. Without English he perhaps could not spread the philosophy of Vedanta and the ideals of Hindu religion.

Narendranath learnt English alphabets and many English words from his mother by sitting on her lap. He heard the story of the *Ramayana* and the *Mahabharata* and stored in his strong memory for ever. This aural practice made him a good story-teller in future.

The pants, what Naren used to put on for school, was mostly found airy in some places. He was so much restless that in school he could not sit on the bench gently. According to his teacher, Naren used to sit almost out of his bench. He was found almost in all that posture between standing and sitting.

Naren was a brilliant student, so the curriculum consumed very little of his time. He used most of his energy in other activities. He was mostly engaged in inventing various kinds of games. He would forget everything when he had his playmates. He used to buy lozenge, marble or cricket bat with the money that he was given for refreshment. He was a good cricketer. Once he absorbed himself in any game, he didn't have sense of other things. It was not so easy to defeat him in any game. After a game was over he would make a plan of a new game for the next day. If ever there was any quarrel among his friends Naren had to settle it. He never liked quarrel for anything, he felt irritated by seeing his friends quarrelling with one another. Sometimes he would also have received one or two blows. He was expert in boxing, he could easily convince anybody to follow his instructions. Later he told his disciples, "From my boyhood I have been a dare-devil; otherwise could I have attempted to make a tour round the world, almost without a penny in my pocket?"[4]

It would not be irrelevant to mention here an excessively bold event of the dare-devil Narendranath. It was an afternoon of April, when a strong wind of *Kalbaishakhi* [a strong wind that rises in the afternoon of April and May] was blowing violently. Thunderbolts and flashes of lightning split the dark sky into Pieces. Boatman was fighting with high waves of the river by clinging to the rudder with his two hands. Young Naren was laughing ha...ha...ha... in enormous delight, thick black hair was fluttering in heavy wind, wide eyes were illuminating in excitement. Other passengers were flinched out of fear, but Naren went on singing loudly.

Viswanath Dutta warned his son, "There are many routes to Dakshineswar, it is better to avoid journey by a boat when the weather is not suitable for the same. Ram goes there by carriage."

Naren went away without any reply. He murmured himself—"Ram Dutta may go to Dakshineswar by carriage to meet Sri Ramakrishna—that is his route, but I'm..."

Narendranath boarded a boat from Ahiritola ghat in the stormy evening—to go to visit Sri Ramakrishna. He would have to brave so many storms to conceive the Master.

Although he was dare-devil or restless in his childhood, he didn't need to spend much time for his lessons; due to his extraordinary talent a study for one or two hours was enough to him. Hence, he had little interest in bookish lesson, most of the time he was engaged in different games. As he grew older, he would start reading his textbooks two or three days before the final examination, rest of the time he would read other books. Reverend Swami Saradananda has mentioned an example:

> ...before his Entrance Examination he read nearly all of the major books in English and Bengali literature and many history books as well. As a result, he sometimes had to work hard on the eve of a final examination. We remember that one day he told us, "Just two or three days before the Entrance Examination, I found I hardly knew anything about geometry. So I began to study the subject, staying awake the entire night, and in twenty-four hours I'd mastered the four books of geometry." He could do this because, by the grace of God, he had a strong body and a wonderful memory.[5]

He was expert in History, Sanskrit and English, but in Mathematics he was mostly similar to his father. Regarding mathematics his father would say, "It is a grocer's craft."

While he was in Metropolitan Institution, he had been suffering from dyspepsia for few years, and became very thin. He then used to eat what would be harmful to him.

He was enough intelligent, and therefore he didn't feel necessary to study much. Hence, he didn't miss any opportunity to have a chat with his classmates; as a result, sometimes he had to face problems. Perhaps the teacher had entered the classroom, his gossiping was still continuing. He was talking about his naughtiness or discussing a topic of the *Ramayana/Mahabharata*. The teacher heard someone was whispering in the class but couldn't identify him. Hence, he started to ask the students about what he was teaching. Many of the students couldn't answer, remained silent.

Although Narendranath was absorbed in chatting with his friends, he could easily understand the subject by hearing a little portion of what the teacher was talking about. When the teacher asked him, he easily pleased him with a correct answer. Then the teacher wanted to know who was whispering while he was teaching in the classroom. Everyone pointed finger to Narendranath. But the teacher couldn't believe them. So he as a punishment told everyone to stand up except Naren, Naren also stood up. Teacher said, "No, you don't have to stand up." Narendranath replied, "No sir, I have to stand up, because I was chatting with my friends." And he remained standing up.

In another event also we can see what had happened between Narendranath and a teacher in his school. There also he was seen raising objection against an injustice. He never could accept any unfairness. There was a teacher, very short tempered. Every now and then he used to treat his students with corporal punishment. One day he was beating a student very badly. Unnecessary excitement and the monstrous appearance of the teacher could not make Narendranath but laugh. That laughter was enough for supplying fuel to his anger. He left the boy, who was being beaten, and immediately started beating Narendranath a sound beating, and said, "Say, you'll never laugh at me." Narendranath didn't agree to promise the same. As a result the teacher continued beating him, threshed his ears and forced him to stand up on the bench. Narendranath felt pain in his ear, wherefrom blood was found oozing out. He became angry and said, "Don't touch my ear. Who are you to punish me? Don't try to touch me again." Suddenly, Iswarchandra Vidyasagar appeared there and saw Narendranath crying. Naren told him everything that had happened and declared that he would not come to school from the next day. Vidyasagar took him to his room and tried to console him. He also made an enquiry on the teacher's behaviour with students and declared—corporal punishment for students would be strictly prohibited in school from next day. When Naren returned home and told everything to his mother, she felt sorry and told in distress that she wouldn't allow his son to continue his studies in that school. But later, when Narendranath was no more in offended state, he again started going to that school. It took him a long time to recover the wound in his ears.

Whenever a new student was admitted to his class, Narendranath would first ask him—"Was any of your ancestors, like grandfather and so on, an ascetic mendicant?" Since his childhood he was seen attracted to an ascetic life. He always wished to be a monk; whenever he saw a monk, he would say, "I'll be a monk too, visit many places and will do a lot of great works." Sometimes his friends would try to read their palms with one another, of course Narendranath was the leader of them. He used to show some lines on his palm and would say, "There is no doubt that I'll be a monk someday and a sign of that is present on my palm." Some old man told him that he had a sign of becoming a saint. Being influenced by the dream of Naren many of his friends wished to be monk in future. They used to discuss the life of great monks and would absorb in different thoughts. Someone would say, "Monks do this and that." Naren said, "No no, you don't know? They live on the Himalayas, where men cannot reach. Every day they meet the Lord Shiva. If you wish to be like them, you have to go there and offer yourselves at the feet of those holy men. They will let you lie on a big bamboo. If anyone is found successful in sleeping on that bamboo, they allow you to wear the loincloth and make you followers of them."

Narendranath was always joyful as he was born with a strong body, a keen intellect, a wonderful memory, and a pure heart. He was carefree in every respect, and participated in physical exercise, instrumental music, singing, dancing, fun and amusements with friends, and so on. He never paid any heed to other's praise or criticism. He also learnt the art of cooking. He often used to arrange materials for cooking with the help of his friends. Sometimes he would collect money from his friends, though he had to spend mostly the maximum part of that. He was a good cook, though he liked to use chili little more than it was usually required.

Joyful Narendranath once organized an amateur theatrical group which used to play in worship hall, but when his uncle raised objection against the same, he started a gymnasium, where he and his friends practiced lessons on different kinds of exercises. One day his avuncular brother got injured and broke his hand while he was exercising. Then Naren's uncle became angry and broke some instruments for exercise, and the gymnasium was stopped.

When the gymnasium at Dutta house was closed, Narendranath took admission into a gymnasium on Cornwallis Street [now Bidhan Sarani] which was close to his home. Navagopal

Mitra, founder of the Hindu Fair, had established it. He was a well-wisher of Hindu and did many things for the development of Hindu society. Narendranath exercised there every day with his friends. There he learnt to fight with sticks, the use of arms, boating, swimming, boxing and so on, and he became expert in each of these exercises. Once in an exhibition, Naren stood first in boxing and won the trophy, a silver butterfly. He was very much interested in fighting with sticks. He learnt the art of fighting with sticks in the gymnasium and became well experienced in the same by practicing it with some Muslim experts outside the gymnasium. Then he was only a boy of ten years, amd a student of Metropolitan school. Once he went to visit an exhibition in a fair and watched the fighting with sticks. When the fighting came to an end, he wanted to show his fighting. One among the fighters, who considered himself the strongest, accepted the challenge and came forward. They started fighting; both the sticks were striking each other and making sound like thak..k.. tha..k. Nobody had any doubt about the result that Narendra's defeat was unpreventable, as his partner was older and stronger than him. Suddenly, Narendranath played such a trick, that his partner couldn't control himself and his stick was found broken into two pieces. Narendranath felt the taste of success and the audience was happy for his success.

Reverend Swami Saradananda has described an event of that time. He said:

> One day the boys were trying their utmost to lift and set up a heavy wooden trapeze frame in the gymnasium, but they kept failing. A crowd gathered to watch, but no one came forward to help them. Seeing a stout English sailor in the crowd, Narendra asked for his help. He gladly agreed to join them. The boys tied a rope to the top of the trapeze and began to pull in up as the sailor tried to set its legs into two sockets. When the frame was almost up, the rope suddenly gave way and the heavy trapeze fell to the ground. One of the legs came out of its socket and hit the sailor's forehead. He fell down unconscious, bleeding profusely from his wound. Seeing the English sailor unconscious, everyone thought that he was dead.
>
> Almost all of the boys ran away for fear of the police. But Narendra and a couple of his close friends stayed behind to try to find a solution to the crisis. Narendra tore a piece from his cloth, soaked it in water, and bandaged the sailor's wound. He then tried to bring him around by splashing water on his face and fanning him. When the sailor regained consciousness, they carried to a room in the Training Academy, a school nearby, and then sent a message to Navagopal, asking him to come immediately with a doctor. When the doctor came to examine the sailor, he told them: "The wound is not serious. He needs a week of rest and nursing, and he will be fine." Narendra tended the sailor, giving him medicine and a good diet, and he recovered. Narendra then collected money from distinguished local people, gave it to the sailor, and bade him good-bye.[6]

We have heard many such stories of Narendra's early life that show how he remained unworried in the midst of dangers and difficulties.

Narendranath was always against laziness. His father bought him a pony; he used to have a tour around the city riding on it in the evening. He was a favourite chap to his neighbours, and he considered them as his kith and kin. He used to call them as uncle, aunt, sister, brother and so on. He always stood by everyone who was in distress. Even a man with solemn gravity couldn't but burst into laughter by his funny actions. He was always welcomed by everyone. Each of his friends thought that he was the most favourite to Naren. He was full of those qualities that attracted everyone of the same age. He was incomparable to any one in hard-working, sportsmanship, craziness, making jokes and so on. He used to search out strange names from mythological tales and call his friends by the same. Everyone was pleased with the new name as it made them feel a smell of kinship.

It is very rare to see a person with head and heart equally developed. Those who are endowed with such quality become prominent in society in their respective fields. In case of Narendranath, we see that the growth of his age influenced him to become calm and his intellects and emotional capacities made him endowed with insight in search of the truth into the superficial world. A gradual change was noticed in his behaviour. He became interested in reading books and newspapers, and in attending different meetings and associations. His memory and the power of understanding were very sharp. His friends were surprised with his ability to judge and sagacity. No one could defeat him in argumentation. Perception of beauty and dexterity in everything is a distinctive side of his character. One day, while Narendranath was teaching music to a friend, he said:

> Mere tune and keeping time are not all of music. It must express an idea. Can anyone appreciate a song sung in a drawling manner? The idea underlying the song must arouse the feeling of the singer, the words should be articulated distinctly, and proper attention be given to tune and timing. The song that does not awaken a corresponding idea in the mind of the singer is not music at all.[7]

Swamiji had experienced many things beyond sense perception. One interesting phenomenon may be mentioned here. He said:

> From my very boyhood, whenever I came in contact with a particular object, man or place, it would sometimes appear to me as if I had been acquainted with it beforehand. But all my efforts to recollect [the particulars] were unsuccessful, and yet the impression persisted. I will give you an instance: One day I was discussing various topics with my friends at a particular place. Suddenly something was said, which at once reminded me that in some time past in that very house I had talked with these friends on that subject and that the discussion had even taken the same turn. Later on I thought that it might be due to the law of transmigration. But soon I decided that such definite conclusions on the subject were not reasonable. No I believe that before I was born I must have had visions somehow, of those subjects and people with whom I would have to come in contact in my present birth. Such memories have come every now and then throughout my life.[8]

Narendranath was an ideal boy in all corners. He used to play like others, but in solitude a stream of high thought would flow in his mind. Then he looked no more an ordinary boy, as if an old traveller in the realm of knowledge. We see this knowledge enlightening through his interest in meditation and attraction towards renouncing the worldly life since his boyhood. Each event of his childhood indicates the rising of unbeatable personality of Swami Vivekananda. In his childhood he felt such strength in himself and had strange visions that are generally not found in any other boys. He was the only owner of these experiences. He was restless but in his mind, he always seemed to look for something else. That is why he would have no sense of anything that had happened around him while he absorbed himself in meditation.

Another experience of his feeling the spiritual world may be mentioned here. Naren's father had to stay at many places of northern and central India for conducting his professional business there. It was 1877 when Narendranath was fourteen years old, reading in class eight, his father lived for some time at Raipur in Madhya Pradesh [in central India]. As he found that he would have to stay there longer than he expected, he sent for his family shortly after he arrived. At that time there was no railway for Raipur. Trains would run up to Nagpur station via Elahabad and Jabbalpur. So to reach Raipur, people had to travel by bullock cart from Nagpur railway station for over a fortnight through a dense forest infested with wild animals. The journey was full of physical hardship, but Narendranath didn't feel it as he was enjoying the beauty of nature. He was overwhelmed by the infinite power and boundless love of God who had adorned the earth with such incomparable beauty.

He said: "What I saw and felt as we passed through that forest has remained imprinted in my memory, particularly a certain event that occurred on the day we skirted the lofty range of the Vindhya Mountains. The peaks on either side of the road rose very high into the sky. The slopes were covered with beautiful trees and creepers that were wonderfully heavy with fruit and flowers. Birds of all colours were flying from grove to grove or swooping to the ground in search of food, filling the gorge with sweet cries. I felt an extraordinary peace of mind as I watched this. The slow moving procession of bullock carts reached a place where two great rocks had come together in a lover's embrace over the narrow forest trail. As I carefully observed the area below the point where they met on one side of the trail, I saw a very deep cleft from the top to the bottom of the rock. Inside that cleft hung an enormous honeycomb, the result of bees' labour throughout many years. Filled with wonder, I thought about the kingdom of the bees—how it had begun and how it had ended—and my mind became so deeply absorbed in thoughts of the infinite power of God, ruler of the three worlds, that I lost all consciousness of my surroundings for some time. I don't know how long I lay in the bullock cart in that condition. When I regained external consciousness, I found that we had passed that place and were already far away. As I was alone in the cart, no one ever knew what happened to me."[9] Swami Saradananda had comment on this occasion, "This was perhaps the first time that Narendranath became completely absorbed in meditation with the help of the intense imagination."

At Raipur no school was found suitable for Narendranath. So he was encouraged by his father in his lessons and to meet notable scholars with whom he used to discuss various intellectual topics usually considered too abstruse for boys of his age. Sometimes the discussion between father and his son would turn into an argumentation, and father would feel happy by getting yielded to his son. On one occasion, when a discussion was going on in full swing, a learned friend of Viswanath Dutta became surprised to know the knowledge of Narendranath as he quoted some lines from the composition of a famous author in Bengali. The gentleman said, "Bravo my boy! We will hear your name someday." That day what the gentleman said, was not out of his overconfidence—Vivekananda in his later life proved the same in his Bengali compositions.

Narendranath had a strong consciousness of self-respect since his boyhood. He didn't allow anybody to neglect him considering his young age. He was aware of the assessment of his intellect. Hence, he didn't find any reason in elevating himself or to allow anybody to disregard him for nothing, and also didn't feel necessary to allow anyone for thinking in that way. Once a friend of his father tried to ignore him, Naren remembered that he had never been ignored by his father, and he became angry as if a snake got excited after being injured by someone. He said to the man, "Many a person thinks that a boy doesn't have any sense of judgment—this type of conception is very much wrong." The gentleman was forced to accept his mistake when he found that Narendranath was angry and didn't like to continue the conversation anymore. In *Kathopanishad*, Nachiketa was also found telling himself, "I'm superior to many, I am inferior to few, but nowhere am I the last, I can also do something."

We have already told about his skill in cooking as a game with his friends. Here at Raipur he had learnt cooking from his father and became expert in it. He also learnt chess and used to play with the experts.

After staying at Raipur for one and half years Viswanath Dutta returned to Kolkata. Pramathanath Bose has said that Viswanath lived at Raipur for two years before he returned to Kolkata [then it was Calcutta]. At that time Narendranath was very much strong and stout, appeared as an adult. In mental development and knowledge he was far ahead of his friends. But the problem arose for his admission to a good school. Teachers didn't consider him eligible for Entrance Examination as he was not in touch with any school for a long time. Finally, after a long request he was allowed to sit in the same class in the same school.

In 1879 Narendranath within a short time passed high school final examination in the first division and was rewarded a silver watch by his father.

In the meantime, he had read many standard books of English and Bengali literature. History was his favourite subject. He also acquired at this time an unusual method of reading a book and acquiring the knowledge of its subject-matter. Here we would like to quote his own words:

> It so happened that I could understand an author without reading his book line by line. I could get the meaning by just reading the first and the last line of a paragraph. As this power developed I found it unnecessary to read even the paragraphs. I could follow by reading only the first and last lines of a page. Further, where the author introduced discussion to explain a matter and it took him four or five or even more pages to clear the subject, I could grasp the whole trend of his arguments by only reading the first few lines.[10]

We would like to present here the percentage of marks obtained by Narendranath in different subjects in Entrance Examination. English—47, Second language—76, History—45, and Mathematics—38, hence the total marks was 206.

Someone, who has obtained a lower standard of marks, may get surprised to know the marks obtained by Narendranath, who became a famous philosopher and the hero of the era. It shows that the quality or intellect of a person cannot be measured properly only by the system of an examination. Few years later this Narendranath became Swami Vivekananda and helped in maintaining the dignity of Hindu religion and regained the pride of India by clearing all comments of bad taste against her through the explanation of the Vedanta in English. It shows the difference between bookish knowledge and wisdom of consciousness.

There are two levels of values designated by the ancient Indian scriptures, *para vidya* [spiritual values] and *apara vidya* [secular values]. This division is merely for practical convenience; otherwise vidya, or learning, is a continuum, leading one towards the ultimate goal which according to Vivekananda is complete freedom of the soul.

Then the theater-hall was very recently introduced to the people of Calcutta. Narendranath often used to watch the show in an auditorium. One day while a play was acted, suddenly a constable appeared there with a warrant for an actor and wanted to arrest him. As a result the show was going to stop immediately, Narendranath stood up said in a thunderous voice, "Get off the stage and wait outside till the show is end. How dare you misbehave and disturb the spectators in this way?" Many of the spectators started shouting—"Get out, get off the stage immediately." Constable realized the situation and moved aside. People, who knew Narendranath, began to pat his back and said, "Bravo brother! Today the show was to be ruined if you were not present here."

We have heard of so many events of boldness, where we are introduced with the courageous act of Narendranath. He was also a good story-teller. His sisters and brothers would request him, "Please tell us a story", and he couldn't be released without telling a story. He told them so many stories—'Ali Baba and Forty Thieves', 'Bangoma-Bangomi' and so on and helped them being educated with the morals of those stories.

We all know about his power of speech. A programme for rewarding the successful students was organized by the Metropolitan school, where a teacher of repute of that school was also rewarded on his farewell. On that occasion Narendranath was requested to deliver a farewell-speech on behalf of the students. At that time Narendranath was familiar to his friend circle as a good reader of English literature and a scholar in English language. But brilliance and delivering speech publicly are not the same, particularly where the seat of the chief guest was occupied by Sir Surendranath Banerjee, one of the earliest Indian political leaders. However, brave Narendranath was ready to deliver the farewell-speech. Then for half an hour on stage he delivered a well-thought speech smoothly in pure English like a seasoned orator and explained how sorrowful the students were for his retirement from teaching, and how his absence might cause an irreparable loss for the school. Later Surendranath Banerjee regarding Swami Vivekananda said, "He was the greatest public orator India had ever known."

God Himself was building him up since his childhood and provided different opportunities for him to reveal his power of intellect. He used to attend all seminars in school in his own interest; telling stories, explaining different subjects to his friends, participating in different debates and so on helped him in escalating the power of revealing his thoughts and experiences. Moreover, he was gifted with a strong and beautiful body by God, and his thunderous voice, musical recitation, praiseworthy oration could easily engulf the heart of his listeners.

When Narendranath lived with his father at Raipur, at that time he was taught different kinds of music by his father. When Viswanath Dutta was in western India for his business, he learnt *Thumri, Tappa, Gazal* [different forms of Indian classical music] and so on, and in leisure time he trained his son in different streams of music. Thus, Narendranath, since his boyhood, earned his skill in different kinds of vocal and instrumental music. He learnt vocal music from Beni Ostad, and Tabla and Pakhoaj from Kasinath Ghoshal. Mr. Ghoshal used to play Pakhoaj in Adi Brahmo Samaj [old Brahmo Society]. In a different opinion the original name of Beni Ostad was Benimadhav Adhikari. He was a Ramayit Vaisnav. Another music teacher was Ahmad Khan. According to Bhupendranath Dutta—Narendranath learnt instrumental music, but his teacher's name was unknown, and in another opinion it is untrue that he learnt Pakhoaj from Kasinath Ghoshal. Bhupendranath said that Narendra's systematic learning period of music was only for three or four years—1879 to 1883. Some people said—he learnt music for a long period.

In the above context we would like to quote a few lines from *Lilaprasanga*, the book composed by Swami Saradananda. He said: "Vishwanath was intelligent and gifted. He loved music and the fine arts. Narendra later said that his father had a sweet voice and that he could sing Nidhu Babu's *Tappa* [light song] beautifully even though he had no formal training. Vishwanath considered music to be a harmless amusement, so he arranged for his eldest son, Narendra, to learn music along with his regular studies. His wife, Bhuvaneswari, was able to master devotional songs—including their tune, measure, and tempo—after hearing them sung only once by Vaishnava minstrels and beggars."[11]

Influence of parents is found more or less to play an important role in their offspring. It was not an exception in Narendra's life. Boys are mostly found to be influenced by the intellect and wisdom of their father and they are guided by the emotional and moral aspects of mother.

Narendranath had more faith in his father's education and intellect than in that of any other person. He would respect his father, but if ever he found any of his father's point of view unjustified he would never hesitate to forward his arguments immediately, and tried to replace the same with his own opinion. He was seen in the same way to explain his view before his Master Sri Ramakrishna Paramhansa. But it doesn't mean that Narendranath always liked to cross swords with others for nothing. This was his intent devotion to truth—a fight between two logical views for the truth. In his later life, he would often say: "Do not believe in a thing because you have read about it in a book. Do not believe in a thing because another man has said it was true. Do not believe in words because they are hallowed by tradition. Find out the truth for yourself. Reason it out. That is realization."[12]

He never accepted anything without searching the truth in it, wherever may it be written or whoever may tell it. He would not acknowledge the thing if it was not supported by any reasonable proof, and in adverse condition he would immediately place his thoughtful opinion. He inherited such disposition from his father. Vishwanath Dutta used to have discussion with his son on different subjects that involved a deep knowledge, high thinking and sharp intellect so that it would help his son in developing his power of intelligence. In course of such discussion he would always allow his son to present his independent opinion. He never ignored his son and didn't force him to accept his ideas as he believed that such actions might interrupt the development of his brain. Narendranath also would respect his father's attitude. He too never liked to advise anybody to follow his ideas foolishly, never tried to force anybody to follow his path. Vishwanath Dutta didn't believe that education is called only to swallow a number of books; to him education is the way to follow, through which one can learn to identify the truth and can develop his intellect. In this way Narendranath learnt the skill of finding out the fundamental rule in each subject and became habituated to accept the truth with his noble mind. He would never feel peace till he reached the ultimate point of any subject by following every possible experiment on the same. His father taught him the lesson how to pick up the synopsis from an argument and present it easily in a beautiful manner. Vishwanath Dutta never regarded the education that had no relation with the reality of practical life. Probably for this reason Vivekananda was damn against any religious or social superstition, rather he was in favour of practical experience instead of materialistic view of rationalism.

Narendranath could never ignore his cordial attraction towards his mother even after he renounced the worldly life. He said about his mother: "I believe that whatever religious culture I have, I owe to that. It was consciously that my mother brought me into the world to be what I am. Whatever good impulse I have was given to me by my mother—and consciously, not unconsciously." He also added: "The love which my mother gave to me has made me what I am, and I owe a debt to her that I can never repay."[13]

He worshipped his mother considering as Goddess. Bhuvaneswari Devi would advise him: "Always follow the truth, be pure, save your dignity, and never ignore the dignity of others, don't poke your nose into the business of others."

He learnt from his parents—"As long as you live, never turn away from doing your duties", and he had maintained the same throughout his life.

Narendranath Entered the College

Narendranath finished his school education by appearing at the Entrance Examination at the age of sixteen years. He was then no more expected to play and make fun with his friends as before, though he felt sad for his Metropolitan school, and for his old classmates. But he had to accept that time always runs in its own course. He had to go ahead. It is very much usual to feel sad when one, on his way to college, looks at the little boys going to school, which makes him remember the days he has passed. It was no more befitting for him to imitate the role of a king that he used to do while playing with his friends in childhood days, now he had to be prepared to be the real king of the spiritual world. Now the time was to begin his work for which he had appeared on the earth. Now he had to be matured enough. Life is no more as smooth as he had in his childhood. Since now he will have to face so many problems in his life. A long journey full of hardship was waiting for him.

On 27 January 1880, young Narendranath was admitted to The Presidency College at Calcutta [now Kolkata]. Admission fee was Rupees ten only. He absorbed himself in studies. His interest in English grew, and he didn't miss any discussion on logic and philosophy. Most of the teachers in government colleges were foreigners. Hence, the students had to follow the European dress code or to wear Indian *chapkan* [a loose and long robe] and *pajamas* in college premises. Narendranath used to wear *chapkan*, *pajamas* and a wristwatch.

Before one year had passed Narendranath was attacked with Malaria. As a result he couldn't continue his studies in college. His percentage of attendance was so low that he was not allowed to appear for F.A. examination. Then he took admission in General Assembly's Institution, founded by Scottish General Missionary Board and later known as the Scottish Church College. According to Bhupendranath when there was an uncertainty of appearing at the F.A. examination, Narendranath wanted to go to England, but his father didn't agree to send him to a country far away from India.

Narendranath passed the first year F.A. examination and got admission for the second year in General Assembly's Institution. Teachers would say about Narendranath, "A great power is hidden in this young man, and one day he will be well-known to the world." Brojendranath Shil, famous philosopher, was also the student of that college, he was senior to Narendra. Whenever Narendra would meet him in any seminar, they would have discussed on philosophy. In 1881, Narendranath passed F.A. examination and B.A. in 1884 from this college, when he was twenty years old. Then he took admission to Metropolitan Institution [now Vidyasagar College] to go in for B.L., but before appearing for the examination he lost his father on 23 February 1884, and he fell into a distress with his family.

After F.A. examination, Narendranath became well acquainted with Western science and philosophy. He had already mastered the doctrines of John Stuart Mill and of other Western logicians. When Narendranath heard of the greatness of German philosophers, he studied the history of philosophy and tried to understand the views of Immanuel Kant, Johann Gottlieb Fichte, Georg Wilhelm Freidrich Hegel, Arthur Schopenhauer, and others. He went to the Calcutta Medical College to learn the formation and function of the nervous system and the brain. He studied the subject and listened to lectures on physiology. He therefore had much knowledge of Western philosophy by the time he passed his B.A. examination in 1884. But this knowledge couldn't give him peace as it could not offer a definite method of knowing God, the absolute Truth that is beyond the limit of the human mind and intellect. When he realized that his study was not adequate to get the Truth, a strange current of restlessness flowed strongly in his mind.

Once he explained his mental state to Swami Saradananda: "from the time I reached my youth, every night when I went to bed two ideal lives appeared before me. One of them was a man of great wealth, surrounded by servants and dependents, enjoying high rank and immense power. I saw myself as foremost among the great men of the world, and I was certain that I had the necessary ability to fulfill that ambition. But the very next moment I'd picture myself as having renounced everything in the world. I was wearing nothing but a loincloth, without anxiety, eating whatever food came my way, sleeping under a tree, and living in complete reliance on God's will. I knew that it was within me to lead the life of the rishis and ascetics if I should choose to do so. These images of the two directions that I could take in life kept appearing before me, but I always ended by choosing the latter. I knew that this was the only path by which a man could achieve true happiness, and I resolved to follow it and not the other. As I dwelt on the happiness of such a life, my mind would become absorbed in God, and I'd fall asleep. Surprisingly, this phenomenon continued every day for a long time."[14]

Thus, Narendranath was getting prepared for his future-life. Developing of physical, mental, intellectual, cordial, and spiritual powers—were included in this preparation. All these different sides were so much entangled with one another that it was impossible to differentiate one from the another. He could never realize religion without relating it to his life. He believed that it is useless to find out the success of a life without knowing God.

At this time, Narendranath felt a strong restlessness that calmed down by reaching at the feet of Sri Ramakrishna, and finally he found out the right path. This will be discussed more elaborately later at right place.

History of Vivekananda's life, when he was 18 to 20 years old, is very much significant for our discussion. The power, with which he appeared on the earth to create a huge stir in human life and philosophy, became restless for being revealed by crossing the limit of his youthful flesh and blood. At this age [adolescence period], everyone is found changed in thinking, great people are also not out of this trend. One is found confused to see the road being multifurcated, and ask, "Which road should I take? How can I reach the goal? I wish to get at the truth, get my life substantially meaningful..." and so on. An ordinary man may do the mistake while choosing the right path, but a great soul never does that. Narendranath also didn't mistake to choose the right path.

Narendranath was always at the top in college, as he was in school. Everyone would acknowledge his leadership. No one could defeat him in any argument. He was habituated in explaining any matter with a reasonable and thoughtful judgment. During conversation, in use of sentences, in making fun and mystery, in enjoyment, in singing—no one was parallel to him. In college-life, he absorbed himself in study, which was not limited to the syllabus only. He was interested in games, in reading novel, monthly magazines and daily newspaper, etc. He began to study history literature, and Eastern and Western philosophy with much heed. His idea on education was very much liberal. He didn't give much attention to examination. With reference to this context, he would say to his classmates: "It is not much important to pass the examination, as it is not the only ambition of a life. Reading books for getting by heart to pass the examination is nothing but misusing the power of memory. You should read books as much as you need to pass the examination."

He would add more, "At present a student is more eager to acquire the degree than knowledge. As a result his education comes to an end just after having the degree. What is called knowledge, and what is its use or how far is it liable to influence the character of a person?—Students should have an idea of the answers to these questions."

As we are talking about the view of Vivekananda on education, we would like to quote few sentences told by him:

> To me the very essence of education is concentration of mind, not the collecting of facts.[15]
>
> The education that you are getting now has some good points, but it has a tremendous disadvantage which is so great that the good things are all weighed down. In the first place it is not a man-making education, it is merely and entirely a negative education. A negative education or any training that is based on negation, is worse than death.[16]
>
> Education is not the amount of information that is put into your brain and runs riot there, undigested, all your life. We must have life-building, man-making, character-making assimilation of ideas. If you have assimilated five ideas and made them your life and character, you have more education than any man who has got by heart a whole library.... If education is identical with information, the libraries are the greatest sages in the world, and encyclopedias are the Rishis.[17]

When Narendranath was in college, he most carefully mastered three subjects of which Mathematics and Astronomy were most remarkable. 'Godfrey's Astronomy' and 'Higher Mathematics' were his favourite subjects. He was inclined to Sanskrit language since his childhood. Since he was only fourteen years old, he could write good essays in Sanskrit. But his most favourite language was Bengali.

We have already told about his strange memory. In this regard people mostly mention the similarity with his mother. If he once would read a poem to his mother, later at any time he could commit the same from his memory. Later this memory-power became stronger. If he wished he could concentrate on a subject, and it would remain always unchanged in his memory. People were surprised to know his memory-power and they considered it a divine power. It was as easy as a game to him to repeat the same if he once had heard it. By the by Swami Saradananda said: "During debate he would listen to a few of his opponent's words to understand the essence of that person's defence and then mentally prepare his reply." When asked how he could spontaneously craft such penetrating arguments to defeat his opponent, he replied, "How many new thoughts are there in this world? If one knows and has mastered those few thoughts together with the reasons for and against them, one need not think too much in order to reply. Any reason the opponent might adduce to support his position must fall within those few thoughts. Rare are those who bring to the world new ideas on any subject."

If he once read forty to fifty pages from a book of history or philosophy, since that day those forty or fifty pages would become his own property for ever.

It is very much usual to him, whose memory-power is so much strong, to acquire a huge knowledge in a short time. He was fond of reading history; not only the story of events or dates, he liked to know and discuss about the environment through which the revolution of a nation or the achievements of its mighty heroes came into light.

Narendranath thoroughly read the *History of French Revolution*, Green's *History of the English People*, and Alison's *History of Europe*, and attentively went through the *Decline and Fall of the Roman Empire* by Gibbon. He hated weakness. His friend, therefore, said, "He was a great admirer of Napoleon and tried to impress upon us that the followers of any great cause must give the unquestioning obedience which Marshal Ney showed to his emperor."[18] He used to say about the famous personalities in Indian history in such a way that he seemed to have met them personally. When he would tell the story of Hindu king of Gupta dynasty or of Mogul emperors, he would have been absorbed so completely that he had been living there for a long time. Later, being an ascetic he travelled those places, and would have been overwhelmed with respect to the memories of that period and felt proud of the ancient history of India.

With reference to the above context, we would like to quote few lines by Sister Christine. She said:

> The Moguls seemed to have cast a spell over Swami Vivekananda. He depicted this period of Indian history with such dramatic intensity, that the idea often came to us that he was perhaps telling the story of his own past. We often wondered whether we saw before us the re-incarnation of the mighty Akbar. How else could he have known the thoughts, the hopes, the purposes of the greatest of the Moguls?
>
> One of his beliefs was that, before one reached the life in which the enlightenment was to be achieved, one must have run the whole gamut of experiences—suffered every tragedy and the direst poverty, and enjoyed to the utmost all that the world has to offer—wealth, adulation, fame, power, ecstatic happiness, dominion. "Millions of times have I been emperor," he would say in his exuberant fashion. Another idea was that, after lives of effort in which complete success had not been reached, there came a final life of worldly attainment, in which the aspirant became a great emperor or empress. This precedes the life in which the goal is reached. Akbar, it is believed in India, was a religious aspirant in the incarnation before he became emperor. He just failed to reach the highest and had to come back for one more life in which to fulfill his desires. There was only one more re-incarnation for him.
>
> "So vividly did Swami depict these historic figures for us—rulers, queens, prime ministers, generals—that they seemed to become for us real men and women whom we had known."[19]

Like other young men Narendranath was also fond of poetry. His most favourite poet was William Wordsworth. He could recite many of his poems from his memory. To him a poem is a colourful pen-picture with beautiful words by the poet. It is the most beautiful art for revealing an ideal, excellence artistry of captivating the heart by the truth. Swamiji said: "True art can be compared to a lily which springs from the ground, takes its nourishment from the ground, is in touch with the ground, and yet is quite high above it. So art must be in touch with nature—and wherever that touch is gone, art degenerates—yet it must be above nature."[20]

As many as the days were gone, Narendranath became more and more restless for acquiring the knowledge of the truth. Eastern or Western philosophy failed to help his search. He realized that it was useless to find out the truth in different books. His feelings came into light through his pen, and he composed a lyric—'Song of Sannyasin', where he said:

> Where seekest thou? That freedom, friend, this world
>
> Nor that can give. In books and temples vain
>
> Thy search....[21]

Sister Christine has explained: "As he grew towards young manhood, he became an agnostic, reading Herbert Spencer with great enthusiasm, with whom he also carried on some correspondence. But agnostic or devotee, the search for God was always uppermost in his mind. It was touching to hear him tell how he went from one religious teacher to another, asking, 'Sir, have you seen God?' and not receiving the answer he hoped for, until he found Shri Ramakrishna at Dakshineswar."[22]

Narendranath read many books on Eastern and Western philosophy. In old books of Indian philosophy, he found some truth, but he felt, that should be recomposed in a new form suitable to modern time. He found some weak points in Hindu philosophy, and therefore, he felt some doubts and had been suffering for tremendous restlessness till he found any fruitful solution of his questions. He realized that the values of Western philosophy are merely the shadows of the same of Hindu philosophy. Western philosophy could approach only a little towards the truth.

Narendranath concentrated in studies, but that didn't mean that he was no more interested in enjoying life, in making fun with friends. Very few students were as witty as he was. If there was anything funny somewhere he would have noticed first. He used to hire a carriage and being overcrowded with friends moved round the city. On Sunday or on any holiday, he used to bathe in the river with many of his friends. Swimming in the river, jumping, playing in water, and enjoying light and lively chat with friends—everything was going on in full swing.

He was full of purity and chastity that he considered the highest quality of a person, and never liked to make any kind of confrontation with this. Purity was the backbone of his character. One of his friends, who didn't care of any morality, said about Narendranath, "Since he grew towards young manhood, he was a living idol of purity. I would often pull his leg by saying 'over puritanical'. Whenever I wished to talk to him, I couldn't find any suitable word—as if words were being obstructed by some unknown causes and could realize how inferior I was to him." More he added, "A smearing of spiritual light was found around him." The same thing was also noticed by his other friends.

We have told about Beni Ostad while we were talking about Narendra's inclination towards music. This Beni Ostad [Beni Gupta or Beni Adhikari] was a student of Ahmed Khan, and he is known to be a scholar in both vocal and instrumental music. Narendranath learnt both vocal and instrumental music for three or four years, but he was more skilled in singing than in playing instrument. We have also come to know that he later learnt *Dhrupad, Khayal, Thumri, Tappa* and the like from Ahmed Khan, and also learnt singing in Hindi, Urdu, and Parsian, which are sung in many festivals of Muslim community. Wherever he went he was appreciated as an expert singer by the listeners, and everyone would request him to sing more. He had earned an adequate knowledge of music. He collected much information by comparing the Eastern music with that of Western and became an experienced critic of music. He wrote a preface to a book on Indian music.

After a few months of the death [Monday, 16 August 1886] of Sri Ramakrishna, Narendranath composed a lyric—'*Ta Thai Ta Thai nache Bhola*' [Bhola dances in rhythm] on the occasion of *Shivaratri*, also composed the tune of the same. Later he composed some lyrics in the pattern of *Dhrupad*.

Swami Pragnyanananda in his book [written in Bengali] titled *Sangeet Sadhonay Swami Vivekananda O Sangeet Kalpataru* explained the talent of Swamiji in music. There he said, "Swamiji was not only a great singer, but also an efficient researcher for truth in music; the art of his vindicated discussion on music in 'Sangeet Kalpataru' illustrates his authenticity in music."

In connection with the book *Sangeet Kalpataru* Swami Gambhirananda said—"In its first edition first 90 pages were used for explaining the tune, time, musical instrument, playing music, lyrics, vocal training, concert, and so on under the title of 'Sangeet O Badyo' [Music and Instrument]. In an appendix with 18 pages were used for briefing the life and works of Bidyapati, Chandidas, Ramprosad and others under the title of 'Sadhok O Kavigoner Jibani' [short biography of worshiper and poets]. In a chapter titled *Sangeet Sangraha* [collection of music] different kinds of lyrics in different languages were represented, where it is to be noticed that Indian National Song was also given. In the third edition, these two articles were written much elaborately and they were printed at the beginning of the book."

Swami Gambhirananda said that Vivekananda wrote a note on the science and philosophy of Indian music in the preface of Bengali book of music. Bhupendranath has written that Narendranath wrote a book on instrumental music and it was published by Vaishnavcharan Basak of Bartala, and a copy of the same is kept in the library of Belur Math. But according to Swami Gambhirananda, Vaishnavcharan was the co-writer of that book, not the publisher. He blamed that he had seen the first and the third editions of the book, which show that it was published by Chandicharan Basak of Arya Pustakalay [Arya Book Store], 118 Upper Chitpur Road, Kolkata; in place of writer's name there was—'A collection by Sri Narendranath Dutta, B.A. and Sri Vaishnavcharan Basak.' At the beginning of the book, co-writer Vaishnavcharan has written in the preface titled 'Bishes Katha'—"The work of collection has been continuing for last one year, most of which was done by Narendranath Dutta, but due to some unavoidable causes he couldn't complete the same. I, therefore, did the rest of his work and published the book."

Swami Gambhirananda has explained the 'unavoidable causes' mentioned by Vaishnavcharan for what Narendranath couldn't complete the book. He said, "...probably he was then busy in some fundamental works at Baranagar Math, and he had to look after the court case after his father's death, and so on." Then he has given thrilling information about when Narendranath started writing the book. He said, "Date of publication of the book was—Bhadra, 1294 as per Bengali calendar, means it was the time in between August and September of 1887. It shows the Narendranath started writing the book just after the death of Sri Ramakrishna or few days before the same. The book was highly appreciated by the people. Vaishnavcharan, in the third edition of the book, has written—"Within six months two thousand copies of the last two editions of *Sangeet Kalpataru* were sold." In those days, it was a matter of pleasure. Later due to a successful business the name of the book was changed and Narendra's name as an author was deleted from the same. Perhaps there was a dispute with the copyright of the book. Someone has written with a pen 'Gayanchandra Basak' on the first page of the first edition of the book, which is kept in the library of Belur Math. Copyright was in the name of Gayanchandra Basak, and the year of edition was 1887. In preface titled 'Sangeet O Badyo' was given a name in English—J.C. Basak followed by the date 1/1/88."

In connection with the above-said incident, we would like to inform something more thrilling. Upendranath Mukherjee, a devotee of Sri Ramakrishna, used to work in a shop at Baranagar. Narendranath often would go there as a customer. Upendranath was poor, hence Narendra wrote a book for earning money to help him. But, when rose a quarrel on its copyright, he took himself away from the site.

Sometimes the students of General Assembly College would request Naren to sing. One day, when an English Professor was found late in coming to the class, everyone forced him to sing a song. The class was then crowded with about two hundred students. Narendra started singing, and everyone in the class was concentrated in his sweet melody. Shortly after that the professor arrived there, and before he entered the classroom he stood still as he heard the singer. When the song came to an end the professor entered the classroom with a sweet smile on his face, and appreciated the singer, though nobody told him the name of the singer.

When Narendra would sing in a gathering of his friends, no one could have any time to look at the clock. Many of his friends said that he sometimes would sing alone and became so much absorbed in singing that he would often forget to take his meal. Sometimes it was seen that he started singing before going for bath, but he forgot to get bath and take his meal. Perhaps he had an urgent work to do but being occupied with the stream of music he forgot to do that. Such was his inclination towards music.

He was equally expert in both singing and dancing. During dancing, he could make his viewers infatuated with joy by the art of his body-language, and if he was accompanied by an elevated music there would have been no bounds of excitement in his dance. In this regard, he was as beautiful as a Greek. He was fond of beauty; and he had beauty of his own in both outside and insight, therefore, his melodious voice and body-movement could easily have a victory over the heart of the spectators. At that time if he was found absent from any function or a gathering that would be considered incomplete, as anyone would except Narendranath could create a storm of joy.

We have already told about those days when Narendranath would imitate the role of king in course of playing a funny game. It shows that he was ever inclined to acting of a role of a dramatic character. At that time public theater was newly introduced, and in aristocrat society many important and respectable persons were found to take part in private theaters. Narendranath also acted with his friends, but he always preferred a positive role in which he would have the privilege of fermentation of his intellect. He acted the role of a yogi in Keshab's *Nava Vrindavan*.

When the day for his B.A. Examination came nearer, he retired to his maternal grandmother's house nearby to avoid the shouting of relatives and hullabaloo of their children. He used to study in a small room on the first floor of that house. It was completely separated from the other part of the house. In later years, he described the room to a friend: "I sat in the room, books in hand, with a pot of strong tea or coffee by my side to keep the brain from getting overtired. I would tie a rope to my foot. Then, if I fell asleep and moved to make myself more comfortable, the rope would jerk me, and I would awake with a start."[23]

At that time Narendranath would go to his house twice a day for having meal or dinner, and rest of the time he would stay at his maternal grandmother's house nearby at Ramtanu Bose Lane for his studies. But this arrangement was not only for his study but also for he liked solitude. There lived many members in his house, noisy; environment was not suitable for his study and meditation. His maternal grandmother's house was comparatively calm and quiet, visitors were very few in number, and they would not break his peace. The room, where Naren used to stay, was on the first floor of outhouse. There was an extra staircase at the entrance of the room, where his friends could easily come to meet him whenever they wished. Naren was in habit of giving name to everyone. He called this small room as 'Tong'. Whenever he would take someone to his room, he said, "Let us go to my Tong." The room was very small—about six feet in width and length was nearly the double of it. A cambric cot and a dirty pillow on it were all is called the furniture of that room. A worn-out mat on was laid on the floor, a Tanpura [stringed musical instrument], a Sitar nearby and a Banya [a small instrument of percussion played along with the Tabla] were kept in a corner of the room. Many a time, the Banya was seen on the mat or under the cot or sometimes Narendra himself was found sitting on it. In another corner of the room, there were a hookah, ball of tobacco and an earthen ashtray. His books were kept on a shelf and scattered about here and there on the floor. His cloths were found hanging from a rope. If he wished he could easily decorate that room with suitable furniture and pictures. He didn't do so because he never felt them necessary. He was never seen inclined to a luxurious life.

For a time Narendranath was busy in his preparation for examination, suddenly a friend came to meet him—it was 11 o'clock in the morning. Narendra had his breakfast before sitting for studies. The friend said, "Brother, will you please leave your studies now, and sing a song for me." Narendra immediately closed the book and put it aside. Tanpura was out of order, so he took the Sitar and after tuning the strings said to his friend, "Then you take the Banya." Friend said, "But, I don't know how to play this instrument, I only have patted on the bench in classroom; how can I play it now?" Naren took the Banya and showed him how to play on it, and said, "Why do you think so? Just follow me carefully. This is not a hard task, just maintain the time of beating," and also told him the sound of music. The friend tried his best and he started singing one after one—khayal, tappa, thumri, dhrupad in Bengali, Hindi and Sanskrit. Each time Narendra told him the new style of rhythm by playing the same. Thus, he forced his friend to learn many types of rhythm in a day. Every after one or two songs they took rest and enjoyed smoking which was only for his friend was tired of playing the Banya. When he sang a Hindi song, he cleared the meaning of that to his friend who was overwhelmed with the knowledge of Narendra in music. Finally, when it was 10 o'clock at night they felt tired and came to consciousness. Narendra went to his house for dinner and his friend set out for his home.

In this way, Narendra's preparation for examination was disturbed by his friends, but he never felt having any antipathy to anything.

While we are talking about the voice of Vivekananda, we must remember what Romain Rolland had said. According to Romain Rolland—"He had a beautiful voice like a violoncello (so Miss Josephine MacLeod told me), grave without violent contrasts, but with deep vibrations that filled both hall and hearts. Once his audience was held, he could make it sink to an intense Piano piercing his hearers to the soul. Emma Calve, who knew him, described it as 'an admirable baritone, having the vibrations of a Chinese gong'."[24]

We would like to mention an important event here. We were talking about the room, which he called 'Tong', where Narendra used to study in his maternal grandmother's house. One day in this room Narendra was singing between his bouts of study. Opposite to this room there was a house across the lane, where lived a young widow. Whenever Narendra would sign, she often used to stand by her window and listen to his song being spell-bound. One evening when Narendranath was absorbed in singing, she crossed over the lane and silently appeared by the door. In the dim light, Narendra saw her standing in the doorway of his room. She was young and beautiful and without his knowledge she had love for him. To her it was romantic. Narendra was startled with wonder. He had never seen the lady before. He fell at her feet. "Mother!" he exclaimed, emphasizing the word; "why have you come? Let me regard you as I would my own mother." The lady understood, and in a moment left the place and since then never came again.

I think we have enough talked about his talent of music. Now we would like to go back to his academic preparation. Only a few days were left for B.A. examination. Every student was busy in paying fees and college dues. Haridas Chattopadhyay, a friend of Narendranath, was poor and he couldn't pay the accumulated college dues for the last one year. It was not easy for him to pay the examination fees. In those days, it was customary for the General Assembly's Institution to help those who, for lack of fund, could not pay the required fees; there was a provision for exemption from paying college dues in special cases.

Rajkumar, an old clerk of the office counter, was given the power in making decision about the exemption of college dues and examination fees. He was a simple and ordinary person, and in the habit of smoking opium, but had compassion on the poor students. Hence, he was a respected person to those who couldn't pay college dues in time. He was reliable to the authority of the college; hence no objection was ever raised against his decision.

Solicitude for others was a remarkable characteristic of Narendranath. He assured his friend that he would see what could be done.

Haridas said, "Brother, I can only manage the examination fees, but cannot pay the college dues."

"Don't worry," Naren assured him, "everything will be managed in time."

After one or two days, when a crowd of students had assembled at the counter in Rajkumar's office to deposit dues and fees, Narendranath made his way through the crowd and said to Rajkumar, "Sir, Haridas is unable to pay his dues. Will you kindly exempt him? If you send him up for the examination, he will be able to pass with credit; otherwise he will be undone."

Rajkumar was an old man, half of his hair was white and half was black, mustache was also similar to his hair but with some marks of tobacco. He didn't get enough time to wear his dress properly, buttons were kept open. He was too busy in collecting fees to listen to anybody carefully. Without looking at Narendra, he replied, "Your presumptuous recommendation is uncalled for, better 'oil your own machine'! I won't send him up unless he pays his dues."

Naren didn't expect such refusal. So rebuffed he left the place, and his friend naturally was disappointed. But Naren consoled him saying, "Why are you giving way to despair? The old man is in the habit of giving such rebuffs. I tell you, I shall find a way out for you; so be at rest."

Haridas had confidence in Narendranath, so a line of smile appeared on his face. He knew that Naren's father was reach, and therefore, he could arrange the required money to pay the college dues, and he felt relief from his tension.

After college hours, instead of returning home, Narendranath went to Simla market, and searched out the opium-smoking den to which Rajkumar usually resorted. As the evening melted into darkness, he saw Rajkumar at the corner of the lane. Narendra rushed to him and stood in his way. Sudden appearance of Narendranath made his face pale with a great surprise. Rajkumar, though puzzled at the sight of Naren at such a place and time, kept his nerve and asked as calmly as he could, "What's the matter, Dutta? You are here!"

Narendranath again presented his plea on behalf of Haridas, and added that, if his request was rejected, he would publicize in the college. Rajkumar's frequenting the opium-smoking den.

"Well, my dear, why are you so angry?" said the old man: "What you want will be done. Can I ever ignore your request?"

Narendranath pretended to be irritated and asked, "Why did you then refuse me in the morning?"

"You know it very well, if I wouldn't refuse you at that time, other students would start demanding for exemption of their fees too, and in that case I would have been in problem. You should have told me privately. You are still a boy, and therefore, don't know how to deal with such a matter. However, the arrears of the college-dues of Haridas would be remitted, but he would be requested to pay the examination fees."

"Well, that can be arranged," Naren replied, "but you have to exempt him from paying the college-dues, he is too poor to pay that." Narendranath took leave of him and tried to control his laughter while he remembered the behaviour of old Rajkumar on his way home.

Haridas lived at Bhuvan Mohan Sarkar Lane which was nearby Naren's house. Early next morning, before sunrise, Narendranath went to Haridas's house and after knocking at the door started singing the song:

In this pure pelucid dawn,
Meditate on Brahman of incomparable glory.
Behold the newly risen sun,
The light of its lovely face
Showing on the mountain top.

The sweet breeze blowing on this auspicious day
Pours nectar while singing His glory.
Let us all go to the abode of God
With offerings of love in our hearts.[25]

Time was very short; at least a month for his B.A. examination was left in hand. Yet he had not read a single page of Green's *History of the English People*, which was one of the textbooks prescribed. He had no interest in any academic competition. He merely cared for a high grade. Only few days before the examination did he busy himself in assigned reading, and then only to pass. Indeed, his academic preparation was generally a last-minute affair and dependent upon his prodigious memory. His inner spiritual urges didn't allow him to set great value on the worldly prosperity. He was not inclined to acquire a university degree. He was mostly busy in singing or gossiping with his friends. To the north of the room, where he used to study in his maternal grandmother's house, was a big room. To the west of this big room, there was a secret chamber. The entrance of the chamber was so small that he had to crawl before getting into it. He vowed that he would not leave the chamber until he had mastered the contents of the history book. In three days, he finished his task and came out of the chamber. But there were other books to read. He confined himself for days at a time, studying day and night.

On the morning before the B.A. examination, Narendranath was found in a strange mood: "fling away all books, for what shall learning be in the presence of the Lord!"—this was how he felt.

On the day of examination, Narendranath woke up before the sun rise and left his bed. Then in the pleasant light of the dawn he went to his friend Dasharathi's [Dasharathi Sanyal, who in his later life became a famous lawyer of High Court] house and stood outside the gate, singing absorbedly while his friends were still in a deep sleep. He began with the opening verse of the song: "We are like children, with little understanding. Shall we not rely upon Him, the Ocean of Wisdom?" Again, it was a song of praise:

Sing ye, O mountains, O clouds, O great winds!

Sing ye, sing ye, His glory!

Sing with joy all ye, the suns and moons and stars!

Sing ye, sing ye, His glory!

As soon as they heard and recognized the voice of Narendranath they left their bed and opened the door. They had a plan to revise their preparation for examination but couldn't do the same in presence of Narendranath. They had no other way than listening to his song till nine o'clock. A friend intervened and reminded him of the examination, but Narendra turned a deaf ear to him.

Narendranath was a flame of spirituality. He always considered purity as the cardinal virtue and made it so in his life. In those days, he practiced the hard life of Brahmachari, used to meditate till late night, and slept on a rug or a mat. He believed that without purity spiritual life is impossible. To him, purity was not a state for avoiding evil, but a passion for good, in each and every aspect. His passion for philosophy grew more. He observed: "By the observance of strict brahmacharya all learning can be mastered in a very short time; one acquires unfailing memory of what one hears or knows but once. The chaste brain has tremendous energy and gigantic willpower." But he never felt necessary to apply any force for remaining pure in mind. He was initiated to honesty and purity by nature since his childhood.

Due to English education, and the impact of Western culture a great transformation was found in the culture of Bengal in the nineteenth century. It was the age of the French Illumination when the spirit of rationalism and individualism dominated European thought. It publicized the supremacy of reason over faith, of individual conscience over outside authority, and brought a new conception of social justice and political rights. A new ideology suddenly burst forth upon the static life, moulded for centuries by a fixed set of religious ideas and social conventions. It gave birth to a critical attitude towards religion and a spirit of inquiry into the origin of State and society with a view to determining their proper scope and functions.

Narendranath's character was made up of a strange harmony of two opposite ideas—one was his inclination towards renunciation of worldly life and the other his interest in enjoying the worldly pleasure. Though he was a preacher of non-dualism, he never advised to stay away from work in practical life. He didn't say to ignore the existence of the world. He has shown in his own life, how to extract joy from a life. One, who has attained divine knowledge, can ignore the world, but others cannot; hence the worldly life is to enjoy. But this enjoyment is not for an unwise person, who for his selfishness makes his life full of sorrow by running unconsciously after happiness. Narendranath believed that a true enjoyment is free from selfishness and free from all ugly desire. Enjoying a true love with ever purity is called true enjoyment.

The spirit of renunciation was awakening in his heart, completely unattached to the worldly life. He realized: "The selfless and unattached man may live in the very heart of a crowded and sinful city; he will not be touched by sin."[26] That is why he could live in a reach family and become sympathetic towards poor.

Narendranath was aware of intellectual diagrams of philosophical system that gives no place to the emotions of man. He didn't want diagrams of Truth, he wanted only the Truth. He became interested in the philosophy of Herbert Spencer, and later on he used the Spencerian mode of reasoning in his discussion of the doctrines of the Upanishads and Vedanta. Thus, he gained a power of thinking, and spirit of search for a scientific basis, that helped him in delivering his message in later years. Once he wrote a letter to Herbert Spencer by criticizing some parts of his book. Spencer, the great philosopher, in his reply praised Narendra for his opinion and assured him that he would try to do the required correction in the next edition of his book. Narendranath obviously was happy with such responsible act of Spencer, and realized that his ideas were not neglected by the great thinkers of the world.

When Narendranath was in General Assembly College, Professor Hastie, the learned philosopher, was the principal of the college. He learnt philosophy from Professor Hastie. One day Professor Hastie told about Narendra, "Narendranath is really a genius. I have travelled far and wide but I have never yet come across a lad of his talents and possibilities, even in German universities, amongst philosophy students. He is bound to make his mark in life!"

Narendranath in Association with Brahmo Samaj

During his tenure in college, Narendranath read much of Western philosophy, as a result of which he was influence by the idea of agnosticism about existence of God. We have already mentioned that he was deeply impressed by the philosophy of Herbert Spencer. But his faith in religion was hurt by *The Science of the First Principles*, the book written by Spencer. He was never in the habit of accepting anything without having any proof of its truthfulness after a long search by his own power of intellect.

He had no orthodoxy or blind-faith in priests, as he knew how religious life of a nation was vitiated by their social hegemony and people's blind adherence to them. This demanded a strong counter-plea very soon. He was not satisfied by the study of Western philosophy that forced him in having a doubt in the existence of God. Moreover, he was irritated by the unholy practices of priests, but couldn't ignore the customs of the society. He read the philosophy of Comte and felt the usefulness of his positivism in practical life. Yet this agnosticism couldn't satisfy him for a long time. There is no creator of this world, and even if He is, no one can see Him—as long as he was thinking so, his mental agony was growing more and more. He became puzzled with different thoughts, became more restless as he had no indication of the Truth. Yet he had no doubt about what he had learnt from his parents, from his daily life since his childhood. He couldn't ignore the necessity of moral life. He believed, even if there is no existence of God, purity in human life should be maintained. One may have the power of thinking, but it is limited, and he can never know everything of the universe. Hence, it cannot be justified to depend on the power of intellect at the cost of demands of the heart. He liked to sleep on a mat or rug and was fond of a life of an ascetic. So he didn't try to remove the idea of renunciation forcefully from his mind—rather, he felt it necessary for the fulfilment of his life.

After a thorough study of Western philosophy, he treated the worldly pleasure with contempt.

Scepticism at least taught him this much lesson, that life is as untruth as a dream and everything in the world is futile. Ultimate success of this unsubstantial life lies only in knowing the Truth—keeping it in mind he tried to go ahead towards the Truth by going through the system of judgment, one after another. He didn't accept that which was not found up to the mark and proved true in his judgment. He tried to understand the future of his life, and he believed that his hard work cannot be fruitless, someday all his doubts will disappear and he will be able to know the Truth. He, therefore, didn't give up his practice of meditation in the midst of these suspicions and deliberations. Whenever he sat in meditation, he would have lost himself somewhere, where doubts and arguments did not find their way in. During meditation he would have felt such a joy or experienced such a thing as was not qualified by his thought or imagination. This was perhaps his experience of the spiritual world.

Agnostic people mostly found missing their path in the darkness. But Narendranath didn't do so; he went on in the direction of light. As many days as he passed, he became more confident in having the knowledge of Truth. But where the knowledge is limited, no one can know more than that. Hence, for how long a man can bear such a pain? Every day his religious nature was being crashed by his doubts and arguments, and his tolerance had no limit; finally he gave up the agnosticism, came back to the hardship of Brahmocharin renouncing the worldly life, and realized the existence of God. God exists, but He cannot be seen with own physical eyes.

Since that day he started spiritual discussion with his friends, sitting in the worship hall, began to explain many spiritual ideas, yet he could not be satisfied. His search for God had no end, he remained thirsty for knowing the Truth. He began to search for such a being, who could understand his pain and show him the right path. He vowed to see God at any cost. So, he had to find out such a man who had seen God and could show him God. Where is that dearest friend? 'Where there's a will there's a way.'—It came true in Narendra's life. But the search was not so easy. He had to move from door to door with a load of thoughts and a heart full of urge to know the God. His search was successful; he met his ever-desired Master after a long wait and endless patience.

How did Narendranath meet his most desired friend?—Let's tell that story now. Let us see how his struggle for the truth was. In this connection, he said:

> At the beginning of this century [19th] it was almost feared that religion was at an end. Under the tremendous sledge-hammer blows of scientific research, old superstitions were crumbling away like masses of porcelain. Those to whom religion meant only a bundle of creeds and meaningless ceremonials were in despair; they were at their wit's end. Everything was slipping between their fingers. For a time it seemed inevitable that the surging tide of agnosticism and materialism would sweep all before it.... When I was a boy, this scepticism reached me, and it seemed for a time as if I must give up all hope of religion. But fortunately for me I studied the Christian religion, the Mohammedan, the Buddhistic, and others, and what was my surprise to find that the same foundation principles taught by my religion were also taught by all religions. It appealed to me this way. "What is the truth? I asked." More he added, "When I was a boy here, in this city of Calcutta, I used to go from place to place in search of religion, and everywhere I asked the lecturer after hearing very big lectures, 'Have you seen God?' The man was taken aback at the idea of seeing God; and the only man who told me, 'I have,' was Ramakrishna Paramahamsa, and not only so, but his said, 'I will put you in the way of seeing Him too'."[27]

Since Narendranath was in school, he was acquainted with Maharshi Devendranath Tagore, who was regarded by many as one of the best spiritual teachers of the time. In this connection, one day he went to meet Maharshi along with some of his friends. He advised them to practice meditation. Later, when the Maharshi was living in retirement in a boat on the Ganga, Narendranath went to him alone. His sudden appearance startled the venerable old man. Before he could say a word, Narendranath, tensed with excitement, asked him, "Sir, have you seen God?" The Maharshi was surprised, and said, "My boy, you have the Yogi's eyes." And then he advised Narendra to practice meditation with great intensity. Narendranath returned with disappointment.

Narendranath started learning music from Beni Ostad since he was a student for Entrance examination. He was familiar to Brahmo Samaj since 1879, when, in Jorasanko Thakur Bari [Tagore's house], a rehearsal of Indian classical music was going on in full swing. Jadu Bhatto, the great performer and researcher of Indian classical music was associated with this family. Maharshi's sons, particularly Jyotirindranath and Rabindranath developed the music department of Brahmo Samaj with their compositions on Dhrupad. Deependranath, grandson of Maharshi Devendranath, was Narendra's classmate. Nadalal Sen, nephew of Keshav Chandra Sen, was also a student of the same class with Narendra. Narendranath had a very close relation with Jorasanko Thakur Bari, and sang many songs composed by Rabindranath Tagore. In those days, Narendranath used to sing for Brahmo Samaj whenever he went there.

Swami Gambhirananda said that, Narendranath, as a learner, went to Maharshi Devendranath Tagore, who advised him about the spiritual world. Though he was personally known to Maharshi, there is no such proof of his intimacy with Adi Brahmo Samaj. His intimacy with Keshav was also at personal level. According to Mahendranath Dutta, Keshav Sen organized a group titled 'Band of Hope', and Narendra registered his name with the group. But Swami Gambhirananda didn't support this statement, rather he said, Narendranath was associated with Thakur Bari for his relatives and classmate. Though he had accepted the opinion of Nalinikumar Bhadra, that Narendranath was associated with Brahmo Samaj since 1879; he said that Narendranath was so busy at that time for his F.A. examination that he could hardly afford much time for the Samaj.

According to Swami Gambhirananda, in 1878, Sadharan Brahmo Samaj [general society of the Brahmos] was established by Shiva Nath Shastri and Vijoykrishna Goswami. Hence, after he returned from Raipur Narendranath appeared for F.A. examination, and there after he was more attracted to the Sadharan Brahmo Samaj than to other two Brahmo organizations. He regularly used to go there, and the registration his name was followed by a ceremony. There is no evidence that Narendra was ever under the leadership of Keshav Sen. Vivekananda, in his later life, wrote in a letter:

> I had connection with Pundit Shiva Nath Shastri's party—but only on points of social reform. Mazoomdar and Chandra Sen—I always considered as not sincere, and I have no reason to change my opinion even now. Of course in religious matters even with my friend Punditji I differed much, the chief being, I thinking Sannyasa or (giving up the world) the highest ideal, and he, a sin. So the Brahmo Samajists consider becoming a monk a sin!![28]

With reference to this context, Swami Saradananda said: "At this time the Brahmos had split into two groups because of the controversial marriage between the Maharaja of Coochbehar and Keshab's daughter. The Sadharan Brahmo Samaj had been formed a few years before the event we describe here. Although Narendra visited Keshab from time to time, he also went regularly to the Sadharan Brahmo Samaj and would sing devotional songs at their Sunday prayer meetings."[29]

We would like to talk something more about Brahmo Samaj to see the situation through which Narendranath passed at that time. According to *Life of Swami Vivekananda* the picture was as follows:

> In brief, the Brahmo Samaj was the outward expression of an endeavour to liberalize and at the same time conserve the evolved traits of the Hindu race. It's coming into existence in the year 1828 was the result of the awakening inspired by the illustrious Raja Rammohan Roy, a man of gigantic intellect and inflexible will; and a man who had the courage and prestige necessary to lead an attack on the evils which threatened the very existence of the nation. He saw that if Hinduism were to survive, it would have to be at the cost of many religious and social customs. Later, Maharshi Devendranath Tagore and Keshab Chandra Sen became his most powerful followers; indeed, it was owing to these two influential persons that the life of the movement was assured.

This movement protested against certain forms and tenets of orthodox Hinduism, such as polytheism, image worship, the doctrine of Divine Incarnations, and the need for a Guru. It offered a monotheistic religion which repudiated all these. On the social side, it demanded the eradication of the caste system, the recognition of the equality of man, the education and emancipation of women, with the raising of the marriageable age. It was a tremendous task which the Brahmo Samaj assigned itself, one requiring endless patience and wisdom. But it lacked the means to carry out these reforms; nor did it recognize that reforms must come from within, that imposing them from outside can have no lasting effect.

The movement, however, was progressive in its views, and it is not to be wondered at that it captured the imagination of young Bengal. In Narendranath, it aroused a tumult of thought and feeling, and he came to regard the Samaj, whose meetings he often attended, as an ideal institution which might help to solve all life's problems, individual or national. He was imbued with the same ideas as the Brahmo leaders. He knew the burden of caste and had chafed under its rigidity; he had no sympathy with polytheism and image worship. He also felt that the women of his nation must be educated. Thus, he espoused the cause of the Samaj with all earnestness, and it was his fervent hope that the strength of thought, depth of feeling, enthusiasm, and personal magnetism, which were characteristics of Keshab Chandra Sen, and through which he influenced his numerous followers, would one day be his.

In 1878, there was a split in the Brahmo Samaj, and a number of its members headed by Pandit Shiva Nath Shastri, and Vijaykrishna Goswami formed a new society on May 15, 1878, called the Sadharan Brahmo Samaj. Narendranath identified himself with the new organization, and his name can still be seen on the roll of the original members. He also joined at this time a movement for the education of the masses, irrespective of caste, creed, or colour. His intense desire for freedom made him willing to identify himself with anything that promised liberation from obsolete methods and willing to cast aside whatever might interfere with his gaining a larger vision. He was not content with passivity; he wanted to know the 'why' and 'how' of every phenomenon, mental or spiritual.[30]

Brahmo Samaj could not help Narendranath in satisfying his desire for knowing the truth. There was a vast difference between his idea of reforming the society and that of Brahmo Samaj; he was far ahead of them. He believed; a true reformation is possible only through education which can bring a change in the way of thinking; a force from outside cannot reform any idea that is being practiced for a long period. He advised to make an effort to remove the bad practices without applying any force from outside to reform a manner and custom or any old faith that has become a tradition. It would be unjustified to apply the Western culture on general public who had already a culture of their own, and in that case the result would be more harmful than benefaction. Before going to reform a culture, we should study the same properly, and then a perfect blending of both the old and new culture can make a true reformation. It means, in any case, no one should ignore his past.

Narendranath, since his childhood, would follow the path fixed by God. He was not completely free from the environment around him, but it could hardly be a cause to stop him in the midway. We have told about Brojendranath Seal, who was a senior to Narendra in college. Narendranath used to discuss philosophy with him. To get a clear view of Naren's personality and the early stage of his mental development, it would be well to quote the observation of Brojendranath Seal, a leading intellect of India in his day. In an article written for the *Probuddha Bharata* (April 1907, and reproduced in the *Brahmavadin* the following month), he says:

> When I first met Vivekananda in 1881, we were fellow-students of Principal William Hastie, scholar, metaphysician, and poet, at the General Assembly's College. He was my senior in age, though I was his senior in the College by one year. Undeniably a gifted youth, sociable, free and unconventional in manners, a sweet singer, the soul of social circles, a brilliant conversationalist, somewhat bitter and caustic, piercing with the shafts of a keen with the shows and mummeries of the world, sitting in the scorner's chair

but hiding the tenderest of hearts under that grab of cynicism; altogether an inspired Bohemian but possessing what Bohemians lack, an iron will; somewhat peremptory and absolute, speaking with accents of authority and withal possessing a strange power of the eye which could hold his listeners in thrall.

This was patent to all. But what was known to few was the inner man and his struggle—the Sturm und drang of soul which expressed itself in his restless and Bohemian wanderings.

This was the beginning of a critical period in his mental history, during which he awoke to self-consciousness and laid the foundations of his future personality. John Stuart Mill's *Three Essays on Religion* had upset his first boyish theism and easy optimism which he had imbibed from the outer circles of the Brahmo Samaj. The arguments from causality and design were for him broken reeds to lean upon, and he was haunted by the problem of the Evil in Nature and Man which he, by no means, could reconcile with the goodness of an All-wise and All-powerful Creator. A friend introduced him to the study of Hume's scepticism and Herbert Spencer's doctrine of the Unknowable, and his unbelief gradually assumed the form of a settled philosophical scepticism.

His first emotional freshness and naïveté were worn out. A certain dryness and incapacity for the old prayerful devotions, an ennui which he concealed under a nonchalant air of habitual mocking and scoffing, troubled his spirit. But music still stirred him as nothing else could and gave him a weird unearthly sense of unseen realities which brought tears to his eyes.

It was at this time that he came to me being brought by a common friend, the same who had introduced him to the study of Hume and Herbert Spencer. I had had a nodding acquaintance with him before, but now he opened himself to me and spoke of his harassing doubts and his despair of reaching certitude about the Ultimate Reality. He asked for a course of Theistic philosophic reading suited to a beginner in his situation. I named some authorities, but the stock arguments of the Intuitionists and the Scotch commonsense school only confirmed him in his unbelief. Besides, he did not appear to me to have sufficient patience for humdrum reading—his faculty was to imbibe not so much from books as from living communion and personal experience. With his it was life kindling life and thought kindling thought.

I felt deeply drawn towards him, for I now knew that he would grapple with difficulties in earnest.

I gave him a course of readings in Shelley. Shelley's Hymn to the Spirit of Intellectual Beauty, his pantheism of impersonal love and his vision of a glorified millennial humanity moved him as the arguments of the philosophers had failed to move him. The universe was no longer a mere lifeless, loveless mechanism. It contained a spiritual principle of unity.

I spoke to him now of a higher unity than Shelley had conceived, the unity of the Para Brahman as the Universal Reason. My own position at that time sought to fuse into one, three essential elements, the pure monism of the Vedanta, the dialectics of the Absolute idea of Hegel, and the Gospel of Equality, Liberty and Fraternity of the French Revolution. The principle of individuation was with me the principle of Evil. The Universal Reason was all in all, Nature, life, history being the progressive unfolding of the Absolute idea. All ethical, social and political creeds and principles were to be tested by their conformity to Pure Reason. The element of feeling speared to me merely pathological, a disturbance of sanity and order. How to overcome the resistance of matter, of individuality and of unreason, to the manifestation of the Pure Reason was the great problem of life and society, of education and legislation. I also held with the ardour of a young inexperienced visionary that the deliverance of the race from the bondage of unreason would come about through a new revolutionary polity of which the watchwords were Equality, Liberty, and Fraternity.

The sovereignty of Universal Reason, and the negation of the individual as the principle of morals, were ideas that soon came to satisfy Vivekananda's intellect and gave him an assured conquest over scepticism and materialism. What was more, they furnished him with the card and compass of life, as it were. But this brought him no peace. The conflict now entered deeper into his soul, for the creed of Universal Reason called on him to suppress the yearnings and susceptibilities of his artist nature and Bohemian temperament. His senses were keen and acute, his natural cravings and passions strong and imperious, his youthful susceptibilities tender, his conviviality free and merry. To suppress these was to kill his natural spontaneity—almost to suppress his self. The struggle soon took a seriously ethical turn—reason struggling for mastery with passion and sense. The fascinations of the sense and the cravings of a youthful nature now appeared to him as impure, as gross and carnal. This was the hour of darkest trial for him. His musical gifts brought him associates for whose manners and morals he had bitter and undisguised contempt. But his convivial temperament proved too strong for him. It was, therefore, some relief to him when I occasionally kept him company of an evening when he went out for a musical soiree.

I saw and recognized in him a high, ardent and pure nature, vibrant and resonant with impassioned sensibilities. He was certainly no sour or cross-grained puritan, no normal hypochondriac; he would indulge cynically in unconventional language except when he would spare my innocence. He took an almost morbid delight in shocking conventionality in its tabernacles, respectability in its booths; and in the pursuit of his sport would appear other than he was, puzzling and mystifying those outside his inner circle of friends. But in the recesses of his soul he wrestled with the fierce and fell spirit of Desire, the subtle and illusive spirit of Fancy. To his repeated quest for some power which would deliver him from bondage and unavailing struggle, I could only point to the sovereignty of Pure Reason and the ineffable peace that comes of identifying the self with the Reason in the Universe. Those were for me days of a victorious Platonic transcendentalism. The experience of a refractory flesh or rebellious temperament had not come to me. I had not sufficient patience for the mood or attitude of mind which surrenders the sovereign right of self-government to artificial props or outside help, such as grace or mediation. I felt no need of conciliating feeling and nature in the cult of Reason, not had had any experience of a will divided in its allegiance to the Self. The experience of a discord between the Ideal and the Real, between Nature and Spirit, had indeed come to me already in an objective way as an outstanding reality and was to come afterwards in subjective fashion, though in forms quite other than what obtained in Vivekananda's case. But at the time, his problems were not mine, not were my difficulties his.

He confessed that though his intellect was conquered by the universal, his heart owned the allegiance of the individual Ego and complained that a pale bloodless reason, sovereign de jure but not de facto, could not hold out arms to save him in the hour of temptation. He wanted to know if my philosophy could satisfy his senses, could mediate bodily, as it were, for the soul's deliverance; in short, he wanted a flesh and blood reality visible in form and glory; above all, he cried out for a hand to save, to uplift, to protect, a Shakti or power outside himself which could cure him of his impotence and cover his nothingness with glory—a Guru or master who by embodying perfection in the flesh would still the commotion in his soul.

At the time, this appeared to me a weakness born of unreason, this demand for perfection in the flesh and for a power out of ourselves to save—this sacrifice of reason to sense. My young inexperienced self, confronted with this demand of a soul striving with itself, knew not wherewith to satisfy it, and Vivekananda soon after betook himself to the ministers and missionaries of the Brahmo Samaj, asking Brahmo with an unconscious Socratic Irony for an ideal made real to sense, for truth made visible, for a power unto deliverance. Here he had enough, he bitterly complained, of moral disquisitions, principles, intuitions for pabulum which to him appeared tasteless and insipid. He tried diverse teachers, creeds and cults, and it was this quest that brought him, though at first in a doubting spirit, to the Paramahansa of Dakshineswar, who spoke to him with an authority as none had spoken before, and by his Shakti brought peace into his soul and healed the wounds of his spirit. But his rebellious intellect scarcely yet owned the Master. His mind misgave him and he doubted if the peace which would possess his soul in the presence of the Master was not illusory. It was only gradually that the doubts of that keen intellect were vanquished by the calm assurance that belongs to ocular demonstration.

I watched with intense interest the transformation that went on under my eyes. The attitude of a young and rampant Vedantist-cum-Hegelian-cum-Revolutionary like myself towards the cult of religious ecstasy and Kali-worship, may be easily imagined; and the spectacle of a born iconoclast and free-thinker like Vivekananda, a creative and dominating intelligence, a tamer of souls, himself caught in the meshes of what appeared to me an uncouth, super-natural mysticism, was a riddle which my philosophy of the Pure Reason could scarcely read at the time. But Vivekananda, "the loved and lost" was loved, and mourned most in what I could not but then regard as his defection; and it was personal feeling, after all, the hated pathological element of individual relationship, which most impelled me, when at last I went on what to a home-keeping recluse like myself was an adventurous journey to Dakshineswar, to see and hear Vivekananda's Master, and spent the greater part of a long summer day in the shady and peaceful solitude of the Temple garden, returning as the sun set amidst the whirl and rush and roar and the awful gloom of a blinding thunderstorm, with a sense of bewilderment as well moral as physical, and a lurking perception of the truth that the majesty of Law orders the apparently irregular and grotesque, that there may be self-mastery in apparent self-alienation, that sense even in its errors is only incipient Reason and that faith in a Saving Power ab extra is but the dim reflex of an original act of self-determination. And a significant confirmation of all this came in the subsequent life-history of Vivekananda who, after he had found the firm assurance he sought in the saving Grace and Power of his Master, went about preaching and teaching the creed of the Universal Man, and the absolute and inalienable sovereignty of the self.

At that time Narendranath was passing through a period of tremendous conflicts, and he was looking for a man who could show him the right part towards the truth. Brojendranath Seal has described this transformation that went on under his eyes. He has told about Narendra's logical firmness perceptible by senses. But Swamiji was not yearning for a cause or any sense perception.

He wanted visible and imperceptible knowledge that comes through Purity attached to God—not through argument or physical sense. Swamiji's opinion was—'Religion realization.' It is "not to know in the ordinary sense of the word, not intellectual understanding, not mere rationalistic comprehension of the real thing, not mere groping in the dark, but intense realization, much more real than this world is to our senses."[31] It doesn't mean, that Swamiji wanted to pay no heed to argumentation under the shadow of perceptible senses or he would search something in philosophy which explains gratification of the senses. He was not satisfied with the association of Brahmo Samaj as it couldn't help him realizing the transcendentalism. Yet, it is true, that he went to Brahmo Samaj in search of truth; he wished to gain something, and Samaj helped him in the manifestation of his personality.

It is very much natural, that a terrible brawl is born during the process of intellectual development of brain. But it is a matter of surprise that Narendranath never lost his self-confidence in the midst of tremendous tussle in mind, rather he acquired more power, more courage to continue his fight for the truth. He began to study Indian history as was written by Marshman, Elphinstone, and other Western historians. William Hamilton, a Western philosopher, said, "Where philosophy ends, there religion begins." After quoting this sentence Swami Saradananda, in his *Lilaprosango*, said, "Narendra was very fond of Hamilton's saying and sometimes referred to it in conversation. Although Narendra concentrated on *sadhana* [meditation], he did not give up study of philosophy. He spent most of his time in meditation, study, and music."[32] But neither books nor theories could satisfy him. When he realized that his learning was utterly inadequate to reveal the Truth, he felt a tremendous current of restlessness flowed more strongly in his mind. He began to search the friend, who can show him the right path—where is that friend, who will help him in realizing the Truth?

General Assembly Institution
(Scottish Church College)

Principal W. W. Hastie

4
At the Feet of the Master

Narendranath had gone through a lot of books on Indian and Western History, on philosophy, discussed with so many scholars, went to Brahmo Samaj, but nothing could satisfy his urge for the Truth. No one could help him in giving relief from his painful but ardent urge. No one could put him into the path of realizing God. No one could tell him that he had seen God. He was in search of the friend, who would take him to the realm of light.

One day in the absence of the professor of English, William Hastie, the noted scholar and principal of General Assembly Institution, was taking English literature class. He was explaining Wordsworth's 'Excursion', where the state of trance is referred to, and of which the poet had had a glimpse while contemplating the beauty of nature. But the students could not understand what is meant by trance. Professor Hastie then said, "Such an experience is the result of purity of mind and concentration on some particular object, and it is rare indeed, particularly in these days. I have seen only one person who has experienced that blessed state of mind, and he is Ramakrishna Paramhamsa of Dakshineshwar. You can understand if you go there and see for yourself."

Haromohan Mitra, a classmate of Narendranath, described this incident to Bhupendranath Dutta as follows: "One day our professor of English was angry with the students as he could not explain Wordsworth's poem. Extremely irritated by the foolishness of the students and he patted on the table, kicked on the floor and went out of the class. That time, while I was passing by the class, I saw, Reverend Hastie was approaching the class. I entered the class and listened to his lecture. He said, 'English professor told me that the students are foolish, they do not understand Wordsworth's poem. Perhaps he could not understand what Wordsworth had experienced as trance.' Then he concluded by saying that there lives a person at Dakshineshwar, and he had experienced that blessed state of mind,—'you may go there to see for yourself.' That day we first heard the name of Sri Ramakrishna."

That day, Narendranath also heard first the name of Sri Ramakrishna along with other students, but that information was kept in his memory for an auspicious and ever-desired moment of future.

Days passed by. Narendranath became more restless for the perceptive knowledge of God. F.A. examination was very near, but he had no consciousness of that, his search for the truth was going unabated. He went on asking, whom ever he came across, "Have you seen God? Where is the friend, who can show me a way out of this state?"—This was the only question wandering in his mind.

It was November 1881, the time, for which Narendranath had been waiting for a long time. The auspicious moment was very near when Narendra would meet his ever desired friend,

Sri Ramakrishna Paramhamsa, who incarnated Himself combining in a single personality the wonderful love and compassion of Buddha and Christ, and the keen intellect of Shankara to demonstrate the true religion. Narendranath was then busy in his preparation for the F.A. examination. Surendranath Mitra, a devotee of Sri Ramakrishna, lived at Simla, nearby Narendra's house. Surendranath invited the Master [Sri Ramakrishna] to his house, and arranged a festival. In this connection, a skilled singer was required. But Surendranath didn't find a professional singer for the day. Suddenly, he remembered the name of Narendranath, who was well known as a good singer in that area. He, therefore, without any delay invited him cordially to sing devotional songs for the Master. When Narendranath came to know the name of Sri Ramakrishna, the memory of that day flashed through his mind—this is He, of whom Professor Hastie told that He has experienced the state of trance, may He be able to help him in realizing God! Only a week was left for the F.A. examination, but he agreed to attend the function only for the opportunity to visit the Master.

Surendranath came in right time to take Narendra to his house. The holy moment, when Narendranath first sang for Sri Ramakrishna, was ever green in his memory. Swami Saradanada said, "Thus the first meeting between the Master and Swami Vivekananda, the chief companion in his divine play, took place." The Master was very much attracted to Narendra at first sight. When Narendranath had finished his song, Sri Ramakrishna called Surendranath and Ramachandra [maternal uncle of Bhuvaneswari Devi] and learned everything about the wonderful singer, and also asked them to bring him to Dakshineswar on some day. He also approached Narendra and carefully watched his features, and after talking with him for some time he invited him to visit Dakshineswar soon.

The Master knew the events in the previous lives of his devotees before they arrived in front of him. The purpose of his present incarnation was to manifest a particular Lila [play] of the Cosmic Mind. He knew that some great souls were born to fulfil that Lila. It was well known to Him who will play what kind of role, and who will be blessed by merely enjoying his association. Revered Swami Saradananda, a direct disciple of Sri Ramakrishan, said, "So it is clear that one who knew all those hidden mysteries while living in the realm of maya must be considered omniscient."

A few weeks after the above event Narendranath appeared for the F.A. examination and he passed in the second division. By this time a proposal came from a rich family for the marriage of Narendranath. Parents of the bride were ready to pay rupees ten thousand as dowry, because the girl's complexion was dark. Viswanath Dutta wished to accept the proposal, but Narendra refused vehemently, and the matter ended. Viswanath Dutta and other members of his family tried to convince Narendra to accept this marriage proposal. But all efforts were in vain. Ramchandra Dutta knew that Narendranath was very much inclined to Sri Ramakrishna, and he used to visit him every now and then, and also advised others to go. Ramchandra was a distant relative of Narendra and had been raised in Viswanath's household. He knew well the mental state of Narendra, and therefore, one day he clearly told him, "Why do you go to Brahmo Samaj and other places? Better visit Sri Ramakrishna at Dakshineswar, if you are really interested in knowing the mysteries of religion and God."

One day Surendranath invited Narendra to accompany him to Dakshineswar in his carriage. Narendra gladly agreed and went to Dakshineswar with him, and also took with him two or three of his friends as well. This was his first visit to Dakshineswar, and the second visit to the Master. Revered Swami Saradananda was in support of the statement. But according to M [Mahendranath

Gupta, the narrator of *The Gospel of Sri Ramakrishna*] this was Narendra's first visit to the Master. The event of festival at Surendranath's house is not mentioned in *The Gospel of Sri Ramakrishna*; perhaps it happened before he came to the Master. In another opinion, Swamiji met the Master second time at Rammohan's house. According to Swami Saradananda, Swamiji first heard the name of Sri Ramakrishna from William Hastie and he first met the Master at Surendra's house, or, during his visit to Brahmo Samaj, might have heard of the Master long ago.

Revered Swami Saradananda heard of Swamiji's first visit to Dakshineswar from the Master, and later he described the same in his *Lilaprosango*, which goes as follows:

The Master said: "Narendra entered the room by the western door, the one that faces the Ganges. I noticed that he was not concerned about his appearance; his hair and his clothes weren't tidy at all. Unlike his companions, he seemed completely detached, as if nothing external appealed to him. His eyes showed that the greater part of his mind was turned inward all of the time. When I saw this, I marveled to myself, 'How is it possible that such a great spiritual aspirant can live in Calcutta, home to such materialistic people?'

"There was a mat spread out on the floor. I asked him to be seated, and he sat down near the jar of Ganges water. A few of his friends were with him that day. I saw that their nature was that of ordinary worldly people, just the opposite of his. They were thinking only of their pleasure.

"I asked him about his singing and found that he knew only two or three songs in Bengali. I asked him to sing them. He began singing this Brahmo song: 'Let us return once more, O mind, to your own abode!'

"He sang that song with his whole soul, as though he were deep in meditation. When I heard it, I couldn't control myself. I went into ecstasy.

"After Narendra left I felt a constant and agonizing desire to see him. At times the pain was so excruciating that I felt as if my heart were being squeezed like a wet towel. When I could no longer control myself, I would run to the pine grove on the northern side of the garden where people seldom go and cry at the top of my voice: 'O my child, come to me! I can't live without seeing you!' After crying this way for a while, I was able to control myself again. This state continued for six months. There were other boys who also came here. I felt greatly drawn to some of them, but nothing like the way I was attracted to Narendra."[1]

We found in *The Gospel of Sri Ramakrishna*: Master said, "At my first meeting with Narendra I found him completely indifferent to his body. When I touched his chest with my hand, he lost consciousness of the outer world. Regaining consciousness, Narendra said: 'Oh, what have you done to me? I have my father and mother at home!'"[2]

Later on, when Swami Saradananda was talking with Narendranath, he gave him his account of the first visit to the Master. Narendranath said:

> "As soon as I finished the song, the Master stood up, took me by his hand, and led me out to the northern veranda. It was winter, so the open spaces between the pillars were covered with screens of matting to keep out the north wind. This meant that anyone standing, on the veranda was completely hidden when the door of the room was closed. The Master closed the door as soon as we were on the veranda. I thought he was going to give me some private instructions. But what he said and did next was something I could never have believed possible. He suddenly caught hold of my hand and began shedding profuse tears of joy. He said to me affectionately, as to an intimate friend: 'You've come so late! Was that right? Didn't you guess how I've been waiting for you? My ears have

> nearly burned off from listening to the talk of these worldly people. I thought I would burst without anyone to tell how I really feel!' He went on like that—raving and weeping. Then he suddenly stood up with his palms folded together and began addressing me as if I were some divine being: 'I know who you are, my Lord. You are Nara, the ancient sage, the incarnation of Narayana. You have come to earth to take away the suffering and sorrow of human beings.'

"I was absolutely dumbfounded by his conduct. I said to myself: 'What kind of a man is this? He must be raving mad! How can he talk like this to me, a nobody—the son of Vishwanath Dutta?' But I didn't answer him, and I let this wonderful madman go on talking as he wished. Presently, he asked me to stay there on the veranda, and he went back into the room. When he returned he brought butter, rock candy, and a few pieces of sandesh, and then he began to feed me with his own hands. I kept asking him to give me the sweets so I could share them with my friends, but he wouldn't. 'They'll get some later,' he said. 'You take these for yourself.' And he wasn't satisfied until I'd eaten all of them. Then he took my hand and said, 'Promise that you'll come back soon, alone.' His request was made so earnestly that I couldn't refuse. I had to say, 'I will.' Then I went back into the room with him and sat down with my friends."[3]

"Beside Narendranath and his friends, there were some other men sitting in the Master's room. Master began to say, "Look, how sparkling is Naren by the wisdom of Saraswati! [Goddess of knowledge]" Everyone got surprised with the words of the Master and stared at Narendranath. They were amazed to think that Master must have seen something special in Narendra. Master asked Narendra, "Do you see light before falling asleep? Narendra replied, "Yes sir." "Oh! Everything is tallying," said the Master. "He is dhyan-sidhya [a dept in meditation]".

Narendranath watched the Master closely, and observed nothing abnormal in his word, movements, or behaviour towards others. He thought, "His [Master] words and ecstasy showed him to be a man of true renunciation who had given up everything for God. He practices what he preaches." The question that he had asked several times to many scholars, rose in his mind. He asked the Master, "Have you seen God?" The Master at once replied, "Yes I've seen God. God can be seen and spoken to, just as I'm seeing you and speaking to you. But who wants to see and speak to God? For wife, children, money, and property people grieve and shed jugs of tears—but who weeps for the vision of God? And yet, if anyone really wants to see God and calls upon Him, God will certainly reveal Himself to that person."

Later on, Narendranath shared what he had experienced that day, with Swami Saradananda. He said: "When I heard these words, I became more and more convinced that he wasn't any of the other religious teachers I had met, so full of poetry and fine figures of speech. He spoke only of what he himself had actually realized by giving up everything and calling on God wholeheartedly. As I tried to reconcile his words with his strange behaviour towards me, I recalled the descriptions of monomaniacs mentioned in books by Abercrombie and other English philosophers, and I concluded that he must be a monomaniac. Yet I could not help acknowledging the magnitude of his renunciation. I thought: 'Well, he may be mad—but this is indeed a rare soul who can undertake such renunciation. Yes, he is mad. But how pure! And what renunciation! He is truly worthy of the reverence, love, and adoration of humankind.' Thinking this, I bowed down at his feet, took my leave of him, and returned to Calcutta that day."[4]

Narendranath returned home with a great change in his mind. Swami Saradananda had experienced that change, and, later on, explained in his *Lilaprosango*, which is as follows:

"When he first met the Master, Narendra was not only spending his time on his education and study of music, but he was also practicing strict brahmacharya and austerities, driven by an intense spiritual impulse. He was a vegetarian, and he slept on the bare floor or on a blanket there. His grandmother had rented a house near his ancestral home. After his Entrance examination, he mainly lived in a front room on the upper floor of that house. When it was inconvenient to stay there for any reason, he rented a room nearby and lived alone, away from his family and relatives, keeping himself busy in pursuit of his spiritual goal. He noble father and other family members thought that he was living alone because he could no study amid the bustle of their extended family.

"During this time, Narendra was visiting the Brahmo Samaj and spending long hours in meditation. He believed in the formless Brahman with attributes, as taught by the Brahmo faith. Unlike others, he was not satisfied with basing his faith formless God on reasoning alone. Driven by the good tendencies of his past lives, he constantly thought to himself: "If God truly exists, He will not conceal His own nature from the human heart that prays sincerely. He certainly must have laid down the path to reach Him. It is meaningless to lead life for any purpose other than to realize God."[5]

After his first visit to Dakshineswar, he frequently thought about the Master's unique character and behaviour. One day about a month after it he returned to Dakshineswar, alone on foot.

He had no idea that the Dakshineswar temple was so far from Calcutta because he had been there only once before, and that was by carriage. He used to visit Dasharathi Sanyal, Satkari Lahiri, and other friends at Baranagore and thought that Rasmani's temple garden was somewhere near their houses. But that time it seemed as if the journey would never end however far he walked. After asking many people the way, he arrived at Dakshineswar at last and went straight to the Master's room. The Master was then sitting, deep in meditation, on the smaller bed that stands beside the bigger one. There was no one with him. When he saw Narendranath, he joyfully called him and made him sit down on one end of the bed. He was in an ecstatic mood. He muttered something to himself that Narendra couldn't understand. The Master looked hard at Narendra, and then arose and approached him. Narendra thought that they were about to have another crazy scene. Before he could realize anything the Master placed his right foot on his body. Immediately he had a wonderful experience. His eyes were wide open, and it seemed to him that everything in the room, including the walls themselves, was rapidly whirling around him and receding. At the same time, it seemed to him that his consciousness and himself, together with the entire universe, was about to vanish into a vast, all-devouring void. He felt, as if he was near to death. He closed his eyes, as he couldn't control himself. He cried out loudly, "Ah, what are you doing to me? Don't you know I have parents at home?" When the Master heard that, he gave a loud laugh. Then he touched his chest with his hand and said: "All right, let it stop now. It needn't be done all at once. It will happen in its own good time." As soon as the Master told this, Narendranath felt that the extraordinary vision vanished in a moment. He returned to his normal state and saw everything was as usual as before.

Narendra felt surprised that it happened actually in a few moments, and yet it changed his whole way of thinking. He was bewildered and he tried to analyze what had happened. He saw how that experience had begun and ended in obedience to the will of this extraordinary man. He had read about mesmerism and hypnotism in books, and he wondered if this was something like that. But he was by no means weak minded. Till that day he was proud of his intelligence and willpower. Ordinary people are overwhelmed and become puppets under the influence of a great personality. When he first met the Master, he had decided that he was mad. Then why should he have suddenly found himself in this state? He couldn't come to any conclusion. He didn't know how to solve the mystery. He remembered the words of Shakespeare, 'There are more things in heaven and earth than are dreamt of in your philosophy.' He thought that this might be one of those things. Finally, he concluded that this mystery could not be solved. He decided to be more cautious to avoid such influence over himself.

Next moment he thought, how he could consider the Master mad when he was able to destroy the strong structure of his mind at will—a mind that was endowed with tremendous will-power. How did he shape his mind as if it were a lump of clay, making it think as he wished? During his first visit the Master took him aside and said so many strange things; how could he believe them to be true, or to be anything other than an eccentric outburst? He couldn't determine the cause of his wonderful experience, and therefore, he couldn't come to a firm resolution about the Master, who was as pure and simple as a child. Since his childhood he had always used observation, investigation, reasoning, and argumentation to form and opinion about a person or a thing. But on that he was dealt with a terrible blow, which distressed his heart. Consequently, he determined to understand the nature and power of this wonderful person by his possible means.

To continue the history of that day we would like to quote from *Lilaprosango*, where revered Swami Saradananda described what he was told by Narendranath:

> Thus was my mind occupied with various thoughts and resolutions throughout the day. After this last incident, the Master became quite a different person. He began to feed me lovingly as he had during my first visit, and he treated me as cordially as if he had known me for a long time. He behaved with me exactly like a man who meets as old friend or a relative after a long separation. But feeding and entertaining me, talking to me and making jokes with me, didn't seem to satisfy him. His affectionate behaviour created a good deal of anxiety in me. As the day was coming to a close, I asked leave to go. This seemed to make him unhappy, and as on the previous occasion he demanded a promise: 'Say that you will come back soon.' So on that day I promised as before, and then I returned home.[6]

According to the author of *Lilaprosango*, he didn't know how long it was before Narendra returned. "After encountering the Master's miraculous power, Narendra had an intense desire to know him, so it seems it must not have been long before he came back to Dakshineswar. His eagerness must have brought him back to the Master as soon as he was able. Because he was attending college, the third visit probably took place on a weekend. When Narendra wanted to investigate something, he lost all interest in food, sleep, or relaxation; he would take no rest until he had mastered the situation. So, quite naturally he was extremely anxious to understand the Master. It is certain that during the third visit Narendra was extremely cautious and very much on his guard lest he fall under hypnotic spell as before. But what happened was inconceivable."[7]

In reference to the above we may say that Narendranath went third time to visit Sri Ramakrishna after a week of his second visit. That day, either because of Rasmani's temple garden was crowded with devotees or for any other reason, the Master invited Narendranath for a walk in Jadu Mallick's garden, just south of the Dakshineswar compound. Jadu and his mother were devoted to the Master, and they left a standing order with the manager that the parlour facing the Ganges should be kept open for the Master whenever he wished to walk in the garden. Master walked with Narendra in the garden. As the Master and Narendra talked about various things and came to the bank of the Ganges, they eventually came to the parlour, where the Master sat down and went into samadhi [trance]. Narendra sat nearby, and closely watched the Master's condition, when the Master suddenly touched him, just as he did on the previous occasion. Although Narendra was on his guard, he lost his consciousness with the power of touch. After a while when he returned to his normal state, he saw the Master passing his hand over his chest and smiling at him, sweetly and gently. He couldn't remember what he experienced during his unconsciousness, and therefore, he couldn't say anything to anybody, or it was a secret. But one day, during conversation the Master disclosed the secret of the event to his devotees, among who revered Swami Saradananda was also present, and realized that Narendranath had no memory of it. Later on, Swami Saradananda in his 'Lilaprosango' said about what he heard from the Master.

The Master said: "That day, after Narendra lost consciousness of his current incarnation, I asked him many questions, such as who he really was, where he had come from, why he had come [been born], how long he would stay in this world, and so forth. He entered his innermost being and found the correct answers to my questions. These answers confirmed what I'd already learned about him in visions. It's forbidden to reveal those things, but I can tell you this: On the day he knows who he really is; he will no longer remain in this world. With a strong effort of will, he will immediately give up his body through the power of yoga. Narendra is a great soul, perfect in meditation."[8]

After this, the Master described one of his earlier visions concerning Narendranath. Here, we would like to quote the description as revered Swami Saradananda has written in his book *Sri Sri Ramakrishna Lilaprosango*.

The Master said: "One day I found that my mind was soaring high in samadhi along a luminous path. It soon transcended the stellar universe and entered the subtle realm of ideas. As it ascended higher and higher, I found the path lined with ideal forms of gods and goddesses on both sides. My mind then reached the outer limits of that region, where a luminous barrier separates the sphere of relative existence from that of the Absolute. My mind crossed that barrier to enter the transcendental realm, where no corporeal being was visible. Even the gods dare not enter that sublime realm and are content to keep their seats far below. But the next moment I saw seven venerable rishis seated there in samadhi. It occurred to me that these rishis must have surpassed not only humans but even the gods in knowledge and holiness, in renunciation and love. Lost in admiration, I was reflecting on their greatness when I saw a portion of that undifferentiated luminous region condense into the form of a divine child. The child came to one of the rishis, tenderly clasped his neck with his lovely arms and, addressing him in a sweet voice, tried to drag his mind down from the state of samadhi. That magic touch roused the rishi from the superconscious state, and he fixed his half-opened eyes upon the wonderful child. His beaming countenance showed that the child was the treasure of his heart. In great joy the divine child spoke to him: 'I am going down. You must go with me.' The rishi remained mute but his tender look expressed his assent. As he gazed at the child, he again became immersed in samadhi. I was surprised to see a fragment of his body and mind then descending to earth in the form of a bright light. No sooner had I seen Narendra than I recognized him to be that rishi."[9]

When at another time, Swami Saradananda asked the Master about the divine child in the vision, he came to know that the Master himself had assumed the form of that child.

Last two incidents dealt terrible blows to his belief. The experience of his visit to the Master forced him to come to a conclusion that on rare occasions some great souls are born in this world whose extraordinary renunciation, austerities, love, and purity exceed what the limited minds of ordinary people conceive of as God. And people would benefit greatly, if the accepted those great souls as gurus. He understood that the Master's will was completely identified with that of God. Narendranath felt a great change in himself, but this change was not yet enough to defeat his practice of investigation before being surrendered completely to the Master. He was in a habit to accept anything only after a long research on it. So it was natural to him to take some more time for an intense observation. Although he agreed to accept the Master as his guru, he declined to follow all his words indiscriminately. Thus the relation between two great souls began to develop through a struggle between investigation and love or faith. Last two meetings had awakened in Narendranath a love and respect for the Master. He wanted to analyze his experience by examining them carefully. So on one hand, he earnestly kept his mind open to receive the novel and so far unknown truths of the spiritual world, and on the other, he engaged himself on in subjecting the Master's visions and his behaviour to meticulous testing. The Master also didn't make any hurry, rather he allowed him to go on his own way—He knew the identity of himself and that of Narendranath, and was well-known about the relation between them.

In connection with the above state, revered Swami Saradananda said:

> Narendra's keen intellect revealed to him that the words spoken by the Master during his first visit—which had led him to consider the Master a monomaniac—could only be understood as meaningful if he believed that the Master was an avatar [incarnation of God]. But how could his truth-seeking and rational mind admit this so quickly? He decided that if God ever gave him the ability to understand those words of the Master, he would consider himself to learning from the Master and discussing with him how to be blessed with God-realization.
>
> When a powerful mind replaces an old idea with a new one, it faces strong resistance from within. Narendra now encountered this situation. Although he realized the wonderful power of the Master, Narendra could not accept him completely; and although he was attracted to the Master, he tried to stay away from him.[10]

Narendranath was identified by the Master as one of the seven venerable rishis, who appeared on the earth for the benefit of people. So it was necessary for Narendranath to identify himself, and he had to know the reason of his birth, before he started his work. He was born with wonderful spiritual tendencies. He said:

> As far back as I can remember, I'd see a marvelous point of light between my eyebrows as soon as I shut my eyes to go to sleep. I watched it and paid great attention as it went through various changes. To see it better, I would lie on my bed like one prostrating before a deity, with forehead touching the ground. That marvelous point of light would change colours and grow bigger and bigger until it took the form of a ball, finally bursting and covering my body from head to foot with a white liquid light. As soon as that happened I lost outer consciousness and fell asleep. I used to believe this was how everybody went to sleep, and I was under that impression for a long time. When I grew older and began to practice meditation, that point of light would appear to me as soon as I closed my eyes, and I'd concentrate upon it. At that time I was practicing meditation with a few friends, following the instructions of Devendra Nath Tagore. We told each other about our visions and experiences, and I discovered that none of them had ever seen that point of light or had gone to sleep as I did.
>
> From my very childhood, whenever I came in contact with a particular object, person, or place, it would sometimes seem as if I were already acquainted with it. I'd try to recall

> when, but couldn't bring it to mind. Nonetheless, I was not convinced that I had never seen it before. This happened quite often. Perhaps I would be discussing various topics with my friends at a particular place. Someone would say something, and immediately the thought would flash in my mind that sometime past, in this very house, I'd had the same discussion with these friends, and on that occasion this person had said the same thing. After long deliberation I couldn't ascertain when I'd had such a discussion with them. When I became aware of the doctrine of reincarnation, I thought that perhaps I might have been familiar with those places and people in a previous life and that partial memories concerning them sometimes surfaced in my mind. Later, I realized that such a conclusion wasn't reasonable. It now seems to me that before I was born I must have somehow seen, as in motion pictures, the people and things I would come in contact with in this life. Those memories now arise in my mind from time to time.[11]

Narendranath described the above experience to Swami Saradananda shortly after they became acquainted, and he told him the cause of the phenomenon towards the end of his life.

According to Swami Saradananda, Narendranath visited the Master after he was told by various people about the Master's pure life and his Samadhi. He never dreamt that his visit to the Master would cause him to undergo any mental change or situation turned out contrary to what he expected. His previous visions and experiences seemed dull and trifling compared to the extraordinary experience he had during his second and third visits to the Master at Dakshineswar. His extreme intellect was bewildered by this mystery, so he faced a problem when he tried to understand the Master's personality. He could find no reason to doubt that those extraordinary experiences had been brought on by the Master's impenetrable divine power. The more he thought about this, the more he became lost in wonder.

Here we would like to quote from 'Lilaprosango' that evaluates the power and strength of Narendranath. Revered Swami Saradananda said:

> One is truly amazed when thinking about the wonderful experience that Narendra had during his second visit to the Master. According to the scriptures, an ordinary aspirant with a limited amount of power attains that rare types of experience by practicing austerities and renunciation over a long period of time. And once it happens, the aspirant becomes overwhelmed by the manifestation of God in the guru and surrenders to the guru completely. It is surprising that Narendra did not do that. His reaction is evidence that he occupied a high position in the spiritual world. He was not overwhelmed by that event because he had such a great capacity for spiritual power. Instead, he was able to maintain self-control and proceed to engage himself in examining and evaluating the Master's divine character and behaviour for a long time. However, although he was not overwhelmed and did not surrender to the Master completely, from that point on he was undoubtedly greatly attracted to him.[12]

Sri Ramakrishna considered Narendranath to be his very own, because he knew that Narendra would be the great educator in the world, and he will help the people to realize the way to the truth. Sri Ramakrishna felt an attraction to Narendra from their first meeting. He became intensely anxious to transmit his life experience to him. He was inclined to use Samadhi to impart the knowledge of Brahman to Narendra on the day he went to Dakshineswar alone. When Narendranath fully surrendered to the Master three or four years later and was imploring him again and again for nirvikalpa samadhi, the Master would refer to the incident of their second meeting at Dakshineswar, and ask him, "Why are you pestering me? Didn't you tell me that you have parents at home and needed to serve them?" At other time the Master told a story of a ghost to his devotees, when Narendra was also present there. He said: "Look, once a man died and became a ghost. He was alone for a long time, so he felt terribly lonely and began to look everywhere for a companion. Whenever he heard that someone had died in a particular place, he would rush there, thinking that he might finally have a companion. But when he saw that the dead person's soul had become liberated by the touch of Ganges water, or by some other means, he would be disappointed and return to his own place to lead his lonely existence. That poor ghost never had a companion." After he had finished the story, he told Narendranath, "My condition was similar to that ghost. When I met you, I thought that I'd finally found a companion, but you cried out that you had parents. So I couldn't have a companion."

We have already discussed about Narendra's second visit to Dakshineswar, when the Master saw him panic-stricken on the verge of entering samadhi, he stopped transmitting it. Revered Swami Saradananda has explained the cause of it. He said, "Because of how this incident turned out, it is no wonder that the Master had some doubt about his earlier visions and experiences regarding Narendra. We think that is why, when Narendra came to Dakshineswar for the third time, the Master overwhelmed him with his power and extracted from him many secrets regarding his life; he was relieved when he found that Narendra's answers confirmed his vision."[13]

According to Swami Saradananda, if his assumption was correct, it proves that Narendranath didn't have the same kind of samadhi on his second and third visits, but had two different kinds of experience.

Revered Swami Saradananda had shared with us an important opinion of Sri Ramakrishna about the extraordinary quality of Narendranath that he discussed with him. He said:

> After questioning Narendra, the Master was relieved of anxious about him to some extent, but not completely. He knew that a man could achieve extraordinary fame and influence if he had but one or two supernatural power or qualities, but Narendra displayed eighteen such powers, and those to their full extent. If Narendra failed to direct these powers through a spiritual channel and use them to realize the ultimate truth about God, humanity, and the world, the result would be undesirable. The Master said that if that happened, Narendra would found a new religion or a sect as other religious leaders had and would become famous throughout the world. But to full the need of the present age, it was necessary to realize and propagate liberal spiritual truths; if Narendra failed to realize this and was unable to help in this pursuit, it would not be possible for him to do real good in the world. So from that point on, the Master was very eager that Narendra should of his own will and without reservation follow him and experience the spiritual truth just as he had.[14]

Sri Ramakrishna used to say: "As watercress and some weeds grow in ponds and small pools where there are no current, so religious cults and narrow-minded sects develop in a religious world where people are satisfied with a partial truth that they think is the whole truth."[15]

From the very beginning Sri Ramakrishna's attraction to Narendranath was based on many factors. Some of them originated from his visions about Narendra, and a fear rose in his mind, if Narendra would accept the bondage of desire for a wife, wealth, or fame, and thereby the purpose of his great life could not be fulfilled.

Sri Ramakrishna is eternally identified with God, the source of the universe. He believed that the Lord's work of doing well to humanity was his duty. He appeared to stop the declination of religion in this present age. His last three meetings with Narendra assured him that Narendra was not born merely to enjoy a selfish worldly life, but that he had come down on the earth because of his intense love for God, and to help him in his mission to benefit humanity. So he considered Narendra to be his very own, and that he was attracted to him.

It is almost impossible for us to describe the extent to which Sri Ramakrishna loved Narendranath. Many devotees had experienced the anxiety that Sri Ramakrishna felt when separated from Narendranath, or joy that he had on seeing him. Nobody could imagine that one could selflessly love another so intensely. They, who had seen that eternal love, are really blessed by God.

Sri Ramakrishna began to express his anxiety for Narendranath to his devotees. He was extremely anxious about him. Swami Premananda went to Dakshineswar for the first time shortly after Narendra's third visit. He was amazed by the Master's deep concern for Narendra. Later on he recalled:

"Swami Brahmananda and I went to Hathkhola ghat in West Calcutta to take a boat to Dakshineswar. We met Ramdayal there. When we learned that he was also going to see Sri Ramakrishna, we got into a boat together. It was almost dusk when we reached Rani Rasmani's Kali temple. We went to the Master's room and were told that he'd gone to the temple to pay obeisance to the Divine Mother. Swami Brahmananda asked us to wait there and went to the Mother's temple to find the Master. Soon I saw them coming. Swami Brahmananda was holding onto the Master very carefully and guiding him, saying: 'Steps. Go up here, down here.' I'd already heard that the Master often became overwhelmed with ecstasy and lost outer consciousness of his surroundings, so I knew that he was in an ecstasy mood when I saw him coming, reeling like a drunken man. He entered his room in this state and sat on a small bedstead. Shortly afterwards he came to normal consciousness and asked me a few question about myself and my relatives. He then began to examine my face, hands, feet, and so on. For some time he held my forearm in his hand to feel its weight, and then he said, 'Good.' He alone knew what he meant by that. Afterwards, he asked Ramdayal about Narendra's health, Hearing that he was all right, the Master said: "It's been a long time since he came here. I want to see him. Please ask him to come sometime."

"We spent a few delightful hours in spiritual talk, then took our supper at 10:00 p.m. and lay down in the southeast veranda of the Master's room. Beds were arranged for the Master and for Swami Brahmananda in the room. Scarcely an hour had passed when the Master emerged from his room, with his cloth under one arm like a boy, and came to our bedside. Addressing Ramdayal, he asked affectionately, 'Are you sleeping?' Both of us quickly sat up in our beds and replied, 'No, sir.' The Master said: 'Look, I haven't seen Narendra for a long time, and I feel as if my whole heart were being wrung forcibly like a wet towel. Please ask him to come at once to see me. He is a person of pure sattva qualities. He is Narayana himself. I cannot have peace of mind unless I see him now and then.'

"Ramdayal had been visiting Dakshineswar for some time, so the childlike nature of the Master was familiar to him. When he saw that childlike behaviour, he knew that the Master was in ecstasy. He tried to console the Master by promising that he would see Narendra first thing in the morning and ask him to come to Dakshineswar. But that night the Master's longing could not be appeased. Knowing that we were getting no rest, he would return to his bed for a time now and then, but after a while he would forget and come back to us to begin speaking of Narendra good qualities, pathetically expressing his terrible anguish because of Narendra's long absence. As I observed his agony, I thought to myself: 'How marvelous is the Master's love! And how hardhearted is that person for whom the Master is in such distress!' We spent the night that way. In the morning we went to pay our obeisance to the Divine Mother in the temple, and then bowed down to the Master and took leave for him before returning to Calcutta."[16]

Baikuntha Nath Sanyal, the devotee of Sri Ramakrishna described the Master's condition that he had experienced: "That day the Master's mind was fully absorbed in thought of Narendra. He spoke of nothing else but what praise he had for him. The Master addressed me, saying: 'Look, Narendra is a man of pure sattva qualities. I saw in my vision that Narendra was one among the four [Sanka, Sanandana, Sanatana, and Santkumara.—Translator] in the indivisible realm and also one of the seven rishis [Marichi, Atri, Angira, Pulaha, Pulastya, Kratu and Vashishtha—Translator]. There is no limit to his good qualities.' After saying that, the Master became restless to see Narendra and began shedding tears profusely like a mother separated from her child. He thought that we might misunderstand him when he could no longer control himself, so he hurried to the northern veranda. We heard him cry in a choked voice, praying, 'Mother dear, I can't live without seeing him,' and so on.

"After a while he controlled himself somehow, returned to his room, and sat near us. He then said plaintively: 'I weep so much, but Narendra does not come. My desire to see him causes a pain as if heart were being wrung like a wet towel. He doesn't understand my spiritual attraction to him.' Saying so, he again became restless and left the room. He returned shortly and said: 'Just see, I'm an old man paining and weeping for Narendra. What will people think of me? You are my own, so I'm not ashamed to express my feelings in your presence. But how will other react? I'm sorry, but I can't control myself.' We were amazed by the Master's love for Narendra. We thought that Narendra must be a godlike person, or why would the Master be so drawn to him? To console him, we said: 'Sir, it is indeed wrong of Narendra. He knows that you feel pain when you can't see him and still he doesn't come.'

"Sometime after this event the Master introduced me to Narendra. I saw that the Master was as anxious when he was separated from Narendra as he was delighted when Narendra visited. Sometime later we went to Dakshineswar to celebrate the Master's birth anniversary. The devotees had adorned him beautifully with a new cloth, a garland, sandal paste, and so on. Kirtan was arranged in the north-eastern veranda of his room. Surrounded by his devotees, the Master listened to the kirtan. Sometimes he was in ecstasy, and sometimes he made the kirtan more interesting by improvising a line or two in his sweet voice. But his joy was not complete because of Narendra's absence. Now and then he would look around and say, 'Well, Narendra has not come!' Narendra arrived about noon and bowed down to the Master. As soon as the Master saw him, he jumped up, sat on his shoulders, and went into ecstasy. When he regained his normal state afterwards, he became busy with talking to Narendra and feeding him. He could not listen to kirtan anymore that day."[17]

It is really amazing that Narendranath received a rare love from associated with Sri Ramakrishna. Yet he remained unperturbed by this and proceeded to test the Master at every step to realize the truth. Sri Ramakrishna was not offended by his conduct. Rather he gladly came forward to help him in realizing the truth. It is beyond our limit to express the relation between these two grate souls.

Revered Swami Saradananda had divided the mode of conduct of the Master towards Narendranath during those five years into five main categories:

(1) At their first meeting the Master's unique insight made him understand that students like Narendra, who was a spiritual aspirant of the highest order, were very rare.

Narendra was born to assist in the mission that the Divine Mother had entrusted to him: to establish the eternal religion as required by the need of the age by alleviating the degradation that had taken place for so long.

(2) He tied Narendra to him permanently with his infinite love and trust.

(3) By subjecting Narendra to various tests, the Master confirmed that his insights about Narendra's greatness and life's goal were valid.

(4) He trained Narendra in many ways, making him a suitable instrument to fulfil the great mission of his life.

(5) When his training was complete, Narendra achieved the knowledge of Brahman. The Master then taught Narendra how to establish the religion for this age, relieving himself of responsibility by handing over to Narendra his mission and his religious order.

From their first meeting, Sri Ramakrishna's life was more connected with Narendranath than with any other devotee. It is said that when Jesus first met one of his main disciples [Simon Peter], he proclaimed, "Upon this immovable rock I shall build my church." Such a feeling also arose in Sri Ramakrishna's mind when he met Narendranath. He had a vision that Narendra was his child, his friend who was born to carry on his mission, and that their lives bound eternally with an unbreakable cord of love from previous lives. In language of 'Lilaprosango'—"This love is an exalted spiritual love in which the lover gives full freedom to the beloved, yet keeps the other as his or her own from age to age. In this love, the lover and the beloved do not seek anything in return from one another and are satisfied instead by offering everything to each other."[18]

Narendranath was attracted to Sri Ramakrishna owing to his one-pointed devotion, purity and renunciation. Sri Ramakrishna observed Narendra's indomitable self-confidence, courage, and passion for truth, and was moved to make him his own.

Narendranath had no fear of what people would thought of him, and never kept anything in secret. People, who didn't see him closely, would think that Narendra was proud, arrogant, and a sign of immature intellect. One day, one of his neighbours told Swami Saradananda about Narendranath: "There's a boy in that house—I've never known anyone so hopelessly spoilt. Since he got his B.A. degree, he's so vain; he thinks that nothing in the whole world matters but him. When his father and other people are present, he'll quite rudely start singing and beating his drum without any respect. He walks through the street smoking cigars in the presence of respected elder neighbours. He is heedless in every respect."

At that time Swami Saradananda didn't meet Narendranath, and therefore, he couldn't ignore any word of the neighbour. But, one day in course of conversation, Sri Ramakrishna said: "I have never seen another boy like Narendra. He's as proficient in vocal and instrumental music as he is in studies, in conversation, and in religious matters. He meditates the entire night and is completely unaware when morning comes. Narendra isn't like a fake coin; if you test him as a money-changer checks a coin [by tapping it], you will hear the right sound. I see other boys pass two or three examinations somehow by working as hard as they can, and there it ends, as if they used up all their energy in accomplishing this. But Narendra isn't like that. He does everything with ease and joy, and passing an examination is a trifling thing for him. He also goes to the Brahmo Samaj and sings devotional songs there. But he isn't like the other Brahmos; he is a true knower of Brahmo. He sees a light when he sits for meditation. Is it for nothing that I love Narendra so much?"[19]

Later on Swami Saradananda came to know that Sri Ramakrishna's highly-praised Narendra was the same young man whom his neighbour had harshly criticized earlier. This is the character of general people who often misjudge a person on the basis of his or her behaviour only.

One day Swami Saradananda met Narendranath at a house that his friend had rented. It was a two-storied building on Gaur Mohan Mukherjee Street, Simla, in front of Narendra's house. He had been classmate with this friend for four or five years. A couple of years before the Entrance examination, his friend decided to go to England and travelled as far as Bombay but couldn't go further. He became a newspaper editor and was preparing some books of collected articles and poems that he had written in Bengali. He had married sometime prior to this incident, and people thought that he was leading a wayward life and earned money by unscrupulous means. Swami Saradananda went to his house to ascertain the truth that day without any information.

When Swami Saradananda was waiting for his friend in the drawing room, he saw a young man entered the room as if he were known to the owner of the house. Without any hesitation, he reclined on a bolster and began to softly sing a Hindi song. The song was connected with Krishna. The young man was well dressed and his hair was nicely combed, although he was not foppish. He was absent-mindedly singing a love song about Krishna and was closely associated with his way-ward friend. Hence Swami Saradananda couldn't come to a favorable opinion. The young man ignored his presence. He watched him smoking tobacco, and concluded that he was a true companion of his wayward friend, who had gone astray by associating with this kind of person. Swami Saradananda didn't try to talk to him.

After a while, his friend came into the living room, and greeted Swami Saradananda with only a few words, then turned joyfully to talk to that young man on various topics. Swami Saradananda didn't like that indifference, but he felt that it would be discourteous to leave abruptly, so he began listening to the conversation between his friend and that young man. The subject was English and Bengali literature. Although both agreed to a great extent that classical literature must correctly express human sentiments, they had a difference of opinion about whether every expression of human feeling should be considered as literature, but the young man refuted that. He tried to convince his friend that while literature might correctly express good or bad sentiments, it could not be considered classical unless it was written with good taste or it set a high ideal. In support of his position, the young man mentioned the books of famous English and Bengali writer, beginning with Chaucer, and showed how each of them had achieved immortality in the literary world by following that principle.

In conclusion the young man said: "Although people experience both positive and negative feelings, they always try to hold to a particular ideal within themselves. The differences that exist among people are based on how completely they realize and manifest their particular ideals. Ordinary people consider the enjoyment of sense objects to be permanent and real, and they are satisfied with achieving those pleasures as the goal of life. They idealize what is apparently real. There's little difference between these people and animals. Writers such as they could never create classical literature. Moreover, there's another kind of human being who isn't satisfied with the enjoyment of pleasure that appear to be real. These people hold the highest ideal within themselves and strive to fit everything they encounter into that mould. They want to realize the ideal. Only people such as they can create true literature. Among these, there are people who are eager to translate the very highest ideal into their lives; they generally have to renounce worldly life. I've seen only Sri Ramakrishna Paramahamsa of Dakshineswar who fully embodies the highest ideal in his life, and that's why I revere him."

In connection with this topic Swami Saradananda said: "Although we were moved by the young man's profound ideas and by his scholarship on that day, we were nonetheless disappointed at seeing his close relationship with our wayward friend, believing his words and actions to be incongruous. We took leave of our friend, A few months after this incident, we were impressed by the praise that the Master had for Narendra, and we visited him at his home. We were dumbfounded when we saw that the Master's highly-praised Narendra was the young man whom we had seen at our friend's house."[20]

Swami Saradananda was of the opinion that, Sri Ramakrishna understood at their first meeting that Narendra's apparent arrogance and vanity originated from his tremendous self-confidence, which arose from his inherent and extraordinary mental power. His bold and carefree behaviour was nothing but a sign of his natural self-control. Sri Ramakrishna knew that in time Narendra's extraordinary character would bloom like a thousand-petalled lotus and become established in its own unparalleled glory and greatness. He knew that when Narendra's life encountered the afflicted world, his arrogance and vanity would melt into infinite compassion, his unique self-confidence would serve to reestablish faith in the broken-hearted, and his carefree conduct, which always remained under his control, would demonstrate to others that self-control was the only way to attain freedom.

If an ordinary man would have heard such praise from Sri Ramakrishna, he would have been overwhelmed and filled with pride. But Narendranath was different. He didn't ignore the good qualities in Keshab and Vijay. He considered himself unworthy of such praise, and vehemently raised an objection: "Sir, why do you say such things? People will think you're mad if you talk like that! Keshab is famous all over the world. Vijay is a saint. I'm an insignificant schoolboy. How can you speak of us in the same breath? Please, I beg of you, never say such things again." Pleased, Sri Ramakrishna responded: "But what can I do about it, my child? You don't suppose I'd say such things of my own accord? It was Mother who showed me the truth about you, and so I had to tell it. Mother has never lied to me."

Narendranath couldn't believe the truth of the Master's visions and said: "How do you know it was Mother who told you? All this may be your imagination. If I were in your position, I would consider such visions to be mere fancies. Western science and philosophy have proven that our senses often deceive us, and that the chances of deception are much greater if our minds hold a constant desire to see a particular thing, you are fond of me and always want to see me become great—this may be why you have such visions."

Thus Narendranath tried to explain with various illustrations how physical science had investigated and verified such visions, which are subjective and proved them to be erroneous. But Sri Ramakrishna considered this explanation as a sign of his love for truth, and he became more pleased with Narendra. Sometimes he was found to be upset with such explanation, and considered it a childlike behaviour. He would think: "Well, Narendra is completely devoted to truth; he isn't one to tell a lie. Also, the scriptures say that no falsehood appears in the mind of a truthful person like him. Could there then be any possibility of error in my visions?" Again, he thought: "I've tested my visions in various ways and have found that the Divine Mother has never revealed anything false to me. I've also received repeated assurances from Her. So why does honest Narendra say that my visions are caused by my imagination? Why doesn't he believe them to be true as I describe them?"

Worried, Sri Ramakrishna finally asked the Divine Mother for an answer. He heard Her voice say: "Who do you listen to Narendra? He will accept the truth before long."

One Sunday, Sri Ramakrishna was extremely restless to see Narendranath. He worried that Narendra might have gone to his friend's house and he might miss meeting him even if he would go to Calcutta. Next moment he concluded that Narendra would certainly sing at the evening service of the Sadharan Brahmo Samaj, so he could see him there. Then he thought if the Brahmo devotees felt disturbed with his presence without any invitation. The next moment he thought: "Well, I visited Keshab's Brahmo Samaj a few times without any invitation, and they were invariably pleased to see me. Moreover, Vijay, Shivanath, and other leaders of the Sadharan Brahmo Samaj have visited Dakshineswar many times." But one important thing he didn't notice that Shivanath and other Brahmo of Sadharan Brahmo Samaj had gradually stopped visiting him when they observed that Keshab and Vijay had changed their religious views under the influence of him. He was not an ordinary man like the leaders of Brahmo Samaj. So he couldn't think like the worldly people, and he decided to go to Brahmo Samaj that evening.

To know what happened next, we must quote the description given by Swami Saradananda: "It was evening. Hundreds of Brahmo devotees were ardently repeating the mantra, *satyam jnanam anantam* Brahma [Brahman is Truth, Knowledge, and infinity], directing their heartfelt devotion to God. Prayer and meditation came to an end, and the preacher began to speak to the congregation from the pulpit on the love of and longing for God. At the moment the Master entered the Brahmo temple in a semiconscious state and moved forward towards the pulpit. Many in the audience had seen him before, so it did not take long for news of the Master's sudden arrival to spread throughout the congregation. Those who had not seen him before stood up, some even standing on the benches to get a better look at him. The noise and disorder in the congregation forced the preacher to interrupt his sermon. Narendra was seated in the choir area. When he realized that the Master was there he immediately rushed to him. But the preacher and other prominent Brahmos did not come forward to receive the Master. They neglected to show him even common courtesy, because they considered him to be responsible for creating dissension among certain Brahmos such as Vijay and others.

"Without glancing to the left or to the right, the Master advanced towards the pulpit, where he went into Samadhi. The congregation, excited to see the Master in that state, made more of a commotion than before. The ushers found that they could not restore order, turned out all the gaslights to force people to leave the building. This caused even more confusion among the crowd as people tried to leave the dark hall.

"Narendra was terribly hurt when he saw that no one in the Sadharan Brahmo Samaj received the Master. Now he was deeply concerned about getting the Master out of the darkened temple. As soon as the Master's Samadhi came to an end, Narendra found a way to lead him out through a back door. He got him into a carriage and rode with him to Dakshineswar."

Narendranath later said: "It's impossible to describe the pain I felt that night when I saw the Master being humiliated like that, and all on my account! How I scolded him for what he'd done! But he didn't care one bit about my scolding or his humiliation. I know that the Master gave no thought to himself because of his love for me, so I didn't hesitate to use harsh words with him on occasion. I said: 'It's written in the Puranas that King Bharata thought so much of his favourite deer that he himself became a deer in his next life. It that's true, you should beware of thinking too much about me!' The Master was as simple as a young boy. He took what I said literally and replied in great distress: 'You're right. So what is going to happen to me, since I can't bear not seeing you?' Then he anxiously went off to consult the Divine Mother. After a while he came back beaming with delight and exclaimed: 'Leave me in peace, you rascal! I'll never listen to anything you tell me again!' Mother said to me: 'You love him so much because you regard him as Narayana [Vishnu] Himself. If the day ever comes when you don't see Narayana in him, then you won't spare him a single glance!' With this short but emphatic statement, he dismissed once and for all everything I'd ever said to him on that subject."[21]

Sri Ramakrishna observed that Narendranath has a pure mind and heart, and he was always motivated by high ideals. So his behaviour with Narendra was quite different from his treatment of other disciples. He used to follow strict rules regarding his food, sleep, japa, meditation, and so on. But there was no such rule for Narendranath; he was allowed to do as he wished. In connection with this topic Sri Ramakrishna said, "Narendra is *nitya-siddha*, eternal perfect"; "Narendra is *dhyana-siddha*, perfect in meditation."; "The fire of knowledge that burns all impurities caused by food is always ablaze in Narendra. That's why his mind will never be distracted or polluted, no matter where or what he eats"; "Narendra is constantly cutting the bonds of maya into pieces with the sword of knowledge, so Mahamaya is incapable of bringing him under Her control."

Once, a Marwari devotee visited Sri Ramakrishna, and presented him with nuts, pistachios, raisins, rock candy, and various sweets. But Sri Ramakrishna neither ate any of these things, nor did he give them to the devotees around him. He said, "They don't know to make gifts without wanting something in return. If they give one roll of betel to a holy man, they attach to it prayers for the fulfillment of sixteen desires. If one eats food from such a materialistic person, one loses devotion." Then, what did he do with the gifts? He said, "Take those things to Narendra. If he eats them, no harm will befall him."

One day Narendranath had a meal in a hotel. Then he went to Sri Ramakrishna, and said, "I have been in a hotel and have eaten food that others consider to be forbidden." The Master knew that it was a warning to him so that he would not touch Narendra or to allow him to use any utensil in his room if he had any reservations. Sri Ramakrishna replied, "It won't do you any harm. If a man keeps his mind on God, eating pork and beef is equivalent to eating the purest havishyanna made of boiled vegetables, rice and ghee. Likewise, if a man is engrossed in worldly desires, eating spinach and vegetables is by no means better than eating pork and beef. I don't mind at all that you've eaten some forbidden food; but if any one of them (pointing to others) cam and told me that, I couldn't touch him."

Sri Ramakrishna didn't take rest until he had blurted all of his innermost thoughts to Narendranath. He used to consult Narendra's opinion in every matter, and to evaluate his visitors' intelligence and intensity of faith he would ask Narendra to engage them in debate. He never asked Narendra to accept anything as true without having fully tested it.

Within a year after their first meeting, Narendranath had dedicated himself to Sri Ramakrishna forever. It seems that he was satisfied with a pure bliss that he had never felt before.

Mahendra Nath Gupta, the recorder of *The Gospel of Sri Ramakrishna*, had the opportunity of visiting Sri Ramakrishna, who removed his pride in learning and made him a humble disciple forever. Narendranath said: "During that period I spent a night with the Master at Dakshineswar, I'd been seated quietly in the Panchavati for a while when the Master suddenly appeared. He took my hand and said, smiling: 'Your learning and intelligence will be tested today. You have only two-and-a-half degrees. Today a schoolteacher [M., Mahendra Nath Gupta] who possesses three and-a-half degrees is here. Come, I want to hear you talk to him.' Like it or not, I had to go with the Master. Reaching his room, I was introduced to M. and we began to discuss various topics. In that manner the Master got us involved in conversation, then remained quietly seated.

He continued listening to what we said and observing us. When M. left, the Master said: 'He might have more degrees, but he's effete. He's too shy; He's not a spirited conversationalist.' In this way the Master enjoyed himself by engaging me in debate with others."

Sri Ramakrishna knew that Narendranath was an aspirant of the highest order, so from the outset he tried to install in him the truths of nondualism. When Narendranath first started coming to Dakshineswar, Sri Ramakrishna would give him the *Ashtavakra Samhita* and other non-dualistic books to read. Narendranath read a little and found fault with the non-dualistic treatises and considered them to be atheistic. He asked Sri Ramakrishna bluntly: "What is the difference between this Advita philosophy and atheism? Should the created jiva think of itself as the Creator? Is there any greater sin than this? I am God; you are God; and everything that is born and dies is God—what could be more absurd? The *munis* and *rishis*, the authors of these books must have been mad—how could they have written such stuff otherwise?" Sri Ramakrishna would smile at Narendra's bluntness, and said mildly: "You may not be able to accept these truths at present, but is that any reason to condemn the great sages who taught them? Why do you try to limit God's nature? Keep calling on Him. He is Truth itself. In whatever way He reveals Himself to you, believe that to be His true nature." But Narendranath at that time paid no heed to Sri Ramakrishna's words. He considered as false anything that had not been verified by reason; it was his nature to stand against any falsehood.

During that period and man named Pratap Chandra Hazra used to live at Dakshineswar temple garden. He was poor, and tried to be religious, but he wished to make money by spiritual practices. So he always sought praise from others by speaking of high philosophy and selfless worship of God. He used to calculate profit and loss in everything. He probably had the idea of achieving some occult powers by which he thought to earn money. Sri Ramakrishna knew Hazar's frame of mind and advised him to give up all worldly desires and call on God. Hazra unwillingly accepted the advice, but was driven by his misguided beliefs and self-interest. He would announce to the visitors that he himself was an extraordinary holy man. Sri Ramakrishna knew all this and sometimes scolded him for it, but he didn't drive him away from Dakshineswar. He would say: "Hazra has a very calculating mind. Don't listen to him."

Hazra was not much educated, but intelligent. He had earned some knowledge on Western philosophy. That's why Narendranath was pleased with him, and whenever he went to Dakshineswar, he would meet Hazra and spend few hours in conversation with him, if it was convenient. Hazra was always humble in presence of Narendranath because he knew well of his intellect. He would listen to Narendra and sometimes prepared a smoke for him. Sri Ramakrishna would say: "Hazra is Naren's fe-rend [friend]."

Revered Swami Saradananda, in his *Sri Ramakrishna and His Divine Play*, has explained a scene that he experienced at Dakshineswar. He said: "When Narendra came to Dakshineswar, the Master quite often went into ecstasy at the very sight of him. When he later regained some consciousness, he would have long spiritual talks with Narendra. At such times the Master would joyfully try to transmit the highest spiritual experiences to Narendra through words and other means. Sometimes the Master wished to listen to devotional songs, and as soon as he heard the sweet melodious voice of Narendra, he would go into Samadhi. But this did not interrupt Narendra's singing. Absorbed, he would continue to sing one song after another for hours. When the Master again regained partial consciousness, he would request Narendra to sing a particular song. He would not be completely satisfied until he heard Narendra sing:

I have joined my heart to Thee: all that exists art Thou;
Thee only have I found, for Thou art all that exists.
O Lord, Beloved of my heart! Thou art the Home of all;
Where indeed is the heart in which Thou dost not dwell?
Thou hast entered every heart: all that exists art Thou,
Whether sage or fool, whether Hindu or Mussalman,
Thou makest them as Thou wilt: all that exists art Thou.
Thy presence is everywhere, whether in heaven or in Kaaba;
Before Thee all must bow, for Thou art all that exists.
From earth below to the highest heaven, from heaven to deepest earth,
I see Thee wherever I look: all that exists art Thou.
Pondering, I have understood; I have seen it beyond a doubt;
I find not a single thing that may be compared to Thee.
To Jafar [the composer] it has been revealed that Thou art all that exists.

After that they would spend some time discussing the various mysteries of Advita Vedanta, such as the difference between the *jiva* and *Ishwara*, the real nature of the *jiva* and of *Brahman*, and so on. Narendra's presence thus created a wave of bliss in Dakshineswar."[22]

One day, during conversation with Narendranath, Sri Ramakrishna talked about various things regarding oneness of jiva and Brahman according to non-dualistic philosophy. After their conversation was over, Narendra went to see Hazra. While smoking and discussing that topic again, Narendranath said: "Can it ever be possible that the water pot is God; that the cup is God, that everything we see and all of us is God?" Hazra joined him in ridiculing the idea, and they both burst into laughter. Sri Ramakrishna was in an ecstatic mood, and when he heard them laughing he came out of his room, holding his cloth under his arm like a boy, "What are you talking about?" he asked them. Smiling, he touched Narendra and went into Samadhi. Narendranath later said: "That day my mind underwent a complete revolution at the marvelous touch of the Master. I was aghast to realize that there really was nothing whatsoever in the entire universe but God. I remained silent, wondering how long this state of mind would continue. It didn't pass away all day. I got back home, and I felt just the same there. Everything I saw was God. I sat down to eat, and I saw that everything—the plate, the food, my mother who was serving it, and I myself—everything was God and nothing but God. I swallowed a couple of mouthful and then sat still without speaking. My mother lovingly asked me: 'Why are you so quiet? Why don't you eat?' That brought me back to everyday consciousness and I began eating again. But from then on I kept having the same experience, no matter what I was doing—eating, sitting, lying down, or going to college. It was a kind of intoxication that I can't describe. If I were crossing a street and saw a carriage coming towards me, I didn't have the urge to get out of its way for fear of being run over, as I would ordinarily. I said to myself: 'I am that carriage. There's no difference between it and me.' During that time, I had no sensation in my hands or my feet. When I ate food, I felt no satisfaction from it; it was as if someone else were eating. Sometimes I would lie down in the middle of a meal and then get up again after a few minutes and go on eating. Thus, it happened on those days that I would eat far more than usual, but this never upset me. My mother became alarmed. She thought I was suffering from some terrible disease. 'He won't live long', she would say.

"When that first intoxication lost some of its power, I began to see the world as though I were dreaming. When I went for a walk around Hedua, or Cornwallis Square [now Azadhind

Bagh], I knocked my head against the iron railings to see if they were dream-railings or real ones. The loss of feeling in my hands and feet made me afraid that I was becoming paralyzed. That overwhelming intoxication didn't leave me for some time. When I did at last return to normal consciousness, I was convinced that the state I'd been in was a revelation of nondualistic experience. And then I knew that what is written in the scriptures about this experience is all true. From that time on, I had no doubts about the truth of nonduality."[23]

On another occasion Narendranath described Swami Saradananda a wonderful incident. It was, as he believed, in the winter of 1884, when they were acquainted. Swami Saradananda described as follows:

> "We remember going to Narendra's house at Gaur Mohan Mukherjee Street in Simla on that day a little before noon and staying till eleven at night. Swami Ramakrishnananda was with us. Since our first meeting, we had felt a divine attraction to Narendra, and this feeling was intensified a thousand fold that day. Before this we understood the Master to be a knower of God or a perfected soul. But on that day Narendra's inspired talks brought a new light to our hearts. We realized that the extraordinary events recorded in the lives of Jesus, Chaitanya, and other great teachers of the world, which we had studied but disbelieved, had parallels in the Master's daily life. With merely a touch, or his desire that it be so, the Master released from bondage those who had taken refuge in him and granted them devotion. He granted them Samadhi, thus endowing them with divine bliss. Or he diverted the course of their lives into a spiritual channel so strong that they attained a vision of God immediately and were blessed forever. We remember that in the evening Narendra took us for a walk in Cornwallis Square. On the way he told us of divine experience that he had experienced by the grace of the Master. He was absorbed within himself for a while and then finally expressed his inner bliss with his heavenly voice:
>
> > Gora* bestows the Nectar of love;
> > Jar after jar he pours it out,
> > And still there is no end!
> > Sweetest Nirai** is susmmoning all;
> > Beloved Gora bids them come;
> > Shantipur*** is almost drowned,
> > And Nadia is flooded with love!
>
> [*Gora is the nickname of Gauranga, or Chaitanya
> **Nitai is the main disciple of Chaitanya
> ***Shantipur and Nadia are places associated with Chaitanya]

"When he had finished singing, Narendra gently soliloquized: "He is actually distributing love. Love, devotion, knowledge, liberation, and whatever one desires—Gora [Sri Ramakrishna] is bestowing upon us whatever he wishes. What wonderful power!" He was silent for a while and then continued, "One night, I was lying on my bed with the door bolted. Suddenly he attracted me—or rather the soul that lives in this body—and drew me to Dakshineswar. He talked with me about various topics, gave me advice, and finally allowed me to return home. He can do anything—this Gora of Dakshineswar can do anything!"

"The evening shadows melted into darkness so deep that we could not see each other. But it was not necessary to so: Narendra's fiery spiritual feelings penetrated our hearts, creating a divine intoxication that left us reeling. We felt as though the real world that we had perceived for so long had disappeared into a dream. We then realized the truth of what worldly people believe to be nothing but a fabrication: the beginningless, infinite God had become manifest as a finite human being out of His unconditional grace and was destroying the bondage of jivas and setting in motion the wheel of dharma. We did not notice how the time passed, but suddenly we heard the bell strike nine. Reluctantly, we prepared to take leave of Narendra, but he said, 'Let us go—I'll accompany you for a short distance.'

"As we walked we began discussing a similar topic, which absorbed us until we reached our home in Champatala. We realized that it was not right for us to have let Narendra come such a long distance. We brought him inside, gave him some refreshment, accompanied him to his home, and then returned home once more."

Swami Saradananda added another incident: "When Narendra entered our house he suddenly stood still, exclaiming: 'I have seen this house before! It's amazing! I'm familiar with its corridors, rooms, and everything!'"[24]

Sri Ramakrishna knew that Narendranath was an aspirant of highest calibre. He bound him to himself with the cord of love, tested him at times, and began to teach him various aspects of spiritual life. It's really amazing how he tested his devotees in various ways, with or without their knowledge. We shall try to describe events as truly as possible and leave the readers to form their own conclusion.

When a certain person first came to Sri Ramakrishna, he observed him very closely. If he liked the visitor, he would talk about spiritual matters with him and ask him to come again. If the visitor continues his visit, Sri Ramakrishna would examine his body and his limbs, his nature of thought, the degree of attachment to lust of money, the magnitude of his worldly desires, and so on. After collecting all these data, he observed his movements, actions and conversations, and then he came to a conclusion about the visitor's spirituality. Thus he was convinced of a man's character. He also tried to know hidden facts about the visitor's inner nature. Sri Ramakrishna said to a devotee: "When I'm alone in the early hours of the morning, I think of your spiritual welfare. The Divine Mother then shows me how far one devotee has advanced on the spiritual path, why another cannot make progress, and so on." Then he added: "Just as by merely looking at a glass case one can see all of its contents, so I can know the inmost thoughts and tendencies—indeed everything about someone—merely by looking at that person."

Sri Ramakrishna was satisfied until he had tested Narendranath in his own way. He used to say about human eyes: "Some people have eyes like lotus petals, some like a bull's eyes, and some possess the eyes of a yogi or of a god. Those who have eyes like lotus petals are endowed with good and spiritual tendencies. Those whose eyes are like a bull's have a strong sex drive. A yogi's eyes have an upward look and a reddish tinge. Divine eyes are not very large but are long and stretched to the ears. Those who glance at the side or look from the corner of their eyes while talking are more intelligent than the average person."

He also told about the formation of the body: "Those who have a devotional temperament have a naturally soft body, and the joints of their hands and feet are flexible. And if their bodies are lean, their muscles and tendons are so shaped that they do not appear angular." He would weigh the person's hand and forearm in his own hand. If he found the weight to be less than usual, he concluded that the man was positive minded. Sri Ramakrishna used to say: "Like the formation of the limbs, physiological functions such as sleep, evacuation, and other ordinary actions, differ according to people's particular mental tendencies. Experienced observers can find indications of human character in those things. For example, people don't all breathe the same way while sleeping. A worldly person breathes one way, a person of renunciation another. While answering the call of nature, the former's urine slants to the left while flowing and the latter's to the right. Pigs will not touch a yogi's faeces."

Sri Ramakrishna also told about the formation of a woman's limbs, similar to what he said about the shape of man's body. He said: "Those with a divine nature eat and sleep little. Their desire for sense enjoyment is also less. Their hearts are filled with joy when they hear about God and when they talk about Him with their husbands. They protect their husbands from base tendencies and sinful acts by giving them spiritual inspiration. They help their husbands in every way so that they may eventually be blessed by realizing God. The character and behaviour of women with a demonical nature are the opposite. They eat and sleep more, and their appetite for physical comfort and enjoyment is greater. Their chief aim is to prevent their husbands from focusing on anything other than giving them happiness. If their husbands talk about spiritual subjects to them, they become angry rather than pleased."

Sri Ramakrishna considered physiognomy to be one of the means for determining human character, and he tested Narendranath and all other devotees with this method to greater or lesser degrees. After examining Narendra he became very pleased and told him: "You have all the good marks on your body; the only defect is that you breathe heavily when sleeping. Yogis say that this indicates a short life."

Sri Ramakrishna examined every action of Narendranath. He hound his mind to be ablaze with spiritual hunger, self-control, courage, strength, self-sacrifice for a noble cause, and other good qualities. He was aware of Narendra's strict adherence to truth and not only trusted him completely, but also was convinced that Narendra would soon reach such a state when he would be unable to utter a falsehood, even accidentally. He always encouraged him saying: "Whoever holds to truth in word, thought, and action is blessed by the vision of God, who is Truth itself" and "One who observes truth in thought, word, and deed for twelve years reaches a state in which whatever he resolves comes to pass."

Once, during conversation, Sri Ramakrishna said: "As the chataka bird drinks only rainwater, it is always looking to the clouds to quench its thirst. It depends completely on them. Similarly, devotees depend on God alone to appease their spiritual thirst and to fulfill other needs as well." Narendra suddenly said: "Sir, although it's a common belief that the chataka bird drinks only rainwater, it isn't true. I've seen these birds drink water from rivers and ponds like the others." Sri Ramakrishna said: "What? Does the chataka bird drink water like other birds? Then this longstanding conviction of mine is false. But because you've seen this, I have no doubt about it." But he became anxious, thinking: "If this conviction of mine happens to be false, others may be the same." This made him sad. Few days later, Narendra called on the Master and said: "Sir, look! a chataka bird is drinking Ganges water." Sri Ramakrishna rushed out of his room and asked: "Where?" When Narendra pointed the bird by his finger, the Master saw a small bat drinking water. He laughed and said: "That's a bat. You rascal! You mistook a bat for a chataka and made me anxious. I won't believe everything you say anymore."

Swami Saradananda described an incident he experienced: "It is often seen that when men come into the presence of women, they become gentler than what can be accounted for a mere sense of politeness, respect, and an appreciation of beauty. According to the scriptures, this is due to a kind of sensibility hidden deep in the heart. When he realized this, the Master was convinced that Narendra would never lose his self-control under the spell of feminine beauty. The Master once compared Narendra with a devotee (Nrityagopal, who later became Swami

Jnanananda) whom we respected highly for his frequent ecstasies. The Master said: "That man loses himself in the loving care of women, but Narendra never does. I've watched him carefully. Though he doesn't say so, I find that he seems rather uncomfortable in their presence. It seems as if by turning his head away, he is asking, 'Why are they here?'"[25]

Although Narendranath possessed knowledge and masculine qualities to a great degree, he didn't lack tenderness and devotion. Sri Ramakrishna examined Narendra and remarked: "Could one who is dry jnani (wise) have such eyes? Knowledge and feminine devotion are blended in you. And those who have only masculine qualities don't have black circles around their nipples. The great hero Arjuna didn't have those marks."

One more method, that Sri Ramakrishna used to test Narendranath, was described by Swami Saradananda: "The Master's heart would swell with divine love whenever he saw Narendra, even from a distance. Many times we saw the Master merge into Samadhi, saying, 'There's Na; there's Na.' After many such visits to Dakshineswar, however, there came a day when the Master treated Narendra with utter indifference. Narendra came, saluted the Master, sat before him, and waited for some time. The Master neither greeted him not asked about his welfare. He glanced at Narendra as one would a stranger, and then remained absorbed within himself. Narendra thought that perhaps the Master was in an ecstatic mood. After a while Narendra left the room and began to smoke and chat with Hazra. When he heard that the Master was talking with others, Narendra returned to him. Even then the Master did not speak to Narendra; instead, he lay down on his bed, turning his face away from him. Thus the whole day passed, and even in the evening the Master's mood did not change. At last Narendra bowed down to the Master and returned to Calcutta.

"A week later Narendra went to Dakshineswar again and found the Master in the same mood, Narendra spent the day talking to Hazra and the other devotees and returned home at nightfall. Narendra came to Dakshineswar a third and fourth time, but found no change in the Master's mood. However, this did not perturb him or make him resentful, and he continued to visit the Master as usual. When Narendra was at home, the Master would sometimes send someone to inquire about his welfare, but now he maintained indifference when Narendra was present. This continued for more than a month. The Master noticed that Narendra did not stop coming to Dakshineswar, so one day he called him to his side and asked: 'Why do you keep coming here when I don't say a single word to you?' Narendra replied: 'Do you think I come here just to talk with you? I love you. I come because I want to see you.' Delighted, the Master said: 'I was testing you to see if you'd stop coming when you didn't receive love and attention. Only a spiritual aspirant of you caliber could have put up with such neglect and indifference. Anyone else would have left me long ago and would never have returned.'"[26]

Before we conclude this topic we should present here another incident that makes clear the intensity of Narendra's longing for God-realization. One day Sri Ramakrishna called him to the Panchavati and said: "Look, as a result of practicing austerities, I have possessed all the supernatural powers. But what shall I do with such powers? I can't even keep a wearing-cloth tied around my own waist! So I'm thinking of asking Mother to transfer them all to you. She has told me that you will have to do much work for Her. So if these powers are transmitted to you, you can use them when necessary. What do you say?"

Narendranath had seen various divine powers in Sri Ramakrishna since their first meeting, so had no reason to doubt him. After serious thought, Narendranath asked: "Sir, will they help me to realize God?"

"No, they won't help you to do that. But they might be useful once you have realized God and have started doing His work" replied Sri Ramakrishna.

Narendranath said: "Sir, I don't need them. Let me realize God first. After that, there will be time enough to decide whether I need them or not. If I get these marvelous powers now, I may forget the whole purpose of my life, and use them to gratify worldly desires. Then they would only become my ruin."

Sometimes, Sri Ramakrishna would say to his devotees: "The person who exists within this (himself) has the nature of a woman, and the person who dwells within Narendra has the nature of a man."

Revered Swami Saradananda in explanation of the above sentence said: "It is difficult to determine what the Master meant when he said that. But we can come to a reasonable understanding if we study the paths that the Master and Narendra followed and the means they adopted to reach God, the ultimate Truth. The Master learned from his gurus all of the spiritual disciplines prescribed by the scriptures for God-realization and then practiced them with complete faith. Narendra's behaviour was just the opposite: He first used his intellect to ascertain whether there was any error in the words of the guru or in the scriptures, and then followed them only when they withstood the test of his reason. As a result of deep-rooted tendencies from previous lives, Narendra had a firm belief in God, but all throughout his life he cherished this thought: Human beings are subject to superstition and error; so why should one indiscriminately accept what they say? Whatever the outcome or origin or reasoning, nowadays people consider it manly to proceed in the spiritual realm, and in all other matters, by keeping faith and devotion under the control of the intellect."[27]

Members of Narendra's household didn't like his frequent visit to Sri Ramakrishna, but no one dared to say anything to him directly because they knew that he was very dear to his parents, and because since his childhood he didn't care for any restriction. He enjoyed complete freedom regarding what he ate, where he went, or what he did. Therefore, no one tried to control his visit to Sri Ramakrishna at Dakshineswar.

We would like to learn about those blessed days of Narendranath with Sri Ramakrishna by going through his memory. He recalled: "It's extremely difficult to describe to others how joyful were the days we spent with the Master. We still wonder at how the Master was constantly training us through play, merriment, and trivial daily activities, thus forming our spiritual lives without our knowledge. When a powerful wrestler trains a boy to wrestle, he controls himself and makes his student appear to be as strong as he is. He awakens his student's self-confidence by feigning to overpower him only with great effort and sometimes allowing himself to be defeated. The Master adopted this method with us. He always saw 'the whole ocean in a drop of water' [in other words, he saw infinite God in each individual]. Because he dwelt in the state of bhava-mukha, he knew how each person's latent spiritual power would manifest itself in the fullness of time. Keeping that bright picture in mind, he would speak highly of us and encourage us. Lest we miss the highest goal of life by becoming entangled in worldly desires, he carefully observed every action of ours and kept us under control with his instructions. But we had no idea that he was watching us so closely and had such control over us. This was his unique technique of training his disciples and moulding our lives.

"Once I felt that although my mind was concentrated to some extent during meditation, it wasn't going any deeper. I asked him what I should do. He told me what he'd done in similar circumstances and gave me additional instructions. I remember that when I meditated in Dakshineswar late at night the whistle of the nearby Alambazar Jute Mill would disturb me and distract my mind. When I reported this to the Master, he advised me to concentrate on the sound of the whistle. I followed his advice and derived much benefit from it.

"On another occasion I found it difficult to forget my body completely during meditation and concentrate my mind wholly on the Ideal. When I told him of my problem, he mentioned how Tota Puri had told him to concentrate between the eyebrows while practicing Samadhi according to Vedanta. He sharply pressed a fingernail into a spot between my eyebrows and said, 'Now concentrate on this painful sensation,' I found that I could easily concentrate on that sensation as long as I liked, and that during that period I completely lost awareness of the other parts of my body, which then caused me no distraction.

"The isolated Panchavati, where the Master had performed his sadhana, was the most suitable place for meditation. But in addition to our spiritual practices, we spent a good deal of time there in sheer fun and merrymaking. The Master sometimes joined us, intensifying our joy. There we used to run, climb trees, swing from the rope-like madhavi vines, and sometimes have a picnic. During our first picnic, the Master noticed that I'd cooked the food, but he partook of it nonetheless. I knew that he couldn't eat food unless it was cooked by Brahmins, so I was planning to obtain Prasad from the kali temple for him. But he prevented me, saying, 'There's no harm in my taking cooked food from a pure and sattvic person like you.' He ignored my repeated objections and ate the food I'd cooked that day."

Meanwhile, Vishwanath Dutta, Narendra's father, died on February, 23, 1884. Narendranath was then of twenty years old. Only twenty-four days ago (30th January) Narendra received the result of his B.A. examination. That day, he went to his friend's house at Baranagor. After having dinner at 11 p.m. they all were busy in chatting in bedroom. Hemali, one of their friends, arrived there at about 2 a.m. with the news that Narendra's father had died of heart-attack. It was a bolt from the blue. Immediately they returned to Calcutta together. In some opinion, Narendranath reached straight to the cremation ground, and performed the funeral rites. His signature is found in the register of the crematorium.

According to the register of Calcutta Corporation, Vishwanath Dutta died on 23rd February, but it was 24th February 1884 on the application made by Bhuvaneswari Devi. On the other hand, Revered Swami Gambhirananda said that, in the afternoon of 25th February 1884, Narendranath went to his friend's house at Baranagor, and there he sang devotional songs until 11 p.m. Thereafter they were busy in chatting, while at about 2 a.m. their friend Hemali arrived to give the news, Narendra's father suddenly had left the world.

Bhavanath Chattopadhyay, a handsome and devout youth, used to visit Sri Ramakrishna at Dakshineswar. During that time he became acquainted with Narendranath and a close friendship developed between them. Bhavanath was also very dear to Sri Ramakrishna because of his humility, modesty, simplicity, faith and devotion. Observing the soft feminine nature and his attraction for Narendra, Sri Ramakrishna would tease him saying: "Perhaps you were Narendra's life-companion in a previous incarnation." Bhavanath lived at Baranagor, whenever he had an opportunity he took Narendra to his house and fed him. Satkari Lahiri and Dasarathi Sanyal were his neighbours. Both of them were close friends of Narendra, and Dasarathi was a classmate as well. Perhaps Narendranath was at Bhavanath's house when he heard the news of his father's death.

While he was engaged in professional work away from Calcutta, Vishwanath Dutta became a diabetic patient. A month before his death he had a mild heart attack, and was advised to take rest. But suddenly a client came and took him to the court. Returning home he felt a pain in chest, and at about 9 p.m. he vomited a little. At about 10 p.m. he had another heart attack which he could not survive. He had plan to go for choosing a bride for Narendra next day; everything was well arranged for the same.

Vishwanath Dutta, Narendra's father, had been spending more than he earned and left nothing but a huge burden of debt on his family. Narendra's relatives, who had benefitted from his father's generosity, became hostile and even tried to evict his family from their home. Narendranath was brought up in comfort, but now he was completely at a loss.

Within a short period after the death of his father there was no end of distress and no relief from his poverty. Desperately he began to search a suitable job, but he met with disappointment everywhere. He described this period: "Even before the prescribed period of mourning [after my father's death] had passed, I began running hither and thither in search of a job. Dizzy from lack of food, I went from office to office barefoot in the blazing sun, carrying my application papers. Some days one or two close friends accompanied me out of sympathy; other days I went alone. But everywhere I met with rejection. That early experience taught me that unselfish sympathy is rare in this world; there is no place here for the poor or the weak. Even those who only a short time ago would have regarded themselves fortunate to do me a favour, now made wry faces and were reluctant to help me, though they could easily have done so had the wished. When faced by all this, the world sometimes seemed to be the handiwork of the devil. I remember that one day when I was walking around in the sun; the soles of my feet became blistered. I was completely exhausted and had to sit down in the shade of the Ochterloney Monument [now Shaid Minar] on the Maidan. A couple of friends were with me, or perhaps they met me there. To console me, one of them sang:

> Here blows the wind, the breath of Brahman—
>
> It is His grace we feel.

When I heard that song I felt as if someone were violently beating me on the head. Thinking of my mother and brothers' helpless condition, I was filled with resentment and despair. 'Be quiet!' I told him. 'That fanciful nonsense is all right for people living in luxury—people who have no idea what hunger is—people whose nearest and dearest aren't wearing rags and starving. Previously this song sounded true and beautiful to me. But now I've seen what life is really like, and that song is nothing but a relentless mockery.'

"I dare say that my friend was terribly hurt by my words. How could he understand the grinding poverty that had made me utter them? Some mornings I'd get up to find that there wasn't enough food for all of us, so I'd tell my mother, 'A friend has invited me to lunch,' and leave home. On such days I had nothing to eat, for I had no money in my pocket. I was too proud to tell anyone about this: Sometimes my wealthy friends would invite me to their houses and pleasure gardens to sing at their parties as before. Unable to avoid them, I sometimes went and tried to entertain them. I had no inclination to tell them how I felt, and they did not try to find out how I was getting along. Rarely would a very few ask, 'Why do you look so pale and sad today?' But only one friend ever found out—and not from me—how things really were. He used to send money to my mother anonymously from time to time. I'm eternally indebted to him.

"Some of my boyhood friends, whose characters had become dissipated in their youth and who had resorted to unscrupulous means to earn money, now became aware of my poverty and tried to drag me into their company. I noticed that those among them who had suddenly fallen into difficult circumstances as I had, and were forced to adopt an ignoble path for their livelihood, actually had empathy for me. Mahamaya, the great enchantress, took advantage of my circumstances and tried to snare me with various temptations. A wealthy woman had been infatuated with me for a long time. When she found an opportunity, she sent a message inviting me to end my poverty by accepting her along with her wealth. Disgusted, I sternly rejected her offer. When another woman approached me with a similar proposal, I told her: 'Look, you've wasted your life seeking the pleasures of your worthless body. Now death is in front of you. Have you done anything to prepare yourself? Shun these filthy desires and call on God.'

"In spite of all these sufferings, I neither lost faith in the existence of God, nor did I doubt the truth of the saying: 'God is merciful.' Every morning I repeated the Lord's name as I got out of bed, and then resumed my search for a job. One day as I was getting out of bed my mother overheard my prayer from. She said bitterly: 'Keep quiet, boy! You've been repeating the Lord's name since you were a child. What has He done for you?' These words hurt me terribly. Stunned, I asked myself: 'Does God really exist? And if He does, does He listen to our fervent prayers? Why do I pray so much and get no answer? Why is there so much woe in His benign kingdom? How could He be merciful when His creation is so full of evil? Afflicted with the sufferings of others, Ishwar Chandra Vidyasagar once remarked, 'If God is compassionate and gracious, why then did millions of people die for want of a morsel of food during the terrible famine?' This harsh and taunting remark reverberated in my ears. My heart was filled with wounded feelings towards God, and at this opportune moment doubt occupied my mind.

"It was against my nature to do anything secretly. Even as a child, I was never able to conceal even the most trivial thought or action from fear or for any other reason. So it wasn't surprising that I now began aggressively to tell people that God did not exist, and that even if He did exist, it was of no use calling on Him because it produced no result. Of course, the rumour soon spread that I'd become an atheist and that I was drinking, mixing with people of bad character, and visiting houses of ill repute. Those lies made me all the more rebellious and aggressive. I began telling everyone—even those who didn't ask my opinion—that I had no objection to any man's drinking wine or going to a brothel if it would help him to forget his hard lot in this world of pain. And I added that I would do these things myself, without the least regard for public opinion, if I believed that they would make me happy even for a single moment.

"Such news travels fast. It didn't take long for a completely distorted version of my words to reach the Master and his devotees in Calcutta. When some of them came to visit me to learn the truth, they made it obvious that they believed at least part of what they had heard, if not all. I was bitterly wounded when I realized that they could think so little of me. I told them that it was cowardice to believe in God merely from fear of hell. Quoting Hume, Mill, Bain, Comte, and other Western philosophers, I fiercely argued that there is no evidence for the existence of God. And they went away, convinced more than ever of my downfall, as I afterwards learned. In my defiant mood, this actually pleased me. Then it occurred to me that perhaps they would tell the Master about this and that he would believe them. I felt terrible pain at the thought. But then I said to myself: 'Let him believe it. If he does, I can't help it, Other's good or bad opinions are worth nothing.' I later discovered that the Master had heard all these lies about me. He made no comment at first. But when Bhavanath tearfully said to him, 'Sir, we never dreamed that Narendra would sink so low!' the Master cried our excitedly: 'Silence, you scoundrel! Mother has told me that he could never do such things. If you talk like this anymore, I won't allow you in my presence again!'

"But what was this atheism of mine? Nothing but egotism and pride. The experiences I'd had since childhood and, more important, since meeting the Master, rose vividly into my mind in bright colours. I said to myself: 'God certainly does exist and there is definitely a way to attain Him. Otherwise, what is life for? What is it worth? The path to God has to be found, no matter how great the struggle.' Days passed, and my mind continued to vacillate between doubt and certainty. Thus I had no respite from my emotional turmoil and financial woes.

"Summer passed, and the rainy season began. I continued looking for work as before. One night as I returned home I was drenched with rain. I hadn't eaten all day, my legs were tired, and my mind was even more exhausted than my body. At length, I grew so exhausted that I couldn't go a single step farther, and I lay down motionless on the open veranda of a neighbour's house. Perhaps I lost external consciousness for a while. I remember that all kinds of thoughts and pictures went through my mind, and I had no power to ignore or concentrate upon any of them. Then I suddenly felt that Providence was lifting up screen after screen in my mind and that all the problems that had been tormenting me—where is the harmony between God's justice and His mercy, why does evil exist within a benign creation—all were resolved. I was beside myself with joy. When I later continued my walk home, I found that there was not a bit of fatigue in my body and that my mind was filled with infinite peace and strength. The day was just breaking.

"I now became absolutely indifferent to the praise or blame of the world. I was firmly convinced that I wasn't born to earn money, support a family, or seek worldly enjoyment like others. I was secretly preparing to renounce the world as my grandfather had done. When the day arrived on which I had decided to start life as a wandering monk, I heard that the Master was coming to a devotee's house in Calcutta. I thought this was very fortunate: I should see my guru before I left home forever. But when I met the Master, he told me imperiously, 'You must come with me to Dakshineswar today.' I offered various excuses, but he wouldn't accept any of them. I had to return with him. We didn't speak much in the carriage. When we got to Dakshineswar, I sat in his room for some time with other devotees. Then the Master went into a state of ecstasy. Suddenly he came over to me, took my hand in his, and sang, with tears pouring down his face:

I am afraid to speak,
I am afraid not to speak,
For the fear rises in my mind
That I shall lose you.

"All this time, I'd fought back the strong emotion I was feeling. I could do so no longer, and my tears poured down like his. I felt sure that the Master knew all about my plans. The others were astonished to see us behaving in this way. After the Master had returned to normal consciousness, one of the devotees asked him what the matter was. He smiled and answered, 'It's just something between the two of us.' That night he sent the others away. Calling me to him, he said in a voice choked with emotion: 'I know you've come to the world to do Mother's work; you can never lead a worldly life. But, for my sake, stay with your family as long as I'm alive.' As he said this, he began to cry again.

"I took leave of him the next day and returned home. A thousand concerns for my family occupied my mind, and with renewed energy I set myself to finding employment. I got a temporary job in an attorney's office translating some books, which brought just enough income to live on. I couldn't find a permanent job, so I had no fixed income with which to maintain my mother and brothers. It occurred to me that God grants the Master's prayers, so I should ask him to pray on my behalf that my family's financial crisis would be overcome, I was sure that he wouldn't refuse, for my sake. I rushed to Dakshineswar and importuned him, saying: 'Sir, you must speak to the Divine Mother so that my family's financial problems can be solved.' The Master replied: 'I can't make such demands. Why don't you go and ask the Mother yourself? You don't accept the Mother—that is why you have all these troubles.' I replied: 'I don't know the Mother. Please tell the Mother for me. You have to, or I won't let you go.' The Master said affectionately: 'My boy, I've prayed many times to the Mother to remove your suffering. But She doesn't listen to my prayers because you don't care for Her. All right, today is Tuesday, a day especially sacred to Mother. Go to the temple tonight and pray. Mother will grant whatever you ask for. I promise you that. My Mother is the embodiment of Pure Consciousness, the Power of Brahman, and She has produced this universe by mere will. What can She not do, if She wishes?'

"When the Master said that, I was fully convinced that all my suffering would cease as soon as I prayed to Her. I waited impatiently for night. At 9:00 p.m. the Master told me to go to the temple. On my way, I was possessed by a kind of drunkenness and began to stagger. I firmly believed that I would see the Mother and hear Her voice. I forgot everything else and became absorbed in that thought alone. When I entered the temple, I saw that the Mother was actually conscious and living, the fountainhead of infinite love and beauty. Overwhelmed with love and devotion, I bowed down to Her and again, praying, 'Mother—grant me discrimination, grant me detachment, grant me divine knowledge and devotion, grant that I may see You without obstruction, always!' My heart was filled with peace. The universe disappeared from my mind and the Mother alone occupied it completely.

"As soon as I returned to the Master, he asked, 'Hello, did you pray to the Mother to relieve your family's needs?' I was taken aback and replied: 'No, sir, I forgot. What shall I do now?' He said, 'Go—go again, and say that prayer.' Again I went to the temple. But when I stood before the Mother, I was again overwhelmed and forgot my intention. I repeatedly bowed down to Her and prayed for knowledge and devotion. When I returned to the Master, he smiled and asked, 'Well, have you prayed for your need this time?' Startled, I said: 'No, sir, I couldn't. As soon as I saw the Mother, I was overwhelmed by a divine power and forgot everything—I asked only for knowledge and devotion. What's to be done now?' The Master said: 'Silly boy! Couldn't you control yourself a little, and remember your prayer? Go back again and tell Mother what you want—be quick!' I went a third time, but as soon as I entered the temple I felt a sense of deep shame. I thought: 'What a trifling thing I am asking of the Mother! As the Master says, "It's like being graciously received by a king and then asking for gourds and pumpkins." It's that kind of stupidity! Am I so smallminded?' I shame and remorse I bowed down to Her again and again and said: 'Mother, I want nothing but knowledge and devotion.'

"When I came out of the temple, I thought that the Master must have played a trick on me: I'd gone to the Mother thrice but hadn't been able to ask for what I needed. I went to the Master and insisted: 'It was certainly you who make me intoxicated and forgetful. Now you must at least say a prayer that my mother and brothers will never lack for food and clothing.' He said: 'My child, you know I could never offer a prayer like that for anyone; the words wouldn't leave my mouth. I told you that you'd get whatever you asked Mother for; but you couldn't do that, either. You aren't destined to have worldly happiness. What am I to do about that?' I said firmly: 'No, sir, I won't let you go. You must say the prayer for my sake. I'm certain my family will be freed from want if only you say they will.' Thus I went on importuning him until at last he said, 'All right—they will never lack for plain food and clothing.'"[28]

The acceptance of God in form was a significant event in Narendra's life. Before that he didn't understand the hidden meaning behind worshipping God as Mother or using symbols and images. So he disregarded the images of gods and goddesses and had never visited their temples with love and respect. Now he had learnt the true mystery of worship, and his spiritual life became more expansive. Sri Ramakrishna was happy with this change in his beloved Naren. Vaikuntha Nath Sanyal, a devotee and friend of Swami Saradananda, visited Dakshineswar the day after this incident. The account of his experience is given here to put a clear and complete picture to the reader.

Sanyal said: "I became acquainted with a person named Tarapada Ghosh, who worked with me in the same office. He was a close friend of Narendra. I'd seen Narendra with Tarapada a few times in our office. Tarapada had told me that Sri Ramakrishna was very fond of Narendra. However, I never tried to get acquainted with him.

"On that day I went to Dakshineswar at noon. The Master was seated alone in his room and Narendra was sleeping on the veranda outside. The Master was beaming with joy. As soon as I bowed down to him, he pointed to Narendra and said: 'Look at that boy—that boy is very good. His name is Narendra. He wouldn't accept the Divine Mother before, but last night he did. He was in need of money, so I advised him to ask Mother for it. But he couldn't; he said he felt ashamed. When he came back from the temple, he asked me to teach him a song in praise of Mother. So I taught him, "Mother, Thou art our sole Redeemer,..." and he sang it all night long. That's why he's sleeping now.' And then the Master smiled with joy and said: 'Narendra has accepted Mother Kali. That's very good, isn't it?' Seeing that he was as happy as a child about this, I answered, 'Yes, sir, it is very good.' A little later he smiled and said again: 'Narendra has accepted the Mother. It's very good. What do you say?' And he kept smiling and saying that, over and over.

"When Narendra awoke at 4:00 p.m., he came and sat near the Master, appearing about to take leave of him and return to Calcutta. But the Master went into ecstasy and moved closer to Narendra. He said: 'What I see is that I'm this body (his own body) and that body (Narendra's body) also. It's true—I see no difference. If you lay a stick on the surface of the Ganges, the water seems to be divided into two parts, but it's really all one; there's no division. The same thing is true here. Can you understand that? What else exists but Mother? Isn't that true?'

"Then he said suddenly, 'I'll smoke.' I hastily prepared the water pipe and gave it to him. After taking a few puffs, he said, 'No, I'll smoke straight from the bowl,' and he took the tobacco bowl in both hands. He puffed again, then held it to Narendra's mouth and said, 'Take a puff or two from my hands.' Narendra hesitated. The Master said: 'What ignorance! Are you and I different? This is I and that is also I.' Saying this, he put his hands to Narendra's mouth and forced him to smoke. Narendra took a couple of puffs and then stopped. Seeing that he had stopped, the Master was about to start smoking again when Narendra said quickly, 'Sir, wash your hands before you smoke!' But the Master wouldn't do so. 'You wretch,' he told Narendra, 'You're too conscious of differences!' The he continued to smoke through his hands although Narendra's lips had touched them. He uttered many spiritual truths from his state of ecstasy. Normally the Master couldn't partake of anything that had been tasted by another—to him it was like refuse. I was amazed when I saw him behave that way with Narendra that day and realized the closeness between them.

"Our conversation continued till 8:00 p.m. When we saw that the Master's ecstasy had come to an end, Narendra and I took leave of him and returned to Calcutta on foot. Later, Narendra told us many times: 'Ever since our first meeting, it was the Master alone who always had faith in me—no one else, not even my own mother and brothers. That faith and that love of his have bound me to him forever. The Master was the only one who knew how to love and who really loved. Worldly people only feign love to gratify their own self-interest.'"[29]

We would like to gladly accept that it is beyond our imagination—how much deep was the love that Sri Ramakrishna had for Narendranath. But it doesn't mean that he would always allow Narendra to cross the limit that was out of his principle. So far the matter is ethical and spiritual; he never liked to move a bit. In this regard Narendranath said: "He loved me so much! But whenever an impure idea crept into my mind he at once knew about it. While going around with Annada, sometime I found myself in the company of evil people. On those occasions the Master could not eat any food from my hands. He could raise his hand only a little, and could not bring it to his mouth. On one such occasion, while he was ill, he brought his hand very close to his mouth, but it did not go in. He said to me, 'You are not yet ready.'"[30]

After his father's death Narendranath tried hard to get a job for the maintenance of his family, but he couldn't find the same. By this time in 1884, with the influence of Mahendra Nath Gupta (M) he had an opportunity of teaching in Vidyasagar's Metropolitan Institution, then situated at Sukia Street, Calcutta. Later in June 1886, he was appointed headmaster of the newly-opened branch of the same Institute in Siddheswar Chandra Lane, Champatala, Calcutta. Vidyasagar's son-in-law was the secretary of the school. He tried to force Narendranath to follow his instruction, but couldn't control him as he was fond of freedom and liked to move on his own way. Finally, Narendranath was compelled by circumstances to leave the post. Bhupendranath Dutta was told by Haramohan Mitra, Narendra's friend that Narendranath later applied for the post of a teacher in City Collegiate School, and he asked Shivnath Sastri for his help in this regard. But he had to be disappointed as Mr. Sastri didn't pay any heed to his request.

Meanwhile, we should remember that M, the recorder of The Gospel of Sri Ramakrishna, also was found not much reliable to Vidyasagar, and after having such an indication he resigned from his service. When Sri Ramakrishna came to know this, he said to M, "That's a right decision. What you have done is very much right."

Revered Swami Bodhananda, an ascetic of Ramakrishna order, was then a student of lower class in Metropolitan Institute, and was one of them who saw Narendranath coming to school, wearing a chapkan (a loose and long robe) and trouser, hanging a long scarf on his neck, an umbrella in one hand, and in the other was a textbook.

During this critical time, Vishwanath's friends, Nimaichandra Basu and W.C. Banerjee, the barrister, were of great help. In these affairs Narendranath himself showed his legal talent, which the English lawyer of the opponent party appreciated and said: "Young man, you will make a very good lawyer." The case was finally decided in favour of Narendranath's family, and they secured their legal share in the property, Later on, they returned to their ancestral house, but by that time Narendranath had renounced the worldly life and became Swami Vivekananda, the most revered ascetic of the world.

One day Narendranath was seated in his study with a few of his friends. He didn't visit Dakshineswar for some time. During conversation a voice was heard calling, "Naren! Naren!" All started to their feet as they recognized the voice. Naren hastened downstairs to receive Sri Ramakrishna. His eyes were filled with tears. "Naren, why did you not come to see me for the last few days?" he asked with a voice as simple as a child. He brought some sweets, and some of it he fed Naren with his own hands. The Lord Himself comes to see him who looks for Him.

"Come" Sri Ramakrishna urged, "sing me one of your songs." Narendranath took the Tanpura and began to sing a song to the Divine Mother. The others sat still. Soon Sri Ramakrishna became unconscious of all outward things. Narendra sang more songs. As soon as Sri Ramakrishna came back to his normal state, he asked: "Will you go to Dakshineswar with me?" Narendra agreed, and went to Dakshineswar with the Master; leaving the Tanpura alone on the floor.

Sometime in 1884, he went to Dakshineswar and found the Master seated in his room surrounded by devotees. Narendranath was also present there. Various spiritual discussions went on, relieved by wit and humour. During conversation, there came the topic of the Vaishnava religion, Sri Ramakrishna briefly explained the quintessence of that doctrine, saying: "This religion advises its followers to practice these three disciplines sincerely: love of God's name, compassion for all living beings, and service of devotees. God and His name are identical. Knowing the Name and the possessor of the Name to be the same, the devotee should always chant His name with love. Knowing God and His devotees, Krishna and the Vaishnavas, to be the same, one should respect, worship, and pay obeisance to monks and devotees. Understanding that this world belongs to Krishna, one should show compassion for all beings." As he said, "compassion for all beings," he suddenly went into samadhi, unconscious of all worldly surroundings. After a while he came down to a semi-ecstatic state and said: "Compassion for all beings? How foolish to speak of compassion! Human beings are as insignificant as worms crawling on the earth—and they are to show compassion to others? That's absurd. It must not be compassion, but service to all. Recognize all as manifestations of God and serve them as such."

Everyone heard these words of Sri Ramakrishna, but no one except Narendranath understood their significance. When Sri Ramakrishna came to his normal plane of consciousness, Narendranath left the room and said to some of his friends: "What a wonderful light I saw today in those words of the Master! How beautifully did he reconcile the simple, sweet, and refreshing ideal of devotion with the knowledge of Vedanta, which people believe to be dry, difficult, and heartless! For so long we've heard that anyone who wants to attain nondual knowledge must retire to the forest, shunning family and friends completely and forcibly uprooting love, devotion, and other sweet sentiments from the heart, driving them away forever. If aspirants who strive to attain that knowledge consider this world and all people within it to be impediments to their spiritual path, they will develop hatred towards them and go astray. But what the Master said today in his ecstatic mood is clear: One can bring Vedanta from the forest to the home and practice it in daily life. Let people continue with whatever they are doing; there's no harm in this. People must first believe and understand that God has manifested Himself before them as the world and its creatures. Whoever people come in contact with in every moment of their lives, whomever they treat with love, respect, and compassion—they all are parts of God, God Himself. If people consider every human being to be God, how can they consider themselves to be superior to others and harbour anger, hatred, an arrogance—or even compassion—towards them? Their minds will become pure as they serve all beings as God, and soon they will experience themselves as parts of the blissful God—by nature pure, illumined, and free.

"The Master's words also shed a special light on the path of devotion. As long as an aspirant can't see God in every being, it isn't possible to attain true and supreme devotion. When true devotees serve human beings as Shiva or Narayana, they see God in others and are soon blessed with supreme devotion. The followers of Karma Yoga and Raja Yoga will also find great light in the Master's words. Embodied being cannot remain without activity for even a moment, so their duty is to perform every action as service to God within human beings; thus they will soon reach the goal. If it's the will of God, I shall proclaim to the world at large the noble truth that

I've heard today. I shall preach this wonderful message to all—the wise and the ignorant, the rich and the poor, the Brahmin and the pariah."

Now we would like to study *The Gospel of Sri Ramakrishna*, recorded by Mahendra Nath Gupta who witnessed many incidents through which grew the relation between Sri Ramakrishna and Narendranath. It will help us to know how Narendra was taught by Sri Ramakrishna, and was prepared for doing his job for what he appeared on the earth. Let us go back to those days, when Narendranath used to learn spiritual lessons sitting at the holy feet of Sri Ramakrishna. We wish to know, what he learnt, and how he was taught and made fit for doing good to human beings.

It was a Sunday of February 1882; when Narendranath visited Sri Ramakrishna at Dakshineswar. Sri Ramakrishna asked Narendra, "If people speak ill of you, what will you think of them?"

Narendra replied, "I shall think that dogs are barking at me."

Master said: "Oh, no! You mustn't go that far, my child! God dwells in all beings. But you may be intimate only with good people; you must keep away from the evil-minded. God is even in the tiger; but you cannot embrace the tiger on that account. You may say, 'Why run away from a tiger, which is also a manifestation of God?' The answer to that is: 'Those who tell you to run away are also manifestation of God—and why shouldn't you listen to them?'

"Let me tell you a story. In a forest there lived a holy man who had many disciples. One day he taught them to see God in all beings and, knowing this, to bow low before them all. A disciple went to the forest to gather wood for the sacrificial fire. Suddenly he heard an outcry: 'Get out of the way! A mad elephant is coming!' All but the disciple of the holy man took to their heels. He reasoned that the elephant was also God in another form. Then why should he run away from it? He stood still, bowed before the animal, and began to sing its praises. The mahut of the elephant was shouting: 'Run away! Run away!' But the disciple didn't move. The animal seized him with its trunk, cast him to one side, and went on its way. Hurt and bruised, the disciple lay unconscious on the ground. Hearing what had happened, his teacher and his brother disciples came to him and carried him to the hermitage. With the help of some medicine he soon regained consciousness. Someone asked him, 'you knew the elephant was coming—why didn't you leave the place?' 'But' he said, 'our teacher has told us that God himself has taken all these forms, of animals as well as men. Therefore, thinking it was only the elephant God that was coming, I didn't run away.' At this the teacher said: 'Yes, my child, it is true that the elephant God was coming; but the mahut God forbade you to stay there. Since all are manifestations of God, why didn't you trust the mahut's words? You should have heeded the words of the mahut God.'

"It is said in the scriptures that water is a form of God. But some water is fit to be used for worship, some water for washing the face, and some only for washing plates or dirty linen. This last sort cannot be used for drinking or for a holy purpose. In like manner, God undoubtedly dwells in the hearts of all—holy and unholy, righteous and unrighteous; but a man should not have dealings with the unholy, the wicked, the impure. He must not be intimate with them. With some of them he may exchange words, but with others he shouldn't go even that far. He should keep aloof from such people."[31]

One day Narendra was seated in front of Sri Ramakrishna along with other devotees. During conversation, Sri Ramakrishna pointed to Narendra and said: "You all see this boy. Narendra and people of his type belong to the class of the ever-free. They are never entangled in the world. When they grow a little older they feel the awakening of inner consciousness and go directly towards God. They come to the world only to teach others. They never care for anything of the world. They are never attached to 'woman and gold'." At this point Narendra left the room, and other devotees remained seated. After a while he returned and started singing:

Meditate, O my mind, on the Lord Hari,
The Stainless One, Pure Spirit through and through.
How peerless is the Light that in Him shines!
How soul-bewitching is His wonderous form!
How dear is He to all His devotees!
Ever more beauteous in fresh-blossoming love
That shames the splendour of a million moons,
Like lightning gleams the glory of His from,
Raising erect the hair for very joy.

The Master shuddered when this last line was sung. His hair stood on end, and tears of joy streamed down his cheeks. Now and then his lips parted in a smile.

The song went on:

Worship His feet in the lotus of your heart;
With mind serene and eyes made radiant
With heavenly love, behold that matchless sight.

Again that bewitching smile. The body motionless as before, the eyes half shut, as if beholding a strange inner vision.

The song drew to a close. Narendra sang the last line:

Caught in the spell of His ecstasy,
Immerse yourself for evermore, O mind,
In Him who is Pure Knowledge and Pure Bliss.[32]

Next day Narendranath again met Sri Ramakrishna at Dakshineswar, where M. (recorder of *The Gospel of Sri Ramakrishna*) was also present. The Master said to Narendra and M., "I should like to hear you speak and argue in English." They both laughed. But they continued to talk in their mother tongue. It was impossible for M. to argue any more before the Master. Later in the afternoon all the devotees except Narendra and M. took leave of the Master. The Master told Narendra, "Look here. Come a little more often. You are a new-comer. On first acquaintance people visit each other quite often, as is the case with a lover and his sweetheart. So please come, won't you?" Narendra was particular about his promises. He said with a smile, "Yes, sir, I shall try."[33]

It was Monday, October 16, 1882, a few days before the Durga Puja, the festival of the Divine Mother. Sri Ramakrishna was in a very happy mood, for Narendranath was with him. Narendra had brought two or three young members of the Brahmo Samaj to the temple garden. Rakhal, Ramlal, Hazra and M. were also present there. Narendra had his midday meal with Sri Ramakrishna. Afterwords a temporary bed was made on the floor. Disciples were taking rest for a while. A few cushions and pillows completed the simple bed. Sri Ramakrishna sat near Narendranath on the bed. He talked with devotees in great delight. A radiant smile was lightening on his face, and his eyes were fixed on Narendra. He was giving them spiritual teachings. Sri Ramakrishna said: "After I had experienced samadhi, my mind craved intensely to hear only about God. I would always search for places where they were reciting or explaining the sacred books, such as the *Bhagavata*, the *Mahabharata*, and the *Adhyatma Ramayana*.

"What tremendous faith Krishnakishore had! Once, while at Vrindavan, he felt thirsty and went to a well. Near it he saw a man standing. On being asked to draw a little water for him, the man said: 'I belong to a low caste, sir. You are a Brahmin. How can I draw water for you?' Krishnakishore said: 'Take the name of Shiva. By repeating His holy name you will make yourself pure.' The low-caste man did as he was told, and Krishnakishore, orthodox Brahmin that he was, drank that water. What tremendous faith!

"Once a holy man came to the bank of the Ganges and lived near the bathing-ghat at Ariadaha, not far from Dakshineswar. We thought of paying him a visit. I said to Haladhari: 'Krishnakishore and I are going to see a holy man. Will you come with us?' Haladhari replied, 'What is the use of seeing a mere human body, which is no better than a cage of clay?' Haladhari was a student of the Gita and Vedanta philosophy, and therefore referred to the holy man as a mere 'cage of clay'. I repeated this to Krishnakishore. With great anger he said: 'How impudent of Haladhari to make such a remark! How can he ridicule as a 'cage of clay' the body of a man who constantly thinks of God, who meditates on Rama, and has renounced all for the sake of the Lord? Doesn't he know that such a man is the embodiment of Spirit?' He was so upset by Haladhari's remarks that he would turn his face away from him whenever he met him in the temple garden, and stopped speaking to him.

"Once Krishnakishore asked me, 'why have you cast off the sacred thread?' In those days of God-vision I felt as if I were passing through the great storm of Aswin (he referred to the great cyclone of 1864), and everything was blown away from me. No trace of my old self on my body, not to speak of the sacred thread! I said to Krishnakishore, 'Ah, you will understand if you ever happen to be as intoxicated with God as I am.'

"And it actually came to pass. He too passed through a God-intoxicated state, when he would repent only the word 'Om' and shut himself up alone in his room. His relatives thought he was actually mad, and called in a physician. Ram Kaviraj of Natagore came to see him. Krishnakishore said to the physician, 'Cure me, sir, of my malady, if you please, but not of my Om.'

"One day I went to see him and found him in a pensive mood. When I asked him about it, he said: 'The tax-collector was here. He threatened to dispose of my bras pots, my cups and my few utensils, if I didn't pay the tax; so I am worried.' I said: 'But why should you worry about it? Let him take away your pots and pans. Let him arrest your body even. How will that affect you? For your nature is that of Kha!' (Narendra and the others laugh) He used to say to me that he was the Spirit, all-pervading as the sky. He had got the idea from the Adhyatma Ramayana. I used to tease him now and then, addressing him as 'Kha'. Therefore I said to him that day, with a smile: 'You are Kha. Taxes cannot move you!'

"In that state of God-intoxication I used to speak out of my mind to all. I was no respecter of persons. Even to men of position I was not afraid to speak the truth.

"One Jatindra (a titled aristocrat of Calcutta) came to the garden of Jadu Malick. I was there too. I asked him: 'What is the duty of man? Isn't our duty to think of God?' Jatindra replied: 'We are worldly people. How is it possible for us to achieve liberation? Even King Yudhishthira had to have a vision of hell.' This made me very angry. I said to him: 'What sort of man are you? Of all the incidents of Yudhishthira's life, you remember only his seeing hell. You don't remember his truthfulness, his forbearance, his patience, his discrimination, his dispassion, his devotion to God.' I was about to say many more things, when Hriday stopped my mouth. After a little while Jatindra left the place, saying he had some other business to attend to.

"Many days later I went with Captain to see Raja Sourindra Tagore. As soon as I met him, I said, 'I can't address you as 'Raja', or by any such title, for I should be telling a lie.' He talked to me a few minutes, but even so our conversation was interrupted by the frequent visits of Europeans and others. A man of rajasic temperament, Sourindra was naturally busy with many things. Jatindra, his eldest brother, had been told of my coming, but he sent word that he had a pain in his throat and couldn't go out.

"One day, in that state of divine intoxication, I went to the bathing-ghat on the Ganges at Baranagore. There I saw Jaya Mukherji repeating the name of God; but his mind was on something else. I went up and slapped him twice on the cheeks.

"At one time Rani Rasmani was staying in the temple garden. She came to the shrine of the Divine Mother, as she frequently did when I worshiped Kali, and asked me to sing a song or two. On this occasion, while I was singing I noticed she was sorting the flowers for worship absentmindedly. At once I slapped her on the cheeks. She became quite embarrassed and sat there with folded hands.

"Alarmed at this state of mind myself, I said to my cousin Haladhari: 'Just see my nature! How can I get rid of it?' After praying to the Divine Mother for some time with great yearning, I was able to shake off this habit.

"When one gets into such a state of mind, one doesn't enjoy any conversation but that about God. I used to weep when I heard people talk about worldly matters. When I accompanied Mathur Babu on a pilgrimage, we spent a few days in Benaras at Raja Babu's house. One day I was seated in the drawing-room with Mathur Babu, Raja Babu, and others. Hearing them talk about various worldly things, such as their business losses and so forth, I wept bitterly and said to the Divine Mother: 'Mother, where have you brought me? I was much better off in the temple garden at Dakshineswar. Here I am in a place where I must hear about 'woman' and 'gold'. But at Dakshineswar I could avoid it.'"[34]

This was one of his methods of teaching his devotees. Sri Ramakrishna used to chat with them, and during conversation he tried to penetrate his spiritual ideas and powers into his disciples.

We have already discussed about Narendranath's talent in music. Sri Ramakrishna was fond of his songs. Many a time, while he listened to his song, he went to samadhi. That day, late in the afternoon Narendra sang for Sri Ramakrishna, when Rakhal, Latu (later he became a monk under the name of Swami Adbhutananda), M., Hazra and Priya, Narendra's Brahmo friend, were present there. The singing was accompanied by the drum:

> Meditate, O my mind, on the Lord Hari,
> The Stainless One, Pure Spirit through and through.
> How peerless is the light that in Him shines!
> How soul-bewitching is His wonderous form!
> How dear is He to all His devotees! . . . .

After this song Narendra sang:

> Oh, when will dawn for me that day of blessedness
> When He who is all Good, all Beauty, and all Truth,
> Will light the inmost shrine of my heart?
> When shall I sink at last, ever beholding Him,
> Into that Ocean of Delight?
> Lord, as Infinite Wisdom Thou shalt enter my soul,

And my unquiet mind, made speechless by Thy sight,
Will find a heaven at Thy feet.
In my heart's firmament, O Lord, Thou wilt arise
As Blissful Immortality;
Ans, as, when the chakora beholds the rising moon,
It sports about for very joy,
So, too, shall I be filled with heavenly happiness
When Thou appearest unto me.
Thou One without a Second, all Peace, the King of Kings!
At Thy beloved feet I shall renounce my life
And so at last shall gain life's goal;
I shall enjoy the bliss of heaven while yet on earth!
Where else is a boon so rare bestowed?
Then shall I see Thy glory, pure and untouched by stain;
As darkness flees from light, so will my darkest sins
Desert me at Thy dawn's approach.
Kindle in me, O Lord, the blazing fire of faith
To be the pole-star of my life;
O Succour of the weak, fulfil my one desire!
Then shall I bathe both day and night
In the boundless bliss of Thy Love, and utterly forget
Myself, O Lord, attaining Thee.

Thus Narendra sang one after another, and sometimes he played drum while singing. Sometimes, Sri Ramakrishna joined him and sang with full of joy: 'With beaming face chant the sweet name of God....'

When the music was over, Sri Ramakrishna held Narendra in his arms a long time and said: "You have made us so happy today!"

Narendra, M., and Priya were going to spend the night at the temple garden. This pleased the Master highly, especially since Narendra would be with him. The Holy Mother (By this name Sri Ramakrishna's wife was known among his devotees), who was living in the Nahabat, had prepared the supper. Surendra bore the greater part of the Master's expenses. The meal was ready, and the plates were set out on the southeast veranda of the Master's room.

Near the east door of his room Narendra and the other devotees were gossiping.

Narendra: "How do you find the young men nowadays?"

M.: "They are not bad; but they don't receive any religious instruction."

Narendra: "But from my experience I feel they are going to the dogs. They smoke cigarettes, indulge in frivolous talks, enjoy foppishness, play truant, and do everything of that sort. I have even seen them visiting questionable places."

M.: "I didn't notice such things during our student days."

Narendra: "Perhaps you didn't mix with the students intimately. I have even seen them talking with people of immoral character. Perhaps they are on terms of intimacy with them."

M.: "It is strange indeed."

Narendra: "I know that many of them form bad habits. It would be proper if the guardians of the boys, and the authorities, kept their eyes on these matters."

They were talking thus when Sri Ramakrishna came to them and asked with a smile, "Well, what are you talking about?"

Narendra: "I have been asking M. about the boys in the schools. The conduct of students nowadays isn't all that it should be."

The Master became grave and said to M. rather seriously: "This kind of conversation is not good. It isn't desirable to indulge in any talk but talk of God. You are their senior, and you are intelligent. You should not have encouraged them to talk about such matters."

Narendra was then about nineteen years old and M. about twenty-eight. Thus admonished, M. felt embarrassed, and the others also fell silent.[35]

Next morning Narendranath said to Sri Ramakrishna: "We noticed several sannyasins belonging to the sect of Nanak in the Panchavati."

Master: "Yes, they arrived here yesterday. I'd like to see you all sitting together on the mat."

As they sat there, the Master looked at them with evident delight. He then began to talk with them. Narendra asked about the spiritual discipline.

Master: "Bhakti, love of God, is the essence of all spiritual discipline. Through love one acquires renunciation and discrimination naturally."

Narendra: "Isn't it true that the Tantra prescribes spiritual discipline in the company of woman?"

Master: "That is not desirable. It is a very difficult path and often causes the aspirant's downfall. There are three such kinds of discipline. One may regard woman (Woman is the symbol of the Divine Mother) as one's mistress or look on oneself as her handmaid or as her child. I look on woman as my mother. To look oneself as her handmaid is also good; but it is extremely difficult to practice spiritual discipline looking on woman as one's mistress. To regard oneself as her child is a very pure attitude."

The sannyasins belonging to the sect of Nanak entered the room and greeted the Master, saying, "Namo Narayanaya (Salutations to God)." Sri Ramakrishna asked them to sit down.

Master: "Nothing is impossible for God. Nobody can describe His nature in words. Everything is possible for Him. There lived at a certain place two yogis who were practicing spiritual discipline. The sage Narada was passing that way one day. Realizing who he was, one of the yogis said: 'You have just come from God Himself. What is He doing now?' Narada replied, 'Why, I saw Him making camels and elephants pass and repass through the eye of a needle.' At this the yogi said: 'Is that anything to wonder at? Everything is possible for God.' But the other yogi said: 'What? Making elephants pass through the eye of a needle! Is that ever possible? You have never been to the Lord's dwelling-place.'"

At nine o'clock in the morning, while the Master was still sitting in his room, Manomohan arrived from Konnagar with some members of his family. In answer to Sri Ramakrishna's kind inquiries, Manomohan explained that he was taking them to Calcutta. The Master said: "Today is the first day of the Bengali month, and inauspicious day for undertaking a journey. I hope everything will be well with you." With a smile he began to talk of other matters.

When Narendra and his friends had finished bathing in the Ganges, the Master said to them earnestly: "Go to the Panchavati and meditate there under the banyan-tree. Shall I give you something to sit on?"

About half past ten Narendra and his Brahmo friends were meditating in the Panchavati. After a while Sri Ramakrishna came to them. M., too, was present.

The Master said to the Brahmo devotees: "In meditation one must be absorbed in God. By merely floating on the surface of the water, can you reach the gems living at the bottom of the sea?"

Then he sang:

Taking the name of Kali, dive deep down, O mind,
Into the heart's fathomless depths,
Where many a pracious gem lies hid.
But never believe the bed of he ocean bare of gems
If in the first few dives you fall;
With firm resolve and self-control
Dive deep and make your way to Mother Kali's realm.
Down in the ocean depths of heavenly Wisdom lie
The wonderous pearls of Peace, O mind;
And you yourself can gather them,
If you but have pure love and follow the scriptures' rule.
Within those ocean depths, as well,
Six alligators lurk–lust, anger, and the rest—
Swimming about in search of prey.
Smear yourself with the turmeric of discrimination;
The very smell of it will shield you from their jaws.
Upon the ocean bed lie strewn
Unnumbered pearls and precious gems;
Plunge in, says Ramprasad, and gather up handfuls there!

Narendra and his friends came down from their seats on the raised platform of the Panchavati and stood near the Master. He returned to his room with them. The Master continued: "When you plunge in the water of the ocean, you may be attacked by alligators. But they won't touch you if your body is smeared with turmeric. There are no doubt six alligators—lust, anger, avarice, and so on—within you, in the 'heart's fathomless depths'. But protect yourself with the turmeric of discrimination and renunciation, and they won't touch you.

"What can you achieve by mere lecturing and scholarship without discrimination and dispassion? God alone is real, and all else is unreal. God alone is substance, and all else is nonentity. That is discrimination.

"First of all set up God in the shrine of your heart, and then deliver lectures as much as you like. How will the mere repetition of 'Brahman' profit you if you are not imbued with discrimination and dispassion? It is the empty sound of a conch-shell.

"There is no use in merely making a noise if you want to establish the Deity in the shrine of your heart, if you want to realize God. First of all purify the mind. In the pure heart God takes His seat. One cannot bring the holy image into the temple if the droppings of bats are all around. The eleven bats are our eleven organs: five of action, five of perception, and the mind.

"First of all invoke the Deity, and then give lectures to your heart's content. First of all dive deep. Plunge to the bottom and gather up the gems. Then you may do other things. But nobody wants to plunge. People are without spiritual discipline and prayer, without renunciation and dispassion. They learn a few words and immediately start to deliver lecture. It is difficult to teach others. Only if a man gets a command from God, after realizing Him, is he entitled to teach."[36]

It was Thursday, November 16, 1882. Sri Ramakrishna had come to Calcutta. In the evening he went to the house of Rajmohan, a member of the Brahmo Samaj, where Narendra and some of his young friends used to meet and worship according to the Brahmo ceremonies. Sri Ramakrishna wanted to see their worship. He was accompanied by M. and a few other devotees.

The Master was very happy to see Narendra and expressed a desire to watch the young men at their worship. Narendra sang and then the worship began. One of the young men conducted it. He prayed, "O Lord, may we give up everything and be absorbed in Thee!" Possibly the youth was inspired by the Master's presence and so talked of utter renunciation. Sri Ramakrishna remarked in a whisper, "Much likelihood there is of that!"[37]

It was the afternoon of 19th August, 1883, when Narendranath and Colonel Viswanath Upadhyay entered the room Sri Ramakrishna was busy in conversation with other devotees. Narendra was then twenty-two years old and was studying in college. They saluted the Master and sat down. The Master requested Narendra to sing. The tanpura hung on the west wall of the room. The devotees fixed their eyes on Narendra as he began to tune the drams.

Master said to Narendra: "The drums don't sound as well as before."

Captain: "They are now full. Therefore they are quite, like a vessel filled with water. Or they are like a holy man, who remains silent when his heart is full of God-consciousness."

Master: "But what about sages like Narada?"

Captain: "They talked because they were moved by the sufferings of others."

Master: "You are right. After attaining samadhi, Narada, Sukadeva, and others came down a few steps, as it were, to the plane of normal consciousness and broke their silence out of compassion for the sufferings of others and to help them."

Narendra began to sing:

> Oh, when will dawn for me that day of blessedness
> When He who is all Good, all Beauty, and all Truth,
> Will light the inmost shrine of my heart?
> When shall I sink at last, ever beholding Him,
> Into that Ocean of Delight?...

No sooner had the Master heard a few words of the song than he went into deep samadhi. He sat with folded hands, facing the east. His body was erect and his mind completely bereft of worldly consciousness. His breath had almost stopped. With unwinking eyes he sat motionless as a picture on a canvas. His mind had dived deep into the Ocean of God's Beauty.

Narendra left the room and went to the east verandah, where Hazra was seated on a blanket, with a rosary in his hand. They fell to talking. Other devotees arrived. The Master came down from samadhi and looked around. He could not find Narendra. The tanpura was lying on the floor. He noticed that the earnest eyes of the devotees were riveted on him.

Master (referring to Narendra): "He has lighted the fire. Now it doesn't matter whether he stays in the room or goes out.

After a little conversation, Sri Ramakrishna left the room abruptly and went to the north-east verandah. Captain and the other devotees remained, waiting for his return. M. accompanied the master to the verandah, where Narendra was talking with Hazra. Sri Ramakrishna knew that

Hazra always indulged in dry philosophical discussions. Hazra would say: "The world is unreal, like a dream. Worship, food offering to the Deity, and so forth, are only hallucinations of the mind. The aim of spiritual life is to meditate on one's own real self." Then he would repeat, "I am He." But, with all that, he had a soft corner in his heart for money, material things, and people's attention.

Sri Ramakrishna smiled and said to Hazra and Narendra, "Hello! What are you talking about?"

Narendra (smiling): "Oh, we are discussing a great many things. They are rather too deep for others."

Master (with a smile): "But Pure Knowledge and Pure Love is one and the same thing. Both lead the aspirants to the same goal. The path of love is much the easier."

Narendra quoted a song:

> O Mother, make me mad with Thy love!
> What need have I of knowledge or reason?

Narendra said to M. that he had been reading a book by Hamilton, who wrote: "A learned ignorance is the end of philosophy and the beginning of religion."

Master (to M.): "What does that mean?"

Narendra explained the sentence in Bengali. The Master beamed with joy and said in English, "Thank you! Thank you!" Everyone laughed at the charming way he said theses words. They knew that his English vocabulary consisted of only half a dozen words.

Narendranath took leave of the Master, and later on, Sri Ramakrishna sat down on the small couch in his room. He said to the devotees: "Narendra, Bhavanath, Rakhal, and devotees like them belong to the group of the nitya-siddhas; they are eternally free. Religions practice on their part is superfluous. Look at Narendra. He doesn't care about anyone. One day he was going with me in Captain's carriage. Captain wanted him to take a good seat, but Narendra didn't look at him. He is independent even of me. He doesn't tell me all he knows, lest I should praise his scholarship before others. He is free from ignorance and delusion. He has no bonds. He is a great soul. He has many good qualities. He is expert in music, both as a singer and player, and is also a versatile scholar. Again, he keeps his passions under control and says that he will never marry. There is a close friendship between Narendra and Bhavanath; they are just like man and woman. Narendra doesn't come here very often. That is good, for I am overwhelmed by his presence."[38]

It was Wednesday, September 26, 1883. There were very few devotees with the Master, for most of them came on Sunday. Rakhal and Latu were living with him the greater part of the time. M. arrived in the afternoon and found the Master seated on the small couch. The conversation turned to Narendra.

Master said to M.: "Have you seen Narendra lately? (with a smile) He said to me: 'He still goes to the Kali temple.' But he will not when the truly understands. His people are very much dissatisfied with him because he comes here now and then. The other day he came here in a hired carriage, and Surendra paid for it. Narendra's aunt almost had a row with Surendra about it."[39]

On Sunday, March 2, 1884, Sri Ramakrishna was sitting on the small couch in his room, listening to devotional music by Trailokya Sannyal of the Brahmo Samaj. He had not yet recovered from the effects of the injury to his arm, which was still supported by a splint. Many devotees, including Narendra, Surendra, and M., were sitting on the floor.

Narendra's father, a lawyer of the High Court of Calcutta, had passed away suddenly. He had not been to make provision for the family, which consequently faced grave financial difficulties.

The members of the family sometimes had to go without food. Narendra was therefore passing his days in great anxiety.

The Master spoke as if piqued because God had not yet shown His kindness to Narendra. Now and then he cast an affectionate glance at his beloved disciple.

Narendra: "I am now studying the views of the atheists."

Master: "There are two doctrines: the existence and the non-existence of God. Why don't you accept the first?"

Narendra didn't reply. Surendra said: "God is just; He must look after His devotees."

Master: "It is said in the scriptures that only those who have been charitable in their former birth get money in this life. But to tell you the truth, this world is God's maya. And there are many confusing things in this realm of maya. One cannot comprehend them.

"The ways of God are inscrutable indeed. Bhishma lay on his bed of arrows. The Pandava brothers visited him in Krishna's company. Presently Bhishma burst into tears. The Pandava said to Krishna: 'Krishna, how amazing this is! Our grandsire Bhishma is one of the eight Venus. Another man as wise as he is not to be found. Yet even he is bewildered by maya and weep at death.' 'But', said Krishna, 'Bhishma isn't weeping on that account. You may ask him about it.' When asked, Bhishma said: 'O Krishna, I am unable to understand anything of the ways of God. God Himself is the constant companion of the Pandavas, and still they have no end of trouble. That is why I weep. When I reflect on this, I realize that one cannot understand anything of God's way.'

"God has revealed to me that only the Paramatman, whom the Vedas describe as the Pure Soul, is as immutable as Mount Sumeru, unattached, and beyond pain and pleasure. There is much confusion in this world of His maya. One can by no means say that 'this' will come after 'that' of 'that' will produce 'that'."[40]

It was Sunday, September 6, 1884. About three o'clock in the afternoon Sri Ramakrishna was seated in Adhar's parlour on the second floor. Narendra, the Mukherjee brothers, Bhavanath, M., Hazra, and other devotees were with the Master.

Arrangements were being made for Narendra to sing. While he was tuning the Tanpura, one of the strings snapped, and the Master exclaimed, "Oh! What have you done?" Narendra then tuned the drums. The Master said to him, "You are beating that drum, and I feel as if someone were slapping my cheek."

Referring to the kirtan, Narendra said: "There is not much rhythm in the Kirtan. That's why it is so popular and people love it so much."

Master: "How silly! People like it because it is so tender and full of pathos."

Narendra sang:

Sweet is Thy name, O Refuge of the humble!
It falls like sweetest nectar on our ears
And comforts us, Beloved of our souls!

Narendra sang one or two more songs. Then sang Vaishnavacharan. The Master began to sing and dance. Devotees couldn't control themselves. They too danced with the Master. Suddenly The Master was in the deepest samadhi, he could not utter a word and his whole body remained transfixed. The devotees danced encircling him. After a while, regaining partial consciousness he danced with the strength of a lion, intoxicated with ecstatic love. When he resumed his seat, still tinged with the lingering glow of divine fervour, he asked Narendra to sing 'O Mother, make me mad with Thy love.'

Narendra sang:

O Mother, make me mad with Thy love!
What need have I of knowledge or reason?

Master said: "And that one—'Upon the Sea of Blissful Awareness'."

Narendra sang: "Upon the Sea of Blissful Awareness waves of ecstatic love arise"...

Master said: "And that one too—'In Wisdom's firmament'. Perhaps it is too long. Do you think so? All right, sing it slowly."

Narendra sang two more songs. The Master improvised, "Be drunk with prema (Love) and weep, chanting Hari's sweet name." And, "Be mad with divine fervour and weep, chanting His name."

Narendra said to the Master in a low voice, "Will you kindly sing that one?"

Master: "My voice has become a little hoarse."

After a few minutes he asked Narendra. "Which one?"

Narendra: "'Gaur, whose beauty delights the world'."

Sri Ramakrishna sang, describing the beauty of Sri Chaitanya:

Who has brought Gaur to Nadia—
Gaur, whose beauty delights the world.
His face, covered with ringlets of hair,
Shines like lightning against a dark cloud....

When the music was over, the Master began to talk with the devotees. He asked Narendra, "Hazra danced?"

Narendra: "A little."

Master: "A little?"

Narendra: "Yes, His belly danced too."

Pandit Shashadhar's host had been thinking of inviting the Master for dinner.

Master: "I have heard that his host is not an honest man. He is immoral."

Narendra: "That is why you didn't drink the water he touched. It happened the first day you met Shashadhar at his house. How did you come to know he was immoral?"

Master (smiling): "Hazra knows of another instance. It happened at Sihore in Hriday's house."

Hazra: "The man was Vaishnava. He came with me to see you [meaning Sri Ramakrishna]. As soon as he sat in front of you, you turned your back on him."

Master said to Narendra: "We learnt later that he led an immoral life. You used to say, at first, that those were all hallucinations."

Narendra: "How was I to know? Now I see that you are always right."

Adhar had prepared a feast for the Master and the devotees, and now he invited them to the meal. The Master said to the Mukherji brothers: "What? Won't you eat?" They said humbly, "Please excuse us."

Master: "But why? You are doing everything else. Why this hesitation only about eating the meal?

Adhar was a low-cast Hindu. Therefore some of the Master's brahmin devotees hesitated to eat at his house. They came to their senses at last when they saw Sri Ramakrishna himself eating.

The Mukherji brothers had arranged with a singer of kirtan to entertain the Master the following day. Sri Ramakrishna asked Narendra to come to Dakshineswar to hear the kirtan. He said, "Come tomorrow, won't you?"

Narendra replied, "I shall try, sir."[41]

Thus, through different ways, Sri Ramakrishna tried to teach Narendra the spiritual ideas. Narendra has learnt each and every lesson with the association of Sri Ramakrishna.

It was Friday, September 19, 1884, when Sri Ramakrishna was busy in talking with devotees, the conversation turned to Narendranath. Then, with reference to Narendra's first visit to Dakshineswar, Sri Ramakrishna said: "When Narendra first came here he was dressed in dirty clothes; but his eyes and face betokened some inner stuff. At that time he did not know many songs. He sang one or two: 'Let us go back once more, O mind, to our own abode!' and 'O Lord, must all my days pass by so utterly in vain?' Whenever he came here, I would talk only with him, though the room was filled with people. He would say to me, 'Please talk to them', and then I would talk with the others. I became mad for the sight of him and for him in Jadu Mallick's garden house. I wept here, too, holding Bholanath's hand. Bholanath said, 'Sir, you shouldn't behave that way for a mere kayastha boy.' One day the 'fat brahmin' (a nickname of Prankrishna, a devotee of the Master) said to me about Narendra, with folded hands, 'Sir, he has very little education; why should you be so restless for him?'"[42]

It was Sunday, September 28, 1884. It was the day of the Mahashtami, the most auspicious day of the worship of Durga, the Divine Mother. At Adhar's invitation Sri Ramakrishna had come to Calcutta to see the holy image at his house. Many devotees, including Narendra, Baburam, M., Niranjan, Vijay, Kedar, Ram and Surendra, were present.

Narendra was seated in front of the Master. While Sri Ramakrishna was talking to Vijay and the others his eyes fell upon his beloved disciple. At once the Master stood up and went to samadhi (trance). He placed one foot on Narendra's knee. He was in a deep spiritual mood, his eyes unblinking, and his mind completely unconscious of the outer world. After a long time he came down to the relative plane of consciousness; but he still appeared dazed, for the intoxication of divine bliss had not altogether left him. Speaking to himself in that ecstatic state, he repeated the name of God. He said: "Satchidananda! Satchidananda! Satchidananda. Shall I repeat that? No, it is the day of the Divine Mother, the Giver of the bliss of divine inebriation. O Mother, full of the bliss of divine inebriation! Sa, Re, Ga, Ma, Pa, Dha, Ni (Do, Re, Mi, Fa, Sol, La, Ti). It is not good to keep the voice on 'Ni'. It is not possible to keep it there very long. I shall keep it on the next lower note.

"There are different planes of consciousness: the gross, the subtle, the causal, and the Great Cause. Entering the Mahakarana, the Great Cause, one becomes silent; one cannot utter a word.

"But an Iswarakoti (manifestation of God Himself), after attaining the Great Cause, can come down again to the lower planes. Incarnation of God, and others like them, belongs to the class of the Iswarakoti. They climb up, and they can come down."

Perhaps this was Sri Ramakrishna's another method of transferring power to make Narendranath aware of himself.

During conversation, Sri Ramakrishna said again: "I become intoxicated at the mere thought of God. I don't have to take any wine. I feel drunk at the very sight of the charanamrita (the water in which the image of the Deity is bather; it is considered very sacred). I feel as if I had drunk five bottles of liquor. When a person attains such a state he cannot help discriminating about food."

Narendra: "As regards food, one should take whatever comes."

Sri Ramakrishna said, "What you say applies only to a particular state of the aspirant's mind. No food can harm a jnani (who realized God). According to the Gita, the jnani himself does not eat; his eating is an offering to the Kundalini. But that does not apply to a bhakta (devotee)." He also added, "With you it is all right. You are in 'this' as well as in 'that'. You can eat everything now" He meant to say, Narendra was attentive both to the world and to the spiritual life. Then he turned to other devotees and said: "Blessed is he who feels longing for God, though he eats pork. But shame on him whose mind dwells on 'woman' and 'gold', though he eats the purest food—boiled vegetables, rice and ghee."[43]

What a strange and close relation was there between Sri Ramakrishna and Narendranath! Sri Ramakrishna used to feel an extraordinary happiness just at the sight of his beloved Narendra. His joy knew no bound whenever Narendra was in front of him. It was Monday, September 29, 1884, the third day of Durga Puja. Sri Ramakrishna was seated with his devotees in his room at Dakshineswar. When Narendra arrived there, he was exceedingly happy. Narendra saluted the Master and began to talk with Bhavanath and other devotees. M. was seated nearby. A long mat was spread on the floor. While talking, Narendra lay on it flat on his stomach. The Master looked at him and suddenly went into trance. He sat on Narendra's back in an ecstatic mood while Bhavanath began to sing: "O Mother, ever blissful as Thou art,".[44]

Sri Ramakrishna was sitting on the small couch in his room. Narendra, Baburam, Bhavanath, and M. were sitting on the floor. Narendra referred to various religious sects—the Ghoshpara, Panchanami, and others. Sri Ramakrishna described their views and condemned their immoral practices. He said that they could not follow the right course of spiritual discipline, but enjoyed sensuous pleasures in the name of religion.

Master (to Narendra): "You need not listen to these things. The bhairavas and the bhairavis of the Tantrik sect also follow this kind of discipline. While in Benaras I was taken to one of their mystic circles. Each bhairava had a bhairavi with him. I was asked to drink the consecrated wine, but I said I couldn't touch wine. They drank it. I thought perhaps they would then practice meditation and japa (chanting the name of God). But nothing of the sort. They began to dance. I was afraid they might fall into the Ganges; the circle had been made on its bank. It is very honourable for husband and wife to assume the roles of *bhairava* and *bhairavi*.

(To Narendra and the others) "Let me tell you this. I regard woman as my mother; I regard myself as her son. This is a very pure attitude. There is no danger in it. To look on woman as a sister is also not bad. But to assume the attitude of a 'hero', to look on woman as one's mistress, is the most difficult discipline. Tarak's father followed this discipline. It is very difficult. In this form of sadhana (worship) one cannot always maintain the right attitude.

"There are various paths to reach God. Each view is a path. It is like reaching the Kali temple by different roads. But it must be said that some paths are clean and some dirty. It is good to travel on a clean path.

"Many views, many paths—and I have seen them all. But I don't enjoy them anymore; they all quarrel.

"No one else is here, and you are my own people. Let me tell you something. I have come to the final realization that God is the Whole and I am a part of Him, that God is the Master and I am His servant. Furthermore, I think every now and then that He is I and I am He."[45]

One day, after his father's death, Narendranath was seated near Sri Ramakrishna at Dakshineswar. He was constantly worried about his financial problem at home. Sri Ramakrishna looked at him intently and said: "Why are you so worried? Don't you know that Sri Krishna said to Arjuna, 'If you have one of the eight siddhis, you may get a little power, but you will not realize Me.' by siddhis one may acquire powers, strength, money and such things, but not God. Let me tell you something else. Go beyond knowledge and ignorance. He who is aware of light is also aware of darkness. He who knows well also knows badly. He who knows happiness also knows misery. So I am asking you to go beyond knowledge and ignorance."[46]

Sri Ramakrishna wanted to explain that one can overcome misery only by going beyond knowledge and ignorance. A man suffers from misery because of his ignorance about God. Spiritual practice can help a man to realize God. That's why he advised Narendra not to be worried, rather he should concentrate himself in spiritual practices.

Once, Girish Ghosh and Narendranath were talking to each other. Meanwhile Girish went out to have a smoke. Then Sri Ramakrishna asked Narendra: "What were you talking about?"

Narendra: "I had a talk with Girish Ghosh. He is indeed a great man. We talked about you."

Master: "What did you say about me?"

Narendra laughed and said: "That you are illiterate and we are scholars. Oh, we talked in that vein!"

Master: "Let me tell you this: really and truly I don't feel sorry in the least that. I haven't read the Vedanta or the other scriptures. I know that the essence of the Vedanta is that Brahman alone is real and the world illusory. And what is the essence of the Gita? It is what you get by repeating the word ten times. Then it is reversed into 'tagi', which refers to renunciation. The pupil should hear the essence of the scriptures from the guru; then he should practice austerity and devotion. A man needs the letter he has received from home as long as he has not learnt its contents. After reading it, however, he sets out to get the things he has been asked to send. Likewise, what need is there of the scriptures if you know their essence? The next thing is the practice of spiritual discipline."[47]

Thus, Sri Ramakrishna taught him the way of living, and to practice the spiritual discipline by going beyond knowledge and ignorance. Book doesn't make a man wise; it only helps to know the way how to be a wise, and one should practice the discipline according to the scripture.

It was Wednesday, February 25, 1885, when Sri Ramakrishna went to the Star Theatre, on Beadon Street, Calcutta, to see a performance of '*Vrishaketu*'. He sat in a box, facing the south, M. and other devotees were near him. When the orchestra stopped playing and Sri Ramakrishna asked Girish Ghosh: "Does this theatre belong to you?"

Girish replied: "It is ours, sir."

Master: "'Ours' is good; it is not good to say 'mine'. People say 'I' and 'mine'; they are egoistic, small-minded people."

Narendra said: "The whole world is a theatre."

Master: "Yes, yes, that's right. In some places you see the play of vidya and in some the play of avidya."

Narendra: "Everything is the play of vidya."

Master: "True, true. But a man realizes that when he has the knowledge of Brahman. But for a bhakta (devotee), who follows the path of divine love, both exist—vidyamaya and avidyamaya.

Then he requested Narendra to sing a little. Narendra sang the words, "Then once mote in the Great Communion all are merged", Sri Ramakrishna said to him, "One realizes this after attaining the knowledge of Brahman; and then all is vidya, Brahman, as you said."[48]

On Sunday, March 1, 1885, Sri Ramakrishna was seated on the small couch in his room. It was the day of the Dolayatra, a Hindu religious festival. Sri Ramakrishna was busy in conversation with devotees, while Narendranath entered the room and saluted him. They began to talk together. Presently the Master came down from the couch and sat on the floor. In the meantime the room was filled with people, both devotees and visitors.

Master said to Narendra: "Are you well? I hear that you often visit Girish Ghosh at his house. Is it true?"

Narendra: "Yes, sir. I go there now and then."

Girish had been visiting Sri Ramakrishna for some months. The Master said that none could fathom the depth of Girish's faith. And his longing for God was as intense as his faith was deep. At home, he was always absorbed in the thought of Sri Ramakrishna. Many of the Master's devotees visited him; they talked only about Sri Ramakrishna. But Girish was a householder who had varied experiences of worldly life, and the Master knew that Narendra would renounce the world, that he would shun 'woman' and 'gold' both mentally and outwardly.

Master said to Narendra: "Do you visit Girish frequently? No matter how much one washes a cup that has contained a solution of garlic, still a trace of the smell will certainly linger. The youngsters who come here are pure souls—untouched by 'woman' and 'gold'. Men who have associated a long time with 'woman' and 'gold' smell of the garlic, as it were. They are like a mango pecked by crows. Such a fruit cannot be offered to the Deity in the temple, and you would hesitate to eat it yourself. Again, take the case of a new pot and another in which curd has been made. One is afraid to keep milk in the second pot, for the milk very often turns sour.

"Householder devotees like Girish form a class by themselves. They desire yoga and also bhoga (enjoying worldly things). Their attitude is that of Ravana, who wanted to enjoy the maidens of heaven and at the same time realize Rama. They are like the asuras, the demons, who enjoy various pleasures and also realize Narayana."

Narendra replied: "But Girish has given up old associates."

Master: "Yes, yes. He is like a bull castrated in old age. In Burdwan I once saw an ox moving about the cows. I asked a bullock-cart driver: 'What is this? An ox? How strange!' He said to me: 'True, sir. But it was castrated in old age, and so it hasn't altogether shaken off the old tendencies.'"

Narendra said: "Nowadays Girish Ghosh thinks of nothing but spiritual things."

Master: "That is very good. But why is he so abusive? Why does he use such vulgar language to me? In my present state of mind I cannot bear such rudeness. When thunderbolt strikes near a house, the heavy things inside the house are not much affected, but the window-panes rattle. Nowadays I cannot bear such roughness. A man living on the plane of sattva (Truth) cannot bear noise and uproar. That is why Hriday was sent away. It was the Divine Mother who sent him away. During the latter part of his stay he went to extremes; he became very rough and abusive. Do you agree with Girish about me?"

Narendra: "He said he believed you to be an incarnation of God. I didn't say anything in answer to his remarks."

Master: "But how great his faith is! Don't you think so?"

After a few minutes silence he said to Narendra tenderly, "My child, you will not attain God without renouncing 'woman' and 'gold'. As he said this, great emotion welled up in his heart. Fixing on Narendra an earnest and tender look, he sang:

> We are afraid to speak, and yet we are afraid to keep still;
> Our minds, O Radha, half believe that we are about to lose you!
> We tell you the secret that we know—
> The secret whereby we ourselves, and others, with our help.
> Have passed through many a time of peril;
> Now it all depends on you.

Sri Ramakrishna seemed to be afraid lest Narendra should leave him. Narendra looked at the Master with tears in his eyes.

A visitor who was there for the first time heard and saw all this. He said to the Master, "Sir, if one must renounce 'woman' and 'gold', then what shall a householder do?"

Master said: "You may enjoy 'woman' and 'gold'. What has passed between us is no concern of yours."

Every now and then the Master cast his gracious look on Narendra. He said: "Have you now become an experienced physician?" Quoting a Sanskrit verse he said, "He who has killed only a hundred patients is a novice in medicine; but he becomes an expert after killing a thousand!"

Did the Master hint that Narendra, even though still young, had had many painful experiences of life?

Narendra smiled and kept silent.[49]

On the morning of Wednesday, March 11, 1885, Sri Ramakrishna and some of his disciples visited Balaram Bose's house. Balaram was one of the householder disciples of the Master. Sri Ramakrishna often called him as a rasaddar, or supplier of stores, appointed by the Divine Mother to take care of his physical needs. Balaram's house in Calcutta had been sanctified many times by the Master's presence. He often asked Balaram to invite young disciples, such as Rakhal, Bhavanath and Narendra to his house. He said: "These pure souls are the veritable manifestations of God. To feed them is to feed God Himself. They are born with special divine attributes. By serving them you will be serving God." And so it happened that whenever Sri Ramakrishna was at Balaram's house the devotees would gather there. It was the Master's chief vineyard in Calcutta. Devotees, who came here, became known to each other intimately.

Sri Ramakrishna loved Narendranath so much that whenever he would have an opportunity to talk about Narendra, he never liked to miss it. He liked to talk about him and as well as to hear of him.

That day Girish Ghosh also came to Balaram's house to see the Master. Narendra didn't understand the incarnation of God as a man. During conversation Sri Ramakrishna said to Girish: "You had better argue this point with Narendra and see what he has to say."

Girish replied: "Narendra says that God is infinite; we cannot even so much as say that the things or persons we perceive are parts of God. How can infinity have parts? It cannot."

Master: "However great and Infinite God may be, His Essence can and does manifest itself through man by His mere will. God's incarnation as a man cannot be explained by analogy. One must feel it for oneself and realize it by direct perception. An analogy can give us only a little glimpse. By touching the horns, legs or tail of a cow, we in fact touch the cow herself; but for us the essential thing about a cow is her milk, which comes through the udder. The Divine Incarnation is like the udder. God incarnates Himself as man from time to time in order to teach people devotion and divine love."

Girish: "Narendra says: 'Is it possible to know all of God? He is infinite.'"

Master: "Who can comprehend everything about God? It is not given to man to know any aspect of God, great or small. And what need is there to know everything about God? It is enough if we only realize Him. As we see God Himself if we but see His Incarnation. Suppose a person goes to the Ganges and touches its water. He will then say, 'Yes, I have seen and touched the Ganges.'" To say this it is not necessary for him to touch the whole length of the river from Hardwar to Gangasagar.

"It I touch your feet, surely that is the same as touching you. (Laughter) If a person goes to the ocean and touches but a little of its water, he has surely touched the ocean itself. Fire, as an element, exists in all things, but in wood it is present to a greater degree."

Girish: "I am looking for firc. Naturally I want to go to a place where I can get it."

Master: "Yes, fire, as an element, is present more in wood than in any other object. If you seek God, then seek Him in man; He manifests Himself more in man that in any other thing. If you see a man endowed with ecstatic love, overflowing with prema (love), mad after God, intoxicated with His love, and then know for certain that God has incarnated Himself through that man.

Girish: "Narendra says that God is beyond our words and thought."

Master: "That is not altogether true. He is, no doubt, unknowable by this ordinary mind, but He can indeed be known by the pure mind. The mind and intellect become pure the moment they are free from attachment to 'woman' and 'gold'. The pure mind and pure intellect are one and the same. God is known by the pure mind. Didn't the sages and seers of olden times see God? They realized the All-pervading Consciousness by means of their inner consciousness."

Girish said with a smile: "I defeated Narendra in the argument."

Sri Ramakrishna immediately protested: "Oh, no! He said to me: 'When Girish Ghosh has so much faith in God's incarnation as man, what can I say to him? It is not proper to meddle with such faith.'"[50]

By that time Narendranath arrived there. Sri Ramakrishna was happy to see him. He wished to continue the discussion on the same topic, and he, therefore, said to Girish, "I should like to hear you and Narendra argue in English."

The discussion began; but they talked in Bengali. Narendra said: "God is Infinity. How is it possible for us to comprehend Him? He dwells in every human being. It is not the case that He manifests Himself through one person only."

Sri Ramakrishna knew that Girish couldn't argue well with Narendra. So, he said tenderly: "I quite agree with Narendra. God is everywhere. But then you must remember that there are different manifestations of His Power in different beings. At some places there is a manifestation of His avidyashakti, at others a manifestation of His vidyashakti. Through different instruments God's Power is manifest in different degrees, greater and smaller. Therefore all men are not equal."

Girish Ghosh joined the Master and said to Narendra: "How do you know that God does not assume a human body?"

Narendra: "God is 'beyond words or thought'."

Master: "No, that is not true, He can be known by the pure intellect, which is the same as the Pure Self. The seers of old directly perceived the Pure Self through their pure intellect."

Girish said to Narendra: "Unless God Himself teaches men through His human Incarnation, who else will teach them spiritual mysteries? God takes a human body to reach men divine knowledge and divine love. Otherwise, who will teach?"

Narendra: "Why, God dwells in our heart; He will certainly teach us from within the heart."

Master said tenderly: "Yes, yes. He will teach us as our Inner Guide."

Gradually Narendra and Girish became involved in a heated discussion. If God is Infinity, how can He have parts? What did Hamilton say? What were the views of Herbert Spencer, of Tyndall, of Huxley? And so forth, and so on.

Master said to M.: "I don't enjoy these discussions. Why should I argue at all? I clearly see that God is everything; He Himself has become all. I see that whatever is, is God. He is everything; again, He is Indivisible. At the sight of Narendra my mind loses itself in the consciousness of the absolute." Then he asked Girish, "What do you say to that?"

Girish: "Why ask me? As if I understood everything except that one point!"

Master: "Again, I cannot utter a word unless I come down at least two steps from the plane of Samadhi (Trance). Sankara's Non-dualism explanation of Vedanta is true, and so is the Qualified. Non-dualistic interpretation of Ramanuja."

Narendra said: "What is Qualified Non-dualism?"

Master: "It is the theory of Ramanuja. According to this theory, Brahman, or the Absolute, is qualified by the universe and its living beings. These three—Brahman, the world, and living beings—together constitute One. Take the instance of a bel-fruit. A man wanted to know the weight of the fruit. He separated the shell, the flesh, and the seeds. But can a man get the weight by weighing only the flesh? He must weigh flesh, shell and seeds together. At first it appears that the real thing in the fruit is the flesh, and not its seeds or shell. Then by reasoning you find that the shell, seeds, and flesh all belong to the fruit; the shell and seeds belong to the same thing that the flesh belongs to. Likewise, in spiritual discrimination one must first reason, following the method of 'Not this, not this': God is not the universe; God is not the living beings; Brahman alone is real and all else is unreal. Then one realizes, as with the bel-fruit, that the Reality from which we derive the notion of Brahman is the very Reality that evolves the idea of living being and the universe. The Nitya and the Lila are the two aspects of one and the same Reality; therefore, according to Ramanuja, Brahman is qualified by the universe and the living beings. This is the theory of Qualified Non-dualism."

Then he said to M.: "I do see God directly. What shall I reason about? I clearly see that He himself has become everything; that He Himself has become the universe and all living beings.

"But without awakening one's own inner consciousness one cannot realize the All-pervading Consciousness. How long does a man reason? So long he has not realized God. But mere words will not do. As for myself, I clearly see that He Himself has become everything. The inner consciousness must be awakened through the grace of God. Through this awakening a man goes into Samadhi. He often forgets that he has a body. He gets rid of his attachment to 'woman' and 'gold' and does not enjoy any talk unless it is about the God. Worldly talk gives him pain. Through the awakening of the inner consciousness one realizes the All-pervading Consciousness."

The discussion came to a close. Sri Ramakrishna said to M.: "I have observed that a man acquires one kind of knowledge about God through reasoning and another kind through meditation; but he acquires a third kind of knowledge about God when God reveals Himself to him, His devotee. If God Himself reveals to His devotee the nature of Divine Incarnation—how He plays in human form—then the devotee doesn't have to reason about the problem or need and explanation. Do you know what it is like? Suppose a man is in a dark room. He goes on rubbing a match against a match-box and all of a sudden light comes. Likewise, If God gives us this flesh of divine light, all our doubts are destroyed. Can one ever know God by mere reasoning?"

Sri Ramakrishna asked Narendra to sit by his side. He tenderly inquired about his health and showed him much affection.

Narendra said to the Master: "Why, I have meditated on Kali for three or four days; but nothing has come of it."

Master: "All in good time, my child. Kali is none other than Brahman. That which is called Brahman is really Kali. She is the Primal Energy. When that energy remains inactive, I call It Brahman, and when It creates, preserves or destroys, I call It Shakti (Energy) or Kali. What you call Brahman I call Kali. Brahman and Kali are not different. They are like fire and its power to burn: If one thinks of fire one must also think of its power to burn. If one recognizes Kali one must also recognize Brahman; again, if one recognizes Brahman one must recognize Kali. Brahman and Its power are identical. It is Brahman when I address as Shakti or Kali."

Then Sri Ramakrishna became busy in talking with Girish.

Girish said to the Master: "I have been thinking of leaving the theatre to the youngsters."

Master: "No, no. It is all right, you are doing good to many."

Narendra said in whisper, "Just a moment ago Girish was calling Sri Ramakrishna God, an Incarnation, and now he is attracted to the theatre!"

Narendra was sitting beside the Master. The Master looked at him intently and suddenly moved closer to his beloved disciple. Narendra didn't believe in God's assuming a human body; but what did that matter? Sri Ramakrishna's heart overflowed with more and more love for his disciple. He touched Narendra's body and said, quoting from a song"

Do you feel that your pride is wounded?
So be it, then; we too have our pride.

Then the Master said to Narendra: "As long as a man argues about God, he has not realized Him. You two were arguing. I didn't like it. How long does one hear noise and uproar in a house where a big feast is being given? So long as the guests are not seated for the meal. As soon as food is served and people begin to eat, three quarters of the noise disappears. When the dessert is served there is still less noise. But when the guests eat the last course, buttermilk, then one hears nothing but the sound 'soop, sup'. When the meal is over, the guests retire to sleep and all is quiet. The nearer you approach God, the less you reason and argue. When you attain him, then all sounds—all reasoning and disputing—come to an end. Then you go into samadhi—sleep,—into communion with God in silence."

The Master gently stroked Narendra's body and affectionately touched his chin, uttering sweetly the holy words, "Hari Om! Hari Om! Hari Om!" He was fast becoming unconscious of the outer world. His hand was on Narendra's foot. Still in that mood he gently stroked Narendra's body. Slowly a change came over his mind. With folded hands he said to Narendra: "Sing a song, please; then I shall be all right. How else shall I be able to stand on my own legs?" Again he became speechless. He sat motionless as a statue. Presently he became intoxicated with divine love and said: "O Radha, watch your step! Otherwise you may fall into the Jamuna. Ah! How mad she is with love of Krishna!"

The Master was in a rapturous mood. Quoting from a song, he said:

Tell me, friend, how far is the grove.
Where Krishna, my Beloved, dwells?
His fragrance reaches me even here,
But I am tired and can walk no further.

Then the Master completely forgot the outer world. He did not notice anyone in the room, not even his beloved Narendra seated by his side. He did not know where he himself was seated. He was totally merged in God.

Suddenly he stood up, shouting, "Deep drunk the Wine of Divine Loves!" As he took his seat again, he muttered, "I see a light coming, but I know not whence it comes."

Now Narendra sang:

Lord, Thou hast lifted all my sorrow with the vision of Thy face,
And the magic of Thy beauty has bewitched my mind;
Beholding Thee, the seven worlds forget their never-ending woe;
What shall I say, then, of myself, a poor and lowly soul? . . .

Listening to the song, Sri Ramakrishna again went into deep samadhi. His eyes were closed and his body was transfixed.[51]

It was Friday, April 24, 1884. Sri Ramakrishna arrived at Balaram's house at about one o'clock in the afternoon. He was ill. He had a sore in his throat. It was the beginning of his throat cancer. Still he had no rest; he used to teach his disciples, and was thoughtful of Narendra, his most beloved disciple. At about four o'clock Narendranath arrived there. The ladies sent a plate of sweets for Sri Ramakrishna. Because of the sore in his throat he could not eat any hard food. He forwarded the plate to Narendra and said, "Ah! This is nice stuff! Eat some! It is good! Eat some!"

Then Sri Ramakrishna went to Girish's house. Girish had arranged a festival to celebrate the Master's coming. Sri Ramakrishna was invited with a large number of devotees to join the festival. Narendranath was also invited. On this occasion a musical party of kirtan was arranged. Sri Ramakrishna and Narendra also joined the party and they sang. After the kirtan was over, Sri Ramakrishna began to talk to the devotees.

Narendra had a friendship with Hazra. Sri Ramakrishna didn't like his character much. He tried to teach Narendra how to avoid such people who don't carry a moral character. During conversation Narendra said to Sri Ramakrishna, "Hazra has now become a good man."

Master: "You don't know. There are people who repeat Rama's name with their tongue, but hide stones under their arms to throw at others."

Narendra: "I don't agree with you, sir. I asked him about the things people complain of. He denied them."

Master: "He is steadfast in his devotions. He practices japa (Chanting the divine name) a little. But he also behaves in a queer way. He doesn't pay the coachman his fare."

Narendra: "That isn't true, sir. He said he had paid it."

Master: "Where did he get the money?"

Narendra: "From Ramlal or someone else."

Master: "Did you ask him all these things in detail? Once I prayed to the Divine Mother, 'O Mother, if Hazra is a hypocrite, then please remove him from here." Later on I told him of my prayer. After a few days he came to me and said, 'You see, I am still here.' (The Master and the others laugh) But soon afterwards he left.

"Hazra's mother begged me through Ramlal to ask Hazra to come home. She was almost blind with weeping. I tried in various ways to persuade him to visit her. I said: 'Your mother is old. Go and see her once.' I couldn't make him go. Afterwards the poor mother died weeping for him."

Narendra: "This time he will go home."

Master: "Yes, yes! He will go home! He is a rogue. He is a rascal. You don't understand him. You are fool. Gopal said that Hazra stayed at Sinthi a few days. People used to supply him with butter, rice, and other food. He had the impudence to tell them he couldn't swallow such coarse rice and bad butter. Ishan of Bhatpara accompanied him there. He ordered Ishan to carry water for him. That made the other Brahmins very angry."

Narendra: "I asked him about that too. He said that Ishan Babu had himself come forward with water. Besides, many Brahmin of Bhatpara showed him respect."

Master: "That was the result of his japa and austerity. You see, physical traits to a great extent influence character. Short stature and a body with dents here and there are not good traits. People with such traits take a long time to acquire spiritual knowledge."

Bhavanath was present there. He said to Sri Ramakrishna, "Let us stop talking about these things."

"Don't misunderstand me," said the Master, and turned to Narendra: "You say, you understand people; that is why I am telling you all this. Do you know how I look on people like Hazra? I know that just as God takes the form of holy men, so He also takes the form of cheats and rogues."

Suddenly the topic of discussion was changed when other devotees asked the Master a different question on a different topic. Sri Ramakrishna began to talk to them.[52]

Next, we see Sri Ramakrishna after about fourteen days on Saturday, May 9, 1885; he was seated in Balaram's drawing room in a happy mood with many devotees. Narendranath was also present there. Balaram was not there. He had gone to Monghyr for a change of air. His eldest daughter had invited Sri Ramakrishna and his devotees and celebrated the occasion with a feast.

Sri Ramakrishna was talking to devotees. Meanwhile, the conversation drifted to Hazra and his egotism. For some reason he had to go away from Dakshineswar.

Narendra said: "Hazra now admits he was egotistic."

Master: "Don't believe him. He says so in order to come back to Dakshineswar." Then he turned to devotees, and said, "Narendra always insists that Hazra is a grand person."

Narendra: "Even now I say so."

Master: "Why? You have heard so much about him, and still you think so?"

Narendra: "He has slight defects but many virtues."

Sri Ramakrishna admitted that Hazra had devotion to his ideal, and he began to describe his other sides that he had experienced. He said: "Hazra said to me, 'You don't care for me now, but later you will be seeking my company.' A Goswami came from Srirampore. He was a descendant of Advaita Goswami. He intended to spend a night or two at the temple garden. I asked him very cordially to stay. Do you know what Hazra said to me? He said, 'Send him to the temple officer.' What crossed his mind was that the Goswami might ask for milk or food, and that he might have to give him some from his own share. I said to Hazra: 'Now, you rogue! Even I prostrate myself before him because he is a Goswami. And you, after leading a worldly life and indulging a great deal in 'woman' and 'gold', have so much pride because of a little japa! Aren't you ashamed of yourself?'

"One realizes God through sattva (balance or wisdom). Rajas (activity or restlessness) and tamas (inertia or dullness) take one away from Him. The scriptures describe sattva as white, rajas as red, and tamas as black. Once I asked Hazra: 'Tell me what you think of the people that come here. How much sattva does each one possesses?' He said: 'Narendra has one hundred per cent and I have one hundred and ten per cent.' 'What about me?' I asked. And he said: 'You still have a trace of pink. You have only seventy-five per cent, I should say.' (All laugh)

"Hazra used to practice japa at Dakshineswar. While telling his beads, he would also try to do a little brokerage business. He has a debt of a few thousand rupees which he must clear up. About the Brahmin cooks of the temple he remarked, 'Do you think I talk with people of that sort?'

"The truth is that you cannot attain God if you have even a trace of desire. Subtle is the way of dharma (religion). If you are trying to thread a needle, you will not succeed if the thread has even a slight fiber sticking out.

"There are people who perform japa for thirty years and still do not attain any result. Why? A gangrenous sore requires very drastic treatment. Ordinary medicine won't cure it.

"No matter how much sadhana (Prayer) you practice, you will not realize the goal as long as you have desire. But this also is true, that one can realize the goal in a moment through the grace of God, through His kindness. Take the case of a room that has been dark for a thousand years. If somebody suddenly brings a lamp into it, the room is lighted in an instant."[53]

We know that Narendranath was in a habit of accepting anything only after a long study on the same. He was a scholar in argument. That day he was arguing with Girish in front of Sri Ramakrishna. He didn't believe the Incarnation of God. He said to Girish: "How can I believe, without proof, that God incarnates Himself as a man?"

Girish Ghosh replied, "Faith alone is sufficient. What is the proof that these objects exist here? Faith alone is the proof."

A devotee: "Have philosophers been able to prove that the external world exists outside us? But they say we have an irresistible belief in it."

Girish said to Narendra: "You wouldn't believe, even if God appeared before you. God Himself might say that He was God born as a man, but perhaps you would say that He was a liar and cheat."

The conversation turned to the immortality of the gods.

Narendra said: "What is the proof of their immortality?"

Girish: "You wouldn't believe it even if the gods appeared before you."

Narendra: "That the immortals existed in the past requires proof."

Meanwhile M. whispered something to Paltu. Paltu smiled and said to Narendra: "What need is there for the immortals to be without beginning? To be immortal one need only be without end."

Sri Ramakrishna smiled and said: "Narendra is the son of a lawyer, but Paltu of a deputy magistrate."[54]

Everyone present there burst into laughter, and all kept silent for a while.

One more scene of argument, where we see Narendranath was arguing on the words of scripture. He said to Girish, M., and others: "How am I to believe in the words of scripture? The *Mahanirvana Tantra* says, in one place, that unless a man attains the knowledge of Brahman he goes to hell; and the same book says, in another place, that there is no salvation without the worship of Parvati, the Divine Mother. Manu writes about himself in the *Manusamhita*; Moses describes his own death in the Pentateuch.

"The Samkhya philosophy says that God does not exist, because there is no proof of His existence.

Again, the same philosophy says that one must accept the Vedas and that, they are eternal.

"But I don't say that these are not true. I simply don't understand them. Please explain them to me. People have explained the scriptures according to their fancy. Which explanation shall we accept? White light coming through a red medium appears red, through a green medium, green."

A devotee replied: "The *Gita* contains the words of God."

Master: "Yes, the *Gita* is the essence of all scriptures. A sannyasi (Ascetic) may or may keep with him another book, but he always carries a pocket *Gita*."

A devotee: "The Gita contains the words of Krishna."

Narendra: "Yes, Krishna or any fellow of Krishna."

Sri Ramakrishna was amazed at these words of Narendra. He said: "This is a fine discussion. There are two interpretations of the scriptures: the literal and the real. One should accept the real meaning alone—what agrees with the words of God. There is a vast difference between the words written in the letter and the direct words of its writer. The scriptures are like the words of the letter; the words of God are direct words. I do not accept anything unless it agrees with the direct words of the Divine Mother."

The conversation again turned to Divine Incarnation, and Narendranath said: "It is enough to have faith in God. I don't care about what He is doing or what He hangs from. Infinite is the universe; infinite are the Incarnations."

As Sri Ramakrishna heard the words, 'Infinite is the universe; infinite are the Incarnations', he said with folded hands, "Ah!"

M. whispered something to Bhavanath. Bhavanath said: "M. says: 'As long as I have not seen the elephant how can I know whether it can pass through the eye of a needle?' I do not know God; how can I understand through reason whether or not He can incarnate Himself as man?"

Sri Ramakrishna replied: "Everything is possible for God. It is He who casts the spell. The magician swallows the knife and takes it out again; he swallows stones and bricks."[55]

The discussion came to an end here as the devotees were egger to listen to Narendra's song. Narendra began to sing.

Sri Ramakrishna at Shyampukur

Sri Ramakrishna's illness was diagnosed as cancer. No proper arrangement for his treatment was possible at Dakshineswar. He needed a constant attention of a physician, which could not be given at the temple garden. Furthermore, the devotees who lived in Calcutta found it inconvenient to attend at Dakshineswar. Therefore, the older devotees had rented a small two-storey house at Baghbazar, and had brought the Master there. Sri Ramakrishna, however, didn't like the place. He preffered Balaram's house and went there. In a few days a new house was selected in Shyampukur, and the Master was taken there. He had been under the treatment of Dr. Mahendra Lal Sarkar. The new building had two big rooms and two smaller one on the first floor. One of the larger rooms was used as the parlour, and in the other the Master lived. Of the two smaller rooms, one was used as a sleeping-room by the devotees, and the other by the Holy Mother when she came there. Near the exit on the roof was a small, covered, square space, where the Holy Mother stayed during the day and prepared the Master's food.

It was the afternoon of October 24, 1885, when Narendranath came to see Sri Ramakrishna at Shyampukur. Sri Ramakrishna was seated in front of Dr. Sarkar, Mahimacharan, M., and other devotees in the room. After a little conversation Sri Ramakrishna asked Narendra to sing. Narendra sang:

> I have made Thee, O Lord, the Pole-star of my life;
> No more shall I lose my way on the world's trackless sea.

He sang four or five songs as he was requested by the Master to sing.

Next day (Sunday, October 25, 1885) also Narendranath arrived at Shyampukur to visit Sri Ramakrishna. Dr. Sarkar, M., Vijay and other devotees were present there. Conversation and singing were being continued one after another. Meanwhile Sri Ramakrishna went into trance. After a long spell the Master regained his consciousness, and said to M.: "Something happens to me in that state of intoxication. Now I feel ashamed of myself. In that state I feel as if I were possessed by a ghost. I cease to be my own self. While coming down from that state I cannot count correctly. Trying to count, I say, 'One, seven, eight', or some such thing."

Narendra said: "It is because everything is one."

Master: "No, it is beyond one and two. There reason withers away. God cannot be realized through scholarship. He is beyond the scripture—the Vedas, Puranas, and Tantras. If I see a man with even one book in his hand, I call him a rajarshi (A rishi, or seer, who appears with outer splendor, like a king). though he is a jnani (One who follows the path of knowledge and discrimination of God; or a non-dualist). But the Brahmarshi (A seer who always dwells in Brahman consciousness) has no outer sign whatsoever."

After more conversation Sri Ramakrishna said to Narendra: "Why don't you sing a little more?" Narendra sang to the accompaniment of the tanpura and other instruments:

Sweet is Thy name, O Refuge of the humble!
It falls like sweetest nectar on our ears
And comforts us, Beloved of our souls!
The priceless treasure of Thy name alone
Is the abode of Immortality?
And he who chants Thy name becomes immortal.
Falling upon our ears, Thy holy name
Instantly slays the anguish of our hearts,
Thou Soul of our souls, and fills our hearts with bliss!

He again sang:

O Mother, make me mad with Thy love!
What need have I of knowledge or reason?
Make me drunk with Thy love's Wine; . . .

A strange transformation came over the devotees. They all turned, as it were, into human beings filled with divine ecstasy. Vijay was the first on his feet, carried away by divine intoxication. Then Sri Ramakrishna stood up, forgetting all about his painful and fatal illness. The doctor, who had been sitting in front of him, also stood up. Both patient and physician forgot themselves in the spell conjured by Narendra's music. The younger Naren and Latu went into deep trance. The atmosphere of the room became electric. Everyone felt the presence of God. Dr. Sarkar, eminent scientist that he was, stood breathless, watching this strange scene. He noticed that the devotees who had gone into trance were utterly unconscious of the outer world. All were motionless and transfixed. After a while, as they came down a little to the plane of the relative world, some were laughing and some were weeping. An outsider, entering the room, would have thought that a number of drunkards had assembled there. Thus M., the recorder of *The Gospel of Sri Ramakrishna*, described.

After a while, during conversation, Vijay Goswami said, "I feel as if someone were always moving with me. He shows me what is happening even at a distance."

Narendra: "Like a guardian angel."

Vijay: "I have seen him [meaning the Master] in Dacca. I even touched his body."

Master (with a smile): "It must have been someone else."

Narendra: "I too have seen him many a time. (to Vijay) How can I say I do not believe your words?"[56]

Next on Tuesday, October 27, 1885, Narendranath was sitting near Sri Ramakrishna. Since his father died he had been very much worried about the family's financial condition. He had to support his mother and brothers. He wanted to make some arrangement for his family and thus get rid of all his worries. Sri Ramakrishna knew all this. He looked affectionately at Narendra. Then he began to talk to M. During this conversation, what he said was nothing but a preface to Narendra's future life. He tried to show him his goal of life.

Sri Ramakrishna said to M.: "Well, I said to Keshab, 'One should be satisfied with what comes unsought.' The son of an aristocrat does not worry about his food and drink. He gets his monthly allowance. Narendra, too, belongs to a high plane. Then why is he in such straitened circumstances? God certainly provides everything for the man who totally surrenders himself to Him."

M.: "Narendra, too, will be provided for. It is not yet too late for him."

Master: "But a man who feels intense renunciation within doesn't calculate that way. He doesn't say to himself, 'I shall first make an arrangement for the family and then practice sadhana.' No, he doesn't feel that way if he has developed intense dispassion. A Goswami said in the course of his preaching, 'If a man has ten thousand rupees he can maintain himself on the income; then, free from worries, he can pray to God.'

'Keshab Sen also said something like that. He said to me: 'Sir, suppose a man wants, first of all, to make a suitable arrangement of his property and estate and then think of God; will it be all right for him to do so? Is there anything wrong about it?' I said to him: 'When a man feels utter dispassion, he looks on the world as a deep well and his relatives as venomous cobras. Then he cannot think of saving money or making arrangements about his property.' God alone is real and all else illusory. To think of the world instead of God!

"A woman was stricken with intense grief. She first tied her nose-ring in the corner of her cloth and then dropped to the ground, saying, 'Oh, friends, what a calamity has befallen me!' But she was very careful not to break the nose-ring."

All laughed. At these words Narendra felt as if struck by an arrow, and lay down on the floor.

M. understood what was going through Narendra's mind and said with a smile: "What's the matter? Why are you lying down?"

The Master said to M., with a smile: "You remind me of a woman who felt ashamed of herself for sleeping with her brother-in-law and couldn't understand the conduct of those women who lived as mistress of strangers. By way of excusing herself she said: 'After all, brother-in-law is one's own. But even that kills me with shame. And how do those women dare to live with strangers?"

M., the recorder of *The Gospel of Sri Ramakrishna*, explained this situation. He has written, "M. himself had been leading a worldly life. Instead of being ashamed of his own conduct, he smiled at Narendra. That was why Sri Ramakrishna referred to the woman who criticized the conduct of immoral women, though she herself had illicit love for her brother-in-law."

Yes, Sri Ramakrishna did the right thing. He never liked that anybody would smile at his beloved Narendra. He advised Narendra to renounce the worldly life which is nothing but an illusory.[57]

Dr. Sarkar didn't believe the incarnation of God as a man. He had a long discussion on this topic with Girish Ghosh, Narendranath, and even with Sri Ramakrishna. But he couldn't win the argument. Finally, he surrendered himself to all of them. But he was worried about Sri Ramakrishna's health. He had great respect for Sri Ramakrishna. He used to shed tears in solitude. He was worried about the state of trance experienced by the Master, because he felt it might be harmful for his health. Narendranath tried to convince him. He said to the doctor: "You may look at the thing from another standpoint. You can devote your life to scientific research without giving a thought of your health or comfort. But the Science of God is the grandest of all sciences. Isn't it natural for him to risk his health to realize Him?"[58]

Narendranath was also against the idea of incarnation of God as a man. But the above statement shows that he became changed. He began to believe the same. He also said to doctor, "We offer worship to him [Sri Ramakrishna] bordering on divine worship."

We cannot come to the conclusion of this episode till we know the views of revered Swami Saradananda. Being one of the disciples of Sri Ramakrishna and well acquainted with

Narendranath he had experienced many things of that period, and Narendra had also shared many of his experiences with him. Swami Saradananda, in his book *Sri Sri Ramakrishna Lilaprasango*, said: "When many devotees firmly believed that the Master was an avatar of the age and were allowing them to be carried away by this sentiment, Vijay Krishna Goswami came from Dhaka to see the Master. In front of all, he declared that one day while he was meditating in his room in Dhaka, the Master had physically appeared before him, and Vijay had confirmed the Master's presence by touching his limbs. This added fuel to the fire, and various emotions arose among the devotees. At that time five or six devotees were experiencing some physical changes and losing partial consciousness when they heard devotional songs. Setting aside common sense and the royal path of discrimination, they now became accustomed to waiting eagerly and in suspense for another miraculous manifestation of the Master's divine power.

"The astute Narendra, whom the Master had made foremost among the devotees, observed that the devotees had come to regard this excessive emotionalism as the culmination of religion and were considering renunciation, self-control, and steadfast devotion as insignificant. Narendra knew that this attitude, if indulged freely, could eventually lead them into great danger. He explained this to the devotees and made a special effort to protect them from any negative consequences.

"One may question why the Master remained aloof when he knew that some of his devotees were going astray. The answer is that he was not indifferent: He knew that genuine devotion was one of the paths to God-realization and that some of those devotees were truly fit for it. He was looking for the right time and opportunity to guide them along that path. We heard him say many times, 'One doesn't attain success suddenly by a mere wish; it happens in the course of time.' And 'Success in a particular matter comes at the proper time.' It may be that he had observed Narendra's determination to remove the devotees' error and was awaiting the result. It may also have been his intention to use Narendra as an instrument to accomplish that task."[59]

Narendra had faith in young devotees that they would understand him easily, because they had strong bodies and resolute minds. So he repeatedly reasoned with them: "An upsurge of emotion that doesn't transform life permanently makes people eager to realize God at one moment, but doesn't give them the power to desist from seeking lust and gold in the next. There's no depth in it, and it's therefore of little value in life. Under its influence people may experience physical reactions—such as tears, goose bumps, and so on—or may temporarily lose partial outer consciousness, but I'm fully convinced that these things are caused by nervous debility. If people can't control themselves through force of mind, they should eat nutritious food and seek medical help.

"There is much artificiality in those physical displays and lapses of outer consciousness. The higher and stronger the dam of self-control, the deeper spiritual emotion becomes. In the lives of a few rare persons, intense spiritual moods take the form of a huge tidal wave, overflowing that dam of self-control and manifesting as physical reaction and a loss of outer consciousness. Foolish people do not understand this and from a mistaken impression. They think that deep spiritual feelings result from those physical displays and lapses of consciousness, so they strive to achieve those signs quickly. This effort of will gradually turns into habit and weakens their nerves day by day. Soon those physical effects appear in them at the slightest awakening of emotion. Consequently, they develop chronic diseases or even become insane by indulging freely in those sentiments. When people try to practice religion, eighty percent of them turn into cheats and about fifteen percent go mad. It's only the remaining five percent who get some direct knowledge of the Truth and become blessed. Therefore, beware!"[60]

At first Swami Saradananda didn't completely believe Narendra's words. But he soon learned accidentally that a devotee had been singing inspiring Vaishnava songs in solitude, practicing to bring on the physical effects that this mood could produce. That devotee also practiced dancing like another devotee who had danced beautifully when he was overwhelmed by emotion and had lost partial consciousness. Shortly after seeing the first devotee dance, a third devotee began to follow the same when absorbed in a religious mood. This proved the truth of Narendra's words. When Narendra saw a devotee having frequent emotional outbursts, talked to him privately and instructed him to control his emotions and to eat nutritious food. The result of this advice was fruitful. Within a fortnight the devotee became healthy and improved his self-control. Many devotees then trusted Narendra's words and no longer considered themselves unfortunate for experiencing physical transformations or unconsciousness as others did.

Narendranath preached against this emotional excitement. If ever he came to know the slightest artificiality in any devotee's religious mood, he would ridicule him in public. He would demonstrate how ridiculous was the Vaishnava practice of men practicing the attitude of a female confidante of Krishna. He would ridicule any of the devotees who had that kind of tendency by referring him as a Sakhi, or a female confidante of Krishna. Narendranath was a true lion among men. He couldn't bear the attitude of a man who had lost his manliness by imitating a woman's mood and gestures, singing Vaishnava lyrics, and weeping. The Master's masculine devotees; who were endowed with knowledge tempered with devotion, Narendra humorously called *Dana* or Shiva's demons, and he called those who had an opposite nature Sakhi or female confidantes of Krishna.

Narendranath was not satisfied by breaking the barrier of sentimentalism with reasoning, jokes, and ridicule. He was aware of the fact that his preaching could not be effective until the old practice was replaced by a new one, and he made special efforts to accomplish that. Narendra would gather them together during leisure time and lead them in songs describing the impermanency of the world and extolling renunciation and devotion to God. Narendra sang these songs and hymns:

O heart, what will you gain by union with a dear one?
Ultimately all this will return to dust....

* * *

O Ocean of nectar and Embodiment of consciousness and bliss,
Life becomes sweet and joyful while singing Your name. . .

* * *

I am neither the mind, the intellect, the ego, nor the chitta [mind-stuff],
Neither the ears, not the tongue, nor the senses of smell and sight;
Neither ether nor air, not fire, nor water, not earth;
I am Eternal Bliss and Awareness—I am Shiva! I am Shiva!

When people came to see the Master and heard Narendra sing those songs and hymns in his sweet and melodious voice, they were so inspired with renunciation and love of God that they would shed tears on their way home.

Swami Saradananda had experienced all these things. He said: "Sometimes Narendra told the devotees wonderful stories of how the Master's sadhana had originated from his deep passion for God, and he charmed them with descriptions of the Master's glory. Quoting from the limitation of Christ [by Thomas a Kempis], Narendra said: "'The life of anybody who truly loves the Lord will be perfectly moulded in His pattern.' Therefore, whether we truly love the Master or not will be proven by this." He reminded the devotees of the Master's teaching: "First tie the knowledge of nonduality in a corner of your cloth, then do as you please." Narendra then explained to them that every one of the Master's ecstatic moods arose from that nondual knowledge; so they should strive to attain that knowledge first.

"Narendra very often encouraged the Master's devotees to verify new ideas before accepting them. We remember that he once heard that one could cure physical ailments by concentrating the mind. He then gathered us in a closed room and engaged us in using that technique to try in curing the Master's illness. However, he always tried to see that the devotees stayed away from practices that were not based on reason."[61]

In support of his statement Swami Saradananda had mentioned the following incident as an example:

"Mahimacharan Chakrabarty's house was across from the place where the south side of Mati Lake met Cossipore Road. Although Mr. Chakrabarty had many good qualities, he always yearned for name and fame. It seems that he was not above resorting to falsehood if it would bring him honour. He arranged every aspect of his life with the expectation that people would call him wealthy, learned, intelligent, virtuous, generous, and so on, which sometimes made him appear ridiculous to others. Once Mr. Chakrabarty founded a free school and called it 'Prachya-Arya-Shiksha-Kendra-Parishat' [The Educational Branch of the Institute of the Oriental Aryans]. He named his only son 'Mriganka-Mauli Patutandi' [One with a beautiful face and the moon on his head]. He gave his pet deer the name 'Kapinjal' [the name of an anchorite]. He was fond of using pompous titles such as these because he felt it unbecoming to a scholar like himself to give short and simple names. He had a large collection of English and Sanskrit books. One day after we became acquainted with him, we went to his house with Narendra. We asked him, 'Sir, have you read all these books?' with due humility he replied that he had. But the next moment Narendra picked up some books from his shelf and found that some of their were uncut. When asked the reason for this, Mahim Chakrabarty replied: "Look, Brother, people borrowed those books that I read, and they did not return them. So I bought those new copies to replace them. Now I no longer allow anyone to borrow my books." Narendra soon discovered that the pages of most of Mr. Chakrabarty's collection were uncut, which convinced him that Mr. Chakrabarty kept those books in his living room for decoration and to solicit respect and admiration from his visitors.

"Once while we were discussing methods of sadhana, Mahim described himself to us as an aspirant of the path of knowledge. Many years before the Calcutta devotees went to the Master, Mahim had visited the Master at Dakshineswar. On some festival days, he put on an ochre cloth and rudraksha beads, held an ektara (a one-stringed musical instrument) in his hand, sat on his tiger skin under the Panchavati, and began his spiritual practices in great pomp. Before returning home, he would hang his tiger skin on a wall in a corner of the Master's room at Dakshineswar. The Master saw right through him with only a cursory examination. One day one of us asked the Master whom that tiger skin belonged to, and he replied: "Mahim Chakrabarty left it there. Do you know why? So people will see it and ask me to whom it belongs. When I mention his name, they'll think Mahim Chakrabarty must be a great aspirant."

"Regarding his initiation, Mahim sometimes said: "My guru's name is Agamacharya Damaruvallabha." But at other times he mentioned that he had taken initiation form Paramahamsa Parivrajaka Tota Puri, as the Master had. He said: "While making pilgrimages in Western India,

I happened to meet him and was initiated. Tota told Sri Ramakrishna to follow the path of devotion and advised me to stick to the path of knowledge and to stay in the world." How far these assertions were true was known only to him and to omniscient God.

"One day Mahim came to Shyampukur and spoke on various topics, attempting to establish that the sadhana he followed was the best and easiest, and that all other sadhanas were inferior. Narendra could not bear to see the Master's young disciples listening to him without protest. Narendra raised counter-arguments and proved that Mahim's position was untenable. He asked, "What proof is there that a person will see God by uttering a mantra while accompanied by an ektara as you are doing?" Mahim replied, "Nada [sound] is Brahman. God is bound to reveal Himself if the mantra is uttered simultaneously with that musical note. One need not practice anything else." Narendra said: "Has God drawn up such a written agreement with you? Will God appear stealthily before you, like a snake charmed by a mantra and an herb, when you raise the pitch of your voice and utter hum-hum?" Unfortunately, because of Narendra's arguments, Mahim's preaching did not gain a following that day, and he quickly took his leave.

Narendra kept a watch on the Master's devotees so that they would pay due respect to genuine spiritual aspirants of other religious communities. He said: "Ordinary people love and respect only those spiritual aspirants of their own faith; they criticize those of other faiths. This attitude shows disrespect for the Master's view 'As many faiths, so many paths,' and therefore to the Master himself."

Swami Saradananda has described a related incident that he had experienced. He said: "Prabhudayal Mishra, a Christian clergyman, came to see the Master. We did not immediately recognize him as a Christian because he was wearing an ochre cloth. When he introduced himself to us, we asked him why he wore ochre cloth if he were a Christian. He replied: "I was born in a Brahmin family. Must I give up the customs and practices of my forefathers because I have established faith in Christ and accepted him as my Chosen Deity? I believe in the yoga scriptures and practice yoga disciplines daily with Christ as my Chosen Deity. I don't believe in the caste system, but I do believe that it is injurious to the practice of yoga if one indiscriminately accepts food from anyone. So every day I eat vegetarian food that I've cooked for myself. Consequently, even though I'm a Christian, I've experienced the results of yoga, such as seeing a light and so on. The devout yogis of India have been wearing ochre cloth from ancient times, so this cloth is dearer to me than any other." Narendra put questions to him one after another and learned about his personal life. When he had determined him to be a yogi and a holy man, Narendra showed great respect for him and asked us to do the same. Many of us took the dust of his feet, and together we had the Master's Prasad of sweets and fruits. He told us that he believed the Master was Jesus Christ himself."[62]

Sri Ramakrishna at Cossipore

When Narendranath was busy in guiding the devotees along the right path, Sri Ramakrishna's illness grew steadily worse. Dr. Sarkar discovered that the medicines that had been producing some good results were no longer working. He became convinced that the Master needed a pollution-free environment. So he recommended Sri Ramakrishna should be moved to a garden house outside the city. The devotees began to search a garden house. They soon located and rented the garden house of Gopal Chandra Ghosh, a son-in-law of Rani Katyayani, at eighty rupees per month. This house is situated at the junction of the northern part of the Mati Lake in Cossipore and the eastern side of the main road leading to Baranagore Bazar. Surendra Nath Mitra of Calcutta, a great devotee of the Master, promised to pay the entire rent.

After securing the house, the devotees fixed an auspicious date and made plans to move the Master's belongings from the Shyampukur house. Finally, the devotees took the Master himself from the Shyampukur house to the Cossipore garden house in the afternoon of 11th December 1885. It was inauspicious to travel during the month of Paush [mid-December to mid-January]. So Sri Ramakrishna moved to the Cossipore garden house just before the last day of Agrahayan [mid-November to mid-December].

The garden was more spacious and secluded than the Shyampukur house. It was full of green trees, flowers of different colours, and the tender green grassy lawns. Sri Ramakrishna found the place pleasant after spending a strech of four months in Calcutta. He was delighted when he entered the garden and breathed in fresh air. He enjoyed the view as he walked slowly towards the house. As he went upstairs to his specious room, he immediately walked to the southern terrace connected to his room and enjoyed the garden's beauty for a while. The Holy Mother was also happy when she saw that she would not have to live here in confinement and suffer any inconvenience.

The garden house was beautiful, but there were many problems too. The place was far away from the doctors who were treating Sri Ramakrishna. It required more men and more money than before. While thinking over this problem, Narendranath quickly calculated that the attendants who volunteered to serve the Master must stay there. Balaram, Surendra, Ram, Girish, Mahendra, and others had been dealing with the financial matters. Narendra took the responsibility of gathering attendants. He decided to spend most of the time at the Cossipore garden house, because he had to set an example to the other young devotees. By seeing the efforts of Narendranath they would be able to work. They also had to face the objections of their guardians for staying away from the house. When Sri Ramakrishna was at Shyampukur, his young attendants went home for their meal and then came back to serve him, but that kind of arrangement was not possible here because of the distance.

Narendra was preparing for his law examination that year. He decided to bring his books with him, so that he could read them whenever he found time. Thus, Narendra resolved to serve his guru first and then appear for the law examination, if possible. He was also worried for his mother and brothers. He had a plan to pass the law examination and work for few years to provide necessities for his family, and then renounce the world and devote himself entirely to spiritual practices. We should know that we can make many plans for our future, but success comes only if they are granted by God. Till now Narendra didn't know what was his goal, or where he had to reach.

Readers may think that here at Cossipore, Sri Ramakrishna was completely dependent on his devotees. It was not unknown to him that a big amount was necessary for the maintenance of all required services. He knew that the type and amount of services he would receive from devotees was intended by the Divine Mother and was for their welfare. Whenever Sri Ramakrishna didn't like the arrangements that the devotees had made, he would make adjustment either with their knowledge or without it, if he felt their feelings would be hurt. Just before going to Calcutta for treatment, he told Balaram: "Look, people collect money for my daily food, but this isn't to my liking. I'm not used to it. If you ask how I'm living in the Kali temple of Dakshineswar at present, when many owners of the temple jointly conduct the worship service, I would respond that I don't receive my food from the money that they pledged. When Rani Rasmani was alive, it was arranged that I would permanently continue to draw my salary as a priest, which was seven rupees per month, and that I would receive Prasad from the temple as long as I lived here. So in a sense I live here on a pencil (he pronounced the English word pension as 'pencil'). I therefore ask that you carry my expenses for food as long as I live away from Dakshineswar for my treatment."

Sri Ramakrishna knew that the Cossipore garden house was rented for him, and he learned that it would cost eighty rupees per month. He was concerned about his devotees, who had to maintain their families. He called his great devotee Surendra, an agent of the Dost Company, and said: "Look, Surendra, these devotees are mostly poor clerks and have large families to maintain. How can they raise so much money to rent this garden house? Please bear the whole of it yourself." Surendra gladly assented, saying, "As you command."

Swami Saradananda had seen all these things before his eyes. He later explained as follows:

> "One day the Master told us that very soon his physical weakness would make it difficult for him to go outside to answer the call of nature. The young devotee Latu (later known as Swami Adbhutananda) was pained when he heard the Master say this. He forthwith responded humbly, with folded hands: "Sir, whatever you order me to do, I will do. I am your sweeper and always ready." Latu uttered those words in his own form of Bengali, which made the Master and us laugh even in that dismal situation. Thus did the Master make his wow arrangements as appropriate, making it easier for the devotees to carry out their respective duties.

"Gradually everything fell into a routine and the young devotees came to Cossipore one after another. When they were not busy caring for the Master, Narendra engaged them in meditation, devotional singing, study, discussion of the scriptures, and spiritual conversation. They were carried away in such a blissful current that they did not notice how the days slipped away. The tremendous attraction of the Master's pure and unselfish love on one hand, and Narendra's wonderful friendship and holy companionship on the other, joined them in such a sweet and strong bond that they truly felt closer to one another than to members of their own families. If someone went home on urgent business, he invariably returned that evening or the next morning at the latest. They lived at Cossipore until the Master passed away and then completed their vow of service by renouncing the world. Although the devotees never numbered more than twelve, they were extremely devoted to their guru and remarkably efficient."[63]

The above-mentioned twelve devotees were—Narendra, Rakhal, Baburam, Niranjan, Jogindra, Latu, Tarak, Brother of Gopal, Kali, Shashi, Sharat, and Hutko Gopal. Sarada could stay only a day or two from time to time because of his father's strong opposition. Hari, Gangadhar, and Tulsi practiced austerities at home and visited the Master occasionally.

Swami Saradananda had described his memory of those days: "One day shortly after the Master arrived at Cossipore; he went downstairs and walked on the garden path for a short time. The devotees were delighted to see this, and hoped that he would soon regain his strength and recover if he could take walks like this every day. However, the next day he felt weaker, having caught a cold from the chilly air outside or for some other reason, so he could not go outside again for many days. His cold subsided in two or three days, but the weakness continued. The doctors prescribed a special broth for him. After taking it for a few days, his weakness lessened to a great extent and he felt better and stronger. This improvement continued for about a fortnight. Dr. Sarkar came to visit and was delighted to find him in better health.

"The young attendants had to go to Calcutta every day to give the doctor a report on the Master's health and to obtain the food he needed. At first both tasks were given to one person, but this arrangement created some inconvenience. So it was decided that two people would go to Calcutta every day for those important errands. If anything else was needed in Calcutta, a third person was sent. In addition, the young devotees began to take turns performing all other duties, such as cleaning the house, shopping for groceries at the Baranagore Bazar every day, and caring for the Master day and night. Narendra supervised their activities and managed other affairs that cropped up.

"As before, the Holy Mother was in charge of preparing the Master's diet. If the doctor prescribed a special diet for the Master in addition to regular food, Brother Gopal or another devotee would learn how to prepare it, and then teach the Holy Mother how to do so. The Holy Mother would converse freely only with Brother Gopal and one or two others. In addition to preparing the Master's meals, the Holy Mother would carry the food tray to him a little before noon and shortly after sunset and wait until he had finished eating. The Master's niece Lakshmi was brought to Cossipore to help the Holy Mother cook and perform other household duties as well as to keep her company. In addition, some of the women devotees who had regularly visited the Master in Dakshineswar began to come to Cossipore and stay with the Holy Mother for a few hours, or sometimes for one or two days. After a week, the whole arrangement worked smoothly.

"The householder devotees were not free from anxiety during that period. They would meet at Ram's or Girish's house, as was convenient, to decide how much time and money they could provide for the Master's service, and then they would act accordingly. They knew that not everyone might be able to contribute an equal amount every month, so they met once or twice a month to make decisions beforehand.

"Most of the young devotees did not visit their homes for even a short while until everything regarding the Master's service was in order. Those who had to go home to handle urgent matters returned within a few hours. They somehow made their guardians understand that they would not be able to visit regularly or live at home as before until the Master had recovered. Of course, no guardian was pleased to hear that, and none of them approved. But what could they do? They thought the boys had been brainwashed and that if they were not handled carefully, more harm than good would result. So the guardians decided to somehow tolerate the boy's behaviour for a time and began to devise some means for bringing them back.

"When the householder devotees and the young disciples jointly undertook their vow of service and everything was orderly and running as smooth as a machine, Narendra was relieved to a great extent and had an opportunity to think about his own affairs. One night he told us that he planned to visit home for a day or two. He then went to bed, but he could not sleep. He soon got up, and finding Gopal and a couple of us awake, he said: "The Master's disease is extremely serious. Who knows whether he has decided to lay down his body? Make your best effort to achieve spiritual enlightenment through service to him and prayer and meditation while there is yet time. If you do otherwise, there will be no end to your repentance after he passes away. We waste out time with the foolish thought that we shall pray to God after finishing this duty, or practice spiritual disciplines after doing that. Thus we entangle ourselves in a net or desires. Those terrible desires lead to destruction—death. Shun those desires! Uproot them!"

"This cold winter night in Paush [mid-December to mid-January] the silence pulsated. Above the blue sky watched the earth steadily with its millions of starry eyes. Below, the sun's scorching rays had dried the ground under the garden trees, and one could sit there because the place had been recently cleaned up. Narendra's detached and meditative mind felt that external silence and began to absorb it within. He stopped walking and sat down under a tree. After a while, he saw a heap of dry straw, leaves, and broken tree branches nearby, and told us: "Set fire to it. This is the hour when monks light their dhuni fires under the trees. Let us also light a dhuni fire and burn up our desires." The fire was lighted and we collected more twigs and piled them around us. As we placed bits of wood on that fire, we pictured ourselves as offering our desires as oblations. We experienced a wonderful bliss and truly felt that our worldly desires were utterly destroyed, our minds were pure and serene, and we were becoming close to God. We thought: "Ah, why didn't we do this before? It has given us so much joy! Henceforth, we shall light a dhuni fire whenever we have the opportunity." After two or three hours we could find no more fuel, so we extinguished the fire and returned to our room to retire again. It was then 4:00 a.m. Those who did not participate in our dhuni ceremony heard the story in the morning and were sad that they had not been called. Narendra consoled them by saying: "We didn't plan to do it, and we didn't know that we would experience such bliss. Don't worry; from now on we shall light the dhuni fire together whenever we find time."

Narendra left for Calcutta in the morning as planned and returned to Cossipore the next day with a few law books."[64]

M., the recorder of *The Gospel of Sri Ramakrishna*, has beautifully described the last chapter of the Master's physical life, which is as follows:

> On Friday, December 11, 1885, Sri Ramakrishna was moved to a beautiful house at Cossipore, a suburb of Calcutta. The house was situated in a garden covering about five acres of land and abounding in fruit-trees and flowering plants. Here the final curtain fell on the Master's life.

At Cossipore he set himself with redoubled energy to the completion of the work of spiritual ministration he had begun long before at Dakshineswar. Realizing that the end of his physical life was approaching, he gave away his spiritual treasures without stint to one and all. He was like one of those fruit-sellers who bring their fruit to the marketplace, bargain at first about the prices, but then toward sunset, when the market is about to close, give away the fruit indiscriminately. Here his disciples saw the greatest manifestation of his spiritual powers. Here they saw the fulfillment of his prophecies about his own end: "I shall make the whole thing public before I go." "When people in large numbers come to know and whisper about the greatness of this body, then the Mother will take it back." "The devotees will be shifted into the inner and outer circles towards the end." And so on. Here he predicted that a band of young disciples, with Narendranath as their leader, would in due course renounce the world and devote themselves to the realization of God and the service of humanity.

"The main building at Cossipore was two storied, with three rooms below and two on the first floor. The Master occupied the central hall of the upper storey; a small room to the left was used at night by his attendants. To the right of the hall was an open balcony where Sri Ramakrishna sometimes used to sit or walked. On the ground floor, a hall just below the Master's and a small room to the right of it were used by the devotees and a small room to the extreme left was occupied by the Holy Mother. In the garden compound were some outbuildings, two reservoirs, and pleasant walks. Sri Ramakrishna breathed more freely in the open air of the new place.

"Almost all the devotees had gathered by this time. They had started coming to him in 1881. By the end of 1884 Sarat and Sashi had become known to the Master, and since their college examinations in the middle of 1885, they had been visiting him almost daily. Girish Ghosh first met the Master in September 1884 at the Star Theatre. Since the beginning of the following December he had been a constant visitor. And it was during the later part of December 1884 that Sarada Prasanna first visited the Master at the Dakshineswar temple. Subodh and Kshirode first visited him in August 1885.

"The young devotees had taken up their quarters at the garden house to tend Sri Ramakrishna, although many of them visited their own homes every now and then. The householders came to see the Master almost every day, and some of them occasionally spent the night with him."[65]

It was the afternoon of Monday, January 4, 1886. Narendranath arrived at Cossipore. Sri Ramakrishna looked at him every now and then, and smiled. It seemed to M., that day the Master's love for his disciple knew no bounds. He indicated to M. that Narendra had wept. Then he remained quiet. Again he indicated that Narendra had cried all the way from his home. Everybody was silent. Narendra broke the silence, and said: "I have been thinking of going there today."

Master: "Where?"

Narendra: "To Dakshineswar. I intend to light a fire under the bel-tree and meditate."

Master: "No, the authorities of the powder-magazine will not allow it. The Panchavati is nice place. Many sadhus have practiced japa and meditation there. But it is very cold there. The place is dark, too."

Again there was a silence for a few moments.

Master smiled and said to Narendra: "Won't you continue your studies?"

Narendra looked at the Master and M., and said: "I shall feel greatly relieved if I find a medicine that will make me forget all I have studied."

The elder Gopal, who was also in the room, said, "I shall accompany Narendra."

Kalipada Ghosh had brought a box of grapes for Sri Ramakrishna; it lay beside the Master. The Master gave Narendra a few and poured the rest on the floor for the devotees to pick up.

It was evening. Narendra was sitting in a room downstairs. He was smoking and describing to M. the yearning of his soul. No one else was there with them.

Narendra: "I was meditating here last Saturday when suddenly I felt a peculiar sensation in my heart."

M.: "It was awakening of the Knudalini (the serpent power)."

Narendra: "Probably it was. I clearly perceived the *Ida* (a nerve in the spinal column) and the *Pingala* (a nerve in the spinal column) nerves. I asked Hazra to feel my chest. Yesterday I saw the Master upstairs and told him about it. I said to him: "All the others have had their realization; please give me some. All have succeeded; shall I alone remain unsatisfied?"

M.: "What did he say to you?"

Narendra: "He said, 'Why don't you settle your family affairs first and then come to me? You will get everything. What do you want?' I replied, 'It is my desire to remain absorbed in Samadhi continuously for three or four days, only once in a while coming down to the sense plane to eat a little food.' Thereupon he said to me: 'You are a very small-minded person. There is a state higher even than that. "All that exist art Thou"—it is you who sing that song.'"

M.: "Yes, he always says that after coming down from Samadhi one sees that it is God Himself who has become the universe, the living beings, and all that exists. The Iswarakotis alone attain that state. An ordinary man can at the most attain Samadhi; but he cannot come down from that state."

Narendra: "He [the Master] said: 'Settle your family affairs and then come to me. You will attain a state higher than Samadhi.' I went home this morning. My people scolded me, saying: 'Why do you wander about like a vagabond? Your law examination is near at hand and you are not paying any attention to your studies. You wander about aimlessly.'"

M.: "Did your mother say anything?"

Narendra: "I went to my study at my grandmother's. As I tried to read I was seized with a great fear, as if studying were a terrible thing. My heart struggled within me. I burst into tears: I never wept so bitterly in my life. I left my books and ran away. I ran along the streets. My shoes slipped from my feet—I didn't know where. I ran past a haystack and got hay all over me. I kept on running along the road to Cossipore."

Narendra remained silent a few minutes and then resumed.

Narendra: "Since reading the *Vivekachudamani* I have felt very much depressed. In it Sankaracharya says that only through great tapasya (religious austerity) and good fortune does one acquire these three things: a human birth, the desire for liberation, and refuge with a great soul. I said to myself: 'I have surely gained all these three. As a result of great austerity I have been born a human being; through great austerity, again I have the desire for liberation; and through great austerity I have secured the championship of such a great soul.'"

M.: "Ah!"

Narendra: "I have no more taste for the world. I do not relish the company of those who live in the world—of course, with the exception of one or two devotees."

Narendra became silent again. A fire of intense renunciation was burning within him. His soul was restless for the vision of God. He resumed the conversation.

Narendra: "You have found peace, but my soul is restless. You are blessed indeed."

M. did not reply, but sat in silence. He said to himself, "Sri Ramakrishna said that one must pant and pine for God; only then may one have the vision of Him."

Immediately after dusk M. went upstairs. He found Sri Ramakrishna asleep.

It was about nine o'clock in the evening. Niranjan and Sashi were sitting near the Master. He was awake. Every now and then he talked of Narendra.

Master: "How wonderful Narendra's state of mind is! You see, this very Narendra did not believe in the forms of God. And now you see how his soul is panting for God!"

This day Sri Ramakrishna's illness was worse. In spite of much suffering he said many things about Narendra—though mostly by means of signs.

At night Narendra left for Dakshineswar. It was very dark, being the night of the new moon. He was accompanied by one or two devotees.[66]

Since his father's death Narendra had been in great distress about his mother and brothers. Now and then they had been on the verge starvation. Narendra was the eldest son. They expected him to earn and feed them. But Narendra couldn't appear at his law examination; he was passing through a state of intense renunciation. He thought to make some provision for his family. A friend had agreed to lend him one hundred rupees. That would take care of the family for three months.

Narendra said to M.: "I am going home. I shall visit Mahimacharan on the way, will you come with me?"

M. didn't want to go. Looking at M. Sri Ramakrishna asked Narendra: "Why?"

Narendra: "I am going that way; so I shall stop at Mahima's place and have a chat with him."

Sri Ramakrishna looked at Narendra intently.

Narendra: "A friend who comes here said he would lend me a hundred rupees. That will take care of the family for three months. I am going home to make that arrangement."

Sri Ramakrishna remained silent and looked at M.[67]

It was Sunday, March 14, 1886. Sri Ramakrishna was seated facing the north in the large room. It was evening. Narendra and Rakhal were gently massaging his feet. M. sat nearby. The Master indicated him to massage his feet. M. obeyed.

The previous Sunday the devotees had observed Sri Ramakrishna's birthday with worship and prayer. His birthday the year before had been celebrated at Dakshineswar with great pomp; but this year, on account of his illness, the devotees were very sad and there was no festivity at all. The Holy Mother was busy day and night in the Master's service. Among the young disciples, Narendra, Rakhal, Niranjan, Sashi, Baburam, Jogin, Latu, and Kali had been staying with him at the garden house. The older devotees visited him daily, and some of them occasionally spent the night there.

That day Sri Ramakrishna was feeling very ill. At midnight the moonlight flooded the garden, but it couldn't wake response in the devotees' hearts. They were drowned in a sea of grief. Everyone was silent. The sight of his suffering was unbearable to them. Sri Ramakrishna lay awake. He said in very low voice: "I have gone on suffering so much for fear of making you all weep. But if you say: 'Oh, there is so much suffering! Let the body die', then I may give up the body."

These words pierced the devotees' hearts.

Next day during conversation, Rakhal said tenderly: "Please speak to God that He may preserve your body some time more."

Master said: "That depends on God's will."

Narendra: "Your will and God's will have become one."

Sri Ramakrishna remains silent. He appears to be thinking about something.

Master said: "And nothing will happen if I speak to God. Now I see that I and the Mother have become one."

Rakhal said in a low voice: "He is referring to God's Incarnation as Gauranga."

The devotees were sitting silently in the room. Sri Ramakrishna looked at them tenderly. Then he placed his hand on his heart and said: "There are two persons in this. One, the Divine Mother" after a little pause he said again: "Yes, one is She. And the other is Her devotee. It is the devotee who broke his arm, and it is the devotee who is now ill. Do you understand?"

Nobody uttered any word.

Master: "Alas! To whom shall I say all this? Who will understand me?" Then after a few minutes, he said: "God becomes man, an Avatar, and comes to earth with His devotees. And the devotees leave the world with Him."

Rakhal: "Therefore, we pray that you may not go away and leave us behind."

Sri Ramakrishna smiled and said: "A band of minstrels suddenly appears, dances, and sings, and it departs in the same sudden manner. They come and they return, but none recognizes them."

The Master and the devotees smiled. After a few minutes he said: "Suffering is inevitable when one assumes a human body. Every now and then I say to myself, 'May I not have to come back to earth again!' But there is something else. After enjoying sumptuous feasts outside, one does not relish cheap home cooking. Besides, the assuming of a human body is for the sake of the devotees."

Sri Ramakrishna looked at Narendra very tenderly, and said: "An outcaste was carrying a load of meat. Sankaracharya, after bathing in the Ganges, was passing by. Suddenly the outcast touched him. Sankara said sharply: 'What! You touched me!' 'Revered sir,' he replied, 'I have not touched you nor have you touched me. Reason me: Are you the body, the mind, or the buddhi? Analyze what you are. You are the Pure Atma (soul), unattached and free, unaffected by the three—*sattva*, *rajas*, and *tamas*.' Do you know what Brahman is like? It is like air. Good and bad smells are carried by the air, but the air itself is unaffected."

Narendra: "Yes, sir."

Sri Ramakrishna advised Narendra in a whisper: "Renunciation is necessary. If one thing is placed upon another, you must remove the one to get the other. Can you get the second thing without removing the first?"

Narendra: "True, sir."

Master again whispered: "When one sees everything filled with God alone, does one see anything else?"

Narendra: "Must one renounce the world?"

Master: "Didn't I say just now: 'When one sees everything filled with God alone, does one see anything else?' Does one then see any such thing as the world? I mean mental renunciation. Not one of those who have come here is a worldly person. Some of them had a slight desire—for instance, a fancy for woman. (Rakhal and M. smiled) And that desire has been fulfilled."

The Master looked at Narendra tenderly and became filled with love. Looking at the devotees, he said: "Grand!"

With a smile Narendra asked the Master: "What is grand?"

Master smiled and said, "I see that preparations are going on for a grand renunciation."

Narendra and the devotees looked silently at the Master. Rakhal resumed the conversation. He said: "Narendra is now beginning to understand you rather well."

Sri Ramakrishna laughed and said: "Yes, that is so. I see that many others, too, are beginning to understand." Then he asked Narendra: "What do you think of me?"

Narendra replied: "You are a hero, a handmade of God, and everything else."

These words filled Sri Ramakrishna with divine emotion. He placed his hand on his heart and is about to say something. He said to Narendra and the other devotees: "I see that all things—everything that exists—have come from this." And then he asked Narendra: "What did you understand?"

Narendra replied: "All created objects have come from you."

The Master's face beamed with joy. He said to Rakhal, "Did you hear what he said?"[68]

Narendranath had just returned from a visit to Bodh-Gaya. Kali and Tarak were also had gone there with him. Narendra had been absorbed in deep meditation before the image of Buddha. He had paid his respect to the Bodhi-tree, which is an offshoot of the original tree under which Buddha attained Nirvana.

It was an evening of Friday, April 9, 1886. Narendra entered the room, when Sri Ramakrishna was seated on his bed. M. was fanning him. Latu came in a little later. Sri Ramakrishna wanted to know about Narendra's visit of Gaya and of Buddha. Narendra said: "He could not express in words what he had realized by his austerities. So people say he was an atheist."

Master: "Why atheist? He was not an atheist. He simply could not express his inner experiences in words. Do you know what 'Buddha' means? It is to become one with Bodha, Pure Intelligence, by meditating on that which is of the nature of Pure Intelligence; it is to become Pure Intelligence Itself."

Narendra: "Yes, sir. There are three classes of Buddhas: Buddha, Arhat, and Bodhisattva."

Master: "This too is a sport of God Himself, a new play of God. Why should Buddha be called an atheist? When one realizes Swarupa, the true nature of one's Self, one attains a state that is something between an *asti*, is and *nasty*, is-not."

Narendra: "It is a state in which contradictions meet. A combination of hydrogen and oxygen cools water, and the same hydrogen and oxygen are used in the oxy-hydrogen blowpipe. In that state both activity and non-activity are possible; that is to say, one then performs unselfish actions. Worldly people, who are engrossed in sense-objects, say that everything exists—*asti*. But the *mayavadis*, the illusionists, say that nothing exists—nasty. The experience of a Buddha is beyond both 'existence' and 'non-existence'."

Master: "This 'existence' and 'non-existence' are attributes of nature. The reality is beyond both." "What did Buddha preach?"

Narendra: "He did not discuss the existence or non-existence of God. But he showed compassion for others all his life. A hawk pounced upon a bird and was about to devour it. In order to save the bird Buddha gave the hawk his own flesh."

Sri Ramakrishna remained silent. Narendra became more and more enthusiastic about Buddha. He said: "How great his renunciation was! Born a prince he renounced everything! If a man has nothing, no wealth at all, what does his renunciation amount to? After attaining Buddhahood and experiencing Nirvana, Buddha once visited his home and exhorted his wife, his son, and many others of the royal household to embrace the life of renunciation. How intense his renunciation was! But look at Vyasa's conduct! He forbade his son Sukdeva to give up the world, saying, 'My son, practice religion as a householder.'"

Sri Ramakrishna was silent; as yet he had not uttered a word.

Narendra: "Buddha did not care for Shakti, or power or any such thing. He sought only Nirvana. Ah, how intense his dispassion was! When he sat down under the Bodhi-tree to meditate, he took this vow: 'Let my body wither away here if I do not attain Nirvana,' Such a firm resolve!"

"This body, indeed, is the great enemy. Can anything be achieved without chastising it?"

Sashi: "But it is you who say that one develops sattva by eating meat. You insist that one should eat meat."

Narendra: "I eat meat, no doubt, but I can also live on rice, mere rice, even without salt."

After a few minutes Sri Ramakrishna broke his silence. He asked Narendra, by a sign, whether he had seen a tuft of hair on Buddha's head.

Narendra: "No, sir. He seems to have a sort of crown; his head seems to be covered by strings of rudraksha beads placed on top of one another."

Master: "And his eyes?"

Narendra: "They show that he is in Samadhi."

Sri Ramakrishna again became silent. Narendra and the other devotees looked at him intently. Suddenly a smile lighted his face and he began to talk with Narendra. M. was fanning him.

Master: "Well, here you find everything—even ordinary red lentils and tamarind. Isn't that so?"

Narendra: "After experiencing all those states, you are now dwelling on a lower plane."

M.: "Yes, after realizing all these ideals, he is now living on a lower plane."

Master: "Someone seems to be holding me to a lower plane."

Saying this, Sri Ramakrishna took the fan from M.'s hand and said: "As I see this fan, directly before me, in exactly the same manner have I seen God. And I have seen—"

With these words he placed his hand on his heart and asked Narendra, by a sign, "Can you tell me what I said?"

Narendra: "I have understood."

Master: "Tell me."

Sri Ramakrishna said again, by a sign, "I have seen that He and the one, who dwells in my heart, is one and the same Person."

Narendra: "Yes, yes! Soham—I am He."

Master: "But only a line divides the two—that I may enjoy divine bliss."

Narendra said to M.: "Great souls, even after their own liberation, retain the ego and experience the pleasure and pain of the body that they may help others to attain liberation. It is like coolie word. We perform coolie work under compulsion, but great souls do so of their own sweet pleasure."

Again all fell into silence. After a time Sri Ramakrishna resumed the conversation.

Master: "The roof is clearly visible; but it is extremely hard to reach it."

Narendra: "Yes, sir."

Master: "But if someone who has already reached it drops down a rope, he can pull another person up. Once, a sadhu from Hrishikesh came to Dakshineswar. He said to me: 'How amazing! I find five kinds of Samadhi manifested in you.'"[69]

Narendranath had been searching for a person who could say to him that he had seen God. More than four years have passed since Narendranath had first met Sri Ramakrishna, who told him that he had seen God, and even he had made him realize the Brahman. Still Narendra had been suffering from his restlessness for the truth. He indeed was searching for his mental peace. But it was not possible till he would realize the truth. He went to Bodh-Gaya, and realized the great renunciation of Buddha. Still he had some questions which were yet to be solved. One thing was clear to him that renunciation was necessary. He didn't care for the job at the Vidyasagar School. He had been thinking of going to Gaya again. He had been told that a zamindar there needed the services of a manager for his estate. He wished to offer himself for the same, only because he would be able to be absorbed in meditation sitting under the Bodhi-tree, whenever there would be an opportunity. He still believed—'There is no such thing as God', and he said the same to M., the recorder of *The Gospel of Sri Ramakrishna*.

M. said to Narendra: "You may say that now, but later on you will talk differently. Scepticism is a stage in the path of God-realization. One must pass through stages like this and go much farther; only thus can one realize God. That is what the Master says."

Narendra: "Has anybody seen God as I see that tree?"

M.: "Yes, our Master has seen God that way."

Narendra: "It may be his hallucination."

M.: "Whatever a person experiences in a particular state is real for him in that state. Suppose you are dreaming that you have gone to a garden. As long as the dream lasts, the garden is real for you. But you think of it as unreal when your mind undergoes a change, as, for instance, when you awake. When your mind attains the state in which one sees God, you will know God to be real."

Narendra: "I want truth. The other day I had a great argument with Sri Ramakrishna himself."

M.: "What happened?"

Narendra: "He said to me, 'Some people call me God.' I replied, 'Let a thousand people call you God, but I shall certainly not call you God as long as I do not know it to be true.' He said, 'Whatever many people say is indeed truth; that is dharma.' Thereupon I replied, 'Let others proclaim a thing as truth, but I shall certainly not listen to them unless I myself realize it as truth.'"

M.: "Your attitude is like that of Western savants—Copernicus and Berkeley, for instance. The whole world said it was the sun that moved, but Copernicus did not listen. Everybody said the external world was real, but Berkeley paid no heed. Therefore, Lewis says, 'Why was Berkeley not a philosophical Copernicus?'"

Narendra: "Can you give me a History of philosophy?"

M.: "By whom? Lewis?"

Narendra: "No, Uberweg. I must read a German author."

M.: "You just said, 'Has anybody seen god as I see that tree?' Suppose God comes to you as a man and says, 'I am God.' Will you believe it then? You certainly remember the story of Lazarus. After his death, Lazarus said to Abraham, 'Let me go back to the earth and tell my friends and relatives that hell and the after-life exist.' Abraham replied: 'Do you think they will believe you? They will say it is a charlatan who is telling them such things.' The Master says that God cannot be known by reasoning. By faith alone one attains everything—knowledge and super-knowledge. By faith alone one sees God and becomes intimate with Him."[70]

In another scene we see Narendranath arguing with Hirananda. It was Thursday, 29th April, 1886; Hirananda came to see Sri Ramakrishna with two of his friends. He was a native of Sindh, about twenty-two hundred miles from Calcutta. After finishing his college education in Calcutta in 1883, he had returned to Sindh and taken charge of editing two papers, the *Sindh Times* and the *Sindh Sudhar*. While studying in Calcutta he had often visited Keshab Chandra Sen and had come to know him intimately. He had met Sri Ramakrishna at the Kali temple at Dakshineswar and had spent an occasional night there with the Master. Hearing of

Sri Ramakrishna's illness, he now came to Calcutta from Sindh to see him. The Master himself had been very eager to see Hirananda.

Sri Ramakrishna pointed to Hirananda and said to M., by signs: "A very fine boy. Do you know him?"

M.: "Yes, sir."

Master requested Hirananda and M. to talk for a little, so that he could hear both of them. When M. remained silent, Sri Ramakrishna asked: "Is Narendra here? Call him."

Narendra entered the room and sat near the Master.

Master said to Narendra and Hirananda: "I want to hear you two talk."

Hirananda was silent a few moments and then after great hesitation began the conversation.

Hirananda: "Why does a devotee of God suffer?"

His words were sweet as nectar. Everyone in the room could feel that his heart was filled with love.

Narendra: "The plan of the universe is devilish. I could have created a better world."

Hirananda: "Can one feel happiness without misery?"

Narendra: "I am not making a plan for a universe, but simply giving my opinion of the present plan. But all these problems are solved if we have faith only in one thing, and that is pantheism. All doubts disappear if one believes that everything is God. God alone is responsible for all that happens."

Hirananda: "Very easy to say that."

Narendra sang Sankara's six stanzas on Nirvana:

Om, I am neither mind, intelligence, ego, nor chitta,
Neither ears not tongue not the senses of smell and sight;
Nor am I ether, earth, fire, water, or air;
I am Pure Knowledge and Bliss; I am Shiva! I am Shiva!

I am neither the prana nor the five vital breaths,
Neither the seven elements of the body not its five sheaths,

Not hands not feet or tongue, or the organs of sex and voiding:
I am Pure Knowledge and Bliss: I am Shiva! I am Shiva!

Neither loathing nor likings have I, neither greed not delusion;
No sense have I of ego or pride, neither dharma nor moksha;

Neither desire of the mind nor object for its desiring:
I am Pure Knowledge and Bliss: I am Shiva! I am Shiva!

Neither right nor wrongdoing am I, neither pleasure not pain,
Nor the mantra, the sacred place, the Vedas, the sacrifice;
Neither the act of eating, the eater, nor the food:
I am Pure Knowledge and Bliss: I am Shiva! I am Shiva!
Death of fear I have none, nor any distinction of caste;
Neither father nor mother nor even a birth have I;
Neither friend nor comrade, neither disciple not guru;
I am Pure Knowledge and Bliss: I am Shiva! I am Shiva!

I have no form or fancy; the All-pervading am I;
Everywhere I exist, yet I am beyond the sense;
Neither salvation am I, nor anything that may be known;
I am Pure Knowledge and Bliss: I am Shiva! I am Shiva!

Hirananda: "Good!"

Sri Ramakrishna said to Hirananda, by a sign: "Give him an answer."

Hirananda: "It is all the same, whether you look at a room from a corner or look at it from the middle. It is the same God-Consciousness that one feels, whether one says. O God, I am Thy servant' or, 'I am He' One may enter a room by several doors."

All sat in silence. Hirananda said to Narendra, 'Please sing some more."

Narendra sang the Five Stanza on the Kaupina (the loin-cloth of the ascetics);

Roaming ever in the grove of Vedanta,
Ever pleased with his beggar's morsel,
Ever walking with heart free from sorrow,
Blest indeed is the wearer of the loin-cloth.
Sitting at the foot of a tree for shelter,
Using the palms of his hands for eating,
Wrapped in a garment fine or ugly,
Blest indeed is the wearer of the loin-cloth.
Satisfied fully by the Bliss within him,
Curbing wholly the cravings of his senses,
Contemplating day and night the Absolute Brahman,
Blest indeed is the wearer of the loin-cloth.

As Sri Ramakrishna heard the line, 'Contemplating day and night the Absolute Brahman', he said in a very low voice, "Ah!" Then, by a sign, he said to the devotees, "This is the characteristic of the Yogi."

Narendra finished the hymn:

Witnessing the change of mind and body,
Naught but the Self within him beholding.
Thinking not of outer, of inner, or of middle,
Blest indeed is the wearer of the lion-cloth.
Chanting "Brahman", the World of redemption,
Meditating only on "I am Brahman",
Living on alms and wandering freely,
Blest indeed is the wearer of the loin-cloth.

Again Narendra sang:

Meditate on Him, the Perfect, the Embodiment of Bliss;

Meditate on Him, the formless, the Root of the Universe,

The hearer behind the ear, the Thinker behind the mind.

The Speaker behind the tongue, Himself beyond all words;

He is the Life of life, the Ultimate, the Adorable! Master said to Narendra: "And that one—'All that exists are Thou.'"

Narendra Sang:

I have joined my heart to Thee: all that exists art Thou;
Thee only have I found, for Thou art all that exists.
O Lord, Beloved of my heart! Thou art the Home of all;
Where indeed is the heart in which Thou dost not dwell?
Thou hast entered every heart: all that exists art Thou.
Whether sage or fool, whether Hindu or Mussalman,
Thou makest them as Thou wilt: all that exists art Thou.
Thy presence is everywhere, whether in heaven or in Kaaba;
Before Thee all must bow, Thou art all that exists.
From earth below to the highest heaven, from heaven to deepest earth,
I see Thee wherever I look: all that exists art Thou.
Pondering, I have understood; I have seen it beyond a doubt;
I find not a single thing that may be compared to Thee,
To Jafar it has been revealed that Thou art all that exists.

As the Master listened to the line—"Thou hast entered every heart", he said by a sign: "God dwells in everybody's heart. He is the Inner Guide."

As Narendra sang the line, "I see Thee wherever I look: all that exists art Thou", Hirananda said to him: "Yes, 'All that exists art Thou'. Now you say: 'Thou! Thou! Not I, but Thou!'"

Narendra: "Give me a one and I'll give you a million. Thou art I; I am Thou. Nothing exists but I."

Narendra recited a few verses from the Ashtavakra Samhita. The room again became silent.

Master said to Hirananda pointing to Narendra: "He seems to be walking with an unsheathed sword in his hand." Then pointing to Hirananda the Master said: "How quiet! Like a cobra, quiet before the charmer, with its hood spread."[71]

Narendranath, in his later life, became a monk and a celibate by his own choice. When he was born, his father had a horoscope taken of his life, but would never tell him what it was. After his father's death, he came across the chart among some papers in his mother's possession and saw from it that he was destined to become a wanderer on the face of the earth.

He had a deep interest in religion and philosophy from his childhood, and was taught renunciation as the highest ideal to which man can aspire. He only needed the meeting with a great teacher—Sri Ramakrishna Paramhamsa—to kindle in him the final determination to follow the path he himself had trod, as in him he found his highest ideal realized.

Who is Sri Ramakrishna? What did he learn from him? What did he realize? Why did he accept Sri Ramakrishna as his teacher? What conclusion he came to? From our previous discussion we have already got some answers of these questions. Now, for the rest, we would like to listen to Narendranath and directly would learn from him. He said:

> "I happened to get an old man to teach me, and he was very peculiar. He did not go much for intellectual scholarship, scarcely studied books; but when he was a boy he was seized with the tremendous idea of getting truth direct. First he tried by studying his own religion. Then he got the idea that he must get the truth of other religions; and with that idea he joined all the sects, one after another. For the time being he did exactly what they told him to do—lived with the devotees of these different sects in turn, until interpenetrated with the particular ideal of that sect. After a few years he would go to

> another sect. When he had gone through with all that, he came to the conclusion that they were all good. He had no criticism to offer to any one; they are all so many paths leading to the same goal. And then he said, "That is a glorious thing, that there should be so many paths, because if there were only one path, perhaps it would suit only an individual man. The more the number of paths, the more the chance is for every one of us to know the truth. If I cannot be taught in one language, I will try another", and so on. Thus his benediction was for every religion.

"People came by thousands to see this wonderful man who spoke in a patois, every word of which was forceful and instinct with light.... I hear of this man, and I went to hear him.

"I sat and watched him. There was nothing wrong in his words, movements or behaviour towards others. Rather, from his spiritual words and ecstatic states he seemed to be a man of genuine renunciation; and there was a marked consistency between his words and life. He used the most simple language, and I thought, "Can this man be a great teacher?" I crept near him and asked him the question which I had asked so often: "Have you seen God, sir?" "Yes, I see Him just as I see you here, only in a much intense sense." "God can be realized," he went on; "One can see and talk to Him as I am seeing and talking to you. But who cares? People shed torrents of tears for their wife and children, for wealth or property, but who does so for the sake of God? If one weeps sincerely for Him, He surely manifests Himself." That impressed me at once. For the first time I found a man who dared to say that he had seen God, that religion was a reality to be felt, to be sensed in an infinitely more intense way than we can sense the world. As I heard these things from his lops, I could not but believe that he was saying them not like an ordinary preacher, but from the depths of his own realizations. But I could not reconcile his words with his strange conduct with me. So I concluded that he must be a monomaniac. Yet I could not help acknowledging the magnitude of his renunciation. "He may be a mad man," I thought, "but only the fortunate few can have such renunciation. Even if insane, this man is the holiest of the holy, a true saint, and for that alone he deserves the reverent homage of mankind!" With such conflicting thoughts I bowed before him."[72]

Sri Ramakrishna loved Narendranath very much, and always thought of him. He used to wait for his arrival. In connection with this situation Swamiji said:

> Seeing that the Master gave me no thought to himself on account of me, I did not hesitate on occasion to use harsh words about his blind love for me. I used to warn him, saying that if he constantly thought of me, he would become like me, even as King Bharata of the old legend, who so doted upon to think of anything else, and as a result, was born as a deer in his next life. At these words, the Master, so simple was he, became very nervous, and said, "What you say is quite true. What is to become of me, for I cannot bear to be separated from you?" Dejected, he went to Kali temple. In a few minutes he returned smiling and said, "You rogue, I shall not listen to you anymore. Mother says that I love you because I see the Lord in you, and the day I no longer do so, I shall not be able to bear even the sight of you." With this short but emphatic statement he dismissed once for all everything that I had ever said to him on the subject.

"One day he said to me, "You can see Krishna in your heart if you want." I replied, "I don't believe in Krishna or any such nonsense!"

"Once I said to him, "The forms of God and things like that, which you see in your visions, are all figments of your imagination." He had so much faith in my words that he went to the

Divine Mother in the temple and told Her what I had said to him. He asked Her, "Are these hallucinations, then?" Afterwards he said to me, "Mother told me that all these are real..."

"Again, he said to me, when you sing, He who dwells here (touching his heart), like a snake, hisses as it were, and then, spreading his hood, quietly holds himself steady and listen to your music.

"We [Sri Ramakrishna and I] talked of our revealed book, the Vedas, of your Bible, of the Koran, and of revealed books in general. At the close of our talk, this good man asked me to go to the table and take up a book; it was book which, among other things, contained a forecast of the rainfall during the year. The sage said, "Read that." And I read out the quantity of rain that was to fall. He said, "Now take the book and squeeze it." I did so and he said, "Why, my boy, not a drop of water comes out. Until the water comes out, it is all book, book. So until your religion makes you realize God, it is useless. He who only studies books for religion reminds one of the fables of the ass which carried a heavy load of sugar on its back, but did not know the sweetness of it."

"I did not believe in anything... At first I did not accept most of what the Master said. One day he asked me, "Then why do you come here?" I replied, "I come here to see you, not to listen to you"... He was very much pleased.

"I used to follow my own whims in everything I did. The Master never interfered.... I became a member of the Sadharan Brahmo Samaj.... The Master knew that women attended the meetings of the Brahmo Samaj. A man cannot meditate with women sitting in front of him; therefore he criticized the meditation of the Brahmo Samaj. But he didn't object to my going there. But one day he said to me, "Don't tell Rakhal about your being a member of the Brahmo Samaj, or he too will feel like becoming one."

"When I found that the Master did not bestow that kind of grace on [my friend] which he had done on me by accepting me and instructing me in spiritual matters, I used to press him to bestow it also on them too. On account of boyish flippancy I was ready on many occasions to argue with him on this point. I said, "Why, Sir? God can never be so partial as to bestow His grace on some and not on others. Why should you then not accept them as you have done me? Is it not certain that one can attain spiritual realization by one's effort forth sufficient effort?" The Master replied, "What can I do, my child? Mother shows me that there is the beastly mental attitude of a bull in them. They cannot realize spirituality in this life. What can I do? And what is it you say? Can anyone become in this life what he wishes to be, by mere will and effort?" But, who lent an ear to the Master's word then? I said, "What do you say sir? Can't one become what one wishes to be, if one wills and makes an effort? Surely one can. I cannot believe what you say about it." At this also the Master said the same thing, "Whether you believe it or not, Mother shows me that." I never accepted then what he said. But, as time passed on, more and more did I understand from experience that What the Master said was right and what I had thought was wrong.

"For the first time I had found a man who dared to say that he saw God, that religion was a reality to be felt, to be sensed in an infinitely more intense way than we can sense the world. I began to go to that man, day after day, and I actually saw that religion could be given. One touch, one glance, can change a whole life. I had read about Buddha and Christ and Mohammed, about all those different luminaries of ancient times, how they would stand up and say, "Be thou whole," and the man became whole. I now found it to be true, and when I myself saw this man, all scepticism was brushed aside. It could be done; and my Master used to say, "Religion can be given and taken more tangibly, more really than anything else in the world...."

"The second idea that I learnt from my Master, and which is perhaps the most vital, is the wonderful truth that the religions of the world are not contradictory or antagonistic. They are but various phases of one eternal religion. That one eternal religion is applied to different planes of existence, is applied to the opinions of various minds and various races.

"Devotion as taught by Narada, he used to preach to the masses, those who were incapable of any higher training. He used generally to teach dualism. As a rule, he never taught Advaitism. But he taught it to me. I had been a dualist before.

"Sri Ramakrishna once told me that not one in twenty millions in the world believed in God. I asked him why, and he told me, "Suppose there is a thief in this room, and he gets to know that there is a mass of gold in the next room, and only a very thin partition between the two rooms; what will be the condition of that thief?" I answered, "He will not be able to sleep at all; his brain will be actively thinking of some means of getting at the gold, and he will think of nothing else." Then he replied, "Do you believe that a man could believe in God and not go mad to get Him? If a man sincerely believes that there is that immense, infinite mine of bliss, and that it can be reached, would not that man go mad in his struggle to reach it?"

"Shortly after meeting the Master, I might not have gained anything else by this practice of religion; but it is certain that I have gained control over my terrible anger by his grace. Formerly I used to loss all control over myself in rage and be seized with repentance afterwards. But now if anyone does me a great harm or even beats me severely, I don't become so very angry.

"One day, during one of my early visits, the Master in an ecstatic mood said to me, "You have come!" "How amazing!" I said to myself. "It is as if he had known me a long time." Then he said to me, "Do you ever see light?" I replied, "Yes, sir. Before I fall asleep I feel something like a light revolving near my forehead."

"When he heard that a proposal had been made about my marriage, he wept, holding the feet of the image of Kali. With tear in his eyes he prayed to the Divine Mother, "O Mother, please upset the whole thing! Don't let Narendra be drowned."

"It is impossible to give others any idea of the ineffable joy we derived from the presence of the Master. It is really beyond our understanding how he could train us, without our knowledge it, through fun and play, and thus mould our spiritual life. As the master wrestler proceeds with great caution and restraint with the beginner, now overpowering him in the struggle with great difficulty as it were, again allowing himself to be defeated to strengthen the pupil's self-confidence—in exactly the same manner did Sri Ramakrishna handle us. Realizing that the Atman, the source of infinite strength, exists in every individual, pigmy though he might be, he was able to see the potential giant in all. He could clearly discern the latent spiritual power which would in the fullness of time manifest itself. Holding up that bright picture to view, he would speak highly of us and encourage us. Again he would warn us lest we should obstruct this future consummation by becoming entangled in worldly desires, and moreover, he would keep us under control by carefully observing even the minute details of our life. All this was done silently and unobtrusively. That was the secret of his training of the disciples and of his moulding of their lives."[73]

Swamiji said about the greatness of the Panchavati, and its significant role in his life:

> The solitude of the Panchavati, associated with the various spiritual realizations of the Master, was also the most suitable place for our meditation. Besides meditation and

> spiritual exercises, we used to spend a good deal of time there in sheer fun and merry-making. Sri Ramakrishna also joined in with us, and by taking part enhanced our innocent pleasure. We used to run and skip about, climb on the trees, swing from the creepers, and at times hold merry picnics. On the first day that we picnicked the Master noticed that I myself had cooked the food, and he partook of it. I knew that he could not take food unless it was cooked by Brahmins, and therefore I had arranged for his meal at the Kali temple. But he said, 'It won't be wrong for me to take food from such a pure soul as yourself.' In spite of my repeated remonstrations, he enjoyed the food I had cooked that day.[74]

Finally, he had expressed the secret of his change under the association of Sri Ramakrishna:

> How I used to hate Kali and all Her ways! That was the ground of my six years' fight—that I would not accept Her. But I had to accept Her at last. Ramakrishna Paramahamsa dedicated me to Her, and now I believe that She guides me in every little thing I do, and does with me what She will!... Yet I fought so long! I loved him, you see, and that was what held me. I saw his marvelous purity... I felt his wonderful love... His greatness had dawned on me then. All that came afterwards, when I had given in. At that time I thought him a brain-sick baby, always seeing visions and the rest. I hated it. And then I too had to accept Her! No, the thing that made me so it is a secret that will die with me. I had great misfortunes at that time... It was an opportunity... She made a slave of me. Those were the very words—"a slave of you." And Ramakrishna Paramahamsa made me over to Her... Strange! He lived only two years after doing that, and most of the time he was suffering. Not more than six months did he keep his own health and brightness.
>
> Let none regret that they were difficult to convince! I fought my Master for six years with the result that I knew every inch of the way! Every inch of the way.[75]

Swamiji had experienced the Nirvikalpa Samadhi at Cossipore. He sat for meditation at ground floor, while Sri Ramakrishna was in his room upstairs. He couldn't feel that he had a body. He could see only his face. He was weeping, saying: "What has happened to me? Where is my body? Where are my limbs?" The elder Gopal saw that, and went to the Master's room and said, "Narendra is crying. He cannot feel his body." After a while he regained his sense and slowly went to the Master's room. The Master said to him, "Now you have known, But I am going to keep the key with me." Narendranath said: "What is it that happened to me?" Turning to the devotees, Sri Ramakrishna said, "He will not keep his body if he knows who he is. But I have put a veil over his eyes." In connection with this incident he said:

> One day in the Cossipore garden, I had expressed my prayer to Sri Ramakrishna with great earnestness. Then in the evening, at the hour of meditation, I lost the consciousness of the body, and felt that it was absolutely non-existent. I felt that the sun, moon, space, time, ether, and all had been reduced to a homogeneous mass and then melted far away into the unknown; the body-consciousness had almost vanished, and I had nearly merged in the Supreme. But I had just a trace of the feeling of ego, so I could again return to the world of relativity from the Samadhi. In this state of Samadhi all the difference between 'I' and 'Brahman' goes away; everything is reduced into unity, like the water of the infinite ocean—water everywhere, nothing else exists—language and thought, all fail there. Then only is the state 'beyond mind and speech' realized in its actuality...
>
> After that experience, even after trying repeatedly, I failed to bring back the state of Samadhi. On informing Sri Ramakrishna about it, he said, "If you remain day and

> night in that state, the work of the Divine Mother will not be accomplished; therefore you won't be able to induce that state again; when your work is finished, it will come again".... Sri Ramakrishna used to say that the Avataras (Incarnations of God) alone can descend to the ordinary plane from that state of Samadhi, for the good of the world. Ordinary Jivas (persons) do not; immersed in that state, they remain alive for a period of twenty-one days; after that, their body drops like a sere leaf from the tree of Samsara (world).[76]

After this incident he realized:

> All philosophy and scriptures have come from the plane of relative knowledge of subject and object. But no thought or language of the human mind can fully express the Reality which lies beyond the plane of relative knowledge! Science, philosophy, etc. are only partial truths. So they can never be adequate channels of expression for the transcendent Reality. Hence viewed from the transcendent standpoint, everything appears to be unreal—religious creeds, and works, I and thou, and the universe—everything is unreal! Then only it is perceived: "I am the only reality; I am the all-pervading Atman (Soul), and I am the proof of my own existence." Where is the room for a separate proof to establish the reality of my existence? I am, as the scriptures say, "*Nityam asmat prasiddham*—always known to myself as the eternal subject." I have seen that state, realized it.[77]

At Cossipore, Sri Ramakrishna transmitted his power to Narendranath. One day, while Swamiji was meditating, he asked Kali [Swami Abhedananda] to hold his hand. Kali said to him, "When I touched your body I felt something like an electric shock coming to my body."

One day Sri Ramakrishna wrote on a piece of paper, "Naren will teach people." But Narendranath said to him, "I won't do any such thing." Thereupon he said, "Your very bones will do it."

We, hereby, would like to conclude the chapter of Narendranath, the first phase of Swami Vivekananda's life. Hereafter we will see how Narendranath did his duties following his Master's command and how he became Swami Vivekananda, the great educator of the world. Before that we must bow down our head at the holy feet of Narendranath, the great disciple of Sri Ramakrishna Paramahamsa.

Sri Ramakrishna (1836-1886)

The Dakshineshwar Temple (founded 1855): Sri Ramakrishna lived and taught here

5
The Baranagore Math

When Sri Ramakrishna fell ill, his devotees requested him to concentrate his mind on the diseased part of the body, so that it would heal. Sri Ramakrishna replied: "What! Bring down the mind that I've given to God to this little body!" He refused to think of body and illness. His mind was dedicated to God.

Towards the end of July, Sri Ramakrishna's health became worse, his throat had become so much affected with cancer that he could speak only in a whisper, or else he would communicate by signs. The disciples were very sad; their grief knew no bound. They were afraid of being orphan. There was no one on the earth, who could love them so much, as their Master loved them.

Narendranath in his later life used to say: "I have not yet found anyone more refined than my Master. His manner of walking, talking, resting, sitting, seeing to the arrangement of things in his room, his practical common sense—all were beautiful and perfect."

In a letter to Mrs. Bull on 23rd May, 1897, J.J. Goodwin wrote:

> When Paramahamsa was passing away he called his disciples but Swamiji [Naren] and gave them an express command that they were always to pay every attention to Swamiji, and never to leave anything undone that could add to his health or comfort. Then sending them out and calling in Swamiji [Naren] he committed all his other disciples into his change.[1]

Let us hear Swamiji what he said:

> Two or three days before Sri Ramakrishna's passing away, She whom he used to call 'Kali' entered this body. It is She who takes me here and there and makes me work, without letting me remain quiet or allowing me to look to my personal comforts. Two or three days before his leaving the body, he called me to his side one day, and asking me to sit before him, looked steadfastly at me and fell into Samadhi. Then I really felt that a subtle force like an electric shock was entering my body! In a little while, I also lost outward consciousness and sat motionless. How long I stayed in that condition I do not remember; when consciousness returned I found Sri Ramakrishna shedding tears. On questioning him, he answered me affectionately, 'Today, giving you my all, I have become a beggar. With this power you are to do many works for the world's good before you will return.' I feel that power is constantly directing me to this or that work. This body has not been made for remaining idle.[2]

One day while Sri Ramakrishna was staying at the Cossipore Garden, his body in imminent danger of falling off for ever, by the side of his bed Narendranath was saying in his mind, "Well, now if you can declare that you are God, then only will I believe you are really God Himself. It was only two days before Sri Ramakrishna passed away. Immediately, he looked up towards

Narendra all of a sudden and said, "He who was Rama, He who was Krishna, verily is He now Ramakrishna in this body. And that not merely from the standpoint of your Vedanta!"

Regarding the incident Swamiji said: "At this I was struck dumb. Even we haven't had yet the perfect faith, after hearing it again and again from the holy lips of our Lord himself—our minds still get disturbed now and then with doubt and despair—and so, what shall we speak of others being slow to believe? It is indeed a very difficult matter to be able to declare and believe a man with a body like ours to be God Himself. We may just go to the length of declaring him to be a 'perfected one', or a 'knower of Brahman'. Well, it matters nothing, whatever you may call him or think of him, a saint, or a knower of Brahman, or anything. But take it from me, never did come to this earth such an all-perfect man as Sri Ramakrishna. In the utter darkness of the world, this great man is like the shining pillar of illumination in this age. And by his light alone will man now cross the ocean of Samsara."[3]

The last two days were very critical for the disciples. They tried hard to control their mourning as they felt that any time their Master would leave his worldly body leaving them behind alone. Only few days ago, Sri Ramakrishna had asked a disciple to read out from the almanac the days of Bengali calendar. When the disciple had reached the end of Sharavan, which fell on August 15, Sri Ramakrishna had asked him to stop. Now, on the evening of August 15, when Dr. Navin Pal came to see him, the Master said, "Today my suffering has become too intense. No medicine is proving of any use. The disease has become incurable." The doctor said, "Yes." The Master said, "I feel like eating barrels full of rice and dal [lentils]." The physician couldn't reply anything. He was hopeless. A little before dusk Sri Ramakrishna complained of difficulty in breathing. Suddenly he entered into Samadhi, which was of rather an unusual kind. Narendranath asked the disciples to chant 'Hari Om Tat Sat'. The chanting continued for a long time. After midnight, Sri Ramakrishna came back to his consciousness and said that he was hungry. He ate a small quantity of porridge and seemed better. Five or six pillows were placed at his back so that he could remain half seated. Leaning against those pillows he talked for a long time with Naren, and gave him his last counsel in a very low voice. Then he uttered the name of Kali three times. He lay back gently on the bed. Suddenly, at two minutes past one that night [August 16], a thrill passed through the Master's body, the hair stood on end, the eyes became fixed on the tip of the nose, a divine smile lit up the face, and the Master again entered into Samadhi.

The disciples had been waiting for his returning to normal consciousness as usual. Narendranath was chanting 'Hari Om Tat Sat' in a loud voice, and the other devotees joined him. The chanting continued throughout the night, but there was no sign of the Master's regaining of physical consciousness. Shashi rubbed the backbone of the Master, but it proved useless. Ramlal, the Master's nephew, was informed, and he came early morning. He examined the Master, and said, "The top of the head is still warm. You better send for the Captain Vishwanath Upadhyay [a devotee of the Master]." The Captain came promptly in the morning. He found that the Master's body was stiff, that the hair all over it was standing on end, and that his eyes were fixed on the tip of his nose but the backbone was still warm. He asked them to apply cow ghee all over the body and to call Dr. Mahendralal Sarkar. The doctor came and, after examination, declared that the Master had left his body. The trance into which he had entered on the previous night thus proved to have been Mahasamadhi, from which there was no return.

When the Holy Mother came upstairs to the bedside of Sri Ramakrishna, she burst into cry, "O Mother Kali! Where have you gone?" The disciples, who witnessed it, could never forget this scene, as it was printed for ever on their memories. They all were overwhelmed in grief. After a while the Mother was helped back to her room downstairs. That evening, when she was removing her ornaments and the other signs of a married woman from her person, as is the custom of the Hindu widow, the Master appeared before him and said: "Where have I gone? I am just here. It is like passing from one room to another." On two subsequent occasions, when the Holy Mother tried to take away her ornaments, Sri Ramakrishna caught hold her hands and forbade her to do so. That's why to the last day of her life she was seen with bracelets on her wrists and a sari with a red border.

Swamiji said, "Those who have seen Sri Ramakrishna are really blessed. Their family and birth have become purified by it.... Nobody has been able to understand who came on earth as Sri Ramakrishna. Even his own nearest devotees have got no real clue to it. Only some have got a little inkling of it. All will understand it afterwards."

He also added:

> Without studying Ramakrishna Paramahamsa first, one can never understand the real import of Vedas, the Vedanta, of the Bhagavata and the other Puranas. His life is a searchlight of infinite power thrown upon the whole mass of Indian religious thought. He was the living commentary to the Vedas and to their aim. He had lived in one life the whole cycle of the national religious existence in India....
>
> Life of Sri Ramakrishna was an extraordinary searchlight under whose illumination one is able to really understand the whole scope of Hindu religion. He was the object-lesson of all the theoretical knowledge given in the Shastras. He showed by his life what the Rishis and Avatars really wanted to teach. The books were theories, he was the realization. This man had in fifty-one years lived the five thousand years of national spiritual life and so raised himself to be an object-lesson for future generations. The Vedas can only be explained and the Shastras reconciled by his theory of Avastha or stages—that we must not only tolerate others, but positively embrace them, and that truth is the basis of all religions.... He had a whole world of knowledge to teach.
>
> The more of such men any country produces, the higher is that country raised. That land where no such men exist, is doomed. Nothing can save it. Therefore my Master's message to the world is, "Be ye all spiritual Get ye first realization!" And to the young and strong of every country he would cry that the time is come for renunciation. Renounce for the sake of humanity! You have talked of the love of man till the thing is in danger of becoming words alone. The time is come to act. The call now is, Do! Leap into the breach and save the world.[4]

That morning (August 16) the news flashed through the air, and the devotees lived in distant places came to know—Sri Ramakrishna had passed away. They assembled at the garden-house of Cossipore. The Master's body was decorated with flowers and garlands, and the devotees sang devotional songs. About five in the afternoon a procession was formed and moved towards the Cossipore crematorium on the bank of the Ganges, a little distance away. Some were holding flags, others the signs of various religious, such as Om, the Cross, the Crescent, and so on. At the cremation ground the Master's body was bathed with the water of Ganges, clad a new ochre clothes, and worshipped again with flowers and garlands. The body was tenderly laid on the pyre prepared for it. The pyre was lighted; clarified butter and incense were poured on it; and in a couple of hours everything was finished.

The ashes and other remains of the body were collected and put into an urn. When the devotees were entering the garden-house with the urn, they all shouted, 'Jai Sri Ramakrishna'—'Glory to Sri Ramakrishna!' The urn was placed on the Master's bed in the room upstairs. The disciples spent the night in discussing the holy life of Sri Ramakrishna, and meditation.

Now, where the ashes should be kept?—Soon after the next day a controversy arose with this question between the young disciples and the householder devotees. Finally with the mediation of Narendranath it was decided to keep a part of the ashes at Kankurgachi, and the other part at Balaram's house at Baghbazar. Few days later the ashes were taken from Baghbazar and kept at Baranagore Math. After 14 years, Swamiji brought the urn to Belur Math, and celebrated a festival on this occasion.

When Sri Ramakrishna was living at Cossipore, Narendranath was accepted as the leader of the young disciples, and an association was formed in the name of the Master. It was rather called '*Sri Ramakrishna Sangha*'. Narendranath indeed began to live his ascetic life since then. The '*Sri Ramakrishna Sangha*' was formed with the young disciples, and among them some remarkable members were: Swami Brahmananda [Rakhal Maharaj], Saradananda [Sarat Maharaj], Ramakrishnananda [Sashi Maharaj], Akhandananda [Gangadhar Maharaj], Abhedananda [Kali Maharaj], Advaitananda [old Gopal], Gopal Ghosh [Hootko Gopal], Trigunatitananda [Sarada Maharaj], Jogananda [Jogen Maharaj], Shivananda [Tarak Maharaj], and so on.

Sri Ramakrishna passed away on 16th August, 1886. The rent for Cossipore garden-house was paid till 31st August. So, at the end of month they had to leave the garden-house. All young disciples wished to continue staying there and to pass their time in spiritual practices and the worship of the Master's relics. But there was no one to pay the rent. It was decided that the urn and some materials used by the Master would be kept at Kankurgachi. Rambabu and others, who used to pay the rent of the Cossipore garden-house, said to the young disciples, "You should go back to your own house." Rambabu also said that the holy ashes would be interred and worshiped at his retreat at Kankurgachi, a suburb of Calcutta. Narendranath and other young disciples were sorry to hear this. They wanted to build a place for the relics on the bank of the Ganges, as the Master had wished.

We have already told about the controversy over the urn. It was somewhat like this: "A controversy arose, but it was then agreed that the ashes would be kept at the Cossipore garden-house until a place had been built on the bank of the Ganges. But this proposal had to be dropped for lack of money. The householders headed by Ramachandra Dutta, Devendranath Mazumdar and Nityagopal then demanded the ashes in order to bury them at Kankurgachi."

However, the young disciples refused to hand them the relics, and the dispute took a serious turn. Shashi and Niranjan had declared themselves guardians of the relics. They were giants, the one in resolution, and the other in appearance; and they were determined not to give the ashes to the householders. Narendranath didn't say anything; he was watching the situation silently. When the situation became worse, Narendranath came forward, and appealed to the young disciples: "Brothers, be reasonable! We should not quarrel like this; otherwise people will think that the disciples of Sri Ramakrishna fought over his relics. Moreover it is not certain where we shall be staying. Let them have the ashes. After all, Rambabu is going to dedicate the retreat in the name of Sri Ramakrishna. Is it not good? We can very well go there and worship the Master. Let us mould our lives according to our Master's teachings. If we are true to his ideals, if we live up to them, we shall have done more than merely worship the relics."

But the young disciples decided that the householder should not be given all of the Master's relics. Then with the permission of Narendranath, they took aside more than half of the ashes and put them in another pot. They made the pot sealed and sent to Balarambabu's house where they would be able to worship regularly. Householder devotees were not told about this. Finally everyone agreed to Rambabu's proposal to install the ashes at Kankurgachi, and the 23rd August, as it was the birthday of Sri Krishna, was fixed for the ceremony. Narendranath also joined the ceremony. Later a temple was built on the spot, where the urn was buried down, and came to be known as the Yogodyana. The place was acquired in 1943 by the Ramakrishna Math, Belur, and recognized as a branch centre.

During this period, Latu, Tarak and Senior Gopal stayed at the Cossipore garden-house, while the other young disciples went their homes. But they and the householder devotees used to come to the garden-house, and spend their time in meditation, singing devotional songs, and discussing on the life of Sri Ramakrishna. Narendranath thrilled them by recounting the incidents in the Master's life, and his teachings.

During this week Narendranath has a vision of Sri Ramakrishna, which he could never forget. He and a brother disciple named Harish were one evening standing near the pond of the garden-house, talking about the loss of the beloved Master. It was about eight o'clock. Suddenly, Narendranath saw a luminous figure covered with a cloth, coming towards them. Who was that? Could it be the Master? He kept quiet, fearing that he was the victim of a hallucination. When he heard his companion say in a whisper, "What is that? Naren, look! Look!" Narendranath called out loudly, "Who is there?" Hearing his voice other disciples rushed to him. But they were too late. The apparition came to a thick Jasmine bush within ten yards where they were standing, and it vanished. Lanterns were brought, and every corner of the garden was searched, but nothing could be found. The vision left a deep impression on Narendranath.

Balaram Bose had taken the Holy Mother with him to his house at Baghbazar, on 21st August. He also arranged for her pilgrimage to Vrindavan. Kali Maharaj, Latu Maharaj, Yogen Maharaj and some women devotees also went with the Holy Mother on 30th August. Tarak Maharaj joined them later. The Holy Mother took the urn containing the young disciples' share of the Master's ashes with her. She used to worship it daily, and felt the presence of the Master. Portions of the relics were sent to Hardwar and other sacred places to be consigned to the Ganges according to Hindu custom. A year later, when she returned to Calcutta, she handed over the urn of relics to Narendranath.

Before leaving the Cossipore garden-house, the Master's relics, his bedding, clothing, furniture, and utensils had been taken to Balarambabu's house. To this day they are devotedly preserved by the monks of the Order at the Belur Math.

By the end of August, Cossipore garden-house was vacated. Some of the young disciples had left for Vrindavan, and others went back to home and resumed their college studies. The Master had already made them monks, and had entrusted them to follow Narendranath. Narendranath was determined that they should lead the life of renunciation; but the householder devotees discouraged them from doing so. Now the question arose—what would be the future of them? Most of the householder devotees said, "How will they get on? We cannot allow them to wander about like ordinary monks. They are still boys, with a bright prospect before them. So, let them go back their homes. It is better for them and for their relatives." Some of them prepared for their B.A. examination. Their guardians said, "They should at least complete their study before going to be a monk. It will help them leading a prestigious life." Thus the young disciples were influenced to return their home.

Swamiji recalled: "Then came the sad day when our old teacher died. We nursed him the best we could. We had no friends. Who would listen to a few boys, with their cranks notions? Nobody, at least, in India, boys are nobodies. Just think of it—a dozen boys, telling people vast, big ideas, saying they are determined to work these ideas out in life. Why, everybody laughed. From laughter it became serious; it became persecution. Why, the parents of the boys came to feel like spanking every one of us. And the more we were derided, the more determined we became."[5]

Some of the parents were against the ideal of renunciation not only for that the boys were too young to do so, but also for they thought that it was not supported by the ideal of Sri Ramakrishna. Their point of view was: "Sri Ramakrishna didn't say to renounce the world; rather he advised that it is more safety to stay in a family and fight against the lust of sex, anger and so on; family is like a fort. He had advised to renounce the world mentally." Some of the householders had the view that they should realize God first, and then take up preaching and other works of service. But Narendranath held that the monks should serve mankind in a spirit of worship for the purification of their hearts, and that this would ultimately lead to the realization of God. In all these controversies, there were some householders who were in favour of Narendranath and other young disciples. They came forward to help them at their best.

Later, in 1895, remembering these critical days, Swamiji wrote to Swami Brahmananda: "Rakhal, you remember, I suppose, how, after the Master's passing away, all forsook us as so many worthless, ragged boys. Only people like Balaram, Suresh [Surendra Mitra], Master [Mahendra] and Chunibabu were our friends in that hour of need. And we shall never be able to repay our debts to them."[6]

When the young disciples found no support from anybody, there was a woman—Sri Sarada Devi, the Holy Mother with them. She understood the situation, and always bestowed Her Blissful hand on the boys—her sons. The Holy Mother prayed to Sri Ramakrishna: "O Lord, You came in human form, played with the devotees, and went away! Should everything end with that? What then was the need to come and undergo so much suffering? I cannot any more bear to see my children, who have given up everything for your sake, going from door to door for food. I pray that those who renounce the world in your name may never be in need of at least coarse food and clothing. They will have together, taking your name and holding to your ideas and ideals; and people afflicted with the suffering of the world will resort to them and get relief by hearing your teachings from them. Was this not what you really came for? I am greatly pained at heart to see them wandering about like this!"

Although the devotees believed that Sri Ramakrishna had come for the regeneration of mankind, and he was the usher of a new age, very few could realize the originality of his message. Very few had understood that this religion for the modern age preached by the Master, though based on the eternal religion of the Vedas, was by no means a repetition or imitation of that religion. They couldn't feel that it would give rise to a new force for the unification of mankind as a whole. Of those few who had understood this, Narendranath was the leader; and they were ready to sacrifice their lives or their vision.

The young disciples were crying for help in this critical time, and became disheartened. But it was unknown to them, that Sri Ramakrishna was making arrangements for the fulfillment of their aspiration. One day, when Surendranath Mitra, the devotee of the Master, who used to bear a part of the expenses at the Cossipore garden-house, returned home from his office and sat for meditation in his shrine, Sri Ramakrishna appeared before him and said: "Oh! What are you doing? My children are wandering in the streets. Look at their sad plight! Make some arrangement for them without delay." Hearing this command of the Master, Surendranath immediately rushed to Narendra's house, and with tearful eyes told him everything that happened. He said: "Brother, where will you go? Let us rent a house. You will live there and make it our Master's shrine; and we householders shall come there for consolation. How can we pass all our days and nights with our wives and children in the world? I used to spend a sum of money for the Master at Cossipore. I shall gladly give it now for your expenses."[7]

Narendranath was overwhelmed with emotion on hearing this. He started out in search of a house, and wrote to Taraknath to be ready to come immediately after receiving the telegram, and take charge of the new Math. Taraknath [Swami Shivananda] accordingly came to Varanasi from Vrindavan, and waited for the next instruction from Narendranath.

After an utmost search by Narendranath and Bhavanath, a house was found at Baranagore, midway between Dakshineswar and Calcutta. The owner of the house was Bhuvan Dutta. It was an old two storied building in a dreary, deserted place, badly in need of repairs, and with reputation of being haunted. The ground floor was engrossed into the land, and it was the resort of snakes, lizards and foxes. Most of the steps of staircase were broken. Floor was badly damaged. The veranda which ran along the front of the upper storey showed signs of decay. The main room where the monks were to live was in a most dilapidated state; indeed, nobody else would have lived there. To the east of the house was another room which had been used as a shrine. To the west was a jungle-like garden overgrown with weeds and shrubs. At the back was a pond covered with green scum which was a breeding place for mosquitoes. People called the building haunted. Ghosts might live there or not, but the house was really very old. No one dared to enter it, because it might collapse any time. But the young disciples of Sri Ramakrishna didn't learn to be afraid of death. It was chosen because of its cheap rent and it was near to the holy Ganga and the Cossipore crematorium where the body of Sri Ramakrishna had been cremated at the bank of the river. The monks were pleased with it, for it was away from the crowed of the city life. Moreover, the solitude of the place would help them in meditation. The house was taken at a monthly rent of ₹ 11 inclusive of tax. A cook was engaged at ₹ 6 per month. For the first few months Surendranath contributed ₹ 30 a month. As the other members joined the monastery one by one, he doubled his contribution, which he later increased to ₹ 100.

It was the beginning of the year 1902; Swamiji was seated in his room at Belur Math, and talking with Sarat Chandra Chakraborty, his disciple. During conversation he told about Surendranath Mitra: "You have doubtless heard Suren Babu's name. He was in a way the founder of this Math. It was this Suren Mitra who used to think most for us in those days. His devotion and faith have no parallel!"

Baranagore Math, as the new monastery was called, became the first headquarters of the monks of the Ramakrishna Order. It was established in the month of September or October of 1886. The monastery remained at Baranagore from 1886 to 1892; then it was shifted to Alambazar, in the neighbourhood of Dakshineswar, where it functioned till 1897. Next it was removed to the garden-house of Nilambar Mukherjee, on the bank of the Ganga across from Baranagore. Finally, the permanent monastery was dedicated in 1898 at the Belur Math, adjacent to Nilambar Mukherjee's garden-house.

After the passing away of Sri Ramakrishna, "The younger Gopal brought the Master's bed and other articles of daily use from the garden-house of Cossipore. The Brahmin who had been cook at Cossipore was engaged for the new monastery. The first permanent member was the elder Gopal. Sarat spent the nights there. In the beginning Sarat, Sashi, Baburam, Niranjan and

Kali used to visit the Monastery every now and then, according to their convenience. Tarak, who had gone to Vrindavan following the Master's death, returned to Calcutta after a few months and soon became a permanent member of the monastery. Rakhal, Jogen, Latu, and Kali were living at Vrindavan with the Holy Mother when the monastery was started. Kali returned to Calcutta within a month, Rakhal after a few months, and Jogen and Latu after a year. The householder devotees frequently visited the monastic brothers and spent hours with them in meditation and study.

"After a short time Narendra, Rakhal, Niranjan, Sarat, Sashi, Baburam, Jogen, Tarak, and Latu renounced the world for good. Sarada Prasanna and Subodh joined them some time later. Gangadhar, who was very much attracted to Narendra, visited the math regularly. It was he who taught the brothers the hymn sung at the evening service in the Siva temple at Benares. He had gone to Tibet to practice austerity; now, having returned, he lived at the monastery. Hari, who was at first only a visitor at the monastery, soon embraced the monastic life and thus completed the band of the Master's sannyasi disciples.

"Surendranath was indeed a blessed soul. It was he who laid the foundation of the Great Order later associated with Sri Ramakrishna's name. His devotion and sacrifice made it possible for those earnest souls to renounce the world for the realization of God. Through him Sri Ramakrishna made it possible for them to live in the world as embodiments of his teaching, the renunciation of 'woman' and 'gold' and the realization of God.

"The brothers lived at the math like orphan boys. Sometimes they would not have the money to pay their house-rent; sometimes they would have no food in the monastery. Surendra would come and settle all these things. He was the big brother of the monks. Later on, when they thought of his genuine love, the members of this first math shed tears of gratitude.

"The new monastery became known among the Master's devotees as the Baranagore Math. Narendra, Rakhal, and the other young disciples were filled with intense renunciation. One day Rakhal's father came to the Math and asked Rakhal to return home. "Why do you take the trouble to come here?" Rakhal said to him. "I am very happy here. Please pray to God that you may forget me and that I may forget you too." The young disciples said to one another: "We shall never return to the worldly life. The Master enjoined upon us the renunciation of 'woman' and 'gold'. How can we go back to our families?"

"Sashi had taken charge of the daily worship in the Math. The Master's relics had been brought from Balaram's house and Sri Ramakrishna was worshiped daily in the worship hall. Narendra supervised the household. He was the leader of the monastery. He would often tell his brother disciples: "The selfless actions enjoined in the Gita are worship, japa, meditation, and so on, and not worldly duties." The brothers at the Math depended on him for their spiritual inspiration. He said to them, "We must practice Sadhana; otherwise we shall not be able to realize God."

"He and his brother disciples, filled with an ascetic spirit, devoted themselves day and night to the practice of spiritual discipline. Their one goal in life was the realization of God. They followed to their hearts' content the injunctions prescribed in the Vedas, Puranas, and Tantras, for an ascetic life. They spent their times in japa and meditation and study of the scriptures. Whenever they would fail to experience the Divine Presence, they would feel as if they were on the rack. They would practice austerity, sometimes alone under trees, sometimes in a cremation ground, sometimes on the bank of the Ganges. Again sometimes they would spend the entire day in the meditation room of the monastery in japa and contemplation; sometimes they would gather to sing and dance in a rapture of delight. All of them, and Narendra particularly, were consumed with the desire to see God. Now and then they would say to one another, "Shall we not starve ourselves to death to see God?"[8]

According to Mahendranath Dutta, Surendranath was against the arrangement of shrine at the Math. He said: "What the hell will you do? Do you want to sit in front of the photo of Sri Ramakrishna, and worship it by playing bell and so on as like the priests do in case of goddess Shitala Devi? I think it is better not to make a shrine." Narendranath also said: "Look! We are monk; we have no fixed place to stay. We don't know when and where we will go and what shall we eat. Don't create a burden by making a shrine. One has to be fixed for the maintenance of shrine, and many other customs are to be followed. Hence, it is better to follow his teachings." But Shashi Maharaj didn't agree with them. He wished to take the charge of the daily worship. So, he was allowed to do the same.

When Sri Ramakrishna was alive, Shashi Maharaj experienced his daily movements, his choice of food, his smoking, and so on. Accordingly, he started worshiping the Master's relics and image with great devotion. He used to chant: "Jay Gurudeva! Jay Gurudeva!" How was the shrine? How did Shashi Maharaj worship? There was a bed for Sri Ramakrishna at the middle of the room—a mat on the floor on which there was a photo of the Master covered with a cloth, along with a cushion, and pillow and so on. A canoe-shaped water container (used in worship by Hindus), and an urn filled with the ashes of the Master's body were also placed near the bed and Shashi Maharaj used to worship by waving a lamp, thurible, incense etc. in front of the deity (adorable Guru). The worship was accompanied with musical instrument of percussion resembling a longish tomtom and cymbals. At the end of greeting he used to fan with a Chamor (a kind of fan or brush made of the hair of a yak's tail) while danced like a mad and roared saying: '*Jay Gurudeva, Sri Gurudeva*'... When he danced with the bit of music and moved around the room, the building seemed to be dangling. Brother disciples would also join the dance and sang with great devotion: '*Jay Gurudeva, Sri Gurudeva*'... Later they saluted the deity (Guru) and read from the *Guru-Gita*. Then they sang the hymn composed by Swami Abhedananda: "*Niranjanang Nitya-Anantarupang Bhaktanucampadhritabigrahang Vai, Ishabatarang Parameshamiddang Tang Ramakrishnang Sirosha Namamoh*" and finally they used to recite "*Jay Guru Maharaj-ji ki Jay*" At first they would sing: "Bhajo Shiva Omkara" and '*Jay Gurudeva, Sri Gurudeva*' during fanning by the Chamor. Thus every day they would enjoy the worship with devotional songs and music.

After Sri Ramakrishna's passing away many young disciples were forced by their parents to return home and continue their studies. At this time, Narendranath started going to the house of those who had resumed their studies, and tried hard to instigate them to join the monastery. It was not prearranged when and to whose house he would go. Being afraid of his arrival everyone would close the door and engage in study. Narendranath would appear like a cyclone and thumped the door till it was opened. When the door was opened, he called his brother disciple and tried to convince him saying: "Have you decided to pass the life for study and examination? Is it the way of following the ideal of Sri Ramakrishna! Did he teach you to do such thing? Is it the reward of his struggle? Don't forget that you are an ascetic; you are initiated for renunciation. How can you wish to be happy with the help of an academic degree? Is it possible to follow both the renunciation and craving for sensual pleasures at a time? What a ridiculous are you! Give up all these futile ideas and come at once to join the monastery." Thus, by reproaching or requesting, he tried to bring them back to Baranagore Math. His enthusiastic words would inspire them to renounce the world for spiritual aspiration. His words made them feel repentant, and immediately would go with him to the monastery. But after two or three days they would return home again. Again Narendranath would go to their house and try to raise the fire of renunciation in them. Narendranath didn't stop until he had gained his point. Such a continuous strike made them strong in taking a solemn vow to renounce the worldly life. They realized the falsehood of academic degree to the aspirants of spiritual path, and willing to know the truth. Gradually the young disciples realized the fabrication of the worldly life and began to gather at the monastery. The seeds, sowed by Sri Ramakrishna in them, began to germinate with the help of Narendranath's enthusiastic words. At the end of December, all the young disciples came to Baranagore and joined the monastery.

The brother disciples of Narendranath looked upon him as their leader, because his personality had become interwoven with their every thought and desire; and also for he seemed to be the true mouthpiece of the Master. Narendranath was their brother and comrade. "He was like a spiritual lion; and hence their love for him amounted almost to reverence. The Master's words about him were constantly in their minds. Did they in their zeal for realization disobey him and go to excess in the practice of austerities, all that he would say was, 'Did not the Master himself give all of you into my charge?' They could not escape the magnetism of his personality. His eyes, his face, his speech, the manner in which he walked, the way in which he showed his confidence in them an cheered and spurred them on, even his methods of admonishing them, made him seem the spirit of the Master incarnate."[9]

The event at Antpur, occurred on 24th December, 1886, was very much significant for the determination of the boys to renounce the world. Matangini Devi, Baburam's mother, invited the young monks to visit her native village, Antpur, during the Christmas vacation.

At first it was decided that Narendranath, Baburam (he was then in Calcutta), and two or more would go; but when the others came to know, they also joined the party. Narendranath, Baburam, Sharat, Shashi, Tarak, Kali, Niranjan, Gangadhar and Sarada boarded the train. They had taken musical instruments with them. The train route was from Howrah to Tarakeswar. As soon as the train left the platform, Narendranath started singing 'Shiva Shankara, bom bom Bhola', and the others joined him. All through the journey they sang continuously. Finally, with full of enthusiasm they got down at Haripal station. Antpur was eight miles away from there. They took a carriage and reached Antpur before the sun set. Matangini Devi became very pleased to see them, and she made every arrangement of their food and shelter, though there were many servants in the house.

In the calm and quiet of the village, the spiritual fire in the young monks blazed up into a conflagration. Narendra's enthusiasm fanned the flames. The spirit of the Master as it were spoke and worked through him. He was intensely possessed by the vision of the sannyasi's life and would cry out, 'Let man-making be the goal of our lives! Let us make this our only spiritual discipline! Away with vain learning! Let not the glamour of the world captivate our minds even for a moment! Realization of God is the one and only thing in life! That is what Sri Ramakrishna's life represented! We must realize God!' Inspired by these thoughts and fired by an oneness of purpose, the young men aware of a sense of unity—a feeling that they were all linked by some wonderful spiritual power. During their stay at Antpur they seemed to grow into one body, one mind and one soul. The days passed in Sadhana (austerity). Ramakrishna was in their minds; his name on their lips. Upon all alike there seemed to descend a spirit of renunciation, a desire to take the sannyasi's vow, each in the presence of the others. The monastic spirit seemed to be intensified in their hearts, both for their own liberation and for the good of the world. Each disciple saw in his brother-disciples a world of spiritual force; and that vision intensified the love among them. This was as it should have been, for the Master's spirit was destined to be perpetuated, no through one or several individual disciples having disciples of their own, which is what happens usually, but in a definite organized form.

Thus at Antpur, in still hours, subtle things were happening, knitting the brothers together. It all found expression one night before a huge Dhuni (sacred fire) in the compound. Overhead was the clear night sky, and all around was quiet. Meditation lasted a long time. When a break was made Narendra began to tell the story of Jesus, beginning with the mystery of his birth, through to his death and resurrection. Through his eloquence, the brother-disciples could catch something of the apostolic fervour that had impelled Paul to spread the Christian gospel far and wide in the face of adversities. Narendra charged them to become Christ themselves, and so aid in the redemption of the world; to realize God and to deny themselves as Jesus had done. Standing there before the sacred fire, their faces lit up by the flames, the cracking of the wood the sole disturbing sound, they took the vows of renunciation before God and one another. The very air was vibrant with their ecstatic fervour. Strangely, the monks discovered afterwards that all this had happened on Christmas-eve![10]

Swami Shivananda recalled this event: "As a matter of fact, our resolve to become organized became firm at Antpur. The Master had already made us sannyasins. That attitude was strengthened at Antpur." After staying there for a week, they all returned to Calcutta. On the way they went to Tarekeswar to visit the famous temple of Shiva, Lord of Monks.

After the foundation of monastery at Baranagore, many young disciples returned home with the excuse of examination and so on. Again they came back to monastery after the event at Antpur. Their parents had tried again to force them for returning home, but this time they failed. When they found no other way of getting their point, they began to blame Narendranath. They said, "This wicked boy is the root of all disasters. Our boys returned home and resumed their study. He has motivated them to join the monastery; he advised them all nonsense." Hearing this Narendranath and other brother disciples laughed and tried to persuade them with reasons. But when they found the parents not paying any heed to their words, they said: "We have renounced the world, and now it is not possible to go back to the family." When Shashi's father came to take him back to home, he replied: "He, who once had renounced the world, considers the home as a tiger's den."

Let us go to the Baranagore Math, where we will see how Narendranath and his brother disciples have been living, what they are doing, and how much difficulties they have been facing in their monastic life. Mahendranath Gupta recorded some events of Baranagore Math in his '*The Gospel of Sri Ramakrishna*'. We would like to see what happened during next four months at the monastery.

Monday, February, 21, 1887.

It was the festival of Shivaratri, the night of Shiva. On this day the devotees observe fast and spend the whole night in meditation, prayer, and other spiritual exercises. Narendra, Rakhal, Niranjan, Sarat, Sashi, Kali, Baburam, Tarak, and Sarada Prasanna were living in the monastery. All day the members had been fasting in observance of the Shivaratri. Sarat, Kali, Niranjan, and Sarada were planning to go to Puri, the following Saturday, on a pilgrimage to the sacred Jagannath. Jogin and Latu were at Vrindavan and had not yet seen the new place.

Narendra had gone to Calcutta that morning to look after a lawsuit in which his family had been involved since the death of his father. At nine o'clock in the morning M. arrived at the Math. Tarak saw him and began to sing a praise of Siva. Rakhal joined him:

There Shiva dances, striking both His cheeks; and they resound, Ba-ba-bom!
Dimi-dimi-dimi! Sounds His drum; a garland of skulls from His neck is hanging!
In His matted locks the Ganges roars; fire shoots from His mighty trident!
Bright shines the crescent moon illumining His gathered locks.

Rakhal and Tarak danced as they sang. Narendra had recently composed the song.

Sashi finished the morning worship in the shrine. Sarat then sang about Shiva to the accompaniment of the tanpura.

Narendra had just arrived from Calcutta. He had not yet taken his bath. Kali asked him, "What about the lawsuit?" "Why should you bother about it?" Narendra replied sharply.

Narendra was smoking and talking to M. and the others. He said: "Nothing can be achieved in spiritual life without the renunciation of 'woman' and 'gold'. 'Woman' is the doorway to hell. All people are under the control of woman. The cases of Shiva and Krishna are quite different. Shiva turned His Consort into His servant. Sri Krishna, no doubt, led a householder's life. But how unattached He was! How quickly He renounced Vrindavan and the gopis!"

Rakhal: "And how He renounced Dwarka, too, where He was king!"

Narendra took his bath in the Ganges and returned to the monastery. He carried his wet cloth and towel in his hand. Sarada prostrated himself before Narendra. He too had been fasting on account of the Shivaratri. He was going to the Ganges for his bath. Narendra entered the worship room and prostrated himself before the picture of Sri Ramakrishna, who was daily worshiped there as the Deity. For a few minutes he was absorbed in meditation.

The devotees assembled in a room and began to converse. The talk turned to Bhavanath. Narendra said, "People like him live like worms in the world."

It was afternoon. Arrangements were being made to worship Shiva in the evening. Leaves of the *bel*-tree were gathered for the worship. Be-wood was chopped for the *homa*.

In the evening Shashi, who was in charge of the worship at the monastery, burnt incense before the pictures of the various gods and goddesses.

The worship of Shiva was to take place under the bel-tree in the monastery compound. The Deity was to be worshipped four times, during the four watches of the night. The brothers assembled under the *bel*-tree. Bhupati and M. were present also. One of the young members of the Math was in charge of the worship. Kali was reading from the Gita. Now and then he argued with Narendra.

Kali: "I alone am everything. I create, preserve, and destroy."

Narendra: "How is it possible for me to create? Another power creates through me. Our various actions—even our thoughts—are caused by the power."

M. told himself: "The Master used to say: 'As long as a man feels that it is he who meditates, he is under the jurisdiction of the Adyasakti. Sakti must be acknowledged.'"

Kali reflected in silence a few moments and then said: "The actions you are talking about are illusory. There is not even any such thing as thought. The very idea of these things makes me laugh."

Narendra: "The 'I' that is implied in 'I am He' is not the ego. It is that which remains after one eliminates mind, body, and so on."

After completing the recital of the Gita, Kali chanted: "Santih! Santih! Santih!"

Narendra and the other devotees stood up and circled round and round the tree, singing and dancing. Now and then they chanted in chorus: "Shiva Guru! Shiva Guru!"

It was midnight, the fourteenth day of the dark fortnight of the moon. Pitch darkness filled all the quarters. Men, birds, and animals were all hushed into silence. The young sannyasis were clad in *gerrua* (ochre) robes. The words "Shiva Guru", chanted in their full-throated voices, rose into the infinite sky like the rumblings of rain-clouds and disappeared in the Indivisible Satchidananda.

The worship was over. The sun, about to rise, was painting the eastern horizon crimson. In this sacred twilight, the conjunction of night and day, the holy Brahmamuhurta, the young worshipers finished their bath in the Ganges.

It was morning. The devotees went to the shrine room, prostrated themselves before the Deity, and gradually assembled in the big hall. Narendra was clad in a new ochre cloth. The bright orange colour of his apparel blended with the celestial luster of his face and body, every pore of which radiated a divine light. His countenance was filled with fiery brilliance and yet touched with the tenderness of love. He appeared to all as a bubble that had risen up in the Ocean of Absolute Existence and Bliss and assumed a human body to help in the propagation of his Master's message. All eyes were fixed on him. Narendra was then just twenty-four years old, the very age at which the great Chaitanya had renounced the world.

Balaram had sent fruit and sweets to the monastery for the devotees' breakfast. Rakhal, Narendra, and a few others partook of the refreshments. After having one or two bites some of them cried out, "Blessed indeed is Balaram!" All laughed.

Narendra now began to joke like a child. He was imitating Sri Ramakrishna. He put a sweet into his mouth and stood still, as if in Samadhi. His eyes remained unwinking. A devotee stepped forward and pretended to hold him up by the hand lest he should drop to the ground. Narendra closed his eyes. A few minutes later, with the sweetmeat still in his mouth, he opened his eyes and drawled out, "I—am—all—right." All laughed loudly.

Refreshments were now given to everyone. M. looked on at this wonderful mart of happiness.

The devotees shouted joyfully, "Jai Gurumaharaj!"[11]

Monday, March 25, 1887.

M. (Mahendra Gupta) arrived at the Baranagore Math to visit his brother disciples. Devendra accompanied him. M. had been coming to the monastery very frequently and now and then had spent a day or two. The previous week he had spent three days at the Math. He was very eager to observe the spirit of intense renunciation of these young men.

It was evening. M. intended to spend the night in the monastery. Shashi lighted the lamp in the worship room and chanted the name of God. Next he burnt incense before all the pictures of gods and goddesses in the various rooms. The evening service began. Shashi conducted the worship. The members of the Math, with M. and Devendra, stood with folded hands and sang the hymn of the *arati*.

When the worship was over, Narendra and M. became engaged in conversation. Narendra was recalling his various meetings with Sri Ramakrishna.

Narendra: "One day during one of my early visits, the Master in an ecstatic mood said to me, 'you have come!' 'How amazing!' I said to myself, 'It is as if he had known me a long time.' Then he said to me, 'Do you ever see light?' I replied: 'Yes, sir. Before I fall asleep I feel something like a light revolving near my forehead.'"

M.: "Do you see it even now?"

Narendra: "I used to see it frequently. In Jadu Mallick's garden house the Master one day touched me and muttered something to himself. I became unconscious. The effect of the touch lingered with me a month, like an intoxication.

"When he heard that a proposal had been made about my marriage, he wept, holding the feet of the image of Kali. With tears in his eyes he prayed to the Divine Mother: 'O Mother, please upset the whole thing! Don't let Narendra be drowned.'

"After my father's death my mother and my brothers were starving. When the Master met Annada Guha one day, he said to him: 'Narendra's father has died. His family is in a state of great privation. It would be good if his friends helped him now with money.'

"After Annada had left I scolded him. I said, 'Why did you say all those things to him?' Thus rebuked he wept and said, 'Alas! For your sake I could beg from door to door.'

"He tamed us by his love. Don't you think so?"

M.: "There is not the slightest doubt about it. His love was utterly unselfish."

Narendra: "One day when I was alone with him he said something to me. Nobody else was present. Please don't repeat it to anyone here."

M.: "No, I shall not. What did he say?"

Narendra: "He said: 'It is not possible for me to exercise occult powers; but I shall do so through you. What do you say?' 'No', I replied 'you can't do that.'

"I used to laugh at his words. You must have heard all these things from him. I told him that his visions of God were all hallucinations of his mind.

"He said to me: 'I used to climb to the roof of the bungalow and cry: "O devotees, where are you all? Come to me, O devotees! I am about to die, I shall certainly die if I do not see you." And the Divine Mother told me, "The devotees will come." You see, everything is turning out to be true.'

"What else could I say? I kept quiet.

"One day he closed the door of his room and said to Devendra Babu and Girish Babu, referring to me, 'He will not keep his body if he is told who he is.'"

M.: "Yes, we have heard that. Many a time he repeated the same thing to us, too. Once you came to know about your true Self in Nirvikalpa Samadhi at the Cossipore garden house. Isn't that true?"

Narendra: "Yes. In that experience I felt that I had no body. I could see only my face. The master was in the upstairs room. I had that experience downstairs. I was weeping. I said, 'What has happened to me?' The elder Gopal went to the Master's room and said, 'Narendra is crying.'

"When I saw the Master he said to me: 'Now you have known. But I am going to keep the key with me.'

"I said to him, 'What is it that happened to me?'

"Turning to the devotees he said: 'He will not keep his body if he knows who he is. But I have put a veil over his eyes.'

"One day he said to me, 'You can see Krishna in your heart if you want.' I replied, 'I don't believe in Krishna or any such nonsense!'

Both M. and Narendra laughed.

"I have noticed a peculiar thing. Some men, objects, or places make me feel as if I had seen them before, in a previous birth. They appear familiar to me. One day I went to Sarat's house in Calcutta, on Amherst Street. Immediately I said to Sarat: 'This house seems familiar to me. It seems to me that I have known the rooms, the passages, and the rest of the house for many many days.

"I used to follow my own whims in everything I did. The Master never interfered. You know that I became a member of the Sadharan Brahmo Samaj."

M.: "Yes, I know that."

Narendra: "The Master knew that women attended the meeting of the Brahmo Samaj. A man cannot meditate with woman sitting in front of him; therefore he criticized the meditation of the Brahmo Samaj. But he didn't object to my going there. But one day he said to me, 'Don't tell Rakhal about your being a member of the Brahmo Samaj, or he too will feel like becoming one."

M.: "You have greater strength of mind. That is why the Master didn't prevent your going to the Samaj."

Narendra: "I have attained my present state of mind as a result of much suffering and pain. You have not passed through any such suffering. I now realize that without trials and tribulations one cannot resign oneself to God and depend on Him absolutely.

"Well, X – is so modest and humble! He is totally self-effacing. Can you tell me how I can develop humility?"

M.: "Speaking about your ego, the Master said, 'Whose ego is it?'"

Narendra: "What did he mean?"

M.: "A friend one day said to Radhika: 'You are egotistic. That is why you insulted Krishna.' Whereupon another friend said to the first: 'Yes, that Radha was egotistic because she regarded Krishna as her Lord. It was Krishna Himself who kept that ego in Radha.

"What the Master meant was that it is God alone who has kept this ego in you, so that He may accomplish many things through you."

Narendra: "But my ego loudly proclaims to all that I have no suffering."

M. smiled and said: "You may loudly proclaim it, if that be your sweet will."

The conversation turned to other devotees.

Narendra: "The Master said about Vijay Goswami, 'He is knocking at the door.'"

M.: "That is to say, he has not yet entered the room. At Shyampukur Vijay said to the Master, 'I saw you at Dacca in this tangible form, in this very body,' You were there too."

Narendra: "Devendra Babu and Ram Babu want to renounce the world. They are trying hard. Ram Babu told me privately that he would give up the world after two years."

M.: "After two years? After making provision for his children?"

Narendra: "Besides, he will rent his present house and buy a small house. Other relatives will arrange his daughter's marriage."

M.: "Nityogopal is in an exalted state of mind, isn't he?"

Narendra: "What do you mean?"

M.: "So much emotion, so much weeping and such exaltation in the name of God!"

Narendra: "Does mere emotion make a man spiritually great? Youngsters like Kali, Sarat, Shashi, and Sarada are more spiritual than Gopal. How great their renunciation is! Gopal does not accept the Master, does he?"

M.: "That is true. The Master remarked that Gopal did not belong to the circle of his devotees. But I saw him show great reverence for Sri Ramakrishna."

Narendra: "What did you see?"

M.: "At that time I was just becoming acquainted with Sri Ramakrishna. One day, after the meeting of the devotees in his room had broken up, I came out and saw Gopal on the foot-path, kneeling with folded hands before the Master. The moon was shining brightly overhead. It was the red path sprinkled with brick-dust, just outside the long verandah north of the Master's room. Nobody else was there. It appeared to me that Gopal had taken shelter at Sri Ramakrishna's feet and the Master was encouraging him."

Narendra: "I didn't see it."

M.: "Further, the Master used to say, 'Gopal is in the state to a paramahamsa.' But I also distinctly remember his forbidding Gopal to be intimate with women devotees. Many a time he warned about it."

Narendra: "Speaking to me about Gopal, the Master asked why, if Gopal was a real paramahamsa, he should hanker after money. 'He doesn't belong to this place', the Master said. 'Those who are my own will always come here.' He used to be angry with T—because he was Gopal's constant companion and didn't come to the Master more often. 'Gopal has spiritual realizations, no doubt,' the Master said to me, 'but he has attained them all of a sudden, without the necessary preparations. He is not one of my own. If he is, why haven't wept for him?'

"Some are proclaiming Gopal as the reincarnation of Nityananda. But times without number the Master said to me: 'In me alone are embodied Advaita, Chaitanya, and Nityananda. I am all these three.'"[12]

Friday, April 8, 1887

About eight o'clock in the morning two devotees, one a householder and the other a monk, were conversing in a room in the Baranagore monastery, when M. came in. The devotees were of the same age—twenty-four or twenty-five years old. M. intended to spend three days at the monastery.

He went to the shrine and saluted the Deity. After visiting Narendra, Rakhal, and the other brothers, he at last came into the room where the two devotees were engaged in conversation. The householder devotee wanted to renounce the world. The monk was trying to persuade him not to do so.

Monk: "Why don't you finish the few duties you have in the world? Very soon they will be left behind. A man was told that he would go to hell. He asked a friend, 'What is hell like?' Thereupon the friend began to draw a picture of hell on the ground with a piece of chalk. No sooner was the picture drawn then the man rolled over it and said; 'Now I have gone through hell!'"

Householder: "I don't relish worldly life. Ah, how happy you are here!"

Monk: "Why don't you renounce the world, if you want to? Why do you talk about it so much? But I repeat, why don't you enjoy the fun once for all?"

Shashi finished the regular worship in the worship hall. About eleven the brothers of the math returned from the Ganges after taking their baths. They put on clean cloths, went to the shrine, prostrated themselves before the Deity, and meditated there a little while.

After the food was offered to the Deity, they had their meal. M. ate with them.

It was evening. Incense was burnt before the pictures of gods and goddesses and the evening service was performed. Rakhal, Shashi, the elder Gopal, and Harish were seated in the big hall. M. also was there. Rakhal warned one of the brothers to be careful about the food to be offered to the Master in the shrine.

Rakhal said to Shashi and the others: "One day I ate part of the Master's refreshments before he took them. At this he said: 'I cannot look at you. How could you do such a thing?' I burst into tears."

The elder Gopal: "One day at Cossipore I breathed hard on his food. At this he said, 'Take that food away.'"

M. and Narendra were pacing the verandah and recalling old times.

Narendra: "I did not believe in anything."

M.: "You mean the form of God?"

Narendra: "At first I did not accept most of what the Master said. One day he asked me, 'Then why do you come here?' I replied, 'I come here to see you, not to listen to you.'"

M.: "What did he say to that?"

Narendra: "He was very much pleased."[13]

Saturday, April 9, 1887

The members of the math were resting a little after their meal. Narendra and M. sat under a tree in the garden to the west of the monastery. It was a solitary place and no one else was present. Narendra was recounting to M. his various experiences with Sri Ramakrishna. Narendra was about twenty-four years old and M. thirty-two.

M.: "You must remember vividly your first visit to him."

Narendra: "Yes. It was at the temple garden at Dakshineswar, in his room. That day I sang two songs."

Narendra sang them for M.:

Let us go back once more, O mind, to our own abode!
Here in this foreign land of earth
Why should we wander aimlessly in stranger's guise?
These living being round about, and the five elements,

Are strangers to you, all of them; none is your own.
Why do you thus forget yourself,
In love with strangers, O my mind?
Why do you thus forget your own?
Ascend the path of Truth, O mind! Unflaggingly climb,
With Love as the lamp to light your way.
As your provision for the journey, bring with you
The virtues, carefully concealed; for, like two highwaymen,
Greed and delusion wait to rob you of your wealth.

And Keep beside you constantly,
Calmness of mind and self-control.

Companionship with holy men will be for you
A welcome rest-house by the road;
There rest your weary limbs awhile, asking your way,
If ever you should be in doubt, of him who watches there.
If anything along the path should frighten you,
Then loudly shout the name of the Lord;
For He is Ruler of that road.
And even Death must bow to Him.

* * * *

O Lord, must all my days pass by so utterly in vain
Down the path of hope I gaze with longing, day and night.
Thou art the Lord of all the worlds, and I but a beggar here;
How can I ask of Thee to come and dwell within my heart?
My poor heart's humble cottage door is standing open wide;
Be gracious, Lord, and enter there but once, and quench its thirst!

M.: "What did he say after listening to your songs?"

Narendra: "He went into Samadhi. He said to Ram Babu: 'Who is this boy? How well he sings!' He asked me to come again."

M.: "Where did you see him next?"

Narendra: "At Rajmohan's house. The Third visit was at Dakshineswar again. During that visit he went into Samadhi and began to praise me as if I were God. He said to me, 'O Narayana, you have assumed this body for my sake.' But please don't tell this to anybody else."

M.: "What else did he say?"

Narendra: "He said: 'You have assumed this body for my sake. I asked the Divine Mother, "Mother, unless I enjoy the company of some genuine devotees completely free from 'woman' and 'gold', how shall I live on earth?"'. Then he said to me, 'You came to me at night, woke me up, and said, "Here I am!".' But I did not know anything of this. I was sound asleep in our Calcutta house."

M.: "In other words, you may be both present and absent at the same time. It is like God, who is both formless and endowed with form."

Narendra: "But you must not tell this to anyone else. At Cossipore he transmitted his power to me."

M.: "Didn't it happen when you used to meditate before a lighted fire under a tree at the Cossipore garden house?"

Narendra: "Yes. One day, while meditating, I asked Kali to hold my hand. Kali said to me, 'When I touched your body I felt something like an electric shock coming to my body.' But you must not tell this to anybody here. Give me your promise."

M.: "There is a special purpose in his transmission of power to you. He will accomplish much work through you. One day the Master wrote on a piece of paper, 'Naren will teach people.'"

Narendra: "But I said to him, 'I won't do any such thing.' Thereupon he said, 'Your very bones will do it.' He has given me charge of Sarat. Sarat is now yearning for God; the Kundalini is awakened in him."

M. "He must be careful that dead leaves do not accumulate there. Perhaps you remember what the Master used to say: 'In a lake the fish makes holes so that they may rest there. But if dead leaves accumulate in the hole the fish do not go there.'"

Narendra: "The Master used to call me Narayana."

M.: "Yes, I know he did."

Narendra: "When he was ill he would not allow me to pour water to wash his hands. At Cossipore he said: 'Now the key is in my hands. He will give up his body when he knows who he is.'"

M.: "Didn't he say it when you were in nirvikalpa Samadhi?"

Narendra: "Yes, at the time it seemed to me I had no body. I felt only my face. I was studying law at home to prepare for the examinations. Suddenly I said to myself, 'What am I doing?'"

M.: "Didn't it happen when the Master was at Cossipore?"

Narendra: "Yes. Like an insane person I ran out of our house. He asked me, 'What do you want?' I replied, 'I want to remain immersed in Samadhi.' He said: 'What a small mind you have! Go beyond Samadhi! Samadhi is a very trifling thing.'"

M.: "Yes, he used to say that vijnana (Science) is the stage after jnana (Knowledge). It is like going up and down the stairs after reaching the roof."

Narendra: "Kali has a craving for knowledge. I scold him for that. Is knowledge so easy to get? Let this bhakti (devotion) first mature. The Master told Tarak at Dakshineswar that emotion and bhakti are by no means the last word."

M.: "What other things did he say about you?"

Narendra: "Once I said to him, 'The forms of God and things like that, which you see in your visions, are all figments of your imagination.' He had so much faith in my words that he went to the Divine Mother in the temple and told Her what I had said to him. He asked Her, 'Are these hallucinations, then? Afterwards he said to me, 'Mother told me that all these are real.' Perhaps you remember that he said to me, 'When you sing. He who dwells here (touching his heart), like a snake, hisses as it were, and then, spreading His hood, quietly holds Himself steady and listens to your music.'

"He has no doubt said many things about me; but what have I realized?"

M.: "Now you have put on the grab of Shiva; you cannot touch money. Do you remember the Master's story?"

Narendra: "Please tell it to me."

M.: "A bahurupi! (a professional impersonator) disguised himself as Shiva and visited a house. The master of the house wanted to give him a rupee, but he did not accept it. Then the polymorphic went home, removed his disguise, came back to the gentleman, and asked for the rupee. 'Why didn't you accept it before?' he was asked. He said: 'I was impersonating Shiva, a monk. I couldn't touch money at that time.'"

When Narendra heard the story, he laughed a long while.

M.: "You have now put on the grab of a physician, as it were. You have become the guardian of these young men. Yours is the entire responsibility. You have to bring up the brothers of the monastery."

Narendra: "Whatever spiritual disciplines we are practicing here are in obedience to the Master's command. But it is strange that Ram Babu criticizes us for our spiritual practices. He says: 'We have seen him (Sri Ramakrishna). What need have we of any such practice?'"

M.: "Let people act according to their faith."

Narendra: "But the Master asked us to practice austerity."

Narendra was again telling M. about the Master's love for him.

Narendra: "How many times he prayed to the Divine Mother for my sake! After my father's death, when I had no food at home and my mother and sisters and brothers were starving too, the Master prayed to the Divine Mother to give me money."

M.: "Yes, I know that. You once told me."

Narendra: "But I didn't get any money. The Master told me what the Divine Mother had said to him: 'He will get simple food and clothing. He will eat rice and dal.'

"He loved me so much! But whenever an impure idea crept into my mind he at once knew about it. While going around with Annada, sometimes I found myself in the company of evil people. On those occasions the Master could not eat any food from my hands. He could raise his hand only a little, and could not bring it to his mouth. On one such occasion, while he was ill, he brought his hand very close to his mouth, but it did not go in. He said to me, 'You are not yet ready.'

"Now and then I feel great skepticism. At Baburam's house it seemed to me that nothing existed—as if there were no such things as God."

M.: "The Master used to say that he too had passed through that mood."

Both M. and Narendra remained silent. Then M. said: "You are all indeed blessed! You think of the Master day and night."

Narendra: "But how little it is! We don't yet feel like giving up the body because we haven't realized God."

It was night. Niranjan had just returned from Puri. The members of the math, and M., greeted him with great joy. Niranjan was telling them his experiences. He was then about twenty-five years old.

The evening worship was over. Some of the brothers were meditating. But many of them assembled in the big all around Niranjan. They were talking. After nine o'clock Shashi offered food to the Deity.

The members of the math finished their supper, which consisted of home-made bread, a little vegetable, and a little hard molasses.[14]

Saturday, May 7, 1887.

It was the full-moon day of the month of Vaishakh (the first month of the Bengali calendar, falling in the summer season). Narendra and M. were seated on a couch in M.'s study in Calcutta. They were talking. Just before Narendra's arrival M. had been studying *The Merchant of Venice, Comus*, and Blackie's *Self Culture*, which he taught at school.

Narendra and the other brothers of the monastery were full of yearning for God-realization. A fire of intense renunciation raged in their hearts.

Narendra: "I don't care for anything. You see, I am now talking with you, but I feel like getting up this minute and running away."

Narendra sat in silence a few minutes. Then he said, "I shall fast to death for the realization of God."

M.: "That is good. One can do anything for God."

Narendra: "But suppose I cannot control my hunger."

M.: "Then eat something and begin over again."

Narendra remained silent a few minutes.

Narendra: "It seems there is no God. I pray so much, but there is no reply—none whatsoever. How many visions I have seen! How many mantras shining in letters of gold! How many visions of the Goddess Kali! How many other divine forms! But still I have no peace. Will you kindly give me six pice?"

Narendra asked for the money to pay his carriage fare to the Baranagore Math. Just then Satkari arrived in a carriage. Of the same age as Narendra, he dearly loved the members of the monastery. He lived near the math and worked in Calcutta. The carriage was his own. Narendra returned the money to M. and said that he would go with Satkari in his carriage. He asked M. to give them some refreshments.

M. accompanied the two friends to the Baranagore Math. He wanted to see how the brothers spent their time and practiced Sadhana. He wanted to see how Sri Ramakrishna, the Master, was reflected in the hearts of the disciples. Niranjan was not at the math. He had gone home to visit his mother, the only relative he had in this world. Baburam, Sarat, and Kali had gone to Puri. They intended to spend a few days there.

Narendra was in charge of the members of the monastery. Prasanna had been practicing austere Sadhana for the past few days. Once Narendra had told him of his desire to fast to death for the realization of God. During Narendra's absence in Calcutta, Prasanna had left the monastery for an unknown destination. When Narendra heard about it, he said to the brothers, "Why did Raja (Rakhal Maharaj) allow him to go?" But Rakhal had not been in the monastery at the time, having gone to the Dakshineswar temple for a stroll.

Narendra: "Just let Raja come back to the monastery! I shall scold him. Why did he allow Prasanna to go away?" Then he said to Harish, "I am sure you were lecturing him then, standing with your feet apart. Couldn't you prevent his going away?

Harish replied in a very low voice, "Brother Tarak asked him not to go, but still he went away."

Narendra said to M.: "You see what a lot of trouble I am in! Here, too, I am involved in a world of maya. Who knows where this boy has gone?"

Rakhal returned from Dakshineswar. Bhavanath had accompanied him.

Narendra told Rakhal about Prasanna's going away from the monastery. Prasanna had left a letter for Narendra. This was the substance of the letter: "I am going to Vrindavan on foot. It is very risky for me to live here. Here my mind is undergoing a change. Formerly I used to dream about my parents and other relatives. Then I dreamt of woman, the embodiment of maya (attachment). I have suffered twice; I had to go back to my relatives at home. Therefore I am going far away from them. The Master once told me, 'Your people at home are apt to do anything; never trust them.'"

Rakhal said: "These are the reasons for his going away. Once he remarked: 'Narendra often goes home to look after his mother, brothers, and sisters. And he supervises the family's lawsuit. I am afraid that I too may feel like going home, following his example.'"

Narendra remained silent.

Rakhal was talking to them about making pilgrimages. He said: "We have achieved nothing by staying here. The Master always exhorted us to realize God. Have we succeeded?"

Rakhal lay down. The other devotees were either lying or sitting.

Rakhal: "Let us go to the Narmada."

Narendra: "What will you achieve by wandering about? Can one ever attain jnana (Knowledge), that you are talking about it so much?"

A devotee: "Then why have you renounced the world?"

Narendra: "Must we live with Shyam because we have not seen Ram? Must we go on begetting children because we have not realized God? What are you talking about?"

Narendra went out, returning after a few minutes. Rakhal was still lying down.

A member of the monastery who was also lying down said teasingly, feigning great suffering on account of his separation from God: "Ah! Please get me a knife. I have no more use for this life. I can't stand this pain anymore!"

Narendra said seriously: "It is there. Stretch out your hand and take it."

Everybody laughed. The conversation again turned to Prasanna.

Narendra: "Even here we are involved in maya (attachment with the world). Why have we become monks, I wonder?"

Rakhal: "I have read in a book that monks should not live together. The author has described a city of monks."

Shashi: "I don't care about sannyas or any such thing. There is no place, where I cannot live."

They were talking of Bhavanath, whose wife had been seriously ill. Narendra said to Rakhal: "I understand that his wife has been snatched from the jaws of death. Is that why he went to Dakshineswar to enjoy the fresh air?"

Ram Babu intended to build a temple in the garden at Kankurgachi, where some of Sri Ramakrishna's ashes were buried.

Narendra said to Rakhal: "Ram Babu has made M. one of the trustees of the garden."

M.: "But I don't know anything about it."

It was dusk. Shashi burnt incense before the picture of Sri Ramakrishna in the worship room and then before the pictures of gods and goddesses in the other rooms.

The evening worship began. The members of the math and the other devotees stood with folded hands near the door of the shrine and witnessed the arati. Then they all sang in chorus the following hymn to Shiva, to the accompaniment of bell and gong:

> Jaya Shiva Omkara, Bhaja Shiva Omkara,
> Brahma Vishnu Sadasiva.
> Hara Hara Hara Mahadev!

Narendra had introduced this song for the evening worship. It is sung in the temple of Shiva in Benaras.

It was eleven o'clock at night when their supper was over. The brothers prepared a bed for M., and all went to sleep.

It was midnight. M. was wide awake. He said to himself: "Everything is as it was before. The same Ayodhya—only Rama is not there." M. silently left his bed. It was the full-moon night of Vaishakh, the thrice-blessed day of the Buddhists, associated with Buddha's birth, realization, and passing away. M. was walking alone on the bank of the Ganges, contemplating the Master.

It was Sunday. M. had arrived the day before and was planning to stay till Wednesday. The householder devotees generally visited the monastery on Sunday.

The *Yogavasishtha* was being studied and explained. M. had heard a little about the teachings of this book from Sri Ramakrishna. It taught the absolute identity of Brahman and the soul, and the unreality of world. The Master had forbidden him and the other householder devotees to practice spiritual discipline following the method of the Advaita Vedanta, since the attitude of the oneness of the soul and God is harmful for one still identified with the body. For such a devotee, the Master used to say, it was better to look on God as the Lord and oneself as His servant.

The conversation turned to the *Yogavasishtha*.

M.: "Well, how is Brahmajnana described in the Yogavasishtha?"

Rakhal: "Hunger, thirst, pain, pleasure, and so on, are all maya. The annihilation of the mind is the only means to the realization of Brahman."

M.: "What remains after the annihilation of the mind is Brahman. Is that not true?"

Rakhal: "Yes."

M.: "Sri Ramakrishna used to say that. Nangta taught him that way. Have you found in the book that Vasishtha asked Rama to lead a householder's life?"

Rakhal: "I haven't yet found anything like that in the book. Rama is not even admitted by the author to be an Incarnation of God."

Presently Narendra, Tarak, and another devotee returned from the bank of the Ganges. They had intended to go to Konnagar, on the other side of the river, but had been unable to find a ferryboat. They sat down. The conversation about the *Yogavasishtha* went on.

Narendra said to M.: "There are many nice stories in the book. Do you know the incident of Lila?"

M.: "Yes, I have read the book here and there. Lila had attained Brahmajnana."

Narendra: "Yes. Do you remember the story of Indra and Ahalya, and the story of how King Viduratha became a chandala (an untouchable)?"

M.: "Yes, I remember."

Narendra: "What a wonderful description of the forest!"

Narendra and the other devotees were going to the Ganges to bathe. M. accompanied them. The sun was very hot; so M. took his umbrella. Sarat, a devotee from Baranagore, was going with them to take his bath. He often visited the monastery.

M. said to Sarat: "It is very hot."

Narendra: "Is that your excuse for taking the umbrella?"

M. laughed.

The members of the monastery were clad in gerrua.

M. said to Narendra: "It is really very hot. One is liable to get a sunstroke."

Narendra: "I see that your body is the obstacle in you path of renunciation. Isn't that so? I mean you, Devendra Babu..."

M. laughed and said to himself, "Is it merely the body?"

After bathing, the devotees returned to the monastery. They washed their feet and entered the worship room. Saluting the Deity, they offered flowers.

Narendra was a little late in coming to the worship room. He found that there was no flower on the tray. There were only a few bel-leaves. He sprinkled the leaves with sandal-paste and offered them to Sri Ramakrishna. He rang the bell, saluted the Deity again, and joined the other brothers in the big hall, which was known as the room of the "Dana's".

The members of the math called themselves the 'Dana' and the 'Daityas', which means the 'Ghosts' and the 'demons', the companions of Shiva. They took these names because of their utter indifference to worldly pleasure and relationships.

A little description of the Baranagore Math: "The southernmost room of the second floor was used for meditation, contemplation, and study, and was known as Kali Tapasvi's room, since Kali used to shut himself in there most of the day. North of this room was the worship room, and north of that, again, was the room where the offerings for the worship were prepared. From this room the devotees used to watch the evening worship. North of the 'offering room' was the room of the 'Dana's', a very long hall where the members of the math used to assemble. Here the householder devotees and visitors were received. North of this hall was a small room where the devotees took their meals. East of the worship room and of Kali Tapasvi's room ran a long verandah, at the south-west corner of which was the library of a society of Baranagore. Between Kali Tapasvi's room and this library was a staircase; and north of the dining room was another staircase, leading to the roof.

Narendra and the other members of the math often spent their evenings on this roof. There they devoted a great deal of time to discussion of the teachings of Sri Ramakrishna, Sankaracharya, Ramanuja, and Jesus Christ, and of Hindu philosophy, European philosophy, the Vedas, the Puranas, and the Tantras.

Narendra, who had a beautiful voice, used to sing in the room of the 'Dana's' and teach music to Sarat and a few others. Kali used to take lessons on the instruments. Many, many happy hours they spent together in that hall, dancing and singing."[15]

That day Narendra was sitting with the devotees in the room of the 'Dana's'. They were talking about religious preaching.

M. said to Narendra: "Vidyasagar says that he does not speak about God to anyone for fear of being caned."

Narendra: "For fear of being caned? What does he mean?"

M.: "This is what Vidyasagar says: 'Suppose that after death we all go to God. The emissaries of Death will have sent Keshab Sen there too. Keshab Sen, no doubt, committed sins while he lived on earth. When that is proved, perhaps God will say, "Give him twenty-five stripes." Then suppose I am taken to God. I used to go to Keshab Sen's Brahmo Samaj in my earthly life. I too have committed many sins; so I too am ordered to be caned. Then suppose I say to God that I acted in that sinful way because I listened to Keshab's preaching. Thereupon God will ask His emissaries to bring Keshab back. When he is brought, the Almighty Lord will say to him: "Did you really preach that way? You yourself knew nothing about spiritual matters and yet you had the hardihood to teach others about God! Emissaries, give him twenty-five stripes more."'"

Everybody laughed.

M.: "Therefore Vidyasagar says: 'I cannot take care of my own self; should I be foolish enough to get an additional caning for misleading others? I myself do not understand God. How shall I lecture to others about Him!'"

Narendra: "He says that he has not understood God. But how, then, can he understand charity and doing good to others? How can he understand about the school? How can he understand about educating boys by establishing schools? How can he understand that it is right to enter the world, marry, and beget children? He who rightly understands one thing understands everything else."

M. said to himself: "Yes, Sri Ramakrishna, too, said that he who knows God knows everything else. Further, he said to Vidyasagar that leading a worldly life, establishing schools, and so on are the outcome of *rajas*. The Master also said the Vidyasagar's philanthropy was due to the influence of *sattva* on *rajas*. Such *rajas* is not harmful."

After the meal the brothers of the monastery rested. M. and Chunilal were conversing. Chunilal told M. of his first visit to Sri Ramakrishna at Dakshineswar. He also told him how at one time he had felt disgusted with the world, had renounced it, and had wandered about in holy places. A few minutes later Narendra came and sat by them. He asked the younger Gopal to prepare a smoke for him. The latter had been meditating. Narendra said to him: "I say! Prepare a smoke. What do you mean by this meditation? First of all prepare yourself for spiritual life by serving God and holy men; then you will be able to meditate. First of all karma, and then meditation." Everybody laughed.

There was a big plot of wooded land to the west of the monastery compound. M. was seated alone under a tree, when suddenly Prasanna appeared. It was about three o'clock in the afternoon.

M.: "Where have you been all these days? Everyone has been so worried about you. Have you seen the brothers? When did you arrive?"

Prasanna: "Just now. Yes, I have seen them."

M.: "You left a note saying that you were going to Vrindavan. We were terribly worried about you. How far did you go?"

Prasanna: "Only as far as Konnagar."

Both of them laughed.

M.: "Sit down. Tell me all about it. Where did you stop first?"

Prasanna: "At the Dakshineswar temple garden. I spent one night there."

M. smiled and said: "What is Hazra's present mood?"

Prasanna: "Hazra asked me, 'What do you think of me?'"

Both laughed.

M. smiled and said: "What did you say?"

Prasanna: "I said nothing."

M.: "Then?"

Prasanna: "Then he asked me to wait on him."

M.: "Where did you go next?"

Prasanna: "By degrees I got to Konnagar. I spent the night in the open. I intended to proceed farther and asked some gentlemen whether I could procure enough money there for a railway ticket to the up-country."

M.: "What did they say?"

Prasanna: "They said, 'You may get a rupee or so; but who will give you the whole fare?'"

Both laughed.

M. said: "What did you take with you?"

Prasanna: "Oh, one or two pieces of cloth and a picture of the Master. I didn't show the picture to anybody."[16]

Thus we saw that Prasanna didn't dare to go farther, and returned to the monastery.

One day Shashi's father came to the Math. He wanted to take his son back home. When Sri Ramakrishna was ill, Shashi had nursed him for nine months with unswerving zeal. He had won a scholarship in the Entrance Examination for his academic ability and had studied up to the B.A. level, but he didn't appear at the examination. His father, a poor Brahmin, was a devout Hindu and spent much of his time in spiritual practice. Shashi was his eldest son. He hopped that his son would complete his education, and earn money for the family. But Shashi had renounced the world for the realization of God. He felt great anguish of heart for his parents. Many a time he said to his friends, with tears in his eyes: "I am at a loss as to my duty. Alas, I could not serve my parents; I could not be of any use to them. What great hope they placed in me! On account of our poverty my mother did not have any jewellery. I cherished the desire to buy some for her. But now all my hopes are frustrated; it is impossible for me to return home. My Master asked me to renounce 'woman' and 'gold'. I simply cannot return home."

After the passing away of Sri Ramakrishna, Shashi's father hopped that his son would come back to his family. Shashi had spent a few days at home, but immediately after the establishment of the new monastery he started visit every now and then, and after a few days, had decided to stay there as one of the members. His father began to come frequently to the monastery and tried to persuade him to come back home; but he failed.

That day, on learning that his father had come, Shashi fled the monastery by another door. He didn't want to meet him.

Shashi's father knew M. They paced the upper verandah together and talked. Shashi's father said: "Who is in charge of this place? Narendra alone is the cause of all the mischief. For a while all these young men returned home and devoted themselves to their studies."

M.: "There is no master here. They are all equals. What can Narendra do? Can a man renounce home against his own will? Have we householders, for instance, been able to give up our homes altogether?"

Shashi's father: "You are doing the right thing. You are serving both the world and God. Can't one practice religion after your method? That is exactly what we want Shashi to do. Let him live at home and come here too. You have no idea how much his mother weeps for him."

M. became sad and said nothing.

Shashi's father: "And if you speak of searching for holy men, I know where to find a good one. Let Shashi go home."

Rakhal and M. were walking on the verandah to the east of Kali Tapasvi's room. Rakhal said, "M., let us practice Sadhana! We have renounced home for good. When someone says, 'you have not realized God by renouncing home; then why all this fuss?' Narendra gives a good retort. He says, 'Because we could not attain Rama, must we live with Shyam and beget children?' Ah! Every now and then Narendra says nice things. You had better ask him."

M.: "What you say is right. I see that you too have become restless for God."

Rakhal: "M., how can I describe the state of my mind? Today at noontime I felt great yearning for Narendra. M., please practice Sadhana; otherwise you will not succeed. Even Sukadeva was afraid of this world. That is why immediately after his birth he fled the world. His father asked him to wait, but he ran straight away."

M.: "Yes, the *Yogopanishad* describes how Sukadeva fled this world of maya. It also describes Vyasa's conversation with Suka. Vyasa asked his son to practice religion in the world. But Suka said that the one essential thing is the Lotus Feet of God. He also expressed his disgust with worldly men for getting married and living with women."

Rakhal: "Many people think that it is enough not to look at the face of a woman. But what will you gain merely by turning your eyes to the ground at the sight of a woman? Narendra put it very well last night, when he said: 'Women exists for a man as long as he has lust. Free from lust, one sees no difference between man and woman.'"

M.: "How true it is! Children do not see the difference between man and woman."

Rakhal: "Therefore I say that we must practice spiritual discipline. How can one attain Knowledge without going beyond maya? Let us go to the big hall. Some gentlemen have come from Baranagore. Narendra is talking with them. Let's go and listen to him:

M. did not enter the room. As he was pacing outside he overheard some of the conversation.

Narendra: "There is no fixed time or place for the sandhya and other devotions."

Gentleman: "Sir, can one realize God through spiritual practice alone?"

Narendra: "Realization depends on God's grace. Sri Krishna says in the Gita:

The Lord, O Arjuna, dwells in the hearts of all beings, causing them, by His Maya, to revolve as if mounted on a machine. Take refuge in Him with all thy heart, O Bharata. By His grace wilt thou attain Supreme Peace and the Eternal Abode.

"Without the grace of God mere worship and prayer do not help at all. Therefore one should take refuge in Him."

Gentleman: "May we come now and then and disturb you?"

Narendra: "Please come whenever you like. We take our baths in the Ganges at your ghat."

Gentleman: "I don't mind that. But please see that others don't use it."

Narendra: "We shall not use your ghat, if that is what you mean."

Gentleman: "No, I don't mean exactly that. But if you see other people using it, then you had better not go."[17]

It was dusk. The evening worship was over. The devotees, as usual, sang in chorus, "Jaya Shiva Omkara". Afterwards they assembled in the room of the 'Danas'. M., too, was seated there. Prasanna was reading from the *Guru Gita*.

Narendra sang:

> I salute the Eternal Teacher, who is the Embodiment of the Bliss of Brahman,
> The Essence of knowledge and liberation, the Giver of Supreme joy;
> Who is all-pervading, like the sky, and is the goal of the Vedanta's teachings:
> Who is One, eternal, stainless, pure, and is the constant Witness of all things;
> Who dwells beyond all moods, transcending the three gunas.

Narendra again sang:

There is none higher than the Guru, none better that the Guru;
This is what Shiva has declared.
I shall sing of the blessed Guru, The Supreme Brahman;
I shall worship the blessed Guru, the Supreme Brahman;
I shall meditate on the blessed Guru, the Supreme Brahman;
I shall bow down to the blessed Guru, the Supreme Brahman.

As Narendra sang these verses from the *Guru Gita* in his melodious voice, the minds of the devotees became steady, like a candle-flame in a windless place.

Rakhal was seated in Kali Tapasvi's room. Prasanna sat near him. M., too, was there.

Rakhal had renounced the world, leaving behind his wife and child. A fire of intense renunciation burnt day and night in his heart. He was thinking seriously of going away, by himself, to the bank of the Narmada or away from the monastery.

Rakhal said to Prasanna: "Where do you want to go, running away from here? Here you are in the company of holy men. Wouldn't it be foolish to run away from this? Where will you find another like Narendra?"

Prasanna: "My parents live in Calcutta. I am afraid of being drawn by their loves. That is why I want to flee to a distant place."

Rakhal: "Can our parents love us as intensely as Gurumaharaj [meaning Sri Ramakrishna] did? What have we done for him, to deserve all this love? Why was he so eager for our welfare in body, mind, and soul? What have we done for him, to deserve all this?"

M. said to himself: "Ah! Rakhal is right. Therefore a person like Sri Ramakrishna is described as the 'Ocean of Mercy without any reason'."

Prasanna said to Rakhal: "Don't you yourself feel like running away from here?"

Rakhal: "Yes, now and then I have a fancy to spend a few days on the bank of the Narmada. I say to myself, 'Let me go to a place like that, and practice Sadhana in a garden.' Again I feel a strong desire to practice the *panchatapa* for three days. But I hesitate to live in a garden that belongs to worldly people."

Tarak and Prasanna were talking in the room of the 'Danas'. Tarak had lost his mother. His father, like Rakhal's father, had lost his wife. Now the monastery was his home. He too was trying to persuade Prasanna to live there.

Prasanna: "I have neither jnana (knowledge) nor prema (love). What have I in the world for a support?"

Tarak: "It is no doubt difficult to attain jnana; but how can you say you have no prema?"

Prasanna: "I have not yet wept for God. How can I say I have prema? What have I realized in all these days?"

Tarak: "But you have seen the Master. And why do you say that you have no jnana?"

Prasanna: "What sort of jnana are you talking about? Jnana means Knowledge. Knowledge of what? Certainly of God. But I am not even sure of the existence of God."

Tarak: "Yes, that's true. According to the jnani, there is no God."[18]

Sri Ramakrishna used to say that those who seek God pass through the state that Prasanna is now experiencing. In that state sometimes one feels doubts about the existence of God. Tarak was now reading Buddhistic philosophy. That is why he said that according to the wise, God does not exist. But Sri Ramakrishna used to say that the jnani (wise) and the bhakta (devotee) will ultimately arrive at the same point.

Narendra and Prasanna were talking in the meditation room. Rakhal, Harish, and the younger Gopal were seated in another part of the room. After a while elder Gopal Arrived.

Narendra was reading from the Gita and explaining the verse to Prasanna.

The Lord, O Arjuna, dwells in the hearts of all beings, causing them, by His maya, to revolve as if mounted on a machine. Take refuge in Him with all thy heart. O Bharata. By His grace wilt thou attain Supreme Peace and the Eternal Abode. Relinquishing all dharmas, take refuge in Me alone. I shall liberate thee from all sins. Grieve not.

Narendra: "Did you notice what Krishna said? 'Mounted on a machine.' The Lord, by His maya, causes all things to revolve as if mounted on a machine. To seek to know God? You are but a worm among worms—and you to know God? Just reflect a moment: what is man? It is said that each one of myriads of stars that shine overhead represents a solar system. This earth of ours is a part of only one solar system, and even that is too big for us. Like an insect man walks about on this earth, which, compared to the sun, is only a tiny ball."

Narendra sang:

We are born, O Lord, in the dust of earth,
And our eyes are blinded by the dust;
With dust we toy like children at play;
O give us assurance, Thou help of the weak!
Wilt Thou cast us out of Thy lap, O Lord,
For a single mistake? Wilt Thou turn away
And abandon us to our helplessness?
Oh, then we shall never be able to rise,
But shall lie for ever dazed and undone.
Mere babes are we, Father, with baby minds;
At every step we stumble and fall.
Why, then, must Thou show us Thy terrible face?
Why, Lord, must we ever behold Thy frown?
Small are we—oh, do not be angry with us,
But tenderly peak to us when we do wrong;
For though Thou dost raise us a hundred times,
A hundred times we shall fall again!
What else can one do with a helpless mind?

Then he said to Prasanna: "Surrender yourself at His feet. Resign yourself completely to His will."

Narendra sang again in an ecstatic mood:

O Lord, I am Thy servant, I am Thy servant! Thy servant am I!
O Lord, Thou art my Master, Thou art my Master! My Master art Thou!
From Thee I have received two pieces of bread and a kaupin;
When I sing Thy name, devotion wells up in my heart and shields me from harm.
Thou art the Master, the All-compassionate; this I repeat, O Lord!
Thy servant kabir has taken refuge at Thy feet.

Narendra said to Prasanna: "Don't you remember Sri Ramakrishna's words? God is the hill of sugar and you are but an ant. One grain is enough to fill your stomach, and you think of bringing home the entire hill! Don't you remember what the Master said about Sukadeva? Even Sukadeva was a big ant at the most. That is why I scolded Kali, saying: 'You fool! Do you want to measure God with your tape and foot-rule?'

"God is the Ocean of Mercy. Be His slave and take refuge in Him. He will show compassion. Pray to Him: 'Protect me always with Thy compassionate face. Lead me from the unreal to the Real, from darkness to Light, from death to Immortality. Reveal Thyself to me and protect me always with Thy compassionate face.'"

Prasanna: "What kind of spiritual discipline should one practice?"

Narendra: "Repeat His name. That's enough. Don't you remember Sri Ramakrishna's song?"

Narendra sang:

O Shyama, my only hope is in Thy hallowed name!
What need have I of kosa and kusi? What need of smiles and conventions?
Thy name dissolves death's bonds, as Shiva has proclaimed.
And I myself am Shiva's servant; whom else should I obey?
O Mother, come what may, I shall repeat Thy name;
Why should I fret myself to death? To Shiva's words I cling.

He sang again:

Mere babes are we, Father, with baby minds;
At every step we stumble and fall.
Why, then, must Thou show us Thy terrible face?
Why, Lord, must we ever behold Thy frown?

Prasanna: "Now you are saying that there is a God. Again, it is you who say that according to Charvaka and many other thinkers the world was self-created."

Narendra: "Haven't you studied chemistry? Who combines the different elements? It is a human hand that combines hydrogen, oxygen, and electricity to prepare water. Everybody admits the existence of an Intelligent Force—a Force that is the essence of Knowledge and that guides all these phenomena."

Prasanna: "How are we to know that God is kind?"

Narendra: "The Vedas say, 'That which is Thy compassionate face.' John Stuart Mill said the same thing. He said, 'How much kindness must He have, who has implanted kindness in the hearts of men.' The Master used to say: 'Faith is the one essential thing. God exists. He is very near us. Through faith alone one sees Him.'"

Narendra sang:

Where are you seeking Me, My servant? I am very close to you.
Far away you still are seeking, though I am so very near.
I am not in skin or hair; I am not in bones or flesh.
Not in mosque and not in temple, nor in Kasi or Kailas.
Never will you come on Me in Ayodhya or Dwarka;
But you will be sure to find Me if you search where faith abides.
Not in pleasant tasks or yoga, not in vairagya or sannyas,
Yet I come without delaying if you only search for Me.

Prasanna: "Sometimes you say that God does not exist, and now you are saying all these things! You are not consistent. You keep changing your opinions."

All laughed.

Narendra: "All right! I shall never change what I have just said. As long as one has desires and cravings, so long one doubts the existence of God. A man cherishes some desire or other. Perhaps he has the desire to study or pass the university examination or become a scholar, and so forth and so on."

Narendra sang again, in a voice choked with emotion:

Hail to Thee, our God and Lord! Hail, Giver of every blessing!
Hail, Thou Giver of good!
O Redeemer from fear, from danger and suffering!
Upholder of the worlds!
Hail, Lord! Victory to Thee!

Unfathomable and infinite, immeasurable, beyond compare,
O God, none equals Thee!
Lord of the Universe! O all-pervading Truth!
Thou the Atman Supreme!
Hail, Lord! Victory to Thee!
O Thou, the All-compassionate One, adored by the whole universe,
I bow before Thy feet!
Thou art the only Refuge in life and death, O Lord;
Before Thy feet I bow!
Hail, Lord! Victory to Thee!

This is our prayer, O Lord! What other boon can we implore?
Thus do we pray to Thee;
Grant us true wisdom here, and in the life hereafter
Reveal Thyself to us.
Hail, Lord! Victory to Thee!

Again Narendra sang, describing how very near God is to us—as near as the musk to the deer—and exhorting his brother disciples to drink deep from the cup of Divine Bliss:

Drinking the Bliss of Hari from the cup of prema,
Sadhu, be intoxicated!
Childhood you spent in crying, and youth in women's control;
Now, in your old age, full of phlegm and wind,
You wait for the funeral couch to beer you to the cremation ground.

Within the musk-deer's navel the fragrant musk is found;
But how can you make it understand?
Without the proper teacher to guide him on his way,
Man, too, is blindly roaming through the world,
Deluded as the foolish deer that wanders round and round the woods.

M. heard all this from the verandah.

Narendra got up. As he left the room he remarked, "My brain is heated by talking to these youngsters."

He met M. on the verandah and said, "Please let us have a drink of water."

One of the members of the math said to Narendra, "Why, then, do you say that God does not exist?"

Narendra laughed.[19]

Next day Narendranath went to Calcutta. He had to attain his lawsuit. He was going to return in the evening; the brothers missed him.

In the afternoon, Rabindra arrived, looking like a mad person. He was barefooted and had only half of his black-bordered cloth round his waist. His eyeballs were rolling like a madman's. All asked him anxiously what the matter was.

"Let me recover my breath!" he said. "I shall tell you everything presently. I am certainly not going back home. I shall stay at this very place with you all. She is certainly a traitor! Let me tell you something, friends. For her sake I gave up my habit of drinking, which I had indulged for five years. I have not taken a drop for the last eight months. And she is a traitor!"

The brothers of the math said: "Be calm, please! How did you come?"

Rabindra: "I have come barefoot all the way from Calcutta."

The brothers asked him where he had lost the other half of his cloth.

Rabindra: "When I was leaving her place she began to pull at my cloth. That is how half of it was torn off."

The brothers told him to bathe in the Ganges and cool off; then they would hear his story.

Rabindra belonged to a respectable kayastha family of Calcutta. He was twenty or twenty-two years old. He had first met Sri Ramakrishna at the Dakshineswar temple and had received his special blessing. On one occasion he had spent three nights with the Master. His disposition was very sweet and tender, and the Master had loved him dearly. Once he had said to Rabindra: "You will have to wait some time; you have to go through a few more experiences. Nothing can be done now. You see, the police can't do much just when the robbers attack a house. When the plundering is almost over, the police make their arrests."

Rabindra had many virtues. He was devoted to God and to the service of the poor. He had many spiritual qualities. But he had walked into the snare of a prostitute. Now suddenly, he had discovered that the woman was being unfaithful to him. Therefore he had come to the math in this disheveled state, resolved not to go back to the worldly life.

A devotee accompanied Rabindra to the Ganges. It was his inmost desire that Rabindra's spiritual consciousness should be awakened in the company of these holy men. When Rabindra finished his bath, the devotee took him to the adjacent cremation ground, showed him the corpses lying about, and said: "The brothers of the math come here every now and then to meditate on God. It is a good place for meditation. Here one sees clearly that the world is impermanent."

Rabindra sat down in the cremation ground to meditate. But he could not meditate long; his mind was restless.

Rabindra and the devotee returned to the math. They went to the worship room to salute the Deity. The devotee said to him, "The brothers of the math meditate in this room."

Rabindra sat there to meditate, but could not meditate long there either.

Devotee: "How do you feel? Is your mind very restless? Is that why you have got up from your seat? Perhaps you could not concentrate well."

Rabindra: "I am sure I shall not go back to the world. But the mind is restless."

M. and Rabindra were talking. No one else was present. M. was telling him stories from the life of Buddha and Chaitanya. M. said to Rabindra that Buddha's spiritual consciousness was first awakened by hearing a song of some heavenly maidens.

M. sang the song:

> We moan for rest, alas! But rest can never find;
> We know not whence we come, nor where we float away.
> Time and again we tread this round of smiles and tears;
> In vain we pine to know whither our pathway leads,
> And why we play this empty play. . .

That night Narendra, Tarak, and Harish returned from Calcutta. They said, "Oh, what a big meal we had!" They had been entertained by a devotee in Calcutta.

The members of the monastery assembled in the room of the 'Danas'. Narendra heard Rabindra's story. He sang by way of giving instruction to him:

> O man, abandon your delusion! Cast aside your wicked counsels!
> Know the Lord and free yourself from earthly suffering!
> For a few days' pleasure only, you have quite forgotten Him
> Who is the Comrade of your soul. Alas, what mockery!

Narendra sang again:

> Drinking the Bliss of Hari from the cup of prema,
> Sadhu, be intoxicated!....

A few minutes later the brothers went to Kali Tapasvi's room. Girish Ghosh had sent two of his new books to the monastery; the *Life of Buddha* and the *Life of Chaitanya.*

Since the founding of the new math Shashi had devoted himself heart and soul to the worship and service of the Master. All were amazed at his devotion. Just as he had tended Sri Ramakrishna's physical body during his illness, so now, with the same unswerving zeal, he worshiped the Master in the shrine room.

A member of the monastery was reading aloud from the lives of Buddha and Chaitanya. He was a little sarcastic while reading Chaitanya's life. Narendra snatched the book from his hand and said: "That is how you spoil a good thing!"

Narendra read the chapter describing how Chaitanya gave his love to all, from the Brahmin to the pariah.

A brother: "I say that one person cannot give love to another person."

Narendra: "But the Master gave it to me."

The brother: "Well, are you sure you have it?"

Narendra: "What can you understand about love? You belong to the servant class. All of you must serve me and massage my feet. Don't flatter yourselves by thinking you have understood everything. Now go and prepare a smoke for me."

All laughed.

The brother: "I surely will not."[20]

Sri Ramakrishna had transmitted valor to all the brothers of the math. It is no monopoly of Narendra's. Is it possible to renounce 'woman' and 'gold' without such inner fire?

It was Tuesday, May 10th 1887. Tuesday is a very auspicious day for the worship of the Divine Mother. Brother disciples made an arrangement for Her special worship at the monastery.

M. was going to Ganges to take his bath. Rabindra was walking alone on the roof. He heard Narendra singing the Sixth Stanza on Nirvana:

> Death or fear I have none, nor any distinction of caste;
> Neither father nor mother nor even a birth have I;
> I am Pure Knowledge and Bliss: I am Shiva! I am Shiva!
> I have no form or fancy; the all-pervading am I;
> Everywhere I exist, yet I am beyond the senses;
> Neither salvation am I, nor anything that may be known:
> I am Pure Knowledge and Bliss: I am Shiva! I am Shiva!

Rabindra went to the Ganges to take his bath. Presently he returned to the monastery clad in his wet cloth.

Narendra said to M. in a whisper: "He has bathed in the Ganges. It would be good to initiate him now into sannyasi."

Both Narendra and M. smiled.

Prasanna asked Rabindra to change his wet cloth and gave him a dry gerrua (ochre) cloth. Narendra said to M., "Now he is going to put on the cloth of renunciation."

M. smiled and said: "What kind of renunciation?"

Narendra: "Why, the renunciation of 'woman' and 'gold'."

Rabindra put on the ochre cloth and entered Kali Tapasvi's room to meditate.[21]

Sri Ramakrishna used to say, "In the morning and evening the mind remains highly imbued with sattva ideas; those are the times when one should meditate with earnestness."

After the passing away of Sri Ramakrishna Narendranath and his brother disciples underwent a lot of religious practice at the Baranagore Math. They used to get up at 3 a.m. and after washing face etc. or after bath they would sit in the worship room and become absorbed in Japa and meditation. Sometimes the Japa and meditation continued from morning till four or five in the afternoon. Ramakrishnananda Maharaj waited and waited with their meal ready, till at last he would come and snatch them from their meditation by force.

They were monks, and whatever they could manage by begging and other means, would be utilized for defraying the Math expenses. Suresh Mitra and Balaram Bose used to bear a great part of expenses. Swamiji said about Suresh Mitra, "It was this Suresh Mitra who used to think for us in those days. His devotion and faith have no parallel!..."

The best description of those days comes from the lips of Swami Vivekananda. Years later, when he was asked by a disciple, he said: "Owing to want of funds I would sometimes fight for abolishing the Math altogether. But I could never induce Ramakrishnananda to accede to the proposal. Know Ramakrishnananda to be the central figure of the Math. There have been days when the Math was without a grain of food. If some rice was collected by begging, there was no salt to take it with! On some days there would be only rice and salt, but nobody cared for it in the least. We were then being carried away by a tidal wave of spiritual practice. Boiled bimba leaves, rice, and salt—this was the menu for a month at a stretch. Oh, those wonderful days! The austerities of that period were enough to dismay supernatural beings, not to speak of men. But it is a tremendous truth that if there be real worth in you, the more are circumstances against you, the more will that inner power manifest itself.... There was the life of Sri Ramakrishna before us, and that was why we did not care much for privations and hardships."[22]

In those days, Narendranath had to fight with another problem, which was very much unfortunate to him. He said: "Then came a terrible time—for me personally and for all the other boys as well. But to me came such misfortune! On the one side was my mother, my brothers. My father died at that time, and we were left poor. Oh, very poor, almost starving all the time! I was the only hope of the family, the only one who could do anything to help them. I had to stand between my two worlds. On the one hand, I would have to see my mother and brothers starve unto death; on the other, I had believed that Sri Ramakrishna's ideas were for the good of India and the world, and had to be preached and worked out. And so the fight went on in my mind for days and months. Sometimes I would pray for five or six days and nights together without stopping. Oh, the agony of those days! I was living in hell! The natural affections of my boy's heart drawing me to my family—I could not bear to see those who were the nearest and dearest to me suffering. On the other hand, nobody to sympathize with me. Who would sympathize with the imagination of a boy—imaginations that caused so much suffering to others? Who would sympathize with me? None—except one [Sri Sarada Devi]. That one's sympathy brought blessing and hope...."

He continued: "Well, that lady [Sri Ramakrishna's] wife, was the only one who sympathized with the idea of those boys.... I believed, as I was living, that these ideas were going to rationalize India and bring better days to my land and foreign races. With that belief, came the realization that it is better that a few persons suffer than that such ideas should die out of the world. What if a mother or two brothers die? It is a sacrifice. Let it be done. No great thing can be done without sacrifice. The heart must be plucked out and the bleeding heart placed upon the altar. Then great things are done."[23]

And thus they went on, that band of boys. Balaram Bose died on 13th April, 1890, and Surendranath Mitra passed away on 25th of the same year. Thereafter, they got support from nobody. They had to beg from door to door for food; got hips and haws—the refuse of everything—a piece of bread here and there. The young disciples were mostly from well to do families, and are of higher casts, and looked beautiful. Hence mostly the people would refuse them giving anything when they would go for begging. Rather they would laugh at them or advice them to earn their livelihood. If ever they could manage some rice from begging, they would boil them and eat with chili-soup. A saucer, two metal water-pots—one for cooking and other for drinking water, an old kettle for preparing tea, and two iron dishes, were all of their utensils. So they had to serve food on banana-leaf or some other leaves like that. Whenever they couldn't manage the leaf, they would spread a cloth on the floor, and pour rice on it, and they all would sit around it to have their meal all together. When they could not manage anything to eat, they would remain with empty stomach. A mat on the floor, and bricks for resting head was their bed. Narendranath would sometimes make joke with his brother disciple, and say, "Give me a soft brick so that I may rest my head." In winter they would lay as close as possible to enjoy the heat of the body of each other, because they had no blanket to protect themselves from cold. This was not all. They had also to fight with the mosquitoes, which didn't care the rule of the British Government. Instead of all these hardship they never stopped worshiping God or spiritual practice. They would remain absorbed in meditation for a long time. They never lost faith in God. They were very much strict to their ideal that they were taught by Sri Ramakrishna.

Sri Ramakrishna said that monks are of three types—first class, middle class and the lower class. Monks, who never search for food, belong to the first class. Middle class monks sing the name of Narayana and move from door to door, but never ask for food. And they, who quarrel with householders, if they are refused, are of lower class. First class monks take the food that comes automatically to them. One day Narendranath and his brother disciples decided: "We all have renounced the world in the name of Sri Ramakrishna. Today we will go nowhere, and let us see whether he gives us food or not. We will neither go for begging nor ask anybody else to give us food." Saying this they all became absorbed in meditation. Hence, the whole day had passed, but nobody came with food. At night they heard someone knocking at the door. Narendranath said, "Open the door, and see who is there. Look, whether the man has something in his hand." A brother opened the door, and saw a man from Lalaji's temple was waiting there with delicious food for them. They all became overwhelmed with joy, and came to know how kind was the Master. They offered the food to the Deity, and then enjoyed the grace of God. They had experienced the same so many times.

Mahendranath Dutta, brother of Narendranath, has informed us that just after the Baranagore Math was established, the young disciples started wearing ochre cloth on going through the scripturally-prescribed ritual for initiation into Sannyasi. According to *The Gospel of Sri Ramakrishna* the disciples were seen in ochre cloth on 21st February 1887, which was the day of *Shivachaturdashi*. Narendranath, Tarak and Kali were in ochre cloth when they went to Gaya from Cossipore. According to the *Life of Swami Vivekananda* by His Eastern and Western Disciples: "Sometime in January 1887, Narendranath sought the opinion of his brother-disciples on going through the scripturally-prescribed ritual for initiation into Sannyasi. They gladly agreed to his proposal that they should observe it. Kali had already obtained from a sannyasi of the Puri denomination information about the performance of the Viraja-homa, and other matters connected with the Sannyasa rite. That he should have this seemed to them nothing but the grace of the Master and a sign of his will. A day was fixed in the third week of January. Early in the morning of that day the young men bathed in the Ganges and then assembled in the shrine-room of the Math, where the Master's photograph and relics were being regularly worshiped. Shashi did the worship of the Master as usual, and then the Viraja-homa was performed. Narendra asked Kali to chant the Mantras prescribed for the occasion. The brothers offered the oblations one by one to the fire as the Mantras were chanted. At first Narendranath, and then Rakhal, Niranjan, Sharat, Shashi, Sarada and others repeated the Mantras and offered the oblations. Afterwards kali did the same. Sri Ramakrishna had already given them ochre cloths at Cossipore, making them monks; this ceremony was the ritual and traditional confirmation of that. It is probable that it was on this occasion that Baburam also went through the ceremony."

Thus they entered into a new life with a name and new identification. Narendranath came to be known as Swami Vividishananda, which he seldom used. Narendranath wanted to take the name Ramakrishnananda for himself; but seeing Shashi's devotion to Sri Ramakrishna, he gave him that name. During those days, when he was a wandering monk, Narendranath changed his name twice—first to Vivekananda (February 1891-October 1892) and then to Sachchidananda (October 1892-May 1893)—to prevent his brother-disciples following him. But on the eve of his departure for the West in May 1893, he took back the name Vivekananda for good, perhaps at the request of the Maharaja of Khetri.

Narendranath liked to make fun by naming others. He had given many new names to many persons. Since his boyhood he was in a habit of such fun. Mockery, fun, love and respect are found being revealed in the new names given by him. He liked to play with names. Once he said—it is hard to overcome the attachment with the name. A young man named Rama (Later became a monk) used to stay at Belur Math every now and then. Swamiji had to milk a goat; he said to Rama, "O, 'Kyabla' (means foolish), hold the goat, I have to milk it." Later he thought that it was not good to call someone as 'Kyabla'; perhaps the boy was hurt by the same. He tried to rectify himself saying: "Name is nothing but a name only, like Vivekananda."

Sri Ramakrishna often called his beloved Narendranath as 'Laren'. Narendranath also used to call him by many names like: 'Mr. Paramahamsa', 'Paramahamsa', 'Gora Roy of Dakshineswar', 'Pagla Bamun (means mad priest)', 'Prist of Dakshineswar', 'Worshiper of idol', 'Old man', and 'Thakur' and so on. But he introduced him to the world as 'Sri Ramakrishna' and 'Thakur' to the devotees.

On the occasion of initiation into Sannyasa, Swamiji gave new name to his brother-disciples. Rakhal or Raja Maharaj, the dearest and dependable brother-disciple of Swamiji, was named as Swami Brahmananda. Baburam Maharaj, overwhelmed with devotion, was named as Swami Premananda; Shashi Maharaj, the founder of the shrine of Sri Ramakrishna, was named as Swami Ramakrishnananda; Sarat Maharaj, the gatekeeper of Holy Mother, became Swami Saradananda; Yogen Maharaj became Swami Yogananda; Latu, the wonderful creation of Sri Ramakrishna, was named as Swami Adbhutananda; Tarak Maharaj, who was also called as Mahapurush Maharaj, was named as Swami Shivananda; Vaidantic Kali Maharaj became Swami Abhedananda; Hari became Turiyananda; Gangadhar, who was as holy as the Ganges, was named as Swami Akhandananda; Niranjan Maharaj became Swami Niranjanananda; Tulsi Maharaj became Swami Nirmalananda; Senior Gopal became Swami Advaitananda, and so many sweet and holy names were given by Swami Vivekananda.

Probably Swamiji couldn't give one name. Sarada Maharaj changed his names as Swami Trigunatitananda, which can hardly be pronounced by the ordinary people so smoothly. In a letter from New York, Swamiji wrote: "You must have an iron will if you would cross the ocean. You must be strong enough to pierce mountains. I am coming next winter. We shall set the world on fire.... In your lips and hands the Goddess of Learning will make Her seat; the Lord of infinite power will be seated on your chest; you will do works that will strike the world with wonder. By the bye, can't you shorten your name a bit, my boy? What a long, long name—a single name enough to fill a volume! Well, you hear people say that the Lord's name keeps away death! It is not the simple name Hari, mind you. It is those deep and sonorous names, such as Aghabhaganarakabinasan (Destroyer of Agha, Bhaga, and Naraka) Tripurmadbhanjana (Subduer of the pride of Tripura, demon of the "Three cities"), and Ashesnihsheshkalyankar (Giver of infinite and endless blessings), and so forth—that put to rout King Death and his whole party. Won't it look nice if you simplify yours a little? But it is too late, I am afraid, as it has already been abroad. But, believe me, it is a world-entrancing, death-defying name that you have got!"[24]

In those days the Baranagore Math was in an intense spiritual atmosphere. Everyone would get surprised at the rigorous life of Narendranath and his brother-disciples. Yet they were not satisfied with their spiritual progress. They would sigh, "Oh, wonderful were Sri Ramakrishna's renunciation and longing for God! We are not able to attain even one-sixteenth part of what he attained."

They would be absorbed in studies of philosophy. The theories of Kant, Hegel, Mill, Spencer, and even those of atheists and materialists, were discussed. They would go through history, religion, sociology, literature, art, science, '*Religion in Social Evolution*', '*India Asks who is Christ*', '*Lawi's History of Philosophy*', and so on. One day Narendranath would prove that God was a myth; the next day he would say to refuge oneself at the feet of God. They would compare their study of Sankhya, Yoga, Naya, Vaisheshika, Mimamsa and Vedanta with each other and their point to agreement and difference were brought out with analytical wisdom. They compared Vedanta with Buddhist philosophy and vice versa. Occasionally Christian missionaries would come to the Math. They argued with the monks. They didn't find words against the strong points of Narendranath, and being defeated they would realize that he had great knowledge about the greatness of Christ. He would develop original lines of thought, bringing out the historical importance of Sri Ramakrishna's life and teachings, and their significance for present and future generation of Hindus. He would show how that life was destined to alter their theological outlook by giving them a truer understanding of Hindu ideals.

One day Swami Yogananda asked Mahendranath, "You read the Bible every now and then, Can you say, which is the best lesson that you have learnt from the Bible? What was the last word that Jesus told his disciples?" Mahendranath couldn't follow the questions, and therefore, he remained silent. Yogen Maharaj laughed and said, "Love each other!" Then he added, "Realizing the meaning of these words is as same as to read the whole of the Bible."

In those days all the young monks were filled with the spirit of the Master. His personality was felt as living among them. They always dwelt in the ecstasy of spiritual zeal. Some would sit motionless for hours plunged in meditation, some sang devotional songs, some would sit at cremation ground deeply absorbed in meditation at night, or they all sit night after night before Dhuni, in their determination of realizing God. Narendra's sense of responsibility for them would keep him watchful. If ever any of them was found practicing austerities too much, he would say, "Do you think you are all going to be Ramakrishna Paramhamsa? That will never be. A Ramakrishna Paramhamsa is born once in an age!"

Swami Sadananda, while speaking of those days, said: "During these years Swamiji would work twenty-four hours at a time. He was like a lunatic in his activity. Early in the morning, whilst it was still dark, he would rise and call the others, singing, 'Awake! Arise, all ye who would drink of the divine nectar!' And long after midnight he and the other monks would still be sitting on the roof of the monastery building, singing hymns of praise. The neighbours expostulated, but to no avail. And the musical voice of Swamiji would lead the chanting of the names of 'Sita-Rama' or 'Radha-Krishna'. Those were strenuous Pandits (learned persons) argued and discussed. But he, the Swami, was never for one moment idle, never dull."[25]

In those days Narendranath and his brother-disciples were busy in study of religious books, arguing on different subjects of spiritual life, meditation and chanting the name of God, and so on; and simultaneously another quality was also found to be revealed in them. They used to serve poor people who had no one to help, and would never let them return without any refreshment who often would come to visit the Baranagore Math. They also tried their level best to nurse them who were ill or in distress.

Sir Nagendra Nath Gupta has told about an incident of those days: "Vivekananda with some of his fellow-disciples was living in a suburb of Calcutta quietly pursuing his studies and rendering such small social service as came his way. One day he met a police officer who was a friend of Vivekananda's family. He was a Superintendent of Police in the Criminal Investigation Department. He greeted Vivekananda cordially and invited him to dinner for the same evening. There were some other visitors when Vivekananda arrived. At length they left, but there were no signs of dinner. Instead, the host spoke about other matters until suddenly lowering his voice and assuming a menacing look he said, 'Come, now, you had better make a clean breast of it and tell me the truth. You know you cannot fool me with your stories for I know your game. You and your gang pretend to be religious men, but I have positive information that you are conspiring against the Government.' 'What do you mean?' asked Vivekananda, amazed and indignant, 'What conspiracies are you speaking of, and what have we to do with them?' 'That is what I wasn't to know,' coolly replied the police officer. 'I am convinced it is some nefarious plot, and you are the ringleader. Out with the whole truth, and then I shall arrange that you are made an approver.' 'If you know everything, why don't you come and arrest us and search our house?' said Vivekananda, and rising he quietly closed the door. Now, Vivekananda was an athletic young man of a powerful build, while the police officer was a puny, wizened creature. Turning round upon him Vivekananda said, 'You have called me to your house on a false pretext and have made a false accusation against me and my companions. That is your profession. I, on the other hand, have been taught not to resent an insult. If I had been a criminal and a conspirator, there would be nothing to prevent me from wringing your neck before you could call out for help. As it is, I leave you in peace.' And Vivekananda opened the door and went out, leaving the redoubtable police officer speechless with ill-concealed fright. Neither Vivekananda nor his companions were ever again molested by this man."[26]

This incident shows the foreign domination of those days in India, and also proved that Vivekananda had started his work what he was told by Sri Ramakrishna to do. Sri Ramakrishna made him the leader of his brother-disciples, and he was given the charge for doing good to the human beings. Being the superintendent of the Master's work he played his role with full responsibility. He prepared his soldiers by teaching his brother-disciples. Each of them was a piece of diamond, and was polished by Swami Vivekananda, who was transformed into an eternal spirit of the world by the magnetic personality of Sri Ramakrishna.

Group at Baranagore Math in 1887
Standing (left to right):
Swami Shivananda,
Swami Ramakrishnananda,
Swami Vivekananda, the monastery cook,
Deven Majumdar, Mahendranath Gupta (M), Swami Trigunatitananda, Mastaphi (maternal uncle of Deven Majumdar)
Sitting (let to right):
Swami Niranjanananda, Swami Saradananda, Hootka Gopal, and Swami Abhedananda

The building was a dreary, deserted place, very old and sadly in need of repairs. It was also said to be haunted. Indeed, nobody else would have lived there. This house was rented at Rs. 10 a month and became the Baranagore monastery.

6
Wandering Monk

Narendranath was transformed into Swami Vividishananda and stepped into the monastic Order of Ramakrishna during his living at Baranagore Math. He had completed the primary phase of the work that he had been given by Sri Ramakrishna to do, with great devotion. He had built a band of young monks who had tremendous faithfulness to each other and tremendous love for one another.

They were ready to plunge into the next phase of the work. The ideal of Sri Ramakrishna got to be carried out. They had to spread the feelings of fraternity among the people of the world, remove the differences between religions. Narendranath and all his brother-disciples were ready to sacrifice their lives for the good of the human beings. They were well aware of antagonism that had to be faced with strong determination. They were well determined—if the whole universe stands against them no one can hurt them. It must crumble before them, because they were pure, strong, sincere and unselfish and the power of the Lord Himself was present in them. Sri Ramakrishna's 'Naren' and the band of young devout monks were ready to spread the message of the Master throughout the world. They had to bring the spirit of the age of the Vedas back to the world. Their mission was for making new human beings bound with the feelings of fraternity. 'No compromise' was the watchword.

The best description came from the lips of Swami Vivekananda himself: "Sri Ramakrishna was a wonderful gardener. Therefore he has made a bouquet of different flowers and formed his Order. All different types and ideas have come into it, and many more will come. Sri Ramakrishna used to say, 'Whoever has prayed to God sincerely for one day, must come here.' Know each of those who are here [the Sannyasin disciples of Sri Ramakrishna], to be of great spiritual power.... When they will go out, they will be the cause of the awakening of spirituality in people. Know them to be part of the spiritual body of Sri Ramakrishna, who was the embodiment of infinite religious ideas."[1] Hence the band of monks went out to fulfil their mission of spreading the message of love and fraternity to the world.

In a lecture Swamiji said about his teacher Sri Ramakrishna: "The teacher is more than my father, and I am truly his child, his son in every respect. I owe him obedience and reverence first, before my own father even; because the father gave me this body, but he [Sri Ramakrishna] showed me the way to salvation, he is greater than father. And we carry this love, this respect for our teacher all our lives. And that is the only organization that exists."[2]

As an introduction to his teacher he said: "I happened to get and old man to teach me, and he was very peculiar. He did not go much for intellectual scholarship, scarcely studied boos; but when he was a boy, he was seized with the tremendous idea of getting truth direct. First, he tried by studying his own religion. Then he got the idea that he must get the truth of the other religions; and with that idea he joined all the sects, one after another. For the time being he did of these different sects in turn, until interpenetrated with the particular ideal of that sect. After a few years he would go to another sect. When he had gone through with all that, he came to the conclusion that they were all good. He had no criticism to offer to anyone; they are all so many paths leading to the same goal. And then he said, 'That is a glorious thing, that there should be so many paths, because if there were only one path, perhaps it would suit only an individual man. The more the number of paths, the more the chance for every one of us to know the truth. If I cannot be taught in one language, I will try another, and so on.' Thus his benediction was for every religion."[3]

Narendranath to Swami Vivekananda via Vividishananda—the tough journey is described by him: "...there at his feet I conceived these ideas—there with some other young men. I was just a boy, I went there when I was about sixteen. Some of the other boys were still younger, some a little older—about a dozen or more. And together we conceived that this ideal had to be spread. And not only spread, but made practical. That is to say, we must show the spirituality of the Hindus, the mercifulness of the Buddhists, the activity of the Christians, the brotherhood of the Mohammedans, by our practical lives. 'We shall start a universal religion now and here,' we said, 'we will not wait'."

He continued: "Our teacher was an old man who would never touch a coin with his hands. He took just the little food offered, just so many yards of cotton cloth, no more. He could never be induced to take any other gift. With all these marvelous ideas, he was strict, because that made him free. The monk in India is the friend of the prince today, dines with him; and tomorrow he is with the beggar, sleeps under a tree. He must come into contact with everyone, must always move about. As the saying is, 'The rolling stone gathers no moss'.

"This handful of boys got hold of these ideas, and all the practical results that sprang out of these ideas. Universal religion, great sympathy for the poor, and all that are very good in theory, but one must practice.

"Then came the sad day when our old teacher died. We nursed him the best we could. We had no friends. Who would listen to a few boys, with their crank notions? Nobody. At least, in India, boys are nobodies. Just think of it—a dozen boys, telling people vast, big ideas, saying they are determined to work these ideas out in life. Why, everybody laughed. From laughter it became serious; it became persecution. Why, the parents of the boys came to feel like spanking every one of us. And the more we were derided, the more determined we became.

"Then came a terrible time—for me personally and for all the other boys as well. But to me came such misfortune! On the one side was my mother, my brothers. My father died at that time, and we were left poor. Oh, very poor, almost starving all the time! I was the only hope of the family, the only one who could do anything to help them. I had to stand between my two worlds. On the one hand, I would have to see my mother and brothers starve unto death; on the other, I had believed that this man's ideas were for the good of India and the world, and had to be preached and worked out. And so the fight went on in my mind for days and months. Sometimes I would pray for five or six days and nights together without stopping. Oh, the agony of those days! I was living in hell! The natural affections of my boy's heart drawing me to my family—I could not bear to see those who were the nearest and dearest to me suffering. On the other hand, nobody to sympathize with me. Who would sympathize with the imaginations of a boy—imaginations that caused so much suffering to others? Who would sympathize with me? None—except one."[4]

That day, a turbulent power was transfused into Narendranath and his brother-disciples under the soothing shade of love of the Mother. With reference to that Holy Mother Swamiji said: "That one's sympathy brought blessing and hope. She was a woman. Our teacher, the great monk, was married when he was a boy and she a mere child. When he became a young man, and all this religious zeal was upon him, she came to see him. Although they had been married for long, they had not seen very much each other until they were grown up. Then he said to his wife, 'Behold, I am your husband; you have a right to this body. But I cannot live the sex life, although I have married you. I leave it to your judgment'. And she wept and said, 'God speed you! The Lord bless you! Am I the woman to degrade you? If I can, I will help you, Go on in your work.'

"That was the woman. The husband went on and became a monk in his own way; and from a distance the wife went on helping as much as she could. And later, when the man had become a great spiritual giant, she came—really, she was the first disciple—and she spent the rest of her life taking care of the body of this man. He never knew whether he was living or dying, or anything. Sometimes, when talking, he would get so excited that if he sat on live charcoals, he did not know it. Live charcoals! Forgetting all about his body, all the time.

"Well, that lady, his wife, was the only one who sympathized with the idea of those boys. But she was powerless. She was poorer than we were. Never mind! We plunged into the breach. I believed, as I was living, that these ideas were going to rationalize India and bring better days to many lands and foreign races. With that belief, came the realization that it is better that a few persons suffer than that such ideas should die out of the world."[5]

We can refer to his remarkable words that help us to get an account of his strong determination. He said: "What if a mother or two brothers die? It is a sacrifice. Let it be done. No great thing can be done without sacrifice. The heart must be plucked out and the bleeding heart placed upon the altar. Then great things are done. Is there any other way? None have found it. I appeal to each one of you, to those who have accomplished any great thing. Oh, how much it has cost! What agony! What torture! What terrible suffering is behind every deed of success in every life! You know that, all of you.

"And thus we went on, that band of boys. The only thing we got from those around us was a kick and a curse—that was all. Of course, we had to beg from door to door for our food: got hips and haws—the refuse of everything—a piece of bread here and there. We got hold of a broken-down old house, with hissing cobras living underneath; and because that was the cheapest, we went into that house and lived there.

"...One thing always to keep us hopeful—the tremendous faithfulness to each other, the tremendous love between us. If I become the devil himself tomorrow, they will say, 'Here we are still! We will never give you up!' That is a great blessing.

"In happiness, in misery, in famine, in pain, in the grave, in heaven, or in hell he who never gives me up is my friend. Is such friendship a joke? A man may have salvation through such friendship. That brings salvation if we can love like that. If we have that faithfulness, why, there is the essence of all concentration. You need not worship any gods in the world if you have that faith, that strength, that love. And that was there with us all throughout that hard time."[6]

During the itinerant days, when Swamiji and his brother-disciples travelled from Baranagore to the rest of India and different countries of the world, this love and faith made them "go from the Himalayas to Cape Comorin, from the Indus to the Brahmaputra."

"This band of boys began to travel about." How was that journey at the beginning? Let us listen to the description of the same from the holy lips of Swamiji. He said: "Gradually we began to draw attention: ninety per cent was antagonism, very little of it was helpful. For we had one fault: we were boys—in poverty and with all the roughness of boys. He who has to make his own way in life is a bit rough, he has not much time to be smooth and suave and polite—"my lady and my gentleman", and all that. You have seen that in life, always. He is a rough diamond, he has not much polish, and he is a jewel in an indifferent casket."[7]

Oh, what a beautiful comparison! "A jewel in an indifferent casket." We know that a piece of diamond glitters only after going through a process of well polish. Here the pieces of diamonds were collected, cut, and polished by Sri Ramakrishna himself in his laboratory at Dakshineswar and Cossipore. If there was anything left unfinished, Narendranath had completed the task while they had been fighting with the pain of poverty at Baranagore Math. He transformed himself into Swami Vividishananda to Sachchidananda, and to Vivekananda, and simultaneously built a band of young monks suitable for the movement of the Ramakrishna Order. Then he said: "And there we were. 'No compromise!'—was the watchword. 'This is the ideal, and this has got to be carried out. If we meet the king, though we die, we must give him a bit of our minds; if the peasant, the same'. Naturally, we met with antagonism."[8]

One, who lives for others, has to face many problems, but finally he wines for his sincerity and strong determination. He, who wants to do good things, only knows the reality of adverse conditions. Swamiji has told about the experience in his life. He said: "This is life's experience; if you really want the good of others, the whole universe may stand against you and cannot hurt you. It must crumble before your power of the Lord Himself in you if you are sincere and really unselfish. And those boys were that. They came as children, pure and fresh from the hands of nature. Said our Master: 'I want to offer at the altar of the Lord only those flowers that have not even been smelled, fruits that have not been touched with the fingers.' The words of the great man sustained us all. For he saw through the future life of those boys that he collected from the streets of Calcutta, so to say. People used to laugh at him when he said, 'You will see—this boy, that boy, what he becomes.' His faith was unalterable: 'Mother showed it to me. I may be weak, but when She says this to so—She can never make mistakes—it must be so.'"[9]

His attitude was: "Twenty times I have died before, and I shall die many times after this. What of that?" Ignoring the fear of death that small band of pure and heroic monks stepped out on the road and started to do the next phase of their work as dictated by Sri Ramakrishna: "The thing, which is mostly desired by others, is not for you. You have come to the world to work for the world. Great work is yet to be done. You cannot leave the world before the work is done."

A monk's life is like a river. A river doesn't become dirty as it goes on flowing continuously. For the same reason a monk remains free from blemish. Hindu monks are fond of pilgrimage. They, who have renounced the world for realizing the God, would like to move from place to place; it is natural to them. The young disciples of Baranagore also would feel hearing the call from distant lands. Being unable to ignore that call many of them every now and then would set out for different places. After the passing away of Sri Ramakrishna some of them went to Vrindavan. Holy Mother also went there and stayed for several months. Once Prasanna (Swami Trigunatitananda) went out for Vrindavan on foot leaving a letter for Narendranath, but he could go only up to Konnagore and next day he returned to monastery for what other brother-disciples laughed at him.

There was a twofold tendency in each member of the Baranagore Math. At this time Narendranath was torn between loyalty to the Math and its mission, and loyalty to the traditional vision of the wandering monks. Once, during conversation, Rakhal Maharaj (Swami Brahmananda) said to Narendranath, "I am thinking for a pilgrimage." Swamiji became angry and said, "Of course you will. Do you think that God will appear in front of you if you move around the world?" There was reason behind his words—the Math was then just established, and the brother-disciples were too young to live the hard life of a wandering monk. They were not yet built so much strong to fight with any kind of adverse condition. They should be built as strong as the thunder so that they could easily overcome any difficult situation. Beside that some of them were required to be present to continue the regular worship of deity and so on. Swamiji would say: "I used to fire them to break it up and go about the world begging. But on no account could I make Shashi yield. He would hear of nothing of the kind. You must know him to be the backbone of the Math." Narendranath, too, wished to enjoy the peace of solitude, and wanted to test his inner strength as well as teach others no to depend upon him always. So he was busy to make his brother-disciples strong with both physical and spiritual power.

As the days went on, the itinerant tendency began to grow among the young monks. Gradually they began to leave the Math for a distant land. Narendranath was very much concerned about his brother-monks, but his attitude was: "Let them have their own experiences. They must break free from the monastery and test their own strength. Their experiences of the new life will make men of them, absolutely fearless and invincible, and spiritually independent; thus they will become giants." And one by one all the brother-monks were to go on pilgrimage, except Shashi (Swami Ramakrishnananda).

From 1887 to 1890 Narendranath went out for different places, but he could never stay out of station for a long. He would return after a short while for he had some urgent work regarding the Math. Every time he would say, "This is the last. Next time I'll not return."

In the summer of 1887 he had fever owing to kidney trouble, and subsequently went to Simultala and Vaidyanath at the request of his brother-monks. They thought that he needed a short rest from the strenuous life of monastery, and a change of environment. Sometimes the serious illness of his brother-monks would bring him back to the monastery.

However, in 1891 he left the monastery and truly became a wandering monk. He didn't come back until February 1897. Very little information is available about where he lived and what he did during the period from 1891 to 1893. He was indifferent to keeping a note of his journeys and doings. Afterwards he spoke of them vaguely and casually. Perhaps he held them too scared to be discussed even with his brother-monks. Little information is found in the reminiscences of some of his brother-monks who were with him for a short period. During this period, he used to change his name, as a result of which it was hard to trace his address. People, who met him in those days, kept records of his stay with them. Some of his letters to his brother-disciples are also considered as an evidence of his movements. Thus it is not possible to record the events of his life from 1887 to 1893 with some accuracy. Many of his brother-monks, excepting Ramakrishnananda and Adbhutananda, were with him when he broke off communication with the Baranagore Math. Particularly Akhandananda was with him longer than any one of the others was. Hereafter we shall call him the "Swamiji".

Itinerant Days in Northern India

According to Swami Gambhirananda, Swamiji left the Baranagore Math probably in 1887, and went to Varanasi. This was his first pilgrimage. He was accompanied by Premananda and Sri Jogyeswar Bhattacherjee (or Fakirbabu), home tutor of Rambabu, the son of Balaram Bose. Varanasi is the home of monks, the centre of learning, and the Seat of Shiva. 'Naren', the beloved disciple of Sri Ramakrishna, was the incarnation of Lord Shiva. Hence Shiva went to visit His own Seat.

He stayed there at Varanasi for a week. The sacred Ganges, thousands of men and women—some are engaged in praying, some are absorbed in meditation; the numerous temples—Visweswara, Vireswara, Annapurna, Durga and idols of many other gods and goddesses—made him overwhelmed with joy, and a vivid impression was imprinted on his mind. In the crowd there were singers, musicians, dancers, literates, illiterates, devotees, poor, rich, monks and householders.

One day, when Swamiji was returning from the temple of Mother Durga, he was surrounded by a troop of large monkeys. They were in a habit to torture innocent people. Swamiji knew the behaviour of those monkeys. So, he became afraid of them and began to run; but the monkeys followed him with the same speed. When he was about to be caught by them, he heard an old man shouting: "Stop and face the brutes." The words brought him to his sense. As soon as he turned and boldly faced the heinous monkeys, they immediately fell back and fled. Swamiji burst into laughter and by that time an old monk came in front of him. With reverence and gratitude Swamiji gave the traditional greeting to the monk, and the monk similarly responded before he walked away. Swamiji understood that he was saved from the monkeys by the advice of that monk.

Later in a lecture in New York Swamiji referred to this incident and said: "That is a lesson for all life—face the terrible, face it boldly. Like the monkeys, the hardships of life fall back when we cease to flee from them. If we are ever to gain freedom, it must be by conquering nature, never by running away. Cowards never win victories. We have to fight fear and troubles and ignorance if we expect them to flee before us."

Swamiji also went to Sarnath, close to Varanasi. At that time, the Stupa of Sarnath and most of its ruins were overgrown with jungle. Buddha had preached the first of his Sermons here. When Swamiji visited the place, most of the Sarnath was ruined, and it seemed to be destroyed by the enemies of the Buddhist monastery. A Stupa was built here during the reign of Ashoka. This Stupa is still in existence, and it was also seen by Huen Sung. At a short distance a big stone was discovered by Mr. Cunningham. Buddha's birth, his attaining Enlightenment, his teachings, and his Nirvana—images of all these events were engraved on this stone.

Sarnath is a city located 13 kilometers north-east of Varanasi near the confluence of the Ganges and the Gomati rivers in Uttar Pradesh, India. The deer park in Sarnath is where Gautama Buddha first taught the *Dharma*, and where the Buddhist Sangha came into existence through the enlightenment of *Kondanna*. During his stay at Kashi, Swamiji used to sit by the river Ganges and would be absorbed in meditation until late night. Being revealed from an iceberg of the Himalayas the holy stream of Ganges flows down towards Calcutta touching many holy places on her way. She is also called the stream of Shiva. Sweet sounds of her waves seem to be chanting holy mantra while she flows by the side of temples of Varanasi. One of her streams touches the holy place of Dakshineswar, where Sri Ramakrishna had played his divine play. Swamiji remembered the history of Varanasi and Sarnath while he was sitting on the bank of the Ganges and watching the beauty of her waves. He was then about twenty-five years old. He was born and he passed his boyhood in the sensualist civilization of Calcutta, the capital of India. Sitting by the Ganges he was thinking about the greatness of Kashi, which is the religious capital of India for the last two thousand years. The place is known only for religious culture. Whereas in Calcutta no such religious practices were found as remarkable as it was found in Kashi. Swamiji had been thinking about this strange land of India, and its history, and the holy Ganges, the life line of this country. The holy Ganges is flowing—from the religious capital to the capital of sensualist civilization. He was thinking how to make a synthesis by mixing these two cultures. Monks of Kashi have no knowledge about what is meant by the modern civilization of the world. They are living in the past. Here, time is motionless; Sarnath is concealed. There in Calcutta, modern people are running after the inane culture of western civilization. They don't like to remember the custom and culture of ancient India. He realized a dark world hidden behind the nobles, saints, temples, the learned community, and schools of Kashi. Hundreds of poor, hungry and widows of different ages thrown away of the society. Lame, crippled, ill and lonely men and women were moving here and there—sinner and pious both are present. He sat on the Ganges and a mighty flow of various such thoughts surged in his mind.

At Varanasi, Swamiji stayed at the residence of Dwarkadas, where he met many monks and scholars. One day the gentleman introduced him to the celebrated scholar and Bengali writer, Bhudev Mukhopadhyaya. Swamiji had a long conversation with him on the merits of various Hindu ideals. When they parted, Mr. Mukhopadhyaya said, "Wonderful! Such a vast knowledge, experience and foresight at such an early age! I am sure he will be a great man."

Swamiji also visited the revered saint Trailanga Swami. He saluted him. Trailanga Swami was mostly found absorbed in meditation, and he didn't talk to any person. Sometime, when he came down to his normal state, he would answer in writing if a question was put to him. Sri Ramakrishna had also visited him, and had put the question whether Jiva and Brahman were one or two entities. Trailanga Swami answered by sign that they were two, so long duality was seen, but that ultimately they are one. It means, so long the perception of difference is present, they are different; otherwise both are same.

Swamiji then went to visit Swami Bhaskarananda, a celebrated ascetic of great learning. He lived almost nude in his cottage. The conversation between them turned to the subject of the conquest of 'lust and gold'. Sri Ramakrishna was a living example of renouncing the 'women' and 'gold'. He used to say that realizing God is impossible without renouncing the 'women' and 'gold'. He has shown this truth throughout his life. Bhaskarananda said, "No one can completely renounce lust and gold." Swamiji replied, "What do you say, sir! There have been many who have done so. This is the very basis of a monk's life and aspiration." Bhaskarananda smiled and declared, "You are but a child. What do you know?" Swamiji replied with more confidence, "And I myself have seen at least one who had completely conquered lust and gold." Bhaskarananda again smiled and paid no importance of his words. Then to avoid any argument Swamiji stood up and immediately left the place. After a few years when Bhaskarananda met Swami Niranjanananda, and came to know that Niranjanananda was a brother-disciple of Swami Vivekananda, he treated him with reverence and made a humble request for having a meeting with Swami Vivekananda. Owing to his illness Swamiji couldn't meet him. He wrote him a letter in Sanskrit, and begged an apology for his inability. Until then Bhaskarananda didn't know, and could never know that Swami Vivekananda was that person with whom he had an argument on the possibility of renouncing lust and gold.

At Dakshineswar Sri Ramakrishna used to talk about Bhaskarananda, and also wanted to know about others of Kashi. Swami Abhedananda visited Bhaskarananda before Swami Vivekananda. He once explained his experience: "He lived in a garden-house completely nude.

When we saluted him and sat in front of him, he asked for our introduction. We said that we are wandering monks and now we have been staying in a garden-house; our next destination is Hardwar, Hrishikesh and so on. He became glad to hear and smiled a little. We had a discussion on some complicated subjects of Vedanta. We saw that he was a Gnostic anchorite. He had vast knowledge in scripture, versed in argumentation.

Holy Mother also went to see Bhaskarananda. Her experience: "I went to see him at Kashi. Some other women were with me. When we reached there, saw—a saint was sitting nude but he was indifferent to that. As we entered the room he said: "Mother! Don't be timorous. All of you are Jagadamba, the Holy Mother. Why do you feel ashamed? For this penis? It is like a finger only. What an indifferent person he was! He never wore even a piece of cloth, whether it is winter or summer; always nude."

In the solitude of night Swamiji sat on the Ganges at Varanasi, and absorbed himself in meditation; realized the cause of his arrival and the direction to fulfil his mission. The time has come to start his work, for what he was appointed by Sri Ramakrishna, and for which purpose he had built a courageous band of young monks. He realized that he should plunge into the field of his work immediately without any delay.

People, who foolishly run after the pleasure and happiness in the world, are followed by the miseries. Our body, made up of five vital elements—earth, water, heat, air and atmosphere or space, is the cause of the irony of life. A good hearted and unselfish man can feel happiness because he loves and lives for others. He, who works for the happiness of others, is truly a happy person. Selfish men do not know the meaning of love; do not know how to live in peace. Camels get injured and suffer from bleeding its mouth, yet they do not give up eating prickly shrubs. He, who is attached to sensual pleasure only, cannot love anybody. If a man works without any selfish motive in view, he gains the highest. Love, truth, and unselfishness are not merely moral figures of speech, but they form our highest ideal.

Swamiji realized: "Pleasure is not the goal of man, but knowledge. Pleasure and happiness come to an end. It is a mistake to suppose that pleasure is the goal. The cause of all the miseries we have in the world is that men foolishly think pleasure to be the ideal to strive for. No one can get anything unless he earns it.... A man may struggle all his life for riches; he may cheat thousands, but his life becomes a trouble and a nuisance to him. We may go on accumulating things for our physical enjoyment, but only what we earn is really ours. We are responsible for what we are; and whatever we wish ourselves to be, we have the power to make ourselves. If what we are now has been the result of our own past actions, it certainly follows that whatever we wish to be in future can be produced by our present actions. Love, truth, and unselfishness are not merely moral figures of speech, but they form our highest ideal."[10]

Sri Ramakrishna, the Holy Mother, and Swami Vivekananda arrived on the earth to teach this lesson to the world.

After spending about a week in spiritual atmosphere of Varanasi, Swamiji suddenly returned to the Baranagore Math, but with a new form and new experience. There he discovered different opinions. His mind was spread to a large extent. He was infatuated with immense joy of the eternal world. His experience of this tour made him feeling a tremendous pressure of work that he was commanded by Sri Ramakrishna. He was restless for spreading the fragrance of love, and teaching the application of the knowledge of Vedanta among the people of every household. His realization became stronger. His heart felt resounded with:

For religion, many creeds have I sought,
Lived in mountain-caves, on cremation-grounds,
By the Ganga and other sacred streams,
And how many days have I passed on alms!

Friendless, clad in rags, with no possession,
Feeding from door to door on what chance would bring.
The frame broken under Tapasya's (Of austerities) weight;
What riches, ask thou, have I earned in life?

Listen, friend, I will speak my heart to thee;
I have found in my life this truth supreme—
Buffeted by waves, in this whirl of life,
There's one ferry that takes across the sea.

Formulas of worship, control of breath,
Science, philosophy, systems varied,
Relinquishment, possession, and the like,
All these are but delusions of the mind—
Love, Love—that's the one thing, the sole treasure.

In Jiva an Brahman, in man and God,
In ghosts, and wraiths, and spirits, and so forth,
In devas, beasts, birds, insects, and in worms,
This Prema (Love) dwells in the heart of them all.

This is Swamiji's realization of life. Hence he invited:

Give away, ne'er turn to ask in return,
Should there be the wealth treasured in thy heart.

Ay, born heir to the Infinite thou art,
Within the heart is the ocean of Love,
"Give", "Give away"—whoever asks return,
His ocean dwindles down to a mere drop.

From highest Brahman to the yonder worm,
And to the very minutest atom,
Everywhere is the same God, the All-Love;
Friend, offer mind, soul, body, at their feet.

These are His manifold forms before thee,
Rejecting them, where sleekest thou for God?
Who loves all beings without distinction,
He indeed is worshipping best his God.[11]

This is Swamiji's philosophy of Hinduism. He wanted to bind the people of the world together with the cord of love, and make them into a wonderful bouquet of worship. To his heart, none was foreign or alien. He wished to spread this philosophy all over the world. Hence he wanted to make this ideal grow in his brother-disciples. They should be wandering like a stream, not to follow the systems of other monasteries. They should go to the people, love everyone from the lowest to the highest without asking for any return. To love all beings is to worship God. Poor and downtrodden people should be worshiped considering them as the manifestation of God. And he strove to inspire his brother-disciples with this new idea of religion. He would urge them to go to the people to preach, but they were quite averse to preaching. They said, "Realization of God is the first and foremost motive of us. The Master said—realization of God is the aim of life, after that, preaching would be done on itself." Earlier Swamiji also had the same ideal, but after returning from Varanasi he changed. He said: "Everyone is preaching; what they do unconsciously I will do consciously. Ay, even if you, my brother-monks, stand in my way, I will go and preach among the Pariahs in the lowest slums. Preaching means expression. Because Trailanga Swami remains silent and never talks, do you think he does not preach? His very silence is a sermon! Even trees and plants are preaching!" Later on, Swamiji preached continuously and made people surprised to realize the power of his speech. His first audience was a small group of monks and devotees at Baranagore Math.

This time Swamiji stayed at Baranagore Math for a short period. He wished to avoid the crowd and to be absorbed in meditative life of a monk. He set out for a journey to North India. His first halt was again at Varanasi, where he met Babu Pramadadas Mitra, a noted Sanskrit scholar, who was well known to Swami Akhandananda. Pramadadas was a rich person of Varanasi. He was introduced to Swamiji by Akhandananda.

Once, Swami Akhandananda had gone to Gaya. There he stayed at the house of Durgashankar, who was a devotee of Sri Ramakrishna. Durgashankar was a wealthy person of Gaya. He often used to go to Dakshineswar to see Sri Ramakrishna and to listen to his devotional songs. Gadashankar, the younger brother of Durgashankar, was also a devotee of Sri Ramakrishna.

Pramadadas, the Zaminder of Kashi, used to visit Durgashankar off and on. He was a scholar in Sanskrit, and a member of Allahabad University. He had some property at Gaya, for which he had to go there every now and then. He heard of Sri Ramakrishna and his life from Durgashankar. Probably relating to this matter he was attracted to Swami Akhandananda, when he was at Gaya. Later they met again at Kashi. Swamiji became a close friend of Pramadadas, and wrote him a number of letters asking his advice on the interpretation of the Hindu scriptures.

Next he went to holy Ayodhya, which had at one time been the capital of the king Ramachandra. In his childhood Swamiji used to worship the idol of Rama and Sita. He had immense respect for them. To him Sri Ramachandra was an ideal personality. He also had a great respect for Sri Hanumana, the great hero, perhaps it was because he himself was a great hero. 'Naren', the great hero and disciple of Sri Ramakrishna, would say: "Only let me say now that if I have told you one word of Truth, it was his and his alone; and if I have told you many things which were not true, were not correct, which were not beneficial to the human race, they were all mine, and on me is the responsibility."

He felt an extreme joy at the sight of Ayodhya. The story of the Ramayana, which he had heard of from his mother, must flash through his mind, and his wide eyes began to search the same in that historical holy place. The sacred land of Ayodhya had again been blessed by the footprints of Swami Vivekananda. We don't have any more details of his movement at Ayodhya.

Then he went to Lucknow, where he was lost in admiration of the splendid history and glorious performance of the Nawabs, and enjoyed the beauty of the garden and mosques of the city. Next, he set out for Agra, of Mughal memories and grandeur. The Taj Mahal and the Agra Fort are the undying fame of the Mughals. What a beautiful mixture of Indian architecture with that of Mughal! This is an example of their living, dying, and freakishness. Swamiji liked the Mughal emperors. What a strange life they had! He enjoyed the artistry and workmanship of the Indian artisans, and became astonished with its beauty. He visited it many times, and watched its beauty from different angles. He used to say, "Every square inch of this wondrous edifice is worth a whole day's patient observation, and it requires at least six months to make a real study of it." The magnificent fort of Agra stimulated his historical imagination. Walking through the streets of the city, he enjoyed the beauty of palaces and tombs of Mughal era unfolded before him.

From Agra he went to Vrindavan in the early part of August 1888. The last thirty miles he had passed on foot with a stick and *kamandalu* (water pot used by Hindu monks) in hand, and two or three books and a blanket. Not a single penny was there with him. He went on walking step by step. When he was about two miles away from Vrindavan, he saw a man cheerfully smoking a pipe by the wayside. Being a smoker he felt to have a smoke. He asked the man to allow him to smoke at his pipe. The smoker shrunk back and said timidly, "It would degrade you, Maharaj (sir). I am a sweeper." Hearing him Swamiji shrunk back by his cast-consciousness and became disappointed for not being able to smoke. He resumed his walking. After going a short distance, the thought struck to him, "What! I have taken the sannyasi's vow and have given up all ideas of caste, family prestige and so forth; yet I fell back into caste ideas when the man told me that he was a sweeper! And I could not smoke the pipe which he had touched! That was due to ages of habit." He turned back and found the man still seated there. He came to him and said, "*Bhaia, hamko bhi ek Chillum bharke do.*"—"Brother, do prepare me a Chillum of tobacco." But the man humbly remonstrated, "*Maharaj, ap sadhu ho; may bhangi.*"—"Sir, you are a holy man; I am a sweeper." Swamiji would not listen to his argument, and insisted him to allow him to smoke from his pipe.

Many days later when Girish Ghosh heard of this incident, he said to Swamiji, "You are addicted to hemp. That's why you could not avoid the temptation of smoking even from a sweeper's pipe." Swamiji replied, "No, G.C., truly, I wanted to test myself. After taking Sannyasa, one should test oneself, whether one has gone beyond the limitation of caste and colour. It is very difficult to observe the vows of Sannyasa strictly; there should be no contradiction between word and deed."

During conversation with a disciple Swamiji said, "Do you think, the ideals of Sannyasa are easy to practice in life, my boy? There is no other path of life so arduous and difficult. Let your foot slip ever so little on the edge of a precipice, and you fall to the valley below. If one has taken the sannyasi's vow, one has to examine oneself every moment to see if one is free from the ideas of caste, colour and so forth. That incident taught me the great lesson that I should not despise anyone, but must think of all as children of the Lord."[12]

Tired with constant walking Swamiji smoked from the sweeper's pipe, and resumed his pilgrimage to Vrindavan. Arriving at Vrindavan he stayed at Kalababu's Kunja, a temple built by the ancestors of Balaram Bose.

Bose family of Baghbazar was well known to the people. Everyone would respect them. Krishnaram Babu from Antpur of Hooghly district came to Calcutta for making business. By the grace of God he earned both money and honour, and built a big house near the terminus of tramway at Shyambazar. He also built a Kali temple and a temple of Shiva. He used to spend money lavishly on charity; helped people in famine. The road behind the tram-depot is known as Krishnaram Bose Street. Guruprasad, son of Krishnaram Bose, was a Vaishnava. There was a shrine of Radhashyamchandji in their house. Shyambazar, the name of the area, derived from the name of this temple. But suddenly Guruprasad lost 14 lac rupees when the 'Thakur Bank' became insolvent. He packed up his business from Calcutta and went to Mahesh at Srirampore, and there he settled down. Later, he built a beautiful temple of Radhashyamji at Vrindavan. This temple is known as the 'Kalababu's Kunja'.

Simple-hearted people, full with devotion, say 'Radhe Radhe' to everyone whom they met on the way—this is the natural style of greeting in Vrindavan. Here Swamiji's heart was flooded with love of Radha-Krishna. There was no argument with anyone. Faith and devotion were only the things that everyone was filled with. Swamiji felt himself absorbed in devotion. The act of Krishna came to life for him; he resolved to visit the environs of Vrindavan.

When Sri Ramakrishna came to Vrindavan, he was found always filled with enormous joy. He went into ecstasy in all temples. He climbed the top of the Govardhan Hill. When he saw the image of Bankebihari [Krishna] he was so overwhelmed with ecstasy that he ran to embrace him. There he met with many great saints. "In the evening when he saw the cowherd boys crossing the Jamuna to return from the pastures with their cows, he beheld among them the cowherd Krishna, dark like a rain cloud, with a peacock feather in his hair. He was then beside himself with feelings of devotion."[13]

After staying at Vrindavan for a few days, Swamiji became restless to visit the places where Sri Krishna played His Divine Play. Brajadham, which includes Vrindavan, Mathura, Gokul, Varsana, Shyamkunda, Radhakunda, and Govardhan Hill, is the field of Krishna's Divine Play. According to the custom of Brajadham, a pilgrim has to visit first the temple of Shiva, and Kali, and then one by one the temple of Govindji, Gopinath, Sheth, Radhavallava, Madanmohan, Sahji, Astha Sakhi, Bankebihari, Kaliadaman, and so on.

While going round the Govardhan Hill, Swamiji vowed that he would eat only what would be offered to him without asking. He would not beg food from anyone. First day he felt tremendous hungry at noon. It was afternoon, but nobody came to offer him food. In addition to his discomfort, it started raining heavily. His pain was ceaseless. Extreme hunger forced him to step out on the road. While walking in the rain, he heard someone calling him from behind; but he didn't turn back to answer him. Gradually the voice came nearer. Swamiji sped up his motion as fast as he could, to test this apparent act of Providence. The man began to run after him, and shouted continuously: "Stop! Stop, sir. I have brought food for you." Food was running after the hungry. But, Swamiji didn't stop. At last, the man overtook him and said breathlessly, "Here is your food. Please accept it." Swamiji accepted the food, but before he could ask him anything, the man disappeared among the trees. Who was that man? Where did he go? Ecstatic with devotion at this miraculous act of God, his eyes filled with tears.

Next he went to Radhakunda, a sacred place associated with Sri Radha. Here he was wearing nothing but a Kaupin [narrow strip of cloth about the loins]. He had no other cloth to wear after his bath. So he took it off, and washed it, and left it on the side of the tank to dry whilst he was bathing. When he finished his bath, he couldn't find the Kaupin anywhere around there. He began to search. Suddenly he looked up in a tree, and saw a monkey sitting with the Kaupin in its hand. He prayed the monkey to return him the Kaupin, but it refused to surrender it. In this situation it was very natural to Swamiji to become angry with Sri Radha, the presiding deity of the place. How could he go to a public place without any cloth? So he vowed that he would go into the recesses of the forest and starve himself to death. As he advanced into the jungle, he saw a man appeared there with a new ochre cloth and some food. Swamiji accepted the cloth and food from him. He went behind a bush to wear the cloth. When he returned after wearing the cloth, he couldn't find the man. He was no doubt surprised with this miraculous act. After having food, when he went to the tank to wash his hand, to his surprise he found his Kaupin lying just where he had put it to dry. This incident made him realize that he had always been protected by God.

According to his letters, published in the *Complete Works* Vol. I to Vol. IX, Swamiji was present at Vrindavan in the month of August 1888. It is not known to us, exactly when he reached Vrindavan. Yogen Maharaj (Swami Yogananda) went to Allahabad, and there he stayed at the house of Dr. Govinda Chandra Bose. After a few days he was attacked with small pox. Dr. Govinda informed the Baranagore Math about the illness of Swami Yogananda. Swamiji reached Allahabad along with Swami Shivananda, Niranjanananda, and Abhedananda. After recovery of Yogananda's illness, they all returned to Baranagore Math. According to his letters, Swamiji was present at Kala Babu's Kunja on 12th August 1888. He wrote in that letter: "Leaving Ayodhya I have reached the holy Vrindavan, and am putting up at Kala Babu's Kunja." From there, he had a mind to proceed very shortly to Haridwar. From another letter dated 20th August 1888, we come to know that, during that time an aged brother-disciple of Swamiji went to visit Kedarnath and Badrinath, and there he met Gangadhar Maharaj [Swami Akhandananda]. Gangadhar Maharaj ascended up to Tibet and Bhutan twice. They were coming back to Vrindavan that very month. So Swamiji postponed his going to Haridwar for some days. Swamiji's first letter was written to Pramadadas Mitra on 12th August 1888. The second letter dated 20th August 1888, was also written to the same man. The third letter was also written to the same person, on 19th November 1888. But the third letter was written from Baranagore Math. It shows that, he returned to Calcutta before 19th August 1888.

Swamiji, in a letter (dated 12th August 1888) from Vrindavan wrote to Pramadadas Mitra: "Leaving Ayodhya I have reached the holy Vrindavan, and am putting up at Kala Babu's Kunja. In the town the mind feels contracted. Places like Radha-kunda, I have heard, are delightful; but they are at some distance from the town."[14] It means Swamiji went to Radha-kunda most probably on some day after 12th August and before 20th August of 1888.

Next we find Swamiji seated in an isolated corner of Hathras Railway station, on his way to Hardwar. He felt tired and hungry too. Assistant Station-master, Sharatchandra Gupta, saw a monk sitting lonely at platform. Sharatchandra was a Bengali, born on 6th January 1865, at Garhpar, in Calcutta. In 1865, his father went with his family to Jaunpur near Varanasi. Sharatchandra passed his student life among the Muslims of Jaunpur. Hence he spoke Hindi and Urdu more fluently than his mother tongue. He was very sweet and humble with manliness in his personality.

Swamiji's brother, Mahendranath Dutta has written: "Someone had bought him a ticket, but nobody made any arrangement of his food. However, Narendranath got down at Hathras Railway station. When the passengers had left the platform for their own destination, Narendranath sat on a bench lonely at platform, looked sad, eyes seemed to be filled with tears, and had no sense of around him. Perhaps he was deeply absorbed in some thought."

Sharatchandra Gupta was the first disciple of Vivekananda, and came to be known as Swami Sadananda. He wrote in his reminiscences about the incident of those days. He was then a young station-master at Hathras station. One day, when a train came to Hathras station, Sharatchandra saw among the third class passengers, a turbaned monk of his own age with a marvellous pair of eyes. Three days before, he dreamt of these very eyes. They had haunted him ever since. As soon as he saw the monk, he remembered that he had been looking for him. He was startled and thrilled.

At first sight he was attracted by the appearance of the young monk. Going up to him, he said, "Maharaj! I am a Bengali. Please leave the train and go with me to my quarters." Swamiji asked him, "But what will you give me to eat?" Promptly quoting from a Persian verse, Sharat replied, "O beloved, you have come to my house! I shall prepare the most delicious dish for you with the flesh of my heart." Swamiji was enchanted to hear this reply and accepted his invitation.

When the station-master's duties were finished, he took Swamiji to his quarters, which was very near to the station. He fetched water from well, and Swamiji took his bath. He prepared food for Swamiji, and arranged bed for his rest. Swamiji started singing:

> "Let us go back once more, O mind, to your own abode!
> Here in this foreign land of earth
> Why should we wander aimlessly in stranger's guise?..."

As he heard this song, Sharat felt a change in himself. His service, his house, his parents, and everything of the world disappeared from his mind. He was a bachelor, but he had his parents, brother and sister in his family. He felt no interest in his family. Everything in the world seemed to be vague. He sat at the holy feet of Swamiji, and said: "Sir, teach me wisdom." Swamiji replied with a Bengali song to the refrain of: "If you wish to attain knowledge, go and cover your moon face with ashes; otherwise find your own way." Sharat was very poor in Bengali. He couldn't get the meaning of the song. He replied immediately: "Swamiji, I am at your service. I am ready to renounce everything and follow you." Saying this he disappeared—to return divested of his official clothes, with ashes on his face.

Tendency of renouncing the world was found in Sharat's family. His elder brother, Adharchandra Gupta, was already a monk. After renouncing the world, he went to Hyderabad of Sindh Pradesh, and stayed there for a long. He had a sweet voice, and often used to sing with clapping. Local people would call him as 'Talibaba'. He also had passed some days at Durgabari in Kashi. Once he met Sister Nivedita in Calcutta. Nivedita said: "The inner man is out." Sharatchandra also had felt the same, renouncing the world was not quite new for him. Swamiji remained silent for the time being.

Swamiji came to know that, a gentleman named Brajenbabu lived nearby. As he heard the name, it seemed to him that the gentleman was an old acquaintance of his. Swamiji went to his residence with Sharatchandra. Brajenbabu recognized him at once, and greeted him gladly, and requested him to stay with him for some days. Swamiji agreed, promising to go back to Sharat's house shortly and stayed with him. During his stay at the house of Brajenbabu, the entire Bengali population of the town poured in to meet Swamiji. Prior to his arrival, there had been some differences of opinion amongst the resident Bengalis; but all these vanished in their longing for visiting and listening to Swamiji. He would talk to them of religion and of their motherland with such oomph, that most of the visitors would not like to return home. During these days Swamiji often visited the quarters of Sarat and his friend Natakrishna. They became more and more attached to him and earnestly begged him to be their guest. He agreed and shortly after that he went to live with them. In a letter Natakrishna wrote about those days:

> "Thus was with others spent the most blessed days of our life in constant spiritual conversations with him. By the power of his holy company, the sectarian quarrels and ill-feeling amongst the different factions of Bengalis vanished. Those who entertained pride of age or high position in society, used to come and sit like children before the young monk, forsaking their conceit of knowledge and position, and asking him questions on religious matters. The evening was generally spent in music, and all the gentlemen who assembled there were simply charmed with his sweet voice, and sat for hours as if spellbound. The more they heard him the more they thirsted in their souls to hear him."[15]

Thus Swamiji created a festive atmosphere at Hathras so long he stayed there. Sharatchandra and other gentlemen were happy in his association. But, one day Swamiji said, "I can't live here anymore. I am a monk; can't stay anywhere for long. I am being attached to your love. This is also a kind of hindrance to a spiritual life. I have to leave now." Many of them requested him in many ways to stay there. But Swamiji's strong determination made them disappointed. Most of them wanted to be his disciple. Swamiji said: "Why? Do you think that you will get everything by becoming my disciple? Remember that God is present everywhere; whatever you will do, will help your religion. I shall try to visit you again." All but Sharatchandra became silent. He said, "I will go with you. Let me have the right to be always at your service by initiating me as a disciple of you." After a pause Swamiji replied: "My son, I have a great mission to fulfil and I am in despair at the smallness of my capacity. I have an injunction from my Guru to carry out this mission. It is nothing less than the regeneration of my motherland. Spirituality has fallen to a low ebb and starvation stalks the land. India must become dynamic and effect the conquest of the world through her spirituality." Sharat became spellbound at these words, and said earnestly, "Here I am, Swamiji; what do you want me to do?" Swami asked, "Are you prepared to take up the begging bowl and the *Kamandalu* and work for the great cause? Can you beg from door to door?" "Yes", Sharat replied boldly. Swamiji became pleased to the courage and determination of Sharatchandra. He spent more few days at Sharat's house.

One morning when Swamiji decided to leave Hathras, Sharat became sad, and said, "Swamiji, make me your disciple." Swamiji replied, "Why, do not think that everything in spiritual life will be gained by becoming my disciple. Remember that God is in everything; and then whatever you do will make for your progress. I shall come and be with you now and then. For the present I must be going to the Himalayas." Sharatchandra repeated his solicitation time and again, and at the end he spoke out: "Swamiji, say what you will, wherever to go I shall follow you." Swamiji realized his determination and sincerity. He said, "Can you really follow me? Then take my begging bowl and go and beg our food from the porters of the station." Sharatchandra immediately went to beg from his own subordinates. After collecting some food he brought it to Swamiji. Swamiji blessed him heartily, and accepted him as his disciple. Sharatchandra became known as Swami Sadananda.

Sharatchandra soon found a substitute to take over his duties, and accompanied Swamiji to Rishikesh. Swamiji had no bag and baggage with him. Sri Ramakrishna used to say, "Monk should not have any baggage with him." But Swami Sadananda had a baggage which contained his cloths, a blanket, and a pair of ammunition boot. He was in a habit of wearing boot. They will go to Saharanpur station by train and from there on foot. Sadananda was not accustomed to a monastic life. He thought that the baggage was not much heavy, so he could easily carry it. Sometime he kept the bag in hand, and then held it on shoulder and vice versa. From right hand to left hand, right shoulder to left shoulder. He felt how much heavy the bag was. Seeing the miserable condition of his disciple Swamiji took the bag from him. He carried the bag by changing his hand from right to left and left to right. And finally he held the bag on his head and went on. While walking on the road, Swamiji began to tell about Slough of Despondency, Castle of Doubt, Giant Despair, and so on from Bunyan's Pilgrim's Progress. Slowly they reached Haridwar and then Rishikesh.

Sharatchandra had never seen such constant spiritual discipline of monastic life, full of uncertainties and hardship. He had described his experience later, "Once in our wanderings in the outlying districts of the Himalayas I fainted with hunger and thirst. The Swami carried me and thus undoubtedly saved me form certain death. On another occasion, like a syce he led the horse, which someone had kindly lent us for the journey, across a mountain river which was very dangerous to ford because of its swiftness and slippery bottom. He risked his life several times for my sake. How can I describe him, friends, except by the word Love, Love, Love! When I was too ill to do anything but stagger along, he carried my personal belongings including my shoes." Such was the Divine play of Swamiji with his disciple, as Sri Ramakrishna had played with him.

Next we see Swamiji and his disciple living in a little cottage like other monks. Swamiji was very happy with the spiritual atmosphere of Rishikesh. He longed to ascend the distant peaks of the Himalayas. The murmuring of the sacred Ganga was a delight to hear. They passed their time in spiritual discipline. One day Swamiji felt hungry, and said to his disciple, "Can you give me something to eat?" Sharatchandra has some money with him. He said, "Yes, Swamiji, I will cook Khichuri (hotchpotch)." Then he became busy in arranging materials for hotchpotch. Swamiji went to the bank of Ganga for a walk. After a while he returned, but in another mood. He became eager to go to Kedar-Badri, but because of poor health of Sharat he kept his desire suppressed. But now, he became restless for wandering, and said to Sharat, "You have become a sort of chain on my feet. I was wandering alone so long. You came and became a source of botheration to me. Now I am going on my own way. I shall stay here no more." He took his staff and water pot, and set out alone on pilgrimage. Sharatchandra was then cooking Khichuri for both of them. He became regretful and sat silently in one corner. He had no idea of what he should do. He said to himself, "How can he leave me alone, for whom I have renounced the worldly life? How can he say that I am a chain on his feet! How can he think that I am a source of botheration to him?" About three or four hours later, Swamiji returned and said, "O Sharat, can you give me something to eat? I am terribly hungry."

Sharat became happy to see him back, and said, "Yes, I shall give you Khichuri just now."

"Did you not take your meal?" asked Swamiji.

"When you were not here, how could I!" replied Sharat.

Swamiji: "You have really become like a chain round my feet. I had gone a long way, but then I remembered that you were alone here and were such a fool. I could not be sure what you might do. Look, it was for you I had to return."

There are so many temples on both the bank of the Ganga. Air is full of fragrance of the holy Ganga. Heart becomes full of joy. This is the heaven. Both the disciples and his master enjoyed Khichuri to their heart's content.

Sharatchandra didn't get afraid of anything when he knew that Swamiji was with him. One day they were going through a jungle, while they came across some bleached human bones, and some pieces of rotting ochre cloth lying here and there. "See," said Swamiji, "here a tiger has devoured a monk! Are you afraid?"

The disciple promptly replied, "Not with you, Swamiji." He knew how Swamiji had saved his life.

Once, Sharatchandra became seriously ill with an unknown disease. When a man is in danger, and he cannot bear his pain, he feels helpless. Sharatchandra also felt the same, and he was afraid whether Swamiji was going to give him up in that misery. He blurted, "Are you finally going to leave me?" Swamiji replied, "Fool, do you not remember that I have carried even your shoes!"

Swamiji was willing to go up into the Himalayas. He wished to go to Kedar-Badri. But suddenly Sharatchandra fell seriously ill, and there was no other choice than taking him to

Hathras. Seeing the Master and his disciple back to Hathras all friends became happy. But then Swamiji himself fell ill, having contracted with malaria from Rishikesh. Someone from Bengali society sent the news of Swamiji's illness to Baranagore Math. Shortly after that a letter came from Baranagore Math, in which they requested Swamiji to return to Calcutta. Just at that time Swami Shivananda, on his way to some holy places in northern India, came to Hathras. He came to know that Swamiji was ill, and immediately brought him back to Baranagore Math. Before leaving Hathras, Swamiji told Sharatchandra to go to Baranagore Math as soon as he felt free from disease.

Swamiji reached Baranagore Math, and found most of his brother-disciples were away on pilgrimage. But those who were present there, and all the householder disciples of Sri Ramakrishna who used to visit the Math, were pleased to have Swamiji back to them. During this period Sharatchandra gave up his job and joined the Baranagore Math.

With the return of Swamiji the atmosphere of Baranagore Math became as it was previously. He experienced so many new things in different places of northern India, and realized the unity in the culture of India. All this he shared with his brother-disciples. He would say, "India, that for the time being seems to be divided in many parts, will soon be united with the benediction of Sri Ramakrishna." Swamiji again started his classes to teach his brother-disciples.

By that time, a young man named Basanta from Allahabad came to Baranagore Math. He was little short of hearing. Swami Sadananda became happy with this new companion, because he could speak to him freely in Hindi. Both were diligent. They used to grow vegetables in the courtyard of the monastery. But few months later Basanta suddenly disappeared; nobody knew where he had gone.

Swamiji returned to Baranagore Math in the month of November of 1888, and became engaged in teaching his brother-disciples. Their view-point had to be widened. They had to be inspired in thinking about the united India. A serious study started. He began to teach—how to realize the underlying implication of religion, how to protect oneself from the selfish rival. They didn't have adequate books for higher study. Who would give them books? One name, Pramadadas Mitra, flashed through Swamiji's mind, because he had already sent some valuable books. He wrote him a letter (on 19/11/1888):

"I have received the two books sent by you and am filled with joy to read your wonderfully affectionate letter which betokens your broad, generous heart. No doubt, it is due to good merit of my previous births that you show, sir, and so much kindness to a mendicant like me who lives on begging. By sending your gift of the 'Vedanta', you have laid under lifelong obligation not only myself but the whole group of Sri Ramakrishna's Sannyasins. They all bow down to you in respect. It is not for my own sake alone that I asked of you the copy of Panini's grammar; a good deal of study, in fact, is given to Sanskrit scriptures in this Math. The Vedas may well be said to have fallen quite out of vogue in Bengal. Many here in this Math are conversant with Sanskrit, and they have a mind to master the Samhita portions of the Vedas. They are of opinion that what has to be done must be done to a finish. So, believing that a full measure of proficiency in the Vedic language is impossible without first mastering Panini's grammar, which is the best available for the purpose, a copy of the letter was felt to be necessity. The grammatical work Mugdhabodha, which we studied in our boyhood, is superior in many respects to Laghukaumudi. You are yourself, however, a deeply learned man and, therefore, the best judge we can have in this matter. So if you consider the Ashtadhyayi (Panini's) to be the most suitable in our case, you will lay us under a debt of lifelong gratitude by sending the same (provided you feel it convenient and feel so inclined). This Math is not wanting in men of perseverance, talent, and penetrative intellect. I may hope that by the grace of our Master, they will acquire in a short time Panini's system and then succeed in restoring the Vedas to Bengal."[16]

At this time, two serious matters drew the attention of Swamiji—(1) social customs and (2) inconsistencies of many scriptural passages. He was searching answers of many questions about the nature of the highest realization, the authority of the Vedas, the law of karma (work), the apparent contradictions in schools of Indian philosophy. While he was wandering, he saw the priest enjoying undue advantage of scriptures, forbidding the study of Vedas by Shudras, caste system and extreme practice of untouchability—all of which made the society a conservative institution. Whatever Swamiji had seen during his visit to a small part of India, he realized that demand of preaching the knowledge of Vedas and Upanishads to the masses. People had to be introduced with the Vedas an Upanishads. Swamiji was trying to find out a solution of these problems. He couldn't think of a society without religion, spirituality, scriptures, and different customs. He believed that there must be a consistency amongst all these elements of human being; and it had been realized by the ancient saints. So, he began to search the argument which could help him to bring a consistency among all contradictory ideas. Hence, he had no time for having a little rest. As a result—28 November, 1888 Swamiji "had an attack of fever again", 4th February, 1889—"I feel now much improved in health", 22nd February, 1889—"I had intended to go to Varanasi, and I planned to reach there after visiting the birthplace of my Master. But unluckily on the way to that village I had an attack of high fever followed by vomiting and purging as in cholera. There was again fever after three or four days—and as the body is now so weak that I can barely walk even two steps", 21st March, 1889—"I am very ill at present; there is fever now and then, but there is no disorder in the spleen of other organs. I am under homoeopathic treatment." Again after three month, on 4th July 1889—"Some relative of my former life (the life he has renounced) has purchased a bungalow at Simultala (near Baidyanath). The place being credited with a healthy climate, I stayed there for some time. But the summer heat growing excessive, I had an attack of acute diarrhea, and I have just fled away from the place."

Continuous working made him attacked with several diseases. Yet he didn't stop his working. He wrote to Pramadadas on 4th July 1889: "I have also found it so very often, that one has to suffer at times for holding in one's brain novel views of all sorts. But with me it is a different malady this time. I have not lost faith in a benign Providence—nor am I going ever to lose it—my faith in the scriptures is unshaken. But by the will of God, the last six or seven years of my life have been full of constant struggles with hindrances and obstacles of all sorts. I have been vouchsafed the ideal Shastra; I have seen the ideal man; and yet fall myself to get on with anything to the end—this is my profound misery."[17]

Swamiji was striving for success in his mission which was bestowed upon him by Sri Ramakrishna. But, as he was near to Calcutta, he felt disturbed by the sight of misery of his mother and brothers. He wrote to Pramadadas: "In Calcutta live my mother and two brothers. I am the eldest; the second is preparing for the first Arts Examination, and the third is young. They were quite well off before, but since my father's death, it is going very hard with them—they even have to go fasting at times! To crown all, some relatives, taking advantage of their helplessness, drove them away from the ancestral residence. Though a part of it is recovered through suing at the High Court, destitution is now upon them—a matter of course in litigation. Living near Calcutta I have to witness their adversity, and the quality of Rajas prevailing, my egotism sometimes develops into the form of a desire that rises to plunge me into action; in such moments, a fierce fighting ensues in my mind, and so I wrote that the state of my mind was terrible. Now their lawsuit has come to an end. So bless me that after a stay here in Calcutta for a few days more to settle matters, I may bid adieu to this place for ever. Bless me that my heart may wax strong with supreme strength Divine, and that all forms of Maya may drop off from me for eye: 'We have taken up the Cross; Thou hast laid it upon us and grant us strength that we bear it unto death. Amen!'—Imitation of Christ. I am now staying in Calcutta. My address is: C/o Balaram Babu, 57 Ramkanta Bose's Street, Bahgbazar, Calcutta."[18]

After ten days Swamiji again wrote a letter to Pramadadas: "I was very glad to get your letter. In such circumstances many give the advice to incline towards the worldly life. But you are truthful and have an adamantine heart. I have been highly comforted by your encouraging and cheering words. My difficulties here have almost come to a close—only I have engaged the services of a broker for the sale of a piece of land, and I hope the sale will be over soon. In that case, I shall be free from all worry and shall at once go straight off to you to Varanasi."[19]

When Swamiji was writing this letter, the wanderer Vivekananda in him became restless. He tried to leave Calcutta every now and then, yet he had to stay for another five months. Thousands of questions were there in his mind yet to be solved. A thorough investigation of everything was his old habit. He would never accept anything without knowing its truth. Though he was taught everything by Sri Ramakrishna himself, he felt his learning was inadequate to clear his doubts, and hence he didn't feel peace in his mind. Pramadadas Mitra was a learned friend, who was scholar in Sanskrit scriptures. So he began to send him many questions with a hope for having a suitable answer. We find many questions sent by Swamiji to Pramadadas in two letters dated 7 and 17 August, 1889. Following list of questions will help the reader to have an idea of his study.

1. Does any narrative occur about Satyakama, son of Jabali, and about Janashruti, anywhere else in the Vedas excepting the Upanishads?
2. In most cases where Shankaracharya quotes Smriti in his commentary on the *Vedanta-Sutras*, he cites the authority of the *Mahabharata*. But seeing that we find clear proofs about caste being based on qualification both in the *Bhishmaparva* of the *Mahabharata* and in the stories there of the Ajagara and of Uma and Maheshvara, has he made any mention in his writings of this fact?
3. The doctrine of caste in the *Purusha-Sukta* of the Vedas does not make it hereditary—so what are those instances in the Vedas where caste has been made a matter of hereditary transmission?
4. The Acharya could not adduce any proof from the Vedas to the effect that the Shudra should not study the Vedas. He only quotes 'Yajnehanabakalupt' (The Shudra is not conceived of as a performer of Yajna or Vedic sacrifices) (Tai. Samhita) to maintain that when he is not entitled to perform Yajnas, he has neither any right to study the Upanishads and the like. But the same Acharya contends with reference to 'Athato Brahmanjigyasa' (Now then commences hence the inquire about Brahman) (Vedanta-Sutras) that the word 'Ath' here does not mean 'Subsequent to the study of the Vedas', because it is contrary to proof that the study of the Upanishad is not permissible without the previous study of the Vedic Mantras and Brahmanas and because there is no intrinsic sequence between the Vedic *Karma-Kanda* and *Vedic Janana-Kanda*. It is evident, therefore, that one may attain to the knowledge of Brahman without having studied the ceremonial parts of the Vedas. So if there is no sequence between

the sacrificial practices and Jnana, why does the Acharya contradict his own statement when it is a case of the Shudras, by inserting the clause 'by force of the same logic'? Why should the Shudra not study the Upanishad?

5. Is the Mukti, which the *Vedanta-Sutras* speak of, one and the same with the Nirvana of the *Avadhuta-Gita* and other tests?
6. What is really meant by Nirvana if, according to the aphorism, 'Without the function of creating etc.' none can attain to the fullest Godhead?
7. Chaitanya-deva is said to have told Sarvabhauma at Puri, 'I understand the Sutras (aphorisms) of Vyasa, they are dualistic; but the commentator makes them, monastic, which I don't understand.' Is this true? Tradition says, Chaitanya-deva had a dispute with Prakashananda Sarasvati on the point, and Chaitanya-deva won. One commentary by Chaitanya-deva was rumoured to have been existing in Prakashananda's Math.
8. In the Tantra, Acharya Shankara has been called a crypto-Buddhist; views expressed in *Prajnāparamitā*, the Buddhist Mahayana book, perfectly tally with the Vedantic views propounded by the Acharya. The author of *Panchadashi* also says, 'What we call Brahman is the same truth as the Shunya of the Buddhist.' What does all this mean?
9. Why has no foundation for the authority of the Vedas been adduced in the *Vedanta-Sutras*? First, it has been said that the Vedas are the authority for the existence of God, and then it has been argued that the authority for the Vedas is the text: 'It is the breath of God.' Now, is this statement not vitiated by what in Western logic is called an argument in a circle?
10. The Vedanta requires of us faith, for conclusiveness cannot be reached by mere argumentation. Then why, has the slightest flaw, detected in the position of the schools of Sankhya and Nyaya, been overwhelmed with a fusillade of dialectics? In whom, moreover, and we to put our faith? Everybody seems to be mad over establishing his own view; if, according to Vyasa, even the great Muni Kapila, 'the greatest among perfected souls', is himself deeply involved in error, then who would say that Vyasa may not be so involved in a greater measure? Did Kapila fail to understand the Vedas?
11. According to the Nyaya, 'Shabda or Veda (the criterion of truth), is the word of those who have realized the highest'; so the Rishis as such are omniscient. Then how are they proved, according to the *Surya-siddhanta*, to be ignorant of such simple astronomical truths? How can we accept their intelligence as the refuge to ferry us across the ocean of transmigratory existence, seeing that they speak of the earth as triangular, of the serpent Vasuki as the support of the earth and so on?
12. If in His acts of creation God is dependent on good and evil Karmas, then what does it avail us to worship Him? There is a fine song of Nareshchandra, where occurs the following: 'If what lies in one's destiny is to happen anyhow, O Mother, then what good all this invoking by the holy name of Durga?'
13. True, it is improper to hold many tests on the same subject to be contradicted by one or two. But why then are the long-continued customs of Madhuparka (a Vedic ceremony, usually in honour of guests, in which a respectful offering was to be made

consisting, among other dainties, of beef.) and the like repealed by one or two such text as, 'The horse sacrifice, the cow sacrifice, Sannyasa, meat-offerings in Shraddha', etc.? If the Vedas are eternal, then what are the meaning and justification of such specifications as 'this rule of Dharma is for the age of Dvāpara,' 'this for the age of Kali', and so forth?

14. The same God who gives out the Vedas becomes Buddha again to annul them; which of these dispensations is to be obeyed? Which of these remains authoritative, the earlier or the later one?
15. The Tantra says, in the Kali-Yuga the Veda-Mantras are futile. So which behest of God, the Shiva, is to be followed?
16. Vyasa makes out in the *Vedanta-Sutra* that it is wrong to worship the tetrad of divine manifestation, expatiates on the great merits of that very Vyasa expatiates on the great merits of that worship in the *Bhāgavata*! Is this Vyasa a madman?[20]

In the second letter dated 17 August, 1889, Swamiji wrote: "I have doubts besides these, and, hoping to have them dispelled from my mind through your kindness, I shall lay them before you in future." It shows that he had so many doubts in his mind, and he was restless for a strong argument that could help him in coming out of this situation. In the same letter he also wrote: "I make no distinction as to householder or Sannyasin in this, that for all time my head shall bend low in reverence wherever I see greatness, broadness of heart, and holiness—Shantih! Shantih! Shantih! My prayer is that among the many people embracing Sannyasa nowadays, greedy of honour, posing renunciation for the sake of a living, and fallen off from the ideal on both sides, may one in a lakh at least become high-souled like you! To you my Brahmin fellow-disciples who have heard of your noble virtues tender their best prostrations." This part of the letter gives us an idea about how much respect Swamiji had for Pramadadas, and how much faith he had on his wisdom, as a result of which he could send so many difficult questions to him.

We don't know how many questions were solved by Pramadadas, and to what extent he was successful to help Swamiji in clearing his doubts; because we see in the same letter: "About one amongst my several questions to which you sent your replies, my wrong idea is corrected." It means Swamiji was not completely satisfied with his replies. Yet he had been searching solution of his questions. On the other side Mr. Mitra became tired of answering. Rather, in two letters, one after one, he advised Swamiji to give up all kind of arguments. Probably it helped Swamiji in coming down his restlessness to some extent. That's why, on 2nd September, 1889, he wrote to Pramadadas: "Some days ago I received your two kind letters. I am very much pleased to find in you a wonderful harmony of Jnana and Bhakti. Your advice to me to give up arguing and disputing is very true indeed, and that is really the goal of life for the individual—'Sundered are the knots of the heart, torn off are all his doubts, and the seeds of his Karma wear off, when the sight of the Transcendent One is gained.' But then, as my Master used to say, when a pitcher is being filled (by immersion), it gurgles, but when full, it is noiseless; know my condition to be the same. Within two or three weeks perhaps, I shall be able to meet you—may God fulfill that wish!"[21] In this way Sri Ramakrishna had been continuously protecting Swamiji.

According to the above letter, Swamiji was in a pleasant mood to some extent. But he didn't stop his study and discussion on spiritual matters. We find another letter that he wrote to Pramadadas from Baranagore Math on 13th December 1889: "I have received the pamphlet written by you. A kind of scientific Advaitism has been spreading in Europe ever since the theory of the conservation of energy was discovered, but all that is Parinamavada, evolution by real modification. It is good you have shown the difference between this and Shankara's Vivartavada (progressive manifestation by unreal superimposition). I can't appreciate your citing Spencer's parody on the German transcendentalists; he himself is fed much on their doles. It is doubtful whether your opponent Gough understands his Hegel sufficiently. Anyway, your rejoinder is very pointed and thrashing."

Beside all these, Swamiji was always aware of his brother-disciples, who were away from the monastery. He would always keep news of their movements, and help them at his best. This is proved by a letter that he wrote on 3rd December 1889, to Mr. Mitra: "Two of my brother-disciples are shortly leaving for Varanasi. One is Rakhal by name, the other is Subodh. The first-named was beloved of my Master and he used to stay much with him. Please recommend them to some Satra (house of alms) during their stay in the city, if you find it convenient." He also added: "Gangadhar is proceeding to Kailas. The Tibetans wanted to slash him up on the way, taking him to be a spy of the foreigners. Eventually some Lamas kindly set him free. We obtain this news from a Tibet going trader. Gangadhar's blood won't cool down before seeing Lhasa. The gain is that his physical endurance has grown immensely—one night he passed uncovered on a bed of snow and that without much hardship."

Swamiji's heart was like an ocean of Love. That's why Sri Ramakrishna made him the leader of his brother-disciples, and told him to take care of them, to guide them in spiritual life so that they do not feel uneasy in renouncing the world. Swamiji had been doing his duty with devotion. This letter proves how much strong they were built by the grace of Sri Ramakrishna and the endless love of Swamiji.

One more thing is cleared in the above that Swamiji was longing for a wanderer's life. He could hear the call from distant lands. At the end of December 1889, he left Calcutta and reached Vaidyanath, on his way to places of pilgrimage in northern India. There from he wrote a letter to Balaram Bose on 25th December 1889: "I have been staying for the last few days in Vaidyanath in Purna Babu's Lodge. It is not so cold, and my health too is indifferent. I am suffering from indigestion, probably due to excess of iron in the water. I have found nothing agreeable here—neither the place, nor the season, not the company. I leave for Varanasi tomorrow. Achyutananda stopped at Govinda Chaudhury's place at Deoghar, and the latter, as soon as he got news of us, earnestly insisted on our becoming his guests. Finally, he met us once again and prevailed on us to accede to his request. The man is a great worker, but has a number of women with him—old women most of them, of the ordinary Vaishnava type.... His clerks too revere us much; some of them are very much ill-disposed towards him, and they spoke of his misdeeds."

Achyutananda Swaraswati was also known by three more names—Achu, Achyuta, and Gunanidhi. Earlier name was Gunanidhi Bhattacharya. He was a preacher of Arya-Samaj established by Swami Dayananda. He travelled Kashmir with Swamiji. Many incidents of Swamiji's life are found in his diary. In this letter Swamiji has told about a woman without referring her name: "Incidentally, I raised the topic of.... You have many wrong ideas or doubts about her; hence I write all this after particular investigation. Even the aged clerks of this establishment highly respect and revere her. She came to stop with...while she was a mere child, and ever lived as his wife.... Everyone admits in one voice that her character is spotless. She was all along a perfectly chaste woman and never behaved with...in any relation but that of wife to husband, and she was absolutely faithful. She came at too early an age to have incurred any moral taint. After she had separated from..., she wrote to him to say that she had never treated him as anything but with a man with a loose character. His old office-bearers too believe him to be satanic in character; but they consider...a Deve (angel), and remark that it was following her departure that...lost all sense of shame."

Then he had concluded this letter with reference to that he realized about the woman: "My object in writing all this is that formerly I was not a believer in the tale of the lady's early life. The idea that there might be such purity in the midst of a relation which society does not recognize, I used to consider as romance. But after thorough investigation I have come to know that it is all right. She is very pure, pure from her infancy—I have not the least doubt about it. For entertaining those doubts, you and I and everyone are guilty to her; I make repeated salutations to her, and ask her pardon for my guilt. She is not a liar. I take this opportunity to record that such courage is impossible in a lying and unchaste woman. I have also been told that she had a lifelong ardent faith in religion also."[22]

In this letter we find Swamiji supporting such a relation which is very much common in many societies at present. But he had supported this only for the chastity of the woman. She was pure from her infancy. The relation between a man and a woman does not depend on marriage; if they remain pure in character, they are respectable. Swamiji had saluted the lady for her chastity. Still it was a courageous act of him, particularly in those days. Swamiji was a great man, who had a heart as wide as the sky. Such a great personality is very rarely found. He is really incomparable to anyone.

Another letter from Vaidyanath to Pramadadas: "After a long attempt, I think, I am now in a position to present myself before you. In a day or some days with a gentleman of Calcutta, but my mind is much longing for Varanasi. My idea is to remain there for some time, and to watch how Vishvanatha and Annapurna deal it out to my lot. And my resolve is something like 'either to lay down my life or realize my ideal'—so help me the Lord of Kashi."[23]

It means, Swamiji wished to go to Varanasi. But the Lord of Kashi sent him to Allahabad. There he took shelter at the house of Dr. Govinda Chandra Bose, and on 30th December 1889, wrote a letter to Balaram Bose: "Gupta (Swami Sadananda) left a slip when coming and the next day a letter from Yogananda gave me all the news and I immediately started for Allahabad which I reached the day after, to find that Yogananda had completely recovered. He had chicken-pox (with one or two small-pox rashes also). The doctor is a noble soul, and they have got a brotherhood, who are all great pious men and highly devoted to the service of Sadhus. They are particularly anxious that I pass the month of Magh here, but I am leaving for Varanasi."[24]

Next day, from Allahabad Swamiji wrote another letter to Pramadadas: "I wrote in a letter to you that I was to go to Varanasi in a day or two, but who can nullify the decree of Providence? News reached me that a brother-disciple, Yogen by name, had been attacked with smallpox after arriving from a pilgrimage to Chitrakuta, Omkarnath, etc., and so I came to this place to nurse him. He has now completely recovered. Some Bengali gentlemen here are of a greatly pious and loving disposition. They are very lovingly taking care of me, and their importunate desire is that I should stay here during the month of Magha (Jan.-Feb.) keeping the Kalpa vow (Special ablutions and worship regularly performed in that holy confluence—a very solemn and sacred practice.). But my mind is very keenly harping on the name of Varanasi and is quite agog to see you. Yes, I am going to try my best to slip away and avoid their importunities in a day or two and betake myself to the holy realm of the Lord of Varanasi. If one of my monastic brother-disciples, Achyutananda Sarasvati by name, calls on you to enquire of me, please tell him I am soon coming to Varanasi. He is indeed a very good man and learned. I was obliged to leave him behind at Bankipore. Are Rakhal and Subodh still there in Varanasi? Please inquire and inform me whether the Kumbha fair this year is going to be held at Haridwar or not."[25]

The remarkable point in this letter is that Swamiji called Achyutananda as one of his brother disciples, and didn't forget to make an enquiry about his brother-disciples who were present there at Varanasi at that time. He also had praised Mr. Mitra: "Many men of wisdom, of piety, many a Sadhu (holy man) and Pundit have I met in so many places, and I have been very much favoured by them, but '*bhinnyaruchirhiloka*—Men are of varying tastes'—(*Raghuvamsham*). I know not what sort of soul-affinity there is between us, for nowhere else does it seem so pleasing and agreeable as with you. Let me see how the Lord of Kashi disposes."[26]

Lord of Kashi confined him in Allahabad for more few days. Wherever He went people would gather around him, this was a very common event. Hence, the house of Govinda Chandra Bose became crowded with people in attraction of Swamiji; as if they were celebrating a festival. When he started preaching, no one would like to leave him. "Continue please, sing that very song once more," they would request. Sometimes they would discuss amongst themselves, "How great he is! How wise! How sweet is his voice and behaviour too! His words are so powerful!" Whenever he would sing or speak, people would become spellbound with surprise and joy. During conversation he would criticize the moral degeneration of people. And sometime, when he would discuss about the Hindu religion, become excited with pride. One day he felt overwhelmed at the sight of a Muslim saint. He said, "Every line and curve of his face showed that he was a Paramahamsa."

One day, Shrischandra Bose, a theosophist, was seated in front of Swamiji at a meeting. Topic of discussion was on the path of knowledge. Swamiji said—doing good to the world and to give salvation should be the aim of religion. Mr. Bose sprang up and shouted, "What have you done? You have spoiled my study for ten years!" Swamiji replied, "So what? Why should I think of your study if you do that for ten years or more?"

Shrischandra Bose was a munsiff (an officer at the lower civil court), and later he became District Judge at Allahabad Court. He and his brother, Major B.D. Bose, opened a publication named 'Panini Press', and published many religious books. They lived in that building called 'Panini Vhavan'. In one sitting with Swamiji, he came back to the main stream of Hindu religion. From a theosophist he became a devotee of Sri Ramakrishna, and began to worship the image of Sri Ramakrishna.

There was an abode of a monk on the bank of Triveni. He was called 'sinduk-sadhu' (A monk who had a wooden chest) and had many devotees. One day, Govinda Babu took Swamiji to him. Sadhu used to sit on a large wooden chest, and also would sleep on the same. When he was asked about the monk, Swamiji said, "He sits on the box keeping his entire possessions in it. Religious practices, God, and asceticism—everything is in that box. This is called a grocery. That's why he has got no promotion."

One day Govinda Bose had taken Swamiji to a hermitage of Dayaram at Jhusi. There they had a lot of fun. Amulya, an acquainted to Swamiji from before, became a Guruji to the people of Allahabad. Swamiji not only loved him but also would respect. People would respect him for his charitable service to the patients of plague and cholera. Then he used to wear common dresses. Later, being a Guru of a group of hemp-smoker, he began to wear ochre cloth. Amulya was Swamiji's classmate in college. He was a brilliant student. He was liberal and liked the Jnan-marg (knowledge considered as the way to salvation), didn't believe in spiritual guide of Guru. He had faith in books and in his own sacrament. He studied medical science in Medical

College, but didn't complete the course. On hearing that Narendranath had renounced the world, he also became a monk.

One day Amulya came to Govinda's house. At dinner, when he saw Swamiji taking chili, he also ate two chilies. Swamiji took three chilies, and thus, they had a competition of eating chilies. Finally Amulya accepted his defeat.

There is a place called 'Jhusi' at the other side of Ganga at Allahabad. It was known as the land of monks for spiritual practices and meditation. Swamiji also went there and had passed few days in meditation. Dr. Nandi, who often used to go to Dakshineswar to see Sri Ramakrishna as a devotee, had seen Swamiji to go to Jhusi to meet other monks. Later he had written in his reminiscence: "Swamiji had passed few months at Jhusi on the other side of the Ganga, where many other monks would live. It was tremendous hot of summer." Dr. Nandi would live five to six miles away from there. Swamiji would go regularly from Jhusi to Dr. Nandi's house on foot for begging, and would return on foot. He would wear half a blanket at his waist and the other half on his shoulder. "Such forbearance was found to be practices by the monks in north-west India. But Swamiji had left them behind in tolerance of hardship." Govindachandra Bose in his reminiscence would say about Swamiji: "I have never seen such renunciation, such stoicism, and such a deep faith in God."

Pavhari Baba at Ghazipur

Swamiji, years earlier at Dakshineswar, heard of Pavhari Baba. At Allahabad he came to know more of him. Since then he had a wish to see him. So he left Allahabad for Ghazipur in the third week of January 1890.

At Ghazipur Swamiji stayed with Babu Satishchandra Mukherjee and Rai Gaganchandra Roy Bahadur. On 21st January 1890 Swamiji wrote in a letter to Pramadadas Mitra: "I reached Ghazipur three days ago. Here I am putting up in the house of Babu Satishchandra Mukherjee, a friend of my early age. The place is very pleasant. Close by flows the Ganga, but bathing there is troublesome, for there is no regular path, and it is hard work wading through sands. Babu Ishan Chandra Mukherjee, my friend's father, that noble-hearted man of whom I spoke to you, is here. Today he is leaving for Varanasi whence he will proceed to Calcutta. I again had a great mind to go over to Kahsi, but the object of my coming here, namely an interview with the Babaji (Pavhari Baba), has not yet been realized, and hence the delay of a few days becomes necessary."[27]

Ishan Chandra Mukherjee's identification: "The Master (Sri Ramakrishna) was very fond of Ishan. He had been a superintendent in the Accountant General's office, and later on his children also occupied high government positions. One of them was a class-mate of Narendra. Ishan's purse was always open for the poor and needy. When he retired from service, he devoted his time to spiritual practices and charity. He often visited Sri Ramakrishna at Dakshineswar."[28]

Babu Satishchandra Mukherjee had left his name behind by founding the 'Dawn Society' in 1902. He had a great respect for Swamiji. At his house many people came to see Swamiji and hear his words. Different subjects would be discussed. There used to be a religious gathering on every Sunday at Gagan Babu's house. They would have been talking about the conduct and behaviour of the society. At that time people at Ghazipur were influenced by the materialistic life of Western countries. As a result of that many of them would not give much importance to their own religion. Swamiji was pained by seeing their aversion to their own religion and the magnetism of the Western culture. He wrote on 21st January, 1890, to Pramadadas Babu:

"Everything here appears good. The people are all gentlemen, but very much Westernised; and it is a pity I am so thoroughly against every affection for the Western idea. Only my friend very little affects such ideals. What a frippery civilization is it indeed that the foreigners have brought over here! What a materialistic illusion have they created! May Vishvanatha save these weak-hearted!" In a postscript to the letter he adds, "Alas for the irony of our fate, that in this land of Bhagvan Shuk's birth, renunciation is looked down upon as madness and sin!"

Swamiji didn't think that social reformation is possible by blaming or criticizing its old customs. His system of reformation is quite different. He realized that mass education with love and patience is necessary. He said, "Wait till the people are educated, till they understand their needs and are ready and able to solve their problems. Instead of frittering away our energies on ideal reforms, which will never become practical, we had better go to the root of the evil and make a legislative body, that is to say, educate out people, so that they may be able to solve their own problems. Until that is done, all these ideal reforms will remain ideals only."[29]

At Ghazipur, Gaganchandra Bose introduced Swamiji to a European named Mr. Ross. Mr. Ross wanted to know about the festival of Holi and Ramalila, and also about other social rituals from Swamiji. He was extremely pleased with Swamiji's answer, and became respectful to the Hindu religion. It is said that Swamiji wrote an essay on the theme of Holi for him. Mr. Ross took Swamiji to Mr. Pennington, the District Judge, and there, Swamiji had a long discussion with him. Swamiji had explained thoroughly the Hindu religion, the scientific value of Yoga, reawakening of Hindu religion, modification of modern India, and so on. He was very much impressed by this discussion and he invited Swamiji to Europe and promised to help him his best. At this time Swamiji met Colonel Mr. Rivett Carnac, and had a long discussion with him. He was overwhelmed by realizing the wisdom of Swamiji.

Swamiji came to Ghazipur mainly to see Pavhari Baba. Let us see, who was Pavhari Baba, and why Swamiji wished to see him? He was born of Brahmin parents in a village near Guzi, about thirty miles from Varanasi. In his boyhood, he came to study and live with his uncle in Ghazipur. His uncle was a lifelong Brahmachari (one who takes the vow of lifelong celibacy), became versed in Vyakarana (grammar) and Naya (logic), and belonged to the Ramajuja or Shri sect. He had a piece of land on the banks of the Ganga, about two miles to the north of Ghazipur, and had established himself there. After his uncle's death he was determined "to supply the gap with a vision that can never change." He wished to find Reality, and wandered throughout the land. On his visit to one place, on the top of mount Girnar in Kathiawar, he was first initiated into the mysteries of practical Yoga. "It was this mountain which was so holy to the Buddhists. At its foot is the huge rock on which is inscribed the first-deciphered edict of the 'divinest of monarchs', Ashoka." From Girnar he returned to Kashi, where he met a great Yogi, who lived in a cave in the high bank of the Ganga. Here he learnt the Advaita system, and then he travelled for years, studying and leading a life of Sannyasi. Finally, he came back to his old home, Ghazipur. He dug a hermitage in the ground, as advised by his teacher, on the high bank of the river. He would remain absorbed in meditation, and at night he crossed the Ganga by swimming, and reached the other shore. There he spent the night in religious practices. His daily diet was a handful of bitter Nimba (margosa) leaves or of a few pods pepper. "Then he gave up going nightly to the woods on the other bank of the river and took more and more to his cave. For days and months, we are told; he would be in the hole, absorbed in meditation, and then come out. Nobody knows what he subsisted on during these long intervals, so the people called him pav-ahari (or air-eater) Baba (or father). When not absorbed in his meditations, he would be living in a room above the mouth of his cave, and during this time he would receive visitors."[30] How did Swamiji get an opportunity to meet Pavhari Baba, and what he had experienced—we will know that directly from him.

"I have visited Pavhari Baba's house—there are high walls all round, and it is fashioned like an English bungalow. There is a garden inside and big rooms and chimneys, etc. He allows nobody to enter. If he is so inclined, he comes up to the door and speaks from inside—that is all. I went and waited and waited in the cold and had to return."[31]

"It is so very difficult to meet the Babaji. He does not step out of his home; and, when willing to speak at all, he just comes near the door to speak from inside. ...People say there are cave-like rooms within where he dwells; and he only knows what he does there, for nobody has had a peep."[32]

"I have obtained an interview with Babaji. A great sage indeed!—It is all very wonderful, and in this atheistic age, a towering representation of marvelous power born of Bhakti and Yoga! I have sought refuge in his grace; and he has given me hope—a thing very few may be fortunate enough to obtain. It is Babaji's wish that I stay on for some days here, and he would do me some good. So following this saint's bidding I shall remain here for some time. ...Unless one is face to face with the life of such men, faith in the scriptures does not grow in all its real integrity."[33]

"I have talked with Pavhari Baba. He is a wonderful saint—the embodiment of humility, devotion, and Yoga. Although he is an orthodox Vaishnava, he is not prejudiced against others of different beliefs. He has tremendous love for Mahaprabhu Chaitanya, and he [Pavhari Baba] speaks of Sri Ramakrishna as 'an incarnation of God'. He loves me very much, and I am going to stay here for some days at his request. Pavhari Baba can live in Samadhi [trance] for from two to six months at a stretch. He can read Bengali and has kept a photograph of Sri Ramakrishna in his room. I have not yet seen him face to face, since he speaks from behind a door, but I have never heard such a sweet voice." In this letter, Swamiji had requested Balaram Babu to send him a copy of *Chaitanys-Bhagavata*. This was for Pavhari Baba. "Send it immediately to the following address: Gagan Chandra Roy, Opium Department, Ghazipur. Please don't forget. Pavhari Baba is an ideal Vaishnava and a great scholar; but he is reluctant to reveal his learning. His elder brother acts as his attendant, but even he is not allowed to enter his room. Please send him a copy of *Chaitanya-Mangala* also, if it is still in print. All remember that if Pavhari Baba accepts your presents, that will be your great fortune. Ordinarily, he does not accept anything from anybody. Nobody knows what he eats or even what he does. Please don't let it be known that I am here and don't send news of anyone to me. I am busy with an important works."[34]

Next, he wrote a letter to Pramadadas Mitra on 7th February 1890. It contains more news: "His dwelling has walls on all sides with a few doors in them. Inside these walls, there is one long underground burrow wherein he lays himself up in Samadhi. He talks to others only when he comes out of the hole. Nobody knows what he eats, and so they call him Pavhari Baba. Once he did not come out of the hole for five years, and people thought he had given up the body. But now again he is out. But this time he does not show himself to people and talks from behind the door. Such sweetness in speech I have never come across! He does not give a direct reply to questions but says, 'What does this servant know?' But then fire comes out as the talking goes on. On my pressing him very much he said, 'Favour me highly by staying here some days.' But he never speaks in this way; so from this I understood he meant to reassure me; and whenever I am importunate, he asks me to stay on. So, I wait in hope. He is a learned man no doubt but nothing in the line betrays itself. He performs scriptural ceremonials, for from the full-moon day to the last day of the month, sacrificial oblations go on. So, it is sure, he is not retiring into the hole during this period. How can I ask his permission, [Evidently for a proposed visit to the saint by the correspondent, Pramadadas Mitra of Varanasi.] for he never gives a direct reply; he goes on multiplying such expressions as 'this servant', 'my fortune', and so on." Towards the end of this letter Swamiji requested Pramada Babu to come to Ghazipur, "Or after his passing away, the keenest regret will be left in your mind. In two days you may return after an interview—I mean a talk with him *ab intra*. My friend Satish Babu will receive you most warmly. So, do come up directly you receive this; I shall meanwhile let Babaji know of you. Even though one can't have his company, no trouble taken for the sake of such a great soul can ever go unrewarded."[35]

From this letter we can guess that Swamiji, by this time, may be staying with Satish Babu, and often used to go to Gagan Babu's house. Swamiji had received the two books, that he asked Balaram Babu to send him, and on 11th February 1890, he acknowledged the same in his reply. It also shows the efficiency of the Postal Department during that time. We know how much Swamiji loved his brother-disciple and how much concerned he was for them. Whatever he would do or wherever he used to be staying, he would always have the news of his brother-disciples. He was suffering terribly from a backache which began in Allahabad. He had recovered from it some time back, but it had recurred. So he would have to stay at Ghazipur, and also for Pavhari Baba had requested it. He was worried for he had not received any letter from Rishikesh, but he came to know about Swami Abhedananda, who in Rishikesh had a relapse and was again suffering from malaria. Yesterday, Swamiji couldn't go out to meet Pavhari Baba due to his pain in loins. Today (14th February 1890) also he has been suffering from lumbago.

For two days (13th & 14th February, 1890) Swamiji couldn't go out to meet Pavhari Baba for his pain in the loins. A man came from him to inquire about Swamiji. Swamiji, in a letter to Pramada Babu, wrote about Pavhari Baba that while he talks, "Fire comes out". Pramada Babu couldn't understand the meaning of it, and he thought it was really 'fire'. Hence, Swamiji wrote him in his reply on 13th February, 1890: "'Fire comes out'—that is, a wonderful devotion to Guru and resignation are revealed; and such amazing endurance and humility I have never seen." Pramada Babu couldn't come to Ghazipur for his illness. So Swamiji assured him: "Whatever good things I may come by, sure, you have your share in them."

Swamiji knew that many of his brother-disciples didn't like his so much interest in Pavhari Baba. But he was determined in his commitment. Perhaps Balaram Babu also was not pleased with his extra attraction towards the Sadhus. Swamiji, therefore, wrote him on 14th February 1890, "I am in receipt of your letter of contrition. I am not leaving this place soon—it is impossible to avoid the Babaji's request. You have expressed remorse at not having reaped any appreciable results by serving the Sadhus. It is true, and yet not true, it is true if you look towards ideal bliss; but if you look behind to the place from which you started, you will find that before you were an animal, now you are a man, and will be a god or God Himself in future. Moreover, that sort of regret and dissatisfaction is very good; it is the prelude to improvement. Without this none can rise. He who puts on a turban and immediately sees the Lord, progresses thus far and no farther."[36]

He had also received a letter from brother Gangadhar (Swami Akhandananda), who was then in Rambag Samadhi, Srinagar, Kashmir. He also had information that "Rakhal and Subodh had gone to Vrindavan after visiting Omkar, Girnar, Abu, Bombay, and Dwarka."[37]

At that time, Swamiji received a letter from an unknown person, who had written something insulting to Pavhari Baba. He wrote about this incident to Balaram Babu: "I have received an anonymous letter which I have been unable to trace back to the gigantic soul who wrote it. Indeed, one should pay homage to such a man. He who considers a great soul like Pavhari Baba to be no more than water in a hoof print, he who has nothing to learn in this world and who feels it a disgrace to be taught by any other man—truly, such a new incarnation must be visited. I hope that if the government should discover the identity of this person, he will be handled with special care and be placed in the Alipore garden (Zoo). If you happen to know this man, please ask him to bless me, so that even a dog or a jackal may be my Guru—not to speak of a great soul like Pavhari Baba. I have many things to learn. My master used to say: 'As long as I live, so long do I learn'. Also please tell this fellow that unfortunately I do not have the time to 'cross the seven seas and thirteen rivers' or to go to Sri Lanka in order to sleep after having put oil in the nostrils."[38]

One of his letters to Swami Sadananda tells us how he built his brother-disciples and what kind of education he gave them. He wrote: "do your own spiritual exercises, and knowing yourself to be the humblest servant of all, serve them. Those with whom you are staying are such that even I am not worthy to call myself their humblest servant and take the dust of their feet,—knowing this, serve them and have devotion for them. Don't be angry even if they abuse or even hurt you grievously. Never mix with women. Try to be hardy little by little, and gradually accustom yourself to maintaining the body out of the proceeds of begging. Whoever takes the name of Ramakrishna, know him to be your Guru. Everyone can play the role of a master, but it is very difficult to be a servant. Especially you should follow Shashi. Know it for certain that without steady devotion for the Guru and unflinching patience and perseverance, nothing is to be achieved. You must have strict morality. Deviate an inch from this, and you are gone for ever."[39] We can never forget that, in his later life, how Swami Sadananda had dedicated himself for the service of people.

Swamiji's sense of duty and love for his brother-disciples was endless, and the same is revealed in this letter to Pramadadas Mitra. He wrote: "I wrote a letter to brother Gangadhar asking him to stop his wandering and settle down somewhere and to send me an account of the various Sadhus he had come across in Tibet and their ways and customs. I enclose the reply that came from him. Brother Kali is having repeated attacks of fever at Rishikesh. I have sent him a wire from this place. So if from the reply I find I am wanted by him, I shall be obliged to start direct for Rishikesh from this place, otherwise I am coming to you in a day or two. Well, you may smile, sir, to see me weaving all this web of Maya—and that is no doubt the fact. But then there is the chain of iron, and there is the chain of gold. Much good comes of the letter; and it drops off by itself when all the good is reaped. The sons of my Master are indeed the great objects of my service, and here alone I feel I have some duty left for me. Perhaps I shall send brother Kali down to Allahabad or somewhere else, as convenient."[40]

At this time, Swamiji suffered from various agonies. He still had been suffering from lumbago, and therefore, couldn't go to Pavhari Baba. Babaji sent his man for making an enquiry of his health. The purpose of his staying at Ghazipur was not yet fulfilled. He was determined not to surrender in despair. He wrote to Swami Akhandananda: "Our Bengal is the land of Bhakti (Devotion) and of Jnana (Knowledge), where Yoga is scarcely so much as talked of even. What little there is, is but the queer breathing exercises of the Hatha-Yoga—which is nothing but a kind of gymnastics. Therefore I am staying with this wonderful Raja-Yoga—and he has given me some hopes, too. There is a beautiful bungalow in a small garden belonging to a gentleman here; I mean to stay there. The garden is quite close to Babaji's cottage. A brother of the Babaji stays there to look after the comforts of the Sadhus, and I shall have my Bhiksha (food obtained by begging) at his place. Hence, with a view to seeing to the end of this fun, I give up for the present my plan of going to the hills. For the last two months I have had an attack of lumbago in the waist, which also makes it impossible to climb the hills now. Therefore let me wait and see what Babaji will give me."[41]

It means, Swamiji's motto was to learn Raja-Yoga from Pavhari Baba, and therefore, he took shelter on the hill. Hence his reply to those, who criticized him for staying at Ghazipur for a long time, was: "My motto is to learn whatever good things I may come across anywhere. This leads many friends to think that it will take away from my devotion to the Guru. These ideas I count as those of lunatics and bigots. For all Gurus are one and are fragments and radiations of God, the Universal Guru."

Swamiji wanted to keep his purpose for staying at Ghazipur in secret, but he had hinted at the same in many letters to many persons. Here at Ghazipur, he had been suffering from pain in the waist, and yet he continued his communication with his brother-disciples. He was very much in the know of every whereabouts of his brother-disciples—what they were doing, how their health was, what they were in need of, when and whom he should write to, and for whom, and so on. Swamiji confined himself to Ghazipur for he wished to get something good from Pavhari Baba, but his mind was wandering around his brother-disciples. He couldn't, even if he would try, think of himself. He would always think of others. Gradually he realized that he had nothing to get from Babaji, on the contrary, he was asked to give something. There was no one else to give him more than what he had received from Sri Ramakrishna.

Swamiji wrote to Pramadadas Babu from Ghazipur on 3rd March 1890: "You know not, sir, I am a very soft-natured man in spite of the stern Vedantic views I hold. And this proves to be my undoing. At the slightest touch I give myself away; for howsoever I may try to think only of my own good, I slip off in spite of myself to think of other peoples' interests. This time it was with a very stern resolve that I set out to pursue my own good, but I had to run off at the news of the illness of a brother at Allahabad! And now comes this news from Rishikesh, and my mind has run off with me there. I have wired to Sharat, but no reply yet—a nice place indeed to delay even telegrams so much! The lumbago obstinately refuses to leave me, and the pain is very great. For the last few days I haven't been able to go to see Pavhariji, but out of his kindness he sends every day for my report. But now I see the whole matter is inverted in its bearings! While I myself have come, a beggar, at his door, he turns round and wants to learn of me! This saint perhaps is not yet perfected—too much of rites, vows, observances, and too much of self-concealment. The ocean in its fullness cannot be contained within its shores, I am sure. So it is not good, I have decided not to disturb this Sadhu (holy man) for nothing, and very soon I shall ask leave of him to go. No help, you see; providence has dealt me my death to make me so tender! Babaji does not let me off, and Gagan Babu (whom probably you know—an upright, pious, and kind-hearted man) does not let me off. If the wire in reply requires my leaving this place, I go; if not, I am coming to you at Varanasi in a few days. I am not going to let you off—I must take you to Rishikesh—no excuse or objections will do."[42]

In spite of the nice weather at Ghazipur Swamiji had been suffering from indigestion though he was saved from malaria. Lumbago forced him to suffer from a great pain. People generally consider money more valuable than God. Swamiji also had such an experience—"Spend money and the owners of temples will fling away the installed god to make room for you; so no anxiety about a resting-place!" At the end of this letter he wrote: "I find wonderful endurance in Babaji, and that's why I am begging something of him; but no inkling of the mood to give, only receiving and receiving! So I also fly off." Again he added: "So now the great conclusion is that Ramakrishna has no peer; nowhere else in this world exists that unprecedented perfection, that wonderful kindness for all that does not stop to justify itself, that intense sympathy for man in bondage. Either he must be the Avatara (incarnation of God) as he himself used to say, or else the ever-perfected divine man, whom the Vedanta speaks of as the free one who assumes a body for the good of humanity. This is my conviction sure and certain; and the worship of such a divine man has been referred to by Patanjali in the aphorism: 'Or the goal may be attained by meditation on a saint.' Never during his life did he refuse a single prayer of mine; millions of offences has he forgiven me; such great love even my parents never had for me. There is no poetry, no exaggeration in all this. It is the bare truth and every disciple of his knows it. In times of great danger, great temptation, I wept in extreme agony with the prayer, 'O God, do save me', but no response came from anybody; but this wonderful saint, or Avatara, or anything else he may be, came to know of all my affliction through his powers of insight into human hearts and lifted it off—in spite of my desire to the contrary—after getting me brought to his presence."[43]

Swamiji had repeatedly tried to leave Ghazipur, but failed. Rather he wrote to Swami Akhandananda to come to Ghazipur, and gave him instruction how to reach there. "If you come to Ghazipur, you have but to inquire at Satish Babu's or Gagan Babu's at Gorabazar, and you know my whereabouts. Or, Pavhari Baba is so well-known a person here that everyone will inform you about his Ashram at the very mention of his name, and you have only to go there and inquire about the Paramahamsa, and they will tell you of me. Near Moghul Sarai there is a station named Dildarnagar, where you have to change to a short branch railway and get down at Tarighat, opposite Ghazipur; then you have to cross the Ganga to reach Ghazipur."[44]

Swamiji had been waiting at Ghazipur to see what the Babaji does. He invited Swami Akhandananda to stay together at the bungalow for some time, and then he wished to start for hills, or for any other place they might decode upon. He also forbade him not to say anybody about his staying at Ghazipur. During this period, Swamiji kept himself hidden somewhere in for some time. On 31st March 1890, he wrote: "I shall continue to stay in secret in a village some distance from this place, and there's no facility for writing any letter from that place, owing to which I could not reply to your letter so long." It means Swamiji had been living somewhere in secret since some days before 31st March. Who knows whether his living in secret was related to the arrival of Swami Premananda at Ghazipur. Monks of Baranagore Math was worried about his absence for a long time, and his intimacy with Pavhari Baba. Perhaps this was the reason of Swami Premananda's arrival at Ghazipur, and he wanted to take him back to the monastery. Swamiji probably didn't like his arrival, and therefore, he went into hiding to a village some distance form Ghazipur. On 15th March, he wrote a letter to Balaram Babu: "Baburam has suddenly come here. He has got fever; he was wrong to start under such circumstances. ...I am leaving this place tomorrow. ...My countless salutations to Mother. You all bless me that I may have sameness of vision, that after avoiding the bondages which one is heir to by one's very birth, I may not again get stuck in self-imposed bondages."[45]

Again on 31st March 1890, he wrote: "Another brother of mine had been with me, but has left for Abhedananda's place. The news of his arrival has not yet been received, and, his health being bad, I am rather anxious for his sake. I have behaved very cruelly towards him—that is, I have harassed him much to make him leave my company. There's no help, you see; I am so very weakhearted, so much overmastered by the distractions of love! Bless me that I may harden. What shall I say to you about the condition of my mind! Oh, it is as if the hell-fire is burning there day and night! Nothing, nothing could I do yet! And this life seems muddled away in vain; I feel quite helpless as to what to do!" It is clear to us, that there was no scarcity in his love towards his brother-disciples, but he didn't like anybody to interfere in his liberty. In that condition he had to be hard, but later he would feel sorry for such a rough behaviour. He wrote: "My Gurubhais (brother-disciples) must be thinking me very cruel and selfish. Oh, what can I do? Who will see deep down into my mind? Who will know how much I am suffering day and night? Bless me that I may have the most unflinching patience and perseverance."

How strange! He, who himself is Lord Shiva, and who arrived on the earth to release the human beings from sorrows, is asking: "Who will know how much I am suffering day and night?" He, who arrived on the earth to encourage the human beings in going to the light from the darkness of ignorance, is saying: "Nothing, nothing could I do yet! And this life seems muddled away in vain; I feel quite helpless as to what to do!" You are really great, and great is your divine play.

Pavhari "Babaji throws out honeyed words and keeps" him from leaving. Hence Swamiji was staying at Ghazipur. On the other hand, he was worried about Baburam Maharaj for he had not received any news from him. On 2nd April 1890, Swamiji wrote to Swami Abhedananda: "Glad to receive your letter as well as Pramada Babu's and Baburam's (Premananda's)." So he got relief from his anxiety. His heart was full of love, which made him write: "You have expressed a desire to see me. I too have a similar longing, and it is this that makes me afraid of going. Moreover, the Babaji forbids me to do so. I shall try to go on a few days' leave from him. But there is this fear that by so doing I shall be drawn up to the hills by the attraction I have for Hrishikesh, and it will be very difficult to shake it off, specially for one weak-minded, you see, like myself. The attack of lumbago, too, will not leave me on any account—a botheration! But then I am getting used to it."[46]

In different times Swamiji had expressed his wish to start for different places. But he could go nowhere. The attraction towards his brother-disciples forced him to return to Calcutta (now Kolkata). Balaram Babu died on 13th April 1890, and Swami Abhedananda was ill—following these two bad news Swamiji left Ghazipur without any delay. 6th July 1890—Swami Saradananda was then in Almora. Swamiji wrote him with an expression of sorrow: "I had no wish to leave Ghazipur this time, and certainly not to come to Calcutta, but Kali's illness made me go to Varanasi, and Balaram's sudden death brought me to Calcutta."

We came to know why Swamiji had returned to Calcutta. What did he do during this period?—Before we come to that point, we have to say something more about what we had left at Ghazipur. We will look into those incidents that had been passed through the life of Swamiji during his staying at Ghazipur.

We have already told about the days at Cossipore garden-house. Swamiji then wished to be absorbed in trance for a long time. But Sri Ramakrishna forbade him to do so, and reproached his selfishness. He was committed to his Gurudev for doing good to the world. But the association with Pavhari Baba at Ghazipur revived his old wish, and he wanted to know the science of Hatha Yoga. But he couldn't disregard the behest of Sri Ramakrishna. His behest to Swamiji was that he should devote himself to the service of the order of all-renouncing devotees founded by him.

Swamiji saw that Pavhari Baba had a photograph of Sri Ramakrishna. He told him that Sri Ramakrishna was an Avatara (incarnation of God). That's why he would respect Babaji. He believed that Pavhari Baba was successful in knowing the truth with the help of Hatha Yoga. He assured Swamiji of giving him some spiritual knowledge. Swamiji, therefore, had been waiting for that holy moment. He wished to be absorbed in trance for a long time like Pavhari Baba. He was so much influenced by Pavhari Baba, that he even wished to be initiated by Babaji.

One day Swamiji had experienced a strange incident. We would better wish to learn the same from his holy lips. It was March 1902, when Swamiji was seated in his room at Belur Math. His disciple asked him, "Have you ever had a vision of Sri Ramakrishna after his passing away?"

Swamiji replied: "After leaving the body, I associated for some time with Pavhari Baba of Ghazipur. There was a garden not far distant from his Ashram where I lived. People used to say it was a haunted garden, but as you know, I am a sort of demon myself and have not much fear of ghosts. In the garden there were many lemon trees which bore numerous fruits. At that time I was suffering from diarrhea, and there no food could be had except bread. So, to increase the digestive powers, I used to take plenty of lemons. Mixing with Pavhari Baba, I liked him very much, and he also came to love me deeply. One day I thought that I did not learn any art for making this weak body strong, even though I lived with Sri Ramakrishna for so many years. I had heard that Pavhari Baba knew the science of Hatha-Yoga. So I thought I would learn the practices of Hatha-Yoga from him, and through them strengthen the body. You know I have a dogged resolution, and whatever I set my heart on, I always carry out. On the eve of the day on which I was to take initiation, I was lying on a cot thinking; and just then I saw the form of Sri Ramakrishna standing on my right side, looking steadfastly at me, as if very much grieved. I had dedicated myself to him, and at the thought that I was taking another Guru I was much ashamed and kept looking at him. Thus perhaps two or three hours passed, but no words escaped from my mouth. Then he disappeared all of a sudden. My mind became upset seeing Sri Ramakrishna that night, so I postponed the idea of initiation from Pavhari Baba for the day. After a day or two again the idea of initiation from Pavhari Baba arose in the mind—and again in the night there was the appearance of Sri Ramakrishna as on the previous occasion. Thus when for several nights in succession I had the vision of Sri Ramakrishna, I gave up the idea of initiation altogether, thinking that as every time I resolved on it, I was getting such a vision, then no good but harm would come from it."[47]

In the summer of 1894, Swamiji wrote a letter to his brother-disciples at Alambazar monastery, in which he sent a part of his poem titled "A Song I Sing to Thee", and promised to send the rest of it later on. Through this long poetry he had spread out all the petals of his lotus-heart. Here we would like to present the reader a part of it, in which one finds a glimpse of his experience.

Servant am I, true servant of Thee Both (Purusha and Prakriti together)
Low at Thy feet, with Shakti, I salute!
Thou standest steadfast, ever at my back,
Hence when I turn me round, I see Thy face,
Thy smiling face. Therefore I sing again
And yet again. Therefore I fear no fear;
For birth and death lie prostrate at my feet.

. . . .

Like to the playing of a little child
Is every attitude of mine toward Thee.

Even, at times, I dare be angered with Thee,
Even, at times, I'd wander far away:—
Yet there, in greyest gloom of darkest night,
Yet there, with speechless mouth and fearful eyes,
Thou standest fronting me, and Thy sweet Face
Stoops down with loving look on face of mine.
Then, instantly, I turn me back to Thee,
And at Thy feet I fall on bended knees.
I crave no pardon at Thy gentle hands,
For Thou art never angry with Thy son.
Who else with all my foolish freaks would bear?
Thou art my Master! Thou my soul's real mate.
Many a time I see Thee—I am Thee!
Ay, I am Thee, and Thou, my Lord, art me![48]

It is already mentioned before that in his letter dated 3rd March 1890, Swamiji wrote to Pramadadas Mitra: "I find wonderful endurance of Babaji, and that's why I am begging something of him, but no inkling of the mood to give, only receiving and receiving! So I also fly off" It means Swamiji decided not to go to anyone else for what he wanted to learn from Babaji. Whatever he had learnt from Sri Ramakrishna was enough to him. In the same letter he added a song, composed by the poet Karnataka, that depicts his mental state. The song explains: "Remain, O mind, within yourself, go not to anybody else's door, only seek for it in the privacy of your heart. There is the supreme Treasure, the philosophers' stone, and He can give whatever you ask for; for countless gems, O mind, lie strewn about the portals of His abode. He is the wishing-stone that confers boons at the mere thought." After this he wrote: "So now the great conclusion is that Ramakrishna has no peer...." It means, Swamiji had experienced the vision of Sri Ramakrishna, of which he later told his disciple, before 3rd March 1890. He had never lost his faith in Sri Ramakrishna. His idea was to learn to recognize good, no matter where he might come across it. After that wonderful vision of Sri Ramakrishna, Swamiji stayed at Ghazipur for a month, and it was only because he wanted to earn more experience. Later, during lectures, with reference to Pavhari Baba he had mentioned many of his advice to the audience. He wrote about Pavhari Baba:

> "Like many others in India, there was no striking or stirring external activity in this life. It was one more example of that Indian ideal of teaching through life and not through words, and that truth bears fruit in those lives only which have become ready to receive. Persons of this type are entirely averse to preaching what they know, for they are for ever convinced that it is internal discipline alone that leads to truth, and not words. Religion to them is not motive to social conduct, but an intense search after and realization of truth in this life. They deny the greater potentiality of one moment over another and every moment in eternity being equal to every other, they insist on seeing the truths of religion face to face now and here, not waiting for death.

"The present writer had occasion to ask the saint the reason of his not coming out of his cave to help the world. At first, with his native humility and humour, he gave the following strong reply:

> 'A certain wicked person was caught in some criminal act and had his nose cut off as a punishment. Ashamed to show his noseless features to the world and disgusted with himself, he fled into a forest; and there, spreading a tiger-skin on the ground, he would

feign deep meditation whenever he thought anybody was about. This conduct, instead of keeping people off, drew them in crowds to pay their respects to this wonderful saint; and he found that his forest-life had brought him once again an easy living. Thus years went by. At last the people around became very eager to listen to some instruction from the lips of the silent meditative saint; and one young man was specially anxious to be initiated into the order. It came to such a pass that any more delay in that line would undermine the reputation of the saint. So one day he broke his silence and asked the enthusiastic young man to bring on the morrow a sharp razor with him. The young man, glad at the prospect of the great desire of his life being speedily fulfilled, came early the next morning with the razor. The noseless saint led him to a very retired spot in the forest, took the razor in his hand, opened it, and with one stroke cut off his nose, repeating in a solemn voice, 'young man, this has been my initiation into the order. The same I gave to you. Do you transmit it diligently to others when the opportunity comes!' The young man could not divulge the secret of this wonderful initiation for shame, and carried out to the best of his ability the injunctions of his master. Thus a whole sect of nose-cut saints spread over the country. Do you want me to be the founder of another such?'

"Later on, in a more serious mood, another query brought the answer: 'Do you think that physical help is the only help possible? Is it not possible that one mind can help other minds even without the activity of the body?'

"When asked on another occasion why he, a great Yogi, should perform Karma, such as pouring oblations into the sacrificial fire, and worshipping the image of Sri Raghunathji, which are practices only meant for beginners, the reply came: 'Why do you take for granted that everybody makes Karma for his own good? Cannot one perform Karma for others?'

"Then again, everyone has heard of the thief who had come to steal from his Ashram, and who at the sight of the saint got frightened and ran away, leaving the goods he had stolen in a bundle behind; how the saint took the bundle up, ran after the thief, and came up to him after miles of hard running; how the saint laid the bundle at the feet of the thief, and with folded hands and tears in his eyes asked his pardon for his own intrusion, and begged hard for his acceptance of the goods, since they belonged to him, and not to himself.

"We are also told, on reliable authority, how once he was bitten by a cobra; and though he was given up for hours as dead, he revived; and when his friends asked him about it, he only replied that the cobra 'was a messenger from the Beloved'.

"And well may we believe this, knowing as we do the extreme gentleness, humility, and love of his nature. All sorts of physical illness were to him only 'messengers from the Beloved', and he could not even bear to hear them called by any other name, even while he himself suffered tortures from them. This silent love and gentleness had conveyed themselves to the people around, and those who have travelled through the surrounding villages can testify to the unspoken influence of this wonderful man. Of late, he did not show himself to anyone. When out of his underground retiring-place, he would speak to people with a closed door between. His presence above ground was always indicated by the rising smoke of oblations in the sacrificial fire, or the noise of getting things ready for worship.

"One of his great peculiarities was his entire absorption at the time in the task in hand, however trivial. The same amount of care and attention was bestowed in cleaning a copper pot as in the worship of Sri Raghunathji, he himself being the best example of the secret he once told us of work: 'The means should be loved and cared for as if it were the end itself.'

"Neither was his humility kindred to that which means pain and anguish or self-abasement. It sprang naturally from the realization of that which he once so beautifully explained to us, 'O King, the Lord is the wealth of those who have nothing—yes, of those', he continued, 'who have thrown away all desires of possession, even that of one's own soul.' He would never directly teach, as that would be assuming the role of a teacher and placing himself in a higher position than another. But once the spring was touched, the fountain welled up with infinite wisdom; yet always the replies were indirect.

"In appearance he was tall and rather fleshy, had but one eye, and looked much younger than his real age. His voice was the sweetest we have ever heard. For the last ten years or more of his life, he had withdrawn himself entirely from the gaze of mankind. A few potatoes and a little butter were placed behind the door of his room, and sometimes during the night this was taken in when he was not in Samadhi and was living above ground. When inside his cave, he did not require even these. Thus, this silent life went on, witnessing to the science of Yoga, and a living example of purity, humility, and love.

"The smoke, which, as we have said already, indicated his coming out of Samadhi, one day smelled of burning flesh. The people around could not guess what was happening; but when the smell became overpowering, and the smoke was seen to rise up in volumes, they broke open the door, and found that the great Yogi had offered himself as the last oblation to his sacrificial fire, and very soon a heap of ashes was all that remained of his body.

"Let us remember the words of Kalidasa: 'Fools blame the actions of the great, because they are extraordinary and their reasons past the finding-out of ordinary mortals.'

"Yet, knowing him as we do, we can only venture to suggest that the saint saw that his last moments had come, and not wishing to cause trouble to any, even after death, performed this last sacrifice of an Arya, in full possession of body and mind.

"The present writer owes a deep debt of gratitude to the departed saint and dedicates these lines, however unworthy, to the memory of one of the greatest Masters he has loved and served."[49]

Let me tell you a funny story of that time, when Swamiji was at Ghazipur. Mahendranath Dutta heard this story in Srishchandra's house at Ghazipur. There lived at Ghazipur a man, who was publicly known as 'Thakurda' (the grandfather). He was Brahmin by cast, and addicted to smoking hemp, opium, hashish. If ever someone would start saying something, he would blurt, "I know this." One day, when Swamiji was seated in Srishchandra's house, suddenly Thakurda appeared there. Everyone started making fun with him. Swamiji started reading from the Veda, and Thakurda, as soon as he heare the name of Veda, began to cry. Swamiji was explaining the verses from the Veda and exclaiming—Ah! How beautiful is the poetry! How wonderful are the words!.... Swamiji was seated on a chair, and Thakurda, being flooded with tears, was rolling about on the floor. He was feigning to be overwhelmed with spirituality. By this time Srishchandra entered the room, and seeing the game of Swamiji, couldn't help laughing. Swamiji beckoned him not to laugh, and said, "Get out of here. Can't you see that I am reading the Veda to Thakurda?" Then he turned to Thakurda and asked, "Do you understand what I am reading?" Srish Babu went into the next room and burst into laughter.

One more incident, the exact time is unknown to us. Perhaps it had happened when Swamiji was returning to Calcutta from Kashi, or on his way to Kashi from Ghazipur.

Swamiji was travelling by train. He got down on the platform when the train halted at Tarighat station on the other side of Ghazipur. It was noon, and the sun was bright just over the head. Swamiji was wearing an ochre cloth, and had nothing but a ticket for a third class compartment and a blanket with him. Even he didn't have any water pot with him. He tried to sit under the shade of the platform, but a policeman drove him away from there. Seeing no alternative he spread his blanket outside the waiting room, and sat on it leaning back to a wooden pillar. A north Indian tradesman was taking rest on a carpet under a shade opposite to Swamiji. Seeing the tired and dry face of Swamiji he threw some taunting words to him. He and his friends were travelling with Swamiji in the same compartment of the train. They, while sitting in the train, also had been laughing at Swamiji and making several jokes at him. It was summer. Swamiji was very much thirsty, but he couldn't buy water, as he didn't have any wallet with him. The trader was a wicked person. He bought water and drank in front of Swamiji showing him the bottle. Swamiji was sitting silently without giving much importance to him. But the trader was not satisfied with his silence, and said, "See, how cold the water is! You are a monk, have renounced everything. You have no money even to buy a water pot. Now feel how hard is living. If you would know how to earn money like me, wouldn't have to face such adversity." Thus the trader continuously disturbed Swamiji during the journey; didn't offer him a drop of water though the day was very much hot. Now at Tarighat station, he again tried to make him excited. Sitting under the shade he began to advise Swamiji, "See the power of money. You have to suffer, because you don't care about money. We earn money so that we can live in comfort." Then he began to eat delicious food one after another, and said, "Look, this is Puri, Kachouri, Petha, Sweets—these are not possible to enjoy without money. Do you think that someone from the sky will drop food for you?"

Swamiji was listening to all these rubbish, and watching all of his miss-behaviour silently with a smiling face. He didn't reproach at all. By that time, suddenly a man appeared in front of Swamiji. He had a small baggage and a mug in his right hand and in other hand a jug of water and a carpet. The man said to Swamiji, "Babaji, why are you sitting in the sun? Come under the shade. I have brought food for you, please take it." What a providential incident! Swamiji looked at the man with a great surprise. The trader was also watching everything. He too got startled with this unexpected incident. The man requested Swamiji repeatedly to take the food. Swamiji said, "Brother, I think you are doing a mistake somewhere. You have come to a wrong person. I am not that person whom you are looking for." The man replied, "No, no; you are that Babaji, whom I had seen." Swamiji got surprised, as he couldn't recognize the man. "How could he recognize me?" Swamiji said to himself, and asked, "What do you mean? When did you see me?" The man replied with a smile, "I am a confectioner, sell sweets. After meal, I had been taking a nap, while I dreamt that Ramaji came to me and said, 'My beloved monk is hungry, and waiting at the station. He hadn't any food since yesterday. Go immediately and serve him.' I woke up, but turned to the other side. Then Sri Ramaji appeared in front of me, and forced me to get up, and repeated the same about the monk. I am not lying. I sprang out of the bed, and as quick as possible I prepared food. Some sweets made in morning were left. I took all of those and left for station." Swamiji asked him, "How do you know that I am that monk?" The man replied, "At first, I too had the same doubt, but when I looked around and found no other monk but you, I realized that you must be that monk of whom I was told by Ramaji." Then the man took him under the shade, and gave him food and water. When Swamiji finished his meal, the man served water for washing his hands, and then he prepared his tobacco pipe. When Swamiji tried to thank him, he said, "No, no. Swamiji, don't thank me, everything is the divine play of Ramaji." The trader, had been watching everything, and listening to their conversation. He didn't have any problem in realizing that Swamiji was not an ordinary monk, but a great soul. Then he felt highly regretted for what he had done before with Swamiji. He also got afraid of getting harm for his sinful act, and thought that Swamiji must have cursed him for the same. Slowly he came to Swamiji and bowed down at his feet, and said with a fearful voice, "Please forgive me. What I did was a sin, and I promise you that I shall never do it again."

We have already told about the illness of Swami Abhedananda, when Swamiji had sent money for him and made every arrangement for his treatment and care. So Swami Abhedananda was staying with Doctor Priya at Varanasi. Swami Premananda went to Varanasi from Ghazipur and met Swami Abhedananda. On 6th July 1890, Swamiji wrote to Swami Saradananda from Baghbazar: "I had no wish to leave Ghazipur this time, and certainly not to come to Calcutta, but Kali's illness made me go to Varanasi, and Balaram's sudden death brought me to Calcutta." It means, Swamiji, after receiving the news of Abhedananda's illness went to Varanasi, and from there he came to Calcutta owing to the sudden death of Balaram Babu. Hence, he went to Varanasi before 13th April 1890, when Balaram Babu died. But in a letter dated 10th May, 1890, Swamiji asked Tulsiram (Tulsi Maharaj): "What is Balaram Babu [Balaram Bose] doing?" [Letter No. 5, C.W. Vol. 9, p. 6] And it is to be noted that the letter was written from Ghazipur. It means there is some mistake in the date of the letter. Most probably it is a printing mistake, because this letter was written before the death of Balaram Babu, and hence, the date should be the 10th April 1890, because on 10th May, 1890, Swamiji wrote a letter to Pramadadas Mitra from Baghbazar [Letter No. 32, C.W. Vol. 6, p. 260]. According to the letter written to Tulsiram, Swamiji was at Ghazipur on 10th May 1890, and according to the letter written to Pramadadas Babu, he was at Baghbazar on the same day. If we consider that Swamiji wrote to Tulsi Maharaj from Ghazipur on 10th April 1890, then the picture should be like this: Swamiji wrote to Tulsi Maharaj from Ghazipur on 10th April 1890, "I too am going off from this place very soon. I go perhaps to Bareilly and up." It means, till then he had no plan for going to Varanasi. After two or three days he went to Varanasi, and there he got the news of the sudden death [13th April 1890] of Balaram Bose, and left for Calcutta. And the incident of Tarighat station occurred on his way to Calcutta from Varanasi. Here we don't find any mistake in this picture.

It is really very hard to find a proper route-map of Swamiji's travelling, because many incidents do not corroborate the dates related to the information. If we once make a mess in the conflicts of dates, it will be difficult for us to go forward. Hence, we should try to focus on the activities and teachings of Swami Vivekananda.

So, we come back to the time (between 10th April and 13th April of 1890), when Swami reached Varanasi from Ghazipur. According to Swami Gambhirananda—Swami Premananda went to Varanasi from Ghazipur and met Swami Abhedananda. Shortly after that Swamiji went to Varanasi and made arrangement for the care of Abhedananda. After that, he settled himself in Pramada Babu's garden house, and devoted his entire time to spiritual practices. When he received the news of Balaram Babu's death, he returned to Calcutta. The news of passing away of Balaram Bose, the great devotee of Sri Ramakrishna, made Swamiji deeply shocked. The memories of those days of sweet companionship made him lament the more. Pramada Babu was struck to see a monk lamenting a death so much. He asked Swamiji, "How can death upset a monk like you? You should be remaining hard and steady." Swamiji said in reply, "Please do not talk that way. We are not dry monks. What! Do you think that because a man is a sannyasi he has no heart?"

10th May 1890, Swamiji was in Calcutta. Balaram Bose passed away on 13th April 1890 and Surendranath Mitra on 25th May of the same year. Swamiji stood face to face with some questions. Who would bear the expenses of Math? Where would the monks live? There was no harm if in that situation the Math was closed, and the monks would travel here and there. In that case, where would the sacred relics of Sri Ramakrishna be preserved? Already the English Law forced them to burn the body of Lord Sri Ramakrishna, which was a heinous act. Swamiji sought help from here and there. Some friends came forward and made some arrangement, Girish Babu and Mahendranath Gupta helped at their best. But they were not so rich. They didn't have enough money to perpetuate the memory of Sri Ramakrishna. Hence the future was misty. Swamiji sought advice of Pramada Babu on May 26 in a long and appealing letter. He wrote:

"I write this to you while caught in a vortex of many untoward circumstances and great agitation of mind; with a prayer to Vishvanatha, please think of the propriety and possibility, or otherwise, of all that I set forth below and then oblige me greatly by a reply.

1. I already told you at the outset that I am Ramakrishna's slave, having laid my body at his feet 'with Til and Tulasi leaves', I cannot disregard his behest. If it is in failure that that great sage laid down his life after having attained to superhuman heights of Jnana, Bhakti, Love, and powers, and after having practiced for forty years stern renunciation, non-attachment, holiness, and great austerities, then where is there anything for us to count on? So I am obliged to trust his words as the words of one identified with truth.
2. Now his behest to me was that I should devote myself to the service of the order of all-renouncing devotees founded by him, and in this I have to persevere, come what may, being ready to take heaven, hell, salvation, or anything that may happen to me.
3. His command was that his all-renouncing devotees should group themselves together, and I am entrusted with seeing to this. Of course, it matters not if any one of us goes out on visits to this place or that, but these shall be but visits, while his own opinion was that absolute homeless wandering suited him alone who was perfected to the highest point. Before that state, it is proper to settle somewhere to dive down into practice. When all the ideas of body and the like are dissolved of themselves, a person may then pursue whatever state comes to him. Otherwise, it is baneful for a practicing aspirant to be always wandering.
4. So in pursuance of this his commandment, his group of Sannyasins are now assembled in a dilapidated house at Baranagore, and two of his lay disciples, Babu Suresh Chandra Mitra and Babu Balaram Bose, so long provided for their food and house-rent.
5. For various reasons, the body of Bhagavan Ramakrishna had to be consigned to fire. There is no doubt that this act was very blamable. The remains of his ashes are now preserved, and if they be now properly enshrined somewhere on the banks of the Ganga, I presume we shall be able in some measure to expiate the sin lying on our head. These sacred remains, his seat, and his picture are every day worshipped in our Math in proper form; and it is known to you that a brother-disciple of mine, of Brahmin parentage, is occupied day and night with the task. The expenses of the worship used also to be borne by the two great souls mentioned above.
6. What greater regret can there be than this that no memorial could yet be raised in this land of Bengal in the very neighbourhood of the place where he lived his life of

Sadhana—he by whose birth the race of Bengalees has been sanctified, the land of Bengal has become hallowed, he who came on earth to save the Indians from the spell of the worldly glamour of Western culture and who therefore chose most of his all-renouncing disciples from university men?

7. The two gentlemen mentioned above had strong desire to have some land purchased on the banks of the Ganga and see the sacred remains enshrined on it, with the disciples living there together; and Suresh Babu had offered a sum of ₹ 1,000 for the purpose, promising to give more, but for some inscrutable purpose of God he left this world yesternight! And the news of Balaram Babu's death is already known to you.
8. Now there is no knowing as to where his disciples will stand with his sacred remains and his seat (and you know well, people here in Bengal are profuse in their professions, but do not stir out an inch in practice). The disciples are Sannyasins and are ready forthwith to depart anywhere their way may lie. But I, their servant, am in an agony of sufferings, and my heart is breaking to think that a small piece of land could not be had in which to install the remains of Bhagavan Ramakrishna.
9. It is impossible with a sum of ₹ 1,000 to secure land and raise a temple near Calcutta. Some such land would at least cost about five to seven thousands.
10. You remain now the only friend and patron of Sri Ramakrishna's disciples. In the North-Western Province great indeed is your fame, your position, and your circle of acquaintance. I request you to consider, if you feel like it, the propriety of your getting the affair through by raising subscriptions from well-to-do pious men known to you in your province. If you deem it proper to have some shelter erected on the banks of the Ganga in Bengal for Bhagavan Ramakrishna's sacred remains and for his disciples, I shall with your leave report myself to you, and I have not the slightest qualm to beg from door to door for this noble cause, for the sake of my Lord and his children. Please give this proposal your best thoughts with prayers to Vishvanatha. To my mind, if all these sincere, educated, youthful Sannyasins of good birth fail to live up to the ideals of Sri Ramakrishna owing to want of an abode and help, then alas for our country!
11. If you ask, 'you are a Sannyasin, so why do you trouble over these desires?'—I would then reply, I am Ramakrishna's servant, and I am willing even to steal and rob, if by doing so I can perpetuate his name in the land of his birth and Sādhanā (spiritual struggle) and help even a little his disciples to practice his great ideals. I know you to be my closest in kinship, and I lay my mind bare to you. I returned to Calcutta for this reason. I had told you this before I left, and now I leave it to you to do what you think best.
12. If you argue that it is better to have the plan carried out in some place like Kashi, my point is, as I have told you, it would be the greatest pity if the memorial shrine could not be raised in the land of his birth and Sadhana! The condition of Bengal is pitiable. The people here cannot even dream what renunciation truly means—luxury and sensuality have been so much eating into the vitals of the race! May God send renunciation and unworldliness into this land! They have here nothing to speak of, while the people of the North-Western Province, specially the rich there as I believe, have great zeal in noble causes like this. Please send me such reply as you think best."[50]

We don't think that this long and appealing letter was as fruitful as expected. This is evident from Swamiji's letter of June 4 to Pramada Babu: "I got your letter. There is no doubt that your advice is very wise. It is quite true that the Lord's will prevail. We also are spreading out here and there in small group of two or three." It means, the monks decided to lead a wandering life. Future of the Math was left on the will of Sri Ramakrishna.

Wandering in the Himalayas

Most of the time, Swamiji was beyond to be understood by his brother-disciples. Some time he was totally introspective, and some time he was restless to redress the misery of the world. When the future of the Math became uncertain, he didn't lose his confidence. He believed that the manifestation of Sri Ramakrishna would surely be fruitful at any cost. He only knows what he wishes. It required the good wishes of the world for the establishment of Ramakrishna Mission on a large scale rather than it was to be founded with the contribution of few persons. Hence, a hard work and vast experience was necessary for the same. Begging was the only means of living until the good time would come, and therefore, they should lead the life of wandering monks. Being seized by these thoughts Swamiji prepared himself for a long journey.

Since he was in Ghazipur, Swamiji was "longing for a flight to the Himalayas." From there he wrote to Swami Akhandananda: "You start immediately on receipt of this. I know the route to Tibet via Nepal that you have spoken of. As they don't allow anyone to enter Tibet easily, so they don't allow anybody to go anywhere in Nepal, except Katmandu, its capital, and one or two places of pilgrimage. But a friend of mine is now a tutor to His Highness the Maharaja of Nepal, and a teacher in his school, from whom I have it that when the Nepal government send their subsidy to China, they send it via Lhasa. A Sadhu contrived in that way to go to Lhasa, China, Manchuria, and even to the holy seat of Tara Devi in North China. We, too, can visit with dignity and respect Tibet, Lhasa, China, and all, if that friend of mine tries to arrange it. You therefore start immediately for Ghazipur."[51]

According to this letter Akhandananda came to Ghazipur, but Swamiji was then in Calcutta. Akhandananda didn't miss this opportunity to visit Pavhari Baba. He fortunately talked to him and became pleased with his sweet words. Pavhari Baba had appreciated the spiritual power of Swamiji. On his way to Calcutta, when, on 9th June 1890, Akhandananda got down at Bali station, he was caught by a police man, who brought him to the police station and from there to Baranagore Math. The police asked for written evidence that Akhandananda was a member of the Math. When Swami Shivananda was about to write it, Swamiji snatched the pen from his hand, and said to the police: "Why should we write?" Seeing the frightful appearance of Swamiji the police left the place.

On 6th July 1890, he wrote to Saradananda: "Girishchandra Ghosh is bearing the expenses of the Math, and for the present the daily maintenance is being managed nicely. ...I intend shortly, as soon as I can get my fare, to go up to Almora and thence to some place in Gharwal on the Ganga where I can settle down for a long meditation. Gangadhar is accompanying me. Indeed it was with this desire and intention that I brought him down from Kashmir. ...I am longing for a flight to the Himalayas. This time I shall not go to Pavhari Baba or any other saint—they divert one from his highest purpose. Straight up!" Swamiji had a plan to go to Tibet via Nepal. Perhaps it was not arranged properly, and therefore, he was thinking for going to Almora.

In the above letter Swamiji advised: "I don't think you ought to be in any hurry about coming down to Calcutta. You have done with roving; that's good, but you have not yet attempted the one thing you should do, that is, be resolved to sit down and meditate. I don't think Jnana is a thing like rousing a maiden suddenly from sleep by saying, 'Get up, dear girl, your marriage ceremony is waiting for you!' as we say. I am strongly of opinion that very few persons in any Yuga (age) attain Jnana, and therefore we should go on striving and striving even unto death. Peace be unto you and strength! Daksha, who is staying at Vrindavan with Rakhal (Brahmananda), has learnt to make gold and has become a *pucca* Jnani, so writes Rakhal. God bless him, and you may say amen! ...How do you find the climate at Almora? Neither S—nor you need come down. What is the use of so many living together in one place and doing no good to one's soul? Don't be fools always wandering from place to place; that's all very good, but be heroes. Who advises you to jump into fire? If you don't find the Himalayas a place for Sadhana, go somewhere else then. So many gushing inquires simply betray a weak mind. Arise, ye mighty one, and be strong! Work on an on, struggle on and on!"

On 15th July 1890, Swamiji wrote to Saradananda: "I will leave this place before this letter reaches you; only I won't go to Almora. I have my own plans for the future and they shall be a secret."

In the third week of July 1890, Swamiji decided to set out again with the same old determination—not to return until he had achieved his spiritual goal. At that time, Holy Mother was living in a rented house at Ghusuree, a village on the other side of the Ganaga. Before leaving Calcutta Swamiji went with Akhandananda to see the Mother and receive her blessings. Swamiji sang a song to please the Mother, and slowly told about his pilgrimage. He said to her, "Mother, I shall not return until I have attained the highest Jnana." The Holy Mother blessed him in the name of the Master. She said, "My son, will you not see your own mother at home before leaving?" "Mother," he replied, "you alone are my mother." Seeing his spirit, the Holy Mother blessed him again and said, "Come back soon. She also blessed Swami Akhandananda, and said, "My son, I am leaving my all [meaning the Swamiji] in your hands. You are familiar with life in the mountains; see that Naren has not to suffer for food."

On returning to the Math Swamiji said to Akhandananda, "Look Ganges, (He used to address him out of affection as 'Ganges') we shall not get down anywhere. We go straight to the North-West Province." Before leaving the Math Swamiji said to his brother-disciples, "I shall not return until I acquire such realization that my very touch will transform a man." Haramohan Mitra, the editor of 'Basumati Patrika' came to station to see them off. It was the morning of a Sunday.

They had to go to Uttarakhand directly. But on the way they halted at Bhagalpur, and took shelter for some days. In the first week of August they reached Bhagalpur, and settled on the bank of Ganga, near the palace of Kumar Nityananda Singh, one of the most prominent people there. They were tired, and looked like other ordinary monks. When Kumar Singh saw them first, he didn't pay much heed to them. But, when he talked to them, he realized that they were learned and intelligent, not ordinary monks. One of them was highly talented. Next day they went to the house of Babu Manmathanath Chowdhury, the tutor and guardian of Kumar Singh. Swamiji explained to him the various aspects of Hindu religion and inspired him by his interpretations of the life of Sri Krishna. In June 1906, Manmathanath wrote to a disciple of Swamiji:

> One morning in August of the year 1890, Swami Vivekananda with Swami Akhandananda came unexpectedly to my house. Thinking them to be ordinary sadhus, I did not pay much attention to them. We were sitting together after our noonday meal; and believing them to be ignorant; I did not enter into conversation with them, but began to read an English translation of a work on Buddhism. After a while, Swamiji asked me what

book I was reading. In reply, I told him the title of the book and asked, 'Do you know English?' He replied, 'Yes, a little.' Then I conversed with him on Buddhism, but after a short time I found out that he was a thousand times more learned then I. He quoted from many English works, and Babu Mathuranath Sinha of Danapur and myself were astonished at his learning and listened to him with rapt attention....

One day Swamiji asked me if I practiced any special Sadhanas, and we conversed on the practice of Yoga for a long time. From this I was convinced that he was not a common man, since what he said of Yoga was exactly the same as that which I had heard from the Swami Dayananda Sarasvati. Besides, he gave out many other important things on the subject which I had not heard before.

Then, to test knowledge of Sanskrit, I brought out all the Upanishads that I had with me and questioned him on many abstruse passages from them. By his illuminating replies I found that his mastery of the scriptures was of an extraordinary kind. And the way in which he recited from the Upanishads was charming. Thus, being firmly convinced of his wonderful knowledge equally in English, Sanskrit and in Yoga, I was greatly drawn towards him. Though he stayed in my house for only seven days, I became so devoted to him that I resolved in my mind that by no means whatever would I let him go elsewhere. So I strongly urged him to live always at Bhagalpur.

Once I noticed him humming a tune to himself. So I asked him if he could sing. He replied, 'Very little.' Being pressed hard by us he sang, and what was my surprise to see that as in learning so in music he was wonderfully accomplished! Next day I asked him if he were willing that I invite some singers and musicians; he consented, and I asked many musicians, several of whom were *ostads*, or adepts in the art, to come. Believing that the music would end by nine or ten at the latest, I did not arrange supper for the guests. Swamiji sang without ceasing till two or three o'clock in the morning. All without exception were so charmed that they forgot hunger and all idea of time! None moved from his seat or thought of going home. Kailashbabu, who was accompanying the Swami [on Tabla?] in his songs, was forced to give up finally, for his fingers had become stiff and had lost all sensation. Such superhuman power I have never seen in anybody, nor do I expect to see it again. The next evening, all the guests of the previous night, and many others, presented themselves without any invitation. The player on the instrument also came, but Swamiji did not sing that evening; so everyone was disappointed.

Another day I proposed that I introduce him to all the rich men of Bhagalpur, and that I myself should take him to them in my carriage so that it would not be any trouble to him. But he declined and said, 'It is not the sannyasi's Dharma to visit the rich!' His fiery renunciation made a deep impression on me. Indeed, in his company I was taught many lessons which have always remained with me as spiritual ideals.

From my boyhood, I was inclined to live in some solitary place and engage in spiritual practices. When I met Swamiji, this desire grew strong. I often told him, 'Let us both go the Vrindavan, and depositing three hundred rupees for each of us in the temple of Sri Govindji we shall have Govindji's Prasad for the rest of our lives as food. Thus, without being a burden to anyone, we shall practice devotion day and night in a sequestered spot on the banks of the holy Jamuna!' In reply to this he said, 'Yes, for a special temperament or nature, this scheme is no doubt good, but not for all', meaning not for himself, who had renounced everything. Amongst his many new ideas, the two most impressive to me were: 'Whatever of the ancient Aryan knowledge, intellect and genius is still left can be mostly found in those parts which lie near the bank of the Ganga. The further one goes from the Ganga, the less one sees them. This convinces one of the greatness of the Ganga as sung in our scriptures.

The epithet mild Hindu, instead of being a word of reproach, ought really to point to our glory, as expressing greatness of character. For see how much moral spiritual advancement, and how much development of the qualities of love and compassion, have to be acquired before one can get rid of the brutish force of one's nature, which actuates the ruining and the slaughter of one's brother-men for self-aggrandizement!'

Swamiji visited only two places while staying at Bhagalpur. The first occasion was when we went to see the holy man of Barari, the late Parvaticharan Mukhopadhyaya; the second was when we paid a visit to the Temple of Nathanagar, one of the holy places of the Jaina community; and there Swamiji talked with the Jaina Acharyas on their religion. He was much pleased with his visits, and was also delighted to see the beauty of the scenery on the banks of the Ganga. He remarked, 'These spots are very suitable for spiritual practices.'

It used to pain me very much when certain detractors criticized him for taking Sannyasa, because he had been born a Kayastha and not Brahmana. They little knew what he was, and that birth had very little to do with the making of a saint. Of course, one has to look to the caste of a sadhu when his only qualification is the grab he wears; otherwise how can the Brahmanas reconcile themselves to offering worship to such a person, unless they have at least the consolation of knowing that the object of their veneration is a Brahmana by birth? The Swami was born with the Brahmanical consciousness, and thus is ten times more a Brahmana than he whose sole claim to Brahmanahood is the fact that he was born of Brahmana parents. And after all, who can resist worshipping what is of true worth and saintliness!

Swamiji well knew in his heart that I would not willingly or easily let him depart from Bhagalpur. So, one day when I was away on some important business, he grasped this opportunity of leaving, after taking farewell of those at home. When I came back I made a strenuous search for him, but could discover no clue of him anywhere. And yet, why should I have thought that my will should prevail? Why should Swamiji be like a frog in the well, when his field of work was the whole wide world?

He had expressed to me his intention of going to Badrikashrama. Therefore, after he had left Bhagalpur, I even went up to Almora in the Himalayas in search of him. There Lala Badri Sah told me that he had left Almora some time before; and knowing that he must have already journeyed a long way in the direction of the Northern Tirtha, I was compelled to give up my idea of following him.

It was my heart's desire to bring him once more to Bhagalpur after his return from America, but he could not come, having then, perhaps, very little leisure or opportunity to do so.[52]

Manmathababu was a staunch Brahmo, but became a follower of Hindu religion by the influence of Swamiji. When Swamiji and Akhandananda were in Bhagalpur, they met Babu Mathuranath Sinha, who was then a home-tutor at Kumar Singh's palace. He wrote in his reminiscences of

Swamiji's visit on the request of one of his disciples. In his letter of August 11, 1905, Mathuranath wrote:

> About fifteen years ago I was at Bhagalpur, as the guest of Babu Manmathanath Chowdhury. One morning I heard of a stir caused by the arrival of two Sannyasins. They were seen by Kumar Nityananda Singh. Something led the Kumar to suppose that they were not of the ordinary type of sadhu; and a short conversation confirmed his view and disclosed the fact that they were highly educated and that one of them, who was later known as Swami Vivekananda, was marvellously gifted. The very sight of them prepossessed me in their favour. I remembered to have seen one of them in my college days at Calcutta, as often leading the choir at the Sadharan Brahmo Samaj. My conversation with him covered much ground, including literature, philosophy and religion. The main topics were the last two. It seemed that learning and spirituality were the very air he breathed. I discovered that the soul of his teaching was an intense and unselfish patriotism with which he invested and vivified his subjects. This was an abiding characteristic with him. When I read the glowing descriptions of the success he had won at the Chicago Parliament of Religions, I felt that in him India had found her man.[53]

After spending about a week in Bhagalpur, they went to Vaidyanath. We don't know whether they reached there by train via Qiul or on foot. At that time most of the pilgrims used to go there on foot. Even now many devotees like to visit Vaidyanath on foot. Babu Rajnarayan Bose, the venerable old Brahmo preacher, veteran social reformer, and national leader, used to live there at Vaidyanath. He embraced Brahmoism, which he considered a part of Hinduism. He was against the use of English language, English dress, or English food. One day Swamiji and Akhandananda went to his house to meet him. They used to live like ordinary monks. Swamiji must have known of the old man's eccentricities, and therefore, he had instructed Akhandananda beforehand not to let it be known that he (Swamiji) knew English. So he was talking in Bengali. In course of conversation, an English word—'plus' slipped out of the lips of Rajnarayan Bose. He thought that Swamiji might not have understood the meaning of the word. So, immediately he made the sign by crossing his fingers. That day Rajnarayanbabu couldn't imagine, when he talked with Swamiji, that the young monk was as fluent in English as in his mother tongue, and was a graduate of Calcutta University. Later on, when Swamiji became famous as Swami Vivekananda, Rajnarayan Bose remembered the day, when he had talked with him. Being surprised he said, "What! I thought that he didn't know English. He must be a wonderful man." Next day they set out for Varanasi.

Nagendra Nath Gupta, in his reminiscences of Vivekananda, wrote about Swamiji's travel in Behar. But it is very hard to discover the time and proper location of his visit. We don't know the exact time when Swamiji went to Bihar, and the incidents that happened to him. Mr. Gupta wrote:

> He (Swamiji) was in Behar when there was great excitement in that Province on account of the marking of mango trees with lumps of mud mixed with vermilion and seed grain. In a number of districts in Behar numerous mango trees were discovered marked in this fashion. The trustees of an empire, as the Government in this country somewhat theatrically call themselves, may have a lofty function; but they have an uneasy conscience; and the official mind was filled with forebodings of some impending grave peril. The wonderful secret police got busy at once, and it was shrewdly surmised that the marks on the mango trees bore a family resemblance to the mysterious *chapattis* which were

circulated immediately before the outbreak of the Mutiny. The villagers, frightened out of their wits by the sudden incursion of armed and unarmed, but not the less terrible on that account, authority in their midst, denied all knowledge of the authorship of these sinister marks. Suspicion next rested upon the itinerant *sadhus* wandering all over the country; and they were arrested wholesale for some time, though they had to be let off for want of evidence, and the recent facilities of regulations and ordinances did not then exist. It was found out afterwards that the marking of mango trees was merely by way of agricultural mascot for a good mango or general crops. Vivekananda had to get up early in the morning and to trudge along the Grand Trunk Road or some village path until someone offered him some food, or the heat of sun compelled him to rest under a roadside tree. One morning as he was tramping along as usual, he heard a shout behind him calling upon him to halt. He turned round and saw a mounted police officer, bearded and in full panoply, swinging a switch and followed by some policemen. As he came up, he inquired in the well-known gentle voice affected by Indian policemen who Vivekananda was.

'As you see, Khan Saheb,' replied Vivekananda, 'I am a *sadhu*.'

'All *sadhus* are *badmashes* (rouges),' sententiously growled the Sub-Inspector of police. As policemen in India are known never to tell an untruth, such an obvious fact could not be disputed. 'You come along with me, and I shall see that you are put in jail,' boomed the police officer.

'For how long?' softly asked Vivekananda.

'Oh, it may be for a fortnight, or even a month.'

Vivekananda went nearer him and in an ingratiating and appealing voice said, 'Khan Saheb, only for a month? Can you not put me away for six months, or at least three or four months?'

The police officer stared, and his face fell. 'Why do you wish to stay in jail longer than a month?' he asked suspiciously.

Vivekananda replied in a confidential tone, 'Life in the jail is much better than this. The work there is not hard compared with this wearisome tramp from morning till night. My daily food is uncertain, and I have often to starve. In the jail I shall have two square meals a day. I shall look upon you as my benefactor if you lock me up for several months.'

As he listened, a look of disappointment and disgust appeared on the Khan Saheb's face, and he abruptly ordered Vivekananda to go away.[54]

Nagendranath has written about another experience that Swamiji related to him. Here also no date is mentioned. At that time Swamiji had undertaken a particular vow that he should steadily walk the whole day without either looking back or begging from any one. He would accept food only if it was offered to him unasked. Sometimes he had to go without any food for even two days. "One afternoon about sunset he was passing in front of a stable belonging to some wealthy person. One of the grooms was standing on the road. Vivekananda had had nothing to eat for two days and was looking weak and weary. The groom saluted him and looking at him asked, 'Sadhu Baba, have you eaten anything today?' 'No,' replied Vivekananda, 'I have eaten nothing.' The groom took him into the stable, offered him water to wash his hands and feet and placed his own food consisting of some *chapattis* (hand-made bread) and a little chutney, before him. The chutney was hot, but in the course of his wanderings Vivekananda had got accustomed to eat chillies, which were often the only condiment he had with his food. I have seen him eating a handful of pungent, green chillies with evident relish. Vivekananda ate the *chapattis* and the chutney, but immediately, afterwards felt a frightful burning sensation in his stomach and rolled on the ground in agony. The groom beat his head with his hands and wailed, 'What have I done? I have killed a *sadhu*.' The pain must have been due to eating the chutney on an empty stomach. Just about this time a man with a basket on his head happened to be passing and halted on hearing the cries of the groom. Vivekananda asked him what he had in his basket, and the man replied it was tamarind. 'Ah, that is just what I want,' said Vivekananda, and taking some of the tamarind he mixed it with water and drank it. This had the effect of allaying the burning sensation and the pain, and after resting for a while Vivekananda resumed his journey."[55]

It is very hard to find out the proper date of these incidents due to non-existence of detailed information. The only evidences are the reminiscences of those, with whom Swamiji had shared his experiences. Moreover, some information is full of controversies. It is not yet discovered whether Swamiji had written any letter between 15th July 1890 and 14th April 1891. We don't have any information of any incident that took place during this long period of about ten months.

Let us back to Varanasi, where Swamiji went with Akhandananda from Vaidyanath. At Varanasi, they stayed with Pramadadas Mitra in his garden-house for a few days. They had long discussion on scriptural topics. But Swamiji was impatient to see the snow-capped Himalayas. On the eve of departure he said to Pramadababu, "I am now leaving Kashi, and shall not return until I have burst on society like a bomb-shell; and it will follow me like a dog." What is this! How confidently the future is declared by the wonderful lips of Swamiji! Pramadababu was surprised as he couldn't understand what Swamiji really meant to say. We can guess that there must be some difference created between the opinions of them on some subject, and finally the situation became so worse that Swamiji was compelled to announce the truth of the future. Pramadababu was a lover of theosophy, and conservative in the field of social activities; whereas Swamiji liked the traditional Hindu religion and had a progressive outlook regarding the human society. He didn't like anything cook-and-bull, and didn't believe in any meaning-less customs and practices. Hence he couldn't support the view of Pramadababu on some topic, and became so much excited that he pronounced the above sentence. And it became true when he returned after stirring the world with new mode of thought and resurrecting the spirit of the Indian sages.

After this incident Swamiji didn't write any letter to Pramadadas Mitra for a long time. On May 30, 1897, Swamiji, when received a copy of the Gita translated in English from Pramadababu, wrote him a letter from Almora. This was the last letter written to Pramadababu. This letter states his sincere depth of love, the power of harmonies, and self-confidence. He wrote:

> I hear some unavoidable domestic grief has come upon you. To you, a man of wisdom, what can this misery do? Yet the amenities of friendly intercourse, incidental to relative existence in this world, require my making mention of it. Those moments of grief, however, very often bring out a better spiritual realization. As if for a while the clouds withdraw and the sun of truth shines out. In the case of some, half of the bondage is loosened. Of all bondages the greatest is that of position—the fear of reputation is stronger than the fear of death; but even this bondage appears to relax a little. As if the mind sees for a moment that it is much better to listen to the indwelling Lord than to the opinions of men. But again the clouds close up, and this indeed is Maya.
>
> Though for a long time I had no direct correspondence with you, yet I have often been receiving from others almost all the news about you. Some time ago you kindly sent

me to England a copy of a translation of the Gita. The cover only bore a line of your handwriting. The few words are acknowledgment of this gift, I am told, raised doubts in your mind about my old affection towards you.

Please know these doubts to be groundless. The reason of that laconic acknowledgement is that I was given to see, during four or five years, only that one line of your handwriting on the cover of an English Gita, from which fact I thought, if you had no leisure to write more, would you have leisure enough to read much? Secondly, I learnt, you were particularly the friend of white-skinned missionaries of the Hindu religion and the roguish black natives were repelling! There was apprehension on this score. Thirdly, I am a Mlechchha (untouchable), Shudra (low caste), and so forth; I eat anything and everything, and with anybody and everybody—and that in public both abroad and here. In my views, besides, much perversion has supervened—one attribute-less absolute Brahman, I see, I fairly understand, and I see in some particular individuals the special manifestations of that Brahman; if those individuals are called by the name of God, I can well follow—otherwise the mind does not feel inclined towards intellectual theorizing such as the postulated Creator and the like.

Such a God I have seen in my life, and his commands I live to follow. The Smritis and the Puranas are productions of men of limited intelligence and are full of fallacies, errors, the feelings of class and malice. Only parts of them breathing broadness of spirit and love are acceptable, the rest are to be rejected. The Upanishads and the Gita are the true scriptures; Rama, Krishna, Buddha, Chaitanya, Nanak, Kabir, and so on are the true Avataras, for they had their hearts broad as the sky—and above all, Ramakrishna, Ramanuja, Shankara, etc. seem to have been mere Pundits with much narrowness of heart. Where is that love, that weeping heart at the sorrow of others?—Dry pedantry of the Pundit—and the feeling of only oneself getting to salvation hurry-scurry! But is that going to be possible, sir? Was it ever likely or will it ever be so? Can anything be attained with any shred of 'I' left anyhow?

Another great discrepancy: the conviction is daily gaining on my mind that the idea of caste is the greatest dividing factor and the root of Maya; all caste either on the principle of birth or of merit is bondage. Some friends advise, 'True, lay all that at heart, but outside, in the world of relative experience, distinctions like caste must needs be maintained.'... The idea of oneness at heart (with a craven impotence of effort, that is to say), and outside, the hell-dance of demons—oppression and persecution—ay, the dealer of death to the poor, but if the Pariah be wealthy enough, 'Oh, he is the protector of religion!'

Over and above, I come to see from my studies that the disciplines of religion are not for the Shudra; if he exercises any discrimination about food or about going out to foreign lands, it is all useless in his case, only so much labour lost. I am a Shudra, a Mlechchha, so I have nothing to do with all that botheration. To me what would Mlechchha's food matter or Pariah's? It is in the books written by priests that madnesses like that of caste are to be found, and not in books revealed from God. Let the priests enjoy the fruits of their ancestor's achievement, while I follow the word of God, for my good lies there.

Another truth I have realized is that altruistic service only is religion, the rest, such as ceremonial observances, are madness—even it is wrong to hanker after one's own salvation. Liberation is only for him who gives up everything for others, whereas others who tax their brains day and night harping on 'my salvation', 'my salvation', wander about with their well-being ruined, both present and prospective; and this I have seen many a time with my own eyes. Reflecting on all these sundry matters, I had no heart for writing a letter to you. If notwithstanding all these discrepancies, you find your attachment for me intact, I shall feel it to be a very happy issue indeed.[56]

Through this letter the difference of opinion between two persons is revealed clearly. Still we cannot forget that Pramadababu was a friend to the disciples of Sri Ramakrishna, and whenever they were in need, he helped them at his best. He had arranged everything for the comfort of Swamiji and his brother-disciples at Varanasi. Whatever he did for the monks of Ramakrishna order is to be always acknowledged with gratitude.

As we know that Swamiji was impatient for going to the Himalayas, but Akhandananda said to him, "Swamiji, you must see the Mahant, Janakibar Saran of Ayodhya. You will find him a great man. He is full of Bhakti (devotion)." Swamiji replied, "What do I care for all this nonsense! I am through now. It will only mean more and more delay. Let me go to the Himalayas." But Akhandananda didn't listen to him. He bought two tickets for Ayodhya, and Swamiji was compelled to board the train for that place. Swamiji didn't speak to Akhandananda while they took a carriage from Ayodhya station. However, Akhandananda took him next day and introduced him to the Mahanta. Mahanta was a scholar in Sanskrit and Persian language, and had charge of a temple with large estates. He was a Vaishnava of great renunciation and devotion. In spite of having lot of money he used to live a very humble life. He cordially welcomed the monks to his Ashrama. They talked a great deal on devotion. Swamiji was impressed with his learning and spiritual fervour, and said to Akhandananda, "I am glad you brought me here. I have seen a man, a real holy man."

Next we see them as guests of Babu Ramaprasanna Bhattacharya in Naini Tal. They reached there on foot through the hills. There they stayed for six days. The word 'Tal' means a lake. Swamiji had a pain in chest as he bathed in the cold water of the lake, but he didn't pay much heed to that, and started for Almora.

On the way from Naini Tal to Almora, Swamiji decided to go on foot the whole distance, and said to Akhandananda, "You go by the foot-path, and I shall go alone by a short-cut through the forest, and meet you later." We don't know when they departed from each other, but we see them again together, when they reached Almora.

One day Swamiji told Akhandananda that he had seen mantra of Gods and Goddesses as glittering as gold and also explained them to him. We find the similar thing in the reminiscence of Sister Nivedita. She wrote: "He (Swamiji) told us of that vision which came to him years ago, while he was still new to the ways of the life of a monk, giving back to him, as he always afterwards believed, the ancient mode of Sanskrit chanting. 'It was evening', he said, 'in that age when the Aryans had only reached the India. I saw an old man seated on the bank of the great river. Wave upon wave of darkness was rolling in upon him, and he was chanting from the Rig-Veda. Then I awoke and went on chanting. They were the tones that we used long ago'."[57]

On the third day they stopped for the night under an old peepal tree, where the Koshi met another mountain river named Suial. This place, known as Kakrighat, is about fourteen and a half miles from Almora by road. Swamiji said to Akhandananda, "This place is charming. What a wonderful spot for meditation!" After having bath in the river Swamiji sat under the tree, and absorbed in deep meditation. After a long time when he returned to normal consciousness, he said to his companion, "Oh, Gangadhar! I have just passed through one of the greatest moments of my life. Here under this peepal tree one of the greatest problems of my life has been solved. I have found the oneness of the macrocosm with the microcosm. In this microcosm of the body everything that is there [in the macrocosm], exists. I have seen the whole universe within an atom." Akhandananda looked at Swamiji, and got surprised with the wonderful glow of joy around his face. Swamiji wrote this experience in his notebook which read:

"In the beginning was the Word etc.

"The microcosm and the macrocosm are built on the same plain. Just as the individual soul is encased in the living body, so is the universal Soul in the Living Prakriti [Nature]—the objective universe. Shiva [i.e. Kali] is embracing Shiva: this is not a fancy. This covering of the one [Soul] by the other [Nature] is analogous to the relation between an idea and the word expressing it: they are one and the same; and it is only by a mental abstraction that one can distinguish them. Thought is impossible without words. Therefore, in the beginning was the Word etc.

"This dual aspect of the Universal Soul is eternal. So what we perceive or feel is this combination of the Eternally Formed and the Eternally Formless."[58]

This realization of his seems to be reflected in his lectures that he gave in the West under the title, 'Cosmos—the Macrocosm and the Microcosm'.

Almora was only two miles away from the monks. But they were very much tired of walking, and they were hungry for not having food for many hours. Swamiji almost fainted, and couldn't walk any more. Swamiji sat down on the road, and Akhandananda went in search of water. There was a Muslim cemetery very near to them. There lived a fakir named Zulfikar Ali in a cottage nearby. He, while going somewhere, saw the plight of Swamiji, and felt sorrow. He immediately offered him a cucumber, which he could provide only in the shape of food. Swamiji asked him to put the cucumber into his mouth. Fakir remonstrated to do so because he was a Muslim. "That does not matter at all," said Swamiji with a smile, "are we not all brothers?" After having been fed by the fakir, Swamiji felt refreshed. With reference to this incident, Swamiji used to say, "The man really saved my life: I had never felt so exhausted." In July 1971, a Vivekananda Resting Hall was built by the efforts of Mr. and Mrs. Boshi Sen of Almora, on the place where the fakir had fed Swamiji with the cucumber.

Seven years later, when Swamiji visited Almora again, he was the world-famous Swami Vivekananda. There he was given a grand reception, and taken in a procession through the town. As the procession was going on, Swamiji happened to see the fakir, and recognized him. Fakir couldn't recognize him. Swamiji immediately called him and introduced him to everyone. Then, with reference to that incident he said, "This man really saved my life that day."

The long journey from the plane to Almora had been full of joy though they didn't have sufficient food and sound sleep. Natural beauty of the mountain made him charmed. Swamiji's mind was quite peaceful. Cool air of the mountain made him free from all weariness. He never felt so much happy that he knew before. Towards the end of August, when they reached Almora, two of his brother-disciples, Swami Saradnanda and Kripananda, were already present there. Akhandananda took Swamiji to the garden of Amba Dutta, and went to inform his brother-disciples of their arrival. When they learnt of the Swamiji's arrival, they hastened to Amba Dutta's garden along with Lala Badri Sah. Before they reached the garden, they met Swamiji on the way. Lala Badri Sah welcomed Swamiji and took him to his house. There Swamiji had a log discussion with one Sri Krishna Joshi, a government official, on the need of becoming monk. Swamiji spoke of the glory of the life of a monk. He said, "Renunciation is the ideal of all religions." He explained the glory of renunciation, with reference to his personal experience. Mr. Joshi struck with the young monk's learning bowed down before him.

While Swamiji was staying in Badri Sah's house, he had experienced a peculiar incident. On day, while Swamiji was busy in conversation with Lala Badri Sah, they heard a sound of beating drum. In a short while, a man came in a hurry and said, "Sir, come soon, someone is captured by ghost." Mr. Sah got up and went out to see the matter. Swamiji also followed him to satisfy his own curiosity. Reaching the spot, he saw a man crying out of pain, and some men were sitting around him holding his hands and legs forcefully. A man (may be a priest or an exorcist) was chanting mantras loudly while searing the victim to parts of his body with a red-hot axe. How strange! No part of his body was found to be burnt! Swamiji got surprised by seeing the treatment. Seeing the ochre cloth of Swamiji they requested him to come forward. One of them said, "Maharaj, please exorcize this man out of your mercy." Swamiji never had dreamt that some time he would have to be an exorcist. He felt himself in a nice fix, but moved to do something; he had to go near the possessed man. At first he wanted to examine the axe closely. As soon as he touched it, he felt his fingers got burnt, although it had been cooled down to blackness. The smarting made him restless and all the theories about the axe phenomenon were spirited away from his mind. In spite of smarting with the burn, he placed his hand on the head of the man and chanted the holy mantra for a while. It was a matter of surprise to find that the man came back to his normal state within ten or twelve minutes. Later on, Swamiji said to his disciple, "Then oh, the gushing reverence the villagers showed to me! I was taken to be some wonderful man! But, all the same, I couldn't make any head or tail of the whole business. So without a word one way or the other, I returned with my host to his hut. It was about midnight, and I went to bed. But what with the smarting burn in the hand and the impenetrable puzzle of the whole affair, I couldn't have any sleep that night. Thinking of the burning axe failing to harm living human flesh, it occurred again and again to my mind, 'There are more things in heaven and earth, Horatio, than are dreamt of in your philosophy'."[59]

Swamiji passed some days at the house of Lala Badri Sah, and he was very much happy with his devotion and hospitality. One day he found a solitary cave above a mountain village, and entered in it to perform spiritual practice day and night. He determined to find the truth. In the silence of the cave he absorbed in deep meditation. When he came out his face shone with a celestial fire. In later years Akhandananda said, "It seemed as though every time the Swami desired to retire into the life of silence and pure monasticism, he was compelled to give it up by the pressure of circumstances. He had a mission to fulfil, and the very essence of his nature would force him into the realization of this line of work."

Three days passed in this manner, and suddenly a telegram came from his brother which carried a tragic news that one of his sisters had committed suicide. Swamiji groamed in anguish. In a moment he seemed to have been rudely awakened to the great problems of Indian womanhood. This pain pushed him towards the solitude of the Himalayas.

On September 5, 1890, Swamiji left Almora for Garhwal. This time he was accompanied by Saradananda, Akhandananda, Kripananda and a coolie to carry their luggage. When they were in Naini Tal, Akhandananda had a pain in chest after he had bathed in the cold water of lake. Since then he had been coughing every now and then. On the way to Badrinarayan they reached Karnaprayag, where they were nicely entertained by a doctor of Government hospital. Saradananda and Kripananda had severe stomach trouble, but fortunately it was soon put right with the help of the doctor.

After leaving Karnaprayag, Swamiji and Akhandananda became ill, and they were compelled to halt in a roadside rest-house for about a week. There they came to know that the road led to Badrinarayan and Kedarnath had been closed by the Government on account of famine in that area. Swamiji cancelled his plan of going to Badrinarayan, and they took the road for Rudraprayag. All along the way they enjoyed the heavenly beauty of the Himalayas. Etymologically Himalaya means "abode of snow" in Sanskrit (from hima "snow", and aalaya "abode"). Swamiji was overwhelmed with the sight of snow-covered peaks. Since he was merely a child, he heard of the beauty of the Himalayas, and he was impatient to experience its beauty with his wide eyes. Scenic view of the river Alakananda charmed him. It seemed to be dancing with joy while flowing through the mountain valleys. Swamiji introduced his brother-disciples to the sweet sound of the stream, and said, "It is flowing in the Raga of Kedar (a tune of Indian classical music)."

At Rudraprayag, they met a Bengali monk, Purnananda by name. That night they stayed with him. Here Swamiji and Akhandananda again had an attack of fever, which was worse than before. Fortunately they met a Sadar Amin (Government official), named Badri Dutt Joshi, who was on tour and had camped there. He gave them some Ayurvedic medicines, and when they were enough improved, sent them by Dandi (a chair-like device carried on the shoulders of coolies) to Srinagar, nine miles off. They had covered 120 miles from Almora by begging their food, having religious discussion, meditating, and suffering from recurring illness. It took them about three weeks to reach Srinagar.

At Srinagar they dismissed the coolies and took shelter in a lonely hut on the bank of the river Alakananda. Swami Turiyananda had once lived in this hut. Here Swamiji would mostly spend his time by explaining the Upanishada to his brother-disciples. Whenever he would explain the meaning of different mantras of old Rishis, he seemed to reach somewhere else. Rest of the time, they would go for begging their food. Beside this they passed the days in prayer, meditation and scriptural study. Here Swamiji met a schoolmaster, a Vaishya by caste. The gentleman was a recent convert to Christianity. Swamiji spoke to him of the glories of Hinduism so eloquently that the gentleman felt highly regretted for changing his religion, and longed to return to the Hindu fold. He became attached to the monks and invited them to his house.

Form Srinagar they moved to Tehri. All the way they didn't have any food, as it was totally desolate. When they reached a village it was quite dark. They sat on a portico, since they were very much hungry and exhausted. Akhandananda and another brother-disciple went into the village in search of food, but nobody opened the door. There is a saying: "There's no giver like a Garhwali (a resident of Garhwal); but he does not give anything unless he is threatened with a stick." Akhandananda remembered this, and began to shout, "Give us food immediately and wood for making fire." Now the villagers opened the door and meekly came forward with foodstuffs and placed them before the monks. After having food they felt quite relaxed. Then they had a long chat with the villagers about their lifestyle and different customs and rituals. Monks were enamored by seeing the simplicity of the villagers.

At Tehri they found two rooms in a deserted garden on the bank of the Ganga. These rooms were specially built for wandering monks. Here they lived by begging, and spent most of their time in spiritual practices. They became acquainted with Babu Raghunath Bhattacharya, the Dewan of the Tehri State and an elder brother of Pundit Haraprasad Shastri of Calcutta. Following his request, they stayed with him for some days. Swamiji was looking for a lonely place for meditation on the bank of the Ganga. Mr. Bhattacharya built a hut for them at Ganeshprayag, at the confluence of the Ganga and Vilagana rivers. But Swamiji couldn't avail himself of this kindness, because Akhandananda had a sever relapse of bronchitis. The local physician advised him to go to the plains, since the mountain air was not suiting his health and winter was very near. Hearing this Swamiji canceled his plan and decided to go to Dehra Dun. He said to Mr. Bhattacharya about the change of his plan. Mr. Bhattacharya gave him a letter of introduction to the Civil Surgeon of Dehra Dun, provided two ponies to take Swamiji and Akhandananda to Mussoorie, and money for their expenses on the way. Hence, after some 15 or 20 days' stay at Tehri, Swamiji set out for Dehra Dun with his brother-disciples.

Akhandananda wrote: "I heard Swamiji several times to say that whenever he wished to absorb in meditation, he was compelled to give up the plan by the pressure of circumstances." Swamiji was entrusted by Sri Ramakrishna to take care of his brother-disciples and to preach the philosophy of the Vedas to the world. He forbade Swamiji to be inclined to the state of trance. He couldn't ignore the command of his Guru.

They went to Rajpur via Mussoorie. There they were surprised to see a monk walking along the road. He looked like Turiananda. When they came closer they cried out together, "yes, it is Hari." This unexpected meeting with their beloved brother-disciple made them extremely happy. They all went down to Dehra Dun. Akhandananda was taken to Dr. Maclaren, the Civil Surgeon, to whom Swamiji had brought the letter of introduction. After a short discussion with Swamiji, Dr. Maclaren was pleased with him. He examined Akhandananda and said, "Don't return to the hills before having a complete medical treatment in the plane."

Now they had to search for a suitable shelter for Akhandananda in Dehra Dun. Swamiji went from door to door to ask for a shelter, but no one was ready to help him. Finally, after much effort, a shelter was found in a newly-built, but incomplete, house of a businessman. While they were searching for a place, they fortunately met one Hridaybabu, a classmate of Swamiji in the General Assembly's Institution in Calcutta. He was a Christian convert, and employed as a teacher in a school. He agreed to accommodate Akhandananda in his house. But Akhandananda, so long accustomed to Hindu mode of life, didn't like Christian ways in that friend's house. He therefore returned to Swamiji. Swamiji again went about the town in search of a suitable shelter for Akhandananda. He asked many houses, "My brother-disciple is ill. Can you give him a little place in your house and arrange for suitable diet for him?" He received cold replies and several excuses. Suddenly one Pundit Ananda Narayan, a Kashmiri Brahmin and an advocate of the town, took charge of Akhandananda. He rented a small house and provided suitable diet and warm clothing for him.

At Dehra Dun, Swamiji met a businessman, who was locally called 'Nanda Ganta' by name. He was stingy person, and considered himself a great follower of Vedanta. Swamiji would often enjoy having conversation with him. One day Swamiji was invited by the son of Nanda Ganta who entertained him with delicious food. On returning home Nanda was surprised to see that Swamiji was served food, but he didn't say anything to his son.

One day at Hridaybabu's house, Swamiji had a hot discussion with some Christian preachers. They tried to teach him the glory of Christianity. Swamiji placed strong argument against their conservativeness, and spoke of the higher criticism of the Bible, something they had never heard. They couldn't withstand the force of his arguments and left the place. He afterwards begged his apology for conducting such a discussion in his house against the Christian faith.

After three days in Dehra Dun, Swamiji advised Akhandananda to go to a friend's house at Allahabad, and Kripananda was entrusted to look after him. Thereafter Swamiji left for Rishikesh with Saradananda and Turiyananda. Kripananda joined them later, when Akhandananda left for Saharanpur on his way to Allahabad.

At Saharanpur Akhandananda took shelter in the house of a lawyer named Bankubihari Chatterjee, who advised him for going to Meerut instead of Allahabad, to meet his friend, Dr. Trailokyanath Ghosh, the Assistant Civil Surgeon. Accordingly Akhandananda was under the treatment of this doctor for a month and a half.

Now we should go to Rishikesh to see what Swamiji and his brother-disciples were doing there? Rishikesh is regarded as one of the holiest places to the Hindus. It is also known as the 'Place of Sages', is the meeting point of the three holy rivers, the Ganga, the Yamuna, and the Saraswati. It lies at the foothills of the Himalayas of the Garhwal region. In those days it was almost a jungle.

At Rishikesh Swamiji and his brother-disciples took shelter in a hut, near the temple of Chandeswar Mahadev. They lived by begging, rest of the time passed by the study of scriptures, specially the '*Brahmasutra*'. Swamiji found the place ideal for the satisfaction of his thirst for spiritual practices. So many sages and saints came here since ancient times to meditate in search of higher knowledge. There Swamiji met a monk named Shankar Giri, who would feel satisfied by his words. He would often say, "Where is that man, who can understand me?" He used to tell many stories of the ancient Rishikesh. He would say: "In those days Rishikesh was a dense forest; many elephants were found moving here and there. This Rishikesh is very much different from what it was before. Now it has become 'Roti-kesh'—there are so many institutions for charitable distribution of food, drink and clothing for monks." Once he told about a wise monk, who was shouting by saying, "Shivoham, Shivoham" or "Soham, Soham" while caught by a tiger.

Swamiji wanted to be engaged in spiritual practice, but before he could plunge into that he became ill. One day his brother-disciples went to jungle to cut bamboo, in order to enlarge the hut. When they returned they found Swamiji had high fever. As his condition grew worse his brother-disciples became fearful. His pulse sank low, and his body became cold. Then his pulse seemed to have stopped, as if he was going to die. He lay unconscious on a couple of blankets laid on the ground. There was neither a medical store nor a physician in that area. The brother-disciples didn't know what to do. They began to weep in grief and anxiety. Turiyananda began to chant some hymns. When they had lost all hope, a monk, clad in a woolen blanket, appeared there and asked, "Why are you all weeping?" Then he took from his wallet some honey and some powdered peepul, and mixing them together, forced the medicine into Swamiji's mouth. It seemed to be the medicine gifted by God. Soon after, Swamiji came back to his consciousness and his body became warm.

After a while he opened his eyes and said: "Cheer up, my boys, I shall not die." Gradually he recovered. Later he told his brother-disciples that, during that unconscious state, he had seen that he had a particular mission in the world to fulfil, and that until he had accomplished his mission, he would have no rest. His brother-disciples noticed a spiritual energy glowing around his face, as if he was restless to find a proper field for its expression.

Swamiji got back to normal state, but his brother-disciples were more cautious about his movement. They realized what Swamiji was to them. After Sri Ramakrishna, Swamiji was the only guardian of them. In absence to Swamiji what would become of the Order? Where would they go? They would become alone in the world. So they decided to stay at Rishikesh for some more days. Few days later, when Swamiji became quite normal, they took him to Haridwar. Once, Saradananda used to stay here in a hut for his spiritual practices. They all took shelter in that hut. In the meantime, Babu Raghunath Bhattacharya, the Dewan of Tehri State, along with Maharaja of Tehri, was passing by that place on his way to Ajmer. He heard of a learned sadhu who had recently been living in a hut at Haridwar. Being curious to see the sadhu he came to the hut and recognized Swamiji who had recently been his guest at Tehri. Swamiji was then still not fully recovered. He gave them some money to repair their hut, and advised Swamiji to go to a particular Hakim (Mohammedan doctor) in Delhi, and gave him a letter of introduction.

At that time, Brahmananda was engaged in spiritual practices at Kankhal. They all went to Kankhal and met Brahmananda. And thence they went to Saharanpur, and stayed at the house of Bankubihari Chatterjee. Here they learnt that Akhandananda had gone to Meerut. Brahmananda was also impatient for meeting with Akhandananda as he had not met him for a long time. Banku Babu also advised that the weather of Meerut would help Swamiji to recover his health. So they immediately set out for Meerut.

Thus we find that Swamiji's trip to the Himalayas came to an end with his departure from Rishikesh. We do not know many things that he had experienced during his stay in the Himalayas. If ever we come to know about some incidents, it is hard to find out the particular dates and the places of occurrence.

It was in Almora that a certain elderly man, with a face full of amiable weakness, came and put him a question about Karma. "What were they to do", he asked, "whose Karma it was to see the strong oppress the weak?" Swamiji turned on him in surprised indignation. "Why, thrash the strong, of course!" he said, "You forget your own part in this Karma: Yours is always the right to rebel!"[60]

In Rishikesh and some other places of the Himalayas, Swamiji met many great monks. He said:

> I saw many great men in Rishikesh. One case that I remember was that of a man who seemed to be mad. He was coming nude down the street, with boys pursuing and throwing stones at him. The whole man was bubbling over with laughter while blood was streaming down his face and neck. I took him and bathed the wound, putting ashes on it to stop the bleeding. And all the time with peals of laughter he told me of the fun the boys and he had been having, throwing the stones, 'So the Father plays', he said.
>
> Many of these men hide, in order to guard themselves against intrusion. People are a trouble to them. One had human bones strewn about his cave and gave it out that he lived on corpses. Another threw stones. And so on....
>
> Sometimes the thing comes upon them in a flash. There was a boy, for instance, who used to come to read the Upanishads with Abhedananda. One day he turned and said, 'Sir, is all this really true?'
>
> 'Oh yes!' said Abhedananda, 'it may be difficult to realize, but it is certainly true.'
>
> And next day, that boy was a silent Sannyasin, nude, on his way to Kedarnath!
>
> What happened to him? you ask. He became silent!
>
> But the Sannyasin needs no longer to worship or to go on pilgrimage or perform austerities. What then is the motive of all this going from pilgrimage to pilgrimage, shrine to shrine, and austerity to austerity? He is acquiring merit and giving it to the world!"[61]

One day Swamiji came across a monk. His savant look and sacred indisposition and behaviour charmed Swamiji and he understood that the monk belonged to the highest level of attainment. After a conversation with that monk he got to know some information that made him spellbound.

The monk said to Swamiji that once he stole some belongings of Pavhari Baba and tried to run away while unfortunately Babaji woke up and caught him after a long chase. But the Babaji didn't ask him for returning those things stolen by him and went back to his abode. Swamiji heard this incident beforehand when he was in Ghazipur. Now after hearing the confession of that 'thief', he got a lively evidence how a dramatic transformation of a thief to a great savant was possible with the association of a great sacred personality. Hence, Swamiji felt a sense of devotion and regard with the greatness of a great man and the awakening of divinity within a human being. The holy man said, "When he (Pavhari Baba) offered me everything considering me as Narayan, I realized my mistake and meanness, and began to wander in search of spirituality renouncing my worldly pursuits." That day, after a long conversation with the monk, Swamiji understood the holy man had realized the truth. Perhaps he never forgot this man. He would say, "The seed of divinity is hidden even in the heart of the criminals."

Once, during his visit to the Himalayas, Swamiji took shelter in a Tibetan family. According to their custom a woman might have more than one husband. There were six brothers in that family but they had only one wife. Swamiji highly reproached that ugly practice. But the brother, who was known to Swamiji, rather asked him, "Swamiji, being a monk how can you suggest someone to be so selfish? Is it not reproachable that I should enjoy this thing alone? Why should we be selfish by keeping one wife for each one? Everything should be enjoyed by all brothers—even the wife."

Although it was a worthless argument, Swamiji was charmed with their innocent nature. He realized that every custom of a society should be judged by different views. With reference to the context of morality and duty Swamiji said, "What is regarded as moral in one country may in another be considered perfectly immoral." He supported this speech with an instance—"In one country cousins may marry; in another, it is thought to be very immoral; in one, men may marry their sister-in-law; in another, it is regarded as immoral; in one country people may marry only one; in another, many times; and so forth. Similarly, in all other departments of morality, we find the standard varies greatly—yet we have the idea that there must be a universal standard of morality."[62]

Now we would like to come back to Meerut, where Swamiji and his brother-disciples reached via Haridwar and Saharanpur. They found Akhandananda at the house of Dr. Trailokyanath Ghosh. It was at the end of autumn, after the time when Mother Kali is offered special worship. Swamiji looked very thin due to his recurring illness. Akhandananda was startled with surprise to see him. With reference to this context he wrote, "I had never seen him thinner. He was worn to a shadow. It seemed that he had not as yet recovered from his terrible illness at Rishikesh." It was decided that Swamiji would stay at the house of the doctor with Swami Akhandananda, while the others would go to stay with one Yajneshwarbabu, who later on embraced the monastic life and became Swami Jnanananda, the well-known leader of the Bharat Dharma Mahamandal. After staying at the doctor's house for about a fortnight, Swamiji and Akhandananda went to stay at a Shethji's garden-house, where other brother-disciples joined them. Shethji was a friend of Yajneshwarbabu. He had arranged everything for the comforts of the monks. The monks cooked their food and spent their time in spiritual practices. Swamiji was still taking his medicine regularly. They had to stay at Meerut for a long period. Swamiji was gradually growing stronger.

At this time Advaitananda (Goplada), also on his pilgrimage, came to Meerut; and Shethji's garden was transformed into a second Baranagar Math, with Swamiji, Brahmananda, Saradananda, Turiyananda, Akhandananda, Kripananda and Advaitananda living there. They passed their time in meditation, prayer, singing devotional songs, and study of the scriptures and other literature in Sanskrit and English. Swamiji would read and explain them the Sanskrit literature like *Mrichhakatika, Kumarsambhab, Meghdut* and *Vishnupuran* and so forth. In the evening they used to go for a walk, and watch the sports and games of the troops on the parade ground. Swamiji asked Akhandananda to bring him the works of Sir John Lubbock. Accordingly Akhandananda would bring him one volume every day from a local library. Swamiji would finish the volume in a day and return it the next day, saying that he had read it. The librarian couldn't believe that it was possible for a man to finish a volume in a day. He argued with Akhandananda that Swamiji had surely returned the volume without reading it. When Swamiji came to know this, he went to the library and said to the librarian, "Sir, I have mastered all those volumes; if you have any doubt, you may put any question to me about them." Then the librarian examined the monk, and became satisfied. His astonishment had no end. He realized that he had done a mistake by measuring the talent of Swamiji. Later Akhandananda asked Swamiji, "How could you do it?" Swamiji replied, "I never read book word by word. I read by sentence, sometimes even paragraph by paragraph, in a sort of kaleidoscope form."

One day Akhandananda brought to Swamiji an Afghan gentleman, who was a refugee Sardar and a relative of the Amir Abdar Rahaman of Afghanistan. He would perform his ablutions, and then come with a basket of sweetmeats in his hand, to present to Swamiji. During conversation he referred to a well-known Muslim fakir of Swat. Many Bengali gentlemen and others also would come to the garden to hear religious discourse from the lips of Swamiji.

In Meerut Swamiji taught many things to his brother-disciples. He used to explain them different Sanskrit literature. One day he cooked pilau and many other delicious foods. When he realized that his brother-disciples were enjoying the food, he served them all without keeping anything for himself. When he was asked, he said, "I have had these enough. I am happy to see you enjoying the food." Though it was a nominal matter, but his brother-disciples could never forget it. They would always feel the greatness of Swamiji—his endless love, his carefulness, his teachings and wandering—everything made their memory glittering forever.

Swamiji wanted to make his brother-disciples dependent on themselves. He knew, if they would always depend on him, it would be hard to do his work that he was bestowed by his teacher Sri Ramakrishna. He had received the command of God regarding his future. So he wished to leave his brother-disciples in order to become a solitary monk. Akhandananda said to him, "It was for you that I cancelled my plan of going to Central Asia, and came to Baranagore Math; and now you are going away leaving me here!" Swamiji replied, "The company of the brother-disciple is a great hindrance to spiritual practices. Just see, it was because of your illness that I could not practice any spiritual disciplines at Tehri. It is not possible to perform any spiritual disciplines, unless the Maya [bondage] of brother-disciples is given up. Whenever I plan to practice disciplines, the Master puts some obstacle in my way. Now I shall go alone. I shall not tell anyone where I am staying." Akhandananda said, "Even if you go to Patal [the nether regions], I shall hunt you out."

One morning in the latter part of January 1891, Swamiji left his devoted brethren and set out for a long journey facing towards Delhi by himself.

Delhi

Delhi is the central point of whole India—may it be the field of politics or of culture or of trade and business. Delhi is famous in history with many stories of joy and woe of Hindu and

Mogul dynasties in its pages. Numerous historical events are associated with almost every part of Delhi and its roads. Delhi had experienced many historical events that made its soil red with the stream of blood since the age of the Mahabharata. Delhi, on the bank of the holy Yamuna, is the eyewitness of many ups and downs of human civilization. People say, *Delhi dil-waloka*, Delhi is for those who are full of humanity. Delhi is the face of Indian civilization and its culture. A visit to Delhi is a visit to India. The royal tombs and palaces, the sites of deserted capitals, the ruins of imperial greatness, make Delhi the ancient Rome of India.

Swamiji, with his small baggage and royal appearance, reached Delhi. In spite of all efforts to hide himself, his intellectual youthful face, wide eyes, stout body and royal style of walking made him attracted to everyone. Whoever came in contact with him, felt attracted to his kind behaviour, and was fortunate for having an opportunity of listening to his sweet words. Seth Shyamaldas, who considered himself such a lucky person, felt grateful to Swamiji for being allowed to receive him at his residence with open arms.

Swamiji went everywhere in Delhi and saw everything. He was impressed by the sight of the ruins of royal and imperial greatness. His spiritual experience and historic perception helped him knowing Delhi as the symbol of the immortal glory of the Indian people, with its grand, composite culture. Delhi as the land of many mythological and historical events, and the evidence of imperial greatness made him realize how the manifestation of the greatness of immortal soul has been developing continuously through the mortal glory of the world. The crisp winter air, the magnificence of the place, its nobility, filled him with physical and spiritual ecstasy.

Since Swamiji had left Meerut, his brother-disciples couldn't live there for a long time. After about ten days, they arrived at Delhi, and after a little search, discovered the address of Swamiji. They were happy to meet him again, but Swamiji was not much pleased for this disturbance in his plan of wandering as a solitary monk. He said to them, "Brothers, I told you that I wanted to be left alone. I said that I had work to do. I asked you not to follow me. Now I insist that you obey me. I do not want to be followed. With this I leave Delhi. And he, who follows me, does so at his peril; for I am going to lose myself to all old associations. Where the Spirit leads, there I shall wander, no matter whether it is a forest or a desert waste, a mountain region or a densely populated city. I am off." The brother-disciples, amazed by his firmness, said, "We did not know that you were staying here. We have come to Delhi to see the old imperial capital. Here we heard of a Swami Vividishananda, an English-speaking monk, and we were curious to see him. It is by accident that we have met you."

It shows that Swamiji had introduced himself in Delhi as Swami Vividishananda, the name which was taken at the time of his formal initiation into Sannyasa. But his brother-disciples seem to have forgotten the name.

Swamiji had to be so much strict to his brother-disciples, because he had to obey the command of his teacher Sri Ramakrishna. He realized the mission of his life, for what he had appeared on this earth. Soon he had to plunge into the field of his work. He should not delay any more in revealing himself as the Swami Vivekananda, the great educator of the world. The holy moment of his triumph was not far away. His plan for wandering as a solitary monk was only for the preparation of plunging into a great struggle, and the second reason for this was to make his brother-disciples self-reliant.

Though he pretended to be angry and told his brother-disciples that he was leaving Delhi, he lingered on in living there for a few days more. Though they were arranged for living apart, they gathered at the Sethji's house to take their food. Shortly afterwards the brother-disciples left Delhi and went in different directions. Swami Saradananda, due to his illness, went to Etawah with Kripananda. Swami Brahmananda and Turiyananda went to Punjab. Swamiji had tonsils, and he went to consult Dr. Hemchandra Sen, a well-known Bengali physician of Delhi. Doctor treated him but didn't pay much heed to his identity, rather his attitude had been little antagonistic. Later, in course of conversation, the doctor expressed to Akhandananda a desire to meet Swamiji again. Accordingly, the doctor invited some professors of the local college to his house, where Swamiji and his two brother-disciples had also been invited. They had a great discussion, and many questions were asked, all of them were highly impressed by the intellect of Swamiji. Dr. Sen was attracted to the small group of monks, and the following day he invited them to a feast at his house. After this two brother-disciples set out for Vrindavan, and Swamiji for Rajputana (now Rajasthan).

Rajasthan

Swamiji wanted to be left alone. So, he was happy after cutting the last attachment of his soul—his love for his brother-disciples. Renouncing all ties, Swamiji went forth, caring for nothing, fearing nothing, towards Alwar, the beautiful and historic land of Rajasthan, the land of Maharana Pratap. Memories of many heroic events flashed through his mind.

It was at the beginning of February 1891. Swamiji alighted at Alwar railway station. Walking along the road, fringed with beautiful gardens and grassy fields, and passing by a row of fine houses, he arrived at the State charitable hospital. There he found a Bengali gentleman standing at the gate. Swamiji asked him, "Do you know any place, where monks can take shelter?" The gentleman was a doctor of that hospital, and his name was Gurucharan Laskar. He was impressed by the wonderful appearance of the monk, and bowed low before him. He said, "Of course there is." Then he accompanied him to the bazaar and showed him a room above a shop. "This is for monks, sir," he said, "will you make yourself comfortable here for the present?" "Gladly!" responded Swamiji with a sweet smile. Swamiji had his belongings consisting of a few books tied up in a blanket, a piece of yellow cloth, a Kamandalu, and a staff. The doctor met the immediate needs of Swamiji, and rushed to a Muslim friend, and said, "O Moulavi Sahib! A Bengali dervish [wandering monk] has just arrived. Come immediately and see him. I have never seen such a Mahatma [great soul] before! Please talk with him while I finish my work, and I shall join you presently."

Moulavi Sahib was a teacher of Urdu and Persian in the High School. As soon as he heard of the monk, he hurried to the bazaar. Before entering the room he took off his shoes outside, and saluted Swamiji. Swamiji called the Moulavi Sahib to his side and discoursed with much love on religious matters. He said, "There is one thing very remarkable about the Koran. Even to this day, it exists as it was found eleven hundred years ago. It retains its pristine purity and is free from interpolations."

The doctor, on his way to the hospital, told everyone of the 'great monk' who had come. The Moulavi likewise informed his Muslim friends. Soon a crowd of people gathered there in the room of Swamiji. Some of them were standing outside the room. Swamiji spoke to them on religious matters and sang Urdu songs, Hindi Bhajana, Bengali Kirtana, and songs of great devotees like, Vidyapati, Chandidas, and Ramprasad. Sometimes he recited from the Vedas and Upanishads, or from the Bible, or from the Puranas. He illustrated the inner significance of all religions with inspiring stories from the lives of Buddha, Shankara, Ramanuja, Guru Nanak, Chaitanya, Tulsidas, Kabir, Ramakrishna and others.

In this way few days passed in Alwar. A number of devotees and admirers began to discuss, if a house could be arranged for Swamiji at the centre of the city, many people would get an opportunity to meet him. Finally, it was arranged for him to stay at the house of Pundit Shambhunathji, a retired engineer of Alwar State. Picture of Swamiji's daily life at this house was: He used to remain absorbed in meditation from early morning until nine. In the mean time, people of different castes, creeds and classes would have been waiting for him in the drawing. Some were Sunnis and Shiahs of the Muslim fold, some were Shaivites and Vaishnavites; some were men of wealth and position and learning, while others were illiterate and poor. Swamiji would treat them all alike and solve their questions on different religious matters. Everyone would frankly speak of their sorrows, and Swamiji, after listening to their problems, would advise them sincerely. If anyone would ask him any irrelevant question, he would not mind it, rather tried to correct him with an adequate reply. Suppose, during a spiritual discussion, someone asked him, "Maharaj, to what caste does your body belong?" He would immediately reply without annoyance, "It is Kayastha!" Some other monks would have evaded a direct reply, hoping to be taken for a Brahmin; but Swamiji was above all that. Again someone would ask him, "Sir, why do you wear ochre cloth?" He would reply, "Because it is the garb of beggars. Poor people would ask me for alms if I were to wear white clothes. Being a beggar myself, most times I do not have even a single piece to give them. It causes me pain to have to refuse one who begs of me. But seeing my ochre cloth, they understand that I also am a beggar. They would not think of begging from a beggar."

Sometimes, when the discussion centered on Mother-worship, Swamiji would be so overwhelmed that he couldn't say anything but "Mother! Mother!" His chanting of the Mother's name, in a voice at first loud and full, would gradually become softer and softer as if it were travelling with his soul—far and far off. Finally, there would be no voice, shed tears of joy. The devotees would have been surprised by seeing his ecstasy and would cry out, "Jai Ma Kali!" Then Swamiji would begin to sing, and it seemed a stream of divine love was flowing in his heart.

In the afternoon, when Swamiji would go out for a walk, many of his devotees would follow him. In the evening, the same crowd would attend the song and prayer and conversation. Many of them would join Swamiji in devotional singing or dancing in joy.

Before singing a Bengali song, Swamiji would explain its meaning to them, and often dictate the words so that they could note down the song in their own script and could sing later on. In Rajasthan, people are mostly devotees of Sri Krishna; hence Swamiji would sing of Sri Krishna's Vrindavan life. When he sang, tears would flow down the cheeks of both Swamiji and the audience. Some of those would feel: "Oh, he is enjoying the vision of Sri Krishna! Oh, how his singing carries away our hearts!" Someone would remark, "His face looked like that of a Gopi, ecstatic with love of Krishna." Swamiji's voice, sometime, would become choked with intensity of feeling and his body motionless; his face would glow with an unexplainable sweetness, radiant with the love of God.

Different men had different opinions on Swamiji. Everyone began to describe according to his own experience. Someone said, "Babaji is always full of joy; a sweet smile is there always on his face." Some said, "I have never heard such a sweet voice, as if a silver string is ringing!" Some said, "He has a thunderous voice." Someone would add, "It contains an electromagnetic power that attracts the listeners' hearts." Some said, "Have you noticed? How beautiful is his nature! He never gets annoyed even if he is asked any foolish question. He treats all alike and replies every question. What a patience!" Another would say, "He has attained divine grace—or why should we feel so attached to him? Wish to sit always at his feet." Thus everyone became attached to Swamiji, and each would think himself the most favourite to him. Swamiji initiated some by giving Mantras.

We have already told about the Moulavi Sahib, who was one of the most devoted to Swamiji. He had a strong desire to invite Swamiji to his house and feed him. He knew that Swamiji was a great monk with no sense of caste; but had a doubt that Pundit Shambhunathji, with whom he was staying, might have an objection. However, after thinking a lot, one evening, he went to Punditji, and with folded hands before all present, said, "Do allow me to have Swamiji in my house for his meal tomorrow. To satisfy you all I shall have all the furniture in my sitting-room washed by Brahmins. The food offered to Swamiji will be bought and cooked by Brahmins in vessels brought from their house." He added, "This Adhama (worthless) will be more than compensated if he can but see Swamiji, at a distance, eating his food."

Everyone present was impressed with the sincerity and modesty of Moulavi's words. On behalf of everyone Punditji clasped his hands and said, "My friend, Swamiji is a monk. What is caste to him! He is a liberated soul. There is no need to take such trouble. I, for my part, have no objection. Any arrangement you may make will satisfy us. Indeed, under such conditions as you propose, I myself can have no qualms of conscience in eating at your house." So, next day the Moulavi Sahib entertained Swamiji in his own house and felt himself blessed. Many other devout Muslims followed the example of Moulavi and cordially invited Swamiji to their homes also. Thus so many people felt themselves gratified by the holy company of Swamiji. Learned, illiterate, old, young, rich, poor and people of different religions, caste and creed—all were happy for having a new idea of living.

Within a few days Major Ramchandraji, the Dewan to the Maharaja of Alwar, heard of Swamiji's presence in the city. He invited Swamiji to his house, and after a little conversation with him he was charmed. He felt that Swamiji would be a good influence on the Maharaja, Mangal Singhji, who had become much anglicized in thought and manners. Hence, without any delay, wrote to the Maharaja, "A great monk with an amazing knowledge of English is here." The Maharaja was at that time living in a palace two or three miles away. Next day he came to the Dewan's house, and bowed down before Swamiji. According to the Hindu tradition, Swamiji closed his hands together and respectfully saluted the Maharaja and urged him to be seated. The Maharaja and his courtiers took their seats.

The Maharaja opened the conversation by saying, "Well, Swamiji Maharaj, I hear that you are a great scholar. You can easily earn a handsome sum of money. Why then do you go about begging?" Swamiji smiled a little, and instead of a reply, asked him, "Maharaja, tell me why you spend your time constantly in the company of Westerners, go on shooting excursions, and neglect your duties to the State?" Those present were taken aback. "What a bold monk! He will repent of this", they thought. But the Maharaja took it calmly; and after a little thought replied, "I cannot say why, but no doubt because I like to." "Well, for the same reason I wander about as a beggar", said Swamiji.

Maharaja, Mangal Singh, again asked, "Well, Swamiji Maharaj, I have no faith in idol-worship. What is going to be my fate?" He smiled while he spoke. Swamiji seemed little annoyed and thought, "How could a Hindu Maharaja say so?" He exclaimed with wonder, "Surely you are joking!" The Maharaja said, "No, Swamiji, not at all. You see, I really cannot worship wood, earth, stone or metal, like other people. Does this mean that I shall fare worse in the life hereafter?" Swamiji answered, "Well, I suppose every man should follow the religious ideal according to his own faith." The devotees of Swamiji were confused at this reply "What did he mean to say? Is he trying to please the Maharaja?" they thought. They knew that Swamiji was not a man of that type, and he sanctioned image-worship. Moreover, they had experienced his devotion to Sri Krishna. But Swamiji had not finished; his eyes lighted on a picture of the Maharaja which was hanging on the wall. He told someone to take down the picture. Holding it in his hand he asked, "Whose picture is this?" The Dewan answered, "It is a portrait of our Maharaja." Everyone present was surprised and had been waiting in suspense—"What is Swamiji going to do?" Swamiji ordered the Dewan, "Spit on it." Those present were trembled with fear. Swamiji continued, "Any one of you may spit on it. What is it but a piece of paper? What objection can you have against doing so?"

The Dewan was dumbfounded, and all eyes glanced in fear and awe from the Maharaja to the monk, from the monk to the Maharaja. But Swamiji continued to insist, "Spit on it, I say. Spit on it." The Dewan cried out, "What, Swamiji! What are you asking me to do? This is the portrait of our Maharaja! How can I do such a thing?" "Be it so," said Swamiji, "but the Maharaja is not bodily present in this portrait. This is only a piece of paper. It does not contain his bones and flesh and blood. It does not speak or behave or move in any way as the Maharaja does; yet all of you refuse to spit on it, because you see in this portrait the shadow of the Maharaja. Indeed, in spitting on the portrait, you feel that you insult your master, the Prince himself." Turning to the Maharaja he continued, "See, Your Highness; though this is not you in one sense, in another sense it is you. That was why your devoted servants were so perplexed when I asked them to spit on it. It is a shadow of you; it brings you into their minds. One glance at it makes them see you in it; therefore they look at it with as much respect as they would have in looking at your own person. Thus it also is with the devotees who worship stone and metal images of gods and goddesses. It is because the image brings to their minds their Ishta (God), or some special form and attributes of the Divinity, and helps them to concentrate, that the devotees worship God in an image. They do not worship the stone or the metal as such. I have travelled in many places, but nowhere have I found a single Hindu worshipping an image, saying, 'O Stone, I worship Thee. O Metal, be merciful to me.' Everyone, Maharaja, is worshipping the same one God who is the Supreme Spirit, the Soul of Pure Knowledge. And God appears to all according to their understanding and their representation of Him. Prince, I speak for myself. Of course, I cannot speak for you."[63]

The Maharaja Mangal Singh had been watching everything and listening to Swamiji attentively. Now, with folded hands, he said, "Swamiji, I must admit that, looking at image-worship in the light you have thrown on it, I have never yet met anyone who worshipped stone, or wood, or metal. Before this I did not understand its meaning. You have opened my eyes. But what will be my fate? Have mercy on me." Swamiji replied, "O Prince, none but God can be merciful to anyone; and He is ever-merciful! Pray to Him. He will show His mercy to you."

After Swamiji had taken leave, Mangal Singh remained thoughtful for a while, and then said, "Dewanji, never have I come across such a great soul! Make his stay with you for some time." The Dewan felt relief, and said, "I shall try my best; but I do not know whether I shall succeed. He is a man of fiery and independent character." After many entreaties Swamiji agreed to live with the Dewan, but only on one condition, that everyone, who wished to see him, should be allowed to come to him without making any discrimination among those poor or rich, learned or illiterate or those of higher positions. The Dewan readily agreed, and Swamiji gladly stayed there with him.

As his desire Dewanji opened the door of his house for all visitors. Many people, who came in contact with Swamiji, found their lives completely changed. One old man would come to Swamiji daily. He constantly asked for his blessings and mercy. Accordingly, Swamiji instructed him in certain practices; but the old man could not follow them properly. Swamiji instructed him again, and the old man would again make some mistakes. Finally, Swamiji made a plan to get himself free from the old man. One day, seeing the man coming at a distance he assumed an attitude of extreme silence. He didn't answer any of the old man's questions; nor did he respond to any of the greetings of the many friends gathered there. No one could understand what the matter with him was. In this way passed an hour and a half, and still Swamiji remained silent like a statue. The old man became angry and left, swearing to himself. As soon as he left the place, Swamiji burst into laughter like a boy. Seeing that everyone present couldn't help laughing. A young man asked him, "Swamiji, why were you so hard on that old man?" Swamiji replied, "Dear sons, I am ready to sacrifice my life for you, for you are willing to follow my advice and have the power to do so. But here is an old man who has spent nine-tenths of his life in running after the pleasures of the senses; now he is unfit for both spiritual and worldly life, and thinks he can have God's mercy for the mere asking! What is needed to attain Truth is personal exertion. How can God have mercy on one who is devoid of such exertion? He who is wanting in manliness is full of Tamas (inertia). It was because Arjuna, the bravest of warriors, was going to lose this manliness that Sri Krishna commanded him to follow the course of life and duty proper to him, so that by fulfilling his duties without attachment to results, he might acquire the Sattvic qualities—purity of heart, renunciation of work, and self-surrender. Be strong. Be manly. I have respect even for a wicked person so long as he is manly and strong, for his strength will some day make him give up his wickedness, and even renounce all work for selfish ends. It will thus eventually bring him to the Truth."[64]

Following Swamiji's advice, many young men of Alwar began to study Sanskrit. At times Swamiji would teach them. He would say, "Study Sanskrit, but along with it study Western science as well. Learn accuracy, my boys. Study and labour, so that the time will come when you can put our history on a scientific basis. Now, Indian history is disorganized. It has no chronological accuracy. The histories of our country written by English writers cannot but be weakening to our minds, for they tell only of our downfall. How can foreigners, who understand very little of our manners and customs, or of our religion and philosophy, write faithful and unbiased histories of India? Naturally, many false notions and wrong inferences have found their way into them. Nevertheless the Europeans have shown us how to proceed in making researches into our ancient history. Now it is for us to strike out an independent path of historical research for ourselves; to study the Vedas and the Puranas and the ancient annals of India; and from this to make it our life-work and discipline to write accurate, sympathetic and soul-inspiring histories of the land. It is for Indians to write Indian history. Therefore set yourselves to the task of rescuing our lost and hidden treasures from oblivion. Even as one whose child has been lost does not rest until he has found it, so do you never cease to labour until you have revived the glorious past of India in the consciousness of the people. That will be the true national education, and with its advancement a true national spirit will be awakened."[65]

Thus, Swamiji became an inspiration to many young men of Alwar. A Brahmin boy used to come to Swamiji, and loved him as a disciple loves his master. He was of the age when he should have been invested with the sacred thread, but he lacked the means. When Swamiji came to know this he spoke the well-to-do among his disciples, "I have one thing to beg of you. Here is a Brahmin boy who is too poor to meet the expenses of his Upanayana [sacred thread ceremony].

As householders it is your duty to help him. Try to raise a subscription on his behalf. It is not proper for a Brahmin boy of his age not to know the obligatory religious duties of his caste. Moreover, it will be very good of you if you can provide for his education also." The devotees began to collect the necessary money.

Shortly after this Swamiji left Alwar, but he didn't forget the boy and the matter of his education. We see him writing a letter from Mount Abu on April 30, 1891, to his disciple Govinda Sahay at Alwar. The letter runs:

> Have you done the Upanayana of that Brahmin boy? Are you studying Sanskrit? How far have you advanced? I think you must have finished the first part.... Are you diligent in your Shiva Puja? If not, try to be so. "Seek ye first the kingdom of God and all good things will be added unto you." Follow God and you shall have whatever you desire... To the two Commander Sahebs my best regards; they being men of high position were very kind to a poor fakir like me. My children, the secret of religion lies not in theories but in practice. To be good and to do good—that is the whole of religion. "Not he that crieth 'Lord', 'Lord', but he that doeth the will of the Father." You are a nice band of young men, you Alwaris, and I hope in no distant future many of you will be ornaments of the society and blessings to the country you are borne in.[66]

Swamiji had gone to Ajmer before he went to Mount Abu, and from Ajmer he wrote to his disciple Govinda Sahay, "Try to be pure and unselfish—that is the whole of religion..."

One day Swamiji asked the devotees, "Is there any sadhus (holy men) nearby?" One of them replied, "There lives an old Brahmachari at some distance." Swamiji wished to see the Brahmachari, and went to see him in the company of a gentleman. But the old Brahmachari was a Vaishnava, who didn't like monks of the Vedantic school. As soon as Swamiji entered, he began, in an obsessive outburst, to criticize the sannyasi life and the wearing of the ochre cloth. As he came close to him, the Brahmachari asked, "Why are you wearing an ochre cloth? I don't like monks wearing an ochre cloth." Swamiji didn't react, but simply asked to be taught something about God and religion. The Brahmachari said, "Well, let it go. I have no anger against you. Have something to eat." Swamiji said that he had had his food just before coming. The old man again became furious and cried, "Then, get out of here." Swamiji bowed down before him and took leave. Coming out of the Brahmachari's Ashrama, Swamiji burst into laughter, and said, "Oh! What a peculiar saint you have shown me! What a grouchy old man!" He laughed more and more, and began to imitate the old Brahmachari's way of speaking. The gentleman also joined in the fun.

Once a disciple invited Swamiji to take food at his house. When Swamiji reached there, the disciple was rubbing oil into his body before taking a bath. He welcomed Swamiji and asked, "Swamiji, is there any advantage in rubbing oil before taking a bath?" Swamiji replied, "Yes, one-sixteenth seer of oil rubbed into the body serves the purpose of eating one-forth seer of ghee."

After finishing the food the disciple said, "Swamiji, you teach us about truthfulness, honesty, courage, purity, selfless work and so on; but it is not possible for one who is in service to follow these teachings strictly. Since we are working in order to earn money, how can we call it selfless service? Service is after all a sort of slavery. Moreover, business life, these days, is such that truth and simplicity are almost impossible for a businessman. Swamiji, it is not possible to keep the moral side sound, if we have to work in this world."

Swamiji replied: "I, too, have thought about this matter a lot, and have at last come to the conclusion that no one really wants to earn money by keeping his character intact. No one even cares to think about the matter or feels it to be a problem, as you do. It is the fault of our present system of education. Personally, I feel that there is no harm if anyone makes agriculture his profession; but if you advise anyone to do so, he retorts, 'Then why have I gone in for so much education? Is it necessary for everyone in the country to be farmers? The nation is already full of them; that is why it has come to such ruin.' But this is not so. Read the *Mahabharata*. The sage Janaka held the plough in one hand and studied the Vedas using the other. Our sages of old were farmers. Not only that: look how America has become so advanced by developing agriculture. I do not mean that we should follow this profession as the ignorant farmers of our country do. We have to learn the science of it, and apply that knowledge to the development of our agriculture. We have to work like intelligent people, after acquiring the necessary knowledge. But these days, no sooner do the village boys read a book or two of English than they run to the cities. In the village they may have plenty of land, but they do not feel satisfied. They want to enjoy city-life and enter service. That is why the Hindus have not progressed like other races. Our death-rate is very high; and if it continues the same, our nation is bound to meet its doom in no time. The main cause of all this is that our agricultural production is not enough. The inclination to go to the cities is noticeable among the villagers. A farmer's son, after getting a little education, leaves his ancestral profession, goes to the city, and takes a job under the white men. Longevity increases by staying in the villages; and disease is almost unknown there. If educated men go to live in the villages, even small villages will become developed; and if agriculture is carried on scientifically, then the yield will be more. In that way the farmers will be awakened to their duty; their intellectual faculties will develop; they will be able to learn more and better things; and *that*, which is very necessary for our nation, will be achieved."

The disciple asked, "What is *that*, Swamiji?"

Swamiji replied, "What else but a sort of brotherly feeling developing between the higher and the lower castes. If educated men like you go to the villages, take up agriculture, mix with the village folk and treat them as your own, without hostility, then you will see, they will be so overwhelmed that they will sacrifice even their lives for you. And what is essential for us today—the education of the masses, the teaching of higher truths to people of the lower castes, and mutual sympathy and love—that also will be achieved."

The disciple asked, "How will that happen, Swamiji?"

Swamiji replied, "Why! Don't you see? If anyone mixes with the villagers, how eager they are for the company of the educated! Thirst for knowledge is in everybody. That is why, when they get the company of an educated man, they sit round him and listen with rapt attention to whatever he says. If educated people take advantage of this tendency of the villagers, invite a group of them to their homes each evening, and teach them with the help of stories and parables, then by means of such a national movement we shall be able to achieve a hundred times more in ten years than we could otherwise achieve in a thousand years."

It is true that Swamiji's dream has become fruitful to some extent. After independence, India has made a great development in many fields. There are many problems yet to be solved. Still it's a long way to go. Swami Vivekananda had envisioned a society with a new type of human being in whom knowledge, action, work, and concentration were harmoniously blended, and he proposed a new type of education for achieving this. The right to education for everyone, guaranteed by the Constitution of India, was Vivekananda's dream, but it is still a far cry from its goal. Still there are many people who cannot complete their education due to poverty. Many schools, colleges and universities have been established, but the education system merely could have been successful in building good human beings as prescribed by Swami Vivekananda. His thought on education ought to be seriously re-examined today.

In Alwar, Swamiji first revealed himself as an educator. Religion, science, patriotism, sociology, Sanskrit, economics, duty, spiritual practice, hospitality, and love—were all he taught them. After staying here for seven weeks, he decided to leave his disciples and admirers. He said to them, "I must be going. A sannyasi must always be on the move." So on March 28, 1891, he took leave, bidding them farewell. They tried their best to stop him, but he, the teacher, had always to be wandering—teaching, preaching, and helping mankind in many places, with the Spirit of God in his heart. Swamiji was going to Pandupol, some eighty miles from Alwar, and he wished to travel this distance on foot. His friends and disciples insisted him for travelling by a covered bullock-cart, so as to avoid the heat and traverse the uninhabited areas. Many of them begged to be allowed to accompany him for the first fifty or sixty miles. At first he objected, but finally couldn't avoid their pleading, and consented.

At Pandupol there was a big temple dedicated to Hanumanji. Swamiji went there and took shelter for the night in the temple-compound. On the following morning he abandoned the bullock-cart, and he and his party went on foot some sixteen miles through a mountainous region, infested with wild beasts, to a village called Tahla. Swamiji entertained them with funny stories, or by singing devotional songs, and some time became serious, and his disciples felt so blessed in his presence, that they had no thought of danger. In this village they spent the night in a temple dedicated to Nilakantha Mahadeva.

The story of Shiva as Nilakantha Mahadeva runs thus. Indra, the King of the Devas (gods), while riding on the elephant Airavata, came across Sage Durvasa who offered him a special garland given to him by the God Shiva. Indra accepted the garland and placed it on the trunk of the elephant as a test to prove that he was not an egoistic god. The elephant, knowing that Indra had no control over his own ego, threw the garland to the ground. This enraged the sage as the garland was a dwelling of Sri (fortune) and was to be treated as a prasada or religious offering. Durvasa cursed Indra and all devas to be bereft of all strength, energy, and fortune.

In battles following the incident, the Devas were defeated and Asuras (demons) led by King Bali, gained control of the universe. The Devas sought help from the Supreme God Vishnu who advised them to treat asuras in a diplomatic manner. The Devas formed an alliance with asuras to jointly churn the ocean for the nectar of immortality and to share it among them. However, Vishnu told the Devas that he would arrange that they alone get the nectar.

The churning of the Ocean of Milk was an elaborate process. Mount Mandara or Mandar Parvat was used as the churning rod, and Vasuki, the king of serpents, who abides on Shiva's neck, became the churning rope. The demons demanded to hold the head of the snake, while the gods, taking advice from Vishnu, agreed to hold its tail. As a result the demons were poisoned by fumes emitted by Vasuki. Despite this, the gods and the demons pulled back and forth on the snake's body alternately, causing the mountain to rotate, which in turn churned the ocean. When the mountain was placed on the ocean, it began to sink. Vishnu, in the form of a turtle Kurma, came to their rescue and supported the mountain on his back.

The *Samudra Manthan* process released a number of things from the Ocean of Milk. One was the lethal poison known as Halahala, which in some versions of the story, escaped from the mouth of the serpent king as the demons and gods churned. This terrified the gods and demons because the poison was so powerful that it could destroy all of creation. Then the gods approached Shiva for protection. Shiva consumed the poison in an act to protect the universe, and his wife Parvati grabbed Shiva's throat in an effort to prevent him from swallowing the poison, which was the most deadly poison in existence, harmful even to a god. As a result, Shiva's throat turned blue. For this reason, Lord Shiva is also called Neelakantha (the blue-throated one; "neela" = "blue", "kantha" = "throat").

To this well-known story Swamiji gave his own interpretation. "All beings," he said, "who dwell within the folds of earthly consciousness, churn the ocean of Maya, that is, human life, and obtain treasures that are pleasing to the senses; but soon the poison, death, must come to end the show. The monk, however, stands apart. Absorbed in the self, he desires none of the enticing gifts which Maya offers; but like Mahadeva, he is ready to come to the assistance of those who lust after sense-pleasures, when, in the presence of death, they come to him (the monk) to save their souls. Then he destroys their Maya—their ignorance—and releases them from the fear of death. He also shows by that the man of Realization has no fear of death."

Next morning Swamiji set out for a village called Narayeani, some eighteen miles away. Here the Mother is worshiped in one of Her forms. Every year a big Mela (fair) is held here, and many people from different parts of Rajasthan come to join the Mela. After a halt for the night Swamiji took leave from his disciples, and went to the next village alone. He walked some sixteen miles and took a train for the city of Jaipur. On the way a devotee, who met him at Alwar, had been waiting for him at Bandikui station. The devotee had come from Jaipur to receive Swamiji. He boarded the train at Bandikui and accompanied him for the rest of the journey to Jaipur. At Jaipur the devotee insisted Swamiji on allowing him to take a photograph. Swamiji consented for the same. This was the first photograph of him as a wandering monk.

Swamiji remained at Jaipur only for two weeks. During this time he met a noted Sanskrit grammarian. He wished to read grammar (Panini's *Ashtadhyayi*) with him. But the Pundit, though very learned, had not the gift of teaching. For three days he tried to explain the commentary on the first Sutra (aphorism), but he failed. On the fourth day, he said, "Swamiji, I am afraid you are not deriving much benefit from studying with me, for in three days I have not been able to make you grasp the meaning of the Sutra." Hearing the Pundit, Swamiji felt ashamed, and resolved to master the commentary by himself. He went through the commentary attentively, and in three hours he accomplished what the Pundit couldn't do in three days. Shortly after, he went to the Pundit and in a casual way explained the commentary and its content. The Pundit was amazed. After this, Swamiji started to master Sutra after Sutra and chapter after chapter. Later he said, speaking of this experience, "If the mind is intensely eager, everything can be accomplished—even mountains can be crumbled into atoms."

During his stay at Jaipur, Swamiji became very intimate with Sardar Hari Singh, the Commander-in-Chief of the State. He passed some days in his house discussing spiritual and scriptural matters. One day the discussion was going on the subject of image-worship. Hari Singh was a strong believer in the doctrines of the Vedanta, and did not believe in the value of image. The discussion went on for hours, but he remained unconvinced. In the evening they went out for a walk. As they were going along the footpath they saw some devotees carrying the image of Sri Krishna and singing devotional songs as they were passing by. Swamiji and Hari Singh watched the procession for a while. Suddenly Swamiji touched Hari Singh and said, "Look there, see the living God!" As Hari Singh looked at the image of the Lord Krishna, he stood there transfixed, with tears of ecstasy trickling down his cheeks. He, when came back to his normal state, said, "Well, Swamiji, that was a revelation to me. What I could not understand after hours of discussion, was easily comprehended through your touch. Truly I saw the Lord in the image of Krishna!" This incident shows that Hari Singh was not an ordinary person. Otherwise he could not continue the argument with Swamiji for hours. Not only this, but also he forced Swamiji to apply his power to comprehend him the idea of image-worship.

Another day when Swamiji was seated with a number of devotees, giving them spiritual instructions, Pundit Suraj Narayan, a learned Sardar, honoured among the society of learned men, came to see him. With reference to the context of Swamiji's conversation he said, "Swamiji, I am a Vedantist. I do not believe in the special divinity of Incarnations—the Avatara of the Hindu mythology. We are all Brahmin. What is the difference between me and an Avatara?" Swamiji replied, "Yes, that is quite true. The Hindus count a fish, a tortoise and a boar as Avataras. You say that you are also an Avatara; but with which of these do you feel yourself one?" There was a din of laughter at this, and the Sardar was silenced.

Swamiji next set out for Ajmer, a holy place for pilgrimage. Ajmer is a popular pilgrimage center for the Hindus as well as the Muslims. As the final resting place of the great Sufi Saint Khwaja Moinuddin Hasan Chisti, Muslims from all over the world revere the Dargah Sharif, where the saint lies buried and equally revered by both the Hindus and the Muslims.

In a picturesque valley surrounded by the hills of the Aravalli Range, 132 kms. west of current state capital—Jaipur lies the historic city of Ajmer—a green oasis, wrapped by barren hills founded by Raja Ajay Pal Chauhan in 7th century AD. Ajmer got its name from name from 'Ajay Meru' or the invincible hill. Here he built India's first hill fort, Taragarh. It continued to be the power center of the Chauhan clan till the end of the 12th century, through times of war and peace, through serenity and sacrifice.

As an aside, Ajmer is also the base for visiting Pushkar about 14 km. away. The abode of Lord Brahma the Pushkar lake is a sacred spot for the Hindus, where they take a dip especially in the month of Kartik (October-November) and considered spiritually motivated.

Swamiji visited the palaces of Akbar and the famous Dargah. He also visited the temple dedicated to the creator, Brahma.

On April 14 Swamiji left Ajmer for Mount Abu, a popular hill station in the Aravalli Range in Sirohi district of Rajasthan state in western India. The mountain is also home to several Hindu temples, including the Adhar Devi Temple (also known as Arbuda Devi Temple), carved out of solid rock; the Shri Raghunathji Temple; and a shrine and temple to Dattatreya built atop the Guru Shikhar peak and a number of Jain temples including Dilwara Temples, a complex of temples carved of white marble that was built between the 11th and 13th centuries AD. The oldest of these is the Vimal Vasahi temple, built in 1021 AD by Vimal Shah and dedicated to the first of the Jain Tirthankaras and they include the Achaleswar Mahadev Temple and the Kantinath Temple. The Dilwara temples of India are located about 2½ kilometres from Mount Abu, Rajasthan's only hill station. These Jain temples were built by Vastupal-Tejpal, two pious brothers, merchant princes. It is one of the most beautiful Jain pilgrimage sites in the world. Although the Jains built some beautiful temples at other places in Rajasthan, some believe that none comes close to these in terms of architectural perfection. The ornamental detail spreading over the minutely carved ceilings, doorways, pillars and panels is simply marvellous.

Swamiji enjoyed the beauty of the place and examined the glories of the temple. There are strange shaped rocks by the lake, one like a praying nun, and another like a toad about to spring into the waters, and so on.

Swamiji was soon attracted by devotees with whom he used to walk in the evening. One day they were walking along Bailey's Walk, which commands a fine view of the hill-station. Swamiji was listening to their stories of this beautiful place. Below them stretched the lake of Mount Abu. Swamiji with his devotees sat down among the rocks and began to sing one after one for hours. Some Europeans were taking an evening stroll. They were charmed with the sweet music and waited for a glimpse of the singer. When Swamiji came down, they congratulated him on his sweet voice and ecstatic song.

Swamiji was then deep in spiritual practices in an abandoned cave. His sole belongings were two blankets, a water-pot, and a few books. One day a Muslim, the pleader of the prince of a Native State, happened to arrive there. He saw Swamiji, and struck with his appearance, and decided to speak to him. After having a little conversation he was charmed with the learning of the recluse, and became attracted to him. He used to visit Swamiji quite often. One day the gentleman asked Swamiji if he could be of any service to him. Swamiji replied, "Look here, Vakil Sahib (Pleader), the rainy season is fast approaching. There are no doors to this cave. You can make a pair of doors for me, if you please." Gratified, the Vakil said, "This cave is a wretched one. If you allow me, I shall make a suggestion. I live here alone in a nice bungalow. If you would condescend to come and live with me, I should feel greatly blessed." Swamiji immediately agreed to the proposal. Then the gentleman said, "But I am a Muslim. I shall, of course, make separate arrangement for your food." Swamiji didn't pay much heed to his words, and moved to the bungalow.

In those days it was not so easy for a Hindu to stay in the house of a Muslim. The Hindu society was very much rigid on this matter. They would consider Muslims as a lower class of people. But Swamiji didn't care of any infamy. During his stay at this Vakil's house Swamiji met the Raja of Khetri, who had an important role in his later life.

Through the Vakil and his brother-officers of other States, Swamiji made many friends in Mount Abu. The Vakil of the Maharao of Kotah, and Thakur Fateh Singh, the Minister of that Prince became his friends. Few days later, the Muslim Vakil invited Munshi Jagmohanlal, Private Secretary to the Raja of Khetri. When he came to the Vakil's house, Swamiji was resting on his bed, having on only a loin-cloth and a piece of ochre cloth. Seeing the monk sleeping, Jagmohanlal thought, "Oh! here is one of those common monks who are no better than thieves and rogues!" Shortly after that Swamiji woke up. Jagmohanlal asked him, "Well, Swamiji, you are a Hindu monk. How is it that you are living with a Muslim? Your food may now and then be touched by him." Swamiji flared up, and said, "Sir, what do you mean? I am a sannyasi. I am above all your social conventions. I can dine even with a Bhangi [sweeper]. I am not afraid of God, for He sanctions it; I am not afraid of the scriptures, for they allow it: but I am afraid of you people and your society. You know nothing of God and the scriptures. I see Brahman everywhere, manifested even in the meanest creature. For me there is nothing high or low. Shiva, Shiva!" A sort of divine fire stretched on his face. Jagmohanlal became silent, but he wished the Raja to make the acquaintance of such a monk. "Swamiji," he said, "do come with me to the palace to meet the Raja Saheb." Swamiji replied, "Very well, I shall go the day after tomorrow."

Jagmohanlal told the Raja everything of what had happened. The Raja became so eager to meet the monk that he said, "I will go myself to see him." When Swamiji came to know this, he went instantly to the palace, where His Highness warmly welcomed him. It was June 4, 1891. After the usual formalities the Raja asked him, "Swamiji, what is life?" Swamiji replied, "Life is the unfoldment and development of a being under circumstances tending to press it down." The Raja was highly impressed with the words of Swamiji, and asked again, "Well, Swamiji, what then is education?" Swamiji responded, "I should say, education is the nervous association of certain ideas." And he went on explaining this statement, "Until some thoughts or ideas had been made instincts they could not be reckoned as real and vital possessions of consciousness." Then in support of this statement he gave an example of the life of Sri Ramakrishna. The Raja, Ajit Singh, was overwhelmed by his words of spiritual nectar, and his soul was absorbed in a burning passion for Truth.

From the Waqyat Register (State Diary) of Khetri State, Swamiji's activities at this time are known in some detail.

June 4, 1891: Swamiji first met Raja Ajit Singh at summer palace at Mount Abu. On this occasion the Raja had a long discussion with him on various subjects, when Hardayal Singhji of Jodhpur was also present. After taking dinner at the palace Swamiji left.

June 6, 1891: Swamiji reached the palace at 10 o'clock in the morning and discussed in English and Sanskrit.

June 11, 1891: This was Swamiji's third visit to the Raja. He discussed on spiritual matter and took lunch at half past ten in the morning. Then he sang few songs and after a discussion on education and philosophy he left at about 2 p.m.

June 15, 1891: Swamiji reached the palace at about 10 a.m. and discussed on various subjects. After having lunch he left at about 3 p.m.

June 22, 1891: Swamiji reached the palace in the morning and took seat in the drawing room. Shortly after that the Raja entered the room and talked with him on education and spiritual matters. At about twelve he took lunch and having a little rest again discussed with the Raja on various subjects till 5 o'clock in the afternoon.

June 23, 1891: Swamiji lunched and had discussion with the Raja, chiefly on education, religion and philosophy.

June 24, 1891: Swamiji reached the palace at about 9.30 a.m. and had discussion with the Raja until lunch time. About 5 p.m. they were joined by Har Bilas Sarda, President of Arya Samaj at Ajmer, and Thakur Mukund Singhji of Jaleswar (near Aligarh).

June 27, 1891: Swamiji lunched and talked with the Raja, and afterwards he sang while the Raja accompanied him on harmonium. More or less the same routine was followed on July 4, 6, 8, 9, 11, 14, and 17.

On July 18, the Raja invited some honoured guests for dinner. Thakur Fateh Singhji Rathor, Thakur Mukund Singhji Chouhan of Jaleswar, and Man Singhji of Jamnagar were present. They listened to the playing of Sitar by one Choubeyji, and afterwards took dinner about midnight.

Har Bilas Sarda, mentioned above, met Swamiji more than once at Mount Abu, and again at Ajmer. He later distinguished himself as a historian of Rajputana, and as the member of the Central Legislative Assembly of India who championed the Child Marriage Restraint Act, popularly known as the 'Sarda Act'. He writes of these days at Mount Abu as follows:

> "...I met Swami Vivekananda four times. The first time I met him was at Mount Abu. It was sometime in the year 1889 or 1890 [June 1891] in the month of May or June (I do not recollect which). I went to Mount Abu to stay with my friend T. [Thakur] Mukund Singh of Chhalasar [Jaleswar], Aligarh district, who was staying at Mount Abu for the hot season. When I reached there, I found Swami Vivekananda staying with T. Mukund Singh. T. Mukund Singh was an Arya Samajist and a follower of Swami Dayananda Saraswati. I stopped with my friend for about ten days and we, Swamiji

and I, was together there and talked on various subjects. I was about 21 years old then and impressed by Swami Vivekananda's personality. He was a most delightful talker and was very well informed. We used to go out for our afternoon walks. After dinner the first day, Swami Vivekananda gave a song at Thakur Sahib's request. He sang in a most melodious tone, which gave me a great delight. I was charmed by his songs, and every day I begged him to give one or two songs. His musical voice and his manner have left a lasting impression on me. We sometimes talked about Vedanta, with which I had some acquaintance... Swami Vivekananda's talks on Vedanta greatly interested me. His views on various subjects were most welcome to me, as they were very patriotic. He was full of love of motherland and of Hindu culture. The time I passed in his company was one of the most pleasant times I have passed in my life. His independence of character particularly impressed me."[67]

One day Raja Ajit Singh said, "Swamiji, please come with me to my State. You will live with me there, and I shall serve you with my whole heart." Swamiji replied, "Well, Your Highness, I shall be glad to accompany you...." Swamiji went to Khetri three times; twice before he went to America and once more after he returned from America.

On July 24, The Raja left Mount Abu with his retinue, and Swamiji went with him. Next morning they reached Jaipur, and stayed at Khetri House. There they stayed for about ten days spending much for their time, as before, in conversation on various subjects. On August 3, they left Jaipur for Khetri by train. They halted at Khairthal for the night, and next day, in the Raja's state carriage, they started for Kot. They stayed for a day at Kot. On August 5, they left for Khetri, and reached on the 7th morning. On the way the Raja had asked many questions to Swamiji and listened to his answers. Khairthal to Khetri, some distance of 90 miles, they travelled on bullockcart.

At Khetri, after some days, the Raja took spiritual initiation from Swamiji, and became his disciple. What a sweet relation was there between the Guru and disciple! The Raja used to be kneeling in reverence before Swamiji, and always was ready to serve him with the whole of his heart. Swamiji not only gave him spiritual lessons but also helped in learning worldly knowledge. He loved him dearly and expected much of him in the way of advancing the well-being of the country. Swamiji stayed there at Khetri for almost three months (August 7 to October 17). During this period the Raja learnt the fundamental principles of physics, chemistry and astronomy from Swamiji. Swamiji spent his time with the Raja and his royal guests, with the pundits and State officers, and others: discussing scriptures, singing songs, studying books and teaching people. At his request the Raja started a small laboratory on the top of his palace. It was equipped with a telescope and a microscope. Swamiji and his disciple put these instruments to good use. Near the palace there was a beautiful pond, on the bank of which Swamiji often used to be seated with the Raja and others, and would discuss various subjects or sang for a long time.

Such was the devotion and reverence of the Raja for his spiritual teacher that he would even rub Swamiji's feet gently while he slept. He also wished to do the acts of service in the day before others, but Swamiji forbade this last. He said, "This will lower the dignity of you (the Raja) in the eyes of others."

October 4, 1891: It was the eve of the Navaratri festival. Swamiji went with the Raja on horseback to visit the temple of Jeen Mata (a well-known deity of Rajputana, in Sikra State).

On the way they visited the Shiva temple on a hill at Gundha, and reached Signore the same day in the evening. They passed the night at Signore, reached Sikra on the 6th. From there they went to visit the temple of Jeen Mata, accompanied by the Maharaja Madho Singhji of Sikra. On 10th they set out for Khetri again and reached the next day. October 12 was Dasera. The day was celebrated by the Raja with a state procession, and special dinner. Swamiji also took part in the celebrations.

At that time Pundit Narayandas was the foremost Sanskrit grammarian in Rajasthan. Swamiji thought this to be a great opportunity to resume his study of the *Mahabhashya* (Patanjali's great commentary) on the Sutra of Panini, which he had left incomplete at Jaipur. The Pundit was pleased to have him as a pupil. One day the Pundit wanted to examine him. He asked him on a very long lesson given the day before. To his surprise Swamiji repeated it verbatim, and added his own comments. After a time the Pundit, realizing that his pupil was able to solve all problems of grammar, said, "Swamiji, there is nothing more to teach you. I have taught you all that I know, and you have absorbed it." Swamiji saluted the Pundit respectfully, and thanked him for his kindness. He became in many respects the teacher of the Pundit.

One day the Raja asked him, "Swamiji, what is Truth" Swamiji replied, "Truth, Your Highness, is One and Absolute. Man travels constantly towards it, from truth to truth, and not from error to truth." On one occasion the Raja asked, "Swamiji, what is Law?" Swamiji instantly replied, "Law is altogether internal. It does not exist outside; it is a phenomenon of intelligence and experience. It is the mind which classifies sense-observations and moulds them into laws. The order of experience is always internal. Apart from the impression received through the sense organs and the reaction of intelligence upon these, in an orderly and consecutive manner, there is no law. The scientists say that it is all homogeneous substance and homogeneous vibration. Experience and its classification are internal phenomena. Thus law itself is intelligent and is born in absolute intelligence." Then with reference to the Sankhya philosophy he showed how modern science corroborated its conclusions.

One day Swamiji was reading a book. The Raja noticed that Swamiji was turning the pages of the book one by one. He became surprised and asked, "Swamiji, how do you read so fast?" Swamiji replied, "When a child starts learning, he repeats each letter and thereafter can read a word. After a time he reads word by word, and gradually learns to read a sentence at a time. Thus with a long and hard practice he can acquire the knowledge of a page at a glance. This is nothing but a matter of practice; any one can do this with the help of deep concentration and Brahmacharya. You too can do this if you wish."

The Raja of Khetri had no son. He believed that he could have a son if he was blessed by Swamiji. One day he expressed sorrows to Swamiji for not having been blessed with a son and heir. "Swamiji," he said, "bless me that a son may be born to me. If you will only do so, there is no doubt that my prayer will be granted." Swamiji couldn't avoid his prayer. Seeing his anxious longing, he blessed him.

At Khetri, Swamiji didn't spend all his time in the palace. He often would visit his poorer devotees, and frequently took food in their house. To him everyone was same. He used to give spiritual instructions to all and would explain the holy words of Sri Ramakrishna and his eternal life. Though they had not seen Sri Ramakrishna, only by listening to his description, they would feel themselves blessed knowledge of his greatness. The whole town of Khetri was fond of Swamiji, and he treated his admirers with the same love and affection as he bestowed on the Raja.

One day the Raja was being entertained with music by a nautch-girl. Swamiji was in his room when the music commenced. The Raja sent a message to Swamiji asking him to come and join the party. Swamiji went to join the Raja. When the Raja ordered the girl-singer to sing, Swamiji stood up and said that as a monk he should not listen to a female singer. The Raja requested him to be seated, saying, "Swamiji, please do listen to her song. She is a good singer; her music can take an ordinary man to a high state. Hop you will be pleased too." Swamiji couldn't avoid his request, and sat down.

The girl started singing. It was dark outside, and the audience was calm and quiet. The sky was full of stars. She sang a song of Surdas, the Vaishnava saint. Through the silence of the evening air, to the accompaniment of music, the girl's melodious voice reached the ear of Swamiji.

> O Lord, look no upon my evil qualities.
> Thy Name, O Lord, is Same-sighted.
> One piece of iron is in the image in the temple,
> And another, the knife in the hand of the butcher;
> But when they touch the philosophers' stone,
> Both alike turn to gold.
> So, Lord, look not upon my evil qualities....

Swamiji was overwhelmed with joy. The girl and her song made him remember that all is Brahman, that the same Divinity is the back of all beings—ay, even of this woman whom he had despised. Speaking of this incident later, he said, "Hearing the song I thought, 'Is this my Sannyasa? I am a sannyasi, and yet I have in me the sense of distinction between myself and this woman!' That incident removed the scales from my eyes. Seeing that all are indeed the manifestation of the One, I could no longer condemn anybody."

Few days before three months at Khetri, Swamiji decided to leave the place again and go forth into the wide world. Towards the end of October, he left Khetri for Ajmer, where he stayed for about three weeks. First he stayed for three or four days with Har Bilas Sarda; and then with Sarda's friend, Shyamji Krishna Varma. Mr. Sarda's reminiscences, relating to Swamiji's visit to Ajmer in November and December 1891, run as follows:

> "The next time I met him (Swamiji) was at Ajmer.... He was my guest, so far as I remember, for two or three days or four: I remember asking him what his name was before he became a sannyasi. He gave it to me.... He left me and went away to Beawar. Mr. Shyamji Krishna Varma, one of the most learned of men I have met, lived in Ajmer in those days, but had gone to Bombay (now Mumbai), when the Swami was with me. On his return, I spoke to him about Swami Vivekananda's learning, eloquence and patriotism, and told him that he had left only two or three days ago and was in Beawar. P. Shyamji Krishna Varma had to go to Beawar the next day and promised to bring Swamiji with him back to Ajmer. The next day he returned to Ajmer with Swami Vivekananda. Swami Vivekananda was his guest for about fourteen or fifteen days and I met him every day at Mr. Shyamji's bungalow. We three used to go out together for our evening walk. I had the happiest time in the company of these two learned men... I remember well that we had most interesting talks with Swami Vivekananda. His eloquence, his nationalistic attitude of mind and pleasant manner greatly impressed and delighted me. Very often I was a listener, when Mr. Shyamji and Swami Vivekananda discussed some Sanskrit literary or philosophic matters....
>
> "He (Swamiji) had large luminous eyes and discoursed eloquently on religious and philosophical subjects. I was charmed by Vivekananda's songs and admired his eloquence and patriotism. We had long conversations and talks on various subjects during the day

> and during our afternoon walks. ...But what delighted me was Vivekananda's singing. He had a musical and melodious voice and I was entranced by his songs. [And in his diary Mr. Sarda wrote of the Swami:] His discourses are most interesting to me. I greatly like him. He is a most pleasant companion. He will be something in the world if I err not greatly."[68]

Swamiji had not yet visited the whole India. He had to touch every part of his motherland. He wished to know the country, its glories, its discredits, and its joy and owe-everything should be in his knowledge and he wished to be acquainted with its variety of cultures. After spending about two weeks in this manner in Ajmer, Swamiji left for Gujarat.

IN WESTERN INDIA

Gujarat

Swamiji reached Ahmedabad, the largest city of Gujarat. After wandering for several days, living on alms, he was received as a guest by Lal Shankar Umia Shankar, a sub-judge of Ahmedabad District. During his stay here, Swamiji visited many places of historic interest. Previously this city was known as Karnavati, and used to be the capital of the Sultans of Gujarat, and came to be known as Ahmedabad. Once it was one of the handsomest cities in India. Tomas Row had compared this city with London. Once the Jainas had mastery over this place, and they had built many beautiful temples here. During Muslim reign many mosques and tombs were built.

Swamiji visited many places of historic interest, both in the city and in its vicinity. He was fascinated by the Jaina temples, and by the magnificence of Muslim culture as manifest in the mosques and tombs. He met many Jain scholars and through a friendly conversation acquired knowledge of Jainism.

After staying for few days in Ahmedabad, he went to Wadhwan in Kathiawar, where he visited the old temple of Ranik Devi. There is a story behind the building of this temple. The story runs thus: "Ranik Devi was a beautiful girl born in the Junagadh territory, when Raja Sidh was ruling Patan State. She was betrothed to him, but the ruler of Junagadh, Ra Khengar, was in love with her. He abducted and married her. This caused a deadly feud between the two chieftains. In time Raja Sidh invaded Junagadh and slew Ra Khengar. When Ranik Devi heard of the death of her husband, and of the invader's wish to marry her, she performed sati; that is, to protect her chastity she offered herself into fire at the cremation of her beloved husband. In her memory the brokenhearted conqueror raised the temple."[69] When Swamiji came to know the story of the temple, he could not but contemplate on the sanctity of the marriage relationship as viewed in the Hindu tradition.

Few days later Swamiji went on to Limbdi, the chief town of the cotton-producing State of that time. He begged his food from door to door, slept where he could get shelter, and lived where he got chance. As he arrived at Limbdi, he heard that there was a place where monks lived. When he reached the place, sadhus welcomed him warmly and urged him to stay with them as long as he wished. Swamiji was very much tired and hungry after his long journey. So, he didn't think of the environment of the place, and accepted the invitation. First two or three days passed in comfort. But after that he found that the inmates belonged to a degenerate group of sex-worshipers. He could hear the prayers and incantations of women as well as of men in the adjoining room. He realized that they were following an ugly culture in the name of spiritual practices, and also thought to leave the place immediately; but to his bafflement he found that he was locked in, and that a guard had been set to prevent his escape. He began to think of a plan to escape. The leader of the sect summoned him and said, "You are a monk with a magnetic personality. Evidently you have practiced Brahmacharya [celibacy] for years. Now you must give us fruit of your long austerity. We shall break your Brahmacharya in order to perform a special type of spiritual practice, and thereby acquire for ourselves certain psychic powers."

Swamiji was shaken with fear; but he didn't lose his presence of mind. So, he didn't show any sign of anxiety, and tried to take the matter lightly. "Now what to do?" Swamiji started thinking after he had been left alone in the room. While praying to the Mother of Universe he made up his mind and his whole personality shook with a terrible resolve, "Not even if they kill me, will I let them break my life long vows!"

Just then, the boy who used to deliver milk to him, and who had become his devotee at first sight, came there. When Swamiji told the boy of this situation, the boy asked him in a whisper if he could be of any help to him. Swamiji thought for a moment and then eagerly said "Yes! Yes! my boy." He had jumped to a sudden conclusion, and seizing a bit of charcoal lying near, he picked up a piece of earthen jar and scribbled as well as he could, few words about his sad plight then putting it into the boy's hand he said, "Here! Hide this beneath your chaddar and run with it as fast as you can to the Maharaja's palace and hand it over to the Maharaja himself and inform him of my situation." The boy hurried to the palace and managed to deliver the note to the Prince himself. The Prince immediately sent some of his guards to Swamiji's rescue. They rescued Swamiji and brought him to the Prince. The Prince invited him to stay in his palace, and Swamiji accepted the same gladly.

Now Swamiji came to stay in the palace of Maharaja. It was a beautiful palace built by Maharaja in 1881 under the supervision of Mr. Brush, the Engineer of Kathiawad Agency at a cost of ₹ 5 lacs from a prototype building plan of a typical town hall of an American city with a unique clock tower with musical chimes. Maharaja had brought special furniture from abroad and decorated the beautiful palace with the help of the famous artist Mr. Vanaruth, well-known all over the country in those days.

Swamiji stayed in this beautiful palace for many days and held discussion in Durbar hall of the palace with Maharaja Thakore Saheb of Limbdi, Shri Yashwantshinji (1859-1907) who was a brilliant, learned and cultured prince. He was the first Kathiawar Chief to visit England (in 1876). During his second trip to England he took part in the Jubilee Celebration of Her Majesty the Queen Empress in 1887, who with her own hands bestowed upon him the decoration of K.C.I.E. He had also visited America. President Cleveland warmly greeted the Maharaja at the White House in Washington DC. Thakore Saheb described in detail what he had learnt from his visits to England and America and requested Swamiji to go to these countries for preaching Sanatana Dharma. Thakore Saheb of Limbdi was the first among the Maharajas to inspire Swamiji to go to the West for preaching work.

Swamiji discussed various topics with Thakore Saheb. Both were young (Thakore Saheb was about four years older than Swamiji. He was born on 23-5-1859) and soon both became intimate friends. Thakore Saheb was astonished to find that Swamiji's knowledge was not only limited to spiritual matters but his extraordinary brilliance could comprehend almost any subject on earth. Swamiji too, started to admire the extra-ordinary genius of Thakore Saheb who did much in the cause of education. Thakore Saheb was of the firm opinion that for the regeneration of India to take place, Indian women must be educated. His adroit handing of the difficult problems that arise between the ruler and the ruled, and his ability to express his views in good English, attracted the attention of His Excellency Sir James Fergusson, who offered him a seat in the local Legislative council. Thakore Saheb, performed his duties in such an efficient manner that His Excellency Lord Reay wrote:

> "My dear friend, now that your term of office in the Legislative Council has expired, I write to say how sorry I am. The Government will be deprived in the future of your service and I must be permitted to add that in you Kathiawar had a most worthy representative."

Efficient in administration and a great philanthropist at heart, he was a pious man, a true Rajarshi. English writer John Houston wrote about him:

> "The purity of his life has elicited for him the title, "Great Janaka" who was an ornament in bygone ages and was endowed with great wisdom."

Most of the discussions between Swamiji and Thakore Saheb were presumably on spiritual matters because Thakore Saheb was a highly spiritual man. He used to spend a lot of time reading and discussing about religion and philosophy. He had already studied a great many Hindu scriptures as well as books of Western writers. Moreover, Thakore Saheb had no children and his younger brother had passed away on 25-8-1891 (just three months before he met Swamiji) so he was in a solemn and receptive mood to discuss about spiritual matters. Having been charmed with the spiritual power of Swamiji, he took mantra-diksha and became his disciple.

During his stay at Limbdi, Swamiji held many discussions in Sanskrit with the local Pundits. His Holiness the Sankaracharya of the Govardhan Math, Puri, had seen this. He was dumbfounded at the young monk's learning, and at his breadth of understanding and sympathy.

After a short stay at Limbdi, Swamiji set out for Junagadh. Thakore Saheb, the Prince of Limbdi, entreated Swamiji to be cautious on his solitary wanderings, and gave him letters of introduction to his friends there and elsewhere. These letters helped him to visit Bhavnagar and Sihor on his way to Junagadh. At Junagadh he was the guest of Haridas Viharidas Desai, the Dewan of the State. The Dewan was charmed with his company and every evening he, with all the State officials, used to meet Swamiji and talked with him on spiritual matters. This conversation would continue until late at night. Swamiji also showed him respect, and a good friendship grew between them which continued for a long time. Swamiji wrote him letters regularly from America. During conversation Swamiji would speak about history and culture of India. Once he spoke of Jesus Christ. He said that he had long since come to understand the influence of Christ in regenerating the ethics of the Western world. With his fiery eloquence, he went on to relate how all the medieval greatness of Europe—the paintings of Raphael, the devotion of Saint Francis of Assisi, the Gothic cathedrals, the Crusades, the political systems of the West, its monastic orders and its religions life—all were interwoven in one way or another with the teachings of the sannyasi Christ. He went on to narrate the excellences of the Sanatan Dharma, and then in a patriotic spirit, made clear to them the nature and extent of the influence exerted by Hinduism on the Western religious imagination, and showed how Central and Western Asia was the scene of this interracial exchanges of ideas. He brought out the values for which their own culture stood, and the essential worth of the Hindu experience in the development of spiritual ideas throughout the world. He also criticized the Christian clergymen who couldn't follow the renunciation of Jesus Christ, but tried to destroy the culture of India. Swamiji also told them about the life and teaching of the Saint of Dakshineswar; and thus Sri Ramakrishna came to be known and appreciated in those distant parts. At Junagadh he had long discussion with many orthodox Hindu pundits. He advised them to respect their own religion.

We have already seen him, while he was in Alwar, revealing as a teacher. We saw him teaching the religious matters along with western science and history to the people at Alwar and Khetri. Here in Junagadh we saw him as a pioneer of the resurrection of Indian culture. He had sharply censured them who were engaged in making the history of India scandalous.

Shri Chhaganlal Harilal Pandya, the manager of the Dewan's office at Junagadh, became a staunch admirer of Swamiji. Swamiji had stayed in his house for a time. He had explained his experience of that time:

> "The Swami's simplicity of life, his unostentatiousness, his profound knowledge of various arts and sciences, his catholicity of views and his devotion to religion, his stirring eloquence and his magnetic powers and extraordinary personality, influenced all of us in Junagadh. Added to these qualities he possessed a great proficiency in music and was conversant with all forms of Indian art.

Ay, withal he was even an artist of the cuisine and could prepare excellent rasogollas (a kind of sweet of Bengal). We were devoted to him."

While giving his opinion about a book on Shri Ramakrishna (in Gujarati) Shri Pandya wrote (in Gujarati) in his letter dated 2-3-1918 to the publisher, "I heard directly from Swami Vivekananda as to how much joy he derived while listening to the nectar-like words of Shri Ramakrishna, how he received special grace of Shri Ramakrishna and how due to his overwhelming love and faith towards him it was possible for him to acquire Brahmavidya. I spent a long time with him at Junagadh."

While giving his opinion about the book of Swami Vivekananda in Gujarati, he wrote (in Gujarati) in his letter dated 9.10.1921 to the publisher, "I had the blessed privilege of coming in contact with Swami Vivekananda, therefore he himself had told me many things about his life... I had come to know as to how many difficulties he had to face for keeping up his vows of Brahmacharya. And when I think, with how much simplicity and humility he used to stay with us, in spite of being such a great scholar, feelings of great regard inevitably fill my mind."

After teaching the people of Junagadh Swamiji went to Girnar, a place of pilgrimage, sacred to Buddhists, Jainas, and Hindus because of its association with the tradition of all three religions. It is about two miles from Junagadh. It is a group of some ten hills, the highest of which, known as Gorakhnath, is about 3,600 feet. Climbing starts from Girnar Teleti. There are more than 10,000 steps cut in the rock, leading to the many Jaina and Hindu temples built on different hills. Swamiji climbed many hills, and visited the Ashoka Stone, on which the Edicts of the Emperor Ashoka and of two other emperors are engraved. There he saw an old Rajput palace, two ancient wells, and the Khapra Khodia caves dating back to the Buddhist period and perhaps used as monasteries. He found a solitary cave, where he practiced meditation for few days. How many hills he climbed is not known to us clearly. While he was there at Girnar, the Dewan took all possible care of him. This is known from the letter Swamiji wrote to him from Girnar:

> "Very kind of you to send up a man inquiring about my health and comfort. But that's quite of a piece with your fatherly character. I am all right here. Your kindness has left nothing more to be desired here. I hope soon to see you in a few days. I don't require any conveyance while going down. Descent is very bad, and the ascent is the worst part of the job, that's the same in everything in the world. My heartfelt gratitude to you. Yours faithfully, Vivekananda."[70] The signature to the letter shows that at Junagadh he used his name as 'Vivekananda'.

Swamiji visited Junagadh many times. During one of the trips he had also stayed with Shri Mansukhram Tripathi, the well-known writer and scholar of Gujarat, a man of high character, who preferred higher values of life. Had he possessed ambition for public and civic honours, his high qualities would have been the means of gratifying it, but being a man of studious disposition he was reluctant to accept honours even if thrust upon him. Owing to these traits of his character he was able to enrich the vernacular literature of India by his contribution in literary, and philosophical subjects through the medium of Gujarati. Swamiji must have enjoyed the company of his host (although he was 23 years elder to him) their common interest being Vedanta. We get confirmation about Swamiji's stay with Shri Mansukhram Tripathi from the account given by Swami Abhedananda in his auto-biography.

"On arrival at Junagadh, I came to hear from people that a Bengali sannyasi with high English education was staying for some days at the house of Mansukhram Suryaram Tripathi, a Gujarati Brahmin, who was the Private Secretary of the local Nawab.... Elated with joy I reached the house of Mansukhram...by enquiry and immediately found that my conjecture was true. Narendranath brightened up with joy to see me unexpectedly. I too could not check my tears to meet him after a long time. Fortunately when I arrived there Narendranath was discussing some topic of non-dualistic Vedanta with Mr. Tripathi.... Mr. Tripathi requested me with courtesy to take rest and sent an order in his house for arranging food for me along with Narendranath.... I gladly stayed in his house for three or four days in the company of Narendranath, and then I got ready to start for Dwarka."[71]

We have noticed that Swamiji spent much of his time in the palaces of Princes of India or with their Dewans. Questions may naturally arise that why did he do so or why did he need any letter of introduction. In reply to these questions Swamiji said that his intention was to influence the princes, and by turning their attention to the religious life, thus to ensure that they were true to their duties, that is, government for the good of the people. They had the power to inaugurate reformation in many fields in the society. They could improve systems of education, establish and foster charitable institutions in their territories. "If I can win over to my cause those in whose power are wealth and the administration of the affairs of thousands, my mission will be accomplished all the sooner; by influencing one Maharaja alone I can indirectly benefit thousands of people." This was the reason of his residing in palaces. We have also seen him many times walking alone without food or taking food from poor devotee's house. Swamiji had tremendous power of intellect and many other good qualities which could easily help him in making both money and reputation in place of the earth. Whatever he did, was only to accomplish his mission for the good of the people.

Shortly after returning from Girnar to Junagadh, Swamiji decided to move again. He proceeded towards Kutch with a letter of introduction from Dewanji Saheb to his bosom friend Motichand Lalchand, Dewanji of Bhuj. Bhuj was the capital of Kutch, situated at the base of a fortified hill on the northern side of the Rann of Kutch. Swamiji stayed with the Dewanji of Bhuj who introduced him to the Maharaja and had long talks with him, both upon the industrial, agricultural and economic problems of the land. He impressed upon them the need for ameliorating the condition of the masses as he had a great faith in the ability of the rulers to do good to their subjects if they could be taught about the ancient Indian ideals of civil government.

Several years later, when the Dewan of Kutch was visited by a disciple of Swamiji, he recalled the extraordinary intellect of Swamiji, his gracious personality, and his power of preaching in such a simple way that all who met him were fascinated.

Maharaja of Kutch—Khengarji Bahadur was one of the most cultured, advanced and enlightened native rulers of India, who had the honour of an audience with Her Majesty during his visit to England (1887) who on this occasion conferred upon him the title of Rao, the Knight Grand Commander of the Indian Empire. He took keenest interest in the subject of female education, got many standard English works translated into Gujarati and carried out considerable improvement in public works.

Swamiji afterwards went to Mandvi when Maharaja of Bhuj made all arrangement for his pilgrimage to various places in Kutch-Narayan Sarovar, Ashapura (Devi Temple), etc.

Later when Swamiji was again at Bhuj with his brother-disciple Swami Akhandananda, he told him, "The Raja is paying us too much attention and that may be an eyesore to many if we stay here long. Twenty five years ago a Bengali sannyasin named Ananda Ashrama came to Bhuj and helped much in the improvement of the State. But such reforms did not find favour in the eyes of the State officers. Ananda Ashrama became their eyesore. His enemies mixed poison with his food and killed him. We may have the same fate. Let us move off even tomorrow."

After returning from his first visit to Bhuj he came back to Junagadh, and took rest for a few days. But he had not much time in hand for having rest or enjoying the life on the earth. He had a mission that he had to fulfil at any cost. Hence he became restless and went on to Veraval and Patan Somnath, popularly known as Prabhas. Sir Henry Elliot records that 10,000 populated villages were held by Somnath temple as an endowment and that 300 musicians were attached to it. There were also 300 barbers to shave the heads of the pilgrims. Several times this temple was destroyed and several times rebuilt. Swamiji paused by this great ruin and pondered over the greatness that had been India's in the past. According to tradition, here Krishna is supposed to have left a mortal body at the end of Krishna avatar (Avatars), enacting the drama of being killed by a hunter who mistook Krishna for a deer and shot him in his foot. He realised that in India religious life forms the centre, the keynote of the whole music of national life. Later (in 1897) he was to address his countrymen, "Some of these old temples of Southern India and those like Somnath of Gujarat will teach you volumes of wisdom, will give you a keener insight into the history of the race than any amount of books." Today at the same spot stands the magnificent renovated temple of Somnath. How happy Swamiji would have been to see it? Or who knows, perhaps he saw it in his mental vision or perhaps it is the fulfilment of his vision!

After seeing the ruins of Somnath temple, the Suraj Mandir, and the new temple of Shiva built by Rani Ahalyabai of Indore (just near Somnath temple) Swamiji bathed at the confluence of three rivers. Being three years younger than Swamiji, Maharaja of Kutch must have entered into intimate friendship with him. During Swamiji's visit to Prabhas he again met Swamiji and had long conversation with him. Maharaja was deeply impressed by Swamiji's magnetic personality and was astonished at his vast knowledge. He used to say: "Swamiji, as after reading may books the head becomes dazed, even so after hearing your discourses my brain becomes dizzy. How will you utilise this talent? You will never rest until you have done wonderful things!"

After a brief stay at Veraval Swamiji returned to Junagadh and leaving it the third time, he came to Porbandar with a letter of introduction to the Administrator Shri Shankar Pandurang Pandit. After Swamiji had visited the ancient temple of Sudama, Shri Shankar Pandurang Pandit introduced him to the Maharaja who took an instant liking to him and urged him to dwell in the palace.

The Dewan, Pandit Shankar Pandurang was a great Vedic scholar and was at that time translating the Vedas. Being acquainted with the wisdom of Swamiji, he often asked his help to explain some of the more abstruse passages of the Vedas. Swamiji helped him with his lucidity. At the request of the Dewan he stayed at Porbandar for some days to help him with his book. He finished his reading of Patanjali's *Mahabhashya* on Panini's *Sutras* and also took up the study of French at the instance of the Dewan, who said, "It will be of use to you, Swamiji."

As he came to appreciate the intellect, liberality and originality of Swamiji's ideas, Pandit Shankar Pandurang said, "Swamiji, I am afraid you cannot do much in this country. Few will appreciate you here. You ought to go to the West where people will understand you and your worth. Surely you can throw a great light upon Western culture by preaching the Sanatan Dharma!" Swamiji was glad to hear these words, for he too had a similar plan, which he had expressed to C.H. Pandya (Shri Chhaganlal Harilal Pandya) at Junagadh.

We remember, once Sri Ramakrishna said that Naren had power enough in him to revolutionize the world. Swamiji was beginning to feel this truth. Since he had left the Baranagor Math, he had been preparing himself to reach his goal. Day by day he was growing stronger. Wherever he travelled and all the courts he visited, the princes and pundits noticed in him "terrible restlessness" to do something for his country. He was beginning to believe that it was necessary to give the world a jerk for taking the people out of the dark of ignorance. The idea uppermost in his mind was the spiritual regeneration of India. He saw the limitations of orthodoxy and those of the reformers too. Everywhere he found petty jealousies, hostility, and lack of harmony. He saw India, potentially supreme, glorious, and rich with its own ancient culture, being degraded by the stupid activities of the so-called "leaders"—demagogues who preached reforms which they were unable to comprehend into their own lives, and who, blinded by the glare of a foreign culture and its momentary power, were trying to throw overboard the experience of the race. He announced a new order of things to the Indian Princes and pundits. His eloquence made them feel that he was a genius, and a man of realization gifted with an irresistible personality. He felt that he should preach the glories of the Sanatan Dharma to the West, and explain them the philosophies of Vedas which the Aryan Rishis had thought out. He also realized that India was truly the Mother of Religions, the fountainhead of spirituality, and the cradle of civilization. He was waiting for the right time and opportunity to leave for a foreign tour.

When Swamiji was at Porbandar a curious thing happened. Swami Trigunatita had been wandering round the pilgrimages. He came from Gujarat to Porbandar, and was staying with some other wandering monks. They wanted to make the pilgrimage to Hinglaj, but it was a tough journey of many miles, and they were weary and had footsore. So they thought of travelling to Karachi by steamer and thence to Hinglaj by camel. But they didn't have money. They were at a loss what to do, when one of the group said, "There is a learned Paramahamsa stopping with the Dewan of Porbandar. He speaks English fluently and is accounted a great scholar. Let Swami Trigunatita go and interview him. Perhaps the Mahatma [great soul] will intercede with the Dewan for us so that our expenses may be paid."

One evening while Swamiji was pacing on the parapeted roof of the palace, he suddenly saw a group of monks proceeding towards the palace. But when he saw his brother-disciple Swami Trigunatitananda among them, he felt a sudden thrill passing through his body, and he went to the ground floor to receive him. But he controlled himself and in an attempt to cast off the golden chain of attachment to his brother-disciple he assumed an attitude of indifference. Noticing this, Swami Trigunatitananda putting aside his joy, told that he had come not to disturb him but only to seek help from an unknown learned monk staying with the Maharaja for pilgrimage to Hinglaj. At first Swamiji dismissed his appeal but later his heart softened and he helped him and his friends while urging him never to follow him again even if he had the slightest suspicion of where he was. Then Swami Trigunatitananda took leave of him and went to the Hatkeswar Shiva temple, where the other monks were waiting for him.

Next morning, while Swami Trigunatitananda was engaged in packing his baggage, Swamiji reached there and took him to the palace of the Dewan. After two days, at the time of departure, Swamiji said to him, "Never say to anyone of the Math, especially to Akhandananda, that I am staying here."

More information about Swamiji in Porbandar has recently been gathered from a centenarian named Acharya Revashankar Anupama Dave, who vividly remembers the happenings of this period. "He had the opportunity of observing and talking with Swamiji when the later was the guest of the Dewan Shankar Pandurang Pandit. Mr. Dave was then a young boy of sixteen. He used to frequent the Dewan's house and the guest-house with his friend Madhav, who had free access there. According to his statement, Swamiji used to stay in the Bhojeshwar Bungalow. His room was in the north-west corner of the building and was reached by turning right at the main staircase. He remembers that the Swami talked mostly in Hindi, but at times many Bengali and Sanskrit words used to creep in. On one occasion, at the request of the Swami, the students of the Sanskrit school were brought to him, among whom were Revashankar, Govindji, and others. The Swami asked Govindji, "How far have you studied?" Govindji replied, "I went to Benaras and have studied the Sama-Veda. I have learnt six Mantras [Shastras?]." The Swami asked him, "Why did you not study further? Why did you come back?" Govindji replied, "I happened to have Karelu; so I had to come back." On hearing the word "Karelu" the Swami had a hearty laugh, and the place seemed to vibrate with it. "Karelu" means bitter gourd, but the boy had meant that he had had an attack of cholera. Then the Swami asked him to recite some Shlokas (verses), which he did. Next, he asked Revashankar, "What are you studying?" Revashankar replied, "*Panchatantra and Aesop's Niti Katha* [Fables]", and recited a verse from each. Swamiji smiled and seemed to be pleased with him. Then the Swami went for a walk. Revashankar remembers that he used to go for walks in the desert of Bhojeshwar with the Dewan. The Swami always had his staff with him, and the Dewan a spear."

After staying at Porbandar for few days Swamiji took a leave of all and set out for Dwarka, holy with memories and legends of Sri Krishna. But of its glories nothing remains at present. Now the ocean roars in tumult over the place where once the powerful Yadava lived and where once stood a great capital of which Shri Krishna was the reigning prince. Gazing all over the ocean, waves of agony raised in the mind of Swamiji at the thought that nothing but ruins remained of great India. He sat on the shore and yearned for fathoming the contents of the future. Then rising as from a dream he went to Sharada Math (a monastery founded by Adi Shankaracharya) where he was assigned a room. There in the silence of his cell, he saw a great light—the resplendent future of India.

We remember that, at the time of Swamiji's departure from Delhi, Akhandananda had said to him, "Even if you go to the nether world, I shall hunt you out." The story of his hunt throws light on the route of wandering Swamiji. At Jaipur, Akhandananda came to know that Swamiji had gone to Ajmer, after staying for few days at Khetri. When he reached Ajmer, he learnt that Swamiji had gone towards Ahmedabad. On his way Akhandananda passed through Beawar, where he learnt that Swamiji had been there, but had returned to Ajmer some time before. However, Akhandananda went on to Ahmedabad, thinking that Swamiji would be going there; but there he learnt that Swamiji had left for Wadhwan. At Wadhwan, he came to know that Swamiji was staying at Junagadh with the Dewan. Akhandananda left for Junagadh, and on reaching there he learnt that Swamiji had left four days previously for Dwarka via Porbandar. On reaching Dwarka he came to know that Swamiji had left for Beyt Dwarka. Akhandananda halted the night at Dwarka, and next day went to Beyt Dwarka; but there he learnt that Swamiji had left for Mandvi in Kutch, on invitation from the Maharaja. Akhandananda went to Mandvi, and heard that Swamiji had gone to Narayan Sarovar, which was eighty miles away. At Mandvi, Akhandananda was cordially received by the Mahant. Swami Akhandananda was warned at Mandvi that the road to Narayan Sarovar was infested with dacoits. But heedless of danger he sped on. On the way he was beaten and robbed by dacoits. At Narayan Sarovar he learnt that the journey to the place, which might have cost him his life, had been fruitless for he was told that Swamiji had left for Mandvi via Ashapuri, a place of pilgrimage. The road lay through desert wastes and was also infested with dacoits and it meant a journey for a hundred miles, yet he heroically marched on in spite of having fallen sick. The Mahant gave him a horse and a guide for going to Ashapuri. There he heard that Swamiji had gone towards Mandvi. Fate at long last looked with a kindly eye at Swami Akhandananda. For after reaching Mandvi this time, he learnt that Swamiji was indeed there staying in the house of a merchant belonging to the Bhatia community.

On reaching Bhatia's house Swami Akhandananda was overwhelmed with the joy to meet Swamiji at last. He was surprised to see a change in Swamiji's face which had a sublime radiance. Swamiji was also astonished and no less glad to meet his beloved brother-disciple but when he heard the story of his chasing him, he got worried that his brother-disciple would not leave him alone as he had come all the way at the risk of his life. He said to Akhandananda, "Look, I have a mission; and if you remain with me, I shall not be able to fulfil it." But Akhandananda was not ready to leave Swamiji alone. It may have been because the Holy Mother had told him on the eve to their departure from Calcutta, "I am leaving my all [Swamiji] in your hands. See that Naren does not suffer on the way for want of food."

Swamiji then told Swami Akhandananda, "Look I have become a spoiled man. You leave me." Swami Akhandananda replied, "What would it matter to me even if you had lost your character? I love you, and that is not in any way affected by your good or bad character. But I do not wish to be in your way. I had a longing to see you, and now I am satisfied. Now you can go alone." Swamiji was happy to hear this and next day left for Bhuj, which Swami Akhandananda reached a day later.

At Bhuj, they stayed for two days. Both of them then went back to Mandvi and halted for a fortnight. There Swamiji made many friends. From there Swamiji went to Porbandar. Swami Akhandananda joined him at Porbandar after about a week and after spending a few days at Porbandar he went to Jamnagar via Jetpur, Gondal, Rajkot and thus spent about a year in Kathiawad. From Porbandar Swamiji alone went to Junagadh.

Swamiji visited Porbandar twice. According to Swami Shivananda, it was the large beautiful library of Shri Sankar Pandurang Pandit which had attracted Swamiji's special notice when he had come to Porbandar at the time of his earlier visit and that Panditji had requested him to stay as long as he liked at his place and utilize the library. Swamiji had consented to do so and hence he came again to Porbandar and this time stayed for about four months. His earlier visit was a short one as confirmed from the autobiography of Swami Abhedananda. During his travels Swami Abhedananda had come to Porbandar and learnt from Shankar Pandurang Pandit that a few days back an English-knowing Bengali Sannyasi named Swami Sachchidananda had come there on a flying visit. Later he found out that he was none other than Swami Vivekananda.

Pandit Shankar Pandurang (1840-94) of Konkan was not only a Sanskrit scholar of eminence, but he was a man of affairs being at the time in high favour with the government. After his return from England in 1874, he was appointed Oriental Translator in Bombay Government as he was proficient in nine languages. In 1886, he was appointed as Registrar in Bombay High Court and shortly afterwards the administrator of Porbandar. Apart from editing 'Atharvaveda' and 'Raghuvansha' of Kalidas he started a journal 'Vedarthyatra' for propagation of Rigveda. His numerous Sanskrit works were appreciated by great scholars all over the world. Prof. Max Mueller had said, "The editions of Sanskrit text published at Bombay by Prof. Bhandarkar and Mr. S.P. Pandit and others need not fear comparison with the best works of European scholars."

Apart from this, he was a great philanthropist. He arranged for irrigation facilities for farmers, started telegraph offices all over the State of Porbandar, started schools for girls as he was a staunch supporter of female education, opened hospitals in the villages and carried out various works for the benefit of the public.

During his long stay at Porbandar Swamiji became very intimate with Pandit Shankar Pandurang and his family. He used to ride with Panditji on horse back to have a look at the distant villages. Being an artist of the cuisine he taught the wife of Panditji, Ushadevi, various delicious preparations. Two sons of Panditji—Madhav and Vaman played with him, learnt swimming from him and became great friends of Swamiji. Three daughters Tara, Kshama and Bhadra who were at first shy, received greater affection and blessings of Swamiji.

Swamiji told about his travelling in Western India: "Once I was travelling in the desert country on the coast of the Indian Ocean. For days and days I used to travel on foot through the desert, but it was to my surprise that I saw every day beautiful lakes, with trees all around them, and the shadows of the trees upside down and vibrating there. "How wonderful it looks and they call this a desert country!" I said to myself. Nearly a month I travelled, seeing these wonderful lakes and trees and plants. One day I was very thirsty and wanted to have a drink of water, so I started to go to one of these clear, beautiful lakes, and as I approached, it vanished. And with a flash it came to my brain, "This is the mirage about which I have read all my life," and with that came also the idea that throughout the whole of this month, every day, I had been seeing the mirage and did not know it. The next morning I began my march. There was again the lake, but with it came also the idea that it was the mirage and not a true lake."[72]

With reference to this experience he said: "So is it with this universe. We are all travelling in this mirage of the world day after day, month after month, year after year, not knowing that it is a mirage. One day it will break up, but it will come back again; the body has to remain under the power of past Karma, and so the mirage will come back. This world will come back upon us so long as we are bound by Karma: men, women, animals, plants, our attachments and duties, all will come back to us, but not with the same power. Under the influence of the new knowledge the strength of Karma will be broken; its poison will be lost. It becomes transformed, for along with it there comes the idea that we know it now, that the sharp distinction between the reality and the mirage has been known."[73]

Next we find Swamiji at Palitana in Gujarat, where the holy mountain Shatrunjaya, sacred to the Jainas, is situated. Palitana is a city of temples many of which date back to the eleventh century. High up on Shatrunjaya mountain sacred to the Jains, is a temple dedicated to Hanuman and a shrine dedicated to Hengar, a Muslim saint. According to Mr. James Fergusson, "The number of temples and small shrines number over 500. It is a city of the Gods and meant for them only. All the peculiarities of Jain Architecture are found in more marked degree at Palitana than at almost any other known place." Swamiji climbed to the top of the mountain to enjoy the view which is magnificent.

At Palitana Swamiji drew the attention of people because of his mastery of singing and playing on instruments. During his stay at Palitana, Shri Chunilal Sarabhai, Dewan of Palitana, had once invited him for meals.

From Palitana Swamiji started for Baroda; but how could he avoid going to Nadiad on the way—which was the home town of his friends Shri Haridas Viharidas Desai, Shri Chhaganlal Pandya and Shri Manasukhram Tripathi? During his short stay here he met Shri Manilal Nabhubhai Dwivedi, the well-known Gujarati writer. His life (1858-1898) was spent in writing many books in Gujarati, English and Sanskrit including 'Imitation of Shankara', 'Rajayoga', 'Siddhanta Sar', 'Bhagavad Gita', etc. He could not go to Chicago Parliament of Religions but his paper was read out there. He was one of the pioneers in spreading Advaita Vedanta in Gujarat hence Swamiji must have enjoyed his company at Nadiad by holding discussions on Vedanta.

From Nadiad, Swamiji came finally to Baroda before leaving Gujarat for Bombay, with a letter of introduction from Dewanji Saheb addressed to his intimate friend Shri Manibhai J. Dewan of Baroda, who was a man of piety and noble character. In 1884-85, he had received the title of Dewan Bahadur from the Government of India along with a medal and gift of ₹ 75,000 while he was the Dewan of Kutch. In Kutch he introduced great and beneficial reform in all departments—collection of revenue, education, sanitation, etc.

At Baroda Dewan Shri Manibhai worked hard and there was spectacular progress in the field of education. Swamiji spent some time with him in discussing about the education system of the State. Swamiji wrote from Baroda on 26th April 1892 to Dewanji Saheb of Junagadh, "I had not the least difficulty in reaching your house from the station Nadiad. And your brothers, they are what they should be, your brothers. May the Lord shower his choicest blessings on your family. I have never found such a glorious one in all my travels. Your friend Mr. Manibhai has provided every comfort for me; but as to his company, I have only seen him twice; once for a minute, the other time for ten minutes at the most when he talked about the system of education here. Of course, I have seen the Library and the pictures of Ravi Varma, and that is about all worth seeing here. So I am going off this evening to Bombay. My thanks to the Dewanji here (or to you) for his kind behaviour. More from Bombay."[74]

Curiously enough, there is no mention in the above letter about Swamiji's meeting with Maharaja Sayajirao Gaekwad. Swamiji had told Prince Martand Varma at Trivandrum that "of all the ruling princes he had met, he had been most impressed with the capacity, patriotism, energy and foresight of H.H. the Gaekwad of Baroda." Swamiji was also perhaps impressed with the Maharani of Gaekwad because he wrote on 17.2.1901 to Miss MacLeod from Belur Math "I hope you will go to Baroda and see Maharani" However, the State records reveal that Maharaja was not in Baroda at the time of Swamiji. He had gone to place called Lonavali (Lonavala?) In all probability Swamiji met him while he was in Mahabaleshwar or Poona. After his return from the West, Swamiji wanted to visit Baroda and meet the Maharaja but it did not materialize.

It appears from the above letter that Swamiji next went to Baroda, the capital of the Gaekwad of Baroda. There he stayed for a short time with Bahadur Manibhai J., one of the minister of the State and a man of piety and noble character. Then, on hearing that the Thakore Saheb of Limbdi was at Mahabaleshwar, he went there to see the prince. V.R. Joshi, in his life of the

Thakore Saheb, writes: "One 24 April 1892, Namdar Thakore Saheb Sri Jasvant Singhji visited Mahabaleshwar. There he stayed for about three months. During this period he had the company of Swami Sri Vivekananda and on several occasions he discussed the subject of philosophy and self-knowledge." From the personal diary (Nondh-Pothi) of the Thakore Saheb, which is published in the same life, it seems that Swamiji reached Mahabaleshwar at the end of April or beginning of May 1892, and that he remained there until the middle of June. The relevant entries in the diary of Thakore Saheb run as follows:

> 4 and 5 May 1892: I have deeply pondered over the discussion which took place four days ago on reincarnation, and have also referred to several books on that subject. 9-11th May: I am pleasantly surprised at Swami Sri Vivekananda's deep knowledge of the Shastras. Whatever knowledge of the Shastras I had, has been much increased through discussions with him. 12 May: At the end of yesterday's discussion it was proved that in ancient times the caste system was based only upon Guna (qualities) and Karma (work).... 18 May: There was a considerable discussion on Adharma or sin. Any action contrary to the ten characteristics (Lakshanas) of Dharma is to be considered as Adharma, that is, sin. Such actions are of three kinds—Bodily, oral and mental. 23 May: Different dispositions of men are caused due to the effect of Satva, Rajas and Tamas... 25 May: Swami Sri Vivekananda has stated that Jivas, Ishvara and Maya are beginningless (Anadi), but according to Vivekananda, Prakriti and Purusha are beginningless and the effect caused by their combination is the Jiva; I believe his opinion to be better.

Apart from his discussions with the Thakore Saheb, Swamiji created a sensation at Mahabaleshwar. Narashimha Chintaman Kelkar, sometime editor of the Maratha of Poona, wrote about Swamiji's visit:

> In 1892, he (Swamiji) had come to our Bombay-Poona side; but he had not become well known then. I was at that time preparing for my LL.B. examination. In summer some pleaders had gone to Mahabaleshwar. On their return they said that they had had an opportunity to see a brilliant Bengali sannyasi there. His command of the English language was wonderful, which used to spellbind the hearers, and his philosophical interpretations were vey lofty befitting a genius. They also said that they had invited the Swami to Satara, but till the end he could not go there, and I also could not see him then.

While Swamiji was at Mahabaleshwar, he was encountered by Abhedananda, who went there from Bombay. The letter writes in his autobiography:

> After having seen Bombay, I went from there to Mahabaleshwar. I heard that Narottam Morarji Gokuldas was a hospitable gentleman in Mahabaleshwar. I went to Gokuldas's house by enquiry and on arrival there I found that Narendranath had already arrived there.... Seeing me Narendranath said with laughter, 'Brother, why are you on my trail for nothing? Both of us have come out with the name of the Master. We had better travel independently.' At this I said, 'Why should I pursue you? I have come here, as you too have, in course of my wanderings. Through the will of the Master we have met again. I assure you that I am not deliberately after you.' Narendranath reacted with loud laughter.... At the request of Gokuldasji, however, I spent three days at his house with Narendranath and on the fourth day I resolved to set out for Poona.

After about two and a half months at Mahabaleshwar, Swamiji left for Poona with the Thakore Saheb. In his letter of June 15, to Haridasbhai, the Dewan of Junagadh, he wrote, "I came down with the Thakore Saheb of Mahabaleshwar, and I am living here with him. I would remain here a week or two more and then proceed to Rameswaram via Hyderabad." The address on this letter was given at Ellapa Balaram's House, C/o Thakore of Limbdi, Neutral Line, Poona. It means the Thakore Saheb had an accommodation at this address. One day he made a request to Swamiji, "Swamiji, do come with me to Limbdi and remain there for good." But Swamiji replied, "Not now, Your Highness. For I have work to do. I cannot rest now. But if ever I live the life of retirement it shall be with you." But before he could carry out this intention, he passed away in the midst of his work.

From his another letter of June 1892 to the Dewan Saheb of Junagadh, it is found that instead of going to Rameswaram via Hyderabad, Swamiji went to Khandwa. As there was no one known to him, he was walking here and there. Walking through the town, he came across the residence of Babu Haridas Chatterjee, a pleader. When the gentleman returned from court, he found Swamiji standing at his door. At the first look he took him as an ordinary monk, who wanders here and there. But after a little talk he realized that this monk was the most learned man he had ever met. He invited him to stay at his house, and treated him as a member of the family. Swamiji was there for about three weeks, and during this time he went on a brief visit of Indore, about forty miles north to Khandwa. Most probably he went to visit the Ujjain, an ancient city situated on the eastern bank of the Shipra River, and to the places of pilgrimage on the bank of the Narmada River. He became dizzy from exhaustion and could not walk any more. The sun was intolerably hot. Managing to reach a tree nearby, he sat down beneath it. A sense of unutterable fatigue came over his limbs. Then, as light shines in the darkness, the thought came to him, "Is it not true that within the Soul resides all power? How can it be dominated by the senses and the body? How can I be weak?" Suddenly he gained energy through his body. His mind was flooded with light; his senses revived. He rose and walked on, determined that he would never again yield to weakness. Many times he had faced a similar condition during his wandering life; but he asserted his higher nature, and strength flowed back to him. Later in one of his lectures in California, Swamiji said:

> Many times I have been in the jaws of death, starving, footsore, and weary; for days and days I had no food, and often could walk no farther; I would sink down under a tree, and life would seem to be ebbing away. I could not speak, I could scarcely think, but at last the mind reverted to the idea: 'I have no fear nor death; never was I born, never did I die; I never hunger or thirst. I am it! I am it! The whole of nature cannot crush me; it is my servant. Assert thy strength, thou Lord of lords and God of gods! Regain thy lost empire! Arise and walk and stop not!' And I would rise up, reinvigorated; and here I am today, living! Thus, whenever darkness comes, assert the reality, and everything adverse must vanish. For, after all, it is but a dream. Mountain-high though the difficulties appear, terrible and gloomy though all things seem, they are but Maya. Fear not, and it is banished. Crush it, and it vanishes. Stamp upon it, and it dies.

Many were the times when Swamiji had to face danger, hardship and want in solitude—with nothing in his possession save perhaps a photograph of Sri Ramakrishna and a copy of the Gita. In central India he had many bitter experiences because people refused to give him food and shelter. In that period he lived with a family of the sweeper caste and saw the priceless worth potentialities that could be found among those who are rejected by the society. It made him realize the distressing condition of his country. Everywhere he saw poverty and misery, and his heart was overwhelmed with compassion.

During this time Swamiji felt that going from place to place and begging for food from door to door was not his aim for the realization of which he had renounced his home. In a letter written about this time to one of his brother-disciples he said disconsolately, "I am going about taking food at other's houses shamelessly and without the least compunction, like a crow.... Let me beg no longer! What benefit is it to the poor to feed me? If they can save a handful of rice, they can feed their own children with it. Anyway, what is the use of sustaining this body if I cannot realize God?" A desperate spiritual dissatisfaction and ascetic mood came upon him. The same thing is found to happen with great souls, who renounce the world for realizing the Truth. In this moment of despair he determined to plunge into the forest and, like some Rishi of old, let the body drop from starvation and exhaustion. While walking through a thick forest he did not have any food. Evening approached. Almost fainted and fatigued, he sank to the ground beneath a tree, fixing his mind on the Lord, and looking vacantly into the distance.

After some time he saw a tiger approaching towards him. He realized that there was no way to escape. He was too tired to walk. He remained silent gazing at the tiger when it stopped at a distant of about ten yards. He thought, "Ah! This is right; both of us are hungry. After all, this body has not been the means of the absolute realization. Therefore by it no good to the world will possibly be done. It is well and desirable that it should be of service at least to this hungry beast." He perhaps could hear the breathing of the death, but he had nothing to do. He was reclining there all the while, calm and motionless, waiting for the tiger to pounce on him at any moment. But for some reason or other the tiger made off of its own accord. Swamiji though that it might yet return, and waited; but it did not. He spent the night in the jungle, and as dawn approached, he felt a sense of great power came upon him. Later he told about this incident, but didn't disclose the content of that spiritual experience.

At Indore, Swamiji stayed with a friend of the Dewan of Junagadh, who perhaps treated him coldly; for on August 22 he wrote to the Dewan from Bombay, "About the kindness and gentlemanliness of your friend Mr. Baderkar of Indore...the less said the better." Here he saw the celebrated Chhattri (umbrella), a monument to Ahalyabai, the famous queen of Indore State, who had been one of the greatest administrators India had ever known. It is said, "Her charitable foundations extended all over India, from the Himalayas to Cape Comorin, and from Somnath to the Temple of Jagannath."

When Swamiji returned to Khandwa, many prominent people, including members of the Bengali community, met him. They all were impressed with his knowledge of the scriptures and English literature. Here Swamiji met Babu Akshay Kumar Ghosh, whose family in Calcutta he had known for a long time. (This young man later became an adopted son of one Miss Muller of England, and on her behalf he invited Swamiji to England in October 1894, when the later was in America.) Haridasbabu, Swamiji's host, described his manner: "There was not the least trace of affection in his conversation. His elevated thought and noble sentiments flowed in the choicest language in an easy and natural way. He had an earnestness about him which made him look as one inspired."

Once Haridasbabu requested Swamiji to give a public lecture, but Swamiji said that he had faith in personal teaching, as found in the traditional guru-disciple system, for in that way the disciple gets opportunity to meet the teacher in an affectionate and personal relationship, like that between father and son. He also said that he had never before given any public lecture, and had no experience of how to modulate his voice on the platform. But being pressed repeatedly he agreed on conditions if a gathering of earnest and sympathetic listeners could be convened; for it would help in creating the atmosphere necessary to motivate the latent power of the speaker. "But as the conditions proposed", writes Haridasbabu, "were not practicable in a backward place like Khandwa, the idea had to be abandoned."

During this period, Babu Madhavchandra Banerjee, the Civil Judge, gave a dinner for the Bengali residents in honour of Swamiji. Swamiji took with him some of the Upanishads, intending to illustrate them before and after the dinner. When the guests arrived, he read out some abstruse passages and explained them in such a way that a child could understand. Among the guests was a Babu Pyarilal Ganguly, a pleader and a scholar in Sanskrit. He had a plan to play the role of a critic; but when he heard the replies and comments of Swamiji, he became silent. Afterwards he told Haridasbabu that Swamiji's very appearance showed greatness.

Haridasbabu wished to fix Swamiji at Khandwa for a long time. But the reply was: "I wish I could do so. Everyone is so kind, but I must be on my way to Rameswaram, to do the pilgrimage I have in mind. But if I go on in this way, halting for weeks in each town, it will never be done." Realizing that he could not stop Swamiji, Haridasbabu gave him a letter of introduction to his brother in Bombay, and said, "He will introduce you to Seth Ramdas Chhabildas, a noted barrister of Bombay. Perhaps he will be able to help you. Really, Swamiji, you have a great future before you." "Well", Swamiji replied, "I myself do not know; but my Master used to predict many things concerning me." Haridasbabu bought him a ticket for Bombay, and Swamiji left Khandwa for Bombay by train.

Bombay [Mumbai]

Swamiji reached Bombay in the last week of July 1892. He was introduced to Ramdas Chhabildas by the brother of Haridas Chatterjee of Khandwa. At the request of the gentleman Swamiji became his guest for few days. Shortly after that Swamiji became well acquainted with the learned society of that place. One day he went to see a noted politician, who gave him a newspaper to read. The paper contained a controversy over the Age of Consent Bill, which was opposed by the learned section of the Bengali community. When he read that his head bent down in shame. Swamiji bitterly criticized the evil practice of early marriage. During that period he used to spend most of the time in further study of the Vedas. On August 22, 1892, he wrote to the Dewan of Junagadh, "...I have got here some Sanskrit books and help, too, to read, which I do not hope to get elsewhere, and am anxious to finish them. Yesterday I saw your friend Mr. Manashukharam who has lodged a Sannyasin friend with him. He is very kind to me and so is his son. After remaining here for 15 to 20 days I would proceed towards Rameswaram, and on my return would surely come to you."

We know that during this time he had deliberately cut himself off from his brother-disciples, for he felt a great need to be alone. Sister Christine (an American disciple of Swamiji), in her reminiscences of Vivekananda, said, "Once after a long search, one of them saw him driving in a carriage somewhere in the Bombay Presidency. "His face shone," he reported, "like the face of a god. It was the face of a knower of Brahman." This witness describes how he came before his adored brother-disciple, but, although kindly received, was sent away again at once." We doubt that the brother-disciple was none other than Swami Abhedananda.

From the "Reminiscences" of Sister Christine we understand that sometime during his stay at Bombay, Swamiji visited Kanheri Caves, about twenty miles north of the city, on the island of Salsette, which is separated from the mainland by a small stream. It is surrounded by the ocean on three sides. In the early years of Christian era this island was inhabited by monastic members of the Buddhist Order. Sister Christine, in her "Memoirs" said: "While he (Swami Vivekananda) was at Thousand Islands he made plans for future, not only for his disciples in India and the work there, but also for those of his followers in America, who were hoping some time to go to India. At that time we thought these plans only day-dreams. One day he said, "We shall have a beautiful place in India, on an island with the ocean on three sides. There will be small caves which will accommodate two each, and between every two caves there will be a pool of water for bathing, and pipes carrying drinking water will run to each one. There will be a great hall with carved pillars for the Assembly Hall, and a more elaborate Chaitya Hall for worship. Oh! It will be luxury." It seemed as if he were building castles in the air. None of us dreamed that this was something which could ever be realized."

Later, when Sister Christine came to India, she tried to discover the place, and to her surprise she was successful in her mission. Her 'Memoirs" continued: "Of all that group I was one who was privileged to go to India, though it was not until several years later. After I had been in India two or three years, I found myself alone in Bombay with two or three days at my disposal. For some time, I had had a desire to visit Kanheri, which I knew was not far from Bombay. I knew nothing of this place except that there were some caves there, one of them a Chaitya Hall, which Fergusson in his *History of Indian and Eastern Architecture* has described as a bad imitation of the one at Karli. Surely there was nothing in this to attract one! I wondered at the intensity of my desire, the more so as there were other groups of caves within easy reach of Bombay, but which I had no special desire to see. I wondered at it.

"No one seemed able to direct me. Those whom I asked had never heard of Kanheri. After a whole day of inquiry, someone said, "I think, if you take the train tomorrow morning at seven and go to a place called Borivali; you will find someone who can tell you where Kanheri is." This I did. I found that Borivali is only twenty-two miles from Bombay. I did not know any Hindustani at that time, but I remembered that the word for cave is *guha*. There were three bullock-carts at the station, one of them in charge of a lad of seventeen or so, whose looks I liked. I went up to him and said, "*Guha*"; he shook his head. I repeated "*Guha, guha*!" He kept on shaking his head. Then a brilliant idea struck me and I said, "Kanheri, Kanheri!" This time he nodded vigorously. Then I said, "*Kitna* (How much)?" and he held up three fingers saying, "*Tin rupiya* (Three rupees)." I was delighted and climbed into his cart.

"The road led first through a field of stubble and from that into a forest. This forest grew denser and darker the farther we penetrated into the interior. Behind trees, I could see the dark aboriginal people of the forest with bows and arrows peering at us. The road had become a mere cow-path and then even this track came to an end. Here my young bullock driver stopped. "From here you must go alone," he startled me by saying. I don't know how, but it seemed that we were able to make ourselves understood. So I answered, "But I can't go on alone. I don't know the way. You must come with me." He replied, "I can't leave my bullocks." I, being at that time ignorant of the fact that there were tigers in the forest which might devour his bullocks, suggested that he tie them to a tree and come with me. This he did after a little hesitation.

"We went only a short distance and then came to a stream which at that season was almost dried up. On the other side was a small hill. Here we found carved stone steps leading to the top. And what a view there was from the crest of the hill! The ocean on three sides, a forest leading down to the water, carved seats on which to rest, sculptured halls of magnificent proportions. Here it all was—the island with the ocean on three sides, a great sculptured Assembly Hall, the Chaitya Hall built in imitation of the one at Karli, the small cells, containing two stone beds each, pools of water between the cells, even the pipes to carry water! It was as if a dream had unexpectedly come true. The place was deserted, not even a caretaker. Coming upon this abandoned site, which answered in detail to the fairytale we had heard before in America, I was profoundly affected."

Coming back to Calcutta, when she told Swami Sadananda the story of the finding of the deserted island with the 109 caves, and explained how Swamiji at Thousand Island had described the place, he said, "Yes, Swamiji in his wanderings in western India before he went to America, found these caves. The place stirred him deeply; for it seems that he had a memory of a previous life in which he lived there. At that time, the place was unknown and forgotten. He hoped that some day he might acquire it and make it one of the centres for the work which he was planning for the future. Later, in my wandering in western India, I too found it, and now you! We have all lived there in the past!"

Being dependent only on God Swamiji wandered all around the country, and realized the culture and civilization of India. This realization was found to be reflected in his later life and it influenced his thought. After the death of his father he had experienced the poverty in his life, and while wandering as a monk, he found the same in innumerable people. He realized that the people are not hostile to religion though they had been living in poverty. But in many places religion became lifeless under the pressure of its customs and practices prescribed by the priests, who had established discrimination among people. In his letter of 22nd August 1892, written to the Dewan of Junagadh, Swamiji described: "I am very sorry to notice in these parts is the thorough want of Sanskrit and other learning. The people of this part of the country have for their religion a certain bundle of local superstitions about eating, drinking, and bathing, and that is about the whole of their religion. Poor fellows! Whatever the rascally and wily priests teach them—all sorts of mummery and tomfoolery as the very gist of the Vedas and Hinduism (mind you, neither these rascals of priests nor their forefathers have as much as seen a volume of the Vedas for the last 400 generations)—they follow and degrade themselves. Lord help them from the Rakshasas in the shape of the Brahmins of the Kaliyuga."[75]

On 20th September 1892, Swamiji wrote to Pandit Shankarlal of Khetri, "The Hindu mind was ever deductive and never synthetic or inductive. In all our philosophies, we always find hair-splitting arguments, taking for granted some general proposition, but the proposition itself may be as childish as possible. Nobody ever asked or searched the truth of these general propositions. Therefore independent thought we have almost none to speak of, and hence the dearth of those sciences which are the results of observation and generalization. And why was it thus?—From two causes: The tremendous heat of the climate forcing us to love rest and contemplation better than activity, and the Brahmins as priests never undertaking journeys or voyages to distant lands. There were voyagers and people who travelled far; but they were almost always traders, i.e. people from whom priestcraft and their own sole love for gain had taken away all capacity for intellectual development. So their observations, instead of adding to the store of human knowledge, rather degenerated it; for their observations were bad and their accounts exaggerated and tortured into fantastical shapes, until they passed all recognition.

"So you see, we must travel, we must go to foreign parts. We must see how the engine of society works in other countries, and keep free and open communication with what is going on in the minds of other nations, if we really want to be a nation again. And over and above all, we must cease to tyrannise. To what a ludicrous state are we brought! If a Bhangi comes to anybody as a Bhangi, he would be shunned as the plague; but no sooner does he get a cupful of water poured upon his head with some mutterings of prayers by a Padri, and get a coat on his back, no matter how threadbare, and come into the room of the most orthodox Hindu—I don't see the man who then dare refuse him a chair and a hearty shake of the hands! Irony can go no further. And come and see what they, the Padris, are doing here in the Dakshin (south). They are converting the lower classes by lakhs; and in Travancore, the most priest-ridden country in India—where every bit of land is owned by the Brahmins...nearly one-fourth has become Christian! And I cannot blame them; what part have they in David and what in Jesse? When, when, O Lord, shall man be brother to man?"[76]

On 22 August, 1892 Swamiji from Bombay wrote to the Dewan of Junagadh, "After remaining here for 15 to 20 days I would proceed towards Rameswaram." But, according to his letter of 20 September, we see him staying in Bombay. Hence, Swamiji remained in Bombay for about two months, and then he went to Poona, on his way to South India. Bombay to Poona—he was travelling by train. He was sitting in a second class compartment, where Lokmanya Bal Gangadhar Tilak and some other gentlemen were his co-passengers. The gentlemen thought that Swamiji was an ordinary uneducated monk, and began to discuss about the monks who had made many damages to India, and so on in English. But Swamiji was sitting silently and listening to their taunt. Mr. Tilak joined their argument and tried to say in favour of monks. Thus the argument went on. After a while Swamiji joined them, and made them convinced with a strong argument in fluent English presenting the other aspect of the subject with strong evidences from history and sociological views. The gentlemen not only felt ashamed of their ill behaviour but also were impressed with the intellect of the monk. We may directly listen to the story from Lokmanya Bal Gangadhar Tilak, the renowned scholar and patriot, who happened to be his fellow passenger. Later, in his reminiscences, Mr. Tilak wrote:

> About the year 1892, i.e. before the famous Parliament of Religions in the World's Fair at Chicago, I was once returning from Bombay to Poona. At the Victoria Terminus a Sannyasin entered the carriage I was in. A few Gujarati gentlemen were there to see him off. They made the formal introduction and asked the Sannyasin to reside at my house during his stay at Poona. We reached Poona, and the Sannyasin remained with me for eight or ten days. When asked about his name he only said he was a Sannyasin. He made no public speeches here. At home he would often talk about Advaita philosophy and Vedanta. The Swami avoided mixing with society. There was absolutely no money with him. A deerskin, one or two clothes and a *Kamandalu* were his only possessions. In his travels someone would provide a railway ticket for the desired station.
>
> The Swami happened to express a strong hope that as the women in the Maharashtra were not handicapped by the *Purdah* system, it was probable that some of the widows in the higher classes would devote their lives to the spread of spirituality and religion alone like the old *yogis* of the Buddhist period. The Swami also believed like me that the *Shrimad Bhagavad Gita* did not preach renunciation but urged everyone to work unattached and without the desire for fruits of the work.
>
> I was at that time a member of the Deccan Club in the Hirabag which used to hold weekly meetings. At one of these meetings the Swami accompanied me. That evening the late Kashinath Govind Nath made a fine speech on a philosophical subject. No one had to say anything. But the Swami rose and spoke in fluent English presenting the other aspect of the subject very lucidly. Everyone there was thus convinced of his high abilities. The Swami left Poona very soon after this.

> Two or three years thereafter Swami Vivekananda returned to India with world-wide fame owing to his grand success at the Parliament of Religions and also after that both in England and America. He received an address wherever he went and on every one of such occasions he made a thrilling reply. I happened to see his likeness in some of the newspapers, and from the similarity of features I thought that the Swami who had resided at my house must have been the same. I wrote to him accordingly inquiring if my inference was correct and requesting him to kindly pay a visit to Poona on his way to Calcutta. I received a fervent reply in which the Swami frankly admitted that he was the same Sannyasin and expressed his regret at not being able to visit Poona then. This letter is not available. It must have been destroyed along with many others, public and private, after the close of the *Kesari* Prosecution of 1897.
>
> Once after this, during one of the Congress sessions at Calcutta, I had gone with some friends to see the Belur Math of the Ramakrishna Mission. There Swami Vivekananda received us very cordially. We took tea. In the course of the conversation Swamiji happened to remark somewhat in a jocular spirit that it would be better if I renounced the world and took up his work in Bengal while he would go and continue the same in Maharashtra. "One does not carry," he said, "the same influence in one's own province as in a distant one.[77]

From Poona Swamiji went to visit the Maharaja of Kolhapur, to whom he had a letter of introduction from the Maharaja of Bhavnagar. The Maharani of Kolhapur became greatly devoted to Swamiji, and requested him to accept a new ochre cloth. One Mr. Vijaipurkar, in his reminiscences, has written of Swamiji's visit to Kolhapur as follows:

> In 1892, when he [the Swami] visited our holy place, each of us felt at the time that he would be a great orator in the future. Not only was he well read, but he had mastered the art of putting his subject in such a manner that it would impress the mind of the hearer. We had invited him to speak in our Rajaramiya Parishad. Had I not had the good fortune of spending about an hour and a half in his company, I should not have understood his power of fascinating his hearers. Before he spoke, we asked him whether he would need any help from our side. He did not take any notes for his lecture. We no doubt knew in general what he said, but when it came through his mouth, it had a unique power of attraction.

"Raosaheb Lakshmanrao Golwalkar was the Private Secretary of the Maharaja. He had arranged for the Swami's stay at the Khasbag. We had learnt that a great sannyasi had come, and that he could speak English. On the way back from our evening walk, we went to see him. When we heard his voice from a distance, we could understand that he had a wonderful personality. When we approached and saluted him, he did not bless us by saying "Narayana" or anything else. He continued his talk without stopping. He would reply promptly when anyone asked a question. We then invited him to come to our Rajaramiya Parishad the next day. There also I witnessed the same thing.... I remember two sentences which he spoke on that occasion. He said, "My religion is that of which Buddhism is a rebel child, and Christianity but a far-fetched imitation.... How will the Europeans understand religion? They are running after luxury." Someone interrupted, saying, "How can flesh-eater understand religion?" The Swami immediately reacted saying, "No, no; your ancient sages were flesh-eaters. Have you not read that in your *Uttara Ramcharita*?" Then he quoted some verses from that epic, in which there are clear references to flesh-eating. After hearing this statement, some doubted his caste; but who would dare to ask him about it?"[78]

After a short stay at Kolhapur Swamiji went to south, and reached Belgaum about October 15, 1892. Here he was the guest of a Maharashtrian gentleman, whose son, Prof. G.S. Bhate, in his reminiscences, wrote about those days. It is as follows:

> "The Swami came to Belgaum from Kolhapur with a note from Mr. Golvalkar, the Khaigi Karbhari [Private seceraty] of the Maharaja.... I remember him appearing one morning about six o'clock with a note from Mr. Golvalkar, who was a great friend of my father's. The Swami was rather striking in appearance and appeared to be even at first sight somewhat out of the common run of men. But neither my father nor anyone else in the family or even in our small town was prepared to find in our guest the remarkable man that he turned out to be.

"From the very first day of the Swami's stay occurred little incidents which led us to revise our ideas about him. In the first place, though he wore clothes bearing the familiar colour of a Sannyasin's garments, he appeared to be dressed differently from the familiar brotherhood of Sannyasins. He used to wear a banyan. Instead of the danda [staff] he carried a long stick, something like a walking-stick. His kit consisted of the usual gourd, a pocket copy of the Gita, and one or two books.... We were not accustomed to a Sannyasin using the English language as a medium of conversation, wearing a banyan instead of sitting bare-bodied, and showing a versatility of intellect and variety of information which would have done credit to an accomplished man of the world.... The first day after the meal, the Swami made a request for betel-nut and pan (betel). Then either the same day or the day after, he wanted some tobacco for chewing. One can imagine the kind of horror which would be inspired by Sannyasin who is commonly regarded as having gone above these small creature comforts, showing a craving for these things. We had discovered by his own admission that he was non-Brahmin and yet a Sannyasin, that he was a Sannyasin and yet craved for things which only householders are supposed to want. This was really topsy-turvydom, and yet he succeeded in changing our ideas. There was really nothing very wrong in a Sannyasin wanting pan and supari (betel-nut) or tobacco for chewing, but the explanation he gave of his craving disarmed us completely. He said that he was a gay young man and a distinguished graduate of the Calcutta University, and that his life before he met Shri Ramakrishna Paramahamsa was entirely different to what he became afterwards. As a result of teachings of Shri Ramakrishna Paramahamsa he had changed his life and outlook, but some of these things he found it impossible to get rid of, and he let them remain as being of no very great consequence. As regards food, when he was asked whether he was a vegetarian or a meat-eater, he said that as a man belonging not the ordinary order of Sannyasins but to the order of the Paramahamsas, he had no option in the matter. The Paramahamsa, by the rules of that order, was bound to eat whatever was offered, and in cases where nothing could be offered he had to go without food. And a Paramahamsa was not precluded from accepting food from any human being irrespective of his religious beliefs. When he was asked whether he would accept food from non-Hindus, he told us that he had several times been under the necessity of accepting food from Mohammedans.

"The Swami appeared to be very well grounded in the old Pandit method of studying Sanskrit. At the time of his arrival, I was getting up the *Ashtadhyayi* by rote, and to my great surprise as a boy, his memory, even in quoting portions of the *Ashtadhyayi* which I had been painfully trying to remember, was much superior to mine. If I remember aright, when my father wanted me to repeat the portions that I had been preparing, I made some slips, which to my confusion the Swami, smilingly, corrected. The effect of this was almost overwhelming as far as my feelings towards him were concerned....

"For a day or two after his arrival my father was busy in trying to take a measure of his guest. In that period he made up his mind that the guest was not only above the ordinary, but was an extraordinary personality. So he got a few of his personal friends together in order to fortify his own opinion of the Swami. They soon agreed that it was quite worthwhile to get all the local leaders and learned men together. What struck us most in the crowded gatherings, which began to be held every day after the presence of the Swami became known to all in Belgaum, was the unfailing good humour which the Swami preserved in his conversations and even in heated arguments. He was quick enough at retort, but the retort had no sting in it. One day we had a rather amusing illustration of the Swami's coolness in debate. There was at that time in Belgaum an Executive Engineer who was the best-informed man in our town. He was one of the not uncommon types among Hindus. He was in his everyday life an orthodox Hindu of the type that I believe Southern India alone can produce. But in his mental outlook he was not only a sceptic, but a very dogmatic adherent of what used to be then regarded as the scientific outlook. He almost appeared to argue in spite of his orthodox mode of life that there was practically no sanction for religion or belief in religion except that the people were for a long time accustomed to certain beliefs and practices. Holding these views he found the Swami rather an embarrassing opponent, because the Swami had larger experience, knew more philosophy and more science than this local luminary. Naturally, he more than once lost temper in argument and was discourteous, if not positively rude, to the Swami. So my father protested, but the Swami smilingly intervened and said that he did not feel in any way disturbed by the methods of show of temper on the part of this Executive Engineer.... He soon nonplussed in argument all the available talent in a mofussil town. But his aim appeared to be not so much victory in debate and argumentation, as a desire to create and spread the feeling that the time had come for demonstration to the country and to the whole world that the Hindu religion was not in a moribund condition. The time had come, he used to say, for preaching to the world the priceless truths contained in Vedanta.... His complaint appeared to be that Vedanta had been treated too much as the possession of a sect competing for the loyalty of the Hindu along with other sects, and not as a life-giving perennial source of inspiration that it really was."

At Belgaum, Swamiji also stayed for nine days with Haripada Mitra, the Subdivisional Forest Officer. In his reminiscences, he wrote:

> Belgaum, Tuesday, October 18, 1892: It was about two hours past evening, when a stout young monk, with a cheerful countenance, came to my house with a lawyer friend of mine of the same locality. The friend introduced him with the words, "Here is a learned Bengali Sannyasin who has come to meet you." I turned back and found a serene figure with eyes flashing like lightning and a face clean shaven. His body was covered with an ochre robe, in his feet he had strapped sandals of Maharashtrian type; and on his head was an ochre turban. The figure was so impressive that it is still vivid in my memory. It pleased me and attracted me, though I did not realize then why it was so. After a while, I saluted him and said, "Sir, do you smoke? I am a Kayastha, and I have but one *hookah*. If you have no objection to smoke from it, I can have some tobacco prepared for you." He replied, "I smoke whatever comes to hand—tobacco from a hookah or cigarette. And I have no objection to smoke from your *hookah*." I ordered for some tobacco.
>
> My belief at that time was that all Sannyasins in ochre robes were cheats, and I naturally thought that this one, too, had come to me with some motive. Besides, the lawyer friend belonged to Maharashtra, while he was a Bengali. It was inconvenient for Bengalis to live with Maharashtrians: and that was why he had come to live with me. Despite all

> such thoughts passing through my mind, I invited him to stay with me and asked him whether his belongings should be brought to my house. He replied, "I am quite at home with the lawyer; and if I leave him just because I have found a Bengali, he will be hurt, for they all love and respect me. But I shall think about it and let you know later on." We did not have much talk that night. But the few words that he spoke convinced me that he was more learned and intelligent than myself. He could have earned a decent sum if he wanted, but he did not touch money. Although he had not the wherewithal to make him happy, he was, in fact, a thousand times happier than myself. It struck me that he had no want, just because he had no thought for any personal gain. When I learnt that he would not come to my house, I said, "If you have no objection to take tea with me, I shall be happy to have you here in the morning." He agreed and went back with the lawyer. At night I was thinking about him for a long time—I had never before met a man so free from wants, so happy and content, and having such a smiling face.[79]

Next morning Haripadababu waited for a long time, but Swamiji did not come. So without waiting any longer, he went to Swamiji's place with a friend. There he was surprised to see a large gathering of lawyers and other learned men. Swamiji was seated amidst the crowd, and was carrying on conversation with them. Saluting Swamiji Haripadababu took his seat among them. He was amazed to see him replying their questions without any hesitation, sometimes in English and sometimes in Hindi or Sanskrit. There were some people, who accepted Huxley's philosophy as their Bible, and started arguing with Swamiji on that basis. But he silenced them all either through repartees or serious dissertation. Haripadababu was thinking, "Is he a man or a god?" Haripadababu later wrote down some of his experiences of that day:

> A very respectable lawyer asked, "The *mantras* we use in our morning and evening prayers are in Sanskrit, and we do not understand a bit of them. Is it of any use to us to go on uttering them?"

Swamiji replied, "They do have good results. Born in a Brahmin family as you are, you can easily learn the meaning of those few *mantras*. If you do not do so, who is to blame? Even if you do not understand the meaning, I hope, when you sit for prayer, you have the feeling that you are doing something virtuous and not sinful. If you have the belief that you are doing something meritorious, then that in itself is enough to yield good results."

Just then somebody said, "Talks on religious matters should not be carried on in a foreign language, since it is prohibited in such-and-such a *purana*."

Swamiji replied, "It is good to talk of religious things, no matter what the language is." In support of this he quoted from the Vedas and added, "A judgment passed by a High Court cannot be set at naught by a lower court."

Haripadababu continued: "Thus it went till it struck nine, when those who had to attend office or court left, while others still sat there. Swamiji's eyes now fell on me, and he said, "My son, I had not the heart to disappoint so many people and go to your place. Please don't mind this." When I pressed him to come and stay with me, he replied at last, "I shall go if you can make my host agree to your proposal". So I persuaded the lawyer friend somehow and returned to my place with Swamiji. His belongings consisted only of a *kamandalu* (a water pot used by monks) and a book wrapped in a piece of ochre cloth. Swamiji was then studding French music. We had our tea at ten o'clock after reaching home. He understood my hesitation in expressing my own doubts, and so he himself gauged my intellectual make-up through a few words.

"Some time earlier, somebody had published a poem in the *Times* asserting that it was extremely difficult to determine what is God, which religion is true, and such other abstruse questions. As that poem had much affinity to my religious ideas of those days, I preserved it carefully. I now produced it before him. He read it and remarked, "The man has become confused". Gradually I got over my hesitation. From the Christian missionaries I had not got any solution to the contradiction involved in holding that God is both just and merciful; and I feared that Swamiji, too, could throw no better light. When I put the question to him, he said, "Methinks you have read much of science. Do not two opposite forces, centripetal and centrifugal—act in each material substance? If such a contradiction can meet in matter, may not justice and mercy be reconciled in God? All I can say is that you have a poor idea of your God." I was silenced. Again, I believed that truth is absolute, and that all religions cannot be true at the same time. In answer to such questions he said, "All we know about things now or may know in future are but relative truths. It is impossible for our limited mind to grasp the absolute truth. Hence, though truth be absolute, it appears variously to diverse minds and intellects. All these facets or modes of truth belong to the same class as truth itself, they being based on the same absolute truth. This is like the different photographs of the same sun taken from various distances. Each of them seems to represent a different sun. The diverse relative truths have the same kind of relation with the absolute truth. Each religion is thus true, just because it is a mode of presentation of the absolute religion."

"When I said that faith is the basis of all religions, Swamiji smiled a little and said, "A man goes beyond all wants once he becomes a king; but the difficulty is how to become one. Can faith be infused from outside? Nobody can have real faith unless he has personal experience." When in the course of talk I called him a *sadhu* (holy man), he said, "Are we really so? There are holy men whose very sight or touch wakes up spirituality in others."

"Again I asked, "Why do Sannyasins idle away their time in this way? Why do they depend on the charity of others? Why don't they undertake some work beneficial to society?" Swamiji said, "Now, look here. You are earning this money with such struggle, of which only a little portion you spend on yourself; and some of it you spend for others who, you think, are your own. But they neither acknowledge any gratefulness for what you do for them, nor are they satisfied with what they get. The balance you save like the mythological *yaksha* who never enjoy it. When you die, somebody else will enjoy it all; and perchance, he will abuse you for not having accumulated more. This is your condition. On the other hand, I do nothing. When I feel hungry, I let others know by gestures that I want food; and I eat whatever I get. Neither do I struggle nor do I save. Now, tell me who among us is the wiser—you or I?" I was astonished, for before this nobody dared to talk to me so boldly and frankly.

"After lunch we had some rest. Then we went to the house of that lawyer friend, where we had more of such discussion. At nine o'clock at night we returned home. On the way I said, "Swamiji, you must have been greatly bored today by all this argumentation." He replied, "My son, would you have offered me even a morsel of food, if I had kept mum, the out and out utilitarians that you all are? I go on chattering like this. People get amused, and so they crowd around me. But know it for certain that people who argue, or put questions like this before an assembly, are not at all eager to know the truth. I also read their motives and answer them accordingly."

"Swamiji," I put in, "how do you get such ready and pointed answers for all the questions?"

"These questions are new to you," he said, "but these have been put to me and I had to answer them times without number."

The conversation continued during dinner. Swamiji told him of the many adventures he had during his travelling through the country under vow and not touching money. When the night had advanced very far, they went to bed. But Haripadababu couldn't sleep. He was surprised to think how the deep-rooted doubts that had haunted him all those years took flight at the very sight of Swamiji! As days passed by, not only his family, but also their servants developed such love and respect for Swamiji, and they served him so meticulously, that he became rather embarrassed.

Haripadababu described his experience of the next day: "October 20, 1892: In the morning I saluted Swamiji. Now I had more boldness as also more devotion. Swamiji, too, was pleased to hear from me many accounts of forests, rivers, hills, and valleys. He had been now in this town for four days. On the fifth day, he said, "A Sannyasin must not live in a town for more than three days, and in a village for more than four days. I want to leave soon." I would not listen to all that; I was determined to argue it all away. After a long discussion he said, "If one stays at one place for long, one develops attachment for others. We left our home and friends. It is but proper for us to be away from all such sources of maya." I entreated him to stay on and argued that he would never fall into maya's snares. At last he agreed to stay for a couple of days more.

"In the meantime I thought that, if Swamiji addressed a public gathering, we would get the benefit of his wisdom and others also would gain thereby. I pressed him for this, but he would not agree on the plea that such platform speeches might generate in him a desire for name and fame. At the same time he intimated that he would have no objection to a public conversazione.

"One day, in the course of a talk, Swamiji quoted verbatim some two or three pages from the *Pickwick Papers*. I wondered at this, not understanding how a Sannyasin could get by heart so much from a secular book. I thought that he must have read it quite a number of times before he took orders. When questioned he said, "I read it twice—once when I was in school, and again some five or six months back." "Then how do you remember," I asked in wonder, "and why can we not remember thus?" "One has to read with full attention," he explained, "and one must not fritter away the energy one draws from food."

"Another day, Swamiji was reading a book all by himself, reclining in his bed. I was in another room. Suddenly he laughed so aloud that I thought that there must be some occasion for such a laughter, and so I advanced to his door to find that nothing special had happened; he continued to read as before. I stood there for some fifteen minutes; till he did not notice me and asked me to walk in. When he heard that I had been standing there for pretty long time, he said, "Whatever one has to do, one must apply to it one's whole attention and energy for the time being. Pavhari Baba of Ghazipur would clean his brass water vessel with the same undivided attention as he used in his meditation, japa, worship, study, etc. He cleaned it so diligently that it shone like gold."

One day Haripadababu asked Swamiji, "Why is stealing considered a sin? Why do all religions prohibit stealing? To me, it seems that to think that one thing belongs to me and another to somebody else is only a figment of the brain. As a matter of fact, it does not amount to stealing if one of my relatives should take away one of my things without informing me. Besides, we do not brand it as stealing when the birds or animals snatch away anything."

"It is true," said Swamiji, "that no act can be regarded as stealing at all times and under all circumstances. Again every act may be considered wrong or even sinful under altered conditions. You should not do anything that brings misery to others, or weakens you physically or morally. That is sinful and its opposite is virtuous. Just think of this: Don't you feel sorry when somebody steals something from you? What is true for you, you should know, is true for the whole world. If you can be so bad as to inflict some pain on some being in this world, though you are fully aware that everything here is evanescent, you will gradually come to such a state that no sin will be too great for you. Again, social life becomes impossible if there is no division of virtue and vice. When you live in society, you have to comply with its rules and regulations. If you retire to a forest, you can go about dancing naked; that harms nobody, and none will stop you. But should you behave so in a town, the reasonable thing to do will be to get you arrested by the police and have you locked up in some solitary place!"

Haripadababu continued: "Swamiji sometimes imparted very valuable lessons through humour or derision. Though he was my *guru*, to sit by him was not just like sitting before a school-master. He would be merry, full of gaiety, fun, and laughter, just like a boy, even when imparting the highest instruction. He laughed and made others laugh with him. Then, suddenly, he would start explaining an intricate point with such seriousness that people wondered at his mastery over the subject and over himself. They used to think, "Did we not find him just now as but one like ourselves?" People would come to him at all hours for learning from him, and his door was always open. They had diverse motives. Some came to test him, some to enjoy his humorous talks, some others to be in closer contact with the rich people of the town who came to Swamiji, and still others to get a few moments' respite from the worries of the world, to hear his spiritual talks, and to be enlightened thereby. Such was his power of diving into others' minds; he understood their motives at once and dealt with them accordingly. Nobody could hide anything from his penetrating eyes."

"Once a boy from a rich family began to frequent Swamiji's place just for the sake of avoiding his university examination, and he gave it out that he would become a monk. He happened to be the son of a friend of mine. I asked Swamiji, "Why does that boy come to you so frequently? Will you advise him to become a monk? His father is a friend of mine."

Swamiji replied, "His examination is near at hand, and he wants to take orders just to avoid the examination. I told him, 'Come for the monastic life after passing the M.A. examination. It is easier to get the M.A. degree than to lead the life of a monk.'"

During Swamiji's stay at Haripadababu's house, so many people used to gather there in the evenings that it all looked like a big meeting. There was a big sandal-tree in that house. Swamiji would sit under that tree resting his back on a pillow while talking to the people.

Haripadababu writes: "Some time earlier my wife had expressed a desire to take initiation from some guru; and I had told her, "Choose a *guru* who will command my respect as well. You will derive no benefit if the very advent of your *guru* in the house should create some adverse feeling in me. We shall both be initiated together if only we come across a good man, otherwise not." She too agreed to this. When Swamiji was with us, I asked her, "Would you like to be a disciple of this *guru*?" "Will he really agree to be a *guru*?" she asked eagerly, and added, "If he agrees, we shall be only too grateful."

"With great hesitation, I asked Swamiji one day, "Swamiji, will you fulfil a desire of mine?" When he wanted to know what it was, I requested him to initiate both of us. He said, "For a householder, it is best to have some householder as his *guru*. It is very difficult to be a *guru*. The *guru* has to take the responsibility of the disciple. Before initiation the disciple must meet the *guru* at least three times." With these and other arguments he wanted to put me off. But when he found that I was not be dissuaded, he agreed. He initiated us on October 25, 1892. Then I had a desire to have his photograph. He would not agree. I persisted, and after a long-drawn tussle, he gave his consent and a photograph was taken on the 28th. As Swamiji had not agreed to be photographed on an earlier occasion, in spite of the earnest request of another gentleman, I had to send two copies of this one to him on request.

"In the course of a talk Swamiji said, "I have a great desire to spend a few day with you in the forest under a camp. But they are holding a Parliament of Religions at Chicago, and I shall go there if I get an opportunity." When I proposed to raise money by subscription, he refused it for some reason best known to himself. At this time, he was under a vow of not accepting or touching any money. After great effort I persuaded him to accept a pair of shoes in place of Maharashtrian sandals as also a cane walking stick. Before this, the Rani of Kolhapur had not succeeded in making him accept any gift, and so she had sent him a pair of ochre clothes. Swamiji accepted these and left behind the pieces he had wearing with the remark, "A Sannyasin must not have a burden about him."

Before he came in contact with Swamiji, Haripadababu had tried to read the Gita more than once. As he could not understand it, he concluded that there was really nothing to know from it, and so he gave up the attempt. One day Swamiji began to explain the Gita to him; then he discovered what a wonderful book it was. He also learnt from him to read the scientific novels of Jules Verne, and *Sartor Resartus* of Carlyle.

At that time Haripadababu used to take medicines rather liberally. Swamiji told him, "When you find that some disease has made you bed-ridden, then only you should take medicines, not otherwise. Ninety per cent of such diseases as nervous debility are mere figments of the brain. The physicians kill more people suffering from such diseases than they save. What do you gain by thinking and talking of all these for ever? Take it easy as long as you live, and be cheerful. Never indulge in pleasures which tax the body or which make you repent. As regards death, what does it matter if one or two like you or me die; that will not make the earth deviate from its axis. We should never consider ourselves so important as to think that the world cannot go on without us."

At that time, for some reason, Haripadababu did not have a good relation with his superiors in office. Any little remark from them would make him lose his balance. Though he had a lucrative job, he could not be happy even for a day, when he told Swamiji about his difficulty. Swamiji replied, "Why are you in service? Is it not for the salary you get? You are getting regularly every month; so why should you be upset? When you are free to resign at any moment you like, and nobody binds you down to it, why should you add to your miseries by thinking, Oh, in what bondage am I placed! Another thing: will you tell me whether, apart from doing the work for which you draw the salary, you ever did anything just to please your superiors? You never did so, and yet you are angry with them that they are not satisfied with you. Is that wise on your part? Know it for certain that the ideas we entertain about others express themselves through our conduct; and even though we may not express these in words, people react accordingly. We see in the external world the same image that we vary in our hearts: nobody realizes how true the saying 'The world is good when I am good' is. From today try to get rid of the habit of finding fault with others, and you will find that, to the extent you succeed in this, the attitudes and reactions of others also change accordingly." Haripadababu writes: "From that day, I got rid of the habit of drugging myself; and a new chapter in my life opened from my effort to give up faultfinding."

He continued: "When the question was raised once as to what constituted good and what bad, Swamiji said, "What is conducive to the goal aimed at is good and what impedes it is bad. Our ideas of good and bad are just like our ideas of elevation and depression. As you rise higher, the distinction becomes obliterated. They say that the moon has mountains and plains; but we see it all as a flat surface. It is just like that." Swamiji had this peculiar power that, whatever might be the question, the answer came so aptly and readily that the hearer stood convinced.

"Words fail to express the sorrow that Swamiji felt another day on reading from the newspaper that a man had died of starvation in Calcutta. Repeatedly he said, "Now the country is about to go to rack and ruin!" Being asked to explain, he said, "Don't you see that in other countries hundreds of people die every year, in spite of their poor-houses, work-houses, charity funds, etc.? But in our country we never heard of death through starvation just because of the system of alms-giving in vogue here. This is the first time I read in a newspaper that man dies of starvation in Calcutta even when there is no famine."

As a result of his English education, Haripadababu thought it was wastage of money to offer a pice or two to beggars. His idea was that such petty help not only did no good to the recipients, but it also brought about their ruin by enabling them to smoke hemp with it. The only gain was that the giver's bill of expenditure went up by that amount! So he concluded that, instead of giving trifling amounts to many, it is better to give somebody a bigger amount. When he asked Swamiji, he replied, "When a beggar comes, it is better to give him something according to your means. After all you will pay a pice or two; and so why should you rack your brain about what the man will do with it—whether he will spend it well or waste? Even if he wastes it on hemp, it is to the advantage of society that he gets those few pice; for unless people like you offer it to him willingly, he will steal it from you. If instead of that, he buys hemp, smokes a little, and then sits quietly, is it not to your own advantage? So even this kind of charity results in nothing but good for society."

From the very beginning Swamiji was against the system of child marriage. He always advised all, and particularly the boys, to stand boldly against this social evil. Such patriotism was very rarely found in other person. Those who met Swamiji after he returned from the West for the first time never knew how he had travelled through the length and breadth of India, observing all the rigorous vows of a monk and not touching money at all. When someone suggested that a man of such a strong will as he had no need to follow so many rules and vows, he replied, "Look here, the mind is so mad, so intoxicated, that it can never sit quiet; if it gets the least opportunity, it will drag you after itself. To keep control over that mind, even a Sannyasin must observe rules. All are under the delusion that they have the fullest control over their minds and that they allow it some freedom knowingly. When one sits for meditation, one can very well understand how much control one really has over the mind. Even when one wants to think of a certain matter for some time, one cannot keep the mind fixed on that subject for so long as ten minutes. All are under the delusion that they are not henpecked and that it is only out of love that they allow their wives to exercise some influence over them. The belief that one has the mind in tether is just like that. Never relax yourself under the false belief that you are the master of your mind."

In the course of a talk one day Haripadababu said to Swamiji, "Swamiji, I think one must be highly educated in order to understand religion." Swamiji replied, "One does not require any high education to understand religion for oneself; but one must have it if one has to explain it to others. Paramahamsa Ramakrishna signed his name as "Ramkesto", but who indeed knew the essence of religion better than he?"

Mr. Haripada Mitra was a fortunate man that he had an opportunity to see Swami Vivekananda, and could talk to him. Reminiscences of such persons are really the priceless wealth to us. While we go through those writings, it takes us to those days, and helps us to see Swamiji and listen to his words of wisdom. They recorded the valuable words of Swamiji for doing well to the people generation after generation, and thus had made their lives immortal.

Haripadababu wrote: "I had an idea that monks and holy men could never be stout and ever contented. One day, when I gave expression to this with a smile and a dig at him, he answered in a bantering tone, "This is my famine insurance fund! Even if I do not get food for days on end, my fat will keep me alive, whereas your vision will be blurred if you do not get food for a day. And a religion that cannot bring peace to men must be shunned as a disease brought on by dyspepsia."

"Swamiji was master in music. One day he started singing. I had no training to appreciate it; besides, how could I have the time to listen to it? We were charmed by his talks and stories. He was well acquainted with several branches of modern science, to wit, chemistry, physics, geology, astronomy, mixed mathematics, and so on, so that he was able to solve our problems about all these in a few words. He would explain intricate religious questions with the help and analogy of science. I never knew anybody else who could prove so convincingly that science and religion had the goal in view and that their progress was also along the same path.

"He liked chillies, pepper, and such other pungent things. When I asked for the reason one day, he said, "During his wanderings a monk has to take all kinds of food, and drink water from all sorts of places; that tells upon the health. To counteract their bad effect, many monks become addicted to hemp and other intoxicants. For the same reason I have taken to chilli."

"Many Princes, including those of Rajasthan and the Deccan, honoured him very much, and he too loved them sincerely. Many could not understand why a monk of such strong principles should mix so much with princes and Rajas. There were fools enough who even hinted at this incongruity. Asked about the reason, Swamiji explained one day, "Just compare the results one can achieve by instructing thousands of poor people and inducing them to adopt a certain line of action on the one hand, and by converting a prince to that point of view on the other. Where will they get the means for accomplishing a good project even if the poor subjects have a will to do it? A prince has the power of doing good to his subjects already in his hands. Only he lacks the will to do it. If you can once wake up that will in him, then, along with it, the fortune of his subjects will take a turn for the better, and society will be immensely benefited thereby."

"To explain that religion does not consist in learned discussion, but in realization, he would say, "The proof of the pudding is in the eating. Realize it. Without that you can understand nothing." He had no kind word for a false monk, and would say, "One should renounce only after one has got control over one's mind while still at home. Else one gets mixed up with the hemp-smoking monks once the first charm wears away." "But it is most difficult to have this at home," I intervened. "For instance, if I start practicing all those virtues like considering all to be equal, giving up likes and dislikes, and so on, which you say are the best means for becoming a man of realization, then from the very next day, my servants, my subordinates, and even the members of my family will not leave me in peace even for a moment." In reply he related the parable of the snake and the holy man, as narrated by Sri Ramakrishna, and then added, "Never give up the hissing. Go on with your work, thinking it to be your duty. Punish others when you have to; but don't be angry when inflicting punishment." Then he resumed the earlier topic and said, "Once I was the guest of a Police Inspector in a place of pilgrimage. He was a religious man, and had some devotion. His salary was only ₹ 125 *per mensem*, whereas his monthly expenditure went up to two hundred or three hundred rupees. When we became more intimate, I asked him, 'Your expenditure seems to exceed your income. How do you manage it?' 'Men like you manage it, sir,' said he with a smile. 'Don't think that all the monks who come to this place of pilgrimage are as good as yourself. Whenever any suspicion arises, I search their belongings; and often enough, much money is found. When any one of them is suspected for theft, he at once takes to his heels leaving behind everything, which then comes to my possession. I do not resort to any other illegal means of satisfaction like bribe.'"

"One day I had a very beautiful talk with Swamiji about infinity. He said, "There can be no two infinites." When I said that time is infinite and so also is space, he replied, "I can understand that space is infinite, but it passes my understanding how time can be infinite. In any case, I can understand that only one thing can be infinite. If there be two infinites, how would you demarcate their respective spheres? If you advance further, you will find that time and space get lost in each other. Still further advance will show you that all things are infinite, but those infinite things are one in essence and not two."

Thus Swamiji stayed in Haripadababu's house till 26th October 1892. On October 27, he said to his host, "I won't stay any more. I have been moving southward with a view to reaching Rameswaram." Haripadababu entreated him to remain for a few more days, but Swamiji resolved to leave. He decided to take the mail train for Marmagao (Margao). Haripadababu bought a ticket for him, and after putting his guru into a railway compartment he fell at his feet and said, "Swamiji, I never saluted anybody in this life with my whole being, but I do so now and feel wholly rewarded."

Haripadababu met Swamiji only three times. The first meeting was before he left for America. That was at Belgaum, about which is already told. The second meeting was some time before he left for the West the second time. The third meeting was some six or seven months before he left this world. Swamiji was a great patriotic person. One of his vows was the welfare of his motherland. But at that time, it was not so easy to the common people to make an adjustment between asceticism and patriotism. Hence many of his listeners felt surprised by hearing the patriotic thoughts from his lips. Even some of them would criticize his words of patriotism. Haripadababu has stated: "Swamiji's patriotism was very profound. This I mentioned even earlier. Once that topic was broached, and somebody told him that though it was a duty for lay people leading a social life to have love for their country, a Sannyasin should be above any attachment for his own country and that he should rather love all countries and pray for the good of all. I shall never forget the burning reply that these words evoked from Swamiji. He said, "How can a man who does not feed his own mother look after other people's mothers?" Swamiji admitted that there were many defects in our current religious practices, habits, and social customs; and he would say, "It is our bounden duty to try to rectify them by all means; but that does not mean that it is necessary to tell the English people about all these things by publishing them in the newspapers. There is no greater fool than one who washes one's dirty linen in public."

"One day we started talking about the Christian missionaries, and I happened to remark that they had done, and had been doing, a great deal of good to our country. At this he said, "But the amount of evil they have done is no less. They have done all in their power to throw to the winds the little faith that our people had in themselves and their own culture. Loss of faith means disintegration of the personality itself. Does anybody understand that? How can the missionaries prove the superiority of their own religion without decrying our deities, without condemning our religion? There is another point to consider. If anyone has to preach a particular religion, he must not only believe in it fully, but also practice it in life with full faith and sincerity. Most of the missionaries say one thing, and do something else. I can never tolerate dishonesty."

Goa

Next Swamiji is found at Margao, in Goa, by the side of Indian Ocean. This was then a Portuguese coastal colony. Which places he visited and what he did at Goa, is not known to us. During his stay at Margao, he wrote a letter to Haripada Mitra. But the date of the letter is not found; only the year 1893 is written, which is possibly not correct. According to the series of letters, it was written in the month of January, 1893. But we find Swamiji in Trivandram in the month of December 1892. Hence, Swamiji, most probably, went to Goa at the end of October or at the beginning of November of 1892. However, Swamiji wrote to Haripada Mitra: "I just now received a letter from you. I reached here (Margao) safe. I went to visit Panjim and few other villages and temples nearby. I returned just today. I have not given up the intention of visiting Gokarna, Mahabaleshwar, and other Places. I start for Dharwar by the morning train tomorrow. I have taken the walking-stick with me. Doctor Yagdekar's friend was very hospitable to me. Please give my compliments to Mr. Bhate and all others there. May the Lord shower His blessings on you and your wife. The town of Panjim is very neat and clean. Most of the Christians here are literate. The Hindus are mostly uneducated. Yours affectionately, Sachchidananda."[80]

In this letter, Swamiji have signed his name as 'Sachchidananda'. Evidently, during this period he changed to his name from 'Vivekananda', which he had used in Rajasthan and Gujarat.

Something of Swamiji's visit to Goa is also known from an article published in the *Hindu* of January 19, 1964. The author, Shri V.S. Sukhthanker, writes:

> "Swami Vivekananda, during his peregrination in India, happened to stop at Belgaum, where he expressed a desire to visit Goa to Dr. V.V. Shirgaonker, a prominent citizen of the city with whom he came into close contact. This was no ordinary visit, for he had a special purpose in mind. Dr. Shirgaonker wrote to Subrai Naik, his learned friend in Margao—Goa, to kindly be at the service of Swamiji.

"The day on which Swamiji alighted at the railway station of Margao, he was received by hundreds of people who had come to accord him welcome. Seated in a horse carriage, he was taken in procession to the house of his host Subrai Naik.

"Subrai Naik who was a scholar in Sanskrit and well versed in Hindu scriptures was naturally charmed by Swamiji's extraordinary intellect and the depth of his religious knowledge. Having come to know that the main object of his distinguished guest in visiting Goa was to study Christian theology from old Latin texts and manuscripts which were unavailable elsewhere in India, Subrai Naik invited a learned Christian friend, J.P. Alvares, and introduced him to Swamiji who had a talk with him on this subject in Latin [?]. Alvares who was greatly impressed by Swamiji's erudition, immediately made special arrangements for him to stay at the Rachol Seminary, the oldest convent-college of theology in Goa, four miles away from Margao, where rare religious literature in manuscripts and printed works in Latin [are] preserved.

"Swamiji spent three days in this seminary assiduously perusing all the important theological works that he found there. His gigantic intellect and original views about Christianity based on sound knowledge were indeed a marvel to the Father Superior and to other Padres and also to all students of this Seminary.

"On his return to Margao, visits to Swamiji from Padres even from distant places became a regular occurrence and they even took part enthusiastically in the farewell meeting organized by the Hindus in the town to honour this Hindu monk on the eve to his departure."

Shri Subrai Naik was a Sanskrit Scholar, and a well-known Ayurveda physician. Swamiji was put up in a room adjoining the temple of Damodarji, the family deity. The room, together with whatever Swamiji used, has been preserved to this day as a memorial of his visit. One day, it is said, Swamiji sang some devotional songs and was accompanied on the Tabla by Kharupji, a reputed Tabla-player. He was called Kharupji for his habit of distorting his face while playing on the Tabla. Swamiji noticed that, and advised him to give up such habit. But Kharupji said, "It is not possible." Then Swamiji himself played on the Tabla and showed that it was possible.

On the eve of Swamiji's departure, Mr. Naik asked him for a photograph of himself, to keep alive the memory of his visit. Swamiji agreed. The photograph of Swamiji is still preserved by the descendants of Mr. Naik. Later, Mr. Naik took Sannyasa and became Swami Subramanyananda Tirtha. He passed away in the same room that had been occupied by Swamiji.

THROUGH SOUTH INDIA

Mysore

From Goa Swamiji went to Dharwar by train and from there direct to Bangalore, in Mysore State. For the first few days he was a guest of Dr. P. Palpu, the Municipal Medical Officer of Bangalore. Dr. Palpu belonged to the Ezhava community, and therefore, he had to suffer at the hands of the higher-caste Hindus. In spite of having necessary qualification, he had not been able to get a Government post in Travancore State, because of the caste prejudice prevalent there. Later he obtained a post in the Mysore State service. When Swamiji came to know about the tyranny of the higher castes over the lower-caste people, he said to him, "Why do you go after the Brahmins? Find out some good noble person from among your own people and follow him." Dr. Palpu took Swamiji's advice seriously and discovered such a person in Shri Narayan Guru, who became well known as the guide and leader of the Ezhava community. Dr. Palpu devoted most of his salary and spare time to the cause of his community.

Soon after his arrival in Bangalore Swamiji became acquainted with the people, and the news about his talent began to spread all over the State. Sir K. Seshadri Iyer, the Dewan of Mysore State, heard of Swamiji. After a conversation for few minutes, he could realize that the magnetic personality and the divine force of Swamiji were destined to leave a mark in the history of his country. We don't know how the Dewan first met Swamiji, but it is known that Swamiji became his guest for three or four weeks in Mysore City. During this time, he met officials and noblemen of the Court of Mysore. Later he became a guest of the Maharaja of Mysore.

Wherever Swamiji would go he was sought after not only by Hindus, but also by people of other faiths as well. Abdul Rahman Saheb, a Muslim Councillor of the State, became surprised to see that the Hindu sannyasi was well acquainted with the Muslim scriptures, and he came to have some doubts concerning the Koran cleared. He didn't know that Swamiji had made the Koran an intellectual and spiritual possession some years earlier.

Being delighted with Swamiji's spiritual knowledge and his powerful explanation of religion Sir Seshadri Iyer said on one occasion, "Many of us have studied much about religion; and yet what has it availed us? Here is this young man whose insight exceeds that of anyone I have ever known. It is simply wonderful. He must have been born a knower of religion, otherwise how could he at such a comparatively young age have gained all this knowledge and insight?" Thinking that the Maharaja of Mysore might be interested in this "young Acharya", he wanted to introduce Swamiji to him. Swamiji, clad in ochre robe, with princely appearance, entered the audience-room of the Maharaja, Shri Chamarajendra Wadiyar. The Maharaja became delighted with his personality. He gazed at the divine face of Swamiji. "Such brilliance of thought, such charm of personality, such wide learning and such penetrating religious insight" quite won him over. Swamiji was then made a State guest and given an apartment in the palace itself. He frequently began to meet the Maharaja, who discussed with him and sought his advice on many important matters. Gradually an intimacy began to grow between them.

One day, in the presence of his courtiers, the Maharaja asked, "Swamiji, what do you think of my courtiers?" Swamiji replied boldly, "Well, I think Your Highness has a very good heart, but you are unfortunately surrounded by courtiers and courtiers are courtiers everywhere!" "No, no, Swamiji," the Maharaja protested, "my Dewan at least is not such. He is intelligent and trustworthy." "But, Your Highness," said Swamiji, "a Dewan is one who robs the Maharaja and pays the Political Agent." The Maharaja, to control the situation, changed the topic. Later he called Swamiji to his private apartments, and said, "My dear Swami, too much frankness is not always safe. If you continue to speak as you did in the presence of my courtiers, I am afraid you will be poisoned by someone." Swamiji replied, "What! Do you think an honest sannyasi is afraid of speaking the truth, even though it costs him his very life? Suppose, Your Highness, your son should ask me tomorrow, 'Swamiji, what do you think of my father?' Am I to attribute to you all sorts of virtues which I am quite aware that you do not possess? Shall I speak falsely? Never!"

Swamiji though was an outspoken man, with love and respect spoke of the Maharaja in his absence. His habit was to take a man to task for his weaknesses; but behind that man's back he would have nothing but praise for his virtues, while his defects would be disregarded.

One day Swamiji was introduced to a noted Austrian musician. He discussed with him on European music. Swamiji's knowledge of Western music made everyone amazed. Another day Swamiji met an electrician who was engaged in installation of electricity in the palace. While Swamiji was talking about electricity, it was found that he had more knowledge on the subject than the electrician.

One day a religious convention of learned men was held in the palace-hall, where Swamiji was also invited to be present. The chair was glorified by the Prime Minister. The topic was Vedanta. The pundits discussed the various theories relating to different aspects of it. At the end of their speech, Swamiji was asked to express his views. He rose, and began to say in Sanskrit fluently. At first he presented a brief note on the topic and then explained the same in detail. He didn't have any book or any paper with him. He explained how the Vedanta can practically be applicable to the society of common people, and how it can bring us peace by harmonizing the same with different religions. All present in the assembly-hall were startled with the originality of his perception and treatment, and in one voice applauded him. Being extremely pleased with Swamiji, the Prime Minister requested Swamiji to accept some presents. He ordered one of his secretaries to take him to the best shop in the market and to buy for him anything that he might like to have. To gratify the Prime Minister Swamiji went with the secretary. The secretary took a cheque-book with him so that he might write a cheque for any amount if required.

Swamiji was like a child: he looked around everything, admired many things, and finally said, "My friend, if the Dewan wishes me to have anything I desire, let me have the very best cigar in the place." The secretary was wondered to hear this. He bought a cigar for Swamiji, which had cost about a rupee only. Coming out of the store, Swamiji lighted the cigar, and got into the carriage with a pleasant face. The Prime Minister, on hearing of this, burst into laughter, and was surprised to think of the monk's apathy towards worldly interests.

One day Swamiji was called to the apartment of the Maharaja, and the Prime Minister went with him. The Maharaja asked, "Swamiji, what can I do for you?" Escaping a direct reply, Swamiji burst forth with an account of his mission. He explained the condition of India. Though India is identified by its philosophical and spiritual wealth, he said, its great needs were of modern scientific ideas and a thorough organic reform. It was for India, Swamiji continued, to give the treasure she possessed to the people of the world. He intended going to America himself to preach the gospel of Vedanta. "And what I want", he added, "is that the West should help us in improving our material condition by providing us with the means of educating our people in modern agriculture, industries and other technical sciences." The Maharaj was spell-bound. Soon he promised the necessary money to defray his travelling expenses, but Swamiji declined this offer for the present. The reason was best known to himself. Perhaps it was for his vow to visit Rameswaram, or he wanted not to be depended on any individual person. But form that day the Maharaja and his Prime Minister regarded him as "the man born for the regeneration of India."

As many as the days went on passing away, the Maharaja became more and more attached to Swamiji. Finally, when Swamiji asked for leaving, the Maharaja felt distressed and entreated him to stay for more few days. He added, "Swamiji, I must have something with me as a remembrance of your personality. So, allow me to take a phonographic record of your voice." Swamiji gave his consent to this, and even now the record is preserved in the palace, though it has long since become indistinct. So great was the Maharaja's admiration for Swamiji that he proposed to worship his feet, as one worships those of one's guru. But Swamiji did not allow it.

After some days Swamiji wanted to take leave. Hearing this, the Maharaja wished to give him costly presents. But Swamiji was not willing to accept anything. When the Maharaja insisted him, he said, "Well, Your Highness, if you persist in offering me something, then please give a nonmetallic Hookah. That will be of some use to me." The Maharaja presented him a rosewood [in another opinion, it was of sandalwood] pipe, delicately carved. At the time of departure, the Maharaja bowed at his feet, and the Prime Minister tried to thrust a roll of currency notes into his pocket, but he failed. Swamiji said, "If you desire to do anything for me, please buy me a railway ticket. I am going to Rameswaram, but on the way I would like to halt at Cochin for few days." Realizing that Swamiji would not allow him to do more, the Prime Minister bought a second-class ticket and gave him a letter of introduction to Shri Shankariah, the acting Dewan of Cochin.

Trichur

The next place Swamiji is known to have visited was Trichur. In those days there was no railway in Cochin and Travancore States. So he got down at Shoranur, the nearest station for Trichur. Then he travelled twenty-one miles by bullock-cart and reached Trichur. When the bullock-cart was passing through the town, Swamiji saw a gentleman standing at the door of a house. Swamiji got down and asked the gentleman, "Is there any suitable place for bathing?" The gentleman was impressed by Swamiji's personality, and invited him to be a guest in an annexe to his house. He arranged for his bath. Swamiji was then suffering from sore throat. The gentleman took him to the District Hospital run by the Government, where a Dr. De Souza treated him. This gentleman was one D.A. Subramanya Iyer, an officer in the Education Department of Cochin State.

At Trichur Swamiji stayed only for few days. He next went to a place called Cranganore or Kodungalloor, famous as a seat of learning and for its Kali temple. When Swamiji went to enter the temple to offer worship to the deity, he was prevented by the temple guards. So he bowed down to the deity from outside, and took shelter under a banyan tree near the temple. His ochre robes and brilliant eyes attracted the attention of a young man. The young man approached him with the intention of having some fun, but he came away disappointed when he found that the monk was not as he had thought to be. By that time two princes of Cranganore palace, Kochunni Thampuran and Bhatta Thampuran, came to the temple, and saw Swamiji sitting under the banyan tree. The two princes were well versed in the scriptures. Seeing the features of Swamiji they realized that he was not an ordinary monk. When they approached him to talk to him, Swamiji asked them why he was not allowed to enter the temple. They replied that this was the custom of that place, because it was difficult to know the caste of people, especially of those who came from outside Kerala. They had an argument in Sanskrit over the issue. Swamiji didn't interfere with their local tradition. They argued with Swamiji for two days, and were defeated. On the third day when they approached Swamiji with the desire to have his holy company, they found him absorbed in meditation. They were surprised to see his glowing face, which reminded them of what scriptures say about the man of meditation. When Swamiji came back to his normal consciousness, he conversed with the princes in Sanskrit. Before they took leave, they bowed at the feet of Swamiji.

Then some of the learned women of the royal family came to meet Swamiji and spoke with him in Sanskrit. Swamiji was surprised to find women speaking Sanskrit so fluently. In no other part of India had he come across such women. On the fourth day the princes came to the temple, but they were disappointed when they did not find Swamiji under the banyan tree. Swamiji had left the town and gone towards Cochin. Some months later, when they saw the picture of Swami Vivekananda in the papers and read about his success in the Parliament of Religion at Chicago, they recognized him to be the monk with whom they had spoken under the banyan tree.

Ernakulam

Swamiji was next found at Ernakulam, the capital of Cochin State. There he met Shri Chattambi Swami, the guru of well-known Narayan Guru of Kerala. This meeting took place during December 1892.

In 1971 Mr. Bodhasharan, who knew Chattambi Swami intimately, gave these reminiscences to Shri Shankari Prasad Basu:

> "I was very intimately connected with the Chattambi Swami. I have often heard from him about his meeting with the Swami (Swamiji).

"It may have been before or after Swamiji's visit to Kanyakumari. At Ernakulam, one Mr. [chandu] Lal and a Brahmin [Shri Ramaiya] used to go for a walk every morning and evening. One day, when they had been for a walk to the seaside as usual, they saw a boat coming. A sannyasi clad in ochre robes, and with staff in hand, got out of it. On seeing him they thought that he must be a great man, and a genuine sannyasi, so they must not miss meeting him. They went forward and approached the monk, who spoke with them in Hindi. One of them took the Swami to his house. They asked him, "Do you know English?" In broken Hindi the Swami replied, "I know a little." But later it was revealed that he was a master of the language. The news soon spread. Many people of Ernakulam flocked round him. At this time Chattambi Swami was also in Ernakulam. Once he came to meet the Swami, but on finding a crowd round him, he left, after seeing him from a distance. The local people told the Swami many things about Chattambi Swami; and some of them promised to bring Chattambi Swami to him so that they could be introduced to each other. At this the Swami said, "If he is really a great man, as you tell me his is, why should he come to me? I shall go to see him." Chattambi Swami was then living at Shankar Menon's house. The Swami went to see him there. They talked in Sanskrit, since Chattambi Swami did not know Hindi. Chattambi took the Swami under a tree so that they could talk together in a secluded place. On the tree was a monkey, which had been reared by the host. When they were talking, the monkey became restless and started shaking the tree. The Swami looked up at the restless monkey and said, "Just like my mind." Chattambi Swami said, "Only a great person like you can say such a thing." Then both of them talked about "Chinmudra". The Swami asked, "Why is the Chinmudra like this?" Chattambi Swami was a scholar learned in Tamil literature; so he gave a proper reply. The Swami was very pleased with it. Catching hold of Chattambi Swami's hands and bending his own head down, he said in Hindi, "Very good." Some may interpret this by saying that the Swami placed Chattambi Swami's hands on his [Swamiji's] head; but Chattambi Swami said, "That [interpretation] is not right. It was a way of showing gratitude."

"Whenever Chattambi Swami saw me, he used to talk of the Swami. He was charmed by the Swami's voice. He used to say, "When the Swami used to sing, it was just like the sound of a golden pot. Oh, how sweet a voice!" He used to praise the eyes of the Swami too.

"Once when the Swami and Chattambi Swami were talking in Sanskrit, a Sanskrit scholar happened to be present. He pointed out a grammatical mistake in the Swami's language. The Swami immediately reacted: "I need not follow grammar; the grammar will follow me."

"Chattambi Swami and Narayan Guru did not approve of the Swami's meat-eating. They used to say, "But for that, he was a divinely-inspired person."[81]

According to K.P.K. Menon, author of the short biography *Chattambi Swamigal*, Swamiji's meeting with Chattambi Swami took place at the house of Rama Iyer, the Dewan's Secretary, who was a great admirer of the latter.

Shri P. Seshadri had researched on Swamiji's visit to Kerala. In the "Vivekananda Centenary Souvenir", published by the Vivekananda Centenary Central Committee of Trichur in 1963, he writes:

> "It is said that Swamiji met the great Chattambi Swami at Ernakulam. Both were impressed with each other and Swamiji asked Shri Chattambi Swami to go over to him alone. He did so and they were talking together one whole night. It is said that one of the topics they discussed was the Chinmudra. It is also said that Swamiji wrote down the name and address of Shri Chattambi Swami in his diary and told him, "I am writing that I have met a real man in Malabar [Kerala]." Shri Chattambi Swami often used to speak of Swamiji with great admiration. In a letter he wrote, with his characteristic modesty: "I doubt whether the difference between Vivekananda Swami and me is merely that between Garuda [the King of Birds] and a mosquito!"[82]

We know that Swamiji was eager to visit Rameswaram. Why did he go to Kerala? We have already told that in Bangalore Swamiji was the guest of Dr. Palpu, who told him of the miserable condition of the lower castes in Cochin and Travancore states. According to Shesadri, Swamiji went to Kerala to see the condition of the people. It was his intention to gain first hand acquaintance with as much of India as he could in the course of his pilgrimage.

Trivandrum

From Ernakulam, the capital of Cochin State, Swamiji went south into Travancore. He was charmed by the natural beauty of the place. It is about 140 miles from Ernakulam to Travancore. In those days the journey took about a week, whether one went by road or waterway. Swamiji reached Travancore on December 13, and stayed there for nine days and left on December 22. Hence he perhaps had left Ernakulam on December 6. In Trivandrum, the capital of Travancore, Swamiji was the guest of Prof. Sundararama Iyer, who was tutor to the First Prince, the nephew of the Maharaja of Travancore. Prof. Iyer writes of Swamiji's nine days' stay with him as follows:

> "I met Swami Vivekananda for the first time at Trivandrum in December 1892, and was then privileged to see and know a good deal of him.... He came to me accompanied by a Mohammedan guide. My second son—a little boy of twelve, who has since passed away—took him for, and announced him to me as, a Mohammedan too, as he well might from his costume which was quite unusual for a Hindu Sannyasin of Southern India. I took him upstairs, entered into conversation, and made him due obeisance as soon as I learnt what he was. Almost the first thing he asked me to do was to arrange for his Mohammedan attendant's meals. His companion was a peon in the Cochin State service, and had been detailed to accompany him to Trivandrum by the Secretary to the Dewan, Mr. W. Ramaiyya.... The Swami had taken almost nothing except a little milk during the two previous days, and only after his Mohammedan peon had been provided with meals and taken leave would he have any thought bestowed on himself.

"Within a few minutes' conversation, I found that the Swami was a mighty man. Having ascertained from him that, since leaving Ernakulam he had taken almost nothing, I asked him what food he was accustomed to. He replied, "Anything you like; we Sannyasins have no tastes." We had some little conversation, as there was yet an interval of a few minutes before dinner. On learning that the Swami was a Bengali, I made the observation that the Bengalis had produced many great men—and, foremost of them all, the Brahmo preacher, Keshab Chandra Sen. It was then that the Swami mentioned to me the name of his guru Shri Ramakrishna, and expatiated briefly on his eminent spiritual endowments, and took my breath completely away by the remark that Keshab was a mere child when compared with Shri Ramakrishna, that not only he, but many eminent Bengalis of a generation past, had been influenced by the sage, that Keshab had in later life received the benefit of his inspiration and had undergone some considerable change for the better in his religious views, that many Europeans had sought the acquaintance of Shri Ramakrishna and regarded him as a semi-divine personage, and that no less a man that the late Director of Public Instruction in Bengal, Mr. C.H. Tawney, had written a paper on the character, genius, catholicity, and inspiring power of the great sage.

"All this conversation had occupied us while the Swami's food was being prepared and during the time he was breaking his nearly two days' fast by a hearty dinner. The Swami's presence, his voice, the glitter in his eyes, and the flow of his words and ideas were so inspiring that I excused myself that day from attending at the palace of the late Martanda Varma, the First Prince of Travancore, who was prosecuting his M.A. studies under my tuition.... I took him in the evening to the house of Prof. Rangacharya, who was then professor of Chemistry in the Trivandrum College, and who was even then at the height of his reputation as a scholar and man of science not only in Travancore, but throughout Southern India. Not finding him at home, we drove to the Trivandrum Club. There I introduced the Swami to various gentlemen present, and to Prof. Rangacharya when he came in later on, to the late Prof. Sundaram Pillai, and others among whom I distinctly remember a late Brahmin Dewan Peshkar and my friend Narayana Menon—who, I believe, is one of the Dewan Peshkars today in Travancore—owing to an incident which, however trifling in itself, brought out a prominent characteristic of the Swami, how he was all eyes and noted closely all that was passing around him and could use them effectively, how he combined with his rare gentleness and sweetness of temper, the presence of mind and the power of retort which could quickly silence an opponent. Mr. Narayana Menon had, while leaving the Club earlier in the evening, saluted the Brahmin Dewan Peshkar and the latter had returned it in the time-honoured fashion in which Brahmins who maintain old forms of etiquette return the salute of Shudras, i.e., by raising the left hand a little higher than the right. Many members of the Club had come and gone, and at last five of us were left, the Swami, the Dewan Peshkar, his brother, Prof. Rangacharya, and myself. As we were dispersing, the Dewan Peshkar made his obeisance to the Swami which the latter returned in the manner usual with Hindu monks by simply uttering the name of Narayana. This roused the Peshkar's ire, for he wanted the Swami's obeisance, too, in the fashion in which he had made his own. The Swami then turned on him and said, "If you could exercise your customary form of etiquette in returning Narayana Menon's greeting, why should you resent my own adoption of the Sannyasins customary mode of acknowledging your obeisance to me?" This reply had the desired effect, and next day the gentleman's brother came to us and conveyed some kind of apology for the awkward incident of the night previous. During the evening, short as his stay had been at the Club premises, the Swami's personality had made an impression on all....

"The Swami paid a visit the next day to Prince Martanda Varma, who, when informed by me of the remarkable intellectual and imposing presence of my visitor, communicated to the Swami his desire for an interview. Of course I accompanied the Swami and was present at the conversation between him and the Prince. The Swami happened to mention his visits to various native princes and courts during his travels. This greatly interested the Prince who interrogated him regarding his impressions. The Swami then told him that, of all the Hindu ruling princes he had met, he had been most impressed with the capacity, patriotism, energy and foresight of H.H. the Gaikwar of Baroda, that he had also known and greatly admired the high qualities of the small Rajput Chief of Khetri, and that, as he came more and more south, he had found a growing deterioration in the character and capacity of Indian princes and chiefs. The Prince then asked him if he had seen his uncle, the ruler of Travancore. The Swami had not yet had time to arrange for a visit to His Highness. I may here mention at once that a visit was arranged two days later through the good offices of the Dewan, Mr. Sankara Subbier. The Maharaja received the Swami, inquired of his welfare, and told him that the Dewan would provide him with every convenience during his stay both in Trivandrum and elsewhere within the State. The visit lasted only for two or three minutes, and so the Swami returned a little disappointed....

"To return to the Swami's conversation with the Prince.... The Swami then made earnest inquiry regarding Prince Martanda Varma's studies, and his aims in life. The Prince replied that he had already taken some interest in the doings of the people of Travancore and that he had resolved to do what he could, as a leading and loyal subject of the Maharaja and as a member of the ruling family, to advance their welfare. The Prince was struck, like all others who had come into contact with him, with the Swami's striking figure and attractive features; and, being an amateur photographer, asked the Swami for a sitting and took a fine photograph which he skillfully developed into an impressive picture and later on sent as an interesting exhibit to the next Fine Arts Exhibition held in the Madras Museum.

"... The Swami found me much inclined to orthodox Hindu modes of life and beliefs. Perhaps that was why he spoke a good deal in the vein suited to my tastes and views, though occasionally he burst out into spirited denunciation of the observance of mere *deshachara* or local usage....

"The Swami once made a spirited attack on the extravagant claims put forth by science on men's allegiance. "If religion has its superstitions," the Swami remarked, "science has its superstitions too." Both the mechanical and evolutionary theories are, on examination, found inadequate and unsatisfying, and still there are large numbers of men who speak of the entire universe as an open secret. Agnosticism has also bulked large in men's esteem, but has only betrayed its ignorance and arrogance by ignoring the laws and truths of the Indian science of thought-control. Western psychology has miserably failed to cope with the superconscious aspects and laws of human nature. Where European science has stopped short, Indian psychology comes in and explains, illustrates and teaches how to render real and practical laws appertaining to higher states of existence and experience. Religion alone—and especially the religion of the Indian sages—can understand the subtle and secret working of the human mind and conquer its unspiritual cravings so as to realize the one Existence and comprehend all else as its limitation and manifestation when under the bondage of matter. Another subject on which the Swami spoke was the distinction between the world of gross matter (*Laukika*) and the world of fine matter (*Alaukika*). The Swami explained how both kept man within the bondage of the senses, and only he who rose superior to both could attain to the freedom which is the aim of all life and raise himself above the petty vanities of the world, whether of men or gods. The Swami spoke to me of the institution of caste, and held that the Brahmin would continue to live as long as he found unselfish work to do and freely gave of his knowledge and all to the rest of the population. In the actual words of the Swami which are still ringing in my ears, "The Brahmin has done great things for India; he is doing great things for India, and he is destined to do still greater things for India in the future." The Swami also declared himself sternly against all interference against the *shastric* (scriptural) usages and injunctions in regard to the status and marriage of women. Women as well as the lower classes and castes must receive Sanskrit education, imbibe the ancient spiritual culture, and realize in practice all the spiritual ideals of the rishis; and then they would take into their own hands all questions affecting their own status and solve them in the light thrown on them by their own knowledge of the truths of religion and the enlightened perception of their own needs and requirements....

"I also asked the Swami for his views on the question of sea-voyage. He replied that the social environment in Western countries must be better prepared than it was and is by the preaching of the Vedanta before Brahmins and other caste Hindus could find it suitable for their accustomed life of ceremonial purity and those time-worn and time-honoured restrictions as regards food, drink, etc., which have made them for ages almost the sole champions of, and channels for, the gospel of mercy. There was not the least objection, however, in the case of Hindus who were already free from, or were prepared to throw aside, all such restrictions.

"On the third and fourth day of the Swami's stay with me, I sent information to a valued friend of mine in Trivandrum... Mr. S. Rama Rao, the then Director of Vernacular Instruction in Travancore... I remember vividly how once Mr. Rama Rao wished the Swami to explain *indriya-nigraha*, the restraint of the senses. The Swami then launched forth into a vivid narration of a story very much like what is usually told of Lila-Shukha, the famous composer of *Krishna-*

Karnamritam. The vivid picture he gave of the last stage in which the hero is taken to Vrindaban and puts out his own eyes when he gets severely handled for his amorous pursuit of a Sett's daughter there, and then proclaims his repentance and his resolve to end his days in unswerving meditation on the divine Shri Krishna at the scene of the Lord's sportive deeds in the days of His childhood on earth, bursts on my mind, even at this distance of twenty-one years, with somewhat of the effect of those irresistibly charming and undying notes on the flute by the late miraculous musician Sarabha Shastriar of Kumbakonam. The Swami's concluding words after mentioning the closing incident of putting out the eyes were: "Even this extreme step must, it necessary, be taken as a preliminary to the restraint of the wandering and unsubjugated senses and the consequent turning of the mind towards the Lord."

"On the third or fourth day of his stay, I made inquires, at the Swami's request, regarding the whereabouts of Mr. Manmatha Nath Bhattacharya, who was then Assistant to the Accountant-General, Madras, and who had come down to Trivandrum on official duty in connection with some defalcations alleged to have taken place at the Resident's Treasury. From that time the Swami used daily to spend his mornings with Mr. Bhattacharya and stay for dinner. One day, however, I complained that he was giving all his time to Mr. Bhattacharya, the Swami made a characteristic reply: "We Bengalis, are a clannish people." He said also that Mr. Bhattacharya had been his school or college mate, and that he had an additional claim for consideration as he was the son of the late world-renowned scholar, Pandit Mahesh Chandra Nayaratna, formerly the Principal of the Calcutta Sanskrit College. The Swami also told me that he had long taken no fish food, as the South Indian Brahmins whose guest he had been throughout his South Indian tour were forbidden both fish and flesh, and would fain avail himself of this opportunity to have his accustomed fare. I at once expressed my loathing for the taking of fish or flesh as food. The Swami said in reply that the ancient Brahmins of India were accustomed to take meat and even beef and were called upon to kill cows and other animals in *yajnas* of for giving *madhuparka* [prepared with honey and meat etc.] to guests. He also held that the introduction and spread of Buddhism led to the gradual discontinuance of flesh as food, though the Hindu *shastras* [scriptures] had always expressed a theoretical preference for those who avoided the use of flesh-foods, and that the disfavour into which flesh had fallen was one of the chief causes of the gradual decline of the national strength, and the final overthrow of the national independence of the united ancient Hindu races and states of India.... The Swami's opinion, at least as expressed in conversation with me, was that the Hindus must freely take to the use of animal food if India was at all to cope with the rest of the world in the present race for power and predominance among the world's communities, whether within the British empire, or beyond its limits.

"Once a visitor detained the Swami from his usual visit to his Bengali countryman, Mr. Bhattacharya. This visitor was one Mr. Piravi Perumal Pillay, the Assistant Dewan or Peshkar in the Huzoor Office, Trivandrum. He seemed to have come on purpose to ascertain what the Swami knew of various cults and religions in India and elsewhere, and began by putting forward various objections to the Advaita Vedanta. He soon found out that the Swami was a master from whose stores it was more important to draw what one could for inspiration without loss of time than to examine what were the depths and heights in which his mind could range. I have seen the Swami exhibit on this occasion...his rare power of gauging in a moment what is the mental reach of a self-confident visitor, and then turning him unconsciously away to ground suitable to him and then giving him the benefit of his guidance and inspiration. On the present occasion, the Swami happened to quote from *Lalita Vistara* some verses descriptive of Buddha's *vairagya* (dispassion), and in such an entrancingly melodious voice that the visitor's heart quite melted, and he speedily fell into a passive listening mood, which the Swami skillfully utilized to carry home to his mind a lasting impression of Buddha's great renunciation, his unflinching search after truth, his final discovery of it and his unwearied ministry of forty-five years among men and women of all castes, ranks, and conditions of life. The discourse occupied nearly an hour, and at its close the Swami's visitor was so visibly affected and acknowledged himself as feeling so much raised for the time being above the sordid realities and vanities of life, that he made many devout prostrations at the Swami's feet and declared when leaving, that he had never seen his like and would never forget the discourse which had impressed him greatly.

"Once I happened to ask him to deliver a public lecture. The Swami said that he had never before spoken in public and would surely prove a lamentable and ludicrous failure. Upon this I inquired how, if this were true, he could face the august assembly of the Parliament of Religions at Chicago at which he told me he had been asked by the Maharaja of Mysore to be present as the representative of Hinduism. The Swami gave me a reply which at the time seemed to me decidedly evasive, namely, that if it was the will of the Supreme that he should be made His mouthpiece and do a great service to the cause of truth and holy living, He surely would endow him with the gifts and qualities needed for it. I said I was incredulous as to the probability or possibility of a special intervention of this kind.... He at once came down on me with a sledge-hammer, denouncing me as one who, in spite of my apparent Hindu orthodoxy so far as my daily observances and verbal professions went, was at heart somewhat of a sceptic, because I seemed to him prepared to set limits of my own to the extent of the Lord's power of beneficent interposition in the affairs of the universe.

"On another occasion, too, some difference of opinion existed in regard to a question of much importance in Indian ethnology. The Swami held that wherever a Brahmin was found with a dark skin, it was clearly a case of atavism, demonstrating the descent of characteristic due to Dravidian admixture. To this I replied that colour was essentially a changeable feature in man and largely dependent on such conditions as climate, food, the nature of the occupation as entailing an outdoor or indoor life, and so on. The Swami combated my view and maintained that the Brahmins were as much mixed race as the rest of mankind, and that their belief in their racial purity was largely founded on fiction. I quoted high authority—C.L. Brace and others—against him in regard to the purity of Indian races, but the Swami was obdurate and maintained his own view.

"During all the time he stayed, he took captive every heart within the home. To every one of us he was all sweetness, all tenderness, all grace. My sons were frequently in his company, and one of them still swears by him and has the most vivid and endearing recollections of his visit and of his striking personality. The Swami learnt a number of Tamil words and took delight in conversing in Tamil with the Brahmin cook in our home. It hardly seemed as if there was a stranger moving in our midst. When he left, it seemed for a time as if the light had gone out of our home.

"Just as he was about to leave, accompanied by his Bengali companion, Mr. Bhattacharya—it was on the 22nd December 1892—an incident happened which is worth recording. Pandit Vanchisvara Shastri—a master of that most difficult branch of learning, Sanskrit grammar, and highly honoured by all who knew him for his piety, learning, and modesty—was a dependent of the first Prince of Travancore, who, at my request, had secured his services as teacher of Sanskrit to my son. During all these days of the Swami's stay he never once came to my house. As the Swami was leaving, he made his appearance and implored me to arrange for an interview, however short.... The Swami and Mr. Bhattacharya were just then descending the stairs to get into their carriage and drive away. The Pandit entreated me in the most pressing manner to ask the Swami for at least a few minutes' delay. On being informed of this, the Swami entered into a brief conversation with him in Sanskrit, which lasted seven or eight minutes only.... The Pandit told me that it related to some knotty and controverted point in *vyakarana* (grammar) and that, even during that brief conversation, the Swami showed that he could display his accurate knowledge of Sanskrit grammar and his perfect mastery of the Sanskrit language.

"With this the Swami's stay of nine days had come to a close. In my recollection of today, it seems to be somewhat of a nine days' wonder; the impression is one which never can be effaced...."[83]

On the day of Swamiji's arrival at Trivandrum, as we have seen, Prof. Sundararama Iyer introduced him to Prof. Rangacharya. S.K. Nair, of Travancore, wrote of these professors' association with Swamiji and of the impression, which is as follows:

> "Both these gentlemen, who were themselves erudite scholars in English and Sanskrit, found great pleasure and derived much benefit by constant conversation with the Swami. Anyone who became acquainted with him could not but be struck with his powerful personality and be drawn to him. He had the wonderful faculty of answering many men on questions at once and the same time. It might be a talk on Spencer, or some thought of Shakespeare or kalidasa, Darwin's Theory of Evolution, the Jewish history, the growth of Aryan civilization, the Vedas, Islam or Christianity—whatever the question, the Swami was ready with an appropriate answer.... Sublimity and simplicity were written boldly on his features. A clean heart, a pure and austere life, an open mind, a liberal spirit, a wide outlook and broad sympathy were the redeeming characteristics of the Swami."

Shri K.S. Ramaswami Shastri, the son of Prof. Sundararama Iyer, wrote in *Prabuddha Bharat* (published in September 1953):

> "It was given to me to meet Swami Vivekananda and spend many days with him at Trivandrum towards the close of 1892... Swamiji stayed in our house for nine days.

"[One day] he said to me and my father: "Practical patriotism means not a mere sentiment or even emotion of love of the motherland but a passion to serve our fellow-countrymen. I have gone all over India on foot and have seen with my own eyes the ignorance, misery and squalor of our people. My whole soul is afire and I am burning with a fierce desire to change such evil conditions. Let no one talk of Karma. If it was their Karma to suffer, it is our Karma to relieve the suffering. If you want to find God, serve man. To reach Narayana you must serve the Daridra Narayana—the starving millions of India."...

It is known that at Trivandrum Swamiji taught about the necessity of many reforms affecting the whole Indian nation, and referred to the need of improving the condition of the poor. Mr. Shastri continued: "On yet another day, Swamiji told me, "You are still a young boy. I hope and wish that some day you will reverentially study the Upanishads, the *Brahma-Sutras* and the *Bhagavad-Gita* which are known as the Prasthana-trya, as also the Itihasa, the Puranas and the Agamas. You will not find the like of all these anywhere else in the world. Man alone, out of all living beings, has a hunger in his heart to know the whence and whither, the whys and wherefores of things...."

Kanyakumari

Mr. Shastri said, "Swami Vivekananda went from Trivandrum to Kanyakumari (Cape Comorin) towards the close of 1892... From Cape Comorin Swamiji went walking to Ramnad and thence to Pondicherry and finally reached Madras...."

It was formerly thought that Swamiji went from Trivandrum to Rameswaram, and from there to Kanyakumari. But the above memories of K.S. Ramaswami Shastri, published in 1953, do not match with the view. In his letter of January 19, 1965, to the General Secretary of the Ramakrishna Math, Mr. Shastri wrote: "On the eve of departure from our house in 1893 [1892] Swamiji Maharaj said that he was going to Kanyakumari...when he came to Madras in January 1897, I met him. He told me that he stayed on the rock overnight."

Many other evidences regarding Swamiji's visit to Kanyakumari are found, but none of them could say the particular date of the same. Apart from the consideration of date, we may come to the conclusion that on 22nd December 1892 Swamiji left Trivandrum for Nagercoil, where from he went to Kanyakumari, and from there to Rameswaram via Madurai.

Kanyakumari, the southern-most tip of India, is around 90 km. away from Trivandrum and is located in Tamil Nadu. It is 20 km. from another famous temple town called Nagercoil. Kanyakumari has now become a famous tourist spot and anyone who goes there does not miss visiting the Vivekananda Rock. Swamiji went to Nagercoil along with Shri Manmatha Bhattacharya. After staying at Nagercoil for a couple of days, he is said to have reached Kanyakumari on the 24th or 25th. It is the meeting-place of three seas, and a place of pilgrimage for Hindus. "Kanyakumari" means virgin girl. The famous temple there is dedicated to the Divine Mother manifest as a virgin girl. Swamiji first visited the temple of Kanyakumari (Parvati) and prayed and meditated for a while. He then came out and stood on the oceanside, gazing at the sea. Some two furlongs away he saw two large rocks. According to the Puranas, the larger and farther of these two rocks is the one that has been sanctified by the blessed feet of the Divine Mother. Swamiji was seized with the desire to reach those rocks. He asked a few boatmen whether he could be ferried to the rock. They were ready to take him there but Swamiji did not have a single paisa to pay them. What happened next was something remarkable. Without much ado, Swamiji plunged into the roaring waves and swam across. The experienced boatmen were shocked to see him do this and screamed out to him to return to the shore. They warned him of the stormy waves and the sharks in the ocean. But Swamiji swam safely across and stepped onto the rock. He spent three days and three nights on that rock. The roaring ocean was all the company he had. There, sitting on the last stone of India, he passed into a deep meditation on the present and future of his country. He sought to understand the root of her downfall. With the vision of a seer, he understood why India had been thrown from the pinnacle of glory to the depths of degradation. He reflected on the purpose and achievement of the Indian world. He perceived the realities and potentialities of Indian culture. He saw religion to be the life-blood of India's millions. He realized in the silence of his heart that India shall rise only through a renewal and restoration of that highest spiritual consciousness that has made her, at all times, the cradle of the Nations and cradle of the Faith. He saw her greatness; he saw her weaknesses as well, the central one of which was that the nation had lost its individuality.

Swamiji's mental state of that time is beautifully described by his Eastern and Western Disciples in the *Life of Swami Vivekananda*:

> The single-minded monk had become transformed into a reformer, a nation-builder and a world-architect. His soul brooded with tenderness and anguish over India's poverty.

> What use is a religion, he thought, from which the masses are excluded? Everywhere and at all times he saw that the poor had been oppressed by whatever power the changes of fortune had set over them. The dominance of the priesthood, the despotism of caste, the merciless divisions which these created in the social body, making outcasts of religion the majority of its followers—these the Swami saw as almost insurmountable barriers to the progress of the Indian nation. His heart throbbed for the masses, great in their endurance. He seemed to enter, in some high mode of feeling, their world. In their sufferings he found himself sharing; by their degradation he found himself humiliated. He longed to throw in his lot with theirs. Agony was in his soul when he thought how those who prided themselves on being the custodians of religion had held down the masses through the ages.

The zeal of his meditation on the rock and the responsibility of his work for the development of India are found reflected in his letter of March 19, 1894, that he wrote to Swami Ramakrishnananda from Chicago:

> In view of all this, especially of the poverty and ignorance, I had no sleep. At Cape Comorin sitting in Mother Kumari's temple, sitting on the last bit of Indian rock—I hit upon a plan: We are so many Sannyasins wandering about, and teaching the people metaphysics—it is all madness. Did not our Gurudeva use to say, "An empty stomach is no good for religion?" That those poor people are leading the life of brutes is simply due to ignorance. We have for all ages been sucking their blood and trampling them underfoot.

What kind of remedy was found by Swamiji, and what was his plan? We find the answer in the same letter:

> Suppose some disinterested Sannyasins, bent on doing good to others, go from village to village, disseminating education and seeking in various ways to better the condition of all down to the Chandala [outcaste], through oral teaching, and by means of maps, cameras, globes and such other accessories—can't that bring forth good in time? All these plans I cannot write out in this short letter. The long and that short of it is—if the mountain does not come to Mohammed, Mohammed must go to the mountain. The poor are too poor to come to schools and Pathashalas, and they will gain nothing by reading poetry and all that sort of things. We, as a nation, have lost our individuality, and that is the cause of all mischief in India. We have to give back to the nation its lost individuality and *raise the masses*. The Hindu, the Mohammedan, the Christian, all have trampled them underfoot. Again the force to raise them must come from inside, that is, from the orthodox Hindus. In every country the evils exist not with, but against, religion. Religion therefore is not to blame, but men.[84]

Swamiji realized the value of money which is necessary in the service of the masses. He has travelled the length and breadth of India, and experienced the nature of people of the country. In the midst of despair, he was sure that from every town he could get ten to fifteen men who would help him to make his plan fruitful. But what could he do without money? "Selfishness personified—are they to spend anything!" exclaimed Swamiji. He, therefore, decided to go to America, where he could earn money by the power of his intellect, and then on returning to India, he would devote the rest of his life to the regeneration of his countrymen—or die in the attempt. He had faith in Shri Ramakrishna who would show him the way, even if nobody in the world would help the work.

Now on this mid-sea rock, he meditated not on God but on Mother India who for Swami Vivekananda was Divine Durga incarnate. What a strange meditation! It was as if all the pages of India's history opened up before him. The vast panorama of his experiences during his travels passed before his mind's eye. He meditated on the past, the present and the future of India, the cause of her downfall and the means of her resurrection.

He felt in his heart of hearts that India would rise only through a renewal and restoration of that highest spiritual consciousness which had made her, throughout her history, the cradle of religions and cultures. He then, sitting on the last bit of rock in the Indian ocean, took the momentous decision to go to the West to give shape to his life's mission of spreading India's religion and culture throughout the whole world and also to seek help for the poor millions of India.

Madurai

Swamiji was perhaps on the rock from December 24 to 26. Next, he set out for Rameswaram, to the north, on foot. On the way he stopped at Madurai, where he met the Raja of Ramnad, Bhaskara Setupati, to whom he had a letter of introduction. Raja Bhaskara Setupati was one of the most enlightened of Indian rulers. He became an admirer and disciple of Swamiji. During conversation Swamiji expressed many of his ideas about the education of the poor, the improvement of agriculture, and about the problem and potentialities of India. The Raja encouraged Swamiji for going to the coming Parliament of Religions at Chicago, and said that it would be an opportunity for drawing attention of the world to Indian spiritual thought, and also for laying foundation of his work in India. The Raja also promised to help him. But Swamiji took leave, saying that he would let him know his decision about going to America in the near future.

Rameswaram

Rameswaram is one of the most sacred Hindu religious sites and a pilgrimage destination for thousands of Hindus every year. The Ramanathaswamy Temple at Rameswaram has the longest corridor in Asia. Rameswaram is situated at the centre of the island, around 11 kilometers from the township of Pamban and 18 kilometers from Dhanushkodi.

Ramanathaswamy Temple is a Hindu temple dedicated to the god Shiva located on Rameswaram island in the state of Tamil Nadu, India. The temple has the longest corridor of all Hindu temples in India. The temple is located in Rameswaram considered a holy pilgrimage site for Shaivites, Vaishnavites and Smarthas. The presiding deity, the Lingam of Ramanathaswamy (Shiva), is believed to have been established and worshiped by Rama, an avatar of god Vishnu, to absolve the sins created during the Ramayana war at Sri Lanka. According to the *Ramayana*, Rama, the seventh avatar of god Vishnu, prayed to god Shiva to absolve sin of killing a brahmin, committed during his war against the demon king Ravana in Sri Lanka. Rama wanted to have the largest lingam to worship Shiva. He directed Hanuman, the monkey lieutenant in his army, to bring the lingam from Himalayas. Since it took longer time to bring the lingam, Sita, the wife of Rama, built a small lingam out of the sand available on the sea shore, which is believed to be the lingam in the sanctum. Two lingams inside the sanctum—one built by Sita, from sand, residing as the main deity, Ramalingam and the one brought by Hanuman from Kailash called Vishwalingam. Rama instructed that Vishwalingam should be worshipped first since it was brought by Hanuman—the tradition continues even today.

Like all ancient temples in South India, there is a high compound wall (madil) on all four sides of the temple premises measuring about 865 feet furlong from east to west and one furlongs of 657 feet from north to south with huge towers (Gopurams) at the east and west and finished gate towers on the north and south. The temple has striking long corridors in its interior, running between huge colonnades on platforms above five feet high.

The second corridor is formed by sandstone pillars, beams and ceiling. The junction of the third corridor on the west and the paved way leading from the western gopuram to Setumadhava shrine forms a unique structure in the form of a chess board and it is popularly known as Chokkattan Madapam where the Utsava deities are adorned and kept during the Vasanthotsavam (Spring festival) and on the 6th day festival in Adi (July-August) and Masi (February-March) conducted by the Setupati of Ramnad.

The outer set of corridors is reputed to be the longest in the world being about 6.9 m height, 400 feet in each in the east and west and about 640 feet in north and south and inner corridors are about 224 feet in east and west and about 352 feet each in north and south. Their width varies from 15.5 feet to 17 feet in the east and west about 172 feet on the north and south with width varying 14.5 feet to 17 feet. The total length of those corridors is thus 3850 feet. There are about 1212 pillars in the outer corridor. Their height is about 30 feet from the floor to the center of the roof. The main tower or rajagopuram is 53 m tall. Most pillars are carved with individual composition. At the beginning, Ramanathaswamy Temple was a thatched shed. The present structure was the work of many individuals spread over a number of centuries. The pride of place in the establishment for the Temple goes to the Setupatis of Ramanathapuram.

The pilgrimage to Rameswaram was the fulfilment of a cherished desire of Swamiji. Thus, he completed his pilgrimage to India herself.

Pondicherry

The year 1892 ended with Swamiji's pilgrimage to India, and he set out for Madras (presently Chennai) from Rameswaram. We remember that Swamiji had parted from Manmathanath Bhattacharya on reaching Kanyakumari (Cape Comorin). Manmathanath chanced to meet Swamiji before he reached Pondicherry. He insisted Swamiji to travel with him to Madras via Pondicherry and be his guest there. Mr. Bhattacharya had some work at Pondicherry. So they stayed at Pondicherry for some days.

One day, at Pondicherry, Swamiji had a heated discussion with a bigoted pandit on topics relating to Hinduism and its reform. The pandit, being of the old school, opposed Swamiji at every turn. He was more pugnacious than learned, and he became fierce in his criticism of Swamiji's progressive ideas. When the conversation turned to the question of going overseas, and Swamiji told that he was thinking of going to the Western world for preaching the glories of Hinduism, the pandit became violent and said, "Hinduism is not in need of any reform. Westerners are all Mlechchhas (untouchable), and the contact with them will spoil the Hindu people." The pandit had seen nothing outside his own province, and knew no better. Hence the argument became bitter, and both became excited. When the pandit found himself defeated, he began to shout, "Never, not at all—not at all." Swamiji tried to explain his point of view, but the pandit didn't like to follow that. Finally, Swamiji said, "My friend, what do you mean? Upon every educated Hindu devolves the responsibility of submitting the contents of Hinduism to the test. For this reason we must come out of the limited grooves of the past and take a look at the world as it moves onwards to progress at the present day. And if we find that there are hide-bound customs which are impeding the growth of our social life or disturbing our philosophical outlook, it is time for us to advance a step by eschewing them." Swamiji also told about the uplift of the masses, and said that the time was at hand when the Sudras (laboring class) would rise and demand their rights. He tried to convince that it was the duty of educated Indians to help the downtrodden classes by giving them education, to spread the ideal of social equality, and to root out the tyranny of priestcraft and the evils of the caste system and the perversion of higher principles of religion should be stopped.

In the end the pandit had to appreciate the force of Swamiji's reasoning, though he still maintained that the Kalapani, or "black water" of the ocean, was the great dividing line between the land of Hindus and the lands of the Mlechchhas, and was never to be crossed. It seems that the pandit had particularly felt annoyed only because Swamiji, being a young man, dared to question his learning and orthodox beliefs. Swamiji was then only a young man of thirty-one years.

Madras [Chennai]

A few days before leaving Pondicherry, Manmathanath had written a letter to a friend in Mysore that Swamiji was with him and would be going to Madras. So when Swamiji arrived with his host in Madras, he found a dozen or so of the city's educated young men were waiting for him. These young men in time became his disciples. Soon the news spread through the city that, "a remarkable English-speaking monk has come." Hence, from the time Swamiji reached Madras, he became acquainted as a public figure. Many progressive young men became his devoted adherents. People began to gather in a large number everyday at Manmathanath's house to meet Swamiji. The group of young men secured a fund for him to go to America. It was in Madras that his formulation of the ideals of Hinduism was really appreciated, and where the people heard the massage of Shri Ramakrishna. It was his Madrasi disciples who were to spread his massage widely even before he returns from the West.

G.G. Narasimhachari was one of them who first met Swamiji on his arrival at Madras. In a paper read at Bangalore in 1906, and published in the *Brahmavadin* the same year, he wrote:

> My first acquaintance with him [the Swami] began at the beginning of the year 1893 of Chicago Religious Parliament, when he came as a wandering sannyasi to Madras, in the company of one Manmathanath Bhattacharya, the then Deputy Accountant-general of Madras. Mr. Bhattacharya picked him up on his way to [from] Rameswaram as a beggarly sannyasi plodding on the road with a staff and a Kamamdalu. Forewarned by a kind Mysore friend of ours of a remarkable English-speaking Sannyasi travelling in the company of Mr. Bhattacharya at Pondicherry, half a dozen picked friends went to meet him at the Babu's on the day of his arrival at Madras. Each one of my friends may be said to have represented a fair knowledge in a branch of modern Western culture, my humble self a large share of the curiosity to see a modern sannyasi of a new type. The very fact that these young men were very good friends was a proof that they all possessed a descent amount of general culture. After we were welcomed by the Babu and left in the presence of the Swami with a bright smiling face and wonderful flashing, rolling eyes, my friends introduced themselves to the Sadhu [monk] through questions. After a few preliminary enquires of ordinary etiquette, he was hemmed in with all sorts of questions literary and scientific, historical and metaphysical. I was the wisest of the lot; I silently sat and enjoyed the fruits of their conversation. The Swami's pithy and melodious answers came like flashes silencing his questioners. Quotations were freely made from all sorts of classical authors, literary and scientific, historical and philosophical. Late in

> the evening when my friends returned home, leaving the travel-worn sannyasi to rest, they began to indulge in all sorts of conjectures about his proficiency.... From that day onward the house of Manmathanath Babu became a place of daily pilgrimage, to the young and old of the city, till the Swami left for America.

Mr. Narasimhachari, in an earlier issue of the *Brahmavadin*, wrote as follows:

> Swamiji was comfortably lodged in Mr. Bhattacharya's residence at St. Thome. Within a few days his intellectual attainments came to be known to all and his first introduction to the madras Public was in the Literary Society at Triplicane, where a conversazione was held. From that day, he became more and more known. Educated men of all ranks and position began to gather in his room and listen with enrapt attention to the mellifluous discourses of the Swami on all matters. His conversational power was marvellous. Even abstruse metaphysical subjects were handled by him in a very pleasing way and in simple language.... Coming again to his discourses in Mr. Bhattacharya's residence, we used to gather there every evening. People whose minds were not settled and who were hating every form of religious faith began to take a peculiarly lively interest in his instructions so much so that from 4 to 10 p.m. there used to be a regular crowd at his residence, people that came to know him being unwilling to miss his company even for a day.

C. Ramanujachari, who was later to devote his life to the work started by Swamiji in Madras, wrote about Swamiji's first visit in these words:

> I had three occasions to meet him [Swamiji] during my life. First in February, 1893, when he was in Madras as a Parivrajaka [wandering monk]. He was then a guest of one Mr. Bhattacharya, the Accountant General of Madras, who lived in a bungalow called "Rahmat Bhag", on the Beach Road, St. Thome. He was given a suite of rooms in the western portion of the house. We, as students then, had heard of a monk called Satchidananda Swami, who had come from the North, who was remarkably intelligent, and had an amazing personality. We had heard of his having met some young men at Madras—Messrs. M. G, Alasinga Perumal of the Pachaiyappa's College, G. Venkataranga Rao, D.R. Balaji Rao...., G.G. Narasimhachari and some young men, who were members of the Triplicane Literary Society—a very virile association of young men, who had been active in inviting prominent men to speak at the Society's premises. The Swami must have been introduced to them through Mr. Bhattacharya. The Swami spoke at the Literary Society of Triplicane first to a small audience. The impression he created then was that he was a remarkable speaker, and by this chiefly young men were first attracted to him. Then followed immediately the realization by the elders that within this magnificent personality were treasured a prodigious intellect, profound learning, fire of sincere patriotism, sparkling wit and above all unbending spirit of renunciation. Soon Madras came to know that here was a man who had power to lift him above all others, and everybody vied with each other to have a glimpse of him. It was one morning, when he, followed by nearly 15 to 20 young men, was walking majestically, with staff in hand, along the Luz Church Road, Mylapore, towards the west, to Sir S. Subramania Iyer's house to see him and to place before him a proposal of sending him to America for the Parliament of Religions, that I saw him for the first and last time on that occasion. I followed him to the end of the road, but, as he proceeded, a large crowd gathered, who, including myself, had to be kept out when the main party entered Sir S. Subramania Iyer's house. I had no chance to see more of the Swami on that occasion, except hearing that he was a great sadhu, who was being sent to America for the Parliament of Religions.

Soon after Swamiji had reached Madras, he was besieged by a large gathering. The discussion would range over religion, literature, history, philosophy, science, social system, psychology, and other subjects. Here one thing is remarkable that at Alwar Swamiji would discuss mostly on religion and devotion, but in Madras, he came forward to take the role of a leader on different subjects. He began to present new ideas and information based on his experience and vast learning. One day someone asked him, "Swamiji, why is it that in spite of their Vedantic thought the Hindus are idolaters?" Swamiji turned with flashing eyes to the questioner and replied, "Because we have the Himalayas!" The questioner seemed to be surprised with this answer, and remain silent looking at Swamiji. Then Swamiji tried to explain him that surrounded by Nature so sublime, man cannot but fall down and adore. Human mind is deeply related with the external world, and therefore, the people of different country are found different in nature due to the structural difference of their minds. Swamiji explained this matter beautifully to his listeners. He seemed to gauge a newcomer's personality at a glance. He would reply according to the personality of the questioner, and everyone was amazed by hearing his readymade answer.

Swamiji's personality seemed to be towered over everything. His thrilling musical voice, his songs, his strength of soul, his power of intellect, his luminous and ready replies, his glittering sense of humor, his epigrams and eloquence—these all held his hearers spellbound. He never used harsh words against anyone; on the other hand he did not refrain from criticism when it was necessary. One day a pandit asked him if there was any harm in giving up Sandhyavandana (ritualistic prayers performed in the morning, noon and evening) due to lack of time. "What!" Swamiji replied immediately, "those giants of old, the ancient Rishis, who never walked but strode, of whom if you were to think but for a moment you would shrivel up into a moth, they, sir, had time—and you have no time!" On the same occasion, when a Westernized Hindu tried to ignore the teachings of the Vedic seers by considering them as "meaningless", Swamiji fell upon him with thunderbolt vehemence, crying out, "How dare you criticize your venerable forefathers in such a fashion! A little learning has muddled your brain. Have you tested the science of the Rishis? Have you even as much as read the Vedas? There is the challenge thrown by the Rishis! If you dare oppose them, take it up; put their teachings to the test."

All who heard Swamiji were amazed. This was the Vedas and Vedanta exhibited as science and at the same time brought to life in personal realization—they didn't hear it before. Each day new gifts and areas of knowledge came to light. One day he would be speaking of Valmiki, Kalidasa, and in the same breath as of Homer and Virgil, Shakespeare and Byron; next day it would be of the Trojans and of the Pandavas, of Helen and of Draupadi. Now he would comment on the glorification of the sensuous in Greek art, and then would go on to contrast it with the whole trend of Hindu art and culture towards the super sensuous.

One day at the palace of the Raja of Ramnad, someone had ridiculed the assertion that it was possible for a human being to see Brahman, the Unknown. At once, Swamiji had exclaimed, "I have seen the Unknown!"

To get relief from the strain by the constant influx of people, Swamiji would often used to walk in the evening on the seashore. One day, when he saw the half-starved children of the fishermen working with their mothers, waist-deep in the water, tears filled his eyes, and he cried out, "O Lord, why dost Thou create these miserable creatures! I cannot bear the sight of them. How long, O Lord, how long!" those who were in his company were overcome and shed tears.

One evening a party was arranged in his honour. The intellectual luminaries of Madras were present. Swamiji boldly, almost challengingly, declared himself to be an Advaitin. A group of intellectuals asked him, "You say you are one with God. Then all your responsibility is gone. What is there to check you when you do wrong, and when you stray from the right path?" Swamiji replied, "If I honestly believe that I am one with God, I shall abominate vice and no check is needed."

Many of the young men who came to meet Swamiji belonged to the social reform movement in Madras. Swamiji saw that they were taking the wrong line, that of sweeping condemnation. He tried to convince them the need to analyse foreign ideals critically and told them to guard against assimilating the materialistic foreign culture. He advised them to preserve the glories of their past to avoid the destruction of the foundation of the national structure. He was not against the social reform; but he believed that it must come from within, not from outside, India; it must be constructive, not destructive.

Swamiji had several conversations at the Literary Society of Triplicane, a noted and flourishing association; and these introduced him to the public. A report of one of them, one which took place in the third week of January 1893, was given in the *Indian Social Reformer*, a weekly edited by Kamakshi Natarajan, one of the most powerful journalist-writer in India at that time. It was extensively quoted in the *Madurai Mail* on January 28, 1893. This latter report (reproduced in *Prabuddha Bharata*, August 1974) began:

> A BENGALI SADHU ON HINDU RELIGION AND SOCIOLOGY
>
> A young Bengali sannyasi of about thirty-two years of age, and a Master of Arts of the Calcutta University was last week interviewed at the Triplicane Literary Society by about a hundred educated Indians among whom was Dewan Bahadur Raghunath Rao. A summary of what was stated by the sadhu is published by the *Indian Social Reformer*, from which we make the following extracts:...

The report then summarizes what the Swami said, under the headings of Vedic Religion, Hindu Ideal of Life, Sradha (i.e. Sraddha) Ceremony, Education of Women, and Emancipation of the Hindus. The chairman of the meeting, Dewan Bahadur Raghunath Rao, was a national figure, and for long General Secretary of the Hindu National Social Conference. He came out strongly in support of the Age of Consent Bill, when even a section of the social reformers had been against it. We have already noted that Swamiji strongly supported this bill.

These days in Madras were referred to by Kamakshi Natarajan, mentioned above, when he spoke at Bombay (presently Mumbai) on the occasion of the Swami Vivekananda Birthday Anniversary in 1920. The relevant portion of the report of his speech (*Prabuddha Bharata*, March 1920) runs:

> Mr. K. Natarajan...said that it was his privilege to meet Swami Vivekananda on the very first occasion on which he appeared in Madras as a poor mendicant monk and he took pride in saying that it was Madras that had discovered Swami Vivekananda, after he had wandered all over India and apparently did not feel that his call had come. He then alluded to the vigorous discourse that Swami Vivekananda, then an obscure sannyasi of 28 [?], gave to an audience preside over by Dewan Bahadur Raghunath Rao, in which he expounded upon the Western interpretation of the Eastern culture. It was here that it was decided that the Swamiji should be sent to the Chicago Congress, where the Swamiji showed that his great interest lay in the application of the great spiritual principles to the interpretation of life in terms of modern civilization....[85]

One day an atheist, named Singaravelu Mudaliar came to Swamiji. He was an Assistant Professor of Science in the Christian College. He saw the practical value of Christianity and criticized Hinduism. He came with an intention to argue, but conversation with Swamiji changed him into a devoted disciple. Swamiji loved him very much, and called him "Kidi". He used to say, "Caesar said, 'I came, I saw, I conquered'. But Kidi came, he saw, and he was conquered!" After a time Kidi devoted his life to his Master's cause. When, at the suggestion of Swamiji, the *Prabuddha Bharata* was started in Madras, Kidi became its honorary manager. Later he renounced the world to lead the life of a monk, and died a saintly death.

V. Subramanya Iyer says that he went with some of his class-fellows to the house of Mr. Bhattacharya, with an idea of having some fun. They wanted to measure the wisdom of Swamiji, and therefore came with some bold questions. They were well prepared with the answers in support of their argument. Mr. Iyer was a student of Christian College and interested in Christianity. Even he once wished to be a Christian too. Reaching the house of Mr. Bhattacharya they found Swamiji smoking his hookah in a sort of half-awake, half-dreamy state. Mr. Iyer and his friends were amazed by the glittering face of Swamiji. One bolder than the others advanced and asked, "Sir, what is God?" Swamiji smoked on as if entirely unconscious of the question. Then he raised his eyes and asked, "Well, my friend, what is energy?" Neither the questioner nor his companions were able to give a suitable definition. Swamiji said, "What is this! You cannot define a simple word like 'energy', which you use every day of your life, and yet you want me to define God!" Then, when he gave a beautiful explanation of those two words 'God' and 'energy' and compared them with his natural eloquence and intellect, the group of boys realized that they were only children to the wisdom of Swamiji. After a time they all left, except the young Iyer. He was greatly impressed and accompanied Swamiji and his disciple on their daily walk to the beach. Casually Swamiji asked Subramanya Iyer, "Well, my boy, can you wrestle?" Iyer nodded his head in the affirmative. Swamiji said in fun, "Come, let us have a tussle." It was with the athleticism of the Swamiji in mind that Iyer used to call him "Pahalwan Swami", that is "Athlete Swami".

Mr. Bhattacharya had a cook in his house. One day Swamiji found the cook looking wistfully at the hookah that he had received as a gift from the Maharaja of Mysore. He asked the cook, "Would you like to have this?" The cook got nervous and remained silent. When Swamiji had repeated the question, he thought that Swamiji would really like to give him the hookah. But he perhaps could not believe it. Then Swamiji called him to come by his side and then and there handed it to him. When the man actually had the hookah in his own hands, he was grateful beyond words. Those who came to know of the incident, Swamiji's renunciation was manifest, for that hookah was his only comfort. Indeed, he was in a habit of giving away whatever was in his possession if that specially was admired by anyone. Once in America, a young Mr. Prince Woods coveted the staff which the Swamiji had used during his wandering days. It was associated with many of his pilgrimage. But Swamiji gave it away, without hesitation, saying, "What you admire is already yours!" And to Prince's mother, Mrs. Kate Tannatt Woods, of Salem, with whom he stayed for a few days in September 1893, he gave his trunk and blanket.

During his stay at Madras, Swamiji had a strange experience. For some days he was bothered by waves of psychic disturbance sent by some spirits. The spirits reported all sorts of false things to make his mind restless. When he remonstrated with them, they explained him of their miserable condition. Swamiji thought over the matter, and went to the seashore, where he took a handful of sand as a substitute for rice and grain, and offered it, praying with his whole heart that these souls might find rest. After that they ceased to disturb him.

Swamiji had another strange experience about this time. Let us listen to it directly from his holy lips:

> Once while I was putting up at Manmatha Babu's place, I dreamt one night that my mother had died. My mind became much distracted. Not to speak to corresponding with anybody at home, I used to send no letters in those days even to our Math. The dream being disclosed to Manmatha, he sent a wire to Calcutta to ascertain facts about the matter. For the dream had made my mind uneasy on the one hand, and on the other, our Madras friends, with all arrangements ready, were insisting on my departing for America immediately, and I felt rather unwilling to leave before getting any news of my mother. So Manmatha, who discerned this state of my mind, suggested our repairing to a man living some way off from town, who having acquired mystic powers over spirits could tell fortunes and read the past and the future of a man's life. So at Manmatha's request and to get rid of my mental suspense, I agreed to go to this man. Covering the distance partly by railway and partly on foot, we four of us—Manmatha, Alasinga, myself, and another—managed to reach the place, and what met our eyes there was a man with a ghoulish, haggard, soot-black appearance, sitting close to a cremation ground. His attendants used some jargon of South Indian dialect to explain to us that this was the man with perfect power over the ghosts. At first the man took absolutely no notice of us; and then, when we were about to retire from the place, he made a request for us to wait.
>
> Our Alasinga was acting as the interpreter, and he explained the requests to us. Next, the man commenced drawing some figures with a pencil, and presently I found him getting perfectly still in mental concentration. Then he began to give out my name, my genealogy, the history of my long line of forefathers, and said that Sri Ramakrishna was keeping close to me all through my wanderings, intimating also to me good news about my mother. He also foretold that I would have to go very soon to far-off lands for preaching religion. Getting good news thus about my mother, we all travelled back to town, and after arrival received by wire from Calcutta the assurance of my mother's doing well.... Everything that the man had foretold came to be fulfilled to the letter, call it some fortuitous concurrence or anything you will... Well, I am not a fool to believe anything and everything without direct proof. And coming into this realm of Mahamaya, oh, the many magic mysteries I have come across alongside this bigger magic conjuration of a universe! Maya, it is all Maya![86]

It is known that the name of this man was Govinda Chetty. After returning from America, when Swamiji again met this man at Kumbhakonam, he hugged him. Since then the man had lost his power and devoted his life in spiritual practices for realizing glimpse of God.

In Madras, Swamiji had many followers. People from all parts of the city came to hear him. His glittering personality captivated their hearts and his ideas fascinated their minds. K. Vyasa Rao has drawn a beautiful pen-picture of the impression Swamiji created:

> A graduate of the Calcutta University, with a shaven head, a prepossessing appearance, wearing the grab of renunciation, fluent in English and Sanskrit, with uncommon powers of repartee, who sang "with full-throated ease" as though he was attuning himself to the Spirit of the universe, and withal a wanderer on the face of the earth! The man was sound and stalwart, full of sparkling wit, with nothing but a scathing contempt for miracle-working agencies...; one who enjoyed good dishes, knew how to appreciate the hookah and the pipe, yet harped on renunciation with an ability that called forth

> admiration and a sincerity that commanded respect. The young Bachelors and Masters of Arts were at their wits' end at the sight of such a phenomenon. There, they saw the man and saw how well he could stand his ground in wrestling and fencing in the arena of the Universal Soul; and when the hour of discussion gave way to lighter moods, they found that he could indulge in fun and frolic, in uncompromising denunciation and in startling *bons mots*. But everything else apart, what endeared him to all was the unalloyed fervour of his patriotism. The young man, who had renounced all worldly ties and freed himself from bondage, had but one love, his country, and one grief, its downfall. These sent him into reveries which held his hearers spellbound. Such was the man who travelled from Hooghly to Tamraparny, who bewailed and denounced in unmeasured terms the imbecility of our young men, whose words flashed as lightning and cut as steel, who impressed all, communicated his enthusiasm to some, and lighted the spark of undying faith in a chosen few.

Vyasa Rao also says that when the world discovered Vivekananda, it discovered Ramakrishna Paramahamsa too: it was through the disciple that the master was known. The people of Madras became followers of Vivekananda not because of what Shri Ramakrishna had said about him, but because of what they themselves saw of this young monk, who had not previously been known to them.

One disciple of Swamiji spoke of him thus:

> The vast range of his mental horizon perplexed and enraptured me. From the Rig-Veda to *Raghuvamsha*, from the metaphysical fights of the Vedanta philosophy to modern Kant and Hegel, the whole range of ancient and modern literature and art and music and morals, from the sublimities of ancient Yoga to the intricacies of a modern laboratory—everything seemed clear to his field of vision. It was this which confounded me, made me his slave.

Another disciple writes:

> He frequently had to descend to the level of his questioners and to translate his soaring thoughts into their language. He would often anticipate several questions ahead and give answers that would satisfy the questioners at once. When asked how he so understood them, he would say with a smile that sannyasis were "doctors of men", and that they were able to diagnose their cases before they administered remedies to them.
>
> At times many men's thoughts were his. He would answer scores of questioners at one time and silence them all.
>
> Soft and forgiving as he was to those on whom his grace rested, one had to live in his presence as in the vicinity of a dangerous explosive. The moment a bad thought entered one's mind, it would flash across his also. One could know it from a peculiar smile that lit his lips and from the words that would causally escape from his mouth in the course of conversation.

During his stay at Madras, Swamiji had announced his intention of going to the West. He said to his followers: "The time has come for the propagation of our Faith. The time has come for the Hinduism of the Rishis to become dynamic. Shall we stand by whilst alien hands attempt to destroy the fortress of our ancient Faith? Are we satisfied with its impregnability? Shall we remain passive, or shall we become aggressive, as in days of old, preaching unto the nations the glory of the Dharma? Shall we remain encased within the narrow confines of our social groups and our provincial consciousness, or shall we branch out into the thought worlds of other peoples, seeking to influence these for the benefit of India? In order to rise again, India must be strong and united, and must focus all its living forces."

Devotees who listened got excited and soon went about to raise subscriptions for Swamiji's sailing for the West. Swamiji himself had it in mind to attend the Parliament of Religions, but he had not taken definite step in the matter; he rather preferred to wait for the will of the Mother to become evident. About this, G.G. Narasimhachari said:

> When it was three [actually eight] months for the Parliament of Religions to commence its sitting at Chicago, the Swami expressed his desire to attend it to represent Hinduism. A few devoted to him went round to collect subscriptions. A philanthropic gentleman whose official position and rank is the pride of Southern India headed the list with ₹ 500, though another gentleman richer than the one mentioned above refused to give a pie, and even suspected the bona fides of Sannyasins in general and Vivekananda in particular....

But Swamiji, when he saw the money, felt uneasy. Question arose in his mind, "Am I following my own will? Am I being carried away by enthusiasm?" He thought for a while and prayed, "O Mother, show me Thy will! It is Thou who art the Doer. Let me be only Thy instrument." He was a monk, and inexperienced in the way of the world. If it was the Mother's will that he would go to distant lands, to meet the strange people and deliver to them a strange message, then it was not necessary to collect money. It should come automatically. And so he said to his disciples, "My boys, I am determined to force the Mother's will. She must prove that it is Her intention that I should go, for it is a step in the dark. If it be Her will, then money will come again of itself. Therefore, take this money and distribute it among the poor." His disciple obeyed him without a word, and Swamiji felt released from a great burden.

Swamiji decided not to think any more of going to the West till he would come to know the Mother's will, and turned his face to Hyderabad.

Hyderabad

People in Hyderabad, who heard of Swamiji from their Madras friends, became restless to see him soon, and invited him to go there on a brief visit. Swamiji readily agreed, considering that there might be a hidden purpose in this unexpected call. Manmathanath Bhattacharya, his host at Madras, telegraphed to a friend, Babu Madhusudan Chatterjee, Superintending Engineer to His Highness the Nizam, saying that Swamiji was to arrive at Hyderabad on February 10 and would be his guest. On the 9th, a public meeting of the Hindus of Hyderabad and Secunderabad was called to arrange a grand reception for Swamiji. When Swamiji arrived at Hyderabad station the following day, he found, to his surprise, about five hundred people assembled on the platform to receive him. Among the people, there were some very distinguished members of the Court of Hyderabad, several on nobility, and many pundits, pleaders, and rich merchants. Notable among them were Raja Srinivas Rao Bahadur, Maharaja Rambha Rao Bahadur, Pandit Rattan Lal, Captain Raghunath, Shamas-ul-Ulema Syed Ali Bilgrami, Nawab Imad Jung Bahadur, Nawab Dula Khan Bahadur, Nawab Imad Nawaz Jung Bahadur, Nawab Secunder Nawaz Jung Bahadur, and Mr. H. Dorabjee, Mr. F.S. Mundon, Rai Hukum Chand, the bankers Seth Chaturbhuj and Seth Motilal, the host, and the host's son, Babu Kalicharan Chatterjee. Kalicharan Babu knew Swamiji since he was in Calcutta; so he came forward and introduced them to him. Garlands of flowers were heaped on the monk. An eye-witness writes:

> The Swami, then a young man of robust health, alighted from a first-class compartment, in the robes of a Paramahamsa, a Kamandalu in hand. He was conveyed to the bungalow of Babu Madhusudan, and was followed thither by many of gentry. Those who could not go to the station came to have interviews at the bungalow. Surely we have not witnessed such crowds before to receive a Swami in Hyderabad. It was a magnificent reception, befitting a reigning Prince.

From Hyderabad, Swamiji wrote to Alasinga on February 11, 1893. He wrote:

> Your friend, the young graduate, came to receive me at the station, so also a Bengali gentleman. At present I am living with the Bengali gentleman; tomorrow I go to live with your young friend for a few days, and then I see the different sights here, and in a few days you may expect me at Madras. For I am very sorry to tell you that I cannot go back at present to Rajputana. It is so very dreadfully hot here already. I do not know how hot it would be at Rajputana, and I cannot bear heat at all. So the next thing, I would do, would be to go back to Bangalore and then to Ootacamund to pass the summer there. My brain boils in heat.
>
> So all my plans have been dashed to the ground. That is why I wanted to hurry off from Madras early. In that case I would have months left in my hands to seek out for somebody amongst our northern princes to send me over to America. But alas, it is now too late. First, I cannot wander about in this heat—I would die. Secondly, my fast friends in Rajputana would keep me bound down to their sides if they get hold of me and would not let me go over to Europe. So my plan was to get hold of some new person without my friends' knowledge. But this delay at Madras has dashed all my hopes to the ground, and with a deep sigh I give it up, and the Lord's will be done! However, you may be almost sure that I shall see you in a few days for a day or two in Madras and then go to Bangalore and thence to Ootacamund to see "if" the M—Maharaja sends me up. "If"—because you see I cannot be sure of any promise of a Dakshini (southern) Raja. They are not Rajputs. A Rajput would rather die than break his promise. However, man learns as he lives, and experience is the greatest teacher in the world.
>
> "Thy will be done on earth as it is in heaven, for Thine is the glory and the kingdom for ever and ever". My compliments to you all.[87]
>
> Yours etc.
>
> Sachchidananda.

The "M—Maharaja", mentioned in the above letter, was none other than the Maharaja of Mysore. And Swamiji signed the letter as Sachchidananda, shows that he used this name before going to America.

On the morning of February 11, a committee of one hundred Hindu residents of Secunderabad approached him with offerings of sweets, milk and fruits, and requested him to deliver a lecture at the Mahaboob College in the city. Swamiji agreed and fixed the 13th as the day. Then he went with Kalicharanbabu to see the fort at Golconda, of historic note and famous for its diamonds. On returning, Swamiji found awaiting him a bearer from the Private Secretary to Nawab Bahadur Sir Khurshid Jah, Amiri-i-Kabir, K.C.S.I., the foremost nobleman of Hyderabad and the brother-in-law of His Highness the Nizam. The bearer gave him a letter, requesting him to come to the palace for an interview the following morning. Next morning Swamiji, accompanied by Kalicharanbabu, went to the palace, where he was received by an aide-de-camp of the Nawab.

Sir Khurshid Jah was noted for religious tolerance and was the first Muslim to visit all the Hindu places of pilgrimage from the Himalayas to Cape Comorin. He received Swamiji warmly and offered him a seat by his side. They had a long conversation for about two hours. Swamiji discussed the contents of Hinduism, Christianity and Islam.

The Nawab was against the form of worship in which deities are conceived as having form. Being a Muslim he believed in the Impersonal Ideal. Swamiji tried to solve the problem. He spoke to him of the evolution of the idea of God, and showed the need for the conception of Him as a person, since human experience was personal by nature, and therefore the highest conception to which human thought could rise had to be personal. He pointed out that every religion but Hinduism depended on the life of some person as its founder: that Vedanta, on the other hand, was based on eternal principles and did not depend on persons: and that it was on this fact that its claim to universality was founded. Swamiji convinced the Nawab how the whole range of religious ideas arrived by mankind had emerged from the depths of human nature as a results of its readings of the Truth. All ideals, he said, are true: the religious systems were paths for the attainment of these various ideals: and every one of them, who practiced intensely, was certain to make manifest the Divinity already in man. Then, about the Vedantic idea of the Absolute, he said that man was the greatest of all beings, for it was by the spiritualized human intelligence that the truths of the universe had been discovered. This idea can help the mankind to cross all limitations and make them divine. At last, he gave out his intention of going to the West to preach the Eternal Religion. The Nawab was deeply impressed by his eloquence and immediately said, "Swamiji, I am ready to help you in your undertaking with one thousand rupees." But Swamiji declined to accept the money just then, saying, "Your Highness, the time has not yet come. When the command comes from the high, I shall make you aware of it." Then he took leave of the Nawab, and went to see the Mecca Masjid, Charminar, Falaknama, Nizam's palaces, Bashirbagh, and other places of interest.

On the morning of 13th Swamiji met by appointment Sir Ashman Jah, K.C.S.I., the Prime Minister of Hyderabad, the Maharaj Norendra Krishna Bahadur, Peshkar of the State, and the Maharaja Shew Raj Bahadur. They all promised to support his proposed preaching in America. In the afternoon he spoke at the Mahaboob College on "My mission to the West". Pandit Rattan Lal was in the chair. More than a thousand people came to hear him, including many Europeans. All were deeply impressed by his command of the English language, his eloquence, his learning, and by his power of exposition. He talked about the greatness of Hindu religion, of the Hindu culture and society in former days, and gave an outline of Vedic and post-Vedic thought. He told about the Rishis who are the great lawgivers, and the authors and arrangers of Shastras. Finally, he spoke of his mission, "which is nothing less than the regeneration of the Motherland". He declared his feeling that it was imperative on him to go out as a missionary from India to the farthest West, to reveal to the world the incomparable glory of the Vedas and the Vedanta.

Next day the well-known bankers of the Begam Bazar, headed by Seth Motilal, came to meet Swamiji, and promised to help him with his passage money for his journey to the West. Some members of the Theosophical Society and of the Sanskrit Dharma Mandal Sabha, also came to see him. On 15th February, Swamiji received a telegram from Poona, signed by the leading citizens in the name of the Hindu societies, asking him to go there on a visit. Swamiji replied, "I cannot go now, but I shall be happy to go if I can in future." The next day he went to see the ruins of the Hindu temples, the famous tomb of Baba Saraf-ud-din, and also the palace of Sir Salar Jung.

In Hyderabad, Swamiji met a yogi famous for his psychic powers. Later In his lecture in America, Swamiji described this experience:

> Another time I was in the city of Hyderabad in India, and I was told of a Brahmin there who could produce number of things from where, nobody knew. This man was in business there; he was a respectable gentleman. And I asked him to show me his tricks. It so happened that this man had a fever, and in India there is a general belief that if a holy man puts his hand on a sick man he would be well. This Brahmin came to me and said, "Sir, put your hand on my head, so that my fever may be cured." I said, "Very good; but you show me your tricks." He promised. I put my hand on his head as desired, and later he came to fulfil his promise. He had only a strip of cloth about his loins, we took off everything else from him. I had a blanket which I gave him to wrap round himself, because it was cold, and made him sit in a corner. Twenty-five pairs of eyes were looking at him. And he said, "Now, look, write down anything you want." We all wrote down names of fruits that never grew in that country, bunches of grapes, oranges, and so on. And we gave him those bits of paper. And there came from under his blanket, bunches of grapes, oranges, and so forth, so much that if all that fruit was weighed, it would have been twice as heavy as the man. He asked us to eat the fruit. Some of us objected, thinking it was hypnotism; but the man began eating himself—so we all ate. It was all right.
>
> He ended by producing a mass of roses. Each flower was perfect with dew-drops on the petals, not one crushed, not one injured. And masses of them! When I asked the man for an explanation, he said, "It is all sleight of hand."
>
> Whatever it was, it seemed to be impossible that it could be sleight of hand merely. From whence could he have got such large quantities of things?[88]

Of another experience he said:

> I once heard of a man who, if any one went to him with questions in his mind, would answer them immediately; and I was also informed that he foretold events. I was curious and went to see him with a few friends. We each had something in our minds to ask, and, to avoid mistakes, we wrote down out questions and put them in our pockets. As soon as the man saw one of us, he repeated our questions and gave the answers to them. Then he wrote something on paper, which he folded up, asked me to sign on the back, and said, "Don't look at it; put it in your pocket and keep it there till I ask for it again." And so on to each one of us. He next told us about some-events that would happen to us in the future. Then he said, "Now, think of a word or a sentence, from any language you like." I thought of a long sentence from Sanskrit, a language of which he was entirely ignorant. "Now, take out the paper from your pocket," he said. The Sanskrit sentence was written there! He had written it an hour before with the remark, "In confirmation of what I have written, this man will think of this sentence." It was correct. Another of us who had been given a similar paper which he had signed and placed in his pocket, was also asked to think of a sentence. He thought of a sentence in Arabic, which it was still less possible for the man to know; it was some passage from the Koran. And my friend found this written down on the paper. Another of us was a physician. He thought of a sentence from a German medical book. It was written on his paper. Several days later I went to this man again, thinking possibly I had been deluded somehow before. I took other friends, and on this occasion also he came out wonderfully triumphant.[89]

On February 17, Swamiji left Hyderabad. More than thousand people came to the railway station to bid him farewell. "His pious simplicity, unfailing self-control and profound meditation", writes Kalicharanbabu, "made an indelible impression on the citizens of Hyderabad."

Thus, Swamiji ended his travelling and surveying India. This journey had made him acquainted with several cultures and customs of people in different places of India and its glorious history. Next, we will see him being prepared for his journey to the world.

7
Preparation for Voyage to the West

When Swamiji returned to Madras, he was warmly accosted at the station by many of his disciples. He seemed full of self-confidence. He came to know his oratorical power when he delivered speech before the assembly at the Mahaboob College, and became confident that he could sway large audience as well as small gatherings. We remember that, at Belgaum, he said to Haripada Mitra that large audience draws out the powers of a speaker; and this was proved in the above occasion.

In Madras, Swamiji continued his discourses and his conversations on religions and many other subjects. Everyday disciples and devotees grew in number. Gradually he became more and more occupied with the idea of going to America. He was filled with eagerness for extending his field of works and for earning new experiences. He would talk to his disciples about his mission to the West, and of his intuition of the opportunity and success that awaited him.

During March and April Swamiji's disciples in Madras started to collect donations for his passage to America. Alasinga Perumal, a devoted follower of Swamiji, was the leader of the fund committee. They went from door to door, to his disciples or his admirers. Some went even to Mysore, Ramnad and Hyderabad for the purpose. Alasinga and the young men under him collected the major portion of the funds. They went mostly to the middle classes, because Swamiji had told them, "If it is the Mother's will that I go, then let me receive the money from the people! Because it is for the people of India that I am going to the West—for the people and the poor!"

From a letter written by Swamiji in May 1893 to the Dewan of Junagadh, it is clear that by the middle of April the people of Madras, in conjunction with the Maharaja of Mysore and the Raja of Ramnad, had contributed the money to send him to Chicago. From a letter of Swami Shivananda dated February 13, 1894, it is known that Swamiji's disciples in Madras "collected through subscription about ₹ 4,000". Swami Shivananda also told to one of his disciples later (January 1925): "Subramanya and Manmathababu paid ₹ 500 each, and then started collecting from other people." When the Raja of Ramnad saw that many big Government officials were contributing, he also sent ₹ 500 at the request of Manmathababu.

We have noted Swamiji, when he was at Madras before going to Hyderabad, to force the Mother to tell him directly Her will. Returning to Madras and finding the eagerness of his disciples to collect funds he thought, "Well, their readiness is perhaps the first sign." Still he seemed to have passed through a period of uncertainty, in spite of being convinced of the necessity of going. Swamiji prayed again to the Mother and to his Master for guidance. He wanted to have an actual vision or a direct command. One night, while he laid half-asleep, the command came in a dream. He saw the figure of his Master, Shri Ramakrishna, walking from the seashore into the waters of the ocean, and beckoning him to follow. He woke up, and felt a great peace in his heart; still the order "go" had been ringing in his mind, as it were. He was satisfied by the vision, and came to know it to be a divine command. All his doubts were deleted.

During his stay in Madras, Swamiji spoke at least twice at the headquarters of the Theosophical Society. The news that appeared in *The Theosophist* of March 1893, though it contains a few factual errors, shows that Swamiji was making an impression on the educated people of Madras.

The report, written by W.R. Old, runs as follows:

> "During the absence of the President-Founder and Mr. Edge, the monotony of routine work has been agreeably broken by several gatherings of Theosophists and friends upon various occasions. The arrival of Sannyasi Sachchidananda Swami in Madras, and his subsequent visits to the Headquarters of the T.S. [Theosophical Society] has [have] been the cause of much local interest. The sannyasi is possessed of great versatility, a thorough knowledge of Pali [*sic*], Sanskrit, English, French [*sic*] and Hebrew [*sic*] being among his many accomplishments. He is also an M.A. [*sic*] of the Calcutta University. To these Nature has added a fine stalwart physique and dignified presence. He has travelled a great deal and, among other places, has visited Lhassa and other cities in Thibet [*sic*]. In his teaching he follows Sri Sankaracharya. But what sets him off from all others of his Holy Order, is the fact that he travels far and wide, mixing freely with the people, holding public meetings and discussions upon religious philosophy. The Sannyasi has had audiences from among the highest intellects in Madras, and has shown himself to be equally facile with arguments from Western philosophy and well versed in modern science.

"Sachchidananda expressed himself pleased with some experiments in "localization" and "impression-reading" conducted at Headquarters...."

In anticipation of his visit to America, Swamiji approached Colonel Olcott, the leader of the Theosophical Society there, for a letter of introduction. This is the account Swamiji gave later:

> Four years ago, when I, a poor, unknown, friendless sannyasin, was going to America, going beyond the waters to America without any introductions or friends there, I called on the leader of the Theosophical Society. Naturally I thought he, being an American and a lover of India, perhaps would give me a letter of introduction to somebody there. He asked me, "Will you join my Society?" "No," I replied, "how can I? For I do not believe in most of your doctrines." "Then, I am sorry, I cannot do anything for you", he answered.

We remember, when Swamiji had first set out on the wandering life, he had sought the blessings of the Holy Mother, Sarada Devi, so now he yearned for her blessings on this longer journey. Accordingly, he wrote to her for her blessings, and requested her at the same time to be silent about his plans. It may well be imagined that the pleasure of the Holy Mother, after receiving the letter from her 'Naren', knew no bounds. For a long time she had not heard from him who had been the most beloved disciple of the Master, and for whom she cherished a special affection. She also had had a similar vision regarding him, in which she saw the form of Shri Ramakrishna entering into the body of Narendra, signifying that the Master would thenceforth work in and through his chief disciple. Still her mind prompted her to prevent her Naren from going to unknown land; but at the same time she realized that it was the will of the Master. She therefore set her personal feelings aside and sent her blessings together with loving counsel.

When Swamiji received the Holy Mother's letter, he became so much glad that he could not stop his tears rolling down from his eyes. He went into his room to conceal his elation, and later on, to the seashore. He said to himself, "Ah! It is all right now. It is the will of the Mother!" When he returned to the house of Manmathababu, his face was glowing with joy. His disciples were waiting as usual to hear his discourse on religious topics. Swamiji entered the room and said, "Yes, now it is the West, the West! Now I am ready. Let us go to work in right earnest. The Mother Herself has spoken!" The disciples were enlightened with joy to see his enthusiasm and within a short while they had collected a substantial amount.

Again at Khetri

It was sometime in the second week of April, when arrangement for sailing had already been made by the disciples at Madras, Munshi Jagmohanlal, the Private Secretary of Raja Ajit Singh of Khetri, unexpectedly, appeared on the scene.

We know that at the end of October 1891 Swamiji had been at Khetri, when the Raja had sought his blessings so that he might be the father of a son. On January 26, 1893, a son had indeed been born to him, and was named Rajkumar Jaisingh. The Raja was excited that through the blessing of Swamiji he had got an heir to the State of Khetri, and therefore wished to celebrate the event, and to have Swamiji on the occasion. Raja Ajit Singh came to know that Swamiji was at Madras, and his disciples were collecting money for his voyage to the West. So he sent Jagmohanlal to bring him to Khetri. The Raja also said that if Swamiji fell short of funds, he promised to contribute from his personal account.

When Jagmohanlal arrived in Madras, he heard that Swamiji was staying at the house of Manmathanath Bhattacharya. After a long search he found the residence to the gentleman, but he was told by a servant that Swamiji had gone to the sea. He felt sad, and cried in despair, "What! has he left for the West? What do you mean?" Meanwhile, he saw Swamiji's ochre robe hanging on the peg, and thought, "He cannot have gone." Just then a carriage drew up at the front of house, and to his delight he saw that Swamiji alighting from it. Instantly the devoted Jagmohanlal prostrated himself full length on the ground. Swamiji was surprised to see him so unexpectedly. After knowing the cause of his arrival Swamiji said, "Dear Jagmohan, I am making preparation to embark for America on May 31st, and hardly a month and a half is left. How can I go to see the Maharaja now?" But the messenger persisted, saying, "Swamiji, you must come to Khetri, even if only for a day. Rajaji will be overwhelmed with disappointment if you fail to come. You need not trouble yourself further about making arrangements for your going to the West. The Maharaja himself will see to it. You simply must come with me." Swamiji realized the situation, and agreed. After some discussion it was decided that he should sail from Bombay [Mumbai].

When Swamiji was about to leave for Khetri, his Madras disciples fell prostrate before him and sought his blessings. They went with him to the railway station. As the train started, they all chanted the name of the Lord, and found him standing at the door with his right hand raised in benediction.

Before reaching Khetri Swamiji wished to stop at Nadiad to meet Haridas Biharidas, but he came to know that the Dewan was not present there. So he did not go there. On the way to Khetri Swamiji stopped at Bombay, Vapingana and Jaipur. In course of their pilgrim travels Swami Brahamananda and Turiyananda came to Bombay from Karachi by boat. At Bombay Swamiji might have met these two brother-disciples at the house of Kalipada Ghosh, a disciple of the Master. Kalipada Ghosh was then living in Bombay because of his employment there. One day Swamiji said to Turiyananda, "Haribhai, I am going to America. Whatever you hear of as happening there [meaning preparations for the Parliament of Religions], is all for this [striking his own chest]. For this [me] alone everything is being arranged."

After staying for few days at Bombay, Swamiji and Jagmohanlal started for Khetri. Brahmananda and Turiyananda also went with them, but they got down at Abu Road station. Most probably on 15th April Swamiji and Jagmohanlal reached Rewari, from where Khetri was still a long journey of about a week. It was evening of April 21, when they reached Khetri they found the palace coruscating with thousands of lights. The festival had already been going on for three or four days, and the whole town was decorated. Singing and dancing were in full swing everywhere. As the carriage bringing Swamiji drew up, the guard presented arms. The Raja was then in his state barge, which was adorned with jewels, and with flowers, garlands and palms. Many guests were seated around him; some of them were princes and chiefs of Rajputana. When Jagmohanlal presented Swamiji, the Raja rose and prostrated himself before his guru. Swamiji blessed him and, taking him by the hand, raised him up. All present rose to their feet and bowed before him. The musicians sang a song of welcome as Swamiji was led to a seat of honour. Then the Raja formally introduced him to all of his guests assembled there, and told them how he was blessed by Swamiji so that a son might be born to him. He told them also of Swamiji's plan of visiting the West to preach the doctrines of the Sanatana Dharma. At this the whole court highly praised. Then the babe was brought to receive the blessings of Swamiji. Swamiji placed his right hand on the head of the babe and uttered holy words. The air filled with the noise of ovation.

This time Swamiji stayed at Khetri for almost three weeks. He spent much of his time with the Raja, talking on various matters. When, in due course, Swamiji told the Raja that he should leave for Bombay to make preparation for the voyage, he said, "Well, Swamiji Maharaj, it wrings my heart to part with you; but I must bow to Providence. I shall, however, accompany you as far as Jaipur." Swamiji remonstrated with him, but the Raja said, "It is a host's duty to see his guest off, at least to the confines of his residence." On 9th May, before his departure, Swamiji was taken to the women's apartments in the palace to bless the Rajkumar, the infant prince.

On May 10, with due ceremony observed, Swamiji made his departure by the state bullock-cart, accompanied by Jagmohanlal. Jagmohanlal was ordered by the Raja to go with Swamiji to Bombay, and had been given sufficient money to meet all the expenses and to provide him with whatever he needed for the voyage. As the Raja requested Swamiji reassumed the name Vivekananda for good, in place of Sachchidananda, that he had been using in South India. From Jaipur Swamiji and Jagmohanlal took a train.

On the way they stopped at Abu Road, and spent the night in the house of a railway employee who had been known to Swamiji since the days of his wandering. Here Swamiji met his brother-disciples Swami Brahmananda and Turiyananda again. They had been staying at Mount Abu, in the summer palace of the Raja of Khetri. They got the information that Swamiji would be passing through Abu Road, and had come all the way by a bullock-cart to meet him. When Swamiji came to know that his brother-disciples had come by a bullock-cart and because of the jolting they had been suffering from pain all through their bodies, he said, "If you would have paid some money to the driver, he would have prepared a soft seat of hay for you. You don't have such simple common sense as that!"

Swami Turiyananda later on told about an incident which indicates the profound love for all men that Swamiji felt in his heart. Although it happened after his first visit to America, it will be in place to mention it now. It took place at Balaram Bose's house in Calcutta, where Swamiji was staying for a time, Swami Turiyananda said:

> I came to see Swamiji and found him walking alone on the veranda lost in such deep thought that he did not perceive my arrival. I kept quiet, lest I should interrupt his reverie. After some time Swamiji, with tears rolling down his cheeks, began to hum a well-known song of Mirabai. Then, with his face in his hands and leaning on the railings, he sang in anguished tones, "Oh, nobody understands my sorrow! Nobody understands my sorrow!" The sad strains, and Swamiji's dejection, seemed to affect even the objects around him! The whole atmosphere vibrated with the sad melody: "No one but the sufferer knows the pangs of sorrows." His voice pierced my heart like an arrow, moving me to tears. Not knowing the cause of Swamiji's sorrow I was very uneasy. But it soon flashed upon me that it was a tremendous universal sympathy with the suffering and oppressed that was the cause of his mood.

Let us return to Abu Road station, where, before resuming his journey, Swamiji had an unpleasant experience with a European ticket-collector. A Bengali gentleman, an admirer of Swamiji, was sitting with him in the compartment, when the ticket-collector appeared there and ordered the gentleman to get out of the carriage, citing an alleged regulation. The gentleman was also a railway employee. He protested and pointed out that there was no regulation requiring him to leave. The ticket-collector got angry and began to shout. Then Swamiji himself intervened. But the ticket-collector became more excited and said sharply, "*Tum kahe bat karte ho*?", which means, "Why do you meddle?" The Hindi word "Tum" is used to address intimate friends or inferiors, while "Ap" is used to one's equals and superiors. So at this Swamiji became annoyed and said, "What do you mean by 'Tum'? Can you not behave properly? You are attending to first- and second-class passengers, and you do not know manners! Why do you not say 'Ap'?" The ticket-collector, realizing his mistake, said, "I am sorry. I do not know the language well. I only wanted this man...." Swamiji interrupted him: "Just now you said you did not know Hindi well. Now I see that you do not even know your own language well. This 'man' of whom you speak is a gentleman!" The ticket-collector, being caught on the wrong foot, left the compartment. Speaking of this incident to Jagmohanlal, Swamiji said, "You see, what we need in our dealings with Europeans is self-respect. We do not deal with men according to their position, and so they take advantage of us. We must keep our dignity before others. Unless we do that, we expose ourselves to insult."

Again at Bombay

When Swamiji, accompanied by Jagmohanlal, reached Bombay, he met Alasinga at the station. Alasinga Perumal, being informed of Swamiji's intention of embarking at Bombay, had come all the way from Madras to see him off to the West. Jagmohan, as we have noted, had been instructed by the Raja of Khetri to make all necessary arrangements. He took Swamiji to the best shop in the city and bought all sorts of things necessary for him. When Swamiji found costly silk materials and suiting being ordered for the robes and turbans that he would wear when lecturing in the West, he protested. A simple ochre robe would do, he said. But Jagmohanlal didn't like to hear anything of the kind. Swamiji felt helpless before the intention of his disciples, and could only surrender. Hence, he was fitted out in royal style, and presented with a handsome purse. Jagmohan bought a first-class ticket for Swamiji on the Japan-bound P. and O. steamer Peninsular, maintaining that the guru of Raja should travel like a Raja.

Finally, May 31, 1893, the day of sailing, arrived. Swamiji looked like a prince in a robe and turban of silk. Jagmohan and Alasinga went up the gangway with him and remained on the board until the ship's gongs gave warning of imminent departure. Their eyes filled with tears as they prostrated themselves at the feet of Swamiji in final salutation, and left the ship. Mr. Chhabildas, who had been one of his hosts in Bombay, sailed for Japan by the same ship.

In a letter from Bombay, dated 22nd May 1893, Swamiji wrote to the Dewan of Junagadh:

> ...Often and often, we see that the very best of men even are troubled and visited with tribulations in this world; it may be inexplicable; but it is also the experience of my life that the heart and core of everything here is good, that whatever may be the surface waves, deep down and underlying everything, there is an infinite basis of goodness and love; and so long as we do not reach that basis, we were troubled; but having once reached that zone of calmness, let winds howl and tempests rage. The house which is built on a rock of ages cannot shake.

Swami Vivekananda was now on his voyage to the West to do his work that was bestowed upon him by his Master. As Sister Nivedita said, "He [Swami Vivekananda] neither used the word 'nationality', not proclaimed an era of 'nation-making'. 'Man-making', he said, was his own task. But he was born a lover, and the queen of his adoration was his Motherland."

In course of his wandering throughout the length and breadth of India Swamiji seems to have touched upon and studied every phase of Indian life. He had talked with saints and scholars and simple souls alike, learnt from all, talked to all, lived with all, saw India as she was and is, and grasped knowledge on various subjects. He received the initiation of the Sikhs, studied both the Indian and Western philosophy, and the Jain Scriptures with Jains. He was accepted as their Guru by Rajput princes, lived for weeks with a family of sweepers in Central India, observed caste-customs of different places, and finally reached Cape Comorin, and in his desire to go outside India swam across the strait to the Island, where he offered the worship and had vowed. The "roaring fire", as he was called by Shri Ramakrishna Paramahamsa, could burn up all impurity. In his Master he found the key to life.

We would like to conclude this chapter with the words of Sister Nivedita:

> These, then—the Shastras, the Guru, and the Motherland—are the three notes that mingle themselves to form the music of the works of Vivekananda. These are the treasure which it is his to offer. These furnish him with the ingredients whereof he compounds the world's heal-all of his spiritual bounty.

8
Voyage to the West

The ship left Bombay and moved on its way facing southwards to Colombo (Ceylon). Destination of the voyage was Chicago port. Swamiji stood on the deck and gazed towards the holy land until it faded from sight. He blessed them who loved him and those whom he loved. His eyes were filled with tears as his heart overwhelmed with emotion. The Master, the Holy Mother, and his brother-disciples flashed through his mind. He thought of India and her culture, of her suffering and her greatness, of Rishis and of the ancient scriptures of Hindu Religion. His heart was rending with love for his native land. Wherever he looked, could see only blue waters of the ocean. He murmured under his breath, "Yes, from the Land of Renunciation I go to the Land of Enjoyment!" But he was not going for enjoyment. It was to be work, hard work ought to be done, tremendous struggle, terrific dubiousness, continuous work attended with much difficulty. That work was to shatter his health; he was not to know rest. Time left in hand was very little, but work to be done was huge. Only nine years of life were left him, and those in service and often in anguish. He was to face many problems. But he didn't have time to think of them. He thought of the Master, and of the Holy Mother of the Universe. Vivekananda, the Seer of the Vedic wisdom, had nothing to worry, because he knew that behind him were the Master and the blessings of the Holy Mother. The ship moved on its way, and Swamiji remained alone with his thoughts and the vastness of the sea.

After boarding the ship Swamiji was worried over taking care of his belongings that his voyage made necessary. He, the wandering monk, going about with his staff and Kamandalu, was now burdened with trunks, portmanteau, and beddings! Gradually he became accustomed to the life on ship, and enjoyed his new experiences. Soon he became friendly with many of his fellow passengers. They admired his orange-robe, glowing face with wide eyes, and commanding personality. His courtly manner and manly bearing made him popular with them. Even the Captain, when at leisure, would join Swamiji on his solitary walks. He showed him the entire ship, and explained to him the working of the engines. Passengers were all foreigners, but Swamiji didn't take much time to accommodate himself to the strange environment and strange food. He observed the manners and customs of the Europeans and soon acquainted himself with them. Swelling and falling of seaweaves, every gush of wind, every cloud, and carefree atmosphere made his poetic mind filled with pleasure. The mighty expanse of ocean, the invigorating air forced his heart dancing with joy.

We remember that once Swamiji said, "I am now leaving Kashi, and shall not return until I have burst on society like a bomb-shell; and it will follow me like a dog." Now standing on the deck he perhaps was thinking as follows:

> I go forth, to preach a religion of which Buddhism is nothing but a rebel child, and Christianity, with all her pretensions, only a distant echo.... I am called by the Lord for

> this. I have been dragged through a whole life full of crosses and tortures, I have seen the nearest and dearest die, almost of starvation; I have been ridiculed, distrusted, and have suffered for my sympathy for the very men who scoff and scorn. Well, my boy, this is the school of misery, which is also the school for great souls and prophets for the cultivation of sympathy, of patience, and, above all, of an indomitable iron will which quakes not even if the universe be pulverized at our feet.... I do not care for liberation, or for devotion; I would rather go to hundred thousand hells, "*Vasantavallokahitam carantah*—doing good to others (silently) like the spring"—this is my religion.... I do not take into any consideration whether people accept [Sri Ramakrishna's] name or not, but I am ready to lay down my life to help his teachings, his life, and his message spread all over the world.... Yes, my own life is guided by the enthusiasm of certain great personality, but what of that? Inspiration was never filtered out to the world through one man!... It is true I believe Ramakrishna Paramahamsa to have been inspired. But then I am myself inspired also. And you are inspired. And your disciples will be; and theirs after them, and so on, to the end of time!... I stand at nobody's dictation. I know my mission in life, and no chauvinism about me; I belong as much to India as to the world.... What country has any special claim on me? Am I any nation's slave?... I see a greater power than man, or God, or devil at my back.... I hate cowardice; I will have nothing to do with cowards or political nonsense. I do not believe in any politics. God and truth are the only politics in the world, everything else is trash.... Truth is my God, the universe my country.... Before proceeding to America I wrote to Mother [Sri Sarada Devi] to bless me. Her blessings came.... The Parliament of Religion is being organized for this [pointing to himself]. My mind tells me so. You will see it verified at no distant date.... I want to give them dry, hard reason, softened in the sweetest syrup of love and made spicy with intense work, and cooked in the kitchen of Yoga, so that even a baby can easily digest it. To put the Hindu ideas into English and then make out of dry philosophy and intricate mythology and queer startling psychology, a religion which shall be easy, simple, popular, and at the same time meet the requirements of the highest minds—is a task only those can understand who have attempted it. The dry, abstract Advaita must become living—poetic—in everyday life; out of hopelessly intricate mythology must come concrete moral forms; and out of bewildering Yogi-ism must come the most scientific and practical psychology—and all this must be put in a form so that a child may grasp it. That is my life's work.[1]

It was after about a month and ten days since the ship had left Bombay, Swamiji wrote a letter [on July 10, 1893] from Yokohama to his disciples of south India. He writes:

> Excuse my not keeping you constantly informed of my movements. One is so busy every day, and especially myself who am quite new to the life of possessing things an taking care of them. That consumes so much of my energy. It is really an awful botheration.
>
> From Bombay we reached Colombo. Our steamer remained in port for nearly the whole day, and we took the opportunity of getting off to have a look at the town. We drove through the streets, and the only thing I remember was a temple in which was a very gigantic Murti (image) of the Lord Buddha in a reclining posture, entering Nirvana.[2]

The next stop was Penang, a strip of land along the sea in the body of the Malaya Peninsula. In the above letter from Yokohama he writes:

> The Malayas are all Mohammedans and in old days were noted pirates and quite a dread to merchantmen. But now the leviathan guns of modern turreted battleships have forced the Malayas to look about for more peaceful pursuits. On our way from Penang to Singapore, we had glimpses of Sumatra with its high mountains, and the Captain pointed out to me several places as the favourite haunts of pirates in days gone by. Singapore is the capital of the Straits Settlements. It has a fine botanical garden with the most splendid collection of palms. The beautiful fan-like palm, called the traveller's palm, grows here in abundance, and the bread-fruit tree everywhere. The celebrated mangosteen is as plentiful here as mangoes in Madras, but mango is nonpareil. The people here are not half so dark as the people of Madras, although so near the line. Singapore possesses a fine museum too.

Next, the ship stooped at Hong Kong, which made him feel that he reached China. He writes his experience as follows:

> You feel that you have reached China, the Chinese element predominates so much. All labour, all trade seems to be in their hands. And Hong Kong is real China. As soon as the steamer casts anchor, you are besieged with hundreds of Chinese boats to carry you to the land. These boats with two helms are rather peculiar. The boatman lives in the boat with his family. Almost always, the wife is at the helms, managing one with her hands and the other with one of her feet. And in ninety per cent of cases, you find a baby tied to her back, with the hands and feet of the little Chin left free. It is a quaint sight to see the little John Chinaman dangling very quietly from his mother's back, whilst she is now setting with might and main, now pushing heavy loads, or jumping with wonderful agility from boat to boat. And there is such a rush of boats and steam-launches coming in and going out. Baby John is every moment put into the risk of having his little head pulverized, pigtail and all; but he does not care a fig. This busy life seems to have no charm for him, and he is quite content to learn the anatomy of a bit of rice-cake given to him from time to time by the madly busy mother. The Chinese child is quite a philosopher and calmly goes to work at an age when your Indian boy can hardly crawl on all fours. He has learnt the philosophy of necessity too well. Their extreme poverty is one of the causes why the Chinese and the Indians have remained in a state of mummified civilization. To an ordinary Hindu or Chinese, everyday necessity is too hideous to allow him to think of anything else.

The ship halted at Hong Kong for three days, and, therefore, the passengers had an opportunity to visit Canton, eighty miles up the Si Kiang River. Swamiji writes his impression in the same letter:

> The river is broad enough to allow the biggest steamers to pass through. A number of Chinese steamers ply between Hong Kong and Canton. We took passage on one of these in the evening and reached Canton early in the morning. What a scene of bustle and life! What an immense number of boats almost covering the waters! And not only those that are carrying on the trade, but hundreds of others which serve as houses to live in. And quite a lot of them so nice and big! In fact, they are big houses two or three storeys high, with verandahs running round and streets between, and all floating!
>
> ...Around us on both sides of the river for miles and miles is the big city—a wilderness of human beings, pushing, struggling, surging, roaring. But with all its population, all its activity, it is the dirtiest town I saw, not in the sense in which a town is called dirty in India, for as to that not a speck of filth is allowed by the Chinese to go waste; but

> because of the Chinaman, who has, it seems, taken a vow never to bathe! Every house is a shop, people living only on the top floor. The streets are very very narrow, so that you almost touch the shops on both sides as you pass. At every ten paces you find meat stalls, and there are shops which sell cat's and dog's meat. Of course, only the poorest classes of Chinaman eat dog or cat.
>
> The Chinese ladies can never be seen. They have got as strict a zenana as the Hindus of Northern India; only the women of the laboring classes can be seen. Even amongst these, one sees now and then a woman with feet smaller than those of your youngest child, and of course they cannot be said to walk, but hobble.
>
> I went to see several Chinese temples. The biggest in Canton is dedicated to the memory of the first Buddhistic Emperor and the five hundred first disciples of Buddhism. The central figure is of course Buddha, and next beneath Him is seated the Emperor, and ranging on both sides are the statues of the disciples, all beautifully carved out of wood.

Swamiji not only learned the lifestyle of the poor Chinese of labouring classes, and their culture, but also acquainted himself with their religion. He noted the points of similarity and dissimilarity between Buddhist and Indian temples, and delighted in the originality that he found there.

Then, as a monk, he wished to visit a Chinese monastery. But in way of thinking the Chinese community were almost similar to the orthodox Christian missionaries. These monasteries were forbidden ground to foreigners. If anybody would go there by mistake, he would surely be maltreated by them. Swamiji felt it unfair, but didn't get frightened at all. He thought that if the monks knew him to be a Hindu sannyasi, they might not molest him. So he persisted, and finally induced the interpreter and his fellow passengers to tread "forbidden land", saying laughingly, "Come, let us see if they will kill us!" Then they forwarded their steps towards the monastery. But they had not gone far when the interpreter cried out, "Away! Away, gentlemen! They are coming, and they are infuriated!" Swamiji found that two or three men with clubs in their hands were approaching rapidly. Frightened at their menacing appearance, all but Swamiji and the interpreter took to their heels. When, in a short while, the interpreter was on the point of fleeing, Swamiji seized him by the arm and said with a smile, "My good man, you must not run away before you tell me the Chinese word for Indian Yogi." The interpreter got surprised with the strange behaviour of Swamiji, and told the word before he could manage to make his escape. Swamiji, the 'roaring fire' of Sri Ramakrishna, found himself alone before those fanatic men. If they would have killed him in that foreign land, there was no one to save him. He loudly called out that he was an Indian Yogi. And lo, the word for "Yogi" acted like magic! The threatening expression of the men changed to that of deep reverence and they fell at his feet. They stretched out their joined palms in most respectful salutation, and said something in their language. Swamiji understood only one word to be "Kabach". He thought that it was surely the Indian word meaning amulet. He looked at the interpreter, who stood at a safe distance; confused at this strange development—for never in his experience had he witnessed such a manifestation as this. He gave an explanation, "Sir, they want amulets to ward off evil spirits and unholy influences. They desire your protection." Swamiji was taken aback for a moment. He did not believe in magic. He was against occultation. Then he took a sheet of paper from his pocket, divided it into several pieces, and wrote on them the word "Om" in Sanskrit, the most holy word of the Vedas and the symbol of the highest truth. He gave them the pieces of paper. They touched them to their head, and led him into the monastery.

They took him to the most isolated portion of the monastery, and had shown many old manuscripts, which were written in Sanskrit and, strange to say, in old Bengali characters. Then he remembered that when he had visited the temple dedicated to the first Buddhist Emperor he was surprised to see that the faces of the Blessed One's five hundred disciples were almost looked like Bengalis. These evidences, as also his previous study of Chinese Buddhism, convinced him that once there was a close communication between Bengal and China, and many Bengali Bhikkhus (Buddhist monks) went to China, when they brought to the distant land the gospel of the Blessed One; and thus Chinese civilization was greatly influenced by Indian thought.

From Canton Swamiji returned back to Hong Kong and from thence to Nagasaki in Japan. He was highly impressed with everything he saw. In the same letter he continues:

> We landed for a few hours and drove through the town. What a contrast! The Japanese are one of the cleanliest people on earth. Everything is neat and tidy. Their streets are nearly all broad, straight, and regularly paved. Their little houses are cage-like, and their pine-covered evergreen little hills from the background of almost every town and village. The short-statured, fair-skinned, quaintly-dressed Japs, their movements, attitudes, gestures, everything is picturesque. Japan is the land of the picturesque! Almost every house has a garden at the back, very nicely laid out according to Japanese fashion with small shrubs, grass-plots, small artificial waters, and small stone bridges.

Leaving Nagasaki the ship stopped at Kobe, where Swamiji left the ship and took the land-rout to Yokohama, with a view to see the interior of Japan. He visited three big cities: Osaka, the great manufacturing town, Kyoto, the former capital, and Tokyo, the present capital. He writes further:

> Tokyo is nearly twice the size of Calcutta with nearly double the population. No foreigner is allowed to travel in the interior without a passport. The Japanese seem now to have fully awakened themselves to the necessity of the present times. They have now thoroughly organized army equipped with guns which one of their own officers has invented and which is said to be second to none. Then, they are continually increasing their navy. I have seen a tunnel nearly a mile long, bored by a Japanese engineer. The Match factories are simply a sight to see, and they are bent upon making everything they want in their own country. There is a Japanese line of steamers playing between China and Japan, which shortly intends running between Bombay and Yokohama.

In all these cities Swamiji visited many important temples and studied the rituals and ceremonies observed in them. To his amazement he found that here also the temples were inscribed with Sanskrit Mantras in old Bengali character. But very few of the priests knew Sanskrit. He found that the modern rage for progress had penetrated even the priesthood; but he was delighted to discover that "to the Japanese, India is still the dreamland of everything high and good."

In this letter from Yokohama to the group of disciples in Madras, we see that the enthusiasm of Japanese, and their industries, streets, houses, sense of beauty—everything made him delighted. He vigorously denounced the evils of his own country and tried to inspire Indians to rise from the lethargy into which they had sunk through priestcraft and social tyranny. He did not rage against the Brahmanical culture, rather, he revered it. The only question that he wished to ask was that why Indians should not be so much active to develop themselves? Why it, which is possible to Japanese, should not be possible to Indians? He wrote in the same letter:

> I want that numbers of our young men should pay a visit to Japan and China every year. Especially to the Japanese, India is still the dreamland of everything high and good. And

> you, what are you? ...talking twaddle all your lives, vain talkers, what are you? Come, see these people, and then go and hide your faces in shame. A race of dotards, you lose your caste if you come out! Sitting down these hundreds of years with an ever-increasing load of crystallized superstition on your heads, for hundreds of years spending all your energy upon discussing the touchableness or untouchableness of this food or that, with all humanity crushed out of you by the continuous social tyranny of ages—what are you? And what are you doing now? . . . promenading the sea-shores with books in your hands—repeating undigested stray bits of European brainwork, and the whole soul bent upon getting a thirty-rupee clerkship, or at best becoming a lawyer—the height of young India's ambition—and every student with a whole brood of hungry children cackling at his heels and asking for bread! Is there not water enough in the sea to drown you, books, gowns, university, diplomas, and all?

These are the words of Swamiji, the 'roaring fire' of patriotism. This letter shows how much he loved India, his Motherland. He tried to inspire Indians to wake up to be "men". That is why he announced:

> Come, be men! Kick out the priests who are always against progress, because they would never mend, their hearts would never become big. They are the offspring of centuries of superstition and tyranny. Root out priest-craft first. Come, be men! Come out of your narrow holes and have a look abroad. See how nations are on the march! Do you love man? Do you love your country? Then come, let us struggle for higher and better things; look out back, no, not even if you see the dearest and nearest cry. Look not back, but forward!
>
> India wants the sacrifice of at least a thousand of her young men—men, mind, and not brutes. The English Government has been the instrument, brought over here by the Lord, to break your crystallized civilization, and Madras supplied the first men who helped in giving the English a footing. How many men, unselfish, thorough-going men, is Madras ready now to supply, to struggle unto life and death to bring about a new state of things—sympathy for the poor, and bread to their hungry mouths, enlightenment to the people at large—and struggle unto death to make men of them who have been brought to the level of beasts, by the tyranny of your forefathers?

Finally, he warned: "Calm and silent and steady work, and no newspaper humbug, no name-making, you must always remember."

Swamiji boarded on the new *Empress of India*, which left Yokohama on July 14 and sailed for Vancouver. There were two more Indians, one Jamshetji Tata who was on a business trip to USA, and the other was Lalubhai. Jamshetji met him when Swamiji was in Japan. In a letter dated October 3, Sister Nivedita wrote: "Mr. Tata told me that when Swamiji was in Japan, everyone who saw him was immediately struck by his likeness to Buddha."

Now some questions usually may crop up in our mind: when and where Swamiji met Mr. Tata, and what did they talk about? What kind of impression had Mr. Tata about Swamiji? And so on.

We can say clearly that in those days Swamiji was the only monk in India who would not like to accept anything without analyzing them with a scientific view. The cause behind his interest in spreading the education on modern science and mechanical skill was to remove the poverty form India, because he was a great patriot. He always would have been thinking for the development of India.

Swami Vivekananda, a robust youth aged around 30 years and wearing saffron attire with a turban usually worn by the Maharajas was found talking to a middle aged gentleman, Jamshetji Tata who was on a business trip to the USA. It was a breezy, sunny afternoon and they were sitting on the deck of *SS Empress of India* which was on its way to Vancouver.

Swamiji and Jamshetji had visited a match manufacturing factory in Japan and were discussing about Japan's progress. Swamiji asked Jamshetji why he instead of setting up his own match manufacturing factory in India was importing match from Japan as this meant draining out of national wealth and in return he got a meager commission. Setting up his own factory will not only increase his profit but at the same time will help Indian youths to get jobs. Swamiji in a letter to his younger brother Mahendranath Dutta had narrated his conversation with Jamshetji.

Jamshetji was amazed to see the burning spirit of this young man. His eyes glittered when he talked about the oppression and torture inflicted by the British on his fellow Indians who did not get a square meal and did not have clothes to put on, education and shelter. Swamiji narrated his own experience which he gathered during his extensive tour in the country. He saw the indifference of the Maharajas and the educated people towards the poor and told Jamshetji that the real hope of India was from the masses. Jamshetji developed affection and respect for Swamiji.

On 11 September 1983 Swamiji, addressed the World Parliament of Religions and created history. He became the central figure at the Parliament. Referring to his speeches *New York Herald* remarked "It was human eloquence at its highest pitch." Another newspaper wrote, "After listening to him we find how foolish it is to send missionaries to his country." From the United States Swamiji went to England for giving lectures and holding classes on Vedanta. The classes became so popular that it became difficult for the organizers to accommodate the ever inquisitive audience. Swamiji came back to India in 1897. People felicitated him and removed the horses from the carriage and drove them. Swamiji lectured in south India and came back to Calcutta. Jamshetji who was in Bombay must have been very happy at the success of his old friend.

In September 1898, Mr. J.N. Tata (Jamsetji Nusserwanji Tata) pledged half of his personal wealth of ₹ 30 lacs (then £ 200,000) to make his dream of a "university or institute of research" a reality. Enthused by this mammoth project, he addressed a letter to Swami Vivekananda on 23 November 1898, which reads as follows:

Esplanade House, Bombay.
23rd Nov. 1898

Dear Swami Vivekananda,

> I trust, you remember me as a fellow-traveller on your voyage from Japan to Chicago. I very much recall at this moment your views on the growth of the ascetic spirit in India, and the duty, not of destroying, but of diverting it into useful channels.
>
> I recall these ideas in connection with my scheme of Research Institute of Science for India, of which you have doubtless heard or read. It seems to me that no better use can be made of the ascetic spirit than the establishment of monasteries or residential halls for men dominated by this spirit, where they should live with ordinary decency and devote their lives to the cultivation of sciences—natural and humanistic. I am of opinion that, if such a crusade in favour of an asceticism of this kind were undertaken by a competent leader, it would greatly help asceticism, science, and the good name of

> our common country; and I know not who would make a more fitting general of such a campaign than Vivekananda. Do you think you would care to apply yourself to the mission of galvanizing into life our ancient traditions in this respect? Perhaps, you had better begin with a fiery pamphlet rousing our people in this matter. I would cheerfully defray all the expenses of publication.

With kind regards, I am, dear Swami

Yours faithfully,
Jamshetji Tata

At that time Vivekananda was busy in starting the Ramakrishna Mission and could not accept the offer, but he promptly sent his disciple Sister Nivedita who met Jamshetji and his advisor, Mr. Padsa. A detailed plan formulated by them was promptly suppressed by the Viceroy, Lord Curzon. However, Tatas persevered and continued to work on their plans.

The effort of Nivedita kindled a new hope in Jamshetji's mind. In 1901, he invited Swami Vivekananda to Bombay through Josephine MacLeod, one of Swamiji's disciples. On 17 February Swamiji wrote a letter to Joe that read: "I am so glad you saw Mr. Tata and find him so strong and good. I will, of course, accept an invitation if I am strong enough to go to Bombay." Swamiji, however, could not go to Bombay because of ill health and Jamshetji's dream to see his friend remained unfulfilled. *Prabuddha Bharat*, in its edition of March 1901, made an editorial comment that read: "It would be an exceedingly happy arrangement if the Tata Research University scheme could be combined along with other schemes for memorials, for the princely gift of the Parsi patriot fully deserves that honour of being associated with Her Majesty's Memorial."

The pressure on the British Government to clear Jamshetji's proposal was mounting both in India and abroad. Swamiji died in July 1902 and Jamshetji died in February 1907. The British Government cleared the proposal in 1905. In 1907, Maharaja of Mysore, a devotee of Swami Vivekananda gave the land to fulfil his guru's dream. The formal vesting was issued in May 1909.

Today the Indian Institute of Science, a premier organization in research stands on 800 acres of land in Bangalore. It is still referred to as the Tata institute.

In conclusion to this matter, we may quote the words of Pandit Nehru: "Rooted in the past and full of pride in India's prestige, Vivekananda was yet modern in his approach to life's problems and was a kind of bridge between the past of India and her present."

In a speech Dr. APJ Abdul Kalam said: "Jamshetji brought two establishments to India, first one was steel plant, and the other was education research institution, based on the vision of Swami Vivekananda. A visionary with his blessings paved the way for a genius to establish Indian Institute of Science in 1899."

Swami Vivekananda had also brought a great change in the life of John D. Rockefeller, a wealthy tycoon of America, who 15 years later, set up his Rockefeller Foundation which did immense charitable work. We will come to this matter later on in time.

Now we should come back to the voyage on *Empress of India*, which left Yokohama on July 14 and sailed for Vancouver. The voyage was not a comfortable one. In a letter of August 20, Swamiji wrote a brief account of this voyage to Alasinga: "From Japan I reached Vancouver. The way was by the Northern Pacific. It was very cold and I suffered much for want of warm clothing." It had not occurred either to him or his disciples that the summer voyage by the Northern Pacific would be cold. From Vancouver, in British Columbia, where the ship landed on the evening of July 25, Swamiji travelled to Chicago. His train passed through the scenic Canadian Rockies to Winnipeg and thence down into the rolling lake country of Minnesota and Wisconsin. It was a beautiful trip, better to see the magnificent view.

References

ANCESTRY

1. *Complete Works of Swami Vivekananda*, seventeenth edition, 1986, 1:8-9
2. Vivekananda: Patriot-Prophet, pp. 91-92
3. Swami Vivekanander Balya Jivon
4. *Sri Ramakrishna and His Divine Play* (Lilaprosango), translated by Swami Chetanananda, first edition, p. 766
5. *Ibid.*, p. 830
6. *Ibid.*
7. *Complete Works of Swami Vivekananda*, fifth edition, 1997, 9:203
8. *Sri Ramakrishna and His Divine Play* (Lilaprosango), translated by Swami Chetanananda, first edition, pp. 768-69

BIRTH AND CHILDHOOD OF VIVEKANANDA

1. *Complete Works of Swami Vivekananda*, seventeenth edition, September 2013, 6:405
2. *Ibid.*, 6:412
3. *Ibid.*, 6:415
4. *Complete Works of Swami Vivekananda*, tenth edition, 1973, 5:128
5. *Sri Ramakrishna and His Divine Play* (Lilaprosango), translated by Swami Chetanananda, first edition, p. 834
6. *Life of Swami Vivekananda*, Eastern and Western Disciples, Vol. 1:36

VIVEKANANDA AS A STUDENT

1. *Complete Works of Swami Vivekananda*, fourteenth edition, March 2016, 4:349
2. *Complete Works of Swami Vivekananda*, seventeenth edition, 1986, 1:28
3. *Complete Works of Swami Vivekananda*, tenth edition, 2016, 7:141
4. *Swami Vivekananda on Himself*, first edition, 1963, p. 5
5. *Sri Ramakrishna and His Divine Play* (Lilaprosango), translated by Swami Chetananada, first edition, pp. 760-61
6. *Ibid.*, pp. 763-64
7. *Life of Swami Vivekananda: Eastern and Western Disciples*, Vol. 1:39
8. *Swami Vivekananda on Himself*, first edition, 1963, p. 6
9. *Sri Ramakrishna and His Divine Play* (Lilaprosango), translated by Swami Chetananada, first edition, pp. 760-61
10. *Swami Vivekananda on Himself*, first edition, 1963, p. 7
11. *Sri Ramakrishna and His Divine Play* (Lilaprosango), translated by Swami Chetananada, first edition, p. 767
12. *Vivekananda: A Biography*, Swami Nikhilananda, first Indian edition 1964, pp. 16-17
13. *Swami Vivekananda on Himself*, first edition, 1963, pp. 1-2
14. *Sri Ramakrishna and His Divine Play* (Lilaprosango), translated by Swami Chetananada, first edition, p. 759

15. *Complete Works of Swami Vivekananda*, seventeenth edition, September 2013, 6:47
16. *Complete Works of Swami Vivekananda*, twenty-fifth reprint, December 2015, 3:301
17. *Ibid.*, 3:302
18. *Life of Swami Vivekananda: His Eastern and Western Disciples*, Vol. 1:51
19. *Reminiscences of Vivekananda*, pp. 188-89
20. *The Complete Works of Swami Vivekananda*, tenth edition, December 1973, 5:258
21. *The Complete Works of Swami Vivekananda*, fourteenth edition, March 2016, 3:301
22. *Reminiscences of Vivekananda*, pp. 175-76
23. *Life of Swami Vivekananda: His Eastern and Western Disciples*, Vol. 1:32-53.
24. *Life of Swami Vivekananda* by Romain Rolland, p. 3
25. *Life of Swami Vivekananda: His Eastern and Western Disciples*, Vol. 1:51
26. *Complete Works of Swami Vivekananda*, seventeenth edition, 1986, 1:60
27. *Swami Vivekananda on Himself*, first edition, 1963, p. 8
28. *Complete Works of Swami Vivekananda*, fifth edition, 1997, 9:448-49
29. *Sri Ramakrishna and His Divine Play* (Lilaprosango), translated by Swami Chetananada, first edition, p. 792
30. *Life of Swami Vivekananda* by Romain Rolland, pp. 55-56
31. *Complete Works of Swami Vivekananda*, fourteenth edition, March 2016, 4:162
32. *Sri Ramakrishna and His Divine Play* (Lilaprosango), translated by Swami Chetananada, first edition, p. 833

AT THE FEET OF THE MASTER

1. *Sri Ramakrishna and His Divine Play* (Lilaprosango), translated by Swami Chetananada, first edition, pp. 756-57
2. *The Gospel of Sri Ramakrishna*, edn-6th, 1974. p. 168
3. *Sri Ramakrishna and His Divine Play* (Lilaprosango), translated by Swami Chetananada, first edition, p. 757
4. *Ibid.*, p. 758
5. *Ibid.*, pp. 758-59
6. *Ibid.*, p. 772
7. *Ibid.*, pp. 772-73
8. *Ibid.*, p. 773
9. *Ibid.*, p. 774
10. *Ibid.*, pp. 775-76
11. *Ibid.*, pp. 777-78
12. *Ibid.*, pp. 778-79
13. *Ibid.*, p. 780
14. *Ibid.*
15. *Ibid.*
16. *Ibid.*, pp. 781-82
17. *Ibid.*, pp. 783-84
18. *Ibid.*, p. 787
19. *Ibid.*, p. 788
20. *Ibid.*, p. 790
21. *Ibid.*, pp. 793-94
22. *Ibid.*, p. 801
23. *Ibid.*, p. 802
24. *Ibid.*, pp. 802-04

25. *Ibid.*, p. 826
26. *Ibid.*, p. 827
27. *Ibid.*, pp. 827-28
28. *Ibid.*, pp. 838-43
29. *Ibid.*, pp. 843-45
30. *Swami Vivekananda on Himself*, p. 32
31. *The Gospel of Sri Ramakrishna*, p. 8
32. *Ibid.*, pp. 12-14
33. *Ibid.*, p. 16
34. *Ibid.*, pp. 44-47
35. *Ibid.*, pp. 47-49
36. *Ibid.*, pp. 51-54
37. *Ibid.*, p. 87
38. *Ibid.*, pp. 216-20
39. *Ibid.*, pp. 216-38
40. *Ibid.*, pp. 243-48
41. *Ibid.*, pp. 266-69
42. *Ibid.*, p. 494
43. *Ibid.*, pp. 523-25
44. *Ibid.*, p. 530
45. *Ibid.*, pp. 533-34
46. *Ibid.*, p. 669
47. *Ibid.*, p. 667
48. *Ibid.*, pp. 678-79
49. *Ibid.*, pp. 683-86
50. *Ibid.*, pp. 700-01
51. *Ibid.*, pp. 708-12
52. *Ibid.*, pp. 739-44
53. *Ibid.*, pp. 747-48
54. *Ibid.*, p. 750
55. *Ibid.*, pp. 751-52
56. *Ibid.*, pp. 768-75
57. *Ibid.*, pp. 786-87
58. *Ibid.*, p. 897
59. *Sri Ramakrishna and His Divine Play* (Lilaprosango), translated by Swami Chetananada, first edition, pp. 904-05
60. *Ibid.*, pp. 905-06
61. *Ibid.*, p. 907
62. *Ibid.*, pp. 908-10
63. *Ibid.*, pp. 921-22
64. *Ibid.*, pp. 922-24
65. *The Gospel of Sri Ramakrishna*, pp. 923-24
66. *Ibid.*, pp. 927-29
67. *Ibid.*, p. 931
68. *Ibid.*, pp. 933-38
69. *Ibid.*, pp. 940-43
70. *Ibid.*, pp. 957-58
71. *Ibid.*, pp. 961-64

72. *Swami Vivekananda on Himself*, pp. 10-13
73. *Ibid.*, pp. 16-24
74. *Ibid.*, pp. 24-25
75. *Ibid.*, p. 33
76. *Ibid.*, p. 36
77. *Ibid.*, p. 37

THE BARANAGORE MATH

1. *Life of Swami Vivekananda: His Eastern and Western Disciples*, sixth edition, 1989, 1:182
2. *Swami Vivekananda on Himself*, first edition, 1963, p. 40
3. *Ibid.*, p. 41
4. *Ibid.*, pp. 64-72
5. *Ibid.*, p. 73
6. *The Complete Works of Swami Vivekananda*, eleventh edition, September 2013, 6:356
7. *The Gospel of Sri Ramakrishna*, p. 971
8. *Ibid.*, pp. 972-73
9. *Life of Swami Vivekananda: His Eastern and Western Disciples*, sixth edition, 1989, 1:195
10. *Ibid.*, pp. 195-96
11. *The Gospel of Sri Ramakrishna*, pp. 973-75
12. *Ibid.*, pp. 976-79
13. *Ibid.*, pp. 979-80
14. *Ibid.*, pp. 980-84
15. *Ibid.*, pp. 984-89
16. *Ibid.*, pp. 989-91
17. *Ibid.*, pp. 992-93
18. *Ibid.*, pp. 993-94
19. *Ibid.*, pp. 994-98
20. *Ibid.*, pp. 1003-05
21. *Ibid.*, pp. 1005-06
22. *Swami Vivekananda on Himself*, first edition, 1963, pp. 74-75
23. *Ibid.*, pp. 75-76
24. *The Complete Works of Swami Vivekananda*, eleventh edition, September 2013, 6:316-17
25. *Life of Swami Vivekananda: His Eastern and Western Disciples*, sixth edition, 1989, Vol. I, p. 208
26. *Reminiscences of Vivekananda*, pp. 8-9

WANDERING MONK

1. *Swami Vivekananda on Himself*, first edition, 1963, p. 79
2. *The Complete Works of Swami Vivekananda*, seventh edition, December 2013, 8:82
3. *Ibid.*, pp. 8:82-83
4. *The Complete Works of Swami Vivekananda*, seventh edition, December 2013, 8:83-85
5. *Ibid.*, pp. 6:85
6. *Ibid.*, pp. 6:85-86
7. *Ibid.*, pp. 6:86-87
8. *Ibid.*, pp. 6:87
9. *Ibid.*
10. *The Complete Works of Swami Vivekananda*, seventeenth edition, 1986, 1:25-32
11. *The Complete Works of Swami Vivekananda*, fourteenth edition, March 2016, 4:493
12. *Life of Swami Vivekananda: His Eastern and Western Disciples*, sixth edition, 1989, Vol. I, p. 218

13. *Sri Ramakrishna and His Divine Play* (Lilaprosango), translated by Swami Chetanananda, first edition, p. 612
14. *The Complete Works of Swami Vivekananda*, eleventh edition, September 2013, 6:225
15. *Life of Swami Vivekananda: His Eastern and Western Disciples*, sixth edition, 1989, Vol. I, p. 221
16. *The Complete Works of Swami Vivekananda*, eleventh edition, September 2013, 6:226
17. *Ibid.*, 6:230
18. *Ibid.*, 6:231
19. *The Complete Works of Swami Vivekananda*, seventh edition, December 2013, 8:293
20. *The Complete Works of Swami Vivekananda*, eleventh edition, September 2013, 6:232-37
21. *Ibid.* 6:237-38
22. *The Complete Works of Swami Vivekananda*, tenth edition, March 2016, 7:423-24
23. *The Complete Works of Swami Vivekananda*, eleventh edition, September 2013, 6:239-40
24. *The Complete Works of Swami Vivekananda*, tenth edition, March 2016, 7:425
25. *The Complete Works of Swami Vivekananda*, eleventh edition, September 2013, 6:240
26. *Ibid.*, 6:240
27. *Ibid.*, 6:242
28. *The Gospel of Sri Ramakrishna*, p. 230
29. *The Complete Works of Swami Vivekananda*, tenth edition, 1973, 5:214
30. *The Complete Works of Swami Vivekananda*, fourteenth edition, March 2016, 4:283
31. *The Complete Works of Swami Vivekananda*, tenth edition, March 2016, 7:425-26
32. *The Complete Works of Swami Vivekananda*, eleventh edition, September 2013, 6:243
33. *Ibid.*, 6:244
34. *The Complete Works of Swami Vivekananda*, first edition, February 1997, 9:3
35. *The Complete Works of Swami Vivekananda*, eleventh edition, September 2013, 6:244-45
36. *The Complete Works of Swami Vivekananda*, tenth edition, March 2016, 7:426-27
37. *The Complete Works of Swami Vivekananda*, eleventh edition, September 2013, 6:246
38. *The Complete Works of Swami Vivekananda*, first edition, February 1997, 9:4-5
39. *The Complete Works of Swami Vivekananda*, tenth edition, March 2016, 7:428-29
40. *The Complete Works of Swami Vivekananda*, eleventh edition, September 2013, 6:246-47
41. *Ibid.*, 6:256
42. *The Complete Works of Swami Vivekananda*, eleventh edition, September 2013, 6:252-53
43. *Ibid.*, 5:254
44. *The Complete Works of Swami Vivekananda*, eleventh edition, September 2013, 6:257
45. *The Complete Works of Swami Vivekananda*, tenth edition, March 2016, 7:429-30
46. *The Complete Works of Swami Vivekananda*, eleventh edition, September 2013, 6:260
47. *The Complete Works of Swami Vivekananda*, tenth edition, March 2016, 7:232
48. *The Complete Works of Swami Vivekananda*, fourteenth edition, March 2016, 4:514-15
49. *Ibid.*, 4:283-87
50. *The Complete Works of Swami Vivekananda*, eleventh edition, September 2013, 6:261-64
51. *Ibid.*, 6:257-58
52. *Life of Swami Vivekananda: His Eastern and Western Disciples*, sixth edition, 1989, 1:244-47
53. *Ibid.*, 1:243-44
54. *Reminiscences of Vivekananda*, pp. 7-8
55. *Ibid.*, pp. 9-10
56. *The Complete Works of Swami Vivekananda*, eleventh edition, September 2013, 6:405-08
57. *The Complete Works of Swami Vivekananda*, first edition, February 1997, 9:360-61
58. *Life of Swami Vivekananda: His Eastern and Western Disciples*, sixth edition, 1989, 1:250
59. *The Complete Works of Swami Vivekananda*, eleventh edition, September, 2013 6:525

60. *The Complete Works of Swami Vivekananda*, seventh edition, December 2013, 8:273
61. *The Complete Works of Swami Vivekananda*, first edition, February 1997, 9:417-18
62. *The Complete Works of Swami Vivekananda*, seventeenth edition, 1986, 1:36-37
63. *Life of Swami Vivekananda: His Eastern and Western Disciples*, sixth edition, 1989, 1:269-70
64. *Ibid.*, 1:271
65. *Ibid.*, 1:271-72
66. *The Complete Works of Swami Vivekananda*, eleventh edition, September 2013, 6:267
67. *Life of Swami Vivekananda: His Eastern and Western Disciples*, sixth edition, 1989, 1:283.
68. *Ibid.*, 1:286-87
69. *Ibid.*, 1:288
70. *Ibid.*, 1:292
71. *Ibid.*, 1:292
72. *Swami Vivekananda on Himself*, pp. 97-98
73. *Ibid.*, p. 79
74. *The Complete Works of Swami Vivekananda*, seventh edition, December 2013, 8:294
75. *Ibid.*, 8:297
76. *The Complete Works of Swami Vivekananda*, tenth edition, December 1973, 5:4
77. *Reminiscences of Vivekananda*, pp. 20-21
78. *The Life of Swami Vivekananda: His Eastern and Western Disciples*, sixth edition, 1989, 1:307-08
79. *Reminiscences of Vivekananda*, pp. 23-24
80. *The Complete Works of Swami Vivekananda*, seventh edition, December 2013, 8:298
81. *The Life of Swami Vivekananda: His Eastern and Western Disciples*, sixth edition, 1989, 1:327-28
82. *Life*, 1:329
83. *Life*, 1:330-37
84. *The Complete Works of Swami Vivekananda*, eleventh edition, September 2013, 6:276-77
85. *Life*, 1:367
86. *Swami Vivekananda on Himself*, pp. 102-03
87. *The Complete Works of Swami Vivekananda*, seventh edition, December 2013, 8:298-99
88. *Swami Vivekananda on Himself*, pp. 104-05
89. *Ibid.*, pp. 103-04

VOYAGE TO THE WEST

1. *Swami Vivekananda on Himself*, pp. 111-13
2. *The Complete Works of Swami Vivekananda*, tenth edition, December 1973, 5:6